1984

BEHAVIOR

Individuals, Groups and Organizations
Second Edition

Melanie Wallendorf
University of Arizona

Gerald Zaltman
University of Pittsburgh

John Wiley & Sons

New York   Chichester   Brisbane   Toronto   Singapore

This book is dedicated to
**Kate Kaiser and
Marjorie Lyles (M.W.)**
and
Kathy Muldoon (G.Z.)

Library of Congress Cataloging in Publication Data:

Wallendorf, Melanie.
   Readings in consumer behavior.

   (Theories in marketing series)
   Includes bibliographies and indexes.
   1. Consumers—United States—Addresses, essays,
lectures. I. Zaltman, Gerald. II. Title. III. Series.
HC79.C6W34 1984   658.8'342   83-21608
ISBN 0-471-09307-6 (pbk.)

Printed in the United States of America

10 9 8 7 6 5 4 3 2 1

ABOUT THE AUTHORS

MELANIE WALLENDORF is an Assistant Professor of Marketing at the University of Arizona. She received her M.A. degree in sociology and her Ph.D. in marketing from the University of Pittsburgh. Professor Wallendorf's research focuses on social structures that hierarchically determine the resources and abilities that consumers bring to the marketplace.

Specifically, her interests include such topics as the adoption and diffusion of innovations, cognitive complexity, social class and ethnic group patterns, and societal modernization and economic development. She is active as a researcher and has served as a consultant in the United States as well as to foreign government agencies. Her research has appeared in such publications as the *Journal of Retailing, Journal of Advertising, Advances in Consumer Research, Perceptual and Motor Skills, American Behavioral Scientist,* and *Journal of Consumer Research.*

GERALD ZALTMAN has a Ph.D. degree in sociology from the John Hopkins University and an M.B.A. degree in marketing from the University of Chicago. He is currently the Albert Wesley Frey Distinguished Professor of Marketing at the University of Pittsburgh. Professor Zaltman is also Co-Director of the newly established University of Pitts-

burgh Program for the Study of Knowledge Use and holds joint appointments in the Graduate School of Public Health, the Department of Sociology, the Graduate School for Public and International Affairs, and the Center for Latin American Studies. He is currently Director of Doctoral Studies in the Graduate School of Business. He previously taught marketing at Northwestern University where he was the A. Montgomery Ward Professor of Marketing and was a visiting professor at the Institute of International Business, The Stockholm School of Economics.

Professor Zaltman is active as a researcher and as a consultant to numerous firms and nonprofit agencies in the United States and abroad. His special interests focus on the responses of individual consumers and organizations to new products and services and the development of product management strategy.

Professor Zaltman is co-author or editor of 25 books and monographs and is a frequent contributor to professional journals and conferences. He is a past President of the Association for Consumer Research and is on the editorial boards of numerous journals in the management and social science areas. Dr. Zaltman has received several awards for his research and writing.

PREFACE

This collection of readings introduces the reader to a sample of the best research in the consumer behavior area. Most readings are presented primarily because of the importance of their findings. Other readings are presented because they are examples of sound research methodology or because they address important issues. Some readings address important but generally neglected topics.

This reader was developed to supplement existing consumer behavior textbooks by providing a detailed look at particular issues or particularly rich and important studies. The readings are current in that they represent, for the most part, not only recent work, but the best extant statements on various topics. In making selections, we had one inflexible criterion: readings had to be meaningful to students who had no substantial prior background in consumer behavior. We intend that the book be used to provide examples of the way in which our knowledge of consumer behavior is built and tested.

Melanie Wallendorf
Gerald Zaltman

ACKNOWLEDGMENTS

First and foremost, we wish to thank the authors of each of the 41 articles for giving us permission to reprint their work. In particular, we wish to thank John Cipkala, who wrote an article especially for this volume. In addition, we would like to express our appreciation to the journals that gave us permission to reprint articles.

We would also like to thank students in our consumer behavior classes at the University of Arizona and the University of Pittsburgh who were helpful in earmarking areas of consumer behavior that they wanted to know more about and what aspects of consumer behavior research they found difficult to understand. Their comments guided us in selecting articles for inclusion in this book, as well as in writing the introductory remarks for each article.

In addition, several of our doctoral students have been extremely helpful in discussing the selected articles with us and assisting us in the process of editing them and preparing introductory comments. In particular, we have enjoyed working with Audrey Federouch and Debbie MacInnis of the University of Pittsburgh, and Barbara Garland and Mark Speece of the University of Arizona.

Several people have reviewed this book at various stages. In particular, we benefitted from the suggestions of David Aaker of the University of California at Berkeley, Barbara Bart of Georgia Southern College, William Bearden of the University of South Carolina, Robert Hughes of the University of Kansas, and Mary Lou Roberts of Boston University.

Finally, we wish to express our appreciation to four people whose assistance was of utmost importance in the physical preparation of the manuscript: Helen Conklin, Leslee Deonarain, Kathy Muldoon, and Martha Wolverton. Their patience and good humor as well as their efficiency have been very helpful.

Of course, we share full responsibility for any errors or omissions.

M.W.
G.Z.

CONTENTS

SECTION I

THE FIELD OF CONSUMER BEHAVIOR

Consumer behavior is one of the most exciting areas of study in marketing today. Perhaps no other field is characterized by such rapid growth and diversity. Marketers and economists have been joined by anthropologists, psychologists, sociologists, lawyers, and political scientists in trying to understand, influence, and predict the behavior of consumers. Government policymakers, business executives, and citizen action agencies are all vitally concerned with the behavior of consumers. The term "consumer" no longer refers only to private individuals buying and using products and services offered by commercial agencies. Organizations are also recognized as consumers. Mothers on welfare, students enrolled in schools, and patients in psychotherapy are viewed as consumers as well. Understanding consumers is the cornerstone not only of marketing but of a responsive society meeting the needs of its citizens.

Despite a blossoming literature and a growing diversity of interests and backgrounds among researchers active in the field, some particular patterns are evident, which should be noted. These patterns refer to both current and emerging trends.

1. The study of consumer behavior is becoming much more rigorous. The incidence of well-conceptualized, well-designed, and well-analyzed research is increasing. From this type of research a sound knowledge base is beginning to develop.

2. There is an increasing focus on the public policy implications of consumer behavior research, particularly on matters pertaining to how consumers process information, such as product ingredients.

3. Psychology and social psychology are the disciplines that have had the greatest influence. This is due largely to the greater acceptance in

these disciplines of consumer behavior as an important context in which to study human behavior.

4. However, in the past few years there has been a substantial renewal of interest in the sociology of consumer behavior by both sociologists and those interested in sociological phenomena.

5. Consumerism has become a major and enduring social institution that has not only triggered public policy concern but has generated concern with providing consumer education. Thus, the audience for consumer research studies has broadened greatly beyond marketing managers to include people in governmental agencies, citizen interest groups, educational institutions, and private not-for-profit social welfare agencies.

6. Attitudes and purchase intentions are perhaps the single most widely studied phenomena, with information-processing issues a close second. However, other topics seem to be on the ascent, including interpersonal processes of social exchange that involve power relationships, influence attempts and negotiation, the buying behavior of organizations, and the impact on consumers of their social roles.

The above observations are only a sample of many that might be offered to the reader. Three articles are selected for this section that will expand the reader's sense of the field. One is authored by a marketing-oriented researcher, the second by two sociologists who are consumer behavior experts, and the third by an economic researcher with a psychological viewpoint. Each of these articles is introduced below.

"THE SURPLUSES AND SHORTAGES IN CONSUMER BEHAVIOR THEORY AND RESEARCH"

Sheth reviews the state-of-the-art in consumer behavior theory and research at the end of the 1970s by asking three questions:

1. *What* has been the focus of understanding in consumer behavior and what should be the future focus?
2. *How* have we researched the consumer behavior phenomenon in the past, and where should we go from here?
3. *Why*, in the past, did we choose to study consumer behavior and what should be the future motivation for our continued interest in the area?

In the first part of his review in which he addresses the first of these questions, he identifies two underlying dimensions for past research: (1) a focus on the individual consumer, and (2) a focus on the decision-making process. To expand the conceptual framework for consumer behavior research, Sheth adds three more dimensions: (1) habit and conditioning, (2) situationalism, and (3) novelty-curiosity. With this expanded framework, he then takes inventory of the past decade's work to highlight areas for future research.

In the middle portion of his review, he reclassifies the decade's work by the ways in which the research has been undertaken. Is it descriptive or normative? Are the constructs borrowed from other fields or self-generated within the marketing field?

Then, in the last portion of his review, he reclassifies past research by its purpose. Has it been conducted to generate empirical knowledge or theoretical foundations? Was its purpose managerial or disciplinary?

The reader should examine the other studies in the collection to determine *what, how,* and *why* their authors have studied these specific topics.

"TOWARD A SOCIOLOGY OF CONSUMPTION"

Since consumer behavior is an interdisciplinary field, different views on the same basic phenomena can be put forth. The fact that they are different does not mean that any of them are wrong. In fact, one reason the field is so exciting is because there is such a diversity of perspectives. Nicosia and Mayer use a sociological approach to the study of consumption. Their article is not meant to deny the importance of the ideas contributed by economists, physiological psychologists, anthropologists, or political scientists. Each of these approaches is needed to fully understand consumer behavior.

This article makes a case for studying consumption in a society as a social indicator, as well as the effect of the society on individual consumer behavior. Nicosia and Mayer cover four main concepts and their relationships to each other. These four concepts are: (1) values, (2) institutions, (3) institutionalized norms, and (4) consumption activities. The basic relationships explored are shown in the following diagram:

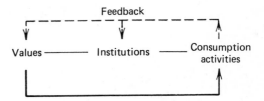

The authors do an excellent job of defining these terms in the first section of the article. The reader is advised to read this section closely and to remember that the definition of consumption activities is broader than is usually reflected in consumer behavior studies. Such studies usually only cover the acquisition phase of consumer behavior.

The authors have a particularly thought-provoking section exploring issues of causality. They ask: Do changes in cultural values lead to increasing briefness of women's swimwear, or does the wearing of brief bathing suits produce changes in cultural values? The point is that it is not so easy to determine which of two events occurring at about the same time caused the other. Also, we can know that the two are correlated, but not know if there is a causal link.

In the next major section, the relationships between these concepts are discussed. The research orientation of the authors and their audience (readers of the *Journal of Consumer Research*) is evident; however, the research questions are also posed in the light of the answers they can provide for government officials and corporate managers.

"ECONOMIC PSYCHOLOGY"

In the last selection, Van Raaij draws upon the disciplines of economics and psychology to provide yet another perspective on consumer behavior. His article inaugurates a new journal, *The Journal of Economic Psychology*. As a first step, Van Raaij begins by defining the domain of economic psychology as "the study of economic behavior," or "the behavior of consumers/citizens that involves economic decisions, and the determinants and consequences of economic decisions." Then, building upon the earlier work of Katona and Strümpel, Van Raaij constructs a new model of economic-psychological relationships. P, or personal characteristics, influence the perceived economic

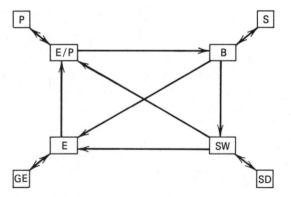

environment, E/P, and GE, or the generalized environment, influences E, economic conditions. E/P is influenced by economic conditions, and the individual's subjective well-being or SW. Economic behavior (B) is influenced by the individual's perceived economic environment and by situational influences. The individual's subjective well-being is also related to his/her societal discontent. There are many possible interactions among the set of variables that Van Raaij has included in his model. The arrow heads indicate the directions of the influences. Clearly, Van Raaij has incorporated both economic and psychological variables.

Unlike the earlier models of Katona and Strümpel, Van Raaij's model represents behavior in cyclical and dynamic terms. Furthermore, the model may focus on four sets of variables, each of which may be treated as dependent or independent. Behavior may be examined on either micro or macro levels. In presenting such a highly flexible model, Van Raaij is laying the foundation for new interdisciplinary research, which will be able to address questions previously ignored.

THE SURPLUSES AND SHORTAGES IN CONSUMER BEHAVIOR THEORY AND RESEARCH

JAGDISH N. SHETH

INTRODUCTION

The purpose of this paper is to take an inventory of consumer behavior theory and research as we end the decade of the seventies. There is no question that consumer behavior as a discipline has displayed a spectacular growth in borrowing concepts from the behavioral and quantitative sciences, in broadening its horizons from traditional marketing problems to social problems, and in generating a body of knowledge about consumers as buyers, users and decision makers. (Sheth, 1972; Jacoby, 1975). It is simply a matter of time before consumer behavior will divorce itself from marketing and stand on its own as a distinct discipline relevant to many other constituents besides marketers and many other disciplines beside marketing. Thus, it appears to be an opportune time to take stock of consumer behavior and research and assess its surpluses and shortages.

Perhaps the most difficult part of taking an inventory of a growing discipline is to decide on where to begin and how to plan assessing the surpluses and shortages in consumer behavior. After some thinking, I have come up with the following three aspects which seem to provide a simple yet comprehensive approach:

1. *What* has been the focus of understanding in consumer behavior and what should be the future focus?
2. *How* have we researched the consumer behavior phenomenon in the past, and where should we go from here?
3. *Why*, in the past, did we choose to study consumer behavior and what should be the future motivation for our continued interest in the area?

Each of the above three aspects will be examined in some depth which hopefully will reveal what we have sufficiently done and where the deficiencies exist in consumer behavior theory and research.

FOCUS OF CONSUMER BEHAVIOR THEORY AND RESEARCH

While consumer behavior theory and research may look very eclectic at first glance, two aspects

Source: Jagdish N. Sheth, "The Surpluses and Shortages in Consumer Behavior Theory and Research," *Journal of the Academy of Marketing Science,* Vol. 7, No. 4, Fall, 1979, pp. 414–427. © 1979.

stand out as the common underlying dimensions with which most research efforts seem to be bonded together. The first aspect is the dominance of focus on the *individual consumer* in many of his roles such as shopper, buyer, decision maker and the user. The second aspect is the dominance of decision making process and the consequent implicit, if not explicit presumption that the buying behavior is a rational problem-solving process (Howard and Sheth, 1969; Sheth, 1976). Accordingly, we seem to have abundance of research studies about the individual consumer and about theories of consumer behavior which are based on decision making processes. This is particularly evident in the recent proliferation of multiattribute attitudes, information processing and brand choice models.

By the same token, research studies on dyads and small groups such as families and organizations are limited. Even larger groups such as market segments, social classes and ethnic groups have been studied more in terms of *aggregates* of individual consumers rather than as distinct group entities.

The situation seems to be decidedly worse with respect to analyzing and understanding those consumers and areas of consumer behavior which do not lend themselves to decision making process approaches. For example, the deviant consumer behavior such as shoplifting, the obsessive consumer behavior such as obesity, alcoholism and drug addiction, and the fads and fashion patronage behavior have not been very successfully understood by the rational problem-solving approaches of the decision making tradition.

It is fairly obvious even to a naive observer that not all consumers or all consumer behavior phenomena can be fully explained or understood by a single perspective especially as elegant and rational as the decision making perspective. I believe that we need to bring at least three additional perspectives to fully comprehend the consumer behavior phenomenon. These are (1) habit and conditioning; (2) situationalism; and the (3) novelty-curiosity or epistemic perspective.

Table 1 represents an attempt at summarizing

Table 1 Surpluses and shortages of focus in consumer behavior theory

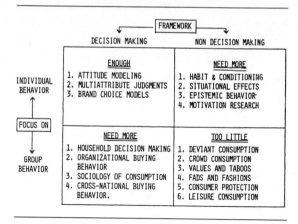

the surpluses and deficiencies with respect to what we have versus what we should focus on in consumer behavior theory and research. What seems to be enough is the decision making framework applied to explain and predict individual consumer behavior. Two classes of research in this interactive combination are: the multiattribute judgments and brand choice models. My own view is what these models now need is more usage and applications by the marketing practitioners and policy makers rather than further theoretical development.

What we need most because too little consumer research or theory effort has been devoted so far is the opposite interactive combination: understanding group behavior which are likely to be based on non-problem solving processes. Examples of such areas of focus for consumer research include crowd consumption, deviant consumption, fads and fashions and understanding values, taboos, and similar clinical mass motivations. This research should be directed at the *macro* (group) rather than at the *micro* (individual) level.

Of course, the above statements do not imply that there is no further need to study the individual consumers or that the decision making framework has outlived its utility. As the table indicates, we still need more research and theory about the individual consumer but in the non-decision making domains of his epistemic behavior, impact of situational effects on his choice behavior, the formation, endurance and utilization of habits (affective predispositions to behave) which may or may not have any underlying cognitive structure, and the whole area of motivation research which was disreputed prematurely in the early days of consumer behavior.

Similarly, there are many areas of group behavior which can be understood by the decision making framework, and where more research and theory are clearly needed. These include the more traditional areas of household decision making, organizational buying behavior, and the newer areas of sociology of consumption and cross-national buying behavior. The important point to come in mind is that we need to develop or borrow more *macro* decision making frameworks rather than simply extend the micro decision making frameworks used in understanding individual consumers. For example, recent literature on cultural aggregates, game theory, jury decision processes, and interorganizational conflict, power and coalitions may prove more relevant than the tenets of social psychology.

PROCESS OF CONSUMER BEHAVIOR THEORY AND RESEARCH

The process of theorizing and researching consumer behavior seems to be at least two dimensional. The first dimension reflects the heavy reliance on, and the consequent dominance of descriptive as opposed to normative process. This is understandable and seems to be due to two reasons. First, we are dealing with very pervasive human or social issues in consumer behavior where it is difficult to impose a common set of normative value-laden judgments or perspectives without being criticized or at least questioned by others. While these two factors explain why we might have leaned toward the descriptive processes in consumer behavior, they cannot justify it.

The second dimension related to how we have gone about researching and theorizing the consumer behavior area is the dominance of borrowed concepts and constructs as opposed to generating our own concepts and constructs unique to consumer behavior. The dominance of borrowed versus self-generated constructs can be attributed to several factors. First, the early pioneers in the discipline of consumer behavior made a fundamental presumption that consumer behavior is not unique but part of a larger syndrome of human and social behavior. Second, when a discipline begins to emerge without a formally defined boundary or at best an ill-defined boundary, it is easier to borrow constructs than create them. This seems very much true of consumer behavior; we still do not precisely know what to include and what to exclude from consumer behavior to make it a distinct discipline. Third, the pervasiveness of the phenomenon itself may have been a contributing factor: It attracted many scholars from a variety of disciplines such as economics, behavioral sciences, social sciences, marketing, and the quantitative sciences. Consequently, there was no single thrust or driving force comparable to what has been true in the pioneering days of economics and psychology. Multitudes of viewpoints and processes were simultaneously applied to understanding consumer behavior as evidenced from reviews of earlier literature (Sheth, 1967). While this was great for the discipline to get off the ground faster and mature quickly, it ended up in the dominance of using borrowed constructs at the expense of self-generating constructs uniquely suited to the discipline.

Having identified the two process dimensions (descriptive vs. normative and borrowed vs. self generated constructs), the task of taking inventory of how we have developed consumer behavior theory and research is made much easier: There is a clear surplus of borrowed constructs and a critical shortage of self-generated constructs in consumer behavior. Similarly, there is a surplus of descriptive constructs and a shortage of normative constructs. In Table 2, I have provided some examples of the types of research and theory processes in consumer behavior which we must discourage and other types which we must encourage to create a balance of processes of researching in consumer behavior.

Table 2 Surpluses and shortages in the process of consumer behavior theory and research

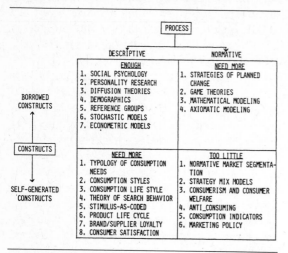

First of all, I think we have borrowed enough constructs from several descriptive disciplines. This includes social psychology, personality research, diffusion of innovations, econometric models as well as stochastic models. On the other hand, we badly need to generate our own constructs related to several normative aspects of consumer behavior. These include developing normative theories of market segmentation, what should be the strategy mix to impact on the consumers without generating negative side effects, how should we protect the consumer *and* which types of consumers, designing anti-consuming policies for certain goods and services, and developing an audit system for measuring consumption indicators which go beyond the recently popular economic and social indicators. The most radical of the proposed areas of future research and theory is the development of marketing policy which would outline rights and obligations of the marketers.

Again, the above analysis does not mean that we should discard descriptive processes altogether or that we should totally stop borrowing constructs from other disciplines. As Table 2 indicates, there are a number of exciting areas of research and theory in consumer behavior which can and should rely upon the descriptive processes. These include self-generating a unique typology of consumption needs/wants, a typology of consumption life styles as opposed to general life styles, and consumption life cycle based on the time dependent covariances of preselected and representative goods and services. It also includes more research on self-generated constructs of brand/supplier loyalty, product life cycle theory, and consumer satisfaction/dissatisfaction research. Finally, we badly need self-generated constructs for the phenomena of information search and the process by which marketing stimuli get internalized in the consumer's mind both in the short and in the long-term memory functions.

Lastly, there are several normative disciplines from which we have neglected to borrow in the past, even though they appear to be useful to consumer behavior. These include the policy literature in sociology related to strategies of planned social change, game theory and normative decision theory, mathematical modeling such as queing theory, inventory control theory and critical path analysis for educating and upgrading the household consumer so that he can better optimize his scarce resources of time, effort and money, and finally axiomatic disciplines such as metatheory, microeconomics, and logic.

PURPOSE OF CONSUMER BEHAVIOR THEORY AND RESEARCH

Looking at the issue of why we have generated consumer behavior knowledge, it would appear that there are at least two underlying dimensions. The first is the dominance of satisfying the managerial as opposed to the disciplinary (meta theory) needs. The second is the dominance of acquiring empirical knowledge (facts and figures) about the consumer as opposed to the theoretical foundations of consumer behavior.

The dominance of managerially oriented research on consumer behavior is clearly due to the following factors. First and foremost, consumer behavior was, and to a large extent it still is, a part of marketing theory and practice. The earliest studies in consumer behavior were undertaken for the marketing managers who wanted to know more about the consumer before deciding on specific marketing strategies. Hence, market research has such a strong overlap with consumer research in content and methodology. Second, research funding by governmental agencies or foundations to study th[...] ry mode has [...]ery recently. [...]essary to rely [...] and conse- [...]e managerial [...]ioned earlier, [...]ost scholars [...]ise in other [...] ng empirical [...]ance can be [...]nductive ap- [...]cipline in its [...]lts in gener- [...]cts and fig- [...]d reporting [...] than on its [...]y is less ex- [...] This tends [...]mpirical as [...] this bias is [...]ation of the [...]cal papers. [...]rlying con- [...]tensify the [...] consumer [...]en looking [...]own theo- [...]says "give [...]onfuse me [...]actor is the [...]competing [...]ostly due [...]enon, and somewhat due to our inability to translate theories into testable hypotheses and to effectively cope with consequent operationalization and analysis problems.

What we have then as a surplus in the why aspect of consumer behavior is the managerial pur-

pose and the empirical knowledge, and what we have as a shortage is the disciplinary (metatheory) purpose and the theoretical knowledge. Table 3 summarizes this point and offers several examples of surpluses and shortages in consumer behavior so far as the purpose of researching and theorizing the area are concerned.

It is obvious that empirical knowledge on an ongoing basis for managerial purposes is probably sufficient by now. In fact, some scholars have openly complained that both the government and the industry collects too much information by way of surveys and audits, consumer demographics, life styles and psychographics as well as his media and shopping habits especially since the start of the age of electronic computers and other electronic devices. It would appear to me that the next progressive step is data analysis. For it is a sad commentary that probably eighty to ninety percent of the information about the consumer goes unanalyzed or at least underanalyzed. In short, data analysis and not data collection should be the further direction in the area of generating empirical knowledge for managerial purposes.

On the other side of the equation, what seems to be in most accute shortage are the theoretical foundations of the discipline itself. While we do have several nice and rich hypotheses (e.g., perceived

Table 3 Surpluses and shortages in the purpose of consumer behavior theory and research

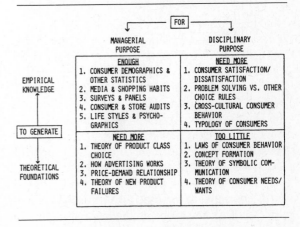

	FOR	
---	MANAGERIAL PURPOSE	DISCIPLINARY PURPOSE
EMPIRICAL KNOWLEDGE	**ENOUGH** 1. CONSUMER DEMOGRAPHICS & OTHER STATISTICS 2. MEDIA & SHOPPING HABITS 3. SURVEYS & PANELS 4. CONSUMER & STORE AUDITS 5. LIFE STYLES & PSYCHOGRAPHICS	**NEED MORE** 1. CONSUMER SATISFACTION/ DISSATISFACTION 2. PROBLEM SOLVING VS. OTHER CHOICE RULES 3. CROSS-CULTURAL CONSUMER BEHAVIOR 4. TYPOLOGY OF CONSUMERS
TO GENERATE ↑	**NEED MORE** 1. THEORY OF PRODUCT CLASS CHOICE 2. HOW ADVERTISING WORKS 3. PRICE-DEMAND RELATIONSHIP 4. THEORY OF NEW PRODUCT FAILURES	**TOO LITTLE** 1. LAWS OF CONSUMER BEHAVIOR 2. CONCEPT FORMATION 3. THEORY OF SYMBOLIC COMMUNICATION 4. THEORY OF CONSUMER NEEDS/ WANTS
THEORETICAL FOUNDATIONS		

risk, buyer attitudes, and stochastic preferences) and some good comprehensive theories in consumer behavior, unfortunately most of them are developed for the managerial perspective. We need discipline-oriented theoretical foundation, especially in the areas of concept formation, symbolic communication and a good theory of consumer needs/wants.

Above all, it would be superb if we can evolve toward some commonly agreed upon and scientifically validated laws of consumer behavior.

This analysis does not mean that we should ignore or even discard the managerial purpose in consumer behavior. However, what the manager needs much more critically are the theoretical foundations of how the marketing mix does or does not work. For example, it would be nice if scholars in consumer behavior can provide him with a single agreed upon explanation as to how advertising works; or provide rich theoretical foundations for the price-demand relationship; or offer a good theory of new product failures.

Finally, the discipline itself needs further empirical knowledge on a number of substantive issues. These include the degree and character of consumer satisfaction/dissatisfaction; prevalence of problem solving versus other methods of making product, brand or store choices; and cross-cultural parallels and contrasts in magnitudes and types of products and services consumed on our planet.

SUMMARY AND CONCLUSIONS

This paper is an attempt to take an inventory of consumer behavior theory and research in order to identify surpluses and shortages of concepts, information and body of knowledge we face today as we say goodbye to the decade of the seventies.

The inventory was taken with respect to the three areas of focus, process and purpose in generating the body of knowledge we call consumer behavior theory and research. The following conclusions were derived in the process:

1. We have focused too much on the individual consumer as opposed to group behavior and similarly too much on the rational models of problem solving (decision making) as op-

posed to other non-problem solving models of choice behavior. The interaction of these two focus factors has resulted in abundance of attitude models, multiattribute judgments, and brand choice models. What we need most is understanding of group phenomena such as crowd consumption, fads and fashions, deviant consumption behavior, and obsessive consumer behavior with the use of more macro and non-problem solving hypotheses and theories of choice behavior.

2. The process of theorizing and researching consumer behavior has been dominated by descriptive as opposed to normative constructs, and by constructs borrowed from other disciplines rather than self-generated constructs unique to consumer behavior. In the process, we seem to have surplus of social psychology, diffusion theory, reference groups, as well as econometric and stochastic modeling of consumer behavior. What we need now are more normative and self-generated hypotheses and theories related to market segmentation, strategy mix models, consumerism and consumer welfare theories, anti-consuming models and a normative marketing policy which defines the rights and obligations of the marketers.

3. Most of the consumer behavior research and theory has been for managerial purposes in contrast to the disciplinary (metatheory) purposes. Similarly, it has been more empirical rather than theoretical. This has resulted in generating lots of facts and figures about the consumer himself, how much does he buy, his media and shopping habits and his demographics, life styles and psychographics. In the process, market research and consumer research have become almost synonymous. What we need, however, are rich theoretical foundations of the discipline itself with respect to many areas such as concept formation, symbolic communication and a theory of consumer needs/wants.

It would be simply exhilarating if we can evolve some agreed upon and properly validated laws of consumer behavior.

REFERENCES

Howard, J. A., and J. N. Sheth (1969) *The Theory of Buyer Behavior,* Wiley & Sons.

Jacoby, J. (1975), "Consumer Psychology as a Social Psychological Sphere of Action," *American Psychologist,* 30, October, 977–987.

Sheth, J. N. (1967) "A Review of Buyer Behavior," *Management Science,* 13, B718–B756.

Sheth, J. N. (1972), "The Future of Buyer Behavior Theory," in *Proceedings of the Third Annual Conference,* Association for Consumer Research, 562–575.

Sheth, J. N. (1976) "Howard's Contributions to Marketing: Some Thoughts," in A. Andreasen and S. Sudman (eds.) *Public Policy and Marketing Thought,* Proceedings of the Ninth P. D. Converse Symposium, American Marketing Association, 17–26.

TOWARD A SOCIOLOGY OF CONSUMPTION

**FRANCESCO M. NICOSIA
AND
ROBERT N. MAYER**

Source: Francesco M. Nicosia and Robert N. Mayer, "Toward a Sociology of Consumption," *Journal of Consumer Research,* Vol. 3, September, 1976, pp. 65–75. Reprinted with permission.

INTRODUCTORY REMARKS

It should not be too controversial to assert that consumer research, as we know it today, was born about two decades ago. We would probably also agree that consumer research is focused primarily on the study of the decision process of an *individual,* although the economic and social events that interact with the psychological attributes of an individual are also frequently included in consumer research.

In the early 1960s, some of us noted that the study of a *society's* consumption might also be useful (e.g., Glock and Nicosia, 1964). So far, however, only a few scholars have considered the consumption of a society (e.g., Bauer, 1966; Felson, 1975; Katona, Strumpel, and Zahn, 1971; Mayer, 1975; Nicosia and Glock, 1968; Nicosia and Witkowski, 1975; Smelser, 1963; Zaltman and Bagozzi, 1975). Even the vast literature on the so-called social indicators has practically ignored a society's consumption as a fundamental social indicator, especially in affluent, post-industrial societies (see, for example, the annotated bibliography by Wilcox et al., 1972).

This lack of attention to a society's consumption is surprising because macroeconomics has shown some of the advantages of studying production and consumption at the societal level rather than at the level of the single firm or the single household. In particular, the conceptual and empirical studies of the "consumption function" in macroeconomics have helped both the private and the public sectors in formulating and implementing policies.

Neither sociologists nor consumer researchers, however, have accepted the challenge of studying a society's consumption in relation to other societal characteristics, despite its potential as a social indicator. Understanding some of a society's characteristics could provide a consumer researcher with the context necessary to help the study of individual consumer choices. For example, understanding the effect of cultural values concerning achievement and the use of time is at least as important as understanding whether consumers process information in an additive or multiplicative manner.

Understanding the interactions among consumption and other societal characteristics would also contribute to the study of consumerism, the social responsibilities of marketing, the involvement of governments in providing consumer information (Mayer and Nicosia, 1974), and the roles of the mass communication systems—including advertising—in a society (Nicosia, 1974a).

More important, such understanding is a necessary input into the difficult decisions of social managers—legislatures, regulatory agencies, and courts—concerning long-term and crucial problems. For instance, it is an understatement to assert that many public policy decisions on management of human and natural resources may affect not only consumption but also institutions, norms, and, eventually, cultural values (Pirages and Ehrlich, 1974). This is true for all societies, regardless of their stage of evolution.

The experiences of societies now struggling to grow past a state of survival imply very difficult decisions for social managers. They must contend with consumption aspirations and activities unknown even half a century ago. The social and economic processes that led to the development of Western societies no longer seem to work. In particular, the visibility of consumption styles in Western societies affects both the kind and the intensity of consumption in developing societies, so that the old cycle of "saving-investment-production and *then* consumption" no longer seems applicable to these societies.

In affluent, post-industrial societies, social management of consumption faces different dilemmas. The recent history of these societies has been an evolution from solving problems of quantity—that is, the delivery of standards of living—to assuring quality of life. The meaning of this evolution for consumers has been the growing expectation that aesthetic as well as functional needs could be fulfilled. Spiraling aspirations to quantity and quality went hand in hand until the energy crunch, stagflation, and unemployment entered the picture. In this new climate, quality is beginning to be perceived not as the handmaiden of quantity but rather as its enemy. To satisfy needs for quantities of goods, we sacrifice qualities of the environment

building a pipeline in Alaska and postponing clean air standards.

Society and consumers had thought that quantity and quality were complementary. Now they are learning that there are conflicts; they are facing trade-offs, and, knowingly or not, they are assuming historical and moral responsibility. What kind of knowledge do social managers have for dealing with this situation? We doubt that either *existing concepts* or *data* are sufficient.

These results are only an initial indication of why we propose to focus on society rather than on the individual consumer (or types of consumers). We shall unfold our arguments gradually—in particular, specifying a *few* characteristics (cultural values, institutions and their norms, and consumption) and their possible relationships—for very little has been dared in this direction.

In the next section of this article we begin the review of the literature in order to define some of the constructs that we believe are basic to a sociology of consumption. We continue the review in the following section, and by using the chosen constructs, work toward the specification of new research directions, hoping to lay the groundwork for future empirical research. In essence, we are proposing a prospectus for basic and applied research, thereby delineating sociology of consumption and its potential contributions.

THE DOMAIN OF A SOCIOLOGY OF CONSUMPTION

The development of empirically based knowledge depends on a process of measuring the words central to the inquiry at hand. To appreciate our efforts, recall that the first step of this process involves mapping of a word's daily meanings. The next step is explication—that is, choosing a number of dimensions, given a research purpose. Thus, a word defined in the space of the chosen dimensions can now be considered a *construct*. The next step involves choices of indicators, measuring instruments, and measurement. The end result is usually a numerical representation of a word.

In the social sciences, even the first step of this

process presents major difficulties because a word's daily connotations are many and confusing. Even key words in social science literature may be vague, for they have not yet been translated into clearly defined constructs. This initial difficulty applies particularly to the literature that we have reviewed.

In this section, we choose cultural values, social institutions and their norms, and consumption activities as central to our domain of inquiry. We then discuss the problems of dimensionalizing these words.

Definition of "Cultural Value"

To transform the term "cultural value" into a measurable construct is more difficult than is the case with either "social institution" or "consumption activities." There is agreement that the term implies *widely held beliefs* as well as a *general guide* for some set of activities. Beyond these, however, many issues have not been settled. We should mention a few that we have found relevant.

To begin with, a cultural value by definition has as its referent an entire population, e.g., all U.S. citizens. The literature has not addressed, however, the problem of how widely held a value must be. Must it be held by a majority or only a plurality of the population? Without an answer to this question, the distinction between cultural values and the frequently used term "subcultural" values is neither conceptually nor operationally clear.

Another unsettled issue is the relationship between the intensity with which a value is held and that value's impact on behavior. An additional issue is that for some authors a cultural value must be considered both desirable *and* essential by a population, while for others it must be desirable but not necessarily essential. An implication for a sociology of consumption is that, for example, if a society believes it *only* desirable that everyone have food, clothing, and shelter, one would expect to see private charitable institutions but not a government welfare apparatus.

A further issue involves the origins and consequences of cultural values. As an example of the ambiguity one faces, recall that the increasing briefness of women's bathing suits over the past 40

years is generally attributed to changes in morality, but to what extent did such fashion changes reinforce or even cause these changes in morality?

We do not intend to resolve these debates. For our purposes, we shall use cultural values in the sense that (a) they are widely held beliefs, (b) they affirm what is desirable, and (c) they have some impact on activities. Some examples of cultural values that might characterize a contemporary society and perhaps bear on its consumption are success through individual achievement, freedom of choice, egalitarianism, active use of time, orientation toward the future (e.g., progress, security), and active mastery of the physical environment.

We must deal with one final difficulty. In the literature, the terms "cultural value" and "norm" are associated but not clearly distinguished. For the purpose of understanding society and its consumption, we find it useful to draw a distinction between the two terms by locating norms in the context of social institutions.

Definition of "Institution"

Understanding society is often based on the study of its organization, namely, its institutions. The term "institution" has different meanings in the literature. Confronted with this variety, we view an institution as a set of specific *activities* performed by specific *people* in specific *places* through *time*. What is important in defining a particular institution is its unique *pattern* of interaction among activities, people, and places through time. Consider, for example, the nuclear and the extended family. They are two different institutions because their patterns of activities, people, and places through time differ.

An institution creates *norms* directing specific activities. For example, when two people marry, norms guiding their financial activities emerge (Ferber and Lee, 1974). Furthermore, norms maintain the pattern of interaction characteristic of a particular institution.

To be viable, an institution must find ways to apply its norms. The primary ways are the creation and implementation of specific *rewards* and *sanctions*. In a work institution, the norm "be productive" may be supported by the reward of wages proportional to productivity and by the sanction of fines for employees found to be intoxicated. Of course, the nature of rewards and sanctions does not need to be financial.

Success in implementing norms depends on at least two facilitating conditions: *communication* and *visibility*. Communication here includes both its amount and content, as well as its channels (e.g., purely visual, mass media, and word of mouth). For example, a story in a company's newsletter for its employees describing how a worker's idea led to both increased productivity and his promotion is an attempt to reinforce the norm "take initiative."

Visibility is usually associated with communication. The aspect that must be emphasized here, however, is the possible influence on a person of knowing that his actions are visible to others. To illustrate, if the norm "do not throw garbage in the street" prevails in a community, it may be adhered to more fully if people live in sight of each other.

At the very least, institutional norms are *bounded* by cultural values. To illustrate, the cultural value "freedom of choice" prevents a private firm from specifying where its employees will live. In addition, some norms *interpret* cultural values into clearer criteria for the performance of specific activities in an institution. For instance, in an American business firm, the cultural value "achieve individual success" is interpreted by norms such as "work hard," "be punctual," and "take reasonable risks." The same cultural value may be translated into different norms in another society. Thus, in a French firm, being successful entails retention of one's own property and the minimization of risk (Landes, 1951; Pitts, 1963).

In searching for norms bearing on *consumption activities,* we should not consider only such institutions as the family, restaurants, department stores, and sports arenas. Work, educational, and religious institutions also create norms bearing on clothes, cars, food, and entertainment.

The important research questions for our purposes, then, are the following:

1. Which institutions create which norms bearing on which consumption activities?
2. How are these norms bounded by cultural values, and how do they interpret cultural values?

Definition of "Consumption Activities"

Conceptual and empirical research implies a classification of activities, with each class concerned with a kind of behavior—e.g., political, occupational, educational, religious. Consumption activities, however, have been either ignored or lumped into the broad class of leisure activities.

We have also found that much social science literature describes some societies as "postindustrial," "materialistic," "service-oriented," or "affluent." Although these adjectives may describe many classes of activities, they seem to stress that consumption activities are relatively more important in distinguishing such societies from those referred to as "pastoral," "developing," or "industrial." An obvious case is the recent value-oriented literature exemplified by the popular writings of Galbraith and Keynes. Yet, curiously enough, there are practically no attempts to study, systematically and comprehensively, a modern society's consumption activities and their possible correlates.

We distinguish three classes of consumption activities: buying, using, and disposing. Why these three instead of some others? What about searching for information? The specific activities implied by information search (e.g., reading ads, asking friends, window shopping) may be performed in the buying, using and disposing of goods. Thus, for the moment, we conceive of information search as a class of activities subordinate (but not hierarchically) to the three we propose.

There remains the problem of operationalizing the term "consumption activity" (Nicosia and Glock, 1968). We can begin with the long-term use and relative success of macroeconomic research on a society's consumption expenditures, which shows that *dollars spent* must be part of the explication, at least for some problems faced by public policy makers.

It is also clear that consumption activities imply goods; thus, the *specific basket of goods* (bought, used, and disposed) is also a salient dimension. The construction, early uses, and refinements of the cost-of-living index are proof of this. One refinement, now routinely implemented, is the computation of the cost of living for different, "typical," baskets, each for a different level of income and for a different geographical area. To the extent that there is a tendency toward an increasing number of typical baskets, a primary contribution of a sociology of consumption is to observe such pluralism and begin analyses not only of the demographic and economic correlates of each typical basket but also of the social processes (involving cultural values, institutions, and norms) that may govern this pluralism.

We should illustrate further the importance of explicating consumption activities not only in terms of dollar expenditures but also in terms of the content of the baskets. Assume that three typical baskets involve the same dollar expenditure for "entertainment." Yet, in one case, the specific entertainment goods are mostly spectator sports events. The second basket includes mostly records, art supplies, and books, while the third consists mostly of outdoor activities such as swimming or backpacking. These differences, and particularly the distribution of people over these three baskets, have implications for resource management and preservation of environmental quality. For instance, the first basket involves transportation and the use of energy, the disposal of food and drink containers, and so on, plus long-term commitments by society to build and operate highways, parking lots, and stadiums.

The explication of consumption activities in terms of baskets is important for understanding the functioning of an institution. Suppose we observe that, within the same family, some members are more committed to spectator sports, others to intellectual entertainment, and others to outdoor pleasures. If this pluralism occurs in an increasing number of families, it may affect the families' abilities to formulate and implement coherent patterns of norms guiding consumption activities.

In addition to dollars spent and goods purchased, *time* should be included in any operational definition of consumption activities. Each activity implies time, but more important, different goods imply different amounts of time allocated to buying, using, and disposing.

It may well be that time is the crucial dimension, since its supply is fixed. The interdependence among all kinds of activities because of the fixed supply of time has strong implications for the study of a society's consumption. How does a society cope with a fixed amount of time available (Nicosia, 1974b)? Whatever social mechanisms lead to greater allocation of time to consumption activities, a net consequence is that some other activities will necessarily receive less time. It is here that cultural values, institutions, and norms may confer meaning to time and thus guide the allocation of time to different activities.

Summary

The domain of a sociology of consumption concerns the study of three classes of variables: cultural values, institutions and their norms, and consumption activities. It also includes the study of the possible interrelationships between these classes of variables—for example, (1) from cultural values to institutions and then to consumption activities, (2) from cultural values directly to consumption activities, and (3) possible feedbacks from consumption activities to institutions and/or cultural values.

We have very little theoretical and empirical knowledge of the processes that govern a society's consumption. In the next section, we shall develop some points of departure for building such knowledge. We shall use as much evidence as exists that is possibly relevant, and, as is always the case in a new venture, we shall make a number of reasonable—common-sense, if you will—speculations.

THE NATURE AND DYNAMICS OF CONSUMPTION IN AFFLUENT SOCIETIES

In reviewing the concepts basic to our inquiry, the emphasis was on the development of operational definitions. In this section, we discuss some new research directions. This is a rather ambiguous undertaking, with few, if any guides.

Our discussion of consumption and its underlying social processes will be organized around three research directions:

1. What are the institutional arrangements— that is, the social organization—of consumption activities in affluent societies?

2. How do cultural values relate to the social organization of consumption activities?

3. How do changes in a society's consumption activities relate to broader social change in cultural values and nonconsumptional institutions, norms, and activities?

Institutional Arrangements of Consumption Activities in Affluent Societies

To understand the social organization of any activity, we must examine the number and types of institutions in which the activity occurs. If we look at an affluent society, we observe that one type of activity primarily occurs in one type of institution— for example, work activities usually occur in work institutions, educational activities in educational institutions. Where do consumption activities take place?

In searching for an answer, let us appreciate the historical background of this association of type of activity with type of institution. In pastoral and agrarian societies, by and large, the institution of the family (or the clan, the immediate community) tended to be the locus of most activities (e.g., production, consumption, education and socialization, procreation, religion, and self-government). During the feudal period, too, the family remained the locus of most of these activities, with the exception of those taken on by the church and the centralized state.

With the advent of industrialization in Western societies, several activities became increasingly organized into specialized institutions outside the family. For example, production moved to the factories; education and increasingly socialization became the job of schools; political legal activities and the control of deviance were performed by the state through its legislatures, police, and growing court system; and medical care was dispensed in hospitals and, recently, also in outpatient clinics and HMOs.

During this industrialization the family was still the main focus of consumption activities, but as affluence spread throughout society, consumption activities also began to move out of the family. It appears, however, that the movement of consumption activities out of the family differs from that of work, education, and other activities. The identification of these differences poses new research questions. What happened to the consumption activities of buying, using, and disposing?

Buying activities.   In agrarian times, buying activities were rare, relegated to ceremonial visits with other families and tribes or to occasional journeys to the village market, for the family tended to be self-sufficient. As production activities became specialized and moved out of the family, however, buying activities increased and moved outside of the family. As production specialized further, industrializing Western societies had to develop ways of facilitating the buying activities of its members. Thus, we have the growth and differentiation of retailing institutions with which consumers can interact directly and of backup institutions such as warehousing, financing, and wholesaling, all attempting to search and match points of original supplies with points of final use (Nicosia, 1962).

The impact of this evolution in retailing institutions is that any consumer faces at least two kinds of choices. First, for most products, a consumer can choose among different types of stores. For example, car engine oil can be purchased in gasoline stations, hardware stores, auto parts stores, and even supermarkets (Nicosia and Mayer, 1973). Secondly, within each type of store, a consumer can also choose one particular store. These two choices are always discretionary and, in principle, at least, they are made for each purchase. These characteristics distinguish buying activities from most nonconsumption activities because work, educational, religious, and other activities, tend to be performed in a particular institution for relatively long periods of time.

The significance of this difference is that norms concerning buying activities cannot be strongly enforced. The exposure to a large number of consumption institutions, combined with the briefness of the stay in each, makes it difficult for norms to be communicated. Furthermore, the ability not to return to any particular consumption institution makes it difficult to enforce its norms through rewards and sanctions.

To the extent that buying activities are performed in a large number of retail institutions, the less likely it is that norms will be consistent for each consumer. To the extent that these institutions are incapable of communicating and enforcing their norms, the more likely it is that the only norm applying to buying activities is "the customer is always right"—as if buying activities were not subject to norms!

Use activities. Use activities may also be gradually moving out of the family in ways different from nonconsumption activities. As in buying activities, one sees an increasing number of use-oriented institutions (e.g., for food, entertainment, and transportation).[1] Here again, consumers choose not only among types (e.g., restaurant, coffee shop, or fast-food outlet) but also within types of use-institution (e.g., McDonald's, Jack in the Box, or Burger King). Moreover, consumers' participation in each institution is brief and changing, with potential implications for the operation of norms similar to those in the case of buying activities.

Use activities are further distinguished by their frequent occurrence in nonconsumption institutions, e.g., at factories, hospitals, schools, and homes of friends. This exposure to a range of institutional types wider than that of buying activities makes it even more problematic that any set of norms can guide use activities.

To what extent, then, are consumers exposed to many differing, often competing, and even contradictory sets of norms? Take, for example, the child who eats dinner at home with his parents one

night, with the babysitter the next night, at a restaurant the next night, and at the home of a friend the night after that (not to mention the diversity of norms governing the conduct at different restaurants and in different homes of friends). This type of social organization of use activities should bear on the socialization of future consumers and on the fate of cultural values such as frugality, cleanliness, and religiosity. Only the analysis of the social organization of use activities leads to the posing of these new questions and, eventually, to the collection of appropriate data.

Disposal activities. Unlike virtually all other activities, disposal activities have remained within the family, but only to the extent that use activities are also performed there. The single corollary in terms of social organization is the birth of the disposal service institution, now practically a legal requirement. Here too, however, it is difficult for norms to emerge and guide disposal activities because of the relative invisibility of these activities and lack of communication concerning them. The content of the garbage can is not made public unless a neighborhood dog intervenes, and the subject is unlikely to come up in daily conversation.

The social organization of disposal activities has begun to change with the timid appearance of public and private recycling efforts. Recent resource management problems emphasize disposal activities, for they bear on the availability of scarce resources and the maintenance of a livable environment. Optimal solutions to these problems require finding the social organization of disposal activities that is most capable of generating and enforcing norms guiding consumers—a fundamental research direction.

Future directions for research. Let us identify the research area that emerges from our understanding of what has happened to the social organization of consumption during industrialization and affluence. Like other activities, buying and use activities have also gradually moved out of the family institution and thus have become less likely to be governed by norms administered by it. However,

---

[1]The $64 billion food service industry, for example, has become the third largest consumer industry, behind the $100 billion retail food business and the $93 billion auto business. The food service industry, moreover, is first in number of outlets (half a million) and in employment (4.7 percent of the labor force) ("America's Eating-out Splurge," 1975, p. 43). At the level of the household, the 1972–73 U.S. Consumer Expenditure Survey showed that 27 percent of the food budget (excluding alcoholic beverages) of the average U.S. family was spent away from home. And a recent report by the Bank of America suggests that by 1980 consumers may be eating half of their meals away from home.

the administration of norms concerning types of nonconsumption activities has been largely absorbed by the corresponding types of nonconsumption institutions. We argue that this has not happened for consumption activities. Instead, they are increasingly dispersed in both consumption and nonconsumption institutions; consumers are thus increasingly exposed to a multiplicity of potentially conflicting norms, none of which can be strongly enforced.

So far, we have stressed only one set of changes that may cause consumers to experience either an overload or an absence of normative regulation. There is an additional set of changes in the very structure of the modern affluent family that further diminishes the ability of the family to administer norms bearing on consumption activities. Some of these changes are well documented: trends in family formation, changes in divorce rates and frequency per person, and the explosion of married women in the work force. By suggesting that these changes affect the family's ability to guide consumption activities, we offer to empirical researchers in these areas a theoretical way to contribute to the synthesis of knowledge of consumer behavior.

Future research should focus on the following themes: changes in the social organization of consumption activities, changes in the family structure, and the consequences of both for private and social management.

Cultural Values and the Social Organization of Consumption Activities

In the previous subsection, we discussed research directions concerning consumption activities, institutions, and norms. Further directions emerge from considering the roles of cultural values in the consumption of affluent societies.

A first research problem is one of identifying which cultural values, if any, are relevant.

The identification of cultural values relevant to consumption poses methodological challenges to future research. There is little empirical work and experience to rely on.

A second research problem concerns the identification of the *social processes* by which cultural values relate to institutions, norms, and activities.

There are many such processes in principle; we shall mention a few.

One possibility is that some cultural values can guide some consumption activities directly rather than through intervening social mechanisms. Little research has addressed this possibility, but applicable findings suggest the absence of a direct relationship (e.g., Heberlein and Black, 1974). In fact, current understanding of society indicates that cultural values relate to activities primarily through institutions and their norms.

As mentioned earlier, activities are related to cultural values through institutions in two ways. First, activities may be guided by institutional norms that are bounded by cultural values. For example, consumption institutions such as restaurants have been generating the norm "any attire is acceptable." Yet, nudity is not acceptable, for the norm is bounded by cultural values concerning morality. Second, activities may be guided by norms that interpret cultural values in clear ways. For instance, the norm "save some of your monthly income" interprets cultural values stressing the importance of the future.

The institutions mediating cultural values and consumption activities may be either consumptional, as in these examples, or nonconsumptionable. As an example of norms interpreting cultural values, some educational institutions may interpret the value "freedom of choice" by generating the norm "select your own course of study," with implications for the consumption not only of books but also of records, films, musical instruments, and pocket calculators (and, ultimately, future consumptional styles).

Another social process comprehends a class of feedbacks. Changes in consumption activities may feed back into institutions and their norms. For instance, as affluence spreads and eating in restaurants becomes more common, the adherence to and enforcement of religious dietary norms become more difficult. This state of affairs may force religious institutions to change these norms, or may ultimately change the nature and extent of member participation.

Changes in consumption activities may also feed back directly into cultural values. Opposition to the purchase and use of alcohol, drugs, and porno-graphic films *assumes the empirical possibility of this feedback.*

So far, we have suggested some of the basic processes that may underlie change in a society's consumption. Empirical research is needed to establish the presence and relative magnitude of these processes. Our discussion has also shown that changes in a society's consumption are part of and interact with social change in general. We thus expect that there are complex processes at work, all of which still require conceptualization. In the following subsection, we shall develop some conceptualizations of more complex processes on the basis of already available evidence.

Changes in a Society's Consumption Activities and Broader Social Change

The relationships between changes in a society's consumption activities and social change in general are the result of numerous and complex social processes. We shall conceptualize one case of social change in which consumption activities may be seen both as results and as causes. In our example, cultural values are "deflected" into consumption activities. Deflection processes can be expected to occur when certain nonconsumption institutions no longer interpret and translate a particular cultural value into activity-specific norms.

The deflection process that we shall map out considers (1) the cultural values of success through individual achievement and of frugality; (2) the institutions of the firm and of the labor union, and their norms; and (3) work and consumption activities. We shall then discuss the interactions among these variables by considering the following questions: What happens when an institution no longer interprets a certain cultural value? Will new institutions emerge capable of interpreting that value, will the value die, or will members of society search for new activities in which to express that cultural value? What are the effects of these possible adjustments on consumption activities?

We begin with the cultural value of getting ahead, i.e., "success through individual achievement." Throughout industrialization, the institu-tional locus for achieving success was the productive sector, and institutional norms specified how an individual could in fact strive for success (e.g., be punctual, come to work alert, show dedication, meet quotas).

Two of the changes in the character of productive activities and institutions that accompanied industrialization had implications for individual achievement. First, increasing specialization and scale of organizations meant a decreasing objective probability of getting ahead, and certainly of reaching the top, in industry. A second change was the birth of the labor union. This latter change has had an impact on working conditions, job security, recruitment and training. However, we want to note its impact on the success ethic. In this regard, labor unions make it increasingly difficult for the worker to distinguish himself and to be rewarded on the basis of his *individual* effort and achievement. The collective bargaining of the union presupposes that rewards are won for a group rather than for specific individuals. Furthermore, unions seek to have job advancement and promotion based on seniority rather than on performance-related attributes of individuals.

If production and labor institutions no longer constitute the primary mechanism by which the cultural value of getting ahead can realistically and feasibly be pursued, what adjustments are likely to occur? Will the cultural value of individual success lose its force? Some counterculture movements may be seen as evidence of this. A second adjustment is also possible—the deflection of the success ethic into consumption activities.

Chinoy (1952) observed this deflection in his study of auto workers. He found that the workers redefined getting ahead in terms of owning certain goods and that this allowed them to continue to believe in the reality of upward mobility. Thus, for Chinoy the major consequence of this deflection process was that consumption activities sustained the success ethic.

We might add that the possible consequences of this process for other values should also be explored. For instance, to what extent does sustaining the success ethic through consumption activities undermine the values of frugality and orientation toward the future? Can this strengthen the societal desirability for egalitarianism to imply not only equal opportunities but also equal economic results? Are we thus observing the birth of the cultural value "the right to consume" beyond the survival level?

An affluent society provides the facilitating conditions for the deflection of the success ethic into the realm of consumption. These conditions include increases in discretionary income *and* time and the reduced physical demands of most jobs, all of which provide the means for pursuing personal achievement in leisure activities and through the acquisition of status-conferring goods. The explosion in hobbies and do-it-yourself activities that began in the 1950s can probably be seen in this light. We may similarly interpret the increase in interest in quasi-cultural activities, from trips to Europe to pottery and jewelry making, which are capable of bestowing distinction on those who experience, rather than own, them.

Finally, this deflection of getting ahead finds expression in the intensity, pace, and efficiency orientation with which some people pursue supposedly relaxing activities, e.g., traveling, entertaining friends, even camping and backpacking. These observations also suggest the possible displacement of another cultural value from the productive sphere, namely, the prescription to derive a high yield from one's use of time and never to waste it (Linder, 1970).

Are there larger socioeconomic consequences of this pursuit of success, achievement, and personal distinction through consumption activities? Does this deflection contribute to an increasing number of consumption styles and a pluralism of market baskets (i.e., the goods, activities, and time implied by one's consumption activities)? The traditional explanations for the increasing differentiation among consumers are differences in income, occupation, education, and psychological predispositions. The presence of deflection processes is an additional explanation to be explored empirically.

Our discussion of the deflection of the success ethic from the sphere of production to that of consumption is only one example of a class of possible deflection processes. We have just mentioned that a similar analysis could be done on cultural prescriptions concerning the use of time. We may add that, in industrializing societies, the value "freedom of choice" was supposed to apply in a variety of institutional spheres. However, developments such as centralization of government and technological complexity have left consumption as the primary area in which a person can exercise some freedom of choice.

In this section, we have suggested research directions for understanding the nature and dynamics of consumption in affluent societies. By using concepts basic to a sociology of consumption, we have explored and often reinterpreted changes in consumption and its related social processes.

Our approach to the study of consumption in affluent societies suggests these research areas:

1. Identification of cultural values, institutions, and norms which are related to consumption activities.
2. Identification of processes of social change which underlie changes in a society's consumption.

We have shown that these areas are points of departure for the specification of testable hypotheses.

We have argued that comprehensive and systematic study of consumption in affluent societies poses research questions that are intrinsically interesting and potentially useful to private and social managers. Our interest in the development of a sociology of consumption goes beyond that of posing new basic and applied research questions. We are asking whether Western history is reaching a crucial point in its evolution. For most of its history, mankind related to its environment by "the sweat of its brow," and its morality was largely based on fear. By trial and error, through victories and defeats, much of humanity has freed itself from toil and reached the opportunity to choose a new kind of morality. It may choose to worship God not out of fear and to organize itself primarily for the satisfaction of social, psychological, and, ultimately, aesthetic and ethical wants (Nicosia, 1966, p. 6).

REFERENCES

"America's Eating-out Splurge," (Oct. 27, 1975), *Business Week,* 2404, 42–46.

Bauer, R. A., ed. (1966), *Social Indicators,* Cambridge: M.I.T. Press.

Chinoy, E. (March 1952), "The Tradition of Opportunity and the Aspirations of Automobile Workers," *American Journal of Sociology,* 57, 453–59.

"Egalitarianism: Threat to a Free Market," (December 1, 1975), *Business Week,* 2409, 62–65.

Felson, M. (1975), "The Differentiation of Material Life Styles: 1925–1966," Working paper, Department of Sociology, University of Illinois at Urbana-Champaign.

Ferber, R., and Lee, L. C. (June 1974), "Husband-Wife Influence in Family Purchasing Behavior," *Journal of Consumer Research,* 1, 43–50.

Glock, C. Y., and Nicosia, F. M. (July, 1964), "Uses of Sociology in Studying 'Consumption' Behavior," *Journal of Marketing,* 28, 51–54.

Heberlein, T. A., and Black, J. S. (August, 1974), "The Land Ethic in Action: Personal Norms, Beliefs, and the Purchase of Lead Free Gasoline," Paper presented at the Annual Meetings of the Rural Sociological Society, Montreal.

Katona, G.; Strumpel, B.; and Zahn, E. (1971), *Aspirations and Affluence: Comparative Studies in the United States and Western Europe,* New York: McGraw-Hill.

Landes, D. S. (1951), "French Business and the Businessman: A Social and Cultural Analysis," in E. M. Earle, ed., *Modern France: Problems of the Third and Fourth Republics,* Princeton, N.J.: Princeton University Press, 334–53.

Linder, S. B. (1970), *The Harried Leisure Class,* New York: Columbia University Press.

Mayer, R. (1975), "Consumer Consciousness and Social Change," Paper presented at the 70th Annual Meeting of the American Sociological Association, San Francisco, August.

———, and Nicosia, F. M. (1974), "Technology, the Consumer, and Information Flows," Vol. 4 in F. M. Nicosia, et al., *Technological Chnage, Product Proliferation, and Consumer Decision Processes,* Washington, D.C.: National Science Foundation.

Nicosia, F. M. (October 1962), "Marketing and Alder-

son's Functionalism," *Journal of Business,* 35, 403–13.

——— (1966), *Consumer Decision Processes: Marketing and Advertising Implications,* Englewood Cliffs, N.J.: Prentice-Hall.

——— (1974a), *Advertising, Management, and Society: A Business Point of View,* New York: McGraw-Hill.

——— (1974b), "Summary Report. Technology and Consumers: Individual and Social Choices," Vol. 1 in F. M. Nicosia, et al., *Technological Change, Product Proliferation, and Consumer Decision Processes,* Washington, D.C.: National Science Foundation.

———, and Glock, C. Y. (1968), "Marketing and Affluence: A Research Prospectus," in R. L. King, ed., *Marketing and the New Science of Planning.* Proceedings of the Fall Conference of the American Marketing Association, August, 1968, Chicago: American Marketing Association, 510–27.

———, and Mayer, R. N. (1973), "Changing a Car's Engine Oil at Home: A Consumer Survey," A report for the U.S. Environmental Protection Agency, Consumer Research Program, University of California, Berkeley.

———, and Witkowski, T. H. (1975), "The Need for a Sociology of Consumption," in G. Zaltman and B. Stemthal, eds., *Broadening the Concept of Consumer Behavior,* Atlanta: Association for Consumer Research, 8–24.

Pirages, D. C., and Ehrlich, P. R. (1974), *Ark II: Social Response to Environmental Imperatives,* New York: Viking.

Pitts, J. R. (1963), "Continuity and Change in Bourgeois France," in S. Hoffmann, et al., eds., *In Search of France,* Cambridge: Harvard University Press, 235–304.

Smelser, N. J. (1963), *The Sociology of Economic Life,* Englewood Cliffs, N.J.: Prentice-Hall.

Wilcox, L. D.; Brooks, R. M.; Beal, G. M.; and Klonglan, G. E. (1972), *Social Indicators and Societal Monitoring: An Annotated Bibliography,* San Francisco: Jossey-Bass.

Zaltman, G., and Bagozzi, R. P. (August, 1975), "Structural Analysis and the Sociology of Consumption," Paper presented at the 70th Annual Meeting of the American Sociological Association, San Francisco.

ECONOMIC PSYCHOLOGY

W. FRED VAN RAAIJ

Source: W. Fred van Raaij, "Economic Psychology," *Journal of Economic Psychology,* Vol. 1, No. 1, March, 1981, pp. 1–24. Reprinted by permission of author and North-Holland Publishing Co., Amsterdam.

INTRODUCTION

Economic psychology is concerned with the study of economic behavior.

Economic behavior is the behavior of consumers/citizens that involves economic decisions, and the determinants and consequences of economic decisions.

Economic decisions involve money, time, and effort to obtain products, services, work, leisure, the choice between product alternatives, spending vs. saving decisions. In fact, all decisions that involve a choice or trade-off of some alternatives or an investment that will bring future profits or benefits may be called an economic decision. Economic decisions are characterized by sacrifices to be made by the actor, an evaluation of present or future benefits of one's expenditure (spending vs. saving), an evaluation of the expected benefits of some alternatives, and a relatively concrete variable of behavior. A customary criterion for an economic decision is the monetary, temporal, or effort sacrifice, for expected present or future well-being of oneself and/or one's household.

The determinants of economic decisions include personal, cultural, situational, and general-economic factors that stimulate or inhibit economic decisions.

Personal factors are personality characteristics of the consumer (e.g., venturesomeness, cognitive style, internal control of reinforcement), life-style characteristics of the household (e.g., traditional vs. modern), and the norms and values of a society or a subculture that stimulate or inhibit certain behaviors.

Cultural and religious *values* forbid certain types of consumption, for instance alcohol consumption with Moslems or birth control devices with Roman Catholics. Norms and values may differ for subcultures, regions, and age groups.

Situational factors are the conditions and circumstances that normally constrain economic decisions within certain boundaries. Disposable income, family size, type of home, market situation determine consumption decisions; the style and color of one's furniture determine new additions to the home interior. Anticipated or unanticipated situations may change one's consumption intentions.

General-economic factors include the perceived fairness of the income distribution, the rates of inflation and interest, the degree of unemployment, the economic policy of the government. These general-economic factors generate optimistic or pessimistic attitudes and expectations with consumers, which influence the desire to spend or to save household income.

The consequences of economic decisions are the satisfactions and the well-being consumers derive from consumption. Dissatisfaction may lead to complaints with the responsible producer or institution. For many purposes, the consequences of economic decisions are employed as criterion measures of economic or consumption policy. We may distinguish the evaluative and behavioral consequences of satisfaction and well-being, and complaints and problems consumers have with products and services. The consequences of economic decisions provide some kind of learning experience for people that may influence further economic decisions.

This article will discuss the relationships between economics and psychology, a number of relevant areas within economic psychology, and areas related to economic psychology. Three models of economic behavior will be discussed. Research on economic behavior can very well be placed in the framework of the third model.

SOCIETAL PROBLEMS

Already at the beginning of this article we want to stress the relevance of economic psychology for the solution of societal problems. In the present time of rising unemployment, stagnating inflation in many countries, rising energy prices and energy shortages, air, water, and soil pollution, food problems and poverty in the third world, the behavior of consumers and citizens is of vital importance. Due to the economic circumstances we have to change our consumption habits and aspirations. We want people to save energy and other resources. The welfare state has become too expensive to main-

tain the extensive present welfare benefits. And we want to develop the third world economies.

The human factor in all these programs of economic and social change cannot be ignored. All programs involve behavioral change. Economic policy measures may change behavior but not always in the desired directions. Information extension as such may change no behavior at all. Research on how people react to altered economic conditions and to policy measures may improve the impact of economic policy. Comparative studies of the relative impacts and efficiencies to change behavior by various methods (information, prompting, feedback, reward or punishment) have already been conducted to promote energy saving among consumers.

Thus, economic measures do not always have the intended effects of the policy maker. Second, policy makers often do not know the relative efficiencies of policy measures to generate behavioral change. Third, satisfaction and well-being of citizens is of great concern, even a criterion measure for economic policy. Fourth, consumer reactions to changed economic conditions, e.g., inflation, have impacts on the continuation or discontinuation of these conditions. The proposed (third) model in this article will serve as a framework for studying the effects of economic policy and marketing policy, the perception and evaluation of economic well-being and satisfaction.

The Journal of Economic Psychology will publish research that hopefully contributes to a better solution of these economic and societal problems of the 1980's.

ECONOMICS AND PSYCHOLOGY

Katona (1963) and Simon (1963) already discuss the relationship between economics and psychology. Katona (1963) argues that psychological variables contribute to a better understanding of the behavior of economic agents. In pure economic research, only the effects of economic behavior are studied, e.g., supply-demand relationships, without considering the intervening psychological processes of evaluation, decision, and choice. Economic "laws" assume one-to-one relationships between economic variables without systematic behavior "disturbances." When economists deal with behavior they either assume that individual tastes and preferences "cancel out" against each other, or they assume a rational behavior of utility maximization, complete knowledge, and control over means. Recent approaches in behavioral economics make more realistic assumptions about economic behavior. Not utility maximization but utility optimalization (Simon 1963) and bounded rationality have become the basic concepts.

Katona (1963) further argues that not the objective economic conditions but the economic conditions as perceived by the consumer/citizen/household determine economic behavior. The perceptions and evaluations of the economic reality and the optimistic or pessimistic expectations regarding personal finances and economic developments in a country determine spending or saving of a household. Psychological variables complement the economic variables for a better description or prediction of economic behavior. For instance, the Index of Consumer Sentiment (Katona 1975), a composite score based on five survey questions about the perception and evaluation of personal finances, inflation, and general economic conditions, adds to a better prediction of consumer expenditure on automobiles and other durable goods than economic variables, such as absolute or relative income, or the price increases of durable goods, alone will do.

Simon (1963) provides a more comprehensive approach. Economics is the science that describes and predicts the behavior of "economic man." Economic people (men and women) are consumers, producers, entrepreneurs, retailers, workers, and investors. All these people make economic decisions about expenditure, expected benefits or profits, expected turnover, income, and career, and expected return on investment. Within the boundaries of their knowledge, aspirations, capacities, and abilities they try to make optimal decisions. In micro-economics, the behavior of an individual consumer or household, or a firm is studied. In normative micro-economics, advice and recommendation is provided to consumers, households, businessmen, and firms. Related to normative micro-economics are management science and operations research. Descriptive micro-economics constitutes the foundation for macro-economics. Two economic principles, rational behavior of "economic man" and perfect competition in markets, in fact eliminate, once accepted and verified, the necessity of studying individual or business behavior. Thus, these principles eliminate the necessity of studying behavior within economics. This might explain why there has been so little interaction between economists and psychologists. Traditional economics is not concerned with the behavior of people but with the "behavior" of commodities (Boulding 1956), stressing that the economist is not really interested in human behavior. Interrelations between objective economic variables are expressed in "laws" of the "behavior" of prices, interest rates, unemployment, perceived as impersonal phenomena of the economic environment (Katona 1975). Behavioral economics or economic psychology, instead, studies the behavior of people who set the prices and whose actions bring about the higher or lower interest rates, inflation rates, or unemployment.

Economic psychology comprises the motivation, perception, evaluation, and cognitive processes of consumers, entrepreneurs, citizens in their economic decisions. In economic psychology, human behavior is studied within the conditions and constraints of the perceived economic environment. Economic behavior is the function of human motives, perceptions, attitudes, expectations, and bounded by the economic conditions.

This paradigm fits very well in the Lewinian function $B = f(P,E)$, that behavior B is a function of personality variables P and environmental (economic) variables E. See Hall and Lindzey (1978: ch. 11).

Economic psychology is both part of psychology and part of economics. It is part of *psychology* in the sense that it employs psychological principles of behavior and psychological methods of measurement in survey, interview, and laboratory research.

Economic psychology is also part of *economics,* in the sense that new (behavioral) variables contribute to a better explanation and prediction of economic phenomena. Behavioral economics is largely inductive, starting from guided observations and leading to empirically determined relationships between concepts, while traditional economics tends to be largely deductive, starting from assumptions about (bounded) rationality and complete knowledge, and leading to testable deductions from the basic assumptions.

KATONA'S MODEL

Katona (1951, 1960, 1964, 1975) may be considered the founding father of psychological economics in the U.S.A. In his writings he states that psychological variables intervene between the economic stimuli and the behavioral responses. See Figure 1. E are the economic conditions and situations, such as a recession, the degree of unemployment, the rates of inflation and interest, contractual obligations of the household, discretionary income, standard of living, tax rates, public transportation modes and frequencies. E stands for the objective economic conditions and opportunities for the individual or the small group (household, management team). P are the personal characteristics, such as aspirations, expectations, internal vs. external control of reinforcement, life style. The economic conditions E and the personal characteristics P influence B, the economic behavior of the individual consumer or entrepreneur. B includes the purchase, use, and disposition of goods and services, investment and savings decisions. On the aggregate level, the behavior of consumers and entrepreneurs influences the fluctuations in and the success of an economic system. Hence, the feedback loop from B to E. For instance, consumers contribute to economic fluctuations through their spending and saving behavior. A tax increase

or a tax cut may have "perverse" consequences of consumers spending more or less, depending upon people's understanding of the situation and expectations elicited by the changed fiscal policy. The virtue of Katona's model is its basic simplicity. The economic stimuli E, in fact, do not influence the personal characteristics, but E and P do influence economic behavior B. Katona's contribution is that psychological variables obtained a place in the thinking of some economists. Katona's Index of Consumer Sentiment (Katona 1975: 92–97) contributes to the prediction of durable good expenditures in predictive time series regressions. Turning points of the index predict economic fluctuations with a time lag of 4 through 6 months.

STRÜMPEL'S MODEL

Strümpel (1972) developed a more elaborate model, as shown in Figure 2. In his model, the determinants of SW, subjective well-being, are the economic environment E and the personal characteristics P, similar to Katona's model. Subjective well-being SW comprises satisfaction with consumption, work, income, marriage, standard of living, sense of opportunities. According to this model, two divergent outcomes, societal discontent SD and economic behavior B are the consequences. Societal discontent includes dissatisfaction with the employment, prices, government policy, and the political system. Economic behavior includes spending, saving, consumer demand, occupational choice, work-leisure trade-offs, investment in education. E, P, and SW not only determine economic behavior B but also create satisfaction and dissatisfaction, and attitudes toward societal issues and problems.

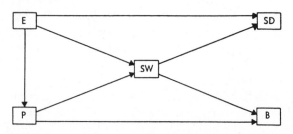

Figure 2   Strümpel's model.

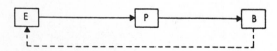

Figure 1   Katona's model.

Although Strümpel's model is richer than Katona's, some critical problems remain. Societal discontent *SD* is not only dependent upon subjective well-being *SW* but also upon economic behavior *B*. Consumers develop satisfactions, dissatisfactions, and even complaints as a consequence of their consumption activities. Another problem is that no or only a very artificial relationship can be thought of between *E* and *SD*. Which economic conditions cause societal discontent without *P* and/or *SW* as intervening variables? A third criticism is the absence of a feedback loop from *SD* and *B* to *E* and *P*. Societal discontent and economic behavior, on the aggregate level, tend to have a strong influence on people's aspirations and expectations and on their perception of the economic reality. Thus, *SD* and *B* influence the performance of the economic system. Strümpel (1974) provides an interesting application of his model in empirical research.

A NEW MODEL

A basic model for economic psychology should include economic and psychological variables; should contain feedback loops from economic behavior to economic conditions and personal aspirations; and should be as simple as possible, grouping variables with a similar function in one category. Figure 3 gives the basic new model, comparable with the model in Van Raaij (1979).

The economic environment *E* of personal finances, market conditions, type of employment, source of income, is influenced by the general environment *GE* of recession or upswing, economic policy of the government, ecological conditions of pollution, war and peace, structural violence. *E/P* is the economic environment as perceived by consumers and entrepreneurs. *E/P* includes business climate, market conditions, expected price developments, perceived opportunity structure, perception of fair income distribution, perceived position of reference groups. Not so much *E* but *E/P* tends to influence economic behavior *B*. The relationship between *E* and *E/P* is a relationship of personal experience, social and mass communication. The objective economic environment is only partly

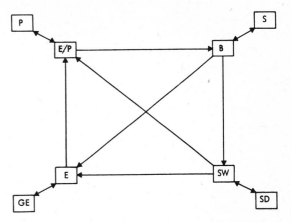

Figure 3 A new model of economic-psychological relationships.

experienced by consumers and entrepreneurs themselves. Consumers experience retail price increases as a sign of inflation. Businesspeople find interest rates acceptable or not for investment credit. Social communication among consumers or among entrepreneurs may influence one's perception of the economic environment. Persons influence each other in determining what are acceptable rates of inflation, interest, unemployment, pollution, and what are acceptable energy prices. From mass communication, as a third factor, people learn facts and evaluations of the economic environment. Newspapers, magazines, radio, and television may even "create" the issues, according to the agenda-setting theory of McCombs and Shaw (1972). Most people only get information about economic events through the mass media. The mass media tend to ignore some and to give disproportionate attention to other economic events thereby "creating" the economic and political issues.

E/P is influenced by the personal factors *P*: goals, values, aspirations, expectations, internal vs. external control of reinforcement, cognitive style, information processing abilities, interest in political and economic affairs. Sociodemographic correlates such as family composition, education, age, occupation may have impact on *E/P*.

The perceived economic environment *E/P* influences economic behavior *B*. The relationship between E/P and B resembles the "effect hierarchies" (Palda 1966). Effect hierarchies postulate a sequence perception-evaluation-behavior, or belief-attitude-intention, or attention-interest-desire-action (AIDA). Engel et al. (1978) give the sequence exposure-attention-comprehension-retention-behavior in their model of consumer behavior. Howard and Sheth (1969) use the sequence attention-comprehension-attitude-intention-purchase. In all of these hierarchies, perceived information from the environment is evaluated (attitude); comprehended and evaluated information leads to behavioral intentions to purchase or to save. In low involvement situations, the sequence may seem to be the reverse. Attitude change comes after the behavior. However, some knowledge and evaluation of the environment is always present before the behavior, while also after the behavior further attitude change and acquisition of knowledge (experience) may take place.

Behavioral intentions lead to behavior, if no anticipated or unanticipated situations S arise and prevent the realization of the behavioral intentions. These situations may be emergencies, accidents, illness, a bank refusing credit, sudden unemployment, marriage, birth of a child. The longer the time lag between behavioral intention and actual behavior, the higher the probability of situational interventions. Economic behavior is also influenced by anticipated situations: a party, a weekend trip, being with your partner. Consumers tend to differentiate their product selection according to anticipated usage situations (Belk 1975).

Subjective well-being SW is the consequence of economic behavior B. Subjective well-being includes the satisfactions and dissatisfactions with the purchase, consumer complaints to the retailer or the producer, and consumer problems with the product or service. After-purchase processes such as learning and reduction of cognitive dissonance contribute to the degree of subjective well-being. External effects of consumption (pollution, noise, other persons' envy) may decrease the subjective well-being of non-consumers. Recreational activities may increase the subjective well-being of the participants, while at the same time they decrease the subjective well-being of the neighboring nonparticipants.

Subjective well-being SW may be defined as the discrepancy between expected and actual performance of a product or a service, or the discrepancy between the expected and actual benefits of an economic decision. The subjective well-being will be lower, if prior expectations were too high or actual performance proved to be too low. Advertising may create too high and irrealistic expectations about product performance, and this may cause dissatisfaction with consumers. Subjective well-being SW is related to societal discontent SD. Consumer satisfaction, along with work and marriage satisfaction, good health, will influence one's general happiness or satisfaction with societal structures and the economic system (capitalism, socialism, communism). Societal discontent, on the other hand, may influence subjective well-being. Persons with a basic discontent or mistrust will probably derive less satisfaction from consumption and other economic decisions.

Subjective well-being SW has impacts on the economic environment E. This closes the cycle of Figure 3. Marketeers study consumer satisfactions and complaints in order to provide better and more competitive products and services. Government policy makers study the well-being of the citizens in order to provide better public programs. Subjective well-being also has impacts on the perceived economic conditions E/P. After experiencing the performance of a product or the quality of a service, consumers may change their perceptions; learning effects are the changes in the belief structure of E/P and the revisions of opinion and attitude.

Note that economic behavior B may have a direct influence on the economic environment E. Spending or saving behavior of consumers or entrepreneurs directly influences economic fluctuations. Consumer preferences and purchases of certain brands directly influence the market share of these brands. However, B and SW together influence repeat purchase of a brand or repeat visits of a store, thus brand or store loyalty.

The main advantage of the new model is its dynamic and cyclical character. The four groups of variables, *E, E/P, B,* and *SW,* are independent variables in one research design and dependent variables in another research design. Most studies in economic psychology involve at least two groups of variables, one group of variables explaining one or more variables of the "following" group. A number of possible research designs emerge:

(1) $E \rightarrow E/P$ Studies how people perceive economic realities; mass communication and agenda-setting studies; the money illusion.

(2) $E/P \rightarrow B$ Studies about perceptions, attitudes, as related to behavior; hierarchy of effect studies.

(3) $B \rightarrow SW$ Studies on consumer satisfaction and complaints, well-being and welfare.

(4) $B \rightarrow E$ Economic research on demand and supply of goods and services.

(5) $SW \rightarrow E$ Studies on the design and development of products, services, and programs based on consumer/participant's satisfactions and experiences; program evaluation studies.

(6) $SW \rightarrow E/P$ Studies how confirmed and disconfirmed expectations change consumer perceptions of the market and products.

(7) $GE \rightarrow E$ Economic studies of the correspondence of general economic conditions and personal finances and opportunities of the household.

(8) $P \rightarrow E/P$ Studies on the effects of personality, cognitive style, and life style on the perception and categorization of economic reality.

(9) $S \rightarrow B$ Studies on situational influences on economic behavior.

(10) $SD \rightarrow SW$ Studies on the correspondence of consumption, economic satisfaction with life, work, and marriage satisfaction.

ORGANIZATIONAL ECONOMIC BEHAVIOR

Compared with consumer economic behavior, organizational economic behavior is a relatively unknown area of economic psychology, although there is a vast amount of research and knowledge. Simon (1963) was one of the first to include "producer behavior" in economic psychology. Managers, entrepreneurs, and business executives control the decision variables in the firm. They decide on make-buy-or-lease, investments, and set goals for short-term and long-term profits. Both economic (financial) and non-economic (power, prestige) motivations direct their behavior. The traditional assumption of profit maximization is now replaced by a satisficing criterion. The firm will take a viable course of action to satisfy the various stakeholder groups: workers, consumers, suppliers, competitors, neighbors, government. Contributions from psychology provide essential clarification of business decision making and entrepreneurial motivation.

Sheth (1977) provides an overview of organizational buyer behavior. He mentions the following reasons why organizational buyer behavior is less well-known than consumer buyer behavior. (1) Most research in organizational buyer behavior has been practice-oriented, and (2) has been scattered across several disciplines such as management science, organizational psychology, political science, and business areas such as production, finance, marketing, personnel management. (3) It is easier for researchers to experience the role of a consumer than a manager's role within an organization. (4) More new approaches and techniques are applied in the study of consumer behavior because consumer behavior is considered to be more complex and irrational than entrepreneur behavior. The latter is not true, especially not for the independent owner-manager of a small firm.

The model of Figure 3 is also applicable to organizational economic behavior. The economic environment E is the environment of the firm or the environment of the department, division, or profit center within the firm, including the type and size of the organization. Organizational climate and style, the role of purchasing within the firm, lateral and vertical involvement, perceptions of one's own role and position within the organization belong to the group of E/P variables. The P correlates pertain to the factors already mentioned and choice criteria, learning, loyalty, and risk perception. The situational correlates S are failures of delivery, strikes, legal-political considerations, and governmental protection measures. Organizational economic behavior B includes the decisions to make, buy, or lease products or components, the choice of facilities, suppliers, distribution channels, the commercialization of new product types, and entering a new market.

Aspects of subjective well-being SW in an organizational context are sometimes called the non-economic motivations of the manager or entrepreneur: power, prestige, and status. Business executives tend to identify themselves very much with their organization, and, consequently, derive subjective well-being from the successes of their company.

Related Disciplines

1. Relationship to organizational psychology.
Organizational psychology is in fact part of economic psychology, as far as workers and managers in an organization make economic decisions about career, work load, promotions, overtime work. However, the separate research tradition of organizational psychology is much older than economic psychology. Research interests and publication outlets of organizational psychology center around worker motivation and satisfaction, the impact of the organizational structure, equity of pay distributions. The model of Figure 3 also applies to

organizational psychology, where E represents the formal organization. P represents employee motivations, personality, goals, and aspirations. B represents employee behavior, while S represents situational constraints and opportunities. SW stands for job satisfaction and employee well-being.

While economic psychology is generally not concerned with research on employee motivation and satisfaction, interesting relationships and parallels exist between organizational and economic psychology. Economic psychology is concerned with the expenditure or saving of income and only partly with the earning of income. Economic psychology is concerned with economic behavior outside the organizational and labor conditions. However, when persons have discretion over the number of hours they work and, hence, their income, and when consumption aspirations and obligations determine one's income, instead of income determining one's consumption, interesting perspectives for economic psychologists emerge. Similarly, when pay increases are seen in relation to inflation rates and other economic conditions, the study of income and inflation becomes part of economic psychology.

2. Relationship with marketing research.
Marketing research studies consumer reactions to marketing mix variables from the producer's viewpoint. The producer's goal is an increase in market share and the fulfillment of consumer needs and wants at a profit. Marketing research is mainly directed toward the specific (brand or type) choice, while economic psychologists are more interested in spending vs. saving, immediate or delayed consumption, and the effects of the economic environment on economic decisions. Van Raaij (1978) presents some differences between marketing research and economic psychology:

1. Marketing research derives its meaning and objectives from marketing. Economic psychology is an autonomous science, directed toward the antecedents and consequences of economic behavior, and the processes and mechanisms underlying economic decisions.
2. Marketing research has a limited interest in consumer behavior, only as far as the relevant

product or service is concerned, and often only the purchase stage of it. Economic psychologists have a broader scope: the total consumption cycle of prepurchase-purchase-use-disposition, and the satisfactions and self-actualization people derive from consuming goods and services.

3. Marketing information and knowledge about the consumer is used to influence that behavior by advertising and promotion. Economic psychology studies consumer behavior as a part of economic behavior from the objective of scientific knowledge and consumer policy (governmental agencies, consumer organizations).

4. Economic psychologists are more interested in the total expenditure in a market than in specific choice of brands and types. Typically for economic psychology is the development of consumer indexes to describe and to predict economic fluctuations in the sales of consumer durable goods.

Marketing research and economic psychology have a number of common interests and research techniques, and may very well contribute to each other's development. The wider scope of economic psychology may provide better insights into the dynamics of consumer demand. Marketing research with a broader scope on consumer behavior (see Arndt 1976) is compatible with the interests of economic psychologists.

3. Research on the adoption of innovations.
The study of the adoption of innovations is related to economic psychology. The model of Rogers and Shoemaker (1971) can be transformed into the model of Figure 3. The economic environment E includes the norms and values of the community regarding change, innovation, and modernization; the tolerance of deviancy; and the communication network among people and between people and mass communication sources. E/P is not only the perception of E by the prospective innovator or non-innovator but also the perceived characteristics of the innovation (relative advantage, compatibility, complexity, trialability, observability, availability). Both the E/P factors and person factors P determine the adoption of an innovation. The person factors P are the personality characteristics (venturesomeness, dogmatism, cosmopolitism), the position in the social network of communication, the perceived need for and the perceived risk of the innovation. The adoption or non-adoption of the innovation is the criterion variable in adoption of innovation research (B). Situational influences S may inhibit the adoption of an innovation, such as lack of money or unavailability of the innovation. Subjective well-being SW of the innovator depends on the relative advantage of the innovation over existing products or procedures, the approval by relevant others of the innovation, and the confirmed expectation with regard to the innovation. The approval of relevant others provides a legitimation of the adoption. Even mass communication sources may provide legitimation of one's adoption. Users of a product tend to read more advertising of that product than of other products. SW factors determine the continued adoption of an innovation.

What are the roles of mass communication in the innovation-adoption process? Mass communication performs three functions in the process: (1) to increase awareness of the innovation, (2) to inform people of the advantages/disadvantages of the innovation, and (3) legitimize the adoption or non-adoption decision. The first and second function operate in the E/P block; the third function in the SW block of variables. Persuasion, in the Rogers and Shoemaker model, refers to the formation of favorable attitudes toward the innovation. In the model of Figure 3 this occurs between E/P and B, although advertising may create biased perceptions of the innovation in E/P.

Adoption of an innovation by an individual consumer or household is only part of the diffusion of an innovation in a social structure. Diffusion theory stresses the social network and the influence of (outside) mass communication sources. Essential are the connections in the social network, through which the diffusion process trickles over time.

4. Sociological concepts. Nicosia and Mayer (1976) have written one of the few contributions of sociology to the study of consumer behavior. They note an overemphasis on individual choice processes, and, consequently, less emphasis on the structural and societal context in which consumers operate. Cultural values are of crucial importance. The traditional values of freedom of choice and success through individual achievement tend to inhibit solidarity between persons, groups, and countries. These values also tend to oppose programs to inform consumers about impending depletion of resources and energy. Do younger generations adhere to less materialistic values? And can we rechannel young people's aspirations and expectations into a non-materialistic direction, instead of frustrating legitimate aspirations of a new generation? (Katona 1975: ch. 25.)

Culture, sub-culture, and social class are also sociological concepts in economic behavior. While the importance of social class for consumption behavior may decrease, subcultures increase in importance. A growing awareness of ethnic background ("roots"), regional, racial, and sexual differences ("liberation") create a rising number of minorities with their own life-style, consumption habits, work and leisure preferences. The most likely future of the advanced industrial societies will be one of *fragmentation*.

The changes in values and life style may create even a third system of production, next to the market (commercial) and planning (collective) system (Galbraith 1973): the household production system. The household or community production system is a non-market form of self-organization to produce vegetables, groceries, children toys, books, energy, and to trade second-hand furniture, clothing, and household utensils.

5. The household production function.

Becker advocates a reformulation of the economic theory of consumer behavior, based on the household production function (Becker 1965; Michael and Becker 1973). In this approach, the household, consisting of one individual to many members, is a production unit, combining purchased market goods and services with inputs from house-

hold members in the form of added value or transformations. A familiar example is the preparation of a dinner, combining purchased meat, vegetables, potatoes, and spices with preparation efforts, time, and energy. Homegrown potatoes and vegetables may be used instead, even increasing the contribution of household production. The household, in this perspective, becomes a small production unit employing capital (household income), raw or prepared materials (food, clothing, detergents), production means (house, household appliances), labor (time and effort of household members and servants) in order to create commodities and benefits for the household members. Or, to say it in another way, to create subjective well-being *SW* for the household members and their guests. A bed, bedroom, time, absence from noise, and (sometimes) sleeping-pills produce the benefits of a sound sleep.

Household production are the unpaid activities carried on by and for household members but which could be replaced by market goods and services. The home-cooked dinner can be replaced by the restaurant dinner. Interesting hypotheses emerge on the trade-offs between time and money. High-income households with high opportunity costs of time are more likely to hire servants. Low-income households with low opportunity costs of time may stretch their income by performing many household tasks themselves, e.g., home improvement and car repair.

Similar to the firm in standard production theory, the household invests in capital assets (savings), capital equipment (durable goods), and human capital (skills and education of the household members). The household decides on family labor supply, time, expenditures on raw materials and services, on family size, marriage, and labor force attachment. Time is a scarce resource in the households. Time-saving equipment is bought to reduce the time spent on household chores (at least for high-income households). On the other hand, the satisfaction of many goods and services depends on the amount of time with which they are consumed (e.g., sports, a fancy dinner, making love).

SUMMARY AND CONCLUSIONS

Economic psychology is concerned with the study of economic behavior, its antecedents and consequences. Economic behavior comprises consumer behavior, employment behavior, fiscal behavior, and the reactions of consumers/citizens to economic conditions. Economic psychology has a micro and a macro aspect. The micro aspects pertain to individual economic behavior including consumer behavior; the macro aspects include aggregate indexes of consumer sentiment, attitudes, and expectations.

A new model is proposed to describe economic behavior. The (perceived) economic environment determines the individual's economic behavior with subjective well-being as its consequence. The results of economic behavior and subjective well-being feed back to the objective and perceived economic environment (Figure 3).

The new model can very well be applied to organizational economic behavior, marketing research with a broader scope, the adoption of innovations, and the theory of the household production function.

Economic psychology or behavioral economics emphasizes the human factor in economic research. Economics, then, becomes a social science richer in its explanation of economic phenomena than the study of the "behavior of commodities." Hopefully, economic psychology contributes to elucidate much of the unpredictability of the human "disturbances" in economic predictions.

REFERENCES

Arndt, J., 1976. 'Reflections on research in consumer behavior.' In: B. B. Anderson (ed.), Advances in consumer research, Vol. 3. Atlanta: Association for Consumer Research.

Becker, G. S., 1965. A theory of the allocation of time. Economic Journal 75, 493–517.

Belk, R. W., 1975. Situation variables and consumer behavior. Journal of Consumer Research 2, 157–164.

Boulding, K. E., 1956. The image. Ann Arbor, MI: University of Michigan Press.

Engel, J. F., R. D. Blackwell and D. T. Kollat, 1978. Consumer behavior. (3rd ed.) Hinsdale, IL: The Dryden Press.

Galbraith, J. K., 1973. Economics and the public purpose. Boston, MA: Houghton Mifflin.

Hall, C. S. and G. Lindzey, 1978. Theories of personality. (3rd ed.) New York: Wiley.

Howard, J. and J. N. Sheth, 1969. The theory of buyer behavior. New York: Wiley.

Katona, G., 1951. Psychological analysis of economic behavior. New York: McGraw-Hill.

Katona, G., 1960. The powerful consumer. New York: McGraw-Hill.

Katona, G., 1963. 'The relationship between psychology and economics.' In: S. Koch (ed.), Psychology: a study of a science. New York: McGraw-Hill.

Katona, G., 1964. The mass consumption society. New York: McGraw-Hill.

Katona, G., 1975. Psychological economics. New York: Elsevier.

Lea, S. E. G., 1978. The psychology and economics of demand. Psychological Bulletin 85, 441–466.

McCombs, M. E. and D. L. Shaw, 1972. The agenda-setting function of mass media. Public Opinion Quarterly 36, 176–187.

Michael, R. T. and G. S. Becker, 1973. On the new theory of consumer behavior. Swedish Journal of Economics 75, 378–396.

Nicosia, F. M. and R. N. Mayer, 1976. Toward a sociology of consumption. Journal of Consumer Research 3, 65–75.

Palda, K. S., 1966. The hypothesis of a hierarchy of effects: a partial evaluation. Journal of Marketing Research 3, 13–24.

Van Raaij, W. F., 1978. 'Economic psychology and marketing.' In: G. Fisk, J. Arndt and K. Grønhaug (eds.), Future directions for marketing. Cambridge, MA: Marketing Science Institute.

Van Raaij, W. F., 1979. 'European consumer research: frontier issues.' In: W. L. Wilkie (ed.), Advances in consumer research, Vol. 6. Atlanta, GA: Association for Consumer Research.

Rogers, E. M. and F. F. Shoemaker, 1971. Communication of innovations. A cross-cultural approach. New York: The Free Press.

Sheth, J. N., 1977. 'Recent developments in organizational buying behavior. In: A. G. Woodside, J. N.

Sheth and P. D. Bennett (eds.), Consumer and industrial buying behavior. New York: North-Holland.

Simon, H. A., 1963. 'Economics and psychology.' In: S. Koch (ed.), Psychology: a study of a science. New York: McGraw-Hill.

Strümpel, B., 1972. 'Economic behavior and economic welfare. Models and interdisciplinary approaches.' In: B. Strümpel, J. N. Morgan and E. Zahn (eds.), Human behavior in economic affairs. Amsterdam: Elsevier.

Strümpel, B., 1974. 'Economic well-being as an object of social measurement.' In: B. Strümpel (ed.), Subjective elements of well-being. Paris: OECD.

SECTION II

SOCIETAL BASES OF CONSUMER BEHAVIOR

Consumers live in large social systems. Examples of large social systems include cultural groups such as Polish, Chinese, or Jewish cultural groups living in the United States; nations such as Sweden, Germany, or Colombia; particular social classes; or a city or town. Cultural groups may influence food preferences; a nation, through its regulatory system and system of services, may influence the price of imported goods and the cost and availability of medical services; a social class may influence the socialization process of a child, what this child's attitudes are toward spending, and the child's aspiration for owning particular products; a city or town may influence whether shoppers will find stores open on Sundays or are able to purchase alcoholic beverages in that community.

The reader will realize that consumers live in, and thus are influenced by, many different large-scale social systems simultaneously. Each of these social systems influences consumer behavior in different ways. A town may influence whether or not adult education classes on consumerism are available, whether through its zoning laws a particular home improvement will be allowed, and whether a particular type of business will be allowed to locate in an area near where many consumers live. A town council may also influence the type of recreational and entertainment facilities available, e.g., whether a theater will be permitted to show "X" rated films.

The influences of culture and social class on consumers are much more familiar to the reader than the effects of a nation or community and are the areas where most consumer studies concerned with large-scale social systems have focused. This is reflected by articles in this section. Before introducing these articles a few observations should be made:

1. The impact of large-scale social systems on consumer behavior is vast. The impact of such systems as culture, class, nation and community may, collectively, be the single most important force influencing consumer behavior. In every respect these systems shape not only what institutions exist but also the very way in which their members perceive the world.

2. Despite the vastness of this influence few studies exist that describe and explain this influence, with the exception of those studies pertaining to social class. One reason for this is that the influence process is difficult to study. It is difficult to separate the influence of a culture from the influence of other social systems. It is especially difficult to separate the influence of several cultures from each other when a consumer participates in or is touched by more than one of them.

3. Understanding social-system influences on consumers is especially important for marketers whose products are distributed broadly, e.g., to different countries or to different regions of a given country. Social systems represent one of the first bases for segmenting markets because they are the most general dimension along which groups of people are differentiated from each other.

4. Public policymakers and consumer educators should realize that their regulatory efforts and educational programs apply to diverse groups. This is often not considered in designing an educational program or in formulating a trade regulation. Instead, the audience or market for these programs is frequently assumed to be homogeneous.

"INTERPRETING CONSUMER MYTHOLOGY: A STRUCTURAL APPROACH TO CONSUMER BEHAVIOR"

In "Interpreting Consumer Mythology," Levy suggests that many products, such as food items, are used in a symbolic way. That is, individuals, families and larger groups use products to describe the particular identities they hold, the values they have, the norms under which they operate, the items they prefer, and the fundamental characteristics that underlie their sociocultural world.

The fact that products are used symbolically suggests some important implications for marketers. Marketers must be sensitive to the ways products are used, the meanings they have, and the ways in which they are incorporated into people's lives. This sensitivity is the key to proper product placement.

How can the meaning of products in consumers' lives be discovered? One method is to conduct a survey to see how many people use a particular product. However, while the information gathered in this manner may be informative, it may tell us little about *why* or *how* this product is important.

Levy suggests that one way of ascertaining such meaning is by attending to the verbal descriptions individuals give of their uses of the product, the situations in which it is used, and how it is used. This qualitative analysis of verbal material is seen as a type of storytelling. The stories are little myths, the symbolic vocabulary that describes how people use products to express their identities. They are a way of organizing perceptions of reality and indirectly expressing people's concerns.

Looking at a sample of families' little myths, Levy finds several myths regarding family food consumption. In the area of food preparation, the laborious efforts of a mother to cook balanced, nourishing meals is symbolic of her warmth, nurturance, and concern for the family. Eating at a gourmet restaurant is symbolic of high status. Eating low calorie foods and engaging in a rigorous exercise program symbolizes identification with the "healthy" crowd. Even the place of dining is symbolic. Eating outside implies freedom from traditional manners and involves less traditional (primitive) methods of cooking.

Levy's central points can be summarized as follows:

1. We incorporate products into our lives and use them in a symbolic way to communicate our broader notions of self, family, and culture.
2. Placing products properly within the interacting social systems requires attention to the symbolic meaning individuals and groups ascribe to these products.
3. Meanings can be ascertained by examining the symbolic vocabulary—the little myths—people use in describing their ways of living, their concerns, and their perceptions of reality.

"CAMPBELL SOUP FAILS TO MAKE IT TO THE TABLE"

Levy's notion of little myths and symbolic consumption surrounding food products is exemplified in the *Business Week* article concerning Campbell Soup. Campbell's products entered the Brazilian market, hoping to capture a large market in that country. However, despite ambitious marketing attempts, the "convenience products" failed to catch on. To some extent, this failure can be attributed to marketers' misunderstanding of the cultural importance regarding food preparation among Brazilian homemakers.

Homemakers were averse to the idea of serving soup they could not call their own, and the products were used primarily as a last resort in "emergency" situations.

As noted earlier, cultural systems can have a pervasive influence on many behaviors, including food preferences. Special attention to these influences is an important aspect of successful product placement.

"AMERICAN JEWISH ETHNICITY: ITS RELATIONSHIP TO SOME SELECTED ASPECTS OF CONSUMER BEHAVIOR"

Elizabeth Hirschman's paper studies the effects of cultural influence on consumer behavior. Hirschman's work is important in several respects. First, it is one of the first marketing studies to suggest ethnic influences beyond those associated with black culture. Second, the author has gone beyond categorization of individuals into ethnic groups by elaborating why and how identification with Jewish ethnicity may lead to differences in consumer behavior. Third, a measure of perceived identification based on the researcher's assignment is used to classify individuals into ethnic categories.

It is hypothesized that ethnic, religious, and developmental experiences among Jewish consumers are different than those for other groups of consumers, and that these differences will show up in such experiences or behaviors as greater childhood information exposure; more adult information seeking; a greater incidence of innovativeness, transfer of information concerning products, and divergent thinking; and a greater capacity for activating consumption information. Two age samples (cohorts), one of college students and another of adults, were employed as respondents.

Consistent with the hypotheses, the results suggest that consumers who identify with the Jewish ethnic and religious tradition are more likely to adopt new products and to transmit information about new products to others. These findings suggest the potential for a faster product life cycle, and less brand and store loyalty. It is also possible that ethnic identification influences consumer competence and ability to arrive at informed decisions.

Although it has traditionally been regarded as a variable for categorizing people, ethnicity, as Hirschman suggests, may have an important causal impact on consumption.

"WIFE'S OCCUPATIONAL STATUS AS A CONSUMER BEHAVIOR CONSTRUCT"

As more and more women enter the labor force, marketers have become increasingly interested in the possible impact of the wife's occupational status on consumer behavior. One's occupation can have a great impact on one's life-style. For example, a high paying job might result in more disposable income and hence allow one to spend money more freely. At the same time, however, a high paying job might require greater time commitments, thus reducing time available for other activities (e.g., helping around the house, meal preparation, vacations). Finally, jobs may pose certain consumer problems such as need for transportation and clothing.

Schaninger and Allen use a three category typology to classify the wife's occupational status: nonworking (NWW), low-occupational status (LSW), and high-occupational status (HSW). Classification of wives into these categories is made on the basis of a widely employed measure of social position, the Hollingshead Index. Schaninger and Allen begin with the assumption that occupational status may affect time pressures, work-related stress, work-related consumption requirements, and family size, and that these differences in occupational-related activities will also lead to differences in consumption patterns. More specifically, they hypothesize differences between the three groups of wives on the use of convenience foods, types of alcohol purchased, amount of TV viewing, number of cars, number of labor saving appliances, and the amount of money spent on clothing and makeup.

Some support for their hypotheses was found. LSW tended to buy more convenience foods, use more makeup, watch more TV, and own more color TVs. HSW tended to buy more imported wine, pay less attention to shopping specials, buy more expensive clothing, and own new, smaller cars.

While reading, keep in mind that there are many possible ways of defining occupational status. The Hollingshead Index is a widely employed measure; however, its popularity does not necessarily guarantee its precision. Also, it is important to ask why some of the observed effects may have occurred. Why is it the case that LSW use more convenience foods? Presumably time pressure is a consideration; however HSW are also under time pressure, yet they do not seem to use convenience foods as much. Why is it that LSW use more makeup, buy domestic wine, and watch more TV? Are there variables other than occupational status taken alone that would explain these effects?

"AN EXPECTATIONAL VIEW OF CONSUMER SPENDING PROSPECTS"

One important aspect of the societal bases of consumer behavior is the way in which economic conditions (e.g., income, inflation) affect consumption (e.g., purchase of durable goods). Generally, this relationship can be inferred through the use of sophisticated statistical techniques using large scale economic data. Often the aim of these analyses is to identify trends in spending patterns. While economic data contribute substantially to the prediction of consumer behaviors, Juster proposes that subjective variables such as consumer plans, attitudes, and expectations may be of added predictive value. He notes that while consumers react behaviorally to economic conditions (e.g., by saving money during inflationary times), they also react subjectively by forming expectations, plans, and attitudes. These subjective estimates can indirectly influence economic conditions by affecting consumer behavior. A recent historical economic trend makes Juster's hypothesis most relevant.

When inflation is high, consumers in the past have reacted by cutting back on spending and waiting for more economically favorable times. However, in the mid 1970s an opposite trend was found. Despite rising inflation, consumers were buying more. Why? Juster believes one reason is tied to the expectations consumers had of the future. Beliefs that prices would only get worse, that inflation would lead to deteriorating business conditions, and that the government would be unable to deal with these conditions became dominant. Juster proposes that these subjective beliefs (expectations, attitudes) probably had an impact on buying behavior. As such, they should be included in economic forecasting models.

Juster indeed found that expectational variables were useful in predicting spending rates. In car sales, some support for his hypotheses was also found. Analyses that contained the expectational variables were better at predicting actual spending rates than were those that excluded them. One other interesting finding was that individuals were more likely to let their own subjective expectations guide their behavior rather than rely on data provided by professional forecasters. This finding casts some doubt on the notion that consumers make choices based on "rational" decisions; that is, that they make decisions based on the best available information.

As economic conditions change, so do consumer expectations, plans, and attitudes. While some economic conditions may lead consumers to save at one point in time, the very same conditions in a different time period may lead to a different behavior. This would be due to differences in consumer expectations. Clearly perceptions of future economic conditions and perceptions of government's ability to deal with these conditions can influence consumer behavior. Attempts to predict the future behavior of consumers must be sensitive to the dynamic relationship between consumer expectations, economic conditions, and consumer behavior.

INTERPRETING CONSUMER MYTHOLOGY: A STRUCTURAL APPROACH TO CONSUMER BEHAVIOR

SIDNEY J. LEVY

. . . The goal of this paper is to explore and illustrate the idea that verbal materials elicited from people in the marketplace are a form of storytelling that can be analyzed as projective. The responses of a consumer telling about the purchase and use of products may be approached from varied viewpoints. Here, the remarks (the protocol) are taken as a literary production we might interpret in ways comparable to those of clinical psychologists, social anthropologists, and literary critics. A recent view of anthropological concepts (Levy 1978) especially stimulated the attempt to use the Lévi-Strauss structuralist approach by likening consumers' household anecdotes to the myths that he has mined so richly.

In open-ended interviewing about the consumption of products, respondents are often asked to describe the product features the family members prefer, to characterize family consumption patterns, to tell about recent instances of using the product, and to explain how and why given products are used. The results of such interviews are commonly reported in a somewhat literal manner, in tabulations of use frequencies, in lists of features cited, in verbal summaries that most people said this or that, or even in lists of verbatim comments without additional comments by the researchers. Ordinarily, the goals are to learn facts of usage and reasons given for and against the product.

Such handling of the data often seems barren and frustrating because it is not sufficiently penetrating, does not tell enough about the meaning of the product in relation to the lives of the users, and its place among other products. The approach suggested here is to avoid accepting the responses as if they are scientific observations to be tabulated as measures. Rather, the assumption is that the products are used symbolically, and that the telling about their uses is a way of symbolizing the life and nature of the family. . . .

. . .

MODES OF ANALYSIS

. . . Projective techniques as research and clinical tools explore the ways people transform and externalize their experience in some narrative form, as a

Source: Sidney J. Levy, "Interpreting Consumer Mythology: A Structural Approach to Consumer Behavior," Journal of Marketing, Vol. 45, Summer, 1981, 49–61. Adapted from the Journal of Marketing, published by the American Marketing Association.

general phenomenon and specifically in response to given materials, in accordance with David Rapaport's formulation of the projective hypothesis, as follows.

> All behavioral manifestations of the human being, including the least and the most significant, are revealing and expressive of his personality, by which we mean that individual principle of which he is the carrier. This formulation of the projective hypothesis implies a specific definition of the term "behavior," which includes all of the following aspects: (a) behavior historically viewed in the life-history; (b) behavior statically viewed as reflected in the environment with which the subject surrounds himself, as the furniture of his house, the clothes he wears, etc.; expressive movements; (d) internal behavior, including percepts, fantasies, thoughts. (Rapaport 1942, p. 213.)

Characteristically, interpretation of projective techniques follows two paths. (1) Specific components of the story (test protocol) are tabulated and used systematically to evaluate either an individual's responses or the empirical validity of generalizations about groups. . . . However, counting popular responses or the length of stories to establish norms for population groups in a purely empirical manner is relatively superficial, compared, say, to having a theory about conformity, rigidity, deviance, and the meanings of the specific perceptions. (2) Qualitative analysis accepts introspection as data and looks for subjective meanings, thus facing the necessity for interpretation. It is phenomenological and interested in symbolic interactionism, trying to see what lies behind or is meant by the manifest behavior. This viewpoint considers social events to be unlike events in the natural sciences. The social events are selected and attended to because of their significance to the people involved, and thus are psychological events in social contexts.

By the logic of the projective hypothesis and the definition of human events as symbolic, interpretation becomes a process of searching for meaning, that is, finding out how mental phenomena—such inner representations of experiences as ideas, imagery, and consumption fantasies as forms of storytelling to the self—are related to interactions with other people and the physical world.

Leslie Stephen wrote that people's doctrines do not become operative in behavior until they have generated an imaginative symbolism. We make distinctions among these imaginative symbolisms by classifying types of narratives. One kind of tale commonly told within a social group is the myth. Formal interpretation of myths is concerned with classifying and explaining grand myths—those tales of the gods, beasts, and heroes that are about the creation of the world, human birth and death, taking form as accounts of floods, supernatural creatures, matings of gods and mortals, heroic family romances, saviors and seers, and cataclysmic physical events. The aim is to demonstrate the similarities and differences among cultures of their grand myths, the sources of the myths, and to explicate the realities to which the mythological symbols referred (Frazer 1927).

· · ·

The fundamental character of a myth points to its universal mode of thought, the way it transcends local culture. As Lévi-Strauss says, "its substance does not lie in its style, its original music, or its syntax, but in the story which it tells" (Lévi-Strauss, 1963, p. 210). When one takes the many versions of the myth (for example, the stories of Oedipus, including the Homeric, Sophoclean, and Freudian), a structural analysis takes account of all the variants, to arrive at the structural law of the myth. That is, what is it really about? The analysis reaches the concusion that the myth struggles with the contradiction between the idea that human beings originate autochthonously and the idea that they are born of the union of man and woman—out of one or out of two.

· · ·

If we take the idea that myths are ways of organizing perceptions of realities, of indirectly expressing paradoxical human concerns, they have consumer relevance because these realities and concerns affect people's daily lives. The issues of male/female, nature/culture, and high/low, for example, are not reserved to story-telling occasions about kings and shepherdesses but are also being acted out in everyday behavior. Some marketing study approaches the same generalized, universal level as the grand myths. In his dissertation on *The Social Construction of Consumption Patterns,* Firat wrestles with the paradox of poor and disadvantaged consumers establishing irrational consumption patterns in cars and expensive foods. He seeks to show how society induces patterns that express such fundamental structural antinomies in consumption as individual/collective, private/public, and passive/active. At this level of analysis, individual choice behavior is almost irrelevant, being interpreted as a manifestation of conformity to the culture's dominant consumption pattern (Firat 1978). In another universal vein, the work of Daniel B. Williams (1976) examines individual consumer purchasing behavior, interpreting the decision making process to a highly generalized level. In analyzing the problem spaces or mediums for problem solving used by the individual purchase problem solver, Williams identifies such space attributes as within the organism/outside the organism, fast/slow, high/low, and phenomenal/transphenomenal.

The idea of taking the consumer protocol as a kind of story to be interpreted draws from various traditions. Robert P. Abelson, for instance, discusses the concept of cognitive script, defining script as "a coherent sequence of events expected by the individual, involving him either as a participant or as an observer" (Abelson 1976, p. 33). Scripts are formed by the linking of chains of vignettes, the latter being "the raw constituents of remembered episodes in the individual's experience." He insists on this holism and criticizes the "elementaristic, stilted, and static" positions common among cognitive and social psychologists, and stresses the way vignettes are "coherently linked." Vignettes in the consumer's script correspond to the mythemes Lévi-Strauss observes in myths, where he similarly insists on the necessity for analysis of clusters or bundles of mythemes. As with scripts, myths may be dealt with particularistically as factual descriptions of recalled events, as traditional marketing research questionnaires typically do; or as revealing basic universal human structures, as Lévi-Strauss seeks to do. In between, we may seek to interpret sufficiently to get below the surface, and concretely enough to apply the ideas to consumer events.

The Present Study

To gather scripts, vignettes, or mythemes as an illustrative instance for this paper, a sample of six consumers was interviewed at length about the various family members, their individual characteristics, and especially their attitudes and behavior in relation to food. The respondents are married, middle-class housewives with young children living at home. Each was asked to talk about her husband and children and how they like and dislike their foods prepared. The women were particularly asked to relate family stories, those little tales or bits of family lore that are repeated to family and friends as ways of typifying the family members. These interviews were interpreted using a background of hundreds of depth interviews from marketing studies of many food products. It should be understood that numbers are not relevant here. The purpose is to illustrate the use of a qualitative, structuralistic approach, not to sample for representativeness, to measure distributions, nor to compute the significance of differences.

The tales that were gathered are taken as susceptible to interpretation at the various levels and in the various modes noted earlier: as descriptions of consumer experiences, as projections of the housewife storyteller, as revealing the family members, as symbolizing the abstracted functions serving the participants and the social unit, and as mundane, secular, little myths that organize consumer reality in accordance with underlying logical structures. . . . Little myths are generalizations about the family and its members, told in the form of anecdotes that use selected facts drawn from the fund of past experiences.

The analysis proceeded by close reading of verbatim transcriptions of the interviews. Observing how respondents project their perceptions of themselves and their families, their language, assumptions, emotional tone, logic, and choice of incidents, the following issues were interpreted.
- Purposes served by the telling of little myths.
- Values preferences portrayed.

- Theories used in accounting for the behavior of family members.
- Structural relationships of characteristics and categories that are used.

Purposes

The stories serve an interwoven set of purposes. Like grand myths, they refer to origins of the group and explain how ancestors came together and what life was like in those days. . . .

The stories act as retrospective affirmations of ties and conflicts when relatives reminisce, and to induct new group members by marriage, birth, and friendship into family traditions by transmitting a fund of important values, ideas, and characteristics. They instruct in the life-style of the lineage, the kind of housing, clothing, transportation, recreation, and food it was and is customary to consume.

The stories illustrate specific relationships and personalities. Often, there is a self-justifying quality: The story proves that the people really are (or were) like that.

. . .

Values and Preferences

In selecting stories to tell, the respondents project their concern with certain values. Middle-class women highlight middle-class values deemed important for transmission through the generations. As telling stories is a method of maintaining family traditions, it is not surprising that the importance of family unity is repeatedly asserted as such a value. One's childhood was part of a close family or regretfully was not; the mother now strives to have a close family, or regrets that maturation and modern life-styles are destroying that closeness. Closeness is evidenced in doing things together, sharing enjoyable experiences such as family picnics, sports outings, travel, hobbies, meals, household projects, in living nearby, in helping one another, showing concern about the children's companions, and occasionally in some special intimacy of emotional communication or understanding.

The dimension of conformity to or deviation from manly norms comes up in relation to food. The traditional husband is a "meat and potatoes man."

His favorite meal is pot roast with potatoes and carrots and onions in a big pot.

He likes roast and gravy. That would be his most special meal. Roast and potatoes, and a vegetable, and lots of bread and butter.

He's kind of a meat and potatoes man.

This pattern reflects the central American diet; therefore, it seems proper and hardly requires explanation. It often goes on in the context of "he eats everything" except perhaps the conventional hatreds (liver) or less usual foods, such as artichokes.

As a cultural subgroup each family also has its local values. It is easy to gather an array of summaries of family tastes. Women generalize that They all love chicken, They're not crazy about fish, We don't eat any raw vegetables, They all like it rare, They like casseroles. Such remarks are usually not literally true (as fuller discussion reveals): but are imaginative generalizations (not imaginary) that symbolize the kind of family being described as stubborn eaters, narrow eaters, easy to feed, and so on, and show what kind of woman the homemaker is to cope with such a family.

Consumers' Theories

The above kinds of behavior may seem conventional but are often left unexplained because they are so taken for granted or seem so easily accounted for as a common learning. But husbands who are not meat and potatoes men require explanation; when a family member departs from the norm of eating what the mother regards as an ordinary diet, a problem is posed. The ideas put forth by the women to explain food handling and preferences or aversions take many forms, as shown by examples in Table 1. . . .

A framework that operates in the thinking of the respondents has such elements as these:

- The process of acquiring and inculcating tastes in the service of health beliefs and propriety is a conflict-filled one. Cooks are motivated to get the family to eat what is served by various moral imperatives, such as that's what people like us eat, the food comprises a healthy diet, and providing it and eating it are ways of showing love (and other emotions). . . . Families do

not harmoniously eat everything, but refuse, resist, or disparage, as well as praise.
- There is a natural hierarchy of desirable to offensive attributes of foods. Any extreme may be troublesome, such as in foods that are too fatty, greasy, spicy, rich, etc.

. . .

- Individuals vary in being physiologically vulnerable, perhaps prone to weight gain or peculiarly sensitive to certain substances. Illness, skin eruptions, respiratory distress, etc., may be explained as simply idiosyncratic reactions or as allergies rooted in either psychological or social factors, or in just that kind of body.
- Taste preferences are explained at all levels—as due to some sheer physiology of the taste buds, as inherited in the genes, as socialized by ethnic context and by family practices, and as due to novel patterns of individual experiences, beliefs, and habituations.

Structural Relations

Food preparation, service, manners, and consumption are all used in symbolic ways. As Lévi-Strauss notes in *The Origin of Table Manners,* "Thus we can hope to discover how, in any particular society, cooking is a language through which that society unconsciously reveals its structure" (Lévi-Strauss 1978, p. 495). The participants communicate through their food behaviors, using the underlying structure both consciously and unconsciously.

The American situation is difficult to interpret in a clearcut way because the available vocabulary is so large. The food products and artifacts come from the whole globe and reflect a mixing of traditions from many societies. The possibilities for different patterns become useful in expressing cultural pride, intergenerational and assimilational conflicts, and individual peculiarities. . . .

Sex and age grading. The roles of sex and age grading are pronounced in distinguishing between the varied suitabilities of foods and methods of preparation. We can distinguish between babies and teenagers, boys and girls, and also observe

Table 1 Consumer explanation

Behavior	Explanation
Chicken liver, calves liver, I don't even prepare.	I think the whole world hates liver.
I used to make tongue quite a bit.	My older son said, "How can you eat tongue with your tongue?" So that was the last time we had tongue.
I learned to modify the wine and butter; I cook very simply now.	My husband got terrible chest pains.
Polish sauerkraut. He hates it.	He says the whole house stinks for weeks after you make it . . . he takes after my father. They both have a queasy stomach and they hate smells.
All of a sudden I find myself taking a piece of cake or something, if it's yummy looking.	I don't even like it, but I've got this idea that it's going to help me bowling. It sounds silly, but that's the truth.
I'm the only one that likes eggplant.	You kind of have to develop a test for it. I like all those weird vegetables.
They like everything.	Probably because I don't give them a choice. Even when they were little kids, I started getting them into all sorts of different vegetables because I like vegetables.
My daughter would not eat meat at all.	A neighbor is a vegetarian, and the woman would tell her they kill that poor little animal, how can you eat their meat?

some of the dimensions at work that affect different food suitabilities. Babies need milk and soft, mushy, undifferentiated foods. Ideas of nurturance, comfort, and easily digested nutrition go in this direction, so that similar foods are regarded as suited to the elderly and the sick. The organisms are weak and should not have strong stimulation in spiciness nor in being too hot or cold. Boys are stereotypically expected to prefer chunky peanut butter, girls the smooth, and gradually, the preference for homogeneous dishes yields to mixtures and combinations. With some maturity the hamburger comes into its own as a youth food, especially appealing to teenagers. A lamb chop or salad is perhaps just right for a woman and a roast or steak for a man. . . .

Social status. Along with age and sex dimensions with their varying degrees of strength and weakness, social class distinctions are pervasive. These are interwoven, thus, there is a tendency to equate higher social position with strength, maturity, and food professionalism, and lower status preferences with softness, greasiness, and sweetness. Going up the scale, conventionality of preparation yields increasingly to elaboration of methods, greater use of herbs and spices, and usage of unusual foods and ingredients. These qualities are not reserved to the upper classes, of course, but form part of the aspirations of lower status groups as well, and are emulated on special occasions. The ability to cook with appropriate sophistication and skill may be achieved through special study or left in the hands of professional chefs, and enjoyed while eating out. . . .

Eating out(side). The in-or-out locus is a structural element that speaks of conventionality and festivity, family unity and separation. . . . The conventional core is the meal at home, maternal, comfortable, familiar, dependent, and routine. To eat away from home carries more exciting meanings. Outdoor, backyard, park, beach, imply freedom from conventions, return to nature, primitive methods of cooking and eating (with fingers), no manners, and lively physical and social activity.

Going out to eat at another home implies some formality, dress-up, a step up in the elaboration of preparation or distinctiveness of the dishes.

The idea of going out to eat at a restaurant interacts with the meanings of the various types of establishments to fit the sex and age grading, and family status dimensions. The choices range from lower class, greasy spoons and forthright EATS cafes, through miscellaneous youthful fast food and family style restaurants, to elegant, cosmopolitan dining rooms. Moving the family unit from the home to the restaurant tends to express a festive attitude and the relaxation of parental responsibility; this attitude becomes even more pronounced for children and adds elements of separation and liberation when they go to fast food restaurants on their own. Lower class cafes and fancy restaurants are adult in meaning, places for adults at work away from home (truck stops, executive business lunches). At the heights, haute cuisine with its subtle sauces and other exotic efforts symbolizes an elite use of leisure, an extreme degree of refinement of the palate, and attendant sybaritic sensibilities. People eat dishes they never have at home and go beyond ordinary meats to expensive cuts and seafoods.

Beyond the cooked. Cooking is aimed at numerous objectives—making substances more chewable, more digestible, safer, warm and comforting, and more interesting to the taste. It is a process of culture, as opposed to the natural, and its degrees of status tend to be equated with distancing from the primitive and animal eating of raw food. As indicated above, these degrees of status are expressed in complexity, subtlety, particular foods, methods of preparation, and settings. Basic qualities range from an infantile, homogeneous, mushy, boiled grossness to a highly differentiated awareness of textures, ingredients, seasonings, and nuances of preparation.

Little myths are dynamic and change as new experiences become available. Recently added in the raw-to-cooked dimension is a new myth of high status consumption that might be termed transcendental or self-conscious rawness. Like a kind of conspicuous underconsumption or like the French court dressing as Watteau shepherds and shepherdesses, one finds elegantly dressed partygoers eating various raw vegetables with their fingers (*crudités*), and exclaiming over their daring in eating raw hamburger (*steak tartar*) or raw fish (*sushi*). With a heightened physicality (exercising, jogging), the sophisticated return to nature goes with natural rather than processed cheeses, live bacterial processes in yogurt, yeasts, and yerba, peasant grains and dark breads. It is a retreat from over-refinement, a cycling down to rescue the effete body and restore its sexual vigor, mingled with the elite cosmopolitanism of imported dishes.

In much of this consumer behavior there is no contradiction; rather, the social group prescribes roles and their accompanying symbols; and consumers participate by adopting the roles and symbols suited to their identities. However, animating the process are the deeper contradictions and conflicts that question whether the physical differences attributed to age and sex differences are properly fitted to the culinary and dietary differences. That is, are we preparing and eating the right things? Women should be good cooks by their maternal nature; but the highest art and science of cookery paradoxically tend to be attributed to male chefs (*pace,* Julia Child). Is hierarchy real? Are the foods, dishes, methods, and deferential service sufficient in their symbolism to reassure the elite that it is truly elevated? Does eating and thinking make it so?

Perhaps even more fundamental to the little myths, given the insistent refinements of gustatory perception and the aesthetic superiorities with which mothers and elites seek to socialize the young and those of lower status, is the struggle with the basic question: Am I an animal or am I a person? How do we reconcile the animal nature of the eaters with the human culture of the cooks, the intractable fact of the body with the refinements of civilization?

MARKETING IMPLICATIONS

This article has been an exploration and stops with some concluding comments. It has demonstrated a qualitative approach to the study of consumer behavior, as follows:

We can enrich our understanding of consumer behavior by taking consumer protocols as stories that use a sociocultural vocabulary. The analysis blends functional-symbolic-structural logics to observe that a dietary behavior is probably not well understood in isolation or by focusing narrowly on product attributes in the way that much marketing research does. Soler reminds us of this.

> It must be placed into the context of the signs in the same area of life; together they constitute a system; and this system in turn must be seen in relation to the other systems in other areas, for the interaction of all these systems constitute the sociocultural system of a people. (Soler 1979, p. 25)

Consumer behavior in the food area uses fundamental generalizations about the meanings of products in a broadly conventional way, within which dynamic processes of individuation and differentiation go on. The little myths show how the basic vocabulary of cooking and eating is used to express identities by males and females, the young and the mature, and people in low, middle, and high status positions. General modeling by age, sex, and social status is a familiar one to marketers; here the analysis observes how specific symbolic distinctions are being made among specific foods, ways of preparing them, and in some of the ideas they represent, such as family unity/dispersion, naivete/sophistication, routine/festivity, sickness/health, grossness/subtlety, conformity/deviation, sacred/profane, etc.

Figure 1 sums up the complex structure of the food mythology. It is drawn to resemble a three-dimensional urban scene, suggesting the cultural sophistication operating to organize biological statuses, sex roles, age gradings, and social positions in terms of both psychological dimensions and food attributes such as taste, texture, appearance, and method of preparation. The marketer works within this complex, using the symbolic vocabulary to define and position the product.

The broad brush strokes indicated above may encourage further study of how families develop their particular little myths; how common cultural

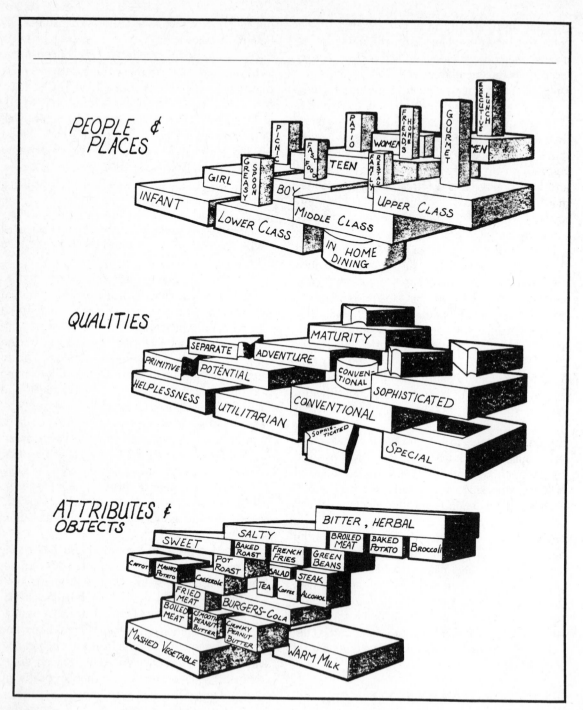

Figure **I**

little myths change over time; how facts of behavior are modified in the telling; what the facts or the modified tellings are being used to say; how marketers participate in creating the symbolic vocabulary; and how they may use the consumers' mythology on behalf of their specific products and brands in their continuing dialog with consumers.

REFERENCES

Abelson, Robert P. (1976), "Script Processing in Attitude Formation and Decision Making," in *Cognition and Social Behavior,* J. Carroll and J. Payne, eds., Hillsdale, NJ: Lawrence Erlbaum Associates.

Firat, A. Fuat (1978), "Social Construction of Consumption Patterns," unpublished Ph.D. dissertation, Northwestern University.

Frazer, James G. (1927), *The Golden Bough: A Study in Magic and Religion,* New York: Macmillan.

Lévi-Strauss, Claude (1963), *Structural Anthropology, Book I,* New York: Basic Books.

———— (1969), *The Raw and the Cooked,* Introduction to a Science of Mythology, 1, New York: Harper and Row.

———— (1978), *The Origins of Table Manners,* Introduction to a Science of Mythology, 3, New York: Harper and Row.

Levy, Sidney J. (1978), "Hunger and Work in a Civilized Tribe," *American Behavioral Scientist,* 21 (March–April), 557–570.

Rapaport, D. (1942), "Principles Underlying Projective Techniques," *Character and Personality,* Vol. X, No. 3 (March), pp. 213–219.

Soler, Jean (1979), "The Dietary Prohibitions of the Hebrews," *New York Review of Books,* 27 (June 14), 24–25.

Williams, Daniel B. (1976), "An Information Processing Theory of Individual Purchasing Behavior," unpublished Ph.D. dissertation, Northwestern University.

CAMPBELL SOUP FAILS TO MAKE IT TO THE TABLE

After three years and an advertising campaign that soaked up $2 million, Campbell Soup Co. is moving its Brazilian canned soup operation to a back burner. The company's production in Brazil, which was sharply curtailed last May following fiscal 1980 losses of $1.2 million, is now limited to packaging soup for Brazil's school lunch program. The Brazilian canned soup debacle is a first for Campbell, which has "never withdrawn from a market anywhere in the world," according to Philip Beach, managing director of its Brazilian subsidiary until mid-1980.

Campbell entered the Brazilian market in 1978, when it joined Brazilian-owned meat producer Swift-Armour S.A. Industria e Comercio to form a company called SOPA (Sociedade Produtora de Alimentos Ltd.). Campbell has a 65% interest in SOPA, with a capital investment of $6 million. Before going into production, Campbell conducted a marketing effort that won two national awards and generated sales of 200,000 cases of canned soup in the first year of operations, says Milton Shayer, SOPA's present managing director.

So what went wrong for Campbell in soup-conscious Brazil? In-depth but belated household interviews by a company-retained psychologist revealed that the Brazilian housewife felt she was not fulfilling her role as a homemaker if she served her family a soup she could not call her own.

Campbell's offerings—mostly vegetable and beef combinations packed in extra-large cans bearing a variant of the familiar red and white label—failed to catch on. Instead, Brazilian housewives seemed to prefer the dehydrated products of competitors such as Knorr and Maggi, which they could use as a soup starter but still add their own flair and ingredients. If one bought Campbell's soup, it was usually to put aside for an emergency, "like when she was late coming home from a tea party," says Shayer.

Poor market tests. Shayer now regrets that market tests were limited to the temperate southern city of Curitiba, and not extended to subtropical areas of Brazil. "We might have seen right away that we needed more than one product," agrees Beach.

Campbell will decide within two months whether it will remain in Brazil, Shayer predicts. Its options include investing in other kinds of equipment to market items such as biscuits and cookies or using existing equipment to turn out "more typical" canned beans and sausage products. It is also possible that Campbell might try to buy a Brazilian food products company and reintroduce a modified soup line as one of several items. "There has to be some option for a company like ours in Brazil," says Shayer. But, he adds: "It's a bad time to start fooling around with new products in Brazil. During bad times people concentrate on basics, which means rice and beans here."

But Campbell has not given up on the Brazilian market, says Richard J. Censits, vice-president for finance at the company's Camden (N.J.) headquarters. Censits points out that while Campbell is "not in a position to go forward on soup" in Brazil, "there is the possibility of marketing other products" there.

Campbell has also encountered difficulty farther south, in Argentina. Swift-Armour SA Argentina, a Campbell subsidiary, reported a $6.1 million loss for the fiscal year ending in August, although nearly half the loss was due to currency translation adjustments.

AMERICAN JEWISH ETHNICITY: ITS RELATIONSHIP TO SOME SELECTED ASPECTS OF CONSUMER BEHAVIOR

ELIZABETH C. HIRSCHMAN

Source: Elizabeth C. Hirschman, ''American Jewish Ethnicity: Its Relationship to Some Selected Aspects of Consumer Behavior,'' *Journal of Marketing,* Vol. 45, Summer, 1981, 102–110. Adapted from the *Journal of Marketing,* published by the American Marketing Association.

INTRODUCTION

Reviews of the marketing literature concerning the interaction of ethnicity with various consumption activities (e.g., Engel, Blackwell, and Kollat 1978; Zaltman and Wallendorf 1979) reveal three generalizations. First, the majority of ethnic group investigations have been post hoc in design and descriptive in nature. Many simply categorize consumers into either an ethnic group of interest category or a general population category, and then test for differences between the two in such areas as brand loyalty, price preference, patronage behavior, and advertising response (e.g., Akers 1968; Solomon and Busch 1977; Solomon, Bush, and Hair 1976). The unique norms and values that characterize a given ethnic group are infrequently considered in development of a priori hypotheses regarding the way(s) the group may be expected to differ from the surrounding society.

Secondly, the ethnic group of interest in the great majority of studies has been black consumers (Bauer and Cunningham 1970, Sexton 1972). Only rarely have investigations been directed towards nonblack ethnic groups such as Hispanics, Italians, or Jews. This condition is unfortunate, for much valuable information on ethnic influence may be obtained by examining groups that are differentiated from society on religious or nationality dimensions, rather than race.

Finally, in many instances subjects have been assigned to the ethnic group of interest or general population category on the basis of researchers' perceptions of their membership in one or the other group. This may, of course, lead to incorrect assignment. Further exacerbating this problem is the fact that subjects are typically not asked the degree of identification they feel with a particular ethnic group. One black consumer may feel an especially strong commitment to black ethnicity, whereas a second may feel much less identification with this group. The degree of identification the individual feels with a given ethnic group may largely determine the level of commitment he/she experiences regarding the norms of the group and, thus, the degree of influence the group has on his/her actions and attitudes (Barth 1969, Glazer and Moynihan 1975, Davidowicz 1977).

. . . The present research addresses these three issues by extending the study of ethnic influences to an examination of Jewish consumers. Several a priori hypotheses are derived from the existing literature on Jewish ethnic characteristics (e.g., Arieti 1976; McClelland 1958, 1961; Veblen 1919; Weber 1952) and serve as a framework for studying the effects of subcultural norms on consumer behaviors. Degree of Jewish ethnicity is assessed using self-designated measures and scaled along two dimensions, religion and culture.

The Multidimensionality of Jewish Ethnicity

When one is born a Jew, he/she is born into a culture and a religion simultaneously (Sklare and Greenblum 1967). Although as an individual a Jew may choose to adhere to one, both, or neither of these two ethnic dimensions, the correlation between the two within Jewish populations has been found to be quite high (Herman 1977). Jewish ethnicity is believed to exert a relatively stronger effect on the individual's behavior because it is multidimensional (Herman 1977). One set of values is promulgated both by informal social interaction and religious instruction; therefore, the individual experiences greater normative consistency. This congruence between culture and religion stands in contrast to conditions prevailing in some other ethnic groups. Irish ethnicity, for instance, may be exhibited quite differently, depending upon whether one is Irish Protestant or Irish Catholic. Jewish ethnicity possesses a unique structure with regard to other ethnic groups that are identified on a unidimensional basis because of its multidimensional nature.

Jewish Ethnicity and Socioeconomic Status

American Jews are predominately found in the upper socioeconomic classes (e.g., Goldscheider 1974, Jencks 1979, Jensen 1973, Kilson 1975, Patai 1977). Because the socioeconomic position held by an individual may be an important deter-

minant of his/her functioning as a consumer, this aspect of Jewish ethnicity is an important one for marketing research. . . .

The Need for Achievement and Ethnic Norms

In *The Achieving Society* McClelland (1961) refers to the need for achievement as the motivation to do well and to complete self-selected tasks successfully. . . . Reasons cited include the emphasis in Jewish religious teachings on individual responsibility for personal actions and extensive self-education. Also, within the Jewish family unit norms have been found that are conducive to the stimulation of high achievement motivation in children (Rosen 1959, Rosen and D'Andrade 1959, Strodtbeck 1958, 1965). Among these are beliefs by the parents that children should be maximally stimulated and strongly encouraged to learn and to develop their talents (Patai 1977, Veroff et al. 1960).

Based upon these norms some expectations may be advanced. First, Jewish children will be exposed to more educating experiences by their parents in order to stimulate their upward mobility. For example, children may be provided with reading material, enrolled in special classes, and encouraged to participate in social activities. It is posited by Veblen (1919) and Arieti (1976) that these externally-imposed norms for self-education and advancement through the acquisition of knowledge will be internalized over time. When the child becomes an adult, it is believed that he/she has adopted these values and continues to acquire educating experiences on a self-motivated basis.

Veblen and Arieti further speculate that with the acquisition of knowledge comes a greater degree of perceived self-control over one's fate and increased reliance on one's judgment. These are believed to provide the essential ingredients for consumer innovativeness as defined by Midgley and Dowling (1978), that is, the willingness to acquire new products independent of the communicated experiences of others. These same characteristics are also believed to enhance the transfer of consumption information to other people. Thus, Jewish consumers may possess more product knowledge, due to their high levels of information seeking and innovativeness, and also the self-confidence necessary to make recommendations to others regarding consumption. This reasoning leads to a set of exploratory propositions:

P1: Jewish ethnicity is positively related to childhood information exposure. Specifically, Jewish children receive more exposure to reading material, special training/instruction, and group participation.

P2: Jewish ethnicity is positively related to adult information seeking. Specifically, Jewish consumers expose themselves to a greater quantity of information sources, for example, the mass media.

P3: Jewish ethnicity is positively related to consumption innovativeness. Jewish consumers are more willing to adopt new products independent of the judgment of others.

P4: Jewish ethnicity is positively related to the transfer of consumption information. Jewish consumers transfer more consumption information to others.

Because Jewish consumers may be exposed to an above average level of cognitively stimulating experiences as children and adults, it is possible that they will display enhanced information processing skills. . . .

. . . The preliminary proposition may be made that Jewish consumers will exhibit enhanced divergent processing ability[1] and active memory capacity as adults. That is, Jewish consumers may have stored and be able to manipulate more cognitive data as a result of their greater exposure to cognitive stimulation. Within the domain of consumption, this proposition would specify that Jewish ethnicity is positively related to divergent processing ability and active memory capacity concerning product information.

P5: Jewish ethnicity is positively related to divergent processing ability and the capacity for activating consumption information.

Jewish consumers have stored and are able to activate more pieces of consumption-relevant information.

METHOD

In investigating the relationship between ethnicity and variables such as consumption innovativeness, information seeking, and information transfer, one must be careful to control for obvious external sources of possible criterion contamination such as age effects, education effects, and occupational effects. To the extent that differences are found between the ethnic group and the population to which it is being compared on such variables, the true effects of ethnicity may be obscured.

One technique for overcoming such external sources of bias is cohort analysis (Glenn 1977). Cohort analysis involves the use of a sample that is invariant with respect to selected sources of potential contamination. A cohort is chosen that contains individuals who are very similar with respect to potentially biasing factors, such as age, but who vary in the level of the primary independent variable of interest, in this case Jewish ethnicity. . . . The use of cohorts is especially recommended in theory-testing behavioral research such as this, because it permits maximum control over extraneous sources of variance, which may threaten the validity of comparisons (e.g., Calder, Philips, and Tybout 1980; Cook and Campbell 1975).

Sample

Two cohorts were used in this research. The source of the first cohort was students attending four universities in different regions of the United States: New York University (n = 98), University of Michigan (n = 40), Georgia State University (n = 145) and University of Southern California (n = 25). Students selected for the research project were between 20 and 29 years old and were majoring in Business Administration. There were no significant differences between Jews and non-Jews in employment status, marital status, educational attainment, or age within any of the four samples.[2] . . .

---

[1]Divergent processing ability is the relative facility the individual possesses to generate multiple dimensions (attributes) for comprehending problems and multiple alternatives (solutions) for solving them.

[2]There were no Jewish subjects contained in the USC sample.

The second cohort was a sample of 363 adult consumers residing in the New York City metropolitan area (including New York, New Jersey, and Connecticut). The consumers selected for this cohort all met an a priori set of socioeconomic criteria: (1) above $20,000 per year in household income, (2) college-educated head of household, and (3) managerial-professional occupational status for head of household.

The adult consumers in this second sample formed a cohort in which socioeconomic status was controlled, an important requirement in examining Jewish ethnicity, since Jewish consumers are predominantly clustered in upper SES strata (Kilson 1975). Subjects in this sample were recruited on a systematic, stratified basis to constitute an SES cohort, hence, they are purposely not representative of the New York City population. There were no significant differences between Jews (n = 120) and non-Jews (243) in this cohort for any demographic features examined—e.g., age, marital status, income, educational attainment, and occupational status.

The non-Jewish religious groups represented in the second cohort were predominately Protestant (n = 114) and Catholic (n = 98). Other religious denominations included Greek Orthodox, Hindu, Muslim, and those with no religious affiliation (n = 31). The primary non-Jewish racial/nationality groups represented were Italian, Greek, Chinese, Irish, and self-labeled WASPs. Thus a diversity of religious and nationality identities is present within the adult cohort sample.

· · ·

Ethnicity

Because ethnicity is a central construct in this research, attempts were made to operationalize it using multiple emic measures. An emic measure of ethnicity is one which permits the individual to ascribe religious and cultural identity to him/herself. It is based on the individual's subjective self-perceptions and not on the perceptions of the researcher, which may be biased by ethnocentrism. This method of measuring ethnicity is the approach deemed most appropriate by cross-cultural behavioral researchers, and especially those in cultural

anthropology and social psychology (e.g., Cohen 1978, Ember 1977, Jorgensen 1979). . . .

Subjects were given four questions to assess their ethnicity. First, they were asked if there were any ethnic or racial group with which they identified.[3] Ten response categories were given for this question: Hispanic, Irish, Greek, Italian, Jewish, Chinese, Japanese, Black, Other,[4] and None. Next, subjects were asked to indicate how strong their identification was with the group they had selected using a five point scale ranging from very strong (5) to very weak (1).

The second set of questions dealt with religious ethnic affiliation. Subjects were asked to indicate with which of five religious categories they were affiliated: Catholic, Jewish, Protestant, Other (specified), and None. Following this was a question asking the subject to indicate how strong the self-designated religious affiliation was on a five point scale ranging from very strong (5) to very weak (1). . . .

Because Jewish ethnicity is posited to be a multidimensional phenomenon, the appropriate measure of it is a combination of self-perceived religious and cultural affiliation strength. Further, because both dimensions are believed to contribute equally to the behavior of the individual, they were summed together to create a composite index of Jewish ethnicity.

· · ·

Childhood Information Exposure

Three types of childhood information exposure were included in the research. First, exposure to print media was measured as the sum of the subject's recall of magazines he/she read regularly as a child. Second, exposure to special training/instruction was measured as the sum of the subject's recall of these experiences. Third, exposure to group interaction was measured as the sum of the subject's

---

[3]The term ethnic/racial was used to operationalize the cultural dimension of ethnicity, as it was found in pretests to more closely connote subjects' perceptions of the meaning of this dimension.

[4]Asked for a specification of ethnic identity by the individual (e.g., Turkish, German, Indian).

recall of participation in groups, clubs, and organizations (Hirschman 1981). . . .

To create an index of these childhood experiences, responses were summed within each question (i.e., print media, special training, group memberships) and the resulting scores were subjected to factor analysis (principal components) using varimax rotation to consolidate the data set. Two factors emerged which together explained 76% of the variance in the student sample and 73% of variance in the adult consumer sample.[5] . . .

Adult Information Seeking

A diversified set of adult information seeking measures was used. These included questions asking the individual to list the different radio stations listened to at least four days per week, television programs watched for at least half the scheduled broadcasts, newspapers read for at least half the issues, magazines read for at least half the issues, and groups in which he/she regularly participated (Hirschman 1981, Hirschman and Wallendorf 1981).

Consumption Innovativeness

Following the conceptualization of innovativeness advanced by Midgley and Dowling (1978), subjects were asked to indicate their willingness to adopt new products in various consumption domains, independent of the judgment of other people who had purchased the product. Fifteen consumption domains were explored ranging from specific personal items (a new hairstyle) to general ideologies (religious and political ideas). A wide variety of topics were included, which were intended to incorporate various levels of economic, social, and attitudinal risk to the individual. A five-point rating scale ranging from very great willingness (5) to very low willingness (1) was used to measure the individual's tendency to innovate in each product area.

Consumption Information Transfer

The operationalization of this construct measured the individual's perceptions of his/her frequency of

providing information to others in a particular domain of consumption. The same 15 consumption domains investigated in the measure of innovativeness were used for information transfer. A five-point rating scale ranging from very great frequency (5) to very low frequency (1) was used to scale responses.

Divergent Processing Ability and Active Memory Capacity

. . .

To operationalize divergent processing ability, subjects in the adult consumer sample were requested to list as many reasonable criteria and solutions as they could for four consumption problems: weekend night entertainment, mode of transportation, place of residence, and a pet.

The measurement of active memory capacity within the student cohort proceeded on the assumption that such capacity could be adequately represented as the number of separate items of information mentally retrieved and manipulated in a given time span (Lachman, Lachman, and Butterfield 1979). Thus, the student respondents were given a product name and required to write as many associations to it as they could in a timed 60 second interval.

Two possible sources of bias may occur in such a procedure. The individual may be given a stimulus word from a consumption domain about which he/she has little knowledge, causing retrieval of associations to be stunted. Also, the individual may be given a stimulus word at a level of generality or specificity that does not correspond to the categorization scheme he/she uses to structure cognitive content. Hence, retrieval may be blocked due to hierarchical incongruence between the stimulus word and encoded content (Cermak and Craik 1979).

To help overcome these two potential sources of bias, stimulus words were chosen from four consumption domains relevant to college students—food, clothing, entertainment, and transportation—at various levels of generality/specificity within each domain. In all, 28 stimulus words were given to each subject; these words represented

---

[5]All factors used in the research had eigenvalues exceeding 1.0.

four consumption domains, cited above, and four levels of generality/specificity within each domain.

. . .

ANALYSIS AND FINDINGS

The relationship between Jewish ethnicity and the consumption variables examined here is posited to be a linear positive function; e.g., the higher one's Jewish ethnicity, the greater the adherence to norms favoring innovativeness and, thus, the higher the level of innovativeness expressed by the individual. . . .

The results are supportive of the general hypotheses advanced, in that Jewish ethnicity was found in all cases positively related to the criteria examined. The correlations were: childhood information exposure ($r = .22S$, $r = .21A$), adult information seeking ($r = .30S$, $r = .34A$), consumption innovativeness, ($r = .23S$, $r = .27A$), consumption information transfer ($r = .21S$, $r = .40A$), active memory capacity ($r = .23S$), divergent processing ($r = .21A$). Thus we may generally conclude that Jewish ethnicity appears to affect consumption behavior largely as expected based upon ethnic norms.

Although this finding is limited in generalizability to consumers in cohorts analogous to those examined here (i.e., college students and upper SES adults), it does tentatively support the position that consumer information gathering, use, and dissemination characteristics may be related to ethnic norms. Of special interest is the possibility that a consumer's receptivity to product information, both as a child and adult, may be related to the ethnic tradition in which that person has been raised. Individual differences in information acquisition and utilization have been detected in many studies, but rarely, if ever, has ethnicity been cited as a possible source of these differences. The present data, albeit limited to two cohorts, suggest such an attribution may be appropriate.

The correlative pattern also indicates that cohort effects are present. That is, the strength of correlation between Jewish ethnicity and a given consumption criterion occasionally varies between the student and adult samples. For example, the correlation between Jewish ethnicity and innovativeness is substantially higher in the adult sample. This suggests that the relationship between ethnicity and the variables examined here may be a dynamic one—or at least one that is manifested differently in separate cohorts.

MARKETING IMPLICATIONS

Bearing in mind the limitation of the samples employed, there are some implications which these findings may have for marketing strategy. Applications of Jewish ethnicity within a pragmatic marketing framework appear possible in at least two areas: innovation diffusion and information transmission. The evidence presented suggests that Jewish consumers may be relatively more innovative, at least within the cohorts examined here. It is possible that in markets having large Jewish populations, a disproportionately high level of consumption innovativeness will be present. This implies not only more rapid awareness and adoption of new products by Jewish consumers, but also the possibility of a faster product life cycle within this subculture.

The potential for less brand and store loyalty and for more rapid advertising campaign wear-out among Jewish consumers may be possible as well. The propensity toward innovativeness may affect not only Jewish consumers in a population, but non-Jewish consumers also. Because innovation diffusion is an inherently social phenomenon, Jewish subcultural innovativeness may carry other consumers along the diffusion curve more rapidly.

It is possible that Jewish consumers may serve as generalized opinion leaders (or more properly, information givers) about products. Marketers, realizing that Jewish consumers may be disproportionately vocal regarding their products, may desire to provide favorable information to them on a targeted basis. For example, mailing lists could be obtained of YMHA/YWHA members, contributors of the United Jewish Appeal, and so forth.

Finally, the results suggest that ethnicity, Jewish or otherwise, should perhaps be viewed as a variable having large potential influence on marketing and consumption. Marketers who desire to understand consumers in a more predictive and comprehensive manner may find it useful to view ethnicity as a cause of consumption patterns, rather than simply as a correlate of item purchasing. For example, the present results suggest that consumers' propensities to adopt new products, to expose themselves to marketing-relevant information sources, and to transfer product information may be tied to their ethnic origins.

Further, public policy makers may take interest in the finding that consumers who were exposed to above average levels of cognitive stimulation as children (due to ethnic norms) exhibited above average levels of two information processing abilities as adults. Ethnic norms may be a factor in influencing consumer competence and ability to arrive at informed choices.

The present research has examined a limited set of consumption characteristics potentially influenced by ethnicity within a limited set of subjects. The domain of ethnic influence may extend beyond the information seeking/processing/transferring phenomena studied here. There is suggestive evidence from other studies (e.g., Patai 1977) that ethnicity affects consumption processes as diverse as voting behavior, fertility levels, demand for educational and medical services, and the types of aesthetic-hedonic products preferred. The present research provides some preliminary clues of what may prove to be one of the most important and pervasive influences on consumption.

REFERENCES

Akers, Fred C. (1968), "Negro and White Automobile Buying Behavior: New Evidence," *Journal of Marketing Research,* 5 (August), 283–290.

Arieti, Silvana (1976), *Creativity: The Magic Synthesis,* New York: Basic Books.

Barth, Fredrick (1969), *Ethnic Groups and Boundaries: The Social Organization of Cultural Difference,* Boston: Little, Brown.

Bauer, Raymond A. and Scott M. Cunningham (1970), "The Negro Market," *Journal of Advertising Research,* 10 (April), 3–13.

Calder, Bobby J., Lynn W. Philips, and Alice M. Tybout (1980) "The Design, Conduct and Application of Consumer Research: Theory vs. Effects Oriented Studies," in *Marketing in the 80's: Changes & Challenges,* R. Bagozzi et al., eds., Chicago: American Marketing Association, 307–311.

Cermak, Laird S. and Fergus I. M. Craik (1979), *Levels of Processing in Human Memory,* Hillsdale, NJ: Lawrence Erlbaum.

Cohen, Ronald (1978), "Ethnicity: Problem and Focus in Anthropology," *Annual Review of Anthropology* (7), 379–403.

Cook, T. and D. Campbell (1975), "The Design and Conduct of Experiments and Quasi-Experiments in Field Settings," in *Handbook of Industrial and Organizational Research,* M. Dunnette, ed., Chicago: Rand McNally.

Davidowicz, Lucy (1977), *The Jewish Presence,* New York: Harcourt, Brace, Jovanovich.

Ember, Carol R. (1977), "Cross-Cultural Cognitive Studies," *Annual Review of Anthropology,* (6), 33–56.

Engel, James, Roger Blackwell, and David Kollat (1978), *Consumer Behavior,* 3rd edition, New York: Holt, Rinehart, and Winston.

Glazer, Nathan and Daniel P. Moynihan, eds. (1975), *Ethnicity: Theory and Experience,* Cambridge: Harvard University Press.

Glenn, Norval D. (1977), *Cohort Analysis,* Beverly Hills, CA: Sage Publications, Inc.

Goldscheider, C. (1974), "Sociological and Demographic Perspective," in *The Jew in American Society,* M. Sklare, ed., New York: Behrmann, 335–384.

Herman, Simon N. (1977), *Jewish Identity: A Social Psychological Perspective,* Beverly Hills, CA: Sage Publications, Inc.

Hirschman, Elizabeth C. (1981), "Social and Cognitive Influences on Information Exposure: A Path Analysis," *Journal of Communication,* 31 (Winter), 76–87.

———, and Melanie Wallendorf (1981), "Media Habits and Variety Seeking," *Proceedings,* Copenhagen: ERRAM.

Jencks, C. J. (1979), *Who Gets Ahead? The Determinants of Economic Success in America,* New York: Basic Books.

Jensen, Arthur R. (1973), *Educability and Group Differences,* New York: Harper & Row.

Jorgenson, Joseph (1979), "Cross-Cultural Comparisons," *Annual Review of Anthropology* (8), 309–331.

Kilson, Martin (1975), "Blacks and Neo-Ethnicity in American Political Life," in *Ethnicity: Theory and Ex-*

perience, N. Glazer and D. P. Moynihan, eds., Cambridge: Harvard University Press.

Lachman, Roy, Janet Lachman, and Earl Butterfield (1979), *Cognitive Psychology and Information Processing,* Hillsdale, NJ: Lawrence Erlbaum.

McClelland, David C. (1958), *Talent and Society,* Princeton, NJ: Van Nostrand.

_____ (1961), *The Achieving Society,* New York: The Free Press.

Midgley, David and Grahame Dowling (1978), "Innovativeness: The Concept and Its Measurement," *Journal of Consumer Research,* 4 (March), 229–242.

Patai, Raphael (1977), *The Jewish Mind,* New York: Charles Scribner's Sons.

Rosen, B. C. (1959), "Race, Ethnicity, and the Achievement Syndrome," *American Sociological Review,* 24 (January), 47–60.

_____, and R. G. D'Andrade (1959), "The Psycho-Social Origins of Achievement Motivation," *Sociometry,* 22 (September), 185–218.

Sexton, Donald (1972), "Black Buyer Behavior," *Journal of Marketing,* 36 (October), 36–39.

Sklare, M. and J. Greenblum (1967), *Jewish Identity on the Suburban Frontier,* New York: Basic Books.

Solomon, Paul J. and Ronald F. Busch (1977), "Effects of Black Models in Television Advertising on Product Choice Behavior," in *Contemporary Marketing Thought,* B. Greenberg and D. Bellenger, eds., Chicago: American Marketing Association, 19–22.

_____, Ronald F. Busch, and Joseph Hair, Jr., (1976), "White and Black Consumer Sales Response to Black Models," *Journal of Marketing Research,* 13 (November), 431–434.

Strodtbeck, Fred L. (1965), "Commentary," in *Productive Thinking in Education,* Washington, DC: National Education Association, 122–127.

_____ (1958), "Jewish and Italian Immigration and Subsequent Status Mobility," in *Talent and Society,* D. C. McClelland, ed., Princeton, NJ: Van Nostrand.

Veblen, Thorstein (1919), "The Intellectual Pre-Eminence of Jews in Modern Europe," *Political Science Quarterly,* 24 (No. 1), 33–42.

Veroff, J., J. W. Atkinson, S. Feld, and G. Gurin (1960), "The Use of Thematic Apperception to Assess Achievement in a Nationwide Interview Study," *Psychological Monographs* (no. 499), 1–31.

Weber, Max (1952), *Ancient Judaism,* Glencoe, IL: The Free Press.

Zaltman, Gerald and Melanie Wallendorf (1979), *Consumer Behavior: Theory and Applications,* New York: John Wiley and Sons.

WIFE'S OCCUPATIONAL STATUS AS A CONSUMER BEHAVIOR CONSTRUCT

CHARLES M. SCHANINGER
AND
CHRIS T. ALLEN

Source: Charles M. Schaninger and Chris T. Allen, "Wife's Occupational Status as a Consumer Behavior Construct," *Journal of Consumer Research,* Vol. 8, September, 1981, 189–196. Reprinted with permission.

Most researchers have attempted to examine the impact of working wives on consumption by comparing the consumption of working-wife families with nonworking-wife families. . . . This paper briefly reviews salient interdisciplinary research, and then proposes and presents empirical support for a trichotomous family classification scheme based on wife's occupational status.

. . .

We propose a three-way family classification scheme based solely on wife's occupation: nonworking wife (NWW), low-occupational-status working wife (LSW), and high-occupational-status working wife (HSW). This measure is operationalized by asking for both wife's occupation and job title in open-ended questions, and then classifying wives into one of the seven occupation categories of the Hollingshead Index of Social Position (Hollingshead and Redlich 1958; Reynolds and Wells 1977). Families with wives in the top three white-collar categories (managerial, professional, administrative and semiprofessional, e.g., doctors, accountants, engineers, teachers, nurses, professional sales) are classified as HSW; those in the lower four categories (secretarial, clerical, retail sales, technicians, and blue-collar and service workers) are classified as LSW families; those not working are classified as NWW. This scheme is straightforward and easy to apply, is based on a standardized and validated component of a widely used social-class scale, and is compatible with abundant sources of secondary data.

Briefly, the following factors are likely to interact to produce lifestyle and consumption differences among NWW, LSW, and HSW families, even after controlling for income:

- Time pressures and work-related stresses, acting on both types of working wives, but believed by researchers in sociology to produce greater adjustment problems in dual career or HSW families (Bebbington 1973; Douglas 1976b; Hunt and Hunt 1977; Rapoport and Rapoport 1971).
- Altered sex-role norms, including greater independence and achievement motivation for the wife, which are particularly likely to cause

HSW families to evidence less traditional husband/wife roles, to have smaller families and postponed progression through the family life-cycle, and more wife influence with conflict and negotiation in decision making (Douglas 1976b; Hayghe 1975; Rapoport and Rapoport 1971; Scanzoni 1976; 1977).

- Social class and social mobility, with HSW families characterized by socially mobile upper-middle-class standing, and LSW characterized by upper-lower- or lower-middle-class standing (Bartos 1978; *Business Week* 1978; Douglas 1976b; Hafstrom and Dunsing 1978; *Wall Street Journal* 1978).
- Work-related consumption requirements, e.g., dress, transportation, day care (*Business Week* 1978; *Wall Street Journal* 1978).

HYPOTHESES

To conserve space and focus principally on the empirical results themselves, the following hypotheses are presented, with a brief rationale:[1]

H1a: Due to upper-lower/lower-middle-class background and time pressures, LSW families will use convenience foods more frequently than other families (Douglas 1976b; Levy 1966).

H1b: The HSW families will tend to avoid instant convenience foods, but use their staple counterparts, due to their upper-middle-class tendencies to put a greater emphasis on the evening meal as a stress-relieving pseudo-leisure activity (Levy 1966).

H2: The HSW families will consume more distilled alcohol and imported wines than other families, due to the interaction of time pressures/stress with social-class backgrounds and social mobility tendencies (Levy 1966; Zaltman and Wallendorf 1979).

H3a: Due to time constraints, both HSW and LSW families will shop at fewer grocery

stores and more convenience stores than NWW families (Anderson 1972; Bartos 1978; Douglas 1976b).

H3b: Due to time constraints, less emphasis on the traditional shopper role, and social-class background, HSW wives will be less deal prone than NWW wives (Levy 1966).

H4: Both HSW and LSW wives will purchase more dresses and use more makeup than NWW wives, due to work requirements (Wells and Tigert 1971).

H5: The LSW families will begin watching television earlier in the evening, watch more television, and score higher on various television ownership variables than HSW families, because they use television as a passive stress-reducing leisure activity (Levy 1966; 1971; Reynolds and Wells 1977).

H6: Both HSW and LSW families will own more labor-saving major and minor appliances, due to time constraints.

H7: Both HSW and LSW families will own more and newer cars than NWW families, due to work transportation requirements.

. . . All income, educational, age, and occupational levels were well represented, although the final sample was somewhat skewed toward higher education, occupation, income, and age categories. . . .

. . .

Of these 225 households, 64 percent were classified as NWW, 22 percent as LSW, and 14 percent as HSW. HSW families were more likely ($p < 0.05$) to be in the top two of Hollingshead's five social-class positions, while LSW families were heavily represented in the lower-middle and upper-lower classes. Approximately 60 percent of the HSW families were in the top-income quartile, while 65 percent of the LSW families were in the top two income quartiles ($p < 0.01$). Wife's occupation and presence of preschool children were not related, although HSW families were marginally less likely, and LSW families were more likely, to have school-age children ($p < 0.10$). Wife's age and occupational status were not related.

---

[1]A more complete rationale of how these factors are likely to interact is provided in Allen and Schaninger (1980).

The Questionnaires

The questionnaires . . . measured comsumption frequency (volume for a few items) for a wide variety of frozen and nonfrozen grocery products, non-alcoholic beverages, and makeup, and purchase frequency for a variety of soft drinks, mixers, and alcoholic beverages. For the most part, seven-point horizontal scales were applied, with verbal frequency descriptions as anchors at the top of each interval column. Footnotes in the data tables describe the actual anchor labels and scale values. Information on shopping behavior, clothing purchases, furniture, automobile, television, and appliance ownership, and media habits were also collected. Age, education, and occupation were collected for husband and wife, along with combined family income and number and ages of children.

RESULTS

Food and Beverage Consumption

Table 1 presents MANOVA results for 30 selected food and beverage items that were chosen to reflect usage of both instant/low-labor products and their staple counterparts. . . .

. . .

The two columns of F values in Table 1 present tests of differences between the two working-wife groups: after removing income effects (in a two-factor classic experimental design), $F_{w/i}$; and by income interaction, F_{wxi}. The multivariate tests were significant ($p < 0.05$) for the single-factor design and after removing income effects ($p < 0.10$). Univariate tests showed that 14 of the 30 items were significant ($p < 0.10$) for the single-factor design, and 12 after removing income effects, with only three demonstrating significant interaction effects.[2]

Differences between the high- and low-status

working wives were consistent with Hypotheses 1a and 1b. The LSW families consumed more of such convenience foods and beverages as instant breakfast, teabags, Tang, bottled juice, frozen pizza, TV dinners, and canned ravioli and spaghetti. They also consumed hot dogs and hamburgers more frequently, and tended (approaching significance) to serve instant tea, instant lemonades, canned soup, and canned vegetables more frequently. Middle-income quartile LSW families also consumed homemade soup less frequently, and middle-income quartile HSW families consumed it more frequently, than working-wife families in other income quartiles. The HSW families consumed more frozen juice, rice, and economy pac and store-brand frozen vegetables (products requiring more time to prepare than the other forms examined). Significance remained for nearly all items after removing income effects, suggesting that income is *not* responsible for these consumption differences.

Significant three-group ($p < 0.10$) multivariate differences in alcohol usage were found only before removing income effects. The HSW families purchased imported red, white, and rosé wines more frequently than either NWW or LSW families.[3] LSW families purchased domestic wines more frequently than the other two groups. Thus, Hypothesis 2 was supported for wine consumption (even after removing income effects), but not for consumption of distilled alcohol.

Grocery Shopping Behavior

Table 2 presents MANOVA results on grocery shopping and deal proneness behavior. Both the single-factor and conditional test of wife's occupation after removing income were significant at the multivariate level. Working wives did not tend to shop at fewer grocery stores and were not significantly more likely to patronize convenience stores, failing to support Hypothesis 3a. Hypothesis 3b was supported only for HSW wives, who tended to pay less attention to grocery specials in the news-

---

[2] The F values and multivariate tests for the single-factor design are not presented in order to conserve table space and to focus the findings on the more conservative, but basically similar, conditional tests. These F tests are directly equivalent to two-tailed r^2 values; thus, an F value significant at 0.10 is equivalent to a one sided t-test significant at 0.05.

[3] In the remaining discussion, statements on group differences are supported by significant t-tests ($p < 0.05$), as well as significant F tests, unless otherwise indicated.

Table 1 MANOVAS on food and beverage items

Food product	Nonworking (n = 143)	Low-status working (n = 49)	High-status working (n = 31)	$F_{w/i}$ (d.f. = 1,68)	F_{wxi} (d.f. = 3,68)
Ground coffee	3.88	4.08	4.16	0.01	1.38
Instant coffee	5.31	5.55	5.13	0.14	1.16
Teabags	5.78	6.33	5.74	1.33	0.74
Instant tea	1.43	1.39	1.13	1.46	1.27
Instant breakfast	1.37	1.25	1.03	4.29[b]	0.47
Frozen juice	4.87	4.84	5.84	2.27	0.36
Bottled juice	2.12	2.06	1.48	3.28[a]	0.57
Frozen lemonade	1.91	1.78	2.03	0.85	0.62
Instant lemonade	1.52	1.49	1.26	2.19	1.91
Tang	2.03	2.16	1.39	4.30[b]	0.32
Homemade soup	3.43	3.37	3.74	1.87	3.10[b]
Canned soup	4.61	4.65	4.16	1.91	3.64[b]
Cup-a-soup	2.15	2.31	2.06	0.63	1.11
Rice	3.59	3.84	4.58	5.19[b]	1.80
Instant rice	2.22	2.35	2.13	0.45	0.98
Instant potatoes	1.52	1.41	1.71	1.13	1.24
Hamburgers	3.93	4.22	3.71	4.89[b]	1.27
Hot dogs	3.43	4.04	3.35	5.76[b]	2.29[a]
Frozen pizza	1.55	1.67	1.32	3.53[a]	0.58
TV dinners	1.45	1.51	1.16	3.12[a]	0.16
Canned ravioli	1.52	1.76	1.32	6.32[b]	0.06
Canned spaghetti	1.71	1.96	1.39	6.21[b]	0.52
Fresh vegetables	5.75	5.86	5.74	0.09	1.14
Canned vegetables	4.39	4.57	3.94	1.90	1.56
Frozen vegetables					
Economy pacs	2.10	1.80	3.32	11.56[b]	1.26
Regular national brands	2.76	2.69	3.10	0.37	0.25
Store brands	3.14	2.80	3.81	4.29[b]	1.39
Boil pouches	1.58	1.43	1.68	0.32	0.49
Casserole entrees	1.37	1.24	1.45	0.50	0.92
International combinations	1.51	1.37	1.26	0.16	0.09
Pillai's criterion				0.55[a]	1.24
Hotelling's trace criterion				1.22[a]	2.39
Wilk's lambda				0.45[a]	0.19

[a] $p < 0.10$.
[b] $p < 0.05$.
NOTE: F values for tests between the two working-wife categories: $F_{w/i}$ presents the conditional tests of wife's occupational status after removing income effects, while F_{wxi} presents the test of their interaction. Mean consumption frequencies are presented based on a seven-point scale (7 = nearly every day, 6 = several times a week, 5 = about once a week, 4 = about once in two weeks, 3 = about once a month, 2 = rarely, 1 = never).

Table 2 MANOVA on shopping behavior, price sensitivity, and deal proneness for grocery items

Grocery shopping variable	Nonworking (n = 140)	Low-status working (n = 48)	High-status working (n = 28)	$F_{w/i}$ (2,190)	F_{wxi} (6,190)
Convenience store patronage	2.62	3.00	2.75	1.48	0.85
Number of grocery stores	1.96	1.90	1.89	0.63	0.60
Look for grocery specials in newspaper	3.54	3.58	2.89	2.53[a]	0.53
Read grocery sale ads carefully	3.54	3.77	3.00	2.60[a]	0.55
Mail coupon usage	3.39	3.88	2.95	3.15[b]	1.72
Newspaper coupon usage	2.71	3.08	2.25	3.62[b]	1.48
Compare grocery prices	3.52	3.58	3.04	1.87	0.96
Pillai's criterion				.124[b]	.175
Hotelling's trace criterion				.135[b]	.184
Wilk's lambda				.879[b]	.835

[a] $p < 0.10$.
[b] $p < 0.05$.
NOTE: F values involve tests among the three groups; $F_{w/i}$ presents the conditional tests of wife's occupational status after removing income effects, while F_{wxi} presents the tests of their interaction. Mean relative frequency values are presented for five-point interval scales for items 3 through 7 (with 5 = almost always and 1 = never); item 2 is the actual number of stores visited per week for groceries; item 1 was coded such that 5 = several times a week or more, and 1 = never.

paper, to read grocery sale ads less carefully, and to utilize mail and newspaper coupons to a lesser degree than NWW or LSW families.

Makeup Usage and Dress Purchases
The top half of Table 3 presents MANOVA results for makeup usage. At the multivariate level, wife's occupation was significant both before and after removing income. The LSW wives used more facial makeup base, contour cream, lipstick, and nail polish than either HSW or NWW wives. They also used more blush/rouge, eyeshadow, and mascara than NWW wives. The HSW wives used more blush/rouge and mascara than NWW wives, but less facial makeup base or eyebrow pencil than either NWW or LSW wives. Thus, the strongest support for Hypothesis 4 is found among LSW wives.

Although the multivariate single-factor, conditional, and interaction tests of women's dress purchases for four price categories were significant, few univariate tests were significant. The LSW wives purchased more $25–$40 dresses than NWW wives ($p < 0.10$), but fewer $41–$60 dresses than either NWW or HSW wives ($p < 0.10$). The HSW wives purchased more $41–$60 dresses than LSW wives, and more dresses over $60 than either LSW or NWW wives ($p < 0.05$). Thus, although both makeup usage and dress purchases support Hypothesis 4, different patterns distinguish the two classes of working wives.

Television Viewing and Ownership
Respondents were asked to indicate when they typically turned their television sets on and off for evening viewing, along with the make, age, and model type (portable versus console, and color versus black and white) for each television set (up to three) owned, and whether or not they subscribed to cable television, owned a converter, or had remote control or instant zoom-in features. The bottom half of Table 3 presents the results of

ANOVAs on these variables. Consistent with Hypothesis 5, HSW families turned their sets on later and watched less television, whereas LSW families turned their sets on earlier and watched more television than NWW families.

The relationships between wife's occupation and television ownership measures were weak, although consistent with Hypothesis 5. The LSW families tended to own more televisions and to own color televisions more than HSW or NWW fami-

Table 3 MANOVA on makeup usage items and ANOVAS on television viewing and ownership

Dependent variable	Nonworking (n = 144)	Low-status working (n = 49)	High-status working (n = 31)	$F_{w/i}$ (2,197)	F_{wxi} (6,197)
Makeup usage[d]					
Facial makeup base	1.49	1.94	.90	4.12[b]	1.24
Blush/rouge	1.19	2.02	1.71	5.44[c]	.89
Contour cream	.44	.76	.29	1.45	.30
Eyeshadow	1.14	1.90	1.48	2.71[b]	.63
Eyeliner	.42	.65	.48	.67	.28
Mascara	1.02	1.53	1.51	4.07[b]	3.66[c]
Eyebrow pencil	.88	1.12	.42	2.90[a]	1.09
Lipstick	2.53	3.24	2.48	2.12	1.32
Lipgloss	.56	.69	1.03	1.44	1.31
Nail polish	1.22	1.65	1.10	2.25[a]	.44
Hairspray	1.11	1.12	.67	.61	.42
Pillai's criterion				.18[b]	.39[a]
Hotelling's trace criterion				.19[b]	.45[a]
Wilk's lambda				.83[b]	.66[a]
Television viewing/ownership[e]					
Time television turned on	6.19	5.48	6.87	6.92[c]	0.34
Time television turned off	10.87	10.85	10.62	0.45	4.79[c]
Hours evening television	4.69	5.12	3.75	4.46[b]	0.88
Number of televisions	1.55	1.71	1.35	3.30[b]	0.61
Number of color televisions	0.78	0.90	0.71	1.91	1.40
Primary television set					
Age	5.37	4.94	6.07	0.41	2.13[a]
Type (none, portable, console/floor)	1.34	1.37	1.23	0.59	0.77
Type (none, black/white, color)	1.50	1.69	1.38	1.55	1.22

[a] $p < 0.10$.
[b] $p < 0.05$.
[c] $p < 0.01$.
[d] Mean frequency of usage is based on a four-point scale (4 = everyday, 3 = several days a week, 1 = evenings out, special occasions, and rarely, 0 = never).
[e] Values presented are means; television types were coded as 0, 1, and 2.
NOTE: F values involve tests among the three groups: $F_{w/i}$ presents the conditional tests of wife's occupational status after removing income effects, while F_{wxi} presents the test of their interaction.

lies. Middle- to lower-income LSW families owned newer televisions (significant interaction).

Major and Minor Appliance Ownership

For major appliances (microwaves, dishwashers, clothes washers and dryers, refrigerators, and freezers) respondents were asked to indicate ownership, brand, age, and features possessed. The total number of features possessed was utilized as a surrogate for quality level of appliances owned. Ownership of 15 minor kitchen appliances was also determined.

Log linear modeling and likelihood ratio Chi squares (Dillon 1979) were applied to examine nominal ownership data on these seven major and 15 minor appliances; microwave ($p < 0.10$) was the only appliance significant for wife's occupation alone, with HSW, followed by LSW, families most likely to own them. The HSW families were most likely to own waffle irons and drip coffee makers ($p < 0.10$), and least likely to own a toaster ($p < 0.10$) or a toaster oven ($p < 0.05$), in tests of the model in which wife's occupation was added to income. Although these findings are consistent with Hypothesis 6, and with the "gourmet" orientation of HSW families, the paucity of significant relationships suggests only weak support of Hypothesis 6.

Separate ANOVAs were run on feature-count indices for five major appliances. Both LSW and HSW families tended to own multifeature washers (even after removing income) and dryers (as well as dishwashers when t-tests were examined, $p < 0.10$), compared to NWW families. Marginally significant interaction effects with income were found for both refrigerator and range feature indices. Higher mean feature counts for refrigerators and ranges were found for high-income HSW families, providing further weak support for Hypothesis 6.

Automobile Ownership

No significant differences were found in number of automobiles owned or in age or type of the family's primary car. The HSW families owned smaller and newer second cars ($p < 0.05$), even after adjusting for income, possibly reflecting stronger wife influence in family auto purchasing. However, Hypothesis 7 is not generally supported.

CONCLUSIONS AND IMPLICATIONS

The results indicate that a three-way categorization of family types based on wife's occupational status holds promise as a summary segmentation construct. Notably, the most prominent type of effect encountered here would be totally lost by a two-way scheme: contrasting or opposite consumption profiles emerged between HSW and LSW families for convenience foods, deal proneness, and emphasis on television.

While it would be inappropriate to advance generalizations based on one exploratory study, this classification scheme seems particularly salient for consumption areas linked to performance of traditional female work tasks. Future research might examine family consumption for a variety of labor-saving services and leisure activities, along with family decision processes. Addition of other categories, such as "plan to work" (Bartos 1978) or "interrupted worker" (Rapoport and Rapoport 1971) wives, to this trichotomous scheme might prove worthwhile, but would require the development of standardized measurement and classification procedures.

Major changes in wives' occupational status also hold implications for traditional consumer behavior constructs. Murphy and Staples (1979) cite smaller family size, postponement of marriage, and rising divorce rates as the demographic trends that justify a reconceptualization of the family life cycle. They might have added the growing number of both career and noncareer oriented working wives to this list. A woman's employment is likely to influence these tendencies as well as delay progression through the family life cycle. Grouping by wife's occupational status within life-cycle stages might enhance explanation of family lifestyle and consumption patterns.

As others have observed (Engel, Blackwell, and Kollat 1978; Zaltman and Wallendorf 1979), social class may be the consumer behavior construct most in need of reevaluation. Haug (1973) concluded that the *majority* of working wife families would be assigned to different social classes if the wife's, rather than the husband's, occupation was used in class assignment; she also demonstrated that using wife's occupation alters conclusions about differences among classes. Incorporating wife's occupation into social-class measurement might change traditional generalizations regarding class differences in consumption and lifestyles.

REFERENCES

Anderson, Beverlee B. (1972), "Working Women versus Non-Working Women: A Comparison of Shopping Behavior," in *1972 Combined Proceedings*, eds. Boris W. Becker and Helmut Becker, Chicago: American Marketing Association, pp. 355–9.

Bartos, Rena (1978), "What Every Marketer Should Know About Women," *Harvard Business Review*, 56, 73–85.

Bebbington, A. C. (1973), "The Function of Stress in the Dual-Career Family," *Journal of Marriage and Family*, 32, 530–7.

Business Week (1978), "Americans Change: How Drastic Shifts in Demographics Affect the Economy," February 20, 64–9.

Douglas, Susan (1976b), "Working Wife vs. Non-Working Wife Families: A Basis for Segmenting Grocery Markets?" in *Advances in Consumer Research: Vol. 3*, ed. Beverlee B. Anderson, Ann Arbor: Association for Consumer Research, pp. 191–8.

Engel, James F., Blackwell, Roger D., and Kollat, David T. (1978), *Consumer Behavior*, New York: Holt, Rinehart, and Winston.

Hafstrom, Jeanne L., and Dunsing, Marilyn M. (1978), "Socioeconomic and Social Psychological Influences on Reasons Wives Work," *Journal of Consumer Research*, 5, 169–75.

Haug, Marie R. (1973), "Social Class Measurement and Women's Occupational Roles," *Social Forces*, 52, 86–93.

Hayghe, Howard (1975), "Marital and Family Characteristics of the Labor Force, March, 1974," *Special Labor Force Report 173*, Washington DC: U.S. Department of Labor Statistics.

Hollingshead, August B., and Redlich, Frederick C. (1958), *Social Class and Mental Illness*, New York: John Wiley & Sons.

Hunt, Janet G., and Hunt, Larry (1977), "Dilemmas and Contradictions of Status: The Case of the Dual Career Family," *Social Problems*, 24, 407–16.

Levy, Sidney J. (1966), "Social Class and Consumer Behavior," in *On Knowing the Consumer*, ed. J. Newman, New York: John Wiley & Sons, pp. 146–60.

Murphy, Patrick E., and Staples, William A. (1979), "A Modernized Family Life Cycle," *Journal of Consumer Research*, 6, 12–22.

Rapoport, Rhona, and Rapoport, Robert N. (1971), "Further Considerations on the Dual Career Family," *Human Relations*, 24, 519–33.

Reynolds, Fred D., and Wells, William D. (1977), *Consumer Behavior*, New York: McGraw Hill.

Scanzoni, John (1976), "Sex Role Change and Influences on Birth Intentions," *Journal of Marriage and Family*, 38, 43–60.

_____ (1977), "Changing Sex Roles and Emerging Directions in Family Decision Making," *Journal of Consumer Research*, 4, 185–8.

Wall Street Journal (1978), "Women at Work," reprint series, August/September.

Wells, William D., and Tigert, Douglas J. (1971), "Activities, Interests and Opinions," *Journal of Advertising Research*, 11, 27–35.

Zaltman, Gerald, and Wallendorf, Melanie (1979), *Consumer Behavior: Basic Findings and Managerial Implications*, New York: John Wiley & Sons.

AN EXPECTATIONAL VIEW OF CONSUMER SPENDING PROSPECTS

F. THOMAS JUSTER

THEORY

Consumer spending decisions are influenced by three sets of factors: changes in real income growth rates, changes in balance sheet position, and changes in "animal spirits," or more prosaically, in consumer expectations, attitudes and plans. Most models of consumer behavior focus heavily on income and balance sheet variables, with particular attention typically paid to changes in transitory and permanent income and income taxes, and to net worth. Recent work has also focused on the asset and liability sides of the balance sheet, on the grounds that liquidity differences are important. Some few models attempt to introduce expectational measures into the econometrics, but such variables typically carry little weight in the models.

The behavior of the variables in these models is especially interesting when viewed over the late 1970s, when the expansion beginning in 1975 was beginning to show signs of weakening. During 1978, most of the financial variables that tend to enter consumption equations were behaving in ways broadly consistent with sluggish to modest growth in consumption. . . .

. . .

. . . The pervasive consumer reaction to general price increases during the postwar period had always (with few exceptions) been retrenchment on spending and increases in saving. But reactions to prospective price increases for specific items like houses and cars can be, and in 1978 was, quite different. The survey data are unambiguous on this point: many consumers thought that this was a good time to buy houses and cars, mainly because they expected housing and car prices to rise substantially in future, and hence felt that it was better to buy now rather than wait until later. Thus anticipatory buying was clearly an important element in consumer behavior, and had been holding up the rate of consumer spending in the face of increasing pessimism about both short- and long-term economic prospects. And consumer skepticism about the ability of policy-makers to cope with macroeconomic solutions underlay their pessimism about general economic prospects.

Source: F. Thomas Juster, "An Expectational View of Consumer Spending Prospects," *Journal of Economic Psychology* 1, March, 1981, 87–103. Reprinted with permission of author and North-Holland Publishing Co., Amsterdam.

. . . Two factors stand out: first, consumers were increasingly less likely to regard effective government economic policies as a reason to expect good business conditions; second, consumers were increasingly more likely to link unfavorable expectations about future business conditions to expectations of increased prices. Thus the decline in optimism about both short- and long-term business conditions was in some significant part due to the expectations that inflation will bring on deteriorating business conditions, and to the expectation that economic policy would fail to cope with deteriorating business conditions.[1]

. . . The proportion of respondents who judge that the present is a good time to buy household durables, houses and cars had risen sharply over several years prior to 1978, and had held up strongly in 1978 largely because an increasing proportion of people report that this was a good time to buy because prices would be higher in future. As a proportion of all favorable opinions about why "this is a good time to buy," the anticipatory buying rationale has almost doubled for household durables since 1975 and had exactly doubled for automobiles.

In a general sense, it can be argued that all of the consumer survey data were signalling prospective weakness. Increasing pessimism based on deteriorating expectations clearly foreshadows future weakness in spending, and while anticipatory buying is a reflection of current strength, it is surely a harbinger of future weakness. At some point, consumers would decide that the risks of deteriorating financial position no longer warranted buying in advance of expected price increases for specific products, and anticipatory buying would come to a halt. When that happened, consumer spending would be expected to be weaker than if such advance buying had not taken place to begin with, and there existed the potential for a significant slide in consumer spending.

MODELLING CONSUMPTION BEHAVIOR[2]

Both the real economic variables that influence consumer behavior and the anticipatory ones can be combined into a set of forecasting models which can be used to view the likely path of future consumption. . . . The set of models presented here have been used in consumption forecast for the last several years, and represent an attempt to combine traditional economic variables with expectational measures in a set of single equation demand models. . . . All the models contain one or more variables reflecting consumer anticipations, and they are consciously designed to allow such variables to play an important role in explaining behavior. . . . The models include an equation predicting the personal saving rate, an equation predicting unit sales of automobiles, and an equation predicting the average "real price" of automobiles.

SAVING RATE

. . . The theory [behind the saving rate model] is relatively straightforward. In the long run, assuming no growth in income or in population, saving would disappear as assets become adjusted to the steady-state long-run income level. Thus saving arises because of disequilibrium between assets and income, or out of population growth. In the short run, changes in various components of income (including personal taxes and social security taxes) will produce positive or negative saving as part of the adjustment process. Finally, uncertainty about real income prospects will have an impact on short-run saving behavior, although uncertainty factors are expected to have little or no long-run effect.

In previous work, the author along with a number of colleagues has used consumer expectations about price changes as a proxy for real income uncertainty. The best proxy in most previous work has proved to be the variation in expected price change among households, rather than the mean

---

[1] These data do not reveal whether judgments about the ineffectiveness of economic policy were due to the perception that policy-makers were less adept now than formerly, or to the perception that the problems were more intractable than they used to be.

[2] The analysis here draws heavily on other work done by the author.

level of price change expected by households. The argument is that wide variation among households in the mean expected price change will tend to be associated with greater uncertainty at the level of individual expected price change, and it is individual uncertainty about price changes expected in the future which is the principal cause of real income uncertainty.

The automobile demand equations differentiate the demand for unit sales and the demand for "quality" per unit. Unit sales are explained within a stock adjustment framework, but the dynamics of the process are subsumed within a measure of automobile purchase probability obtained from the surveys. The transitory effects of income change and expectations on automobile sales are reflected by another survey measure of optimism/pessimism, and by real income change and the rate of unemployment. The unit sales equation has several dummy variables reflecting special factors in the automobile market—strikes, rebates, and inventory cleanup prior to the introduction of new models.

Automobile "real price" or quality is basically explained by the level of real per-family income. . . . In these equations, automobile unit sales are dominantly explained by expectational variables reflecting cyclical swings in income and optimism, while automobile real price (quality) is dominantly explained by the level of income.

EMPIRICAL ESTIMATES

The basic empirical estimates for the personal saving rate are shown in Table 1, while estimates for the automobile purchase rate and the average real price of automobiles are shown in Table 2.

In the top panel of Table 1, the first equation shows the basic Houthakker-Taylor saving rate equation. The remainder of the rows show the results of estimating equations which add alternative measures of the uncertainty effect to the basic model. Equation 2 adds the filtered[3] changes in the Index of Consumer Sentiment (ICS), while the

other equations add both the filtered ICS and a set of lagged variables reflecting either prices or some dimension of expected price change. The price measures presented here include actual price change as measured by the Consumer Price Index, both the mean and the standard deviation of the Michigan data on price changes expected by consumers, and both the mean and the variance of price changes expected by the panel of professional economic forecasters surveyed by the financial columnist, J. A. Livingston.

In the bottom panel of Table 1, a number of constrained regressions are shown. All the data in the top half of the table imply very long lags in the response of consumer saving to changes in income components or in uncertainty. These lags seem unreasonably long on *a priori* grounds, and the bottom half of the table constraints the coefficient of the leg term to imply a quicker response of saving to changes in income or uncertainty.

Several features of these results are worth noting in detail. First, while the basic Houthakker-Taylor model produces reasonably good fits to the data, the addition of the uncertainty measures cuts the residual unexplained variance significantly—by about 20 percent, for the best of the equations involving uncertainty variables. Next, while the survey measures of expected price changes are slightly superior to the Consumer Price Index in unconstrained equations, the expectations do quite a bit better in the constrained regressions in the lower part of the table. If the constrained regressions convey a more accurate picture of the true lag structure in the model, the data suggests that expectations about price change contain significant information not contained in actual price change, although the actual change is not a bad proxy for price expectations. . . .

One of the most interesting results in the table is the relatively poor performance of the Livingston data on the price expectations held by professional economic forecasters, relatively to the price expectations held by consumers. The Livingston data have been used in a number of studies concerned with the structure of price expectations, partly because they have been widely available and partly because they have a very long history going back

[3]The filter eliminates changes in the ICS which are neither large nor systematic. The methodology is explained in Juster and Wachtel 1972.

Table 1 Regression equations explaining personal saving behavior

Panel A: Unconstrained equations

	Regression coefficients (t-ratios)						Price variables							
Eq.	S_{-1}	ΔSI	ΔTX	ΔTR	ΔLPY	$ZICS_{-1}$	Name	P_{-1}	P_{-2}	P_{-3}	P_{-4}	$\overline{SE}$	R^2	DW
1	0.985 (99)	−0.71 (1.8)	−0.91 (11.4)	0.78 (3.9)	0.31 (5.3)							0.052	0.912	2.16
2	0.981 (106)	−0.91 (2.4)	−0.87 (11.7)	0.77 (4.2)	0.41 (6.9)	−0.0058 (3.9)						0.048	0.928	2.24
3	0.911 (29)	−0.61 (1.7)	−0.84 (11.3)	0.82 (4.8)	0.40 (6.8)	−0.0038 (2.5)	SRC $E(\sigma p)$	0.029 (3.3)	−0.008 (0.7)	0.000 (0.3)	−0.013 (1.6)	0.045	0.941	2.32
4	0.971 (51)	−0.63 (1.7)	−0.93 (11.9)	0.84 (4.7)	0.39 (6.6)	−0.0042 (2.8)	SRC $E(\bar{P})$	0.013 (2.5)	−0.011 (1.7)	0.012 (1.9)	−0.013 (2.5)	0.046	0.935	2.39
5	0.961 (51)	−0.86 (2.2)	−0.86 (11.1)	0.77 (4.2)	0.45 (6.7)	−0.0059 (3.8)	LIV $E(\sigma_p^2)$	0.018 (1.2)	−0.016 (0.6)	0.008 (0.3)	−0.000 (0.2)	0.048	0.930	2.23
6	0.970 (57)	−0.91 (2.4)	−0.87 (10.6)	0.76 (3.9)	0.44 (7.0)	−0.0056 (3.7)	LIV $E(\bar{P})$	0.018 (0.7)	−0.012 (0.2)	−0.017 (0.3)	−0.021 (0.8)	0.048	0.930	2.26
7	0.964 (53)	−0.83 (2.2)	−0.87 (11.8)	0.76 (4.2)	0.44 (7.2)	−0.0047 (3.1)	CPI	0.0086 (2.2)	−0.0044 (1.0)	0.0065 (1.5)	−0.0084 (2.2)	0.046	0.935	2.38

Panel B: Constrained regressions

	Regression coefficients (t-ratios)						Price variables							
Eq.	S_{-1}	ΔSI	ΔTX	ΔTR	ΔLPY	$ZICS_{-1}$	Name	P_{-1}	P_{-2}	P_{-3}	P_{-4}	$\overline{SE}$	R^2	DW
1	0.85	−0.47 (1.3)	−0.80 (11.0)	0.86 (4.9)	0.41 (6.9)	−0.0041 (2.6)	SRC $E(\sigma p)$	0.032 (3.6)	−0.005 (0.5)	0.002 (0.2)	−0.013 (1.6)	0.045	0.755	2.07
2	0.80	−0.35 (0.9)	−0.76 (10.0)	0.88 (4.8)	0.42 (6.8)	−0.0044 (2.7)	SRC $E(\sigma p)$	0.034 (3.7)	−0.003 (0.3)	0.004 (0.4)	−0.013 (0.14)	0.048	0.739	1.80
3	0.70	−0.12 (0.3)	−0.70 (7.8)	0.94 (4.3)	0.45 (6.2)	−0.0049 (2.6)	SRC $E(\sigma p)$	0.038 (3.5)	0.001 (0.1)	0.007 (0.6)	−0.012 (1.2)	0.056	0.698	1.32
4	0.85	−0.40 (0.9)	−0.77 (8.8)	0.92 (4.3)	0.57 (8.2)	−0.0043 (2.4)	CPI	0.015 (3.5)	−0.000 (0.1)	0.001 (1.7)	−0.007 (1.5)	0.056	0.681	1.56
5	0.80	−0.21 (0.4)	−0.73 (7.2)	0.98 (3.9)	0.63 (7.7)	−0.0042 (2.0)	CPI	0.018 (3.6)	0.000 (0.1)	0.011 (1.7)	−0.0077 (1.2)	0.066	0.637	1.26
6	0.70	0.16 (0.2)	−0.65 (4.7)	1.12 (3.3)	0.74 (6.8)	−0.0038 (1.4)	CPI	0.024 (3.5)	0.004 (0.5)	0.013 (1.6)	−0.006 (0.8)	0.089	0.571	0.94

NOTES:

All dollar variables are deflated per household.

S is personal savings, ΔSI the change in social insurance contributions made by employees, ΔTX is change in personal tax and non tax payments, ΔTR is change in transfer payment, and ΔLPY change in labor and property income.

$ZICS$ is the filtered change in the Index of Consumer Sentiment.

The SRC price variables are the mean and standard deviation of the distribution of expected price change obtained from the Michigan Survey of Consumers, the Livingston price variables are the mean and the variance of the distribution of expected price change obtained by J. A. Livingston, and the CPI is the Consumer Price Index.

Other variables included in the regression and not shown in Table 1 are three dummies reflecting automobile strikes (in 1964:4, 1967:4 and 1970:4), and dummy variables reflecting the anticipation of tax cuts—one in the first quarter of 1975 prior to the massive tax cut in the second quarter, and the other in 1977: 1 prior to the abortive tax cut planned for the second quarter of 1977.

Table 2 Automobile demand equations

Panel A: Unit sales of automobiles

Time period	CAR/HH$_{-1}$	P*	MAZICS$_{-1}$	ΔYD/HH	U	Const.	R²	$\overline{SE}$	DW
			Regression coefficients (t-ratios)						
1954–1978	0.52	0.69	0.0018	0.020	−0.0024	0.018	0.814	0.0096	2.10
	(7.3)	(5.0)	(4.8)	(2.0)	(2.6)	(1.5)			
1954–1974	0.47	1.03	0.0019	0.017	−0.0020	−0.005	0.850	0.0091	2.67
	(6.4)	(6.0)	(4.2)	(1.3)	(1.6)	(0.3)			

Panel B: Average real price of automobiles

Time period	V$_{-1}$	YD/HH		Const.	R²	$\overline{SE}$	DW
	Regression coefficients (t-ratios)						
1954–1978	0.75	0.056		0.040	0.941	0.079	2.67
	(11.3)	(3.3)		(0.5)			

NOTES:

CAR/HH is the new passenger car purchase rate deflated by households.

*P** is new car purchase probability, obtained from the Michigan Survey.

MAZICS is a two-quarter moving average of the filtered Index of Consumer Sentiment (see *ZICS* in Table 1 Notes).

ΔYD/HH is change in real disposable income per household.

U is the general unemployment rate.

V is the average dollar price of new cars deflated by an index of new car prices.

YD/HH is real income per household.

to the late 1940s.[4] In addition, some would argue on theoretical grounds that the Livingston series is the right data to include in models of consumer or business decision making.

The last point is of some methodological as well as practical interest. One school of thought with substantial influence in many current policy discussions takes the view that decisions are made on the basis of "rational" expectations, by which is meant simply that decision makers act on the basis of the best available information including forecasts of the probable impact of economic activity on policymaking. In a world with zero information dissemination costs, the professional efforts of economic forecasters are presumably worth more weight than the unguided guesses of a representative sample of consumers. But there is no evidence from Table 1 that consumers act in that way: their personal saving behavior is not at all well explained by the guesses of professional forecasters, which

[4]See John A. Carlson 1977; and Mullineaux 1978.

ought to be the proper ingredient in a rational expectations world. Rather, they act on the basis of their own expectations, which differ significantly and often vary sharply from the expectations of professional forecasters. Thus, however relevant the rational expectations model may be for commodity markets and other market in which professional speculative activity is a dominant force, that seems not to be true of the formation of consumer expectations about price change nor of the behavior relationship between price expectations and savings. I find those results both plausible and sensible—and enlightening about the appropriate role of the rational expectations theory in economic modeling and in the formulation of economic policy.

Comparison of the SRC data on expected price change and actual price change are interesting and potentially illuminating, . . . in that they suggest that a rise in either actual prices or expected prices (means or standard deviations) will result in higher saving.

One explanation for the roughly equivalent impact of actual or expected price changes on savings in the top half of the table is that the unconstrained equation essentially fits a very long moving average of all the independent variables to actual savings. If the moving average is long enough, there can hardly be much difference between the explanatory power of expected price changes and actual price changes, provided the two bear a reasonably close resemblance to each other, as of course they do. But in the constrained regressions in the bottom half of the table, one would expect to find greater discriminating power, and that comparison clearly favors the role of expected price change in determining saving behavior.

Other tests with the saving model shown in Table 1 were also conducted, primarily to see if the very large coefficients of personal tax change, social security tax change, and change in transfer payments could be due to the presence of poorly measured seasonal variation. . . . But neither straightforward seasonal dummies themselves, nor seasonal dummies interacted with particular tax or transfer items, proved to be of any use in the equation. . . . Hence, whatever is accounting for these

very strong impacts of tax and transfer changes on saving, it appears not to be poor seasonal adjustment of the series themselves.

The basic saving rate equation does contain a set of dummy variables not shown in Table 1, which are included to adjust for the effects of particular events that the equation should not be expected to reflect. Specifically, dummy variables are included for the three automobile strike quarters—the fourth quarters of 1964, 1967, and 1970. Automobile strikes are associated with low levels of automobile sales, and since automobile sales are an extremely important determinant of change in consumer installment credit, they also have a significant impact on the measured personal saving rate. . . .

In addition, there is some indirect survey evidence to suggest that the 1975 cut in personal income taxes had an effect on personal saving prior to its implementation, and similar (but less persuasive) evidence that the abortive 1977 second quarter tax cut also had an anticipatory impact on saving behavior. Thus the equation has first quarter 1975 and first quarter 1977 dummy variables, designed to reflect anticipation of a tax cut.

AUTOMOBILE SALES

The automobile purchase rate model . . . implies a stock adjustment framework, with transitory changes in income having a strong effect on automobile sales. For the empirical implementation, a good bit of evidence suggests that a survey measure of automobile purchase probability is a good substitute for the entire stock adjustment process, while other survey measures of optimism tend to be superior to objective measures of income change. The idea is that consumers reported probability of vehicle purchase must reflect the mechanism implied by a stock adjustment process, and hence can replace that part of the model.

The equations summarized in Table 2 are basically driven by the two survey measures of vehicle purchase probability and the Index of Consumer Sentiment, but the present version of the model provides room for a couple of conventional financial variables—the change in real per-household income, and the general unemployment rate. . . .

One interesting aspect of the model fitted through the first quarter of 1978 is the reemergence of financial variables as having some independent influence on purchase rates. In the version estimated through 1974, neither level of real per household income, change in income, nor the unemployment rate made significant contributions to an explanation of purchase rates. But in equations fitted through 1978, both real income change and unemployment become significant at conventional levels, while the estimated influence of the survey variables is a bit less.

A possible interpretation of this shift of power in the equation from expectational to real financial varibles is that the uncertainty which has characterized the economy during recent years has meant that consumers are more apt to behave in accordance with actual events than with events that they anticipate, because the anticipations themselves are less firmly held and therefore less closely linked to actual behavior. Given the notorious sensitivity of time series to minor shifts in data occasioned by revisions, as well as to the presence or absence of other variables, that must be regarded as speculative. But it seems an interesting speculation, and is in accord with what does seem clearly the case— that consumers are much more volatile in their expectations and attitudes now than they were back in the 1960s and early 1970s, and the increased volatility could mean that the link between expectations and behavior has become modified.

The equation explaining real car price (average quality per car) is straightforward. Average car quality appears to be a simple function of permanent income, and is reflected by an equation with real per-family income and a distributed lag. The equation is also shown in Table 2.

USING MODELS TO FORECAST

One can use the set of models described above to make predictions of the saving rate, the level of automobile sales, the level of real automobile price (i.e., quality), and automobile demand in constant dollars, provided estimates of the relevant inde-

pendent variables, such as changes in real income components and the future values of the survey measures, can be obtained. Inserting plausible values of the independent variables into these models would have yielded 1979 predictions of an increase in the rate of personal saving, and a decline in the automobile sales rate. The second of these events would have been accurately foreshadowed, but the first would not—the rate of personal saving continued to drop throughout 1979, and reached historically low levels during the latter part of that year.

It is instructive to ask: why would the saving rate model have produced estimates that were wide of the mark during 1979? The answer lies in the analysis described earlier in the text, where the growing divergence between the current conditions and expectations components on the index of the consumer sentiment were discussed. While it was clear enough that expectations were getting more pessimistic, and while they actually became more pessimistic during 1979, it was also true that speculative buying, which is reflected by the survey measures of current market conditions, grew in strength. But the role of price expectation in the above model is to measure uncertainty about future changes in real income, and the model contains no provision for the role of anticipatory buying in the determination of saving behavior. Thus during a period when anticipatory buying forces reached record levels in the U.S. economy, a model which behaved quite sensibly during most of the postwar period would have provided estimates of saving behavior that turned out to be quite far off the mark.

The basic message from this exercise is that one has to be very chary in using time-series models that may reflect shifting relationships. Implicitly, the models discussed in this paper could be expected to hold in economic environments where the dominant reaction of consumers to expectations in rising prices is the conservatism and caution induced by the uncertainty associated with changes in future real income. While that was true throughout virtually all of the postwar period in the U.S., it was clearly not true of developments in 1978 and 1979, where the dominant reaction to the expectation of rising prices was speculative buying and debt acquisition centered in housing, cars, and durables.

We may ask: why did U.S. consumers react with a speculative buying response to the inflation of 1978–79, while they failed to react in that way to the inflation of 1973–74? The likely answer is that consumers learned from experience. In 1973–74, when the first bout of double-digit inflation associated with rising oil and other raw material prices was experienced in the U.S. and the western world generally, consumers reacted with the view that those volatile price rises would not be associated with gains in money income, hence would be reflected in sharply declining real incomes. While real income did in fact decline as a consequence of a severe recession, consumers discovered that they survived the crisis and that neither their financial status nor the economy fell apart in the face of inflationary stresses. Thus, when the next episode of double-digit inflation began to appear in the late 1970s, they were more impressed by the gains to be obtained from acquiring goods via expanded debt than by the prospective losses resulting from the uncertainties associated with an overextended financial position. And the proposition that consumer spending would collapse when the speculative buying fever finally burst was strikingly demonstrated during the early spring of 1980, when the speculative buying measures collapsed, and with them consumer spending, in the aftermath of the vigorous anti-inflation and credit control measures announced by the Federal Reserve Board and the President in March of that year.

REFERENCES

Carlson, John A., 1977. A study of price forecasts. Annals of Economic and Social Measurement 6 (Winter), 27–56.

Juster, F. Thomas, 1973. Savings behavior, uncertainty and price expectations. The economic outlook for 1974. Papers presented to the 21st Conference on the Economic Outlook at the University of Michigan, Nov., 1973.

Juster, F. Thomas, 1975. Inflation and consumer savings behavior—some time-series and cross-section results. Prepared for the CIRET conference, Stockholm, Sweden, June 1975 (mimeo).

Juster, F. Thomas and Lester Taylor, 1975. Toward a theory of saving behavior. Papers and Proceedings of the American Economic Association, May, 1975.

Juster, F. Thomas and Paul Wachtel, 1972. A note on price inflation and the savings rate. Brookings Papers on Economic Activity 3, 765–778.

Mullineaux, Donald, J., 1978. On testing for rationality: another look at the Livingston price expectations data. Journal of Political Economy 86, 329–335.

SECTION III

GROUP NORMS AND ROLES IN CONSUMER BEHAVIOR

Consumers participate in numerous groups within the larger social systems to which they belong. The consumer belongs to two particular formal groups, the family and a firm or work group. Such groups are called *affiliative groups*. Other groups to which consumers do not belong still influence their behavior because they would like to join them. These groups are called *aspiration groups*. There are still other groups consumers may not wish to join but that somehow influence their behavior because they want to show they do *not* belong. These groups are called *dissociative groups*. All three types of groups are called *reference groups;* they are groups consumers may think about and hence may be influenced by when forming an attitude or behaving in a certain way. The reader will probably encounter these terms when studying consumer behavior and the terminology is introduced for this reason.

An illustration of these groups might be helpful. Consider a teenager choosing new clothing. Two important affiliative groups would be the teenager's family and immediate circle of friends. The family may influence what is purchased by controlling the amount of financial resources provided to the teenager. The friendship group may influence how much of the wardrobe is comprised of very informal leisure clothes as opposed to dressier items. The style of clothes displayed by an in-group in the teenager's school may also influence clothing selection. By choosing clothing compatible with the style displayed by this group to which the teenager doesn't belong (we'll assume), the teenager may feel the chances of acceptance by this group are increased. This in-group is an aspiration group. A dissociative group may be a group that is thought of negatively or positively, and membership in that group is not desired. The dress behavior of a disliked group may serve as clear clues to the teenager about what clothing behavior to avoid.

Consumers need not interact regularly with a group for it to be influential in their buying behavior. Nor is it necessary for face-to-face interaction to ever occur for a group to be influential. Examples include movie stars, leaders of a consumer advocate group, or a legislative subcommittee holding a hearing on food quality. There are many ways in which groups are influential regardless of their type (e.g., affiliative group versus dissociative) or the degree of interaction and face-to-face contact. Groups influence such phenomena as:

1. Product preferences
2. Brand preferences
3. Deliberate avoidance of products and brands
4. The allocation of income across product categories
5. Price sensitivity
6. Store patronage
7. Sensitivity and susceptibility to nonprice promotional activities such as advertising and cents-off coupons
8. How consumers process information

It is one thing to know what kind of groups may influence consumers and what attitudes and behaviors can be influenced by social groups. It is another matter to know how and why groups influence consumers. In addressing this latter issue we will consider only groups to which consumers belong. Individual consumers have goals that are often best achieved in collaboration with other people usually seeking the same goals or compatible goals. Individuals in the group reward a group member to the extent that the group member contributes toward the achievement of the collective goals of the group. Similarly, individuals are punished if they detract from the achievement of group goals.

Through the application of rewards and punishments, certain behaviors emerge that are important for achieving goals. These behaviors represent what the group as a whole believes are appropriate behaviors. Such collective evaluations of behavior in terms of what is appropriate are called *norms*. Some norms reflect the values and goals of the group. These are called *expressive norms*. A purchasing agent who is constantly seeking information about new technological developments by reading the relevant literature in his or her area and attending professional meetings and trade shows reflects the firm's goals of being a leader in the field and being up-to-date. The purchasing agent seeking the best price-quality combination for a component part from a supplier is following the firm's goal of obtaining profit while maintaining a reputation for quality products. This price-quality concern is an instrumental norm encouraged by the firm for all its members, perhaps especially those in the purchasing department.

Thus norms are specifications of behaviors that group members are expected to show or approximate. The task of the marketing manager is to identify these norms and to establish in the minds of the consumer just how a particular product fits with important norms, and also how a product may help the consumer conform to these norms. This brings us back to the earlier discussion of the various influences groups have on consumers. The influence of a group, say a family, on a teenager's price sensitivity may be exerted by the family rewarding the teenager for being frugal and punishing the teenager for being extravagant. A salesperson serving this particular teenager might want to know that the family group in this example has a norm about frugality. Thus each of the phenomena identified earlier as being influenced by groups is really influenced by the norms of groups. Group norms prescribe appropriate behaviors for each of those phenomena. Social groups often have a division of labor among their members to facilitate the achievement of group goals. Often these norms apply differentially. They may be more relevant to some people in a group and less relevant to other people, depending on the division of labor. Thus some people in a group for whom a norm is especially relevant are expected to behave somewhat differently. These expectations actually apply to any person who has a particular position assigned by the division of labor in a group. This position is called a *role*. A role is a set of expected behaviors for individuals who occupy a certain position as they interact with other people. The interaction may involve many people from diverse groups.

While it is important to determine what groups affect consumers and through what norms, it is also important to understand what roles individuals occupy. Knowing that social roles are important helps identify the set of norms that are most important in a group. If we know that the mother's role is the most important in a family with regard to the use of credit cards for nonbusiness reasons, then to understand household credit card usage we would want to study social norms pertaining to mothers' usage of credit cards.

It is important to remember that roles are social in nature; they involve a relationship between two or more individuals. Thus the role of mother really refers to relationships between mothers and children and probably mothers and fathers as well. The behavior of a mother will vary as a result of interaction with various children as the mother encounters their expectations and their efforts to influence her, and as she expresses her own expectations and attempts to influence. Moreover, the role relationship between a mother and child may be influenced by the relationship the mother has with the father, by a school teacher, and by friends who have children.

Similarly, the behavior of a puchasing agent is a result of expectations held by other people such as salespeople from other firms and various individuals in the company such as the production manager and vice-president for finance. The expectations of these people may actually create conflict for the purchasing agent. The production manager may demand high-quality materials while the financial officer demands purchasing at the lowest cost possible.

Many products and services are purchased as a symbolic expression of a role relationship. An engagement ring expresses the formation of a new role relationship. A gold watch given at a retirement ceremony expresses a change in another role relationship. Other products and services are required for the performance of a role. Medical equipment for medical personnel is an example of this. Food served to a dinner guest would be another illustration. The reader may well imagine numerous other situations where the purchase and use of products and services directly pertain to a role relationship.

Identical roles in different settings may vary. This is important to the marketer. A purchasing agent in one firm may have much less influence on a purchase decision than his or her counterpart in a competing firm. Similarly, the role of parent may vary substantially from culture to culture or even over time within the same family. Thus variation in roles exists and must be considered in the formulation of marketing strategy.

"STUDENTS AND HOUSEWIVES: DIFFERENCES IN SUSCEPTIBILITY TO REFERENCE GROUP INFLUENCE"

An individual may be motivated to follow the direction of a reference group for any of several reasons. First, if one finds that additional information is needed in order to make a decision, he/she may try to gather this information from a group with that kind of knowledge or expertise either by asking for this information directly or by inferring it from their behavior indirectly. This type of motivational influence is called informational reference group influence. Second, one may feel pressure to comply with the directives of the reference group, because he/she desires the rewards that the group may mediate. This second type of motivational influence is called utilitarian reference group influence. Third, he/she may either like the members of the reference group or use one's association with the reference group to enhance his/her ego, whether or not the group administers rewards and punishments. This third type of motivational influence is called value-expressive reference group influence.

Park and Lessig examine the differences between students and housewives for these three types of motivational reference group influence for twenty products. They found that there are significant differences between housewives and students for all three types of motivational reference group influences. Their results call into question the practice of generalizing findings from consumer research studies using business students as subjects to the general population.

"WORKING WIVES AND CONVENIENCE CONSUMPTION"

Because individuals belong to many different social groups, each with its own division of labor, an individual's assigned positions or roles may vary considerably from group to group. Again, depending on one's position, the groups to which one belongs will demand variable amounts of time and energy. When the multiple demands arising from membership in different groups become burdensome so that the individual's roles conflict, the individual experiences what is called role overload.

Because of the sharp increase in the employment of married women, consumer researchers have hypothesized a parallel increase both in the use of convenience foods and in the ownership of time-saving durables. Although family income and social status appear to correlate with convenience consumption, paradoxically, there appears to be no direct correlation with the wife's employment. To resolve this puzzle, Reilly has hypothesized an indirect relationship between wife's employment and convenience consumption that is mediated by role overload. To test this theory of such an indirect relationship, a structural equation model is employed that is based on three exogenous ("causes") constructs—wife's work involvement, family's social status, and wife's education—and four endogeneous ("effects") constructs—wife's earnings, wife's role overload, the number of convenience foods served to the family, and the number of time-saving durables owned by the family.

The model is then tested using a sample of Milwaukee housewives. The results of this test support role overload as a mediator between wife's employment and convenience consumption.

STUDENTS AND HOUSEWIVES: DIFFERENCES IN SUSCEPTIBILITY TO REFERENCE GROUP INFLUENCE

**C. WHAN PARK
AND
V. PARKER LESSIG**

Much of the experimental research conducted in psychology and consumer behavior has used college students as respondents. This raises a question concerning the external validity of the experimental results. The response differences between students and housewives have been examined in several studies (Sheth 1970; Khera and Benson 1970; Enis, Cox, and Stafford 1972; Shuptrine 1975; Copeland et al. 1973; Enis and Stafford 1969). None of these studies provided unequivocal conclusions regarding differences between the two populations.

Arndt (1971) reported that college students and their parents differ along "perceptual variables" where it is not clear whether the difference is a function of (a) the different kinds of items examined or (b) the differences in the usage of these items across the students and their parents. In addition to the inconclusive findings, there has been no systematic treatment of the locus of the level of response differences, that is, process related differences, or specific situation bounded response differences between the two types of groups.

The objective of the present study is to examine differences between students and housewives with respect to process-related differences, specifically, to examine differences between the two populations in terms of their susceptibility to reference group influence. The degree of reference group influence is examined for each of 20 products, and for three different types of reference group influence.

REFERENCE GROUP INFLUENCE

In the present study, a reference group is defined to be an actual or imaginary individual or group conceived of having significant relevance upon an individual's evaluations, aspirations, or behavior. Within this definition, three motivational influences of reference groups will be examined—informational, value expressive, and utilitarian.

Informational Reference Group Influence
This reference group influence is similar to the informational or comparative influence suggested by Deutsch and Gerard (1955), although their defini-

Source: C. Whan Park and V. Parker Lessig, "Students and Housewives: Differences in Susceptibility to Reference Group Influence," *Journal of Consumer Research*, Vol. 4, September, 1977, pp. 102–110. Reprinted with permission.

tion is not specific. An influence is accepted (internalized) if it is perceived as enhancing the individual's knowledge of his environment and/or his ability to cope with some aspect of this environment, e.g., purchasing a product.

An individual may use an informational reference group in two different ways. One is to actively search for information from opinion leaders or from a group with the appropriate expertise. Second, the individual makes an inference by observing the behavior of significant others.

Utilitarian Reference Group Influence

This reference group influence is similar to the normative influence (Deutsch and Gerard 1955), the conformity concept of "it-is-dangerous-not-to-conform" (Asch 1952), and the compliance process (Kelman 1961; Jahoda 1972). An individual in a product purchasing situation would be expected to comply with the preferences or expectations of another individual or group if:

1. He perceives that they mediate significant rewards or punishments;
2. He believes that his behavior will be visible or known to these others; and
3. He is motivated to realize the reward or to avoid the punishment.

A crucial difference between the utilitarian reference group influence examined in this paper and the normative social influences just cited is that most of these other social influences are derived from explicit rewards and punishments which accompany specific group memberships and specifically defined norms.

Value-Expressive Reference Group Influence

This reference group influence relates to an individual's motive to enhance or support his self-concept. Such an individual would be expected to associate himself with positive referents and/or dissociate himself from negative referents (Kelman 1961).

The value-expressive reference group influence is characterized by two different processes. First, an individual utilizes reference groups to express himself or bolster his ego. In this case, there should be a

consistency between the desire to express one's self and the psychological image attached to the reference group.

Second, an individual is influenced by a value-expressive reference group because of his simple affect (liking) for that group. This does not require consistency between one's self image and the psychological image attached to the reference group. Thus, an individual responds (e.g., adopts the recommendations) to the reference group although the content of responses (e.g., acceptance of recommendations) is irrelevant to the group.

REASONS FOR REFERENCE GROUP DIFFERENCES BETWEEN STUDENTS AND HOUSEWIVES

Motivational factors were emphasized as one of the determinants of perceptual processes (Bruner 1958) and as a critical element in explaining cognitive consistence theories (e.g., Katz 1968; Davis 1968; Kelman and Baron 1968). This leads to the speculation that if there are differences in needs or motivation among different people, there should also be process related differences among them. There is theoretical support for the existence of need differences between the two samples (students and housewives) in terms of their response to reference group influence.

First, need differences may exist due to differences in their age distributions. An age difference quite often accompanies a difference in (a) the amount of learning (i.e., the degree of familiarity with the product), (b) the accommodation of information (Jacoby et al. 1974), and (c) risk handling (Kogan and Wallach 1967). Another factor is that young people, such as college students, may be more susceptible to reference group influence since they would be expected to have more limited capacity to cope with uncertainty and risk than more mature individuals, such as housewives.

Second, need differences may exist between students and housewives due to differences in their immediate social surroundings and their daily activity patterns. We suspect that substantial differences may exist between students and housewives in terms of the frequency of informal social contacts, the intensity of peer pressure on one's choice behavior, the visibility of social approval in a group, and the rigidity of the group structure in which they interact. For example, we would expect students to have more frequent social contacts than housewives; we would also expect the group structure in which students interact (e.g., sororities, fraternities, and dormitories) to impose more rules and norms than is the case of groups in which housewives interact. The visibility of one's behavior in a rigid group structure would make students more responsive to group influence (Deutsch and Gerard 1955).

Also, the availability of frequent informal social contact (to which students are exposed perhaps more than housewives) facilitates obtaining information from others and aids in the social confirmation and legitimization of one's behavior. These informal groups play an important role in risk reduction. Several studies support the position that peers are a dominant influence on the behavior of young adults (Teter 1966; Kanter 1970; Scott 1974).

Third, need differences between students and housewives may exist due to differences in their stages in the socialization process. Specifically, hedonism (Rosenberg 1968) may be stronger among students than among housewives. Young people, like students, are in a continuous socialization process in which they are forming an ego, expressing themselves to an outside world, and testing their acceptability to others. Doing these things involves trial and error learning of ego expression and self-realization, both of which are part of the socialization process (Scott 1974). Ego-related consumption and a peer group's influence on it is perhaps best described by Reisman and Rosenborough (1955) who state that children learn "consumption necessities" from their parents but "affective consumption [styles and moods of consumption]" from peers.

An additional point is that although socialization is a lifelong process, the intensity of socialization in terms of the amount of learning should be much stronger at an earlier age than at a later age (Brim 1968). Two specific implications from this are that (a) socialization is a more active process among students than among housewives, and (b) students are more likely to have yet-to-be-solidified cognitive structures than housewives, thus making students more susceptible to changes in attitude and behavior (Feather 1971).

METHOD

Manifestation Statements

The authors and a graduate assistant exchanged ideas concerning the probable behavior which consumers manifest in conjunction with significant others. Furthermore, one of the authors conducted intensive informal interviews with one graduate and five undergraduate students relating to probable reference group behavior. Specifically, each student was instructed on the theoretical nature of each type of reference group influence and then asked to describe the behavior which he and others have likely exhibited in conjuction with each type of influence. Based upon these interviews and from general inferences in the literature, 18 statements relating to reference group influence were written. These statements were designed to be general enough to encompass different forms of behavior underlying a given type of reference group influence, yet specific enough to reflect only *one* motivational function.

The 18 statements were examined in a pretest using 22 consumer behavior students who were already familiar through class lectures with the different types of reference group influence. For 14 statements, the students' responses were consistent with our expectations. Since the 14 statements covered all three forms of reference group influence, only these statements were used in the main study, though some were changed slightly based upon pretest feedback. Of these revised 14 statements (see exhibit), five of these statements relate to the informational reference group influence, four to the utilitarian influence, and five to the value-expressive influence.

To test the validity of the revised statements, the student pretest was followed by a similar pretest consisting of 42 adult subjects living in the Kansas City metropolitan area, randomly selected from a telephone directory. After being informed through

Exhibit Statements manifesting reference group functions

Informational influence

A_1 The individual seeks information about various brands of the product from an association of professionals or independent group of experts.

A_2 The individual seeks information from those who work with the product as a profession.

A_3 The individual seeks brand related knowledge and experience (such as how Brand A's performance compares to Brand B's) from those friends, neighbors, relatives, or work associates who have reliable information about the brands.

A_4 The brand which the individual selects is influenced by observing a seal of approval of an independent testing agency (such as Good Housekeeping).

A_5 The individual's observation of what experts do influences his choice of a brand (such as observing the type of car which police drive or the brand of TV which repairmen buy).

Utilitarian influence

B_1 To satisfy the expectations of fellow work associates, the individual's decision to purchase a particular brand is influenced by their preferences.

B_2 The individual's decision to purchase a particular brand is influenced by the preferences of people with whom he has social interaction.

B_3 The individual's decision to purchase a particular brand is influenced by the preferences of family members.

B_4 The desire to satisfy the expectations which others have of him has an impact on the individual's brand choice.

Value-expressive influence

C_1 The individual feels that the purchase or use of a particular brand will enhance the image which others have of him.

C_2 The individual feels that those who purchase or use a particular brand possess the characteristics which he would like to have.

C_3 The individual sometimes feels that it would be nice to be like the type of person which advertisements show using a particular brand.

C_4 The individual feels that the people who purchase a particular brand are admired or respected by others.

C_5 The individual feels that the purchase of a particular brand helps him show others what he is, or would like to be (such as an athlete, successful businessman, good mother, etc.).

---

printed descriptive material of the three different forms of reference group influence, the subjects in this adult pretest were able to correctly associate the manifestation statements with the appropriate influence.

Subjects

Subjects from two different populations were selected for examination in the main study. For the first set of subjects, 162 housewives living in Topeka, Kansas area were randomly selected (from the telephone directory) as possible study participants. Each prospective respondent was contacted by telephone and informed that they would be paid two dollars for their participation. A total of 145 individuals indicated a willingness to cooperate and were therefore sent a questionnaire and a cov-

er letter; of these, 100 completed and returned all questions.

The second set of subjects consisted of unmarried junior and senior marketing students at the University of Kansas. Each student's participation was under one of two different response situations. Specifically, 51 students responded to the questionnaire in class. In order to examine the possible impact of two different response settings, an additional 52 students were asked to complete the questionnaire at home. Of these 52 students, 37 returned responses to all questions.

Measuring Reference Group Influence

Influences associated with a number of different types of products were examined. The products selected vary along two types of product classification (Enis 1974): loyal (to brand) vs. not loyal (to brand) and shopping vs. convenience. This set also includes representative products from Bourne's (1956) study in which he presented a matrix categorizing reference group influences upon products and brands. Specifically, the following 20 products were examined in this study: automobiles, beer, canned peaches, cigarettes, clothing, coffee, color television, facial soap, furniture, hamburger substitute, headache remedy, home air conditioner, insurance, laundry soap, low phosphate detergent, magazine or book selection, mouthwash, refrigerator, physician selection, and transistor radios.

The subjects were presented the 14 reference group manifestation statements with a listing of the 20 products, and asked to indicate, for each product, the extent to which the situation described by the statement is relevant to a consumer's alterna-

tive (e.g., brand) selection. In doing this, they were to assume that the individual has decided to purchase the product but has not yet decided which brand of the product to buy. The following response categories were provided for each statement-product combination: highly relevant (H), medium relevance (M), low relevance (L), and not relevant (NR).

For each subject, three scores were obtained for each of the 20 products indicating the relevance of each of the three types of reference group influence. To illustrate the group influence scores, consider the information reference group influence. For a given subject, the degree of that group influence associated with a particular product is defined as the highest response for that product given on any of the five statements of that influence. This produced, for each product, a distribution of 100 responses for the housewife sample and of 88 re-

Table 1 Comparison of reference group influence scores

Product	Informational			Utilitarian			Value-expressive		
	Students in-class	House-wives	Students at-home	Students in-class	House-wives	Students at-home	Students in-class	House-wives	Students at-home
Headache remedy	3.76	3.38	3.59	3.49	2.98	3.08	2.88	2.42	2.51
Beer	3.07	2.60	2.84	3.72	3.08	3.62	3.53	2.71	3.62
Color television	3.90	3.84	4.00	3.75	3.51	3.51	3.67	3.43	3.73
Clothing	3.50	3.45	3.32	3.88	3.59	3.86	3.94	3.61	3.92
Laundry soap	3.23	2.99	3.05	2.80	2.53	2.68	2.64	2.42	2.22
Hamburger substitute	2.98	2.56	2.92	3.09	2.33	2.59	2.33	1.93	2.19
Automobile	3.96	3.85	3.92	3.90	3.70	3.95	3.96	3.65	3.97
Furniture	3.50	3.51	3.35	3.60	3.59	3.59	3.67	3.52	3.70
Facial soap	3.21	2.89	2.84	2.98	2.94	2.76	3.29	2.85	3.00
Air conditioner	3.74	3.75	3.84	3.33	3.21	2.95	3.27	3.14	3.11
Insurance	3.80	3.71	3.81	3.55	3.38	3.22	3.29	3.08	3.14
Mouthwash	3.17	2.92	2.86	3.33	3.02	3.11	3.35	2.57	3.05
Coffee	3.23	2.88	2.86	3.43	3.28	3.27	2.80	2.58	2.62
Refrigerator	3.66	3.70	3.68	3.35	3.23	2.89	3.12	3.14	3.22
Physician selection	3.86	3.72	3.95	3.76	3.50	3.54	3.27	3.18	3.30
Canned peaches	2.47	2.49	2.49	2.84	2.54	2.51	2.02	1.99	1.89
Radio	3.31	3.16	3.38	3.04	2.79	2.81	2.88	2.64	2.81
Detergent	3.05	2.88	2.87	2.57	2.35	2.24	2.63	2.17	2.24
Books or magazines	3.29	3.00	3.03	3.47	3.36	3.43	3.41	3.08	3.49
Cigarettes	3.01	2.49	2.97	3.10	2.68	3.19	3.31	2.51	3.35

sponses for the student sample. Coding individual responses within a distribution as 4 for H, 3 for M, 2 for L, and 1 for NR, the relevance of that group influence for a given product is found by averaging across the subjects, in a manner identical to that just described, scores for the 20 products were calculated which reflect the influence on brand (or alternative) selection of utilitarian and by value-expressive reference groups and appear in Table 1.

FINDINGS

The informational, utilitarian, and value-expressive reference group influence scores of the 51 in-class students were compared to the corresponding scores of the 100 housewives by 60 *t* tests (three reference group influence scores on each of 20 products). The same comparison procedure was also followed in comparing the 37 at-home students and the 100 housewives. This examination was critical since, in most cases, housewives respond to questionnaires at home while students typically provide responses in class. Fifteen of the 60 comparisons between the at-home students and the housewives and 22 of the 60 comparisons between the in-class students and the housewives showed significant differences at the 0.05 level. These differences are presented in Tables 2 and 3. Fifteen and 22 significant *t* tests are significantly greater (well beyond the 0.00001 level) than the expected number of 3 under the hypothesis of no difference. Thus, across all three types of reference group influence, the alternative hypotheses are accepted which state that the reference group influence scores of housewives differ from those of students at-home and from those of the in-class students. Furthermore, if each type of reference group influence is examined separately, the number of significant *t* tests for each influence type (i.e., informational, utilitarian, and value-expressive) for both the housewife vs. at-home student comparisons and the housewife vs. in-class student comparisons is significantly greater than that expected if, for that type of reference group influence, the scores of housewives and students were the same.

Table 2 Areas of significant difference between student at-home and housewife reference group influence

Product	House-wife	Student	t value
Informational influence			
Color television	3.84	4.00	−2.46[a]
Hamburger substitute	2.46	2.92	−2.33[b]
Physician selection	3.72	3.95	−2.27[b]
Cigarettes	2.49	2.97	−2.32[b]
Utilitarian influence			
Beer	3.08	3.62	−2.72[a]
Clothing	3.59	3.86	−2.07[b]
Automobiles	3.70	3.95	−2.38[a]
Cigarettes	2.68	3.19	−2.31[b]
Value-expressive influence			
Beer	2.71	3.62	−4.36[a]
Color television	3.43	3.73	−2.05[b]
Clothing	3.61	3.92	−2.44[a]
Automobiles	3.65	3.97	−2.61[a]
Mouthwash	2.57	3.05	−2.20[b]
Books or magazines	2.57	3.49	−2.23[b]
Cigarettes	2.51	3.35	−3.63[a]

[a]Significant at .01 level.
[b]Significant at .05 level.

The informational, utilitarian, and value-expressive reference group influence scores of the 51 in-class students were compared to the corresponding scores on the 37 at-home students. Nine of the 60 comparisons showed significant differences at the 0.05 level. Response differences were found for the following product-reference group sets: informational reference group influ-

Table 3 Areas of significant difference between student in-class and housewife reference group influence

| Product | Reference group influence score | | |
	House-wife	Student	t value
Informational influence			
Headache remedy	3.38	3.76	−2.83[a]
Beer	2.60	3.08	−2.72[a]
Hamburger substitute	2.46	2.98	−3.02[a]
Coffee	2.88	3.23	−2.12[b]
Cigarettes	2.49	3.01	−2.79[a]
Utilitarian influence			
Headache remedy	2.98	3.49	−2.99[a]
Beer	3.08	3.72	−3.77[a]
Clothing	3.59	3.88	−2.56[a]
Hamburger substitute	2.33	3.09	−3.93[a]
Automobile	3.70	3.90	−2.22[b]
Physician selection	3.50	3.76	−1.98[b]
Cigarettes	2.68	3.09	−2.10[b]
Value-expressive influence			
Headache remedy	2.42	2.88	−2.46[a]
Beer	2.71	3.53	−4.39[a]
Clothing	3.61	3.94	−3.02[a]
Hamburger substitute	1.93	2.33	−2.18[b]
Automobile	3.65	3.96	−2.83[a]
Facial soap	2.85	3.29	−2.47[a]
Mouthwash	2.57	3.35	−4.12[a]
Detergent	2.17	2.63	−2.46[a]
Book or magazines	3.08	3.41	−2.05[b]
Cigarettes	2.51	3.31	−3.99[a]

[a]Significant at .01 level.
[b]Significant at .05 level.

ence—facial soap and coffee; utilitarian reference group influence—headache remedy, hamburger substitute, air conditioner, insurance, and refrigerator; value-expressive reference group influence—laundry soap and detergent. Nine significant differences are significantly greater than that which would be expected (i.e., 3) if location had no effect on the student responses. Although there were no consistent directional response differences for these nine products, the significant differences do suggest that response setting does have some effect upon subject responses.

Finally, both of the student samples, i.e., in-class and at-home, were combined to form a single sample; the reference group influence scores of this combined student sample were compared to the corresponding housewife scores. As Table 4 reveals, 22 of the 60 comparisons showed significant differences at the 0.05 level.

SUMMARY AND CONCLUSIONS

The results of this study reveal that, regardless of response setting, significant differences exist between students and housewives in terms of the influence of reference groups on brand (or other product alternative, e.g., model) selection. Where significant differences exist between students and housewives, students are without exception consistently more susceptible to reference group influence. This observation is consistent with the expectations drawn from the paper's theoretical section.

It should also be noted that significant differences (9 out of 60 comparisons) were found between the responses of students at home and those of the in-class students. Unlike the two cases where student and housewife responses were compared, these differences were not consistent and did not lead to meaningful interpretation. Identification of the factors causing response differences between the two locations is beyond the scope of this study and at this point would only be speculation. Observation of these differences does, however, illustrate the importance of response setting control in comparing the responses of two populations.

Table 4   Comparison of reference group influence scores

Product	Informational		Utilitarian		Value-expressive	
	Students[a]	Housewives[b]	Students[a]	Housewives[b]	Students[a]	Housewives[b]
Headache remedy	3.69	3.38[c]	3.32	2.98[c]	2.73	2.42
Beer	2.78	2.60[c]	3.68	3.08[c]	3.57	2.71[c]
Color television	3.94	3.84[c]	3.65	3.51	3.69	3.43[c]
Clothing	3.43	3.45	3.87	3.59[c]	3.93	3.61[c]
Laundry soap	3.16	2.99	2.75	2.53	2.47	2.42
Hamburger substitute	2.96	2.56[c]	2.89	2.33[c]	2.27	1.93[c]
Automobile	3.94	3.85	3.92	3.70[c]	3.97	3.65[c]
Furniture	3.44	3.51	3.60	3.59	3.68	3.52
Facial soap	3.06	2.89[c]	2.89	2.94	3.17	2.85[c]
Air conditioner	3.78	3.75	3.17	3.21	3.21	3.14
Insurance	3.81	3.71	3.41	3.38	3.23	3.08
Mouthwash	3.05	2.92	3.24	3.02	3.27	3.57[c]
Coffee	3.08	2.88	3.64	3.28	2.72	2.58
Refrigerator	3.67	3.70	3.16	3.23	3.16	3.14
Physician selection	3.89	3.72[c]	3.67	3.50	3.28	3.18
Canned peaches	2.47	2.49	2.71	2.54	1.97	1.99
Radio	3.34	3.16	2.94	2.79	2.85	2.64
Detergent	2.98	2.88	2.43	2.35	2.47	2.17
Books or magazines	3.18	3.00	3.46	3.36	3.44	3.08[c]
Cigarettes	3.00	2.49[c]	3.14	2.68[c]	3.33	2.51[c]

[a]This score is based upon examination of the *entire* student sample.
[b]This score is based upon examination of the 100 housewives sample.
[c]*t* test is significant at the .05 level.

Some may be surprised by finding reference group influences on housewives significantly greater than that on students for products like furniture, where presumably housewives are more likely to be making purchases. The measures used were designed to indicate the degree of reference group influence in selecting the appropriate alternative *given* that the product is to be purchased. In the theoretical section of this paper, three reasons were presented for expecting the reference group influence upon students to be greater than that upon housewives. We believe that these arguments are in no way diminished for products (like furniture) where housewives are likely to have more experience and information than students.

The findings do not suggest that reference group influence differences between students and housewives should hold across all types of situations. Rather, the results suggest that students, when compared to housewives, are (a) more likely to be receptive to reference group influence given the particular product, or (b) more receptive to reference group influence for a larger number of product cases.

Much of the experimental research conducted in psychology and consumer behavior has used college students as respondents. The results of this study illustrate the danger in generalizing the findings of studies using business students as subjects to other populations.

REFERENCES

Albert, Bernard (1967), "Non-Businessmen as Surrogates for Businessmen in Behavioral Experiments," *Journal of Business,* 40, 203–7.

Arndt, J. (1971), "A Research Note on Intergenerational Overlap of Selected Consumer Variables," *Markeds Kommunikasjon,* 3, 1–8.

Asch, S. (1952), *Social Psychology,* Englewood Cliffs, N.J.: Prentice Hall.

Bourne, E. S. (1956), "Group Influences in Marketing and Public Relations," in *Some Applications of Behavioral Research,* eds. R. Likert and S. P. Hayes, New York: UNESCO.

Brim, O. G. (1968), "Adult Socialization," in *Socialization and Society,* ed. J. Clausen, Boston: Little, Brown & Co.

Bruner, J. S. (1958), "Social Psychology and Perception," in *Readings in Social Psychology,* eds. E. F. Maccaby, T. M. Newcomb, and E. L. Hartley, New York: Holt, Rinehart and Winston, 85–93.

Copeland, Ronald M., Francia, Arthur J., and Strawer, Robert H. (1973), "Students as Subjects in Behavioral Business Research," *Accounting Review,* 48, 365–72.

Davis, Keith E. (1968), "Needs, Wants, and Consistency," in *Theories of Cognitive Consistency: A Sourcebook,* eds. R. P. Abelson et al., Chicago: Rand McNally & Co., 327–30.

Deutsch, M., and Gerard, H. B. (1955), "A Study of Normative and Informational Social Influences upon Individual Judgment," *Journal of Abnormal and Social Psychology,* 51, 624–36.

Durkheim, Emile (1951), *Suicide,* trans. George Simpson, New York: Free Press.

Enis, Ben M. (1974), *Marketing Principles,* Pacific Palisades, Calif.: Good Year Publishing Company, Inc.

———, Cox, Keith K., and Stafford, James E. (1972), "Students as Subjects in Consumer Behavior Experiments," *Journal of Marketing Research,* 9, 72–4.

———, and Stafford, James E. (1964), "Consumer's Perception of Product Quality as a Function of Various Informational Inputs, *Proceedings,* Fall Conference, American Marketing Association, 340–4.

Feather, N. T. (1971), "Organization and Discrepancy in Cognitive Structures," *Psychological Review,* 178, 355–79.

Hyman, H. H. (1942), "The Psychology of Status," *Archives of Psychology,* 38, 15.

Jacoby, Jacob, Speller, D. E., and Kohn, Carol A. (1974), "Brand Choice Behavior as a Function of Information Load: Replication and Extension," *Journal of Consumer Research,* 1, 33–42.

Jahoda, Marie (1972), "Conformity and Independence: A Psychological Analysis," in *Behavioral Science Foundations of Consumer Behavior,* ed. Joel Cohen, New York: Free Press, 339–54.

Johnson, Harry M. (1960), *Sociology: A Systematic Introduction,* New York: Harcourt Brace Jovanovich, 557–8.

Kanter, Donald L. (1970), "Pharmaceutical Advertising and Youth," unpublished paper, Coronada Unified School District, Coronado, Calif.

Katz, Daniel (1978), "Consistency for What? The Functional Approach," in *Theories of Cognitive Consistency: A Sourcebook,* eds. R. P. Abelson et al., Chicago: Rand McNally & Co., 179–91.

Kelman, H. C. (1961), "Processes of Opinion Change," *Public Opinion Quarterly,* 25, 57–78.

———, and Baron, Reuben M. (1968), "Determinants of Modes of Resolving Inconsistency Dilemmas: A Functional Analysis," in *Theories of Cognitive Consistency: A Sourcebook,* eds. R. P. Abelson et al., Chicago: Rand McNally & Co., 670–83.

Khera, Inder P., and Benson, James D. (1970), "Are Students Really Poor Substitutes for Businessmen in Behavioral Research?" *Journal of Marketing Research,* 7, 529–32.

Kogan, N., and Wallach, Michael A. (1967), "Risk Taking as a Function of the Situation, the Person, and the Group," in *New Directions in Psychology III,* New York: Holt, Rinehart & Winston.

Levitt, Theodore (1965), *Industrial Purchasing Behavior,* Boston: Harvard University.

Reisman, D., and Roseborough, H. (1955). "Careers and Consumer Behavior," in *Consumer Behavior*

Vol. II, The Life Cycle and Consumer Behavior, ed. Lincoln Clark, New York: New York University Press.

Rosenberg, M. J. (1968), "Hedonism, Inauthenticity, and Other Goals Toward Expandion of a Consistency Theory," in *Theories of Cognitive Consistency: A Sourcebook,* eds. R. P. Abelson et al., Chicago: Rand McNally & Co., 73–111.

Scott, Ward (1974), "Consumer Socialization," *Journal of Consumer Research,* 1, 1–14.

Sheth, Jagdish N. (1970), "Are There Differences in Dissonance Reduction Behavior Between Students and Housewives?" *Journal of Marketing Research,* 7, 243–5.

Shuptrine, F. Kelly (1975), "On the Validity of Using Students as Subjects in Consumer Behavior Investigations," *Journal of Business,* 48, 383–90.

Teter, J. W. (1966), "The Family, Peers and Media Influence on Youth's Present and Future Consumption Preferences," unpublished thesis, Oklahoma State University, Stillwater, Okla.

WORKING WIVES AND CONVENIENCE CONSUMPTION

MICHAEL D. REILLY

The dramatic rise in employment of married women outside the home has prompted consumer researchers to investigate the hypothesis that one result of the wife's employment would be an increase in the use of convenience foods and greater incidence of time-saving durable ownership. Yet, studies to date have failed to support either of these hypotheses, regardless of the size or type of sample, or the statistical technique used. In spite of these findings, it may be premature to conclude that there are no differences in the consumption of convenience items as a result of the wife's employment. Family income and family social status both have been found to correlate with convenience consumption. To the extent that these are affected by the wife's employment, an indirect relationship between working and convenience consumption might be expected.

In the research reported here, these factors are included in a structural-equation model of the determinants of consumption of convenience foods and the ownership of time-saving durables. Additional insights into the structure of the relationships between the wife's employment and convenience consumption are gained from a closer and more formal examination of the thinking underlying the initial hypotheses. Role overload, a type of role conflict that results from excessive demands on the time and energy supply of an individual, is postulated as mediating the relationship between wife's employment and family convenience consumption. Accordingly, role overload is included in the model.

Before detailing the model, let us consider role theory as an explanation of why researchers might have expected convenience consumption to accompany the wife's employment and why their expectations might have been incorrect. For this purpose we begin with an analysis of the influence of social structure on behavior.

ROLE THEORY

Role theory attempts to explain how social structure influences behavior.[1] In sociology, social

[1]For a general treatment, the interested reader is referred to Sarbin and Allen (1968). Ostlund (1973) has provided the most complete discussion of role theory in the marketing literature.

Source: Michael D. Reilly, "Working Wives and Convenience Consumption," Journal of Consumer Research, Vol. 8, March, 1982, pp. 407–418. Reprinted with permission.

structure is typically conceptualized as consisting of five types of social institutions: the family, the economic system, the political system, the educational system, and the religious institutions.

Each institution contains a number of interrelating positions (Bates and Harvey 1977; Davis 1948; Goode 1960; Gross, Mason and McEachern 1958; Levy 1952; Linton 1936). A position can be defined as the behavior expected of an institutional member. For example, one position in the family institution might be called the husband-father. The occupant of this position is typically expected to work outside the home, be a sexual partner for the wife-mother, aid in child rearing, and do much of the yard work.

Each individual in society occupies positions in a number of institutions. Following Merton (1957), we might say that each person has a position set, which consists of all positions occupied by a given individual across social institutions.

Role Enactment

The behavior of an incumbent in a position is usually defined as that individual's role enactment. Different individuals enact similar positional expectations differently. Not all husband-fathers behave identically, nor would we expect that they might. Differences exist even in the role enactment of positions with rigidly defined expectations, such as supreme court justices, who might differ in age, race, political group membership, religious affiliation and—most recently—sex. Since behavior, even on the bench, simultaneously reflects the expectations of these positions as well, two justices might behave quite differently. Further, some latitude in individual interpretation of positional expectations is allowable because of innate individual differences.

A third explanation for discrepancies between positional expectations and actual behavior recognizes that some positional expectations conflict. This notion has generated extensive research in sociology, psychology, and organizational behavior (Beehr 1976; Beehr, Walsh and Taber 1976; Child 1943; Gross, Mason and McEachern 1958; Hammer and Tosi 1974; House and Rizzo 1972; Kahn, Wolf, Quinn, Snoek, and Rosenthal 1964; Marks 1977; Miles and Perreault 1976; Rizzo, House and Lirtzman 1970; Sarbin and Allen 1968; Schuler 1975; Sieber 1974; Turner 1962).

Role Conflict

Role conflict, the presence of conflicting or inconsistent expectations, has been investigated in several forms. Most relevant to our analysis of convenience consumption is role overload, i.e., conflict that occurs when the sheer volume of behavior demanded by the positions in the position set exceeds available time and energy. The role-overload notion formalizes the thinking which led earlier researchers to the hypothesis that working wives would presumably be more convenience-oriented in their consumption.

One might expect a working wife to experience more role overload than a nonworking wife, since the work would create additional demands on her time and energy supplies. The working wife might try to minimize her role overload by saving time and energy in the performance of household chores, including serving convenience foods and/or buying time-saving appliances. Accordingly, the family in which the wife works should exhibit greater convenience consumption than a family in which the wife is not employed outside the home. Yet, the data consistently fail to indicate any differences in convenience-consumption patterns by wife's employment. Clearly, one of the two premises is incorrect. Either working does not necessarily lead to role overload, or convenience consumption is not used by working wives to reduce their role overload.

Some theoretical support exists for the first of these possibilities. Sieber (1974) suggested that the positive outcomes from occupying an additional position might well outweigh any additional role conflict and role overload that such occupancy creates. He described four basic positive outcomes: role privileges, status security, status enhancement, and personality involvement. Because of these benefits, working wives might not perceive additional role overload, even though their total workload has increased.

Marks (1977) suggests that the time and energy devoted to a particular position may reflect the individual's commitment to that position, as well as the availability of time and energy. In some cases, excuses offered by uncommitted individuals for their lack of participation may be mistaken for role overload. The role overload expressed by working wives in their family role might be low because of their commitment to that role.

A third argument against increased role overload follows directly from the position set. The time and energy demands of all positions in the position set contribute to role overload. Working might not cause role overload for a wife if the rest of the positions in her position set are not demanding. She may experience less role overload than a nonworking counterpart with several children in diapers. In fact, many women may work because they are bored and, thus, may experience very little role overload.

Any or all of these arguments might explain the lack of empirical evidence linking working-wife families with differential consumption of convenience products and ownership of time-saving durables. There are fewer arguments that convenience consumption may not be used to reduce overload. Prior to this research, role overload and convenience consumption had not been measured simultaneously.

MODEL DEVELOPMENT

The foregoing discussion suggests that if role overload, wife's employment, and convenience consumption were measured simultaneously, an indirect relationship between working and convenience consumption might be found. It could be that working causes role overload, which in turn causes increased use of convenience goods and/or likelihood of owning time-saving durables. Each of these effects may be weak enough that no direct effect is observable between work status and consumption. However, any model would be incomplete without considering other factors which have previously been related to convenience consumption.

With this in mind, a structural-equation model was developed with three exogenous constructs: wife's work involvement, family's social status, and wife's education. (Figure 1 diagrams the proposed causal flows.) Five endogenous constructs are included: the wife's earnings, the wife's role overload, total family income, the number of convenience foods served to the family, and the number of time-saving durables owned by the family.

The wife's work behavior has two links with convenience consumption, both of which are indirect. First, the wife's work involvement may cause mildly increased levels of role overload, due to the increased time and energy demands. As discussed earlier, the relationship between work and role overload is then expected to be linked positively to use of convenience foods and ownership of time-saving durables, two possible strategies for reducing role overload.

The second indirect link concerns the wife's earnings. Working wives contribute income to the family. Total family income has been related to the ownership or purchase of durable items in several instances (Anderson 1971; Strober and Weinberg 1977, 1980). Income has been less successful in predicting the use or purchase of convenience goods (Anderson 1971), with an exception reported by Douglas (1976). It has further been established that the wife's income relates to durable ownership because it raises total family income (Strober and Weinberg 1980). Based on these results, the model positively links the wife's employment to her earnings, and her earnings to total family income. Total family income is then positively related to ownership of time-saving durables, as suggested by Strober and Weinberg (1980).[2]

The remaining constructs in the model are family social status and wife's education. Anderson (1971) found a significant relationship between the ownership of convenience durables and the household head's educational level, occupational status, and socioeconomic status. The same study

---

[2]It might be argued that it would make sense to look for a relationship between income and the *value* of time-saving durables owned, rather than the *numbers* of these durables. However, it is doubtful that expensive durables would save significantly more time than cheaper models of the same item. Thus, for the purpose of the study, the critical dimension is ownership rather than value. This may result in underestimating the efficacy of income for understanding the market for time-saving durables.

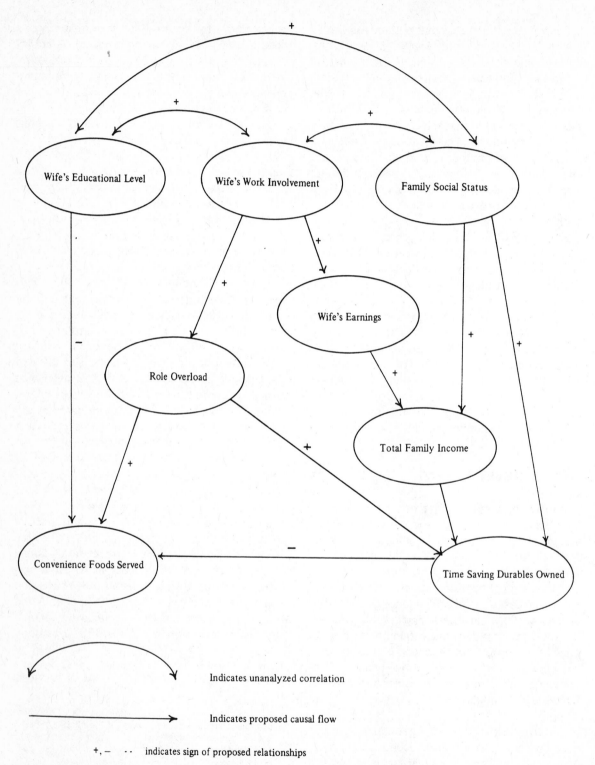

Figure 1   Proposed causal model.

found that the convenience goods usage patterns were not related to the occupation or socioeconomic status of the household head and only weakly related to the education of the household head. On the basis of these findings, family social status was included in the model, with positive causal flows toward time-saving durable ownership and family income. Because strong evidence was absent, the social-status construct was not causally linked to consumption of convenience foods.

Douglas (1976) discovered a negative link between the wife's educational status and the family's propensity to purchase convenience products and services. Accordingly, the wife's educational level is posited as being negatively related to serving of convenience foods and allowed to correlate freely with family social status.

The last proposed causal flow deserves special comment. Durable ownership and convenience-food use are hypothesized as competing strategies for reducing role overload. Wives who own many time-saving durables probably feel less need to serve convenience foods. Similarly, wives who serve convenience foods frequently may not need time-saving durables. The negative relationship restores consistency to the model. The wife's educational level should be positively related to status, and status should relate positively to durable ownership. Since the wife's education is negatively related to convenience-food use, the model would be inconsistent unless durable ownership and convenience-food use are negatively related. This suggests that housewives, particularly those from different educational strata, may decide to opt for one of the two possible strategies for reducing their role overload. Presumably the less educated engage in increased convenience-food consumption, while the more educated buy time-saving durables.

METHOD

Sample Procedure

The data used to test the structural-equation model resulted from personal interviews and self-administered questionnaires, using an area cluster sample of the Milwaukee, Wisconsin SMSA. The questionnaires were collected by a professional market-research organization in August 1979. Since a final sample size of 200 was targeted, ten experienced interviewers were each given two randomly selected starting points and told to proceed either south or west, depending on which direction the street ran. From each starting point, the interviewer was instructed to use the first ten dwellings as an initial target sample. If one of the initial ten dwellings could not be contacted after three callbacks at different times, was not the home of a married couple of less than retirement age, or refused to participate, then the dwelling was deleted, and the next dwelling on the street was added to the target group. One exception to this procedure occurred because one selected starting point was in the urban core, and police orders forbid survey research in that part of Milwaukee.

Sample Description

The procedure yielded 186 completed responses. Of the total target dwellings, 41 percent were not contacted after three callbacks. Another 18 percent were not the home of a married couple of working age. Finally, 13 percent refused to participate. Assuming that a comparable number of the refusals were not qualified, the response rate among qualified, contacted respondents was about 73 percent. Comparisons of the sample with the Milwaukee SMSA and the U.S. population show that the major underrepresented groups in the sample are nonwhites—probably because of the removal of the urban core—and working-wife families (in 1979, approximately 50 percent of married women worked outside the home).[3]

Data Collection

The data collection combined interviews, questionnaires, and interviewers' judgments. All instruments were pretested on a convenience sample of respondents, similar to those in the study.

The interviewer conducted a personal interview that measured the wife's employment, educational levels, and family social-status measures. Following the interview, the respondent was left with a

[3]Detailed comparisons are available from the author.

questionnaire measuring role overload, durable ownership, and convenience-food service behavior. As the interviewer left, she made judgments about the quality of the dwelling and the neighborhood for the status indices. The interviewer returned later to collect the completed questionnaires, debrief the respondents, and pay them for their participation. Respondents who provided incomplete information were recontacted. After the data were collected, 20 percent of the interviews were randomly selected and validated over the phone by the research supervisor.

Construct Operationalization

Multiple measures of family social status and work involvement were taken. The only nonstandard measure was role overload. A special scale was developed to measure the role overload of the wife, based on the House and Rizzo (1972) role-conflict and role-ambiguity scales. However, since these scales were developed for use in organizational settings, it was necessary to modify them for this application. To do this the author and several doctoral students wrote a number of potential role-overload items which were administered to a convenience sample of 106 married women. Items with low item-to-total correlations were eliminated. The result was a set of 13 items in Likert-scale format. The reliability of the scale was estimated using the coefficient alpha, as well as the results of administering some of the items twice in the final instrument. The computed value of Chronbach's (1951) alpha was 0.88, whereas the two items that were administered at different locations in the final scale produced correlations of 0.74.

Analysis Procedure

The structural-equation parameters were estimated using the LISREL IV computer program (Jöreskog and Sörbom 1978). This estimation procedure provides full-information maximum-likelihood estimates of the parameter for the structural-equation system defined by the equation:

$$\beta\eta = \Gamma\xi + \zeta \qquad (1)$$

where

β a coefficient matrix of causal relationships among endogenous constructs

η a vector of endogenous constructs

Γ a coefficient matrix of causal relationships from the exogenous constructs to the endogenous constructs

ξ a vector of exogenous constructs

ζ a vector of structural errors

The LISREL procedure also estimates two measurement models which link the latent, unobserved constructs with their observed, operational indicators. The measurement models can be expressed in two equations:

$$Y = \Lambda_y \eta + \epsilon \qquad (2)$$
$$X = \Lambda_x \xi + \delta \qquad (3)$$

where

Λ_x, Λ_y = coefficient matrices relating observed indicator to latent constructs for exogenous and endogenous constructs, respectively

η, ξ = vectors of endogenous and exogenous constructs, respectively

ϵ, δ = measurement error vectors for indicator variables

X, Y = vectors of indicator variables

The uses of LISREL IV procedures have been well explicated, so only the unusual features of the current analysis will be described.[4] Since only one indicator was available for each endogenous construct, Λ was specified as an identity matrix and θ_ϵ, the variance-covariance matrix of ϵ, was constrained to be a zero matrix. The variance-covariance matrix of δ, θ_λ, was initially constrained to be a diagonal matrix with the diagonal elements associated with single indicator constructs assumed to be zero. Figure 2 presents the proposed model LISREL form. Figure 2 is similar to Figure 1 in that the latent constructs are linked in the same pattern. The difference is that the relationship between

---

[4]Baggozzi (1977a; 1977b; 1980) has covered the basics of using LISREL IV in marketing-theory construction.

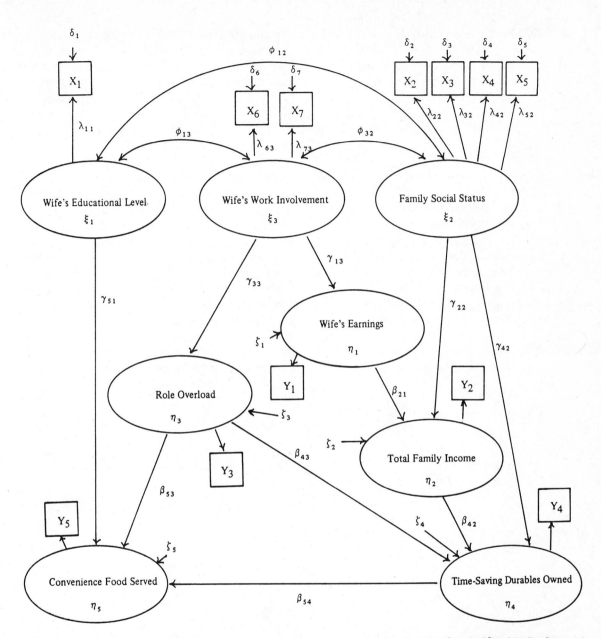

Figure 2   Proposed Model in LISREL Format

NOTE: Explanation of multiple measures: X_2 = Warner Index of Status Characteristics; X_3 = Hollingshead Two-Factor Index; X_4 = Duncan Occupational-Status Index; X_5 = Coleman and Neugarten Index of Urban Status; X_6 = 0 = not working, 1 = works part time, 2 = works full time; X_7 = 0 = not working, 1 = considers employment just a job, 2 = considers employment a career.

these latent constructs and their observed indicators is diagrammed. Following standard practice, latent constructs are diagrammed as ovals and observed measures as rectangles.

The correlation matrix from Table 1 was input to the LISREL IV program. Each correlation coefficient is based on 186 cases. The initial iteration produced a model with $\chi^2 = 192.5$, $df = 45$, $p = 0.0000$. The large value of χ^2, relative to the degrees of freedom, indicates that the proposed model did not fit the data well. The difference between the observed correlation matrix and that resulting from the hypothesized model was statistically significant. The accepted procedure in such a case is to iteratively relax constrained parameters which cause stress in the fit. Effectively, this is the same as fitting a less restrictive model. As each constraint is relaxed, the χ^2 associated with the model will decrease. At the same time, degrees of freedom will decrease. This iterative procedure is continued until the decrease in χ^2 is not adequate to compensate for the degrees of freedom lost.

In this application, several constraints needed to be relaxed to achieve better model fit. Initial indications pointed to correlated measurement error among the indicator variables for the exogenous constructs. Although these correlations were not expected, they seem logical. Each of the status measures is a different composite of the same underlying variables. Measurement errors for these variables should appear in all indices. Thus we might expect some correlated measurement errors within the family social-status indicators. Also, since the wife's education (X_1) is used in the computation of the Coleman and Newgarten Index of Status (X_5), we might expect some cross-construct measurement errors to be correlated between these variables.

The stress measures also suggested the relaxation of three structural constraints. Accordingly, prediction errors for the wife's role overload were allowed to correlate with prediction errors for total family income and time-saving durables owned. The model was further modified to allow a causal

Table 1 Input correlation matrix

Variable	Y_1 Wife's income	Y_2 Family income	Y_3 Role over-load	Y_4 Time-saving durables	Y_5 Conve-nience foods	X_1 Wife's educa-tion	X_2 Warner ISC	X_3 Hollings-head two-factor index	X_4 Duncan	X_5 Index of urban status	X_6 Work status	X_7 Work atti-tude
Y_1 Wife's income	1.0											
Y_2 Family income	0.22[b]	1.0										
Y_3 Role overload	−0.14[a]	0.04	1.0									
Y_4 Durables	0.07	0.25[c]	0.13[a]	1.0								
Y_5 Foods	0.09	−0.04	0.08	−0.19[b]	1.0							
X_1 Wife's education	0.13	0.17[a]	0.04	0.21[b]	−0.19[b]	1.0						
X_2 Warner ISC	0.03	0.42[c]	−0.12[a]	0.26[c]	−0.03	0.34[c]	1.0					
X_3 Hollingshead two-factor index	0.01	0.18[b]	−0.10	0.12[a]	−0.02	0.14[a]	0.75[c]	1.0				
X_4 Duncan	0.00	0.32[c]	−0.06	0.20[b]	0.08	0.30[c]	0.64[c]	0.53[c]	1.0			
X_5 Index of urban status	0.07	0.40[c]	−0.03	0.29[c]	−0.05	0.60[c]	0.85[c]	0.53[c]	0.62[c]	1.0		
X_6 Work status	0.66[c]	0.07	0.17[b]	0.00	−0.06	0.00	−0.03	−0.02	0.02	−0.01	1.0	
X_7 Work attitude	0.55[c]	0.06	0.15[a]	0.08	−0.11	0.09	−0.07	−0.08	−0.01	0.01	0.85[c]	1.0

[a]$p < 0.05$.
[b]$p < 0.01$.
[c]$p < 0.001$.

flow from the wife's educational level to her income. After these constraints were relaxed, the model fit was substantially improved ($X^2 = 49.08$, $df = 41$, $p = 0.18$),[5] suggesting a successful fit between the proposed causal structure and the observed correlation matrix.

DISCUSSION

Interpretation of Results

Figure 3 reports the LISREL IV estimates of the parameters in the final model. The coefficients linking the X variables with the latent constructs, shown as λ's in Figure 2, can be interpreted as the loadings of the indicator variables on the unobserved constructs. The coefficients linking the three exogenous constructs, shown as ϕ's in Figure 2, can be interpreted as the amount of unanalyzed correlation among these constructs. The coefficients linking the constructs with causal flows, shown as γ's and β's in Figure 2, are path coefficients and detail the causal flows among the constructs.

The final model, as estimated, supports the proposition that the wife's work involvement relates indirectly to the family's consumption through work overload. Working wives were somewhat more likely to report role overload. Wives who reported role overload were somewhat more likely than others to serve convenience food and to own time-saving durables, although the former relationship did not achieve statistical significance at the 0.05 level. Both the relationship between work status and role overload and that between role overload and the two types of convenience consumption are fairly weak. Wife's work involvement causes about three percent of the variance of role overload. This finding supports the conclusion that working does not necessarily result in role overload. Role overload stems from the totality of the position set, and the presence of a work position is not sufficient to cause role overload in all cases. To completely account for role overload, it would be

necessary to measure the time and energy demands of all positions occupied, as well as the time and energy available to each individual.

Role overload is a weakly positive, statistically significant cause of the ownership of time-saving durables, and a weakly positive, nonsignificant cause of serving convenience foods. In both cases, the relationship might be expected to be weak to the extent that convenience consumption is effective in reducing role overload. These findings support the theory developed earlier. As indicated by the correlation matrix in Table 1, working-wife families were not significantly greater consumers of convenience foods, nor were they more likely to own convenience durables. When role overload is measured and allowed to mediate the relationship, the relationship between working and convenience consumption becomes more logical.

A more complete explication of the determinants of role overload is the next step. For example, it seems likely that role overload experienced would be determined by a number of factors not considered in the current study. To the extent that children are present in the home, we would expect the time and energy demands of the wife's family role to increase. Activities outside the home, for example church participation, club membership, and volunteer work, might all be positively related to role overload. Working is only one position in the position set, and role overload results from the totality of demands on time and energy. For a better picture of the relationships among role overload, working behavior, and convenience consumption, future research should further explore the determinants of role overload.

By the same token, the impact of role overload on consumption behavior deserves further consideration. Convenience consumption and ownership of time-saving durables are only two ways to reduce the demands of the family position. Other possibilities include redivision of household labor assignments, eating out frequently, buying fast food for home consumption, and hiring household help. Each of these can significantly reduce the time and energy demands of the wife's family role, and each would be an alternative to owning time-saving durables or serving convenience foods.

[5]δ_2 and δ_6 were constrained to zero to prevent the estimation of negative variance.

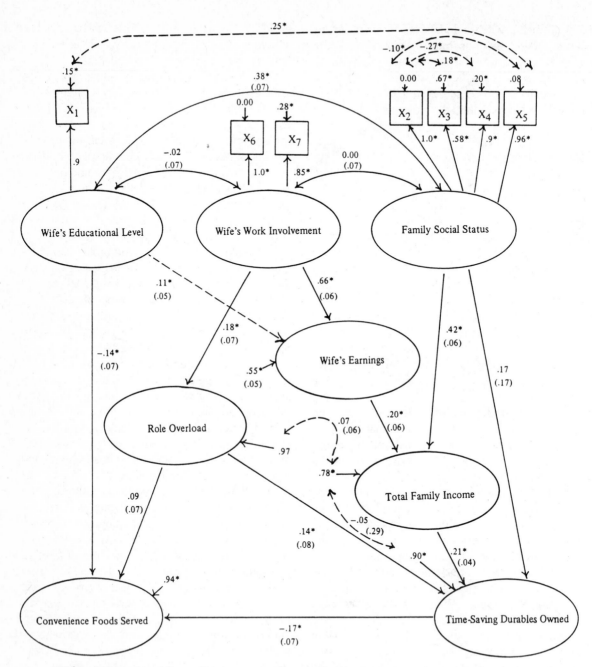

Figure 3   Final Model After Estimation[a]

NOTE.[a] $X_2 = 49.06$. $df = 41$, $p = 0.18$; * = statistically significant coefficient ($t \geq 1.65$); standard errors shown in parentheses; and indicators for $Y_1 - Y_5$ are omitted.

Income, Status, and Durable Ownership

As hypothesized, the wife's income contribution to the total income for the family was related to the family's ownership of time-saving durables. The relationship between family social status, as measured by the four indices, and durable ownership was in the predicted direction, but was not statistically significant. Income was positively related to family status as predicted. Thus the data support the thesis, presented in Strober and Weinberg (1980), that the critical determinant of durable ownership is total family income and that the wife's labor-force participation is significant only as it contributes to total family income. Seemingly, the findings linking time-saving-durable ownership to family social status are an artifact of the high correlation between family social status and income. Further research is needed using structural-equation methodology to clarify the relationships among status and income for ownership of other types of durables.

As expected, the wife's educational level was negatively related to the number of convenience foods served. Convenience foods served were negatively related to the number of time-saving durables owned. Perhaps the most surprising finding was the lack of relationships among the wife's education, the family's status, and the wife's work involvement. In the current sample, working wives were not from any identifiable educational or social strata. This is contrary to research findings that have profiled working wives as more educated and from higher status families. This finding is puzzling and suggests a need for caution in generalizing the findings. However, the wife's educational level was causally related to her income, indicating that highly educated wives who choose to work are likely to earn more than their less educated counterparts.

Limitations of the Study

The most serious limitation of the study is the size of the sample used to fit the structural-equation model. The rule of thumb for determining minimum sample size for LISREL IV application is that the number of cases should exceed the number of indicator variables by at least 50. In this case, there were 12 indicator variables and 186 cases, so the minimum requirements were met, but a larger sample would increase our confidence in the stability of the results. Also, the sample was entirely from the Milwaukee SMSA, omitting the urban core. A more geographically diverse sample would have been desirable.

Another limitation reflects the distributional assumption of the LISREL procedure. In the hypothesis-testing procedure, multivariate normality is assumed. The LISREL estimates are maximum-likelihood estimates and, therefore, fairly robust to violation of the normality assumption. Despite this, the measurement of work involvement with two trichotomies is probably a source of nonnormality.

SUMMARY AND CONCLUSIONS

This paper examined the use of convenience foods and the ownership of time-saving durables for working wife and nonworking wife families. Past research suggested several factors that might be related simultaneously to labor-force participation and these types of consumption behaviors. Role theory also provided the concept of role overload as a possible mediating variable.

A structural-equation model was developed and fitted to a sample of data from the Milwaukee, Wisconsin SMSA. Role overload and increases in family income were posited as indirect links between the wife's work involvement and the use of convenience foods and ownership of time-saving durables. Family social status and the wife's educational level also were included in the model, as suggested by past research. After relaxing some model constraints, a satisfactory fit was achieved. As predicted, role overload was causally related to working and convenience consumption.

The hypothesized relationships were in the predicted directions, and all were statistically significant, with the exception of that between family social status and durable ownership and that between role overload and convenience foods served. On this basis, it is reasonable to conclude that the proposed model of the relationships between the wife's work status and the family's consumption behavior accurately represents the data. The major problem is in the amount of variance explained. Taken together, the constructs in the model explain about ten percent of the variance in ownership and about six percent of the variance in convenience food use. Although these levels of explanation are not much different from past research results, considerable variance remains unexplained.

It may be that the measure of convenience consumption used in this and similar research is not particularly sensitive. Individuals may or may not use the measured convenience foods for a number of reasons other than a desire to save time. Similarly, the ownership of time-saving durables may be motivated by considerations other than work-load reduction. Some measurement research is needed to identify behavioral measures of convenience consumption which are not confounded with other factors.

A second possibility is that the factors which influence the use of convenience foods and the ownership of time-saving durables are not well explicated. It may be that one or more important factors were omitted here. Further research is needed to identify these factors, so that our knowledge of convenience-consumption determinants might be more complete.

REFERENCES

Anderson, W. Thomas (1971), *The Convenience Oriented Consumer,* Austin, TX: Bureau of Business Research, Graduate School of Business, University of Texas at Austin.

Bagozzi, Richard P. (1977a), "Structural Equation Models in Experimental Research," *Journal of Marketing Research,* 14, 209–26.

———— (1977b), "Convergent and Discriminant Validity by Analysis of Covariance Structures: The Case of the Affective, Behavioral and Cognitive Components of Attitude," in *Advances in Consumer Research, Vol. 4,* ed. William D. Perreault, Jr., Atlanta: Association for Consumer Research, pp. 11–18.

———— (1980), *Causal Models in Marketing,* New York: John Wiley & Sons.

Beehr, Terry A. (1976), "Perceived Situational Moderators of the Relationship Between Subjective Role Ambiguity and Role Strain," *Journal of Applied Psychology,* 61, 35–40.

————, Walsh, Jeffery T., and Taber, Thomas T. (1976), "Relationship of Stress to Individually and Organizationally Valued States: Higher Order Needs as a Moderator," *Journal of Applied Psychology,* 61, 41–7.

Child, Irving L. (1943), *Italian or American? The Second Generation in Conflict,* New Haven: Yale University Press.

Chronbach, Lee J. (1951), "Coefficient Alpha and the Internal Structure of Tests," *Psychometrica,* 16, 297–334.

Coleman, Richard P., and Neugarten, Bernice L. (1971), *Social Status in the City,* San Francisco: Josey Bass.

Davis, Kingsley (1948), *Human Society,* New York: The Macmillan Company.

Douglas, Susan P. (1976), "Cross-National Comparisons and Consumer Stereotypes: A Case Study of Working and Nonworking Wives in the U.S. and France," *The Journal of Consumer Research,* 3, 12–20.

Duncan, Otis D. (1961), "A Socioeconomic Index for all Occupations," in *Occupations and Social Status,* eds., Albert J. Reiss, Otis D. Duncan, Paul K. Hatt, and Cecil K. North, New York: Free Press, pp. 109–38.

Goode, William J. (1960), "A Theory of Role Strain," *American Sociological Review,* 25, 483–96.

Gross, Neal, Mason, Ward, and McEachern, Alexander (1958), *Explorations in Role Analysis,* New York: John Wiley & Sons, Inc.

Hammer, W. Clay, and Tosi, Henry L. (1974), "Relationship of Role Conflict and Role Ambiguity to Job Involvement Measures," *Journal of Applied Psychology,* 59, 497–99.

Hertzler, Joyce O. (1972), *American Social Institutions: A Sociological Analysis,* Boston: Allyn & Bacon.

Hollingshead, August B. (1949), *Elmtowns Youth, The Impact of Social Classes on Adolescents,* New York: John Wiley & Sons.

House, Robert J., and Rizzo, John R. (1972), "Role Conflict and Ambiguity as Critical Variables in a Model of Organizational Behavior," *Organizational Behavior and Human Performance,* 7, 467–505.

Jöreskog, Karl G., and Sörbom, Dag (1978), *LISREL IV Analysis of Linear Structural Relationships by the Method of Maximum Likelihood,* Chicago, IN: International Educational Services.

Kahn, Robert L., Wolf, D. M., Quinn, R. P., Snoek, J. D., and Rosenthal, R. A. (1964), *Organizational Stress,* New York: John Wiley & Sons.

Levy, Marion J. (1952), *The Structure of Society,* Princeton, N.J.: Princeton University Press.

Linton, Ralph (1936), *The Study of Man,* New York: Appleton-Century-Crofts, Inc.

Marks, Stephen R. (1977), "Multiple Roles and Role Strain: Some Notes on Human Energy, Time and Commitment," *American Sociological Review,* 42, 921–36.

Merton, Robert F. (1957), *Social Theory and Social Structure,* New York: Free Press.

Miles, Robert H., and Perreault, William D. Jr. (1976), "Organizational Role Conflict: Its Antecedents and Consequences," *Organizational Behavior and Human Performance,* 17, 19–44.

Ostlund, Lyman E. (1973), "Role Theory and Group Dynamics," in *Consumer Behavior: Theoretical Sources,* ed. Thomas S. Robertson, Englewood Cliffs, NJ: Prentice Hall, pp. 230–75.

Reynolds, Fred D., Crask, Melvin R., and Wells, William D. (1977), "The Modern Feminine Life Style," *Journal of Marketing,* 41, 38–45.

Rizzo, John R., House, Robert J., and Lirtzman, Sidney I. (1970). "Role Conflict and Ambiguity in Complex Organizations," *Administrative Science Quarterly,* 15, 150–63.

Sarbin, Theodore R., and Allen, Vernon L. (1968), "Role Theory," in *The Handbook of Social Psychology,* eds. George Lindzey and Elliot Aronson, Reading, MA: Addison-Wesley Publishing Company, pp. 488–567.

Schuler, Randall S. (1975), "Role Perceptions, Satisfaction and Performance: A Partial Reconciliation," *Journal of Applied Psychology,* 60, 683–87.

Sieber, Sam D. (1974), "Towards a Theory of Role Accumulation," *American Sociological Review,* 39, 567–78.

Strober, Myra H., and Weinberg, Charles B. (1980), "Strategies Used by Working and Nonworking Wives to Reduce Time Pressures," *Journal of Consumer Research,* 6, 338–48.

——— (1977), "Working Wives and Major Family Expenditures," *Journal of Consumer Research,* 4, 141–47.

Turner, Ralph H. (1962), "Role Taking: Process Versus Conformity," in *Human Behavior and Social Processes,* ed. A. M. Role, Boston: Houghton-Mifflin.

Warner, William L., Meeker, Marcia, and Eells, Kenneth (1957), *Social Class in America: A Manual of Procedure for the Measurement of Social Status,* Glouchester, MA: Peter Smith.

SECTION IV

THE CONSUMER BEHAVIOR OF FAMILIES AND ORGANIZATIONS

There are two types of formal organizations that are central to consumer behavior. One is the family. Although the family is not often referred to as a formal organization, it is a legally constituted group. The second type of formal organization is usually associated with a business firm, although non-business organizations are also formalized through the law. Families as consuming groups have received considerable attention by consumer behavior researchers. Other organizations have received far less attention as consumers, although this is changing now as consumer behavior researchers begin to view the term *consumer* broadly.

The family and other organizations are especially interesting because they highlight the fact that there is often a division of labor in the overall consumption process. This division of labor is important to marketers and consumer educators. An organization or a family usually assigns different activities to different members. This may be done very explicitly, as is likely in the case of a business firm, or it may be done without any real awareness of a division of responsibility occurring. In a given instance of buying and consuming the following responsibilities are assigned:

1. Gatekeeping. Someone in the family or firm determines whether or not information about a product or a supplier is passed along to other members of the group. A mother learning of a new restaurant determines whether or not her family also hears about it, and therefore whether the family has a chance to try it.
2. Opinion leadership. Someone in the group provides information about the desirability of a restaurant, for example, or the quality of industrial cable provided by a particular supplier.

3. Decision making. The task of deciding to actually try a restaurant or sign a contract with a supplier is made by an individual or subgroup.
4. Implementor. This task of carrying out a decision may be made by the mother in the case of the restaurant or by a purchasing agent in the case of industrial cable.
5. User. This is the person or group that consumes the product. It may be the entire family or those not on a diet or it may be the production department of a firm.

A single person may perform more than one task or responsibility although usually not more than two or three. Who assumes which responsibilities will very likely differ from product to product. This is especially true for families and somewhat less true in business and public organizations. There will also be some variation across different families and firms for a given product. For example, in one family the husband may be the decision maker for a restaurant, while in another family the children may be the dominant decision makers. In one firm the purchasing agent's role may be limited to soliciting bids from suppliers, while in another firm the purchasing agent may have a major role in selecting the supplier.

We now consider some other dynamics among families and firms as consumer units.

"GIFT DECISIONS BY KIDS AND PARENTS"

Unfortunately, many studies of family consumer decision processes are actually studies of husband-wife interactions only. The effects of children on consumer behavior patterns are ignored too often. Caron and Ward investigated the effect of children's requests for Christmas gifts on the gifts actually chosen by the parents. Note that there are multiple roles that apply in this situation. The parent is the purchaser but the child is the user of the product. Due to this particular division of responsibility, the child is then an influencer in the parent's decision process.

Figure 1 in the article gives an explicit model of the relationships between variables that are studied. In addition to these variables, social class and age are studied for their relation to purchase processes. However, only middle and upper social classes are sampled; the article's results thus cannot be used to make generalizations about child influence patterns in lower-class families.

The Caron and Ward article presents several findings that raise new questions about family decision processes. Why are older children more likely than younger children to use the mass media as a source of product information? Caron and Ward suggest that over time children may learn to use the media as an information source. Why do upper-class children prefer competitive and interactive toys? Why do middle-class children receive more gifts? Caron and Ward suggest that the differences might be due to different value orientations.

Although these suggested explanations sound plausible, they can only be validated through additional research. The suggested explanations are not the findings of the research. This problem occurs whenever research investigates the differences between groups of people (e.g., social classes or age groups). This points out that much research discovers what relationships exist, but researchers must then construct explanations about why these relationships hold. The statistical analyses in research reports give a sense of how valid and reliable the findings are. Only additional research can validate explanations about why certain differences between groups of people exist.

"A MODERNIZED FAMILY LIFE CYCLE"

A popular concept in family research in sociology as well as in consumer behavior concerns the family life cycle. In its broadest forms, the theory indicates that families go through a number of distinct stages in a sequential manner: marriage without children, family with children, the empty nest (children married), and old age. Considerable disagreement in sociology has centered on specifying the number of stages of a family life cycle. The broad stages, enumerated above, have been further subdivided, sometimes with as many as seven substages within each general stage.

Murphy and Staples argue that the concept of family life cycle has failed to develop with historically changing family conditions. Declines in family size and growth in divorce rates have altered the very nature of the family itself. They develop a conceptual model that takes into account the various family stages one might pass through depending on whether one is married, divorced, or remarried, and depending on whether one's children are living with the parent(s). This model represents the heart of their paper, so pay close attention to it while reading. Further, the authors elaborate upon the types of buying behaviors one might anticipate for members in each family stage. According to the authors, knowing whether an individual is young, middle-aged or old, with or without children, married or divorced tells us much about a family's needs and life-styles.

The model of family life cycle offers some interesting perspectives for marketers. However, it is important to keep in mind that family life cycle theorists assume individuals pass through each stage sequentially. Part of this argument is undoubtedly correct since the family life cycle implicitly accounts for age as a stage differentiating variable (we all grow old in an age sequential manner!). However, there undoubtedly exist other family forms, some of recent historical development, that are not captured by their model. Consider, for example, an individual who has children, but who has never married. Also consider a family whose children are fully grown and working, but who find it necessary to come back and live at home. Recent research shows this to be a growing trend among American households. Also, some parents move back with their children, thus eliminating the stage of older unmarried without children. Furthermore, there are some issues regarding age as a criterion for stage boundaries, such as where to place the couple who marries at age 38 and has a child at age 40. According to the model, they should be classified as middle-aged with teenage children. Thus, they have completely missed the sequentially earlier stage. What is the difference between "middle-aged, married, without dependent children" and "older, married"?

Family composition is indeed changing. It may therefore be unrealistic to assume that we can place families in a sequential pattern and assume that their movements through various stages are fixed.

"ENVIRONMENTAL UNCERTAINTY AND BUYING GROUP STRUCTURE: AN EMPIRICAL INVESTIGATION"

Spekman and Stern examine the effects of an organization's structural characteristics on its buying decisions under uncertain situations. Like families, organizational members make group decisions, sometimes in light of uncertain consequences.

Spekman and Stern note that members involved in organizational decisions often have different jobs. They are also the holders of different forms of information. The most informed decision makes maximum use of all available information. This pooling of data is especially crucial under uncertain situations. The authors speculate that the degree to which information can be pooled varies as a function of the organizational structure.

The interpersonal relations occurring in a decision-making context can also be influenced by organizational structure. While most organizations normally make decisions in a relatively bureaucratic manner, less centralization is to be anticipated in an uncertain decision when information pooling is critical.

The central hypotheses propose that firms under low environmental uncertainty will (1) have more centralized (bureaucratic) buying groups, (2) will have greater division of labor, (3) more rules, and (4) will engage in less participative decision making than will firms under high environmental uncertainty. It is also hypothesized that (5) under environmental uncertainty the purchasing agent will hold greater power in his/her ability to influence a purchase decision than she/he will under low environmental uncertainty.

Using a sample of individuals from 20 firms, the authors found support for the hypothesis that greater participative decision making occurs under uncertainty. The results also suggest that the purchasing agent's influence is greater when decision making is taking place in uncertain environmental conditions. Presumably, the purchasing agent is in a unique position, between the boundaries of other groups, and can facilitate information transfer.

Certainly structural characteristics of the organization can affect information transfer and interpersonal power relations within the decision-making unit. How information is gathered, how it is utilized, and how decisions are made are central issues, not only at the micro level of individual consumer decisions, but also at the more complex and interactive systems of families and organizations. It is in these latter instances that the complexities and dynamics in identifying decision-making processes abound. Partly these complexities relate to diverse individual orientations of problems and solutions and the information to which they are exposed.

GIFT DECISIONS BY KIDS AND PARENTS

**ANDRE CARON
AND
SCOTT WARD**

Consumer groups, government officials, and marketers have debated the possibly deleterious effects of television advertising on pre-teenage children. While the issues are complex, perhaps the single fact with which all the involved parties can agree is that research is needed as a basis for valid and effective government or industry regulation.

One major issue concerns children's ability to process information in television advertising. Critics imply that a wide range of techniques in television commercials render children unable to effectively process information—that is, to fairly evaluate information about products and brands and to make decisions based on this information. Younger children, and perhaps especially children from disadvantaged family backgrounds, are thought to be particularly limited in their information-processing abilities and, consequently, may be more "vulnerable" to advertising's persuasive influences.

Defenders of advertising to children, on the other hand, imply that even if children make poor consumer choices due to their limited ability to process information in advertising, such consequences are rarely lasting. They may even be beneficial, since children will be less likely to repeat the error.

A related issue concerns the effects of television advertising on family life—for example, does television advertising cause children to influence their parents to buy various products for them? And are some families (especially low-income families) less able to cope effectively with these influence attempts than other kinds of families?

Previous research has shown that the frequency of children's in-family purchase influence attempts varies with the child's age and with the particular product. Children are more likely to influence their parents to purchase products which are frequently consumed by them (e.g., breakfast cereal) and which are of particular interest to them (e.g., toys for younger children, records for older children). The frequency of children's purchase influence attempts generally decreases among older children, but parental acceding to such attempts increases with age. A modest correlation ($.18$, $p < .05$) has

Source: Andre Caron and Scott Ward, "Gift Decisions by Kids and Parents," *Journal of Advertising Research*, Vol. 15, August, 1975, pp. 15–20. Reprinted with permission.

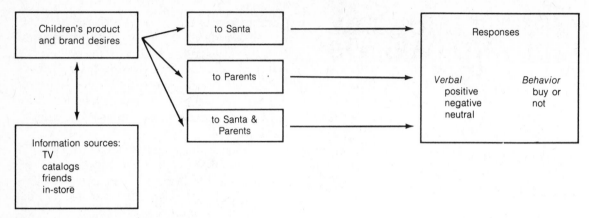

Figure 1   Model of relationships investigated in study.

been found between frequency of children's asking for products and patterns of intra-family conflict (Ward and Wackman, 1972).

It is not possible to isolate effectively the singular influence of television advertising on children's attempts to influence parental purchasing, since the products children most want are those which are most advertised. However, it is possible to examine differences in these patterns of intra-family influence among families in different social classes—a question not addressed in previous research.

PILOT STUDY

This reports initial analyses of an extensive research project. The study examines certain aspects of the relative influences of mass media and interpersonal sources on children's product desires and parental decision-making regarding their children's product desires. In the study, these desires were explored in the setting of children expressing their wants for Christmas gifts, expressed to mothers or in a letter to Santa. An attempt was made to trace children's desires for Christmas gifts from the initial idea to influencing parents to purchase the product, to parental responses—initial verbal response (e.g., "yes," "no," "maybe") and ultimate behavioral response (buying or not).

The various relationships investigated in the overall study are displayed in Figure 1.

METHODOLOGY

Data were gathered from a total of 84 mother-child pairs from an initial random sample of third graders (n = 54) and fifth graders (n = 52) in Montreal. Samples were drawn from two different socioeconomic areas: middle-class (average family income $9,000) and upper-class (average family income $14,500). Essentially we were interested in understanding where children get ideas for things they request, what kinds of things they request, and what kind of reception their request is likely to get inside the family.

The procedures were as follows: Approximately four weeks before Christmas, children were asked to write a letter to Santa, telling him what they wanted for Christmas. Information sources were ascertained by asking children to tell where they got the idea for each gift they requested of Santa. Meanwhile, mothers were trained to unobtrusively record each Christmas gift request during a seven-day period and to note their verbal response (if any) to the child. Also during this period we conducted a content analysis of television commercials directed to children in these age groups. Following the Christmas vacation, we ascertained the specific gifts which children received.

FINDINGS

Mothers registered a total of 360 requests during the seven-day period. From letters to Santa written outside the home, we tabulated requests made exclusively to Santa (total requests = 677). By comparing letters to Santa with requests to mothers, we found 117 common requests made both to mothers and to Santa.

Children requested much the same kinds of items (to Santa, parents, or both) regardless of age or social class. Most requested were non-interactive toys (23 per cent of all requests). These are toys such as dolls, models, etc., which children normally play with alone, or at least do not require others in order to enjoy them. Second most requested were sports items (18 per cent), followed by competition toys (e.g., slot-racing sets, 14 per cent) and clothing (13 per cent).

Regarding information sources about the gifts requested, children most often cited television as the source of gift ideas, closely followed by friends (Table 1). Minor variations to these patterns were observed by social class and by sex, but older children were considerably more likely to cite television as the idea source and considerably less likely

to cite friends than were younger children. Older children were also more likely to cite catalogs. These findings suggested that older children have learned to use a variety of mass media as sources of product ideas. This age-related finding was similar to patterns found for kindergarten, third, and fifth grade children when they were asked how they would find out about new products (Ward and Wackman, 1973).

Gift Requests

Data in Table 2 show that younger children asked for more gifts than older children; however, their conversion rate (i.e., receiving specifically-requested gifts) was not as high as that for older children. More important were the social class differences. Middle-class children requested more gifts than upper-class children, and they directed more requests to Santa only than did upper-class children. Middle-class children in the sample fantasized more than upper-class children, or were perhaps more intimidated at the prospect of directing purchase influence attempts at their parents; they preferred to cast their lot with Santa instead. On the other hand, they received more gifts, requested or not, although the conversion rate of requests to gifts was very similar in both economic groups (all proportions considered).

Table 1 Sources of gift ideas*

Information Source	Total	Grade 3	Grade 5	Middle-class	Upper-class	Sex M	Sex F
Television	27%	23%	31%	26%	27%	28%	25%
Catalog	19	14	24	17	21	22	15
Store	22	21	22	24	18	15	29
Friends	26	34	17	27	24	27	24
Other	7	8	6	6	10	8	7
Total	100%	100%	100%	100%	100%	100%	100%
n =	(320)	(172)	(148)	(186)	(134)	(180)	(140)

*Cell entries are percentages of all requests cited in letter to Santa, in response to the question: "Where did you get the idea that you wanted (each item requested)?"

Table 2   Summary of mean number of gift requests, receipts, and proportion of requests to parents, and/or Santa, by social class and grade

	Middle-class n = 45	Upper-class n = 39	Grade 3	Grade 5
Total requests (mean)	8.7	7.3	8.5	7.5
Gifts received (mean)	5.7	4.7	5.0	5.5
Requested (Santa or Parent) and received (mean)	2.7	2.5	2.6	2.6
Received without requesting (mean)	3.0	2.2	2.4	2.9
% Requests to Parents only	32%	41%	38%	34%
% Requests to Santa only	54	37	48	45
% Requests to Santa and Parents	14	22	14	21

Types of Gift Requests

Data in Table 3 show significant differences in the type of gift requested by children of different social class groups. Middle-class children prefer noninteractive toys, followed by sport items; upperclass children request more competition games, toys, clothing, and sport items. Our data also showed significant age differences (p < .008) with younger children requesting overall more noninteractive toys (27 per cent), and older children preferring more sport items (20.7 per cent). Sex differences were not found to be significant.

Parents' Responses to Requests

When children asked for specific items as Christmas gifts, parents most often responded verbally in neutral terms (e.g., "we'll see"). This finding was reasonably consistent, regardless of the specific item asked for, although requests for clothing, books, and records were somewhat more likely to elicit positive verbal responses. Data in Table 4 show few age differences, although middle-class parents were slightly more likely to respond negatively than were upper-class parents. Differences in the total number of requests (middle-class request-

Table 3   Total requests by type of gift and by social class

Types of items	% Middle-class	n =	% Upper-class	n =
Non-interactive Toys	27.4	(107)	15.7	(45)
Creative Games/Toys	10.5	(41)	9.4	(27)
Competition Games/Toys	10.2	(40)	18.5	(53)
Sport Item	18.9	(74)	17.5	(50)
Clothing	10.0	(39)	17.5	(50)
Books & Records	7.4	(29)	9.4	(27)
Others	15.6	(61)	11.9	(34)
Total	100.0	(391)	100.0	(286)

$X^2 = 28.13$ d.f. = 6,   p < .001

Table 4 Parents' verbal responses to children's overt gift requests

	Grade		Social class	
	3	5	Middle	Upper
Positive	32%	32%	29	35%
Negative	19	21	22	18
Neutral	48	47	48	47
	100%	100%	100%	100%
n =	(182)	(160)	(170)	(172)
	X^2 = n.s.		X^2 = n.s.	

ing more) might be explained by the fact that upper-class children received more positive responses and less negative ones.

Total Gifts Received Whether or Not Requested by the Child

In terms of gifts received, data in Table 5 indicate that both groups (middle- and upper-class) receive mostly what they requested—that is, noninteractive toys for the middle-class children and competition games/toys for the upper-class children. Per-

centages of items requested are repeated from Table 3 to compare kinds of gifts received and frequency of requests for each gift item. Significant differences for age ($p < .01$) show younger children received mostly non-interactive toys (23 per cent) and competition games/toys (15.4 per cent), while older children receive more creative games/toys (21 per cent) and clothing (17 per cent). Not unexpectedly, girls received different items than did boys; clothing (17.4 per cent) and "other" (i.e., jewelry, musical instruments, etc.) were most likely to be given to girls; non-interactive toys (19 per cent) and competition games/toys (17.1 per cent) were received in the most part by boys. Further data analysis indicates that approximately 50 per cent of the gifts received had not been explicitly requested either in the letter to Santa Claus or to the parents. The majority of these unsolicited gifts were of the following nature: creative games/toys (22.9 per cent), competition games (17 per cent), others (16.6 per cent), and clothing (14.8 per cent). No significant differences were found for social class or for age; differences for sex ($p < .004$) were similar to those previously indicated.

Table 5 Total gifts requested and total received (requested or not)* by type of gift and by social class

	Middle [n = 45]				Upper [n = 39]			
	Requested		Received requested or not		Requested		Received requested or not	
Types of Items	%	n	%	n	%	n	%	n
Non-interactive Toys	27.4	(107)	21.5	(55)	15.7	(45)	11.4	(21)
Creative Games/Toys	10.5	(41)	18.4	(47)	9.4	(27)	15.3	(28)
Competition Games/Toys	10.2	(40)	10.5	(27)	18.5	(53)	22.3	(41)
Sports Items	18.9	(74)	11.7	(30)	17.5	(50)	13.0	(24)
Clothing	10.0	(39)	14.1	(36)	17.5	(50)	15.8	(29)
Books & Records	7.4	(29)	6.6	(17)	9.4	(27)	9.2	(17)
Other	15.6	(61)	17.2	(44)	11.9	(34)	13.0	(24)
Total	100	(391)	100	(256)	100	(286)	100	(184)

*X^2 = 18.93   d.f. = 6   p = < .0043

Table 6 Percentage of gift requests fulfilled by parents, by recipients of gift request, social class, and grade

Recipients of gift request	Social class		Grade	
	Middle	Upper	3	5
Parents				
Only	28%*	34%	33%	30%
Common	51	52	53	50
Santa				
Only	27	23	21	32
Total	31	34	30	35
N =	(120)	(97)	(110)	(107)

*Should be read: "Among middle-class children, 28% of specific gift requests made to parents were fulfilled—the specifically requested item was received."

Fulfillment of Gift Requests

Data in Table 6 show the percentage of requests which were and were not fulfilled. For example, 28 per cent of middle-class children's requests were fulfilled (i.e., the specific gift requested was received); thus, 72 per cent were not. The percentage of specific gift requests that were received is somewhat higher for upper-class children. For both groups of children, requests made to both Santa and parents ("common requests" in Table 6) were most likely to be fulfilled. This finding probably reflects the intensity of children's desires. That is, there may have been qualitative differences in the requests of children, and the more intense desires may have been reflected in the child's asking both Santa and his parents for the particular item.

Data in Table 7 examine patterns of parental yielding to children's purchase influence attempts by item requested and by social class. Middle-class families are shown to be somewhat more likely to yield to requests for non-interactive toys; however, upper-class parents are more likely to yield to requests for sports items, clothing, books, and records, and slightly more likely to yield to requests for creative games. Again, the context of these data

Table 7 Purchase requests and parental acceding by gift items and social class

Items	Middle Class					Upper Class				
	Asked		Asked and received		% Acceding	Asked		Asked and received		% Acceding
	%	n	%	n		%	n	%	n	
Non-Interactive Toys	27.4*	107	33.3	40	37.3	15.7	45	11.3	11	24.4
Creative Games/ Toys	10.5	41	11.7	14	34.1	9.4	27	10.3	10	37.0
Competition Games/Toys	10.2	40	9.2	11	27.5	12.5	63	19.6	19	30.2
Sports Items	18.9	74	15.0	18	24.3	17.5	50	16.5	16	32.0
Clothing	10.0	39	10.8	13	33.3	17.5	50	19.6	19	38.0
Books & Records	7.4	29	5.0	6	20.7	9.4	27	9.3	9	33.3
Others	15.6	61	15.0	18	29.5	11.9	34	13.4	13	38.2
Total	100.0	391	100.0	120	30.6	100.0	286	100.0	97	33.9

*To be read: "Of all gifts children requested, 27.4% of requests were for non-interactive toys. Of all gift requests which were fulfilled, 33.3% were requests for non-interactive toys. Of all requests for non-interactive toys, parents acceded 37.3% of the time."

should be kept in mind: while middle-class children made more requests, they were more likely to get "neutral" verbal reactions from their parents and slightly less likely to get positive reactions when compared to upper-class children. In any case, the proportion yielding is quite similar for the two social class groups.

CONCLUSION

Interpretations of these data are highly speculative, as the sample was small. However, this study could be a prototype for larger-scale work, which would permit more definitive conclusions about the relative influences of mass media advertising on children and how children's desires for advertised products are handled in the family environment.

The data do suggest that the family environment is indeed a mediator of television advertising's effects. In fact, the differences in children's product desires and parents' patterns of responding to requests for particular types of toys may reflect fundamental value orientations of parents and children. Middle-class children exhibited less interest in competition toys than did upper-class children; parents of upper-class children were more likely to buy competition toys for their children. While care must be taken in interpreting the data on this point, it seems reasonable to conclude that both middle- and upper-class children were exposed to roughly the same level of advertising for competition games/toys. However, the two groups of children were apparently differentially interested in receiving them, perhaps reflecting different value orientations already formed by third and fifth grade.

The fact that parents mediate gift requests, regardless of social class, is seen in the data. For example, middle-class parents are less likely to respond to requests for sporting goods than are parents of upper-class children. This may reflect high cost, or it may reflect the fact that middle-class children may already possess many sporting goods items. In any case, middle- and upper-class parents selectively yield to purchase requests. Also reflective of different family environments are the different numbers of requests. Middle-class children did

indeed make more gift requests than upper-class children. A number of explanations could be advanced for this finding—e.g., norms in upper-class homes mediate against frequent asking for products; upper-class children receive more positive responses to their requests, so the need to repeat them is not great.

A final, highly suggestive finding in the study is that children cite a variety of sources for gift (product) ideas. It is particularly interesting to note that fifth grade children are more likely to cite television as a source of gift ideas than are third grade children. This finding is consistent with larger scale research (Ward and Wackman, 1973), and it suggests that older children learn to use television as a source of product information. Younger children are more bound to their perceptual environment, and are more likely to find out about products by actually seeing them in stores.

Some further analyses will be done on these data in an effort to relate content of commercials—including stylistic variables—and patterns of interpersonal relationships, as determined by sociometric data, to children's product desires and subsequent parental behavior.

Aside from the small sample sizes, an obviously limiting factor is that the differences between our age and social class groupings are not large. The income variations are not that great, and neither are the age differences. High proportions of third and fifth graders are probably in the concrete operational stage of development, although at different ends of the developmental continuum. Consequently, our age-related differences are not great.

REFERENCES

Ward, Scott, and Wackman, D. (August, 1972), "Children's Purchase Influence Attempts and Parental Yielding," *Journal of Marketing Research,* 9, 316–19.

Ward, Scott, and Wackman, D. (1973), "Effects of Television Advertising on Consumer Socialization," Marketing Science Institute Research Report, Cambridge, Mass.

A MODERNIZED FAMILY LIFE CYCLE

**PATRICK E. MURPHY
AND
WILLIAM A. STAPLES**

. . .

One aspect of the family that has been studied by sociologists and consumer and marketing researchers is the "family life cycle" (FLC). It has been shown to be a valuable concept for these three gropus of researchers (Lansing and Kish 1957; Rich and Jain 1968; Spanier, Lewis, and Cole 1975). Unfortunately, the life cycle has not been examined in light of current demographic trends. The purpose of this paper is to review the family life cycle concept, discuss prior research concerning its impact on consumer behavior, and suggest a new, more appropriate FLC with research implications.

THE TRADITIONAL FAMILY LIFE CYCLE

Approach and Eras

The family life cycle is derived from the "developmental" approach to studying the family (Hill and Rodgers 1964; Hill 1970; Rodgers 1964; Rodgers 1973), an interdisciplinary approach drawing from rural and urban sociology, child psychology, and human development. Consequently, alternative views have been expressed about the number, as well as the determinants, of the "stages" in the FLC.

. . .

Family life cycles can be characterized as ranging from simple to complex. . . . Despite the differences in number of stages and the factors causing movement through them, agreement exists on one central idea—each family progresses through a number of distinct phases from point of formation to death of both spouses.

. . .

CHANGES IN FAMILY COMPOSITION AND LIFE STYLE

A number of recent demographic shifts have altered the composition of the "typical" American family and, in some cases, changed its life style significantly. One of the most influential factors is

Source: Patrick E. Murphy and William A. Staples, "A Modernized Family Life Cycle," *Journal of Consumer Research,* Vol. 6, June, 1979, 12–22. Reprinted with permission.

the overall decline in the average family size. The fertility rate by 1976 had decreased to 1.8 children per woman.[1] With the number of children in the family declining and likely born within a few years of one another, the middle FLC stages (i.e., those with children present) will tend to last fewer years. Therefore, the time with children living at home may no longer be the predominant portion of the FLC.

A related trend is the tendency for delay of time of first marriage. The annual rate of first marriages has declined almost continuously for two decades. Postponement of marriage has been especially prominent among women in their early 20's. The proportion of women still single at ages 20 to 24 has increased by nearly one-half since 1960, from 28 percent to 43 percent. Continuation of this trend would indicate an increase in the amount of time women and, as a result, men spend in the single FLC stage.

A third important demographic development affecting the FLC is increasing incidence of divorce in the United States. From 1965 to 1976 the divorce rate doubled, from 2.5 to 5.0 per 1,000 population. Also, initial divorces are occurring about six months to one year earlier than they did ten years ago, and those who remarry are doing so sooner. Clearly, marital events are being compressed into a shorter span of years.

Although in 1975 four of every five divorced persons remarried by middle age, the decrease in remarriages since 1972 suggests that this proportion may decline in the near future. For example, for persons 35 to 54 years old, the proportion of persons currently divorced increased by one-third between 1970 and 1975. It appears, then, that the middle and older age segments of the family life cycle may be increasingly composed of divorced individuals who are living alone or with children. Divorce projections indicate further increases in the divorce rate. Among women in their 20's today, 40 percent can expect their first marriage to end in divorce. Although it cannot be stated with certainty that this high rate of divorce will proceed unabated,

these statistics emphasize the current necessity of recognizing "divorce" as an option within the FLC.

A MODERNIZED FAMILY LIFE CYCLE

Before delineating the steps of the proposed family life cycle, a few exceptions that will not be taken into account in this revised concept need recognition. Although cohabitation as an alternative to marriage is becoming increasingly popular with some segments of society and is beginning to draw research attention (Danzier and Greenwald 1977; Satow 1977), less than one percent of all couples are living together and maintaining a quasi-familial relationship out of marriage (Carter and Glick 1976).

In addition, women who have never been married but are raising a family are also excluded. Individuals who remain single throughout their life are by definition not included in forming a family. Furthermore, married couples who are separated are not explicitly dealt with in this revised FLC. It appears, however, that most persons who separate eventually divorce because it is now easier to afford, and the social stigma of divorce is rapidly lifting (Glick and Norton 1977, p. 15). Finally, young and middle-aged widowed husbands and wives and their families are not taken into account.

Table 1 presents the modernized (i.e., revised) family life cycle; it contains five major stages with 13 sub-categories. To provide a sense of continuity for the following elaboration, the Figure depicts the flow of families through the revised FLC stages. . . .

. . .

The efficacy of this revised family life cycle should not be judged exclusively by the absolute numbers of people that it accounts for, but rather by its ability to reflect changing demographic trends. Wells and Gubar (1966) and other traditional FLC formulations do not take into account the divorced or childless families and, therefore, are not reflective of recent major demographic shifts. Even if the divorce rate subsides somewhat and family size increases in the future, the modern-

[1]The statistics reported in this section were taken or derived from Glick and Norton (1977).

Table 1 Comparison of population distributions across the stages of two family life cycles, 1970[a]

	Murphy and Staples			Wells and Gubar	
Stage	No. individuals or families (000's)	% Total U.S. population[b]	Stage	No. individuals or families (000's)	% Total U.S. population[b]
1. Young single	16,626	8.2	1. Bachelor	16,626	8.2
2. Young married without children	2,958	2.9	2. Newly married couples	2.958	2.9
3. Other young					
a. Young divorced without children	277	0.1			
b. Young married with children	8,082	17.1	3. Full nest I	11,433	24.2
Infant[c]					
Young (4–12 years old)[c]					
Adolescent[c]					
c. Young divorced with children	1,144	1.9	4. Full nest II	6,547	13.2
Infant					
Young (4–12 years old)					
Adolescent					
4. Middle-aged					
a. Middle-aged married without children	4,815	4.7			
b. Middle-aged divorced without children	593	0.3			
c. Middle-aged married with children	15,574	33.0	5. Full nest III	6,955	14.7
Young					
Adolescent					

(continued)

ized FLC sufficiently covers these potential changes.

Young Stages

Although "young single" is not technically a family stage, almost everyone passes through it before beginning a family. For most individuals, this stage would begin at about 18 years of age or the time they graduate from high school. Those who marry at 18 or before will skip this stage, but the number

of teen-age marriages has been declining (Glick 1977). One study (Bomball, Primeaux, and Pursell 1975) found that as the number of college graduates increases, marriage is temporarily postponed. College enrollments, especially on the part of women, are continuing to grow (VanDusen and Sheldon 1976). Therefore, with the postponement of marriage until the mid-twenties by more individuals, young singles will establish some amount of financial independence and may experience

Table 1 *(Continued)*

	Murphy and Staples			Wells and Gubar	
Stage	No. individuals or families (000's)	% Total U.S. population[b]	Stage	No. individuals or families (000's)	% Total U.S. population[b]
d. Middle-aged divorced with children Young Adolescent	1.080	1.8			
e. Middle-aged married without dependent children	5,627	5.5	6. Empty nest 1	5,627	5.5
f. Middle-aged divorced without dependent children	284	0.1			
5. Older					
a. Older married	5,318	5.2	7. Empty nest II	5,318	5.2
b. Older unmarried Divorced Widowed	3,510	2.0	8. Solitary survivor-in labor force	428	0.2
			9. Solitary survivor-retired	3,510	2.0
All other	34,952 203,210[e]	17.2	All other[d]	46,738 203,210[e]	23.3

[a]Figures for this Table were taken or derived from U.S. Bureau of the Census 1973, Tables 2 and 9.

[b]As there are single and divorced individuals in some of the stages, the numbers were calculated as a percentage of the entire population, not just the number of families. Also, the percentages of the total for families were determined by multiplying the number of families by 2.3 (average number of children per family in 1970) and adding the parents (or parent, in divorced instances) to the number. For example, the 17.1 percent in the young married with children was computed as follows:

$$\frac{8,082 \ (2.3 \text{ children}) \ + \ 16,164 \ (\text{parents})}{203,210} = 17.1\%.$$

[c]As many families have children at more than one of these age levels, it is not meaningful to compute the numbers for each of these ages independently.

[d]Includes all adults and children not accounted for by the family life cycle stages.

[e]Source: U.S. Bureau of the Census 1970. The numbers do not add to this total because of the calculations explained in Footnote b.

several life styles, e.g., student, employee, dropout.

The second FLC stage is the young (under 35) marrieds without children. . . . This period of establishment, or "honeymoon" stage was traditionally rather short, lasting less than two years before the first child was born (Glick and Park 1965, p. 190). Currently, because of the widespread use of contraception, changing attitudes toward parenthood, and more working wives for financial or career reasons, this stage may be extended for several years. This decision usually allows the young married to establish a degree of financial security.

In addition to those who consciously decide not

to have children, there are two options for the next stage of the revised FLC. One option is "young divorced." According to recent statistics, one of every three marriages will end in divorce, and, as mentioned previously, divorces are occurring at earlier points in the marriage (Glick and Norton 1977, pp. 25–6).

. . . Life styles of divorced individuals may revert back to the single stage, but sometimes they are psychologically unprepared to begin the "mating game" again. Both are usually financially worse off, unless the wife receives a large alimony settlement or has a career of her own. As most men and women remarry after an early divorce, they would then "recycle" through the young married stage again.

The stage that traditionally follows young married without children is young married with children . . . As shown in Table 1, the subsections of this stage are infant, young (4–12 years old), and adolescent children. The existence of children usually alters drastically the life style and financial situation within the family. Commitment to child rearing in terms of years will probably not be as extensive as in earlier generations.

Divorce within the young-married-with-children FLC stage, although traumatic, is becoming more prevalent. In fact, over 60 per cent of divorces in 1976 occurred when the woman was under age 30, and in about two-thirds of these cases children were present (Glick and Norton 1977). Whether the divorce happens when the children are in the infant, young, or adolescent subcategory, both life style and financial implications are significant. Almost always the wife retains custody of the children and, although child support is usually required of the husband, it is frequently inadequate. The wife must then look for employment—sometimes several years after being out of the labor force. The cost of maintaining a separate household leaves many men without much discretionary income.

Middle-Aged Stages

As shown in Table 1, the middle-aged stages contain six possibilities. The range for this category is approximately 35–64 years of age for the family head.[2] One possibility within the middle-aged group is marriage without children. Although this group has historically been a very small segment, it will likely increase in the future because more couples are making a conscious decision not to have children. Urban highly-educated women (Kerckhoff 1976), who are presently growing in number, show the greatest tendency to remain childless. The life style of middle-aged couples without children will probably not be as hectic as when they were younger, but the freedom will remain. If the couple is healthy and financially comfortable, these families could be characterized as occupying the "carefree stage."[3]

The middle-aged divorced situation without children (stage 4b in Table 1) may occur at this time in the family development, or as a continuation of those in young divorced stage not remarrying. A divorce in this stage is less common (Kerckhoff 1976), and when it occurs may present a major life style adjustment for both the spouses. The financial condition of the divorced individual is likely dependent on occupation and socioeconomic status. For some it may be quite comfortable, but for others financially strained. These persons may remarry (see Figure 1), but the likelihood that they would ever have children is small.

The more traditional middle-aged group (stage 4c in Table 1) comprises those with young and adolescent children. The number of families in this stage is large and will continue to be significant. The predominant family life style is one that revolves around the children and their school activities. However, the father's and/or mother's career and its concomitant social and time obligations may alter this life style. Today's family in this stage is better off financially because a larger percentage of the wives are working. Sometimes, it is neces-

---

[2]The U.S. Bureau of the Census divides ages ending in the digit five according to ten-year intervals (i.e., 25–34, 35–44, etc.). Therefore, the lower limit of middle-age was set at 35 to correspond with these data. Reasons for the upper limit are provided in the "older stages" section.

[3]Of course, race, socioeconomic status, and occupation may affect the degree to which this stage may be characterized as carefree.

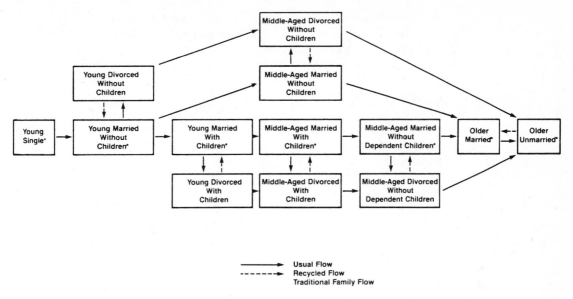

Figure 1 Family life cycle flows.

sary for the wife to work to meet family financial needs (Oppenheimer 1974).

Middle-aged divorced with children (4d in Table 1) can be arrived at either by a divorce occurring at this time or an extension of the young-divorced-with-children stage. If divorce takes place at this time, life style changes are significant. Both parents and children must adapt. This may mean that the wife and often the children have to take on additional responsibilities for the family's livelihood. On the other hand, families that have experienced a divorce at an earlier stage have likely undergone the adaptive process and are settled in this life style. The procedure for getting to this stage makes little difference in financial terms, however. The divorced father has financial constraints as long as the children are still eligible for child support. Likewise, the mother with children present is saddled with financial burdens.

The final two categories within the middle-aged group are married without dependent children (4e in Table 1) and divorced without dependent children (4f). These represent what Wells and Gubar (1966) and others have described as the "empty nest" stage. Since the age at which children are

born is lower for non-whites and those of lesser education, income, and job status (United States Census 1974), these families or divorced individuals would probably experience a longer empty nest period. The trend toward smaller families in all socioeconomic levels may mean more time in this stage for middle and upper socioeconomic classes in the future, also (Glick 1977). In any event, once the children are on their own the married couple or the divorced man and woman not only experience financial relief, but also many life style options become available.

Older Stages

The final FLC stages (Table 1) are simply labeled "older." The family head's age is about 65 years old, and this category begins at retirement. It might happen at age 60, 62, 65, or possibly later. The recent legislation postponing mandatory retirement may defer this category for some. As retirement represents a major life style and financial change for most, it seems logical that the older stages would start here.

The two major distinctions within the older category are married or unmarried, i.e., divorced or widowed. Older retired couples have few time commitments, but also may have to reduce their standard of living. Those with past savings and good health may have an active retirement, e.g., travel and recreation; others less financially solvent or with infirmities will probably experience an unpleasant final stage.

The "solitary survivor" stage (5b in Table 1), like the young single, is not technically part of the "family" life cycle, but is included to complete the process. For the previously divorced individual, this stage represents only an occupational and possibly a life style change, but not an emotional one. However, the person who was married for most of his/her lifetime may experience emotional as well as physical and financial hardships when losing his/her spouse. Of course, it is possible that an older widowed or divorced person will remarry (see Figure 1).

The major stages and their subsections shown in Table 1 attempt to depict a more thorough conceptualization of the modern American family's life cycle. It is possible to follow the flow through the stages as shown in Figure 1. For instance, the "typical" family would progress through stages 1, 2, 3b, 4c and 4e, and 5a and 5b (see Table 1). On the other hand, a woman divorced at age 30 with one child and not remarried would follow the sequence 1, 2, 3b, 3c, 4d, and later 4f and 5b. Those divorced individuals who remarry may recycle through one or more stages, depicted by the dotted lines in Figure 1.

RESEARCH IMPLICATIONS

The objective of this section is to specify areas that may be studied by family sociologists and consumer and marketing researchers. For each of these groups, topics that may be researched, as suggested by recent demographic trends, are examined—e.g., postponement of marriage and declining family size. These might be analyzed by either the traditional or modernized FLC. More significantly, two important areas (divorced persons and childless couples) can be studied using only the revised FLC categories.

. . .

Consumer Researchers

Family decision-making patterns have been extensively analyzed by consumer researchers using the decision process (i.e., problem recognition, search, evaluation, purchase, and postpurchase behavior) and family role structure (i.e., initiator, decider, buyer, etc.) approaches (Davis 1976; Davis and Rigaux 1974; Ferber and Lee 1974). These approaches can be applied in both the traditional and modernized FLC context. In examining the age of family members, the earlier findings (Blood and Wolfe 1960; Granbois 1963; Wolgast 1958) that joint involvement in decision making decreases over the stages of life cycle might be reexamined. For example, those not marrying until the middle or late twenties could have already established strong decision-making patterns or time constraints that may preclude young husbands and wives from extensive joint decision making. Furthermore, those couples spending an extended time in the empty nest stage might become more oriented to joint decision making again.

Another important research area that can be best analyzed by employing the revised FLC concerns family size. For instance, the differences in husband and wife influence in families with children may no longer follow Kenkel's (1961) findings that joint decision-making involvement decreases with the presence of children. Young, middle-aged, or older married couples *without* children might currently differ substantially from families with children, with respect to husband and wife influence in the decision process stages and/or the extent of role specialization. Joint decision making of couples never having children could be analyzed over the revised FLC stages.

The area of future FLC research most obvious from the modernized family life cycle, and most absent in the literature, is a comparison between the decision-making patterns of traditional and nontraditional (those headed by a divorced parent) households. Specifically, does the divorced person engage in more or less external search than married couples? Possible role structure differences in families of married versus divorced parents with one or more children deserve attention. In addition, the role children play in household decision making in divorced families appears to be an important research topic. For example, is the teen-age daughter the primary supermarket products decision-maker? The degree of husband, wife, or child dominance could vary widely depending on the family composition or the stage in the revised family life cycle. Also, the "gatekeeper" effect for information acquisition and purchase deliberation may not be operable in divorced families.

Marketing Researchers
Those engaged in marketing products and services will be interested in how consumption is affected by the FLC. In fact, Cox (1975) found the tradi-tional FLC stage superior to "length of marriage" in determining consistency between husbands' and wives' attitudes toward automobiles. Hisrich and Peters (1974) also determined that life cycle stage was more significantly correlated with the use or nonuse of several entertainment activities than age or social class.

The changing family size and age profile of the United States population implies that researchers using either the traditional or modernized FLC should investigate the marketing implications of these trends. For example, declining family size affects marketers who sell products appealing to large families, such as station wagons, several-bed-room homes and large size packages. In addition, the quantities of products purchased by families in stages containing children will likely decline. The extended "empty nest" stage identified by Glick (1977) may also be a segment for marketers to study and cultivate. Even if the family is not wealthy, the length of this stage may allow couples to save for vacations, better furniture, and possibly a different home.

The young divorced stage might be a promising segment for marketers of small appliances rather than large ones, because the individual may view this stage as temporary. Within the service area, personal enhancement services, such as health spas and tennis clubs, would seem to be in demand by the more affluent in this group. Also, life insur-ance marketers may find the divorced woman in-terested in buying insurance for herself and possi-bly the children. Moreover, most divorced women

with children from middle and lower social classes would probably be seeking inexpensive clothing for herself and the children.

In the middle-aged categories of the revised FLC, those who remain childless may represent a good market for luxury goods, e.g., expensive res-taurants, extended vacation packages, high quality furniture. Divorced individuals who hold good jobs and have no dependents may also be classified as part of this same market. Middle-aged divorced parents, on the other hand, would seem to be seek-ing more low-priced and functional products, such as used cars, inexpensive furniture, and fast food restaurants.

CONCLUDING COMMENT

Although the traditional family life cycle has proven to be a valuable tool for researchers, recent changes in family composition and life style suggest that a revision of the concept is needed. The mod-ernized FLC proposed in this paper utilizes the age of household head, marital status, and, to a less extent, children's ages to determine the length of the stages. Recognition of divorce and remaining childless as options (Table 1) are its major dis-tinguishing features. An explanation of life style and financial characteristics for each stage is given to clarify this conceptualization, and research im-plications are drawn for family sociologists and consumer and marketing researchers.

REFERENCES

Blood, Robert O., Jr., and Wolfe, Donald M. (1960), *Husbands and Wives: The Dynamics of Married Liv-ing*, New York: The Free Press, pp. 41–4.

Bomball, Mark R., Primeaux, Walter J., and Pursell, Donald E. (1975), "Forecasting Stage 2 of the Family Life Cycle," *Journal of Business*, 48, 65–73.

Carter, Hugh, and Glick, Paul C. (1976), *Marriage and Divorce: A Social and Economic Study*, 2nd ed., Cambridge MA.: Harvard University Press.

Cox, Eli P. III (1975), "Family Purchase Decision Mak-ing and the Process of Adjustment," *Journal of Mar-keting Research*, 12, 189–95.

Danziger, Carl, and Greenwald, Mathew (1977), "An Overview of Unmarried Heterosexual Cohabitation and Suggested Marketing Implications,'' in *Advances in Consumer Research,* Vol. 4, ed. William D. Perreault, Jr., Atlanta: Association for Consumer Research, pp. 330–4.

Davis, Harry L. (1976), ''Decision Making Within The Household,'' *Journal of Consumer Research, 2,* 241–60.

———, and Rigaux, Benney P. (1974), ''Perception of Marital Roles in Decision Processes,'' *Journal of Consumer Research, 1,* 51–62.

Ferber, Robert, and Lee, Lucy C. (1974), ''Husband-Wife Influence in Family Purchasing Behavior,'' *Journal of Consumer Research, 1,* 43–50.

———, (1977), ''Updating the Life Cycle of the Family, *Journal of Marriage and the Family, 39,* 5–13.

Glick, P. and Norton, Arthur J. (1977), ''Marrying, Divorcing, and Living Together in the U.S. Today,'' *Population Bulletin, 32,* Washington, D.C.: Population Reference Bureau, Inc.

———, and Parke, Robert, Jr. (1965), ''New Approaches in Studying the Life Cycle of the Family,'' *Demography, 2,* 187–202.

Granbois, Donald H. (1963), ''The Role of Communication in the Family Decision-Making Process,'' in *Proceedings,* ed. S. Greyser, Chicago: American Marketing Association, pp. 44–57.

Hill, Reuben (1970), *Family Development in Three Generations,* Cambridge, MA: Schenkman Publishing Company, Inc.

———, and Rodgers, Roy H. (1964), ''The Developmental Approach,'' in *Handbook of Marriage and the Family,* ed. Harold T. Christensen, Chicago: Rand McNally and Company, pp. 171–211.

Hisrich, Robert D., and Peters, Michael P. (1974), ''Selecting the Superior Segmentation Correlate,'' *Journal of Marketing, 38,* July, 60–3.

Kenkel, William F. (1961), ''Family Interaction in Decision Making on Spending,'' in *Household Decision-Making,* ed. Nelson N. Foote, New York: New York University Press, pp. 140–64.

Kerckhoff, Alan C. (1976), ''Patterns of Marriage and

Family Formation and Dissolution,'' *Journal of Consumer Research, 2,* 261–75.

Lansing, John B., and Kish, Leslie (1957), ''Family Life Cycle As An Independent Variable,'' *American Sociological Review, 22,* 512–9.

Oppenheimer, Valerie K. (1974), ''The Life Cycle Squeeze: The Interaction of Men's Occupational and Family Life Cycles,'' *Demography, 11,* 227–45.

Rich, Stuart U., and Jain, Subhash C. (1968), ''Social Class and Life Cycle as Predictors of Shopping Behavior,'' *Journal of Marketing Research, 5,* 41–9.

Rodgers, R. (1973), ''The Family Life Cycle Concept-Past, Present, and Future,'' paper presented at Thirteenth International Family Research Seminar, Committee on Family Research, International Sociological Association, Paris, France.

Satow, Kay (1977), ''Some Comments on Changing Life Styles Among Single Young Adults,'' in *Advances in Consumer Research,* Vol. 4, ed. William D. Perreault, Jr., Atlanta: Association for Consumer Research, pp. 335–6.

Spanier, Graham B., Lewis, Robert A., and Cole, Charles L. (1975), ''Marital Adjustment Over the Family Life Cycle: The Issue of Curvilinearity,'' *Journal of Marriage and the Family, 37,* 263–75.

U.S. Census Bureau (1974), *Fertility Histories and Birth Expectations of American Women: June 1971.* Current Population Reports, Population Characteristics, Series P-20, No. 263, Washington, D.C.: U.S. Government Printing Office.

VanDusen, Roxann A., and Sheldon, Eleanor B. (1976), ''The Changing Status of American Women: A Life Cycle Perspective,'' *American Psychologist,* February, 106–16.

Wells, William C., and Gubar, George (1966), ''Life Cycle Concept in Marketing Research,'' *Journal of Marketing Research, 3,* 355–63.

Wolgast, Elizabeth H. (1958), ''Do Husbands or Wives Make the Purchasing Decisions?'' *Journal of Marketing, 23,* 151–8.

ENVIRONMENTAL UNCERTAINTY AND BUYING GROUP STRUCTURE: AN EMPIRICAL INVESTIGATION

**ROBERT E. SPEKMAN
AND
LOUIS W. STERN**

Source: Robert E. Spekman and Louis W. Stern, "Environmental Uncertainty and Buying Group Structure: An Empirical Investigation," *Journal of Marketing,* Vol. 43, Spring, 1979, 54–64. Adapted from *Journal of Marketing,* published by the American Marketing Association.

As the study of organizational buying behavior matures, there is a noticeable increase in research reflecting the dynamics and complexities of multiperson decision processes. . . . Consistent with this growing stream of research, the authors have accepted as fact that organizational buying is primarily a multiperson, decision making process in that most organizational purchasing decisions are influenced by various members of the buying center (Robinson, Faris, and Wind 1967; Webster and Wind 1972). However, the degree to which buying center members are actively involved in the procurement process can vary from a fairly routine situation where the purchasing agent attempts to take into consideration the preferences of the other buying center members to extremely complex situations in which the final purchase decision is truly a group decision. The point is that in an organizational context an individual (usually, the purchasing agent) rarely makes a procurement decision independent of the influence of others (Wind 1976). Espousing the view that the "buying group" is the appropriate unit of analysis, our focus will be to examine the structure of the group itself.

Our emphasis on the structure of the buying group reflects a current stream of organizational research which suggests that organizational structure is central to (1) the capability to solve problems effectively (Leavitt 1951); (2) the ability to differentiate interpersonal communication patterns (Hage 1974); and (3) the determination of power relationships within organizations (Hickson et al. 1971). In fact, several organizational theorists (e.g., Duncan 1972; Galbraith 1973; Lawrence and Lorsch 1967) conceptualize structure as the critical variable determining the effectiveness or ineffectiveness of a decision unit's information processing potential. From this body of literature emerges four conceptually unique dimensions of structure which will guide our investigation of buying group organization. For example, a rather rigid, highly bureaucratized buying group can be described as highly centralized, bound by strong rules and procedures and a strict division of labor, and with little member participation in decision making. Conversely, less bureaucratic buying groups (i.e., with low levels of centralization, rules and procedures, division of labor, and a great deal of participation in decision making) are likely to be more flexible and, thus, more open to adaptation and change. From such structural profiles, it is then possible to infer certain interpersonal characteristics of the buying group with respect to its decision making style, patterns of informal communication flows, and so forth. Moreover, an analysis of this structural profile allows a richer description of the buying group as an information processing, decision making entity.

. . .

A critical variable which has been found by students of organization theory to affect the structure of departments and divisions within companies is the extent of environmental uncertainty facing the department or division under study. So-called "contingency" theorists (e.g., Duncan 1972; Galbraith 1973) have shown that the more uncertain a department's environment is perceived to be by its members, the more likely it is that the department will be structured in a more flexible, less bureaucratic way in order to permit the free flow of generally novel and nonroutine information regarding the environment. Static and simple environments do not require a continuous gathering and processing of such information, and therefore, the structure of departments facing them will, according to the contingency theorists, be more rigid and bureaucratic. By adapting its structural configuration to match the level of uncertainty in its environment, a firm can facilitate the gathering and processing of information crucial to its decision making; thereby reducing uncertainty to a manageable level. Here, we also will examine whether such findings hold for the groups responsible for organizational buying decisions. That is, we will determine whether the extent of perceived environmental uncertainty is related to the structure of organizational buying groups. Specifically, four hypotheses can be formally stated:

Firms operating under conditions of low environmental uncertainty will have:

H_1: more highly centralized buying groups than firms operating under conditions of higher environmental uncertainty,

H_2: a more highly specified division of labor in

their buying groups than firms operating under conditions of higher environmental uncertainty,

H_3: a higher degree of rules and procedures in their buying groups than firms operating under conditions of higher environmental uncertainty,

H_4: less participation in decision making in their buying groups than firms operating under conditions of higher environmental uncertainty.

Inherent to the hypotheses regarding structure is the role of the purchasing agent within the buying group. From a marketing perspective, it is useful to know whether or not the purchasing agent's influence within a buying group increases or decreases as the amount of perceived environmental uncertainty varies. Thus, not only should one be curious as to the level of influence exerted by a purchasing agent, he/she also should seek to ascertain whether the agent performs an even more critical function as the need for additional information regarding prices, availability of supply, quality of sources, and the like increases. Therefore, the more dynamic and complex the buying group's environment, the more likely it may be that the purchasing agent's influence heightens as he/she assumes increased data gathering (i.e., uncertainty absorbing) activities for the buying group as a whole. A final hypothesis is

H_5: buying group members operating under conditions of higher environmental uncertainty will attribute greater influence to purchasing agents than those buying group members operating under conditions of low environmental uncertainty.

METHODOLOGY

The Sample
The sample employed in this study consisted of 20 firms from the greater Chicago area. These firms represented 11 different industries of which 70% served mainly industrial markets and the remainder served mainly consumer markets. Specifically, firms were drawn from the food, steel and nonferrous metals, pharmaceutical, environmental

controls, electronics, agricultural and transportation equipment, medical supply, industrial gases, industrial and automotive parts, printing and duplication equipment, and chemical industries. As this research reflected a universalistic (or theory-centered) approach (Kruglanski 1975), no attempt was made to select the sample on a random basis. Rather, care was exercised in collecting a representative cross section of large manufacturing companies in diverse kinds of industries. During March-April 1976, 400 respondents were either personally administered or mailed questionnaires. Of the 360 returned questionnaires, 38 were either unopened or invalidated by the respondent. In total, there were 322 usable questionnaires (an 80.5% response rate).

Determination of Buying Group Membership

Unlike a formal structural subunit (i.e., a marketing department or purchasing department), the buying group is a more nebulous construct, reaching across functional boundaries, whose composition, hierarchical levels, lines of communication, etc., are not strictly prescribed by an organization chart or official document. The buying group evolves as an informal communication network which does not derive its structural configuration from the formal organization per se, but rather from the regularized patterning of interpersonal communication flows among the various group members. Thus, the buying group construct defines an informal, cross-departmental decision unit (Spekman 1977) in which the primary objective is the acquisition, importation, and processing of relevant purchasing-related information. . . . An important point to note is that buying group membership evolves during the procurement process and is a function of the information requirements and needs of a particular buying context.

Operationally, membership in a buying group was ascertained by asking a purchasing agent (PA) the names and titles of those organization members with whom he/she interacts in making purchasing-related decisions for the particular commodity (i.e., a product, service, component, etc.) for which he/she was responsible. If, for example, a

PA sought advice and/or received purchasing-specific information from persons in quality assurance, production, R&D, and sales forecasting, these organizational actors became members of the buying group for the particular commodity in question. This sociometric procedure does not imply that the PA's position is central to the buying group in terms of status or importance. It does permit, however, the anchoring of a buying group's purchasing-related responsibility to a particular commodity.

. . . Since purposive participation was an explicit criterion for membership, only those organization members who perceived themselves to be active in a particular buying group were included in the final sample. In this fashion, 52 buying groups, representative of 21 different commodities, were empirically determined.

Research Instruments

The scales employed in this study were based on perceptual measures. . . .

Perceived environmental uncertainty. In an attempt to capture the relevant task environment, the environmental uncertainty scale ($\alpha = .68$) focused exclusively on purchasing-related decisions and reflected the entire range of information inputs impinging on the buying groups. Specifically, attention was given to purchasing-related factors external to the buying group, but internal to the firm as well as factors external to both the buying group and the firm. It can be seen, therefore, that purchasing decisions can be affected by such external factors as government regulations and economic conditions as well as by internal considerations with respect to material tolerances, production estimates, sales forecasts, and so on.

Buying group structure. Each dimension of buying group structure was derived empirically by a factor analysis with varimax rotation. . . . Embodying the implicit focus of the definition of a buying group, each dimension of structure reflected a concern for the lateral, interpersonal relationships which evolve during the procurement process. For example, *centralization* ($\alpha = .63$) referred to whether purchasing authority was dispersed among buying group members or closely held by one member regardless of his/her formal hierarchical position. Similarly, *participation in decision making* ($\alpha = .70$) examined the extent to which the various buying group members were involved in purchasing-related decisions. *Rules and procedures* ($\alpha = .68$) measured the degree to which purchasing activities were conducted in a routine and formal fashion. Finally, the *division of labor* construct ($\alpha = .39$) examined the extent to which purchasing-related activities were shared by the buying group members.

Power.   The power construct ($\alpha = .78$) focused on the degree to which the purchasing agent was perceived by the other buying group members to influence the purchasing decision making process. Consistent with other power theorists (e.g., March 1955), attributed power was utilized to measure the influence of the purchasing agent within the buying group. Specifically, the power scale examined the purchasing agent's influence in an eight-step succession of purchasing-related events adapted from the Robinson, Faris, and Wind (1967) "BUYPHASE."

. . .

FINDINGS

Environmental Uncertainty and Buying Group Structure

. . . The results indicate that there is no statistically significant relationship between either centralization ($F = 1.28$, $p = .262$) or rules and procedures ($F = .044$, $p = .547$) *and* environmental uncertainty. However, there is strong support for the hypothesized relationship between uncertainty and participation in decision making ($F = 8.87$, $p. = .005$) as well as weak support for the relationship between uncertainty and division of labor ($F = 2.12$, $p = .152$).

Despite these inconsistent results, there is an interesting pattern emerging from the data. The constructs depicting division of labor and participation in decision making appear to be more amenable to measures of informal structure and, in fact, seem to

be more descriptive of the information processing potential of buying groups. As the information needs of buying groups increase in response to conditions of higher environmental uncertainty, the various tasks within them become less routine and less differentiated (i.e., less division of labor). The resultant increase in shared purchasing responsibility contributes to a more flexible organizational design, thereby permitting buying group members to react more quickly, and more easily, to the increased contingencies of a more highly uncertain environment. Similarly, greater participation in decision making connotes the emergence of additional lateral communication networks, replacing the rigid vertical paths of a more bureaucratized buying group. These networks facilitate the acquisition of more extensive and intensive purchasing-related information. It can be seen that both constructs serve to highlight the process of joint decision making and the sharing of purchasing responsibilities within the buying groups.

Conversely, it is likely that the constructs measuring centralization and rules and procedures are more highly interwoven with the formal structure of the various companies which participated in the study. Indeed, these two structural dimensions appear to embody those organizational mechanisms which ensure that individuals conform to the requirements of the organization. Theoretically, it would not be surprising to find the formal structure of the companies circumscribing the informal relationships of their buying groups because it has been found elsewhere that organizations strive to minimize variance in the behavior of their members (Rogers and Agarwala-Rogers 1976). That is, the formal hierarchy may be used to limit individual discretion through supervision (i.e., centralization) and/or the formalization of rules and procedures may be employed to guide the behavior of buying group members. Because the actions of the buying groups are central to the uninterrupted flow of material in the production process, it is conceivable that firms would attempt to routinize much of the behavior within these groups.

These findings suggest that while the buying groups seemingly adapted their structural configuration (i.e., greater participation in decision making and less division of labor) in response to greater levels of environmental uncertainty, equal consideration was given to retaining a degree of control over individual discretion. Herein lies the existence of a potential managerial dilemma—whether to promote a flexible buying group structure so as to facilitate information gathering or processing in the face of environmental uncertainty *or* whether to constrain the group's activities so as to coordinate the flow of industrial goods into the production process. As the composite profile of buying groups tends to cluster at the "bureaucratic" end of the structural continuum, it would appear that the overriding concern among all buying groups was minimizing the impact of individual variations. . . .

Given the wide variety of commodities purchased, such a narrow range in buying group structure was not anticipated. If one recalls, however, the historical development of the purchasing function, this result is not totally surprising. That is, each buying group, regardless of the commodity purchased, was, to a greater or lesser extent, linked to the production technology (Perrow 1972; Woodward 1965) of the firm in question. Thus, a more bureaucratic configuration would tend to enhance coordination among the various organizational units and actors. As the resultant coordination and control improves workflow efficiency, one can appreciate more easily the fairly bureaucratic profile across the present sample of manufacturing companies.

Environmental Uncertainty and the Purchasing Agent's Influence

The bivariate regression analysis . . . indicates a statistically significant relationship between environmental uncertainty and the influence of purchasing agents ($F_{1,50} = 5.42$, $p < .05$). This finding is consistent with research by organizational theorists (e.g., Adams 1976) who have hypothesized that as a firm's external environment becomes more turbulent and unstable, the information processing function of boundary role persons (here, the purchasing agent) becomes central to a firm's ability to effectively gather, analyze, and act on relevant environmental information.

As purchasing agents are able to effectively

"cope with" or "absorb" uncertainty for other buying group members, they have an excellent opportunity to enhance their position of influence (Spekman 1979). No doubt some of this influence is attributable directly to the centrality of the purchasing function in the production workflow. However, as the level of uncertainty increases, the need for environmental information becomes crucial to buying group members, and the coping ability of the purchasing agent contributes, conceptually at least, to a strengthening of his/her influence. Clearly, one can envision purchasing agents utilizing their contacts with outside sales personnel and their knowledge of potential or actual problems in the marketplace as a power resource. Moreover, an examination of disaggregated (i.e., individual level) data, . . . reveals that as the environment becomes more uncertain, the purchasing agent's influence is felt by the other buying group members to extend beyond those issues directly germane to the procurement decision ($F_{1,203} = 10.46$, $p < .01$). These findings add credence to the growing anecdotal evidence reporting the purchasing agent to have input into such diverse areas as product design, long range planning, and other traditionally nonpurchasing-related areas (*Business Week* 1975).

SUMMARY AND CONCLUSION

Marketers seeking to influence the industrial procurement process have had to rely heavily on individual level research regarding the decision inputs of purchasing agents or on data describing the function of purchasing departments. To a significant extent, this reliance on somewhat simplistic data is due to the fact that little systematic study has been undertaken to understand the structure of the multiperson buying groups responsible for major purchase decisions (Nicosia and Wind 1977). In this respect, then, this study represents an important step forward. Specifically, it contributes a conceptually rigorous research paradigm which facilitates an examination of aspects of organizational buying behavior from other than the individual level of analysis. Structure is viewed as a central variable, for it not only shapes the nature and degree of interpersonal interaction within the buying group, but also it is a primary determinant of the buying group's information acquisition and processing capabilities.

While sweeping generalizations beyond this sample must be cautioned, several points can be highlighted. It is interesting to note that regardless of the level of uncertainty associated with the purchase of a particular commodity, the composite profile of buying group structure tends to reflect a fairly bureaucratic structure. One explanation hinges on the possibility that the formal organization's mechanisms of control and coordination influence the perceptions of the buying group members with respect to aspects of their informal interactions within the buying groups. However, the greater the uncertainty and the concomitant need for greater information, the more likely it is that role prescriptions will be relaxed and joint participation in decision making will be emphasized.

It also is noteworthy that the purchasing agent's influence is shown to increase, relatively speaking, as the level of environmental uncertainty increases. Conceptually, this increased influence is viewed as a result of the unique boundary-spanning position occupied by the purchasing agent. The PA sits at the junction of many communication paths and, therefore, is able to monitor, if not control, the quality and amount of information received by the other buying group members. The likelihood is that, as the environment becomes even more uncertain, the purchasing agent may be able to increase his/her potential influence.

Moreover, these findings add credence to the participative and interactive nature of organizational buying. Consistent with recent strategies for industrial market segmentation (Wind and Cardoza 1974), this research suggests that knowledge of a buying group's decision making behavior is useful in the development of microsegmentation strategies. Clearly, the successful marketer is cognizant of the need to develop communications programs which address the joint decision making properties and differential information requirements of the various buying group members. The need and desire for increased information will in-

tensify as environmental uncertainty increases and, given the results reported above, it can be expected that the structure of buying groups will become somewhat more flexible in order to search for, accommodate, and utilize relevant purchasing-related information.

REFERENCES

Adams, J. S. (1976), "The Structure and Dynamics of Behavior in Organizational Boundary Roles," in *Handbook of Industrial and Organizational Psychology,* M. Dunnette, ed., Chicago: Rand McNally.

Business Week (1975), "The Buyer Gains More Clout," (January 13), 42–43.

Duncan, R. (1972), "Characteristics of Organizational Environments and Perceived Environmental Uncertainty," *Administrative Science Quarterly,* 17 (June), 313–327.

Galbraith, Jay (1973), *Designing Complex Organizations,* Reading, MA: Addison-Wesley.

Hage, J. (1974), *Communication and Control,* New York: John Wiley and Sons.

Hickson, D., C. Hinings, C. Lee, and R. Schneck (1971), "A Strategic Contingencies' Theory of Intraorganizational Power," *Administrative Science Quarterly,* 16 (June), 216–229.

Kruglanski, A. (1975), "The Two Meanings of External Invalidity," *Human Relations,* 28, 653–659.

Lawrence, P. and J. Lorsch (1967), *Organization and Environment,* Homewood IL: Richard D. Irwin.

Leavitt, H. (1951), "Some Effects of Certain Communication Patterns on Group Performance," *Journal of Abnormal and Social Psychology,* 46 (February), 38–40.

March, J. (1955), "An Introduction to the Theory and Measurement of Influence," *American Political Science Review,* 49 (June), 433–451.

Nicosia, F. and Y. Wind (1977), *Behavioral Models for Market Analysis.* Hinsdale, IL: Dryden Press.

Perrow, C. (1972), *Complex Organizations: A Critical Essay,* Belmont CA: Wadsworth Publishing.

Robinson, P., C. Faris, and Y. Wind (1967), *Industrial Buying and Creative Marketing.* Boston: Allyn and Bacon.

Rogers, E. and R. Agarwala-Rogers (1976). *Communication in Organizations.* New York: Academic Press.

Spekman, R. E. (1977), "A Contingency Approach to Power Relationships within the Industrial Buying Task

Group," unpublished Ph.D. dissertation, Evanston: Northwestern University.

Webster, F. and Y. Wind (1972), *Organizational Buying Behavior,* Englewood Cliffs, NJ: Prentice-Hall, Inc.

Wind, Y. and R. Cardoza (1974), "Industrial Marketing Segmentation," *Industrial Marketing Management,* 3 (February), 153–166.

Woodward, J. (1965), *Industrial Organization: Theory and Practice,* London: Oxford University Press.

SECTION V

COMMUNICATION PROCESSES IN CONSUMER BEHAVIOR

Communication is the process of establishing a commonness of thought between two or more persons. It is, in effect, the "glue" of social interaction. Without communication, interaction could not occur and hence buyer-seller relationships could not develop.

The communication process involves five key factors. First, there is the *source* of a communication. An important issue in the study of consumer behavior concerns the credibility of various sources of information. Does a communication about a product have more of an impact on consumers when the source of communication is an acknowledged expert rather than when it comes from a trusted friend who is not an expert? Second, it is necessary to consider the particular *message* being conveyed. Should the message be of a threatening nature, i.e., should it stress the bad consequences of not using a particular product or brand? Should the message be highly persuasive or should it merely try to convey information without interpretation or evaluation? A third consideration involves the *channel* of communication. What channel is most likely to catch the attention of consumers for a particular product? Are some channels such as informal word-of-mouth discussions better than more formal channels such as newspapers for disseminating information about a new product? Channels such as print, broadcast, and interpersonal media may vary greatly in their possible persuasive effects, their speed in disseminating information, their ability to overcome biases among consumers, and the number and type of people reached. A fourth important consideration in communication is the *receiver* or the intended audience. Here research has focused on the relative susceptibility to influence of consumers with different personalities, levels of formal education, and perceptions of themselves and others. A final consideration concerns *destination* effects. What happens after a communication is received? How is it remembered by the consumer? If the communication changes consumers' attitudes, will those attitudes fade quickly, especially if competitive advertising occurs?

It is important to consider key communication roles as they may occur in formal groups. There appear to be four key communication roles in any type of group. The gatekeeper may or may not belong to a particular group. The gatekeeper tries to prevent too much information from entering a group by filtering communications. Too much information can cause an overload and result in a breakdown in the channels of communication. For example, if a consumer receives too much information, there may be a tendency to "turn off" that channel altogether. A second role, that of *liaison,* integrates the information into the group and thus interconnects various parts of an organization or different informal groups. The liaison role is thus very important for rapidly disseminating information from a gatekeeper. The *opinion leader* is the person who helps evaluate the reliability of communications. The opinion leader is able to informally influence the attitudes and behaviors of others more or less frequently. Finally, the *cosmopolite* role relates a social system to its environment. The cosmopolite person is often in contact with sources of information outside the group, but also belongs to the group. This is what differentiates the cosmopolite from a gatekeeper who may not belong to the group for which he or she serves as gatekeeper. Also a gatekeeper is likely to function with respect to only one type of channel or one type of product. A cosmopolite, on the other hand, is likely to be in contact with diverse channels dealing with diverse topics.

"A CONTROLLED STUDY OF THE EFFECT OF TELEVISION MESSAGES ON SAFETY BELT USE"

One of the most common misperceptions about consumer behavior relates to the persuasive effect of television advertisements. Most people overestimate the power of a television advertising campaign. In particular, even the best-designed campaign is likely to have little or no impact if it is attempting to persuade people to do something they do not want to do. It is one thing to encourage a person to try a new brand of soap when that person already uses and has a positive attitude toward soap in general. It is quite another thing to try to persuade people to change a negative attitude into a positive attitude and thereby change their action patterns.

These contentions are well illustrated by the Robertson article. The researchers followed practices that are usually suggested for those planning communication messages. The content and basic message of the ads were based on preliminary research to determine differences between seat belt users and nonusers. Viewer involvement was high and the emotional reactions (particularly to the "girl at the window" ad) were strong. The emotions evoked included sympathy, fear, horror, regret, anger, and resolution to act differently. Not all of the messages, of course, can be classified as high-fear appeals.

Yet, these ads still had no effect on seat belt use. How can one know that this experimental result accurately reflects people's actual responses to the ads? This question can only be answered by examining the research methodology.

The research methodology used in this study is very strong. Actual behavior was observed rather than relying on self-claimed use of seat belts. Observations were made before the message campaign, continuously during the campaign, and after the campaign. This made it possible to determine whether or not there was a change in behavior. The importance of the use of a control group is demonstrated by this article. Without the control group, the researchers would have concluded that belt use decreased as a result of the television messages. However, since the control group also showed this decline, their conclusion is that the messages had no effect.

The researchers thus conclude that certain strategies will not change behavior in certain situations. In particular, they advocate the use of passive approaches. These are strategies that bring about change without relying on action on the part of the unprotected persons. The passive alternative to seat belts (which are an active strategy) is air bags or other passive restraint systems. Other consumer-related examples include required nutritional levels in foods rather than nutritional labels and fixed finance charges rather than finance charge disclosures. Thus, in addition to demonstrating the persuasive potential (or rather, persuasive failure) of television messages in certain situations, this article offers strategy recommendations for successful change programs.

"THE BUYING CENTER: STRUCTURE AND INTERACTION PATTERNS"

Communications theory affords additional insights into the industrial buying process. The group of individuals within an organization who collectively decide upon the purchase of a good or service is called the buying center. The nature of that group's structure and interaction patterns is of primary concern to the industrial marketer. Even though the participants in the buying center may be expected to vary from product to product, insights into the group's functioning may be expected to carry over across products. The buying center is essentially a small social system within the organization. As such, it forms a communications network, which builds its own structure out of the regular patterns of communication of the group members. These patterns can be described in terms of five communications concepts: (1) vertical involvement, (2) lateral involvement, (3) extensivity, (4) connectedness, and (5) centrality. Vertical involvement specifies the number of levels of authority within the organization. Lateral involvement specifies the number of separate functional areas within the organization. Extensivity specifies the total number of people within the buying network. Connectedness specifies the degree of linkage between individuals in the buying center. Centrality specifies the position of the purchasing manager within the buying center.

Johnston and Bonoma first build a model of the buying center as a communications network with the above five dimensions. They then address the question of the differences in the buying center to be expected across both organizations and product situation purchases. To what extent would such common product situation attributes as the importance of the purchase, the complexity of the product, the novelty, or the purchase class have an impact on the above five dimensions of the buying center? To what extent would such common organizational structural variables as size of the organization, complexity of the organization, formalization or centralization have an impact on the buying center? Johnston and Bonoma then test their buying center model with survey data. For all buying center dimensions except centrality, either organizational structural variables or purchase situation attributes have a statistically significant ($p \leq .05$ or better) impact on the buying center dimensions.

"SUBLIMINAL ADVERTISING: WHAT YOU SEE IS WHAT YOU GET"

One of the consumer's most persistent fears is the violation of his/her mind by subliminal advertising. Moore carefully reviews both the theory and the research concerning subliminal advertising. Can minds be "broken and entered" or not?

Although Moore cites some findings supporting the linkages between positive affect or liking for a given stimulus and the prior subliminal presentation of that same stimulus, he agrees with McConnell (1977) overall that "all things considered . . . secret attempts to manipulate people's minds have yielded results as subliminal as the stimuli used."

A CONTROLLED STUDY OF THE EFFECT OF TELEVISION MESSAGES ON SAFETY BELT USE

LEON S. ROBERTSON, PhD
ALBERT B. KELLEY
BRIAN O'NEILL
CHARLES W. WIXOM
RICHARD S. EISWIRTH
WILLIAM HADDON, Jr., MD

Source: Leon S. Robertson, Albert B. Kelley, Brian O'Neill, Charles W. Wixom, Richard S. Eiswirth, and William Haddon, Jr., "A Controlled Study of the Effect of Television Messages on Safety Belt Use," *American Journal of Public Health,* Vol. 64, November, 1974, p. 1074. Reprinted with permission of the American Public Health Association.

INTRODUCTION

The use of safety belts in automobiles greatly reduces the probability of death and injury in crashes (Tourin and Garrett, 1960; Bohlin, 1967; Campbell, 1968; Levine and Campbell, 1971). As a result of legislation in several states, lap belts have been standard equipment in at least the front outboard seating positions of 1964 and later models of American made cars (Seat Belt Accidents, 1965).

However, the availability of safety belts does not guarantee their use. In October, 1970, a study was conducted which included actual observation of drivers in their automobiles. In a metropolitan area, only 7 percent of drivers of 1968 and later models were using lap and upper torso belts and an additional 16 percent were using lap belts only. Lap and upper torso belts were used by 1 percent of drivers of 1968 and later models in smaller cities and 9 percent of such drivers used lap belts only (Robertson, O'Neill, and Wixom, 1972). Belts even when present, were used less often in earlier models. In spite of a number of campaigns urging safety belt use, the proportion of vehicle occupants using them is so low that much of the reduction in death and injury that should be achieved by their use is not being realized.

Campaigns promoting the use of safety belts have been based on inadequate knowledge of the factors contributing to lack of use. If the campaigns have been evaluated at all in terms of effectiveness, the evaluations have been faulty in design and execution (Haskins, 1969; Haskins, 1970).

In the present work, we have avoided some of the problems of previous studies and have tried to design and implement as definitive a study as present knowledge and technology allow. First, a survey was conducted of actually observed safety belt users and nonusers to determine the factors which distinguished the two groups (Robertson, et al., 1972). Second, television messages based partially on the preliminary study were developed and produced. These messages were then shown on one cable of a dual cable television system designed for marketing studies. The second cable as well as noncable groups allows comparison with groups not exposed to the messages to determine the effect of the messages relative to the effect of other factors which may influence belt use. The messages were shown for 9 consecutive months. For 1 month before and throughout the campaign, drivers were observed as to safety belt use and were matched through license plate numbers to the households on a given cable. In addition to being controlled, the study was "double blind," that is, the television viewers did not know that they were being studied and the observers did not know the purpose of the study or that the persons being observed were in experimental or control groups.

THE TELEVISION MESSAGES

The preliminary survey consisted of interviews with actually observed safety belt users and a random sample of nonusers observed at the same sites and times. The higher the respondent's education, the greater the likelihood that he was observed wearing safety belts. Those who rated safety belts as relatively more comfortable and convenient, those who said that they did not smoke while driving, and those who had a friend or relative injured, but not killed, in an automobile crash were also more likely to use belts. Furthermore, these factors were additive, that is, the presence of each factor increased the probability of use independent of the other factors (Robertson, et al. 1972).

The finding that a friend's injury, but not death, increased the probability of use indicates the likelihood that fear of being disfigured or disabled is more conscious and motivational in the use of safety belts than fear of death in a crash. Thus, we decided to emphasize the efficacy of safety belts in decreasing the probability of disfigurement and disability.

We were more wary of the comfort and convenience factor. Realizing that the safety belts in many automobiles are uncomfortable and inconvenient because of poor deisgn, we did not want to reinforce the tendency not to use belts because of this factor. Smoking while driving and education probably reflect a number of differences in personal characteristics such as risk-taking behavior and self-esteem. Since we do not believe that these characteristics are readily manipulable by televi-

sion messages, these factors were not considered in the creation of the messages. Techniques which are said in the industry to be successful in product marketing—for example, physician endorsement and a family responsibility theme—were employed in addition to the disfigurement-disability theme.

The television messages were written and produced in collaboration with an advertising agency which had a record of success in advertising commercial products as well as experience with public service material. Six basic messages were eventually developed and filmed. The following are brief descriptions of these messages:

1. A father (Figure 1) is shown lifting his teenaged son from a wheelchair into a car. As they ride along, safety belts obviously fastened, the father's thoughts are voiced off-camera intermixed with the son's on-camera expressions of excitement at going to a football game. The father expresses guilt for not having encouraged his son to use safety belts before the crash in which he was injured. The analogy to the protection that the son wore when he played football is drawn.

2. A teenaged girl (Figure 2) is shown sitting in a rocking chair looking out a window. She says, "I'm not sick or anything. I could go out more but since the car crash, I just don't. . . . The crash wasn't Dad's fault. I go for walks with my father after dark . . . that way I don't get, you know, stared at." She turns enough to reveal a large scar on what was the hidden side of her face. She continues, "It doesn't hurt anymore." An announcer says off-camera, "Car crashes kill two ways: right away and little by little. Wear your safety belts and live!"

3. A woman whose face cannot be seen (Figure 3) is shown in front of a mirror applying makeup. A full face picture on her dressing table shows her as a beautiful woman. Her husband enters the scene and suggests that they go to a party. She asks him not to look at her without makeup as she turns to reveal a scarred face. An off-camera announcer describes a crash in which the wife was driving slowly and carefully. The announcer con-

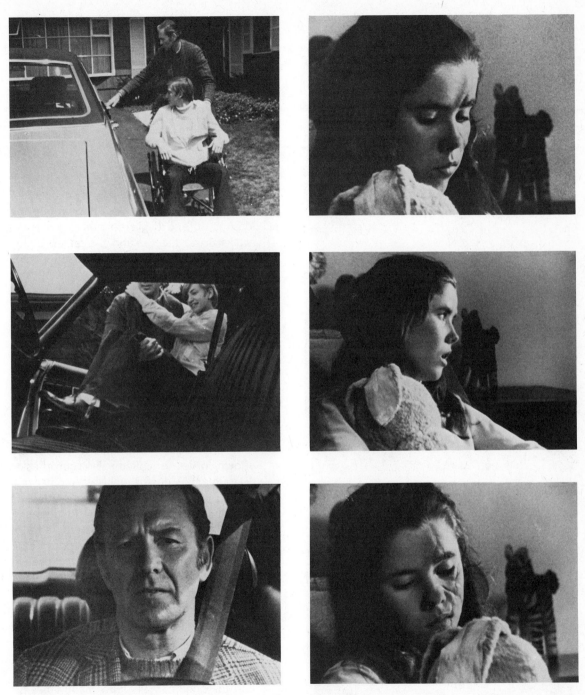

Figure 1   Father and son advertising messages.   **Figure 2**   Girl at the window advertising message.

Figure 3   Woman at the mirror advertising message.

tinues, as the picture on the table is shown, "Terry would still look like this if she had been wearing safety belts." Safety belts are shown through a shattered windshield. Announcer: "It's much easier to wear safety belts than to hear your husband say . . ." Husband: "Honey, I love you anyway."

4. A father and mother (Figure 4) are shown riding in the front seat of a car, their 8-year-old daughter seated between them. The father must brake hard to avoid another car entering from a side road. The daughter bumps her head as she is thrown into the dashboard and begins to cry. A policeman walks up to the car and the father angrily says: "Did you see what that guy just did? That jerk. I had to jam on my brakes. My little girl hit her head." The policeman asks the father why the child wasn't wearing safety belts. Over the father's protestations about the other driver, the policeman emphasizes the father's responsibility to protect his child. The scene closes with the policeman walking away saying: "When are people gonna learn?" and the announcer following with: "It doesn't take brains to wear safety belts. But it sure is stupid not to."

5. Two physicians and a nurse (Figure 5) are shown ordering coffee. The nurse asks: "Trouble?" A doctor replies: "Another guy driving home not wearing his safety belts." Nurse: "Gonna live?" Doctor: "Guess you could call it living." Nurse: "You've had a lot of car crash cases lately." Doctor: "Yeah, and I'm getting sick of it. They've got safety belts in the cars. Why . . . why in the name of God don't they put 'em on?" Waitress: "Do safety belts really make a difference?" The doctor shows her how a thermometer case can be hit and the thermometer inside not broken, but it shatters when hit out of the case. The waitress expresses further doubt and the doctor says: "How many times do you have to tell 'em?"

6. A car is shown in a driveway (Figure 6). From a puff of smoke steps a witch who announces: "Ha, ha, ha. I'm the Wicked Car

Figure 4 Family and policeman advertising message.　　**Figure 5** Physicians and nurse advertising message.

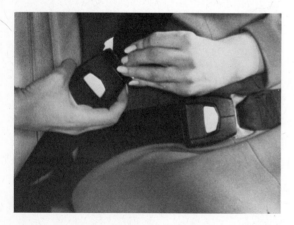

Figure 6 Witch and fairy: childrens advertising message.

Witch. Your Mommy and Daddy cannot see me but I make them drive without their safety belts. That's how they get hurt in car crashes.'' The mother gets into the car and the witch hides some belts in the seat and tangles others. A Good Car Fairy appears and says: ''Children! I am the Good Car Fairy. When your Mommy and Daddy get in the car, say 'Mommy! Daddy! If you love me, wear your safety belts!' '' The Wicked Witch and the Good Fairy argue as the father enters the car. A little girl calls from the porch: ''Mommy! Daddy! Wear your safety belts.'' The parents fasten the belts, the Wicked Witch disappears in a puff of smoke, and the Good Fairy again admonishes the children to urge their parents to demonstrate their love by wearing their safety belts.

By industry standards, the messages were of high quality. The ''father and son'' was judged the best among 30 entries in the public service category of the TV-Radio Advertisers Club of Philadelphia. The ''teenaged girl at the window'' was among the 10 finalists of 400 entries in the public service category of the Advertising Club of New York. It was also chosen as a finalist among the public service entries in the American TV and Radio Commercials Festival and National Print Advertising Competition. An informal opinion was obtained from the Director of the National Association of Broadcasters Code Authority that the messages were in compliance with the code.

The messages were not shown indiscriminately. Each was placed on or adjacent to a program likely to have an audience to whom the message would most likely appeal. For example, the witch was shown on network children's programs, the father and son on National Football League games, and the scarred faces on popular ''soap operas.'' No attempt was made to control what was shown in addition to our messages. For example, a number of automobile manufacturers had ''tag lines'' urging safety belt use at the end of their commercials throughout the study period. Of course, these additional messages were shown to both experimental and control groups and were thus constant for both audiences.

STUDY DESIGN

The messages were shown on one cable of a dual cable television system designed for marketing studies (Brown and Gatty, 1969). Located in a county of 230,000 people (1970 census), the two cables feed television signals to 13,800 households. There were 6,400 of these households on Cable A, on which our messages were shown, and 7,400 on Cable B, which was, in this case, the control cable. Each cable contains the full range of channels available from local stations as well as special movie and weather channels.

The two cables are distributed in a checkerboard fashion among blocks of homes in the community that have chosen to pay for the improved signal which the cable provides. Although the assignment of households to one or another cable was not strictly random, the various marketing studies done in the community have found no significant differences between the two in demographic characteristics, ownership of automobiles and other consumer goods, and pretest purchasing behavior for a large number of products (Adler and Kuehn, 1969).

In all, 14 observation sites were chosen. Using maps of the cable distribution among the streets and traffic flow maps obtained from the local traffic engineer, we chose observation sites at points which maximized the likelihood of observing automobiles from the neighborhoods where the cables were installed. Observers were assigned to a particular site for a given number of hours on a given day. No deviation from the observation sites was allowed. From May 10 through October 15, the observers were rotated among the sites daily. Observation periods were 7 a.m. to 10 a.m., 10 a.m. to 1 p.m., 1 p.m. to 4 p.m., and 4 p.m. to 7 p.m. Because of shortened daylight, the periods were changed to 8 a.m. to 12:30 p.m. and 12:30 p.m. to 5 p.m. after October 15. Half of the sites allowed observation of cars going into the center of the city and were observed during morning hours. The remaining sites, situated so as to observe drivers leaving the center of the city, were observed during afternoon hours. A morning and an afternoon site each was observed each weekday in the May to October 15 period. Observations were also obtained on Saturdays and Sundays but on a separate rotation among the sites. After October 15, only one site per day was observed, alternating morning and afternoon sites every other weekday. Thus, 14 weekdays were required to observe all of the sites in each time period in a given rotation during both summer and winter months. The sites remained constant and the observers were rotated among them in the same order throughout the study.

The observers were hardly noticed by persons being observed. The occasional motorist or pedestrian who stopped and asked, "What are you doing?" was satisfied with the answer "Taking a traffic survey."

Observing the driver only, observers stood at designated sites on the opposite side from the driver of an approaching automobile. The driver's sex, racial appearance, and approximate age were tape recorded as the vehicle approached the observer. The driver's use or nonuse of lap and lap-and-shoulder belts was observed as the automobile passed the observer. The automobile license number was then obtained as the automobile moved away.

The license plate numbers were matched with owner's names and addresses using the files of the state department of motor vehicles. The names and addresses were then matched to the file specifying which cable was assigned to given households. In those cases where the household was not on a cable, the household was specified as to whether or not it was in the same county as the cable groups.

Thus, there are four groups for comparison: Cable A households where the messages were shown, Cable B households which constitute a control group, noncable households in the same county as the cable households, and out-of-county households.

The messages were shown for 9 months on Cable A exclusively. Table 1 presents the distribution of the messages by time of day over the 9-month period, June 7, 1971, through March 5, 1972. For the first few months, the messages were shown mainly in daytime hours. In the late fall and winter,

Table 1   Number of safety belt messages shown by month and time of day

| | 1971 | | | | | | | 1972 | | |
Times	June	July	August	September	October	November	December	January	February	Total
Sign-on—noon										
No.	30	31	40	53	32	32	12	14	33	277
%	21*	28	29	48	30	33	17	19	34	
12:01—6:00 p.m.										
No.	105	68	78	43	50	25	26	41	43	479
%	73	62	57	39	48	26	38	55	45	
6:01 p.m.—signoff										
No.	8	11	19	15	23	40	31	20	20	187
%	6	10	14	13	22	41	45	27	21	
Total	143	110	137	111	105	97	69	75	96	943

*Percentages are based on the total number of messages in a given month.

more "prime" evening time became available through the courtesy of insurance companies and other advertisers who were willing to have public service advertising in lieu of their scheduled commercials on Cable A. These arrangements were made with the parent companies so that local affiliates of the companies were unaware of the experiment. The local television station managers were aware of the campaign, as they are of all tests on the experimental cable system. Since their stations receive extra income for some of the tests, it is in their interest not to reveal the experimental nature of the cable system to the population in the city. Special arrangements were made with the station managers to forward complaints to us—which were anticipated because of the strong themes—but none occurred.

There were fewer exposures in the later months because a greater number of people can be reached by fewer exposures in prime time. We estimate on the basis of ratings of the audience of the program on which the messages were shown that the average television viewer saw one or another of the messages two to three times per week. Of course, high frequency viewers saw the messages more often and low frequency viewers saw them less often than the average. In total, the campaign was equivalent to the type of major advertising effort which companies use to promote a new product. If this campaign had been sponsored on a national basis, it would have cost approximately $7,000,000.

RESULTS

The campaign had no measured effect whatsoever on safety belt use. Table 2 shows the percentage of observed male drivers using lap or lap-and-shoulder belts for each of the time periods necessary to observe drivers at all of the designated sites.

There is no significant difference between drivers from households on the experimental cable and drivers from households on the control cable in any of the observation periods. Also, there is no difference in use between those on the cables and other drivers observed at the same sites whether from in or out of the county. The same conclusion must be reached when the data for females are viewed in Table 3.

There is a downward drift in safety belt use from the spring through the winter months, more remarkable among male than female drivers. However, this decline occurs in the control and noncable groups as much as in the experimental group. Therefore, it cannot be argued that the messages had a deleterious effect on safety belt use. Some

Table 2 Percentage of male drivers using safety belts in experimental, control, and nonstudy groups

Dates	Experimental cable A		Control cable B		No cable, same county		No cable, out of county	
	% use	No. observed	% use	No. observed	% use	No. observed	% use	No. observed
Preexperimental	15	461	16	552	14	4343	14	1672
5/28–6/16	14	372	14	469	13	3840	12	1521
6/17–7/6	13	338	15	511	14	3706	9	1551
7/7–7/26	8	370	11	456	11	3825	9	1764
7/27–8/13	11	332	11	465	11	3785	8	1641
8/16–9/2	12	356	10	442	9	3458	8	1455
9/3–9/22	7	312	9	439	8	3367	7	1861
9/23–10/12	7	343	6	372	7	3322	5	1776
10/13–10/29	13	199	8	287	12	2005	7	1151
11/1–11/16	9	304	10	428	8	3207	8	1725
11/17–11/30*	9	124	10	164	10	1301	9	723
12/13–12/30	5	274	7	278	5	3271	5	1704
12/31–1/18	5	382	4	447	5	4154	4	2091
1/19–2/7	6	355	5	457	4	4497	6	2544
2/8–2/25	5	408	5	564	4	5139	4	2903
2/28–3/16	4	308	4	478	5	4270	4	2889
3/17–3/31	5	297	6	371	5	3474	4	2400

*Some sites missing due to observer illness.

unknown factor or factors contributed to a decreased use of safety belts in the winter months in all of the groups studied. The overall use rates were significantly lower for black persons (3 per cent) than for whites (10 per cent) as found in earlier studies (Council, 1969). Age differences were not statistically significant.

DISCUSSION

It must be concluded that the television campaign did not affect the use of safety belts. The decrease in belt use observed during the study occurred in the control and noncable groups as well as the group exposed to the campaign. It is clear that safety belt use did not increase during that campaign. The observed reduction in safety belt use in winter could be a result of other factors. For example, belt systems (which are at present in the U.S. usually designed without inertia reels, long known

devices that allow free movement until an impact occurs) are often rated as inconvenient (Robertson, et al., 1972). Having to adjust them to fit over bulky winter clothing could deter some persons from using them in winter.

The failure of these campaigns to increase safety belt use adds evidence to the argument that approaches directed toward changing behavior are inefficient and often ineffective means of reducing highway losses (Klein and Waller, 1970). "Passive" approaches, i.e, those which reduce the frequency or severity of damage to people and property, or both, irrespective of voluntary action on their part (Haddon and Goddard, 1962), show greater promise toward reducing the deaths and injuries in crashes, as they have historically in closely analogous public health situations. Some passive devices, e.g., energy-absorbing steering columns and windshields that perform like firenets, have been required by federal standards since

Table 3   Percentage of female drivers using safety belts in experimental, control, and nonstudy groups

Dates	Experimental cable A		Control cable B		No cable, same county		No cable, out of county	
	% use	No. observed	% use	No. observed	% use	No. observed	% use	No. observed
Pre-experimental	15	273	13	374	17	2760	15	772
5/28–6/16	13	238	16	301	14	2310	6	639
6/17–7/6	12	240	13	276	13	2139	11	685
7/7–7/26	13	197	11	273	13	2193	11	769
7/27–8/13	13	226	12	277	11	2105	13	753
8/16–9/2	12	187	10	273	11	1933	11	641
9/3–9/22	12	150	13	288	8	1948	10	696
9/23–10/12	10	206	8	259	7	1935	5	724
10/13–10/29	13	118	10	173	12	1136	12	455
11/1–11/16	16	192	14	324	11	2029	10	717
11/17–11/30*	14	74	15	103	14	743	12	227
12/13–12/30	8	196	8	232	7	1933	6	720
12/31–1/18	7	248	8	342	10	2494	9	1088
1/19–2/7	12	259	8	368	8	2731	8	1130
2/8–2/25	7	272	5	354	7	2727	6	1318
2/28–3/16	8	232	7	336	7	2565	7	1333
3/17–3/31	10	170	7	222	7	2006	7	1114

*Some sites missing due to observer illness.

1968 and have been shown to produce large reductions in fatalities and injuries (Levine and Campbell, 1971; Haddon, 1972).

The apparent failure of a number of mass media safety belt campaigns to increase use beyond precampaign levels may not mean that it is impossible to create a campaign which will increase safety belt use. However, the evidence on lack of effect of past efforts is sufficiently strong that the burden of proof of substantial further gains in belt usage resulting from such campaigns is on those who advocate use of mass media to promote use of safety belts.

REFERENCES

Adler, J., and Kuehn, A. A. (1969), "How Advertising Works in Market Experiments," Fifteenth Annual Conference of the Advertising Research Foundation.

Bohlin, N. I. (1967) , "A Statistical Analysis of 28,000 Accident Cases with Emphasis on Occupant Restraint Value," Eleventh Stapp Car Crash Conference Proceedings, 299–309.

Brown, N., and Gatty, R. (1969), "Designing Experiments with TV Advertising Laboratories," Proceedings of the Business and Economic Statistics Section, American Statistical Association, 120–29.

Campbell, B. J. (1968), "Seat Belts and Injury Reduction in 1967," University of North Carolina Highway Safety Research Center, Chapel Hill.

Council, F. M. (1969), "Seat Belts: A Follow-up Study of Their Use under Normal Driving Conditions," University of North Carolina Highway Safety Research Center, Chapel Hill.

Haddon, W., Jr., and Goddard, J. L. (1962), "An Analysis of Highway Safety Strategies in Passenger Car Design and Highway Safety," Association for the Aid of Crippled Children and Consumers Union of the U.S., New York.

———. (1972), "A Logical Framework for Categorizing Highway Safety Phenomena and Activity," *Journal of Trauma,* 12, 193–207.

Haskins, J. B. (1969), "Effects of Safety Communication Campaigns: A Review of the Research Evidence," *Journal of Safety Research,* 1, 58–66.

———. (1970), "Evaluative Research on the Effects of Mass Communication Safety Campaigns: A Methodological Critique," *Journal of Safety Research,* 2, 86–96.

Klein, D., and Waller, J. A. (1970), "Culpability and Deterrence in Highway Crashes," U.S. Government Printing Office, Washington, D.C.

Levine, D. N., and Campbell, B. J. (1971), "Effectiveness of Lap Seat Belts and the Energy Absorbing Steering System in the Reduction of Injuries," University of North Carolina Highway Safety Research Center, Chapel Hill.

Robertson, L. S., O'Neill, B., and Wixom, C. W. (1972), "Factors Associated with Observed Safety Belt Use," *Journal of Health and Social Behavior,* 13, 18–24.

Seat Belt Accidents (1965), *American Jurisprudence,* Rochester, N.Y.: Lawyers Cooperative Publishing Co., 355.

Tourin, B., and Garrett, J. W. (1960), "Safety Belt Effectiveness in Rural California Automobile Accidents," Automotive Crash Injury Research of Cornell University (now Cornell Aeronautical Laboratory, Inc.), Buffalo.

Westland, J. G. (1971), "Progress of Victorian Seat Belt Legislation to 30th September, 1971," Road Safety and Traffic Authority, Victoria, Australia.

THE BUYING CENTER: STRUCTURE AND INTERACTION PATTERNS

**WESLEY J. JOHNSTON
AND
THOMAS V. BONOMA**

Source: Wesley J. Johnston and Thomas V. Bonoma, "The Buying Center: Structure and Interaction Patterns," *Journal of Marketing,* Vol. 45, Summer, 1981, pp. 143–156. Adapted from *Journal of Marketing,* published by the American Marketing Association.

INTRODUCTION

The concept of the buying center refers to all those members of an organization who become involved in the buying process for a particular product or service (Robinson et al. 1967). While the major buying roles (e.g., initiator, influencer) remain constant over all purchases, the participants can and do change over purchase types and categories. The buying center notion has been one of the most important conceptual contributions made in the study of industrial buying behavior. Yet progress in moving from the abstract buying center concept toward a research topic or management aid has been slow (Wind 1978b; Gronhaug and Bonoma 1980).

Nonetheless, the need to examine the group and other social aspects of the buying center remains a central one:

- To the extent that the buying center includes more than one member, any analysis . . . should include an explicit examination of the relevant characteristics of the group, i.e., the cohesiveness of the buying center, the leadership pattern, and the formal and informal network of communications among the center's members (Wind 1978a).
- The development of organizational (as distinct from individual) characteristics (such as group cohesiveness, autonomy, intimacy, polarization, stability, flexibility, etc.) is the least advanced area of organizational studies (Wind 1978c).

This paper develops some structural and interaction-based system concepts to examine the functioning of corporate buying centers from a small group perspective, to develop compatible methods that can be used to measure these relational concepts, and to conduct an investigation of the buying center as a small social system in a number of organizations. The practical implications of this kind of approach to the buying center are numerous from an industrial marketer's perspective. They include understanding the involvement and interaction of organizational members in the buying decision process, information transmission and processing in the buying center, and the importance of purchasing management in the buying center.

Previous Research on the Buying Center

Although the term buying center was first used by Robinson et al. (1967), the first citation recognizing that a number of managers other than the purchasing staff were regularly involved in buying decisions was Cyert et al. (1956). Since then many articles examining the buying center have appeared.

The frequency of buying involvement of different functional areas in the firm like engineering, production, and purchasing has been investigated on a number of occasions (Buckner 1967, *Scientific American* 1969). These studies typically employed a large cross-sectional survey of industrial firms, from which aggregate frequencies of functional area involvement were computed on an industry or product basis. No attempt was made in any of these studies to group or systematically investigate characteristics of organizations or groups with similar buying involvement.

More recent research has turned to the perceived influence of various functional roles in the buying process (Fortin and Ritchie 1980, Grashof and Thomas 1976, McMillan 1973, Patchen 1974). The results of these studies show that these are significant differences in the perceived influence of major participants in the buying process, but that every participant or group reports that it is one of the most important and central. Little or no consensus on who is the most influential party has been obtained (Silk and Kalwani 1979). However, when the question is restricted to who participates in the buying center, high consensus is achieved (Gronhaug 1977, Kelly 1974, Patchen 1974). Apparently, it is quite easy to identify buying center participants in any given purchase situation, but quite difficult to understand their dynamics and power relationships.

Power, politics, and influence may be central social variables in the buying center. Strauss (1962) found the work behavior of purchasing agents to be strongly influenced by lateral negotiations, or formal and informal interactions with peers to influence the terms of purchases. In another study, Pettigrew (1975) examined the communications entering and exiting the buying firm. He found that certain individuals acted as gatekeepers to structure the outcome of the purchasing situation in the buying firms through control of information. Martilla (1971) found that word-of-mouth communication within firms is an important influence in the later stages of the adoption process. Opinion leaders were found to be more central to the verbal communication network than were other buying influentials in the firm.

The results of the research conducted to date depicts the buying center as a complex, multiperson group within the buying organization. The characteristics of this group, its structure, operation, and dynamics, remain largely unknown.

The Buying Center from a Systems Perspective

While researchers have conceptually examined the buying center from a small group or systems perspective (Anyon 1963, Bonoma and Johnston 1978, Bonoma et al. 1977, Choffray and Lilien 1978, Cyert and MacCrimmon 1968, Cyert and March 1963), and others have called for work in the area (Nicosia and Wind 1977), only a very limited amount of empirical work has actually been done.

Only a few studies that actually take a system or small group perspective could be found in the industrial buying behavior area (Choffray 1977, Corey 1978, Hillier 1975, Wind 1978b, Spekman 1978, Spekman and Stern 1979).

Table 1 summarizes the research on the buying center, illustrating which studies have examined the various characteristics of the phenomenon.

Using this foundation, and adding to it from the area of psychological and general management work in communications theory, Johnston (1979) identified a set of buying center dimensions that could be used to describe industrial purchases. These dimensions, their associated measurements, and the underlying theoretical notions are outlined below. To check on the validity of the notions, and to develop some data on how purchases of capital equipment differ from those of industrial services, extensive interviews with buying center members

Table 1   Research studies on the buying center

Study	Buying characteristic examined	Size—number of people involved	Responsibilities—tasks of various functions	Participation in various stages	Perceived influence of various functions and individuals	Frequency of involvement of different functions	Correlates of involvement	Vertical/lateral influence dimensions	Communication process	Group characteristics (systems perspective)
Cyert et al.	1956	X	X	X						
Strauss	1962		X	X	X			X	X	
Buckner	1967					X				
Weigand	1968		X		X					
Scientific American	1969					X				
Martilla	1971				X		X		X	X
Brand	1972			X	X					
McMillan	1973		X		X					
Kelly	1974		X	X						
Patchen	1974	X	X	X	X		X			
Gronhaug	1975	X					X			
Hillier	1975	X	X				X	X		X
Pettigrew	1975	X	X	X				X	X	
Calder	1976	X	X	X				X	X	X
Grashof and Thomas	1976	X	X		X					
Choffray	1977		X	X			X	X	X	X
Gronhaug	1977		X	X						
Corey	1978		X	X				X		
Spekman	1978	X	X	X				X		X
Silk and Kalwani	1979				X					
Fortin and Ritchie	1980		X	X	X			X		

were conducted in 62 purchases across 31 corporations. First the theory and method will be developed, and then the data will be presented.

STRUCTURAL AND INTERACTIVE DIMENSIONS OF THE BUYING CENTER

No two buying decisions in any given company are likely to be exactly alike, nor will any two companies follow exactly the same procedures in even highly similar purchase situations. However, there may be some general patterns of interaction and social behavior which will be the same, even across moderately dissimilar purchase situations.

Industrial buying behavior has been viewed as a system composed of many dyadic (two-person) in-

teractions within the context of a formal organization (Bonoma, Bagozzi, and Zaltman 1978; Bonoma, Zaltman, and Johnston 1977). By mapping the social interrelationships that take place during a purchase, as expressed by communications between various buying group dyads, the social dynamics of the buying center for that purchase should become clear. In this view, the buying center exists as a communication network that does not necessarily derive its configuration nor operation from the formal organization, but rather from the regularized patterns of communication that reflect the individuals involved and their relationships. We set out to develop some aspects of this communication structure to serve as measures of the social operations of a buying group.

From our theoretical perspective, the work on the buying center reviewed above, and especially the social psychological literature on communications and small groups (see Shaw 1976 for a good review), we hypothesized that five dimensions of the buying center be specified and measured. These dimensions are:

- *Vertical involvement* in the buying center's communications. This dimension is characterized by the number of levels of the organization's authority hierarchy exerting influence and communicating within the buying center. Six levels of authority were defined for the purpose of this study: ownership (board of directors), top management (CEO, president, executive vice president), policy level management (functional vice presidents, general managers), upper level operating management (e.g., directors, managers), lower level operating management (e.g., supervisors, product managers), and production work/clerical employees.
- *Lateral involvement* of different departments and divisions in the buying communications. This dimension can be operationalized as the number of separate departments, divisions, or firm functional areas involved in the purchase decision (see Strauss 1962 on the relevance of lateral involvement).
- *Extensivity,* or the total number of individuals involved in the buying communication network. Communication and information processing systems can be described in terms of the number of parts (e.g., people, departments) at work in a system. Schroder et al. (1966) referred to this property as "differentiation." We operationalized buying center extensivity as the total number of individuals involved in the buying process; this measure has been previously shown to correlate positively with decision quality by Schroder.
- *Connectedness* of those involved in the buying communication network. This concept and its associated measure indicates the degree to which the members of the buying center are linked with each other by directed communications concerning the purchase. The de-

gree of connectedness can be empirically expressed as a percentage of the total possible connectedness in a particular buying center. Only communications about the purchase under consideration were included in this percentage. Others were disregarded.

- *Centrality* of the purchasing manager in the buying communication network. The centrality of the purchasing manager was expressed as the sum of his/her purchase communications, both sent and received, weighted by the total number of individuals in the buying center. Previous studies in psychology found centrality correlated highly with perceived leadership, status, and influence (Shaw 1976).

These five communication concepts can be shown diagramatically. Figure 1 presents a conceptual picture of an organization buying center for a specific hypothetical purchase. The communication links between those persons both within the firm and external to it are shown. In addition, the five interactive dimensions we have proposed can be measured. Five levels of vertical hierarchy are involved (vertical involvement), 11 different divisions or departments are implicated in communications (lateral involvement), a total of 25 different people within the firm are involved (extensivity), the degree of connectedness is slightly less than 10%, with 56 communication links existing out of a possible 600, and the purchasing manager's centrality is 17%, with eight communication links versus 48 possible (centrality). This graphic summary of the buying center offers some interesting possibilities to purchasing management or sales management in addition to its research uses. These are discussed in the section on implications.

EXPECTED CORRELATES OF THE BUYING CENTER'S DIMENSIONS

In order to gain a view of how the communications model and measures would perform, we measured certain more traditional structural characteristics of firms and purchase situation attributes shown to have an influence on buying center participation in preview studies (e.g., Johnston 1979). Using these

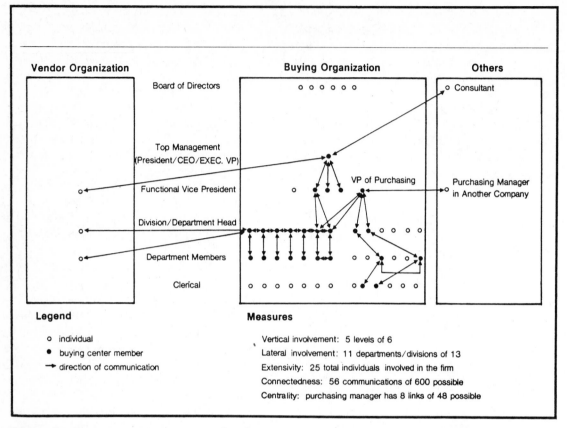

Figure 1 A communications picture of a buying center.

structural and situational variables, we could observe how the communications measures behaved under different firm conditions and buying situations.

STRUCTURAL VARIABLES OF THE FIRM

Research on organizational structure has concentrated on five aspects of the firm as often important in firm and buying center performance (Spekman 1978; Zaltman, Duncan, and Holbeck 1973):

- Centralization—the degree to which authority, responsibility, and power are concentrated within an organization or buying unit.
- Formalization—the extent to which activity in an organization or buying group is formally prescribed by rules, policies, and procedures.

- Complexity—the degree to which the organization is compartmentalized and pursues functional specialization.
- Size—organizational revenues, employees, or some other measure.
- Participation—the extent to which various organizational members are involved in decision making

Since the communication dimensions specified above measure several aspects of participation, this variable was not included as an independent measure. The other structural variables were employed.

Purchase Situation Attributes

In addition to the structural variables, we looked at purchase communications concerning two kinds of buying situations: capital equipment and services.

Table 2 Independent (predictor) variables and their operationalization

Organizational structure	Measure	Label
Size	Annual sales in dollars	SALES
Complexity	Number of divisions/subsidiaries	DIVSUB
Formalization	Percentage of the buying process communication that was written	WRITTEN
Centralization	Organization and operation of the purchasing function in the firm (Centralized/Decentralized/Combination)	ORGPRCH

Purchase situation attribute	Measure	Label
Importance	Average of entire buying center's perceived importance (1–10 scale)	IMPORT
Complexity	Time required to complete the buying process	TIME
Novelty	Buy grid categorization (New task, modified rebuy, straight rebuy)	NEWNESS
Purchase class	Type of purchase (capital equipment or industrial service)	PURCLS

We used such a gross buying situation categorization because it has been relatively difficult to identify primary purchase situation attributes that are independent of the organization that buys (see, e.g., Downs and Mohr 1972). In fact, research has demonstrated clearly (Gronhaug 1975, Robinson et al. 1967) that what is bought influences how it is bought. Therefore, in addition to collecting data on capital goods and service purchases, we collected data on managers' impressions of the purchase's importance, novelty, and complexity. Table 2 lists the independent variables measuring the buying organizations' structure and the purchase situations' attributes and their operationalization.

Research Propositions

Since buying center communications have not been measured before in the way we advocate, we did not attempt to advance a series of complex hypotheses for this study. However, a general examination of the available literature would suggest:

1. Higher purchase importance, complexity, and novelty ought to lead to more involved vertical and horizontal decision making communication nets that are more connected and extensive in their composition (Robinson et al. 1967).

2. Local variables, such as those having to do with the purchase situation, ought to have more influence on buying center communications than structural aspects of firms (Spekman 1978).

3. Product and service purchases should differ reliably on a number of the structural and interactive dimensions, but services should probably not present any radically different buying center dynamics from those of equipment purchases (Johnston and Bonoma 1981).

In order to assess these exploratory propositions, and more importantly, the communications perspective offered above, data were collected on 62 purchases.

METHOD

The sample consisted of interviews examining the purchase of capital equipment and industrial services in different organizations. Each organization from which data was collected was a for-profit firm in the private sector of the economy.

We initially identified one individual in each firm who was involved in some way in the communication network generated by a purchase situation. This individual was usually from the purchasing or materials management department. Semistructured interviews were conducted to identify all those individuals with whom the initial contact person communicated as well as the perceived content of these communications. The individual's role and tasks in the purchasing process were also recorded. Protocol analysis was used as part of the interview process.

After identifying and structuring the entire part this individual played in the purchasing process, the other individuals identified as having had contact with this initial person were interviewed to determine their part in the buying process. This interview technique has been referred to as snowball interviewing and for this type of multiperson research is superior to alternative methods, such as Bale's (1950) Interaction Process Analysis, which require visual observation of all group members throughout the entire problem-solving period (something seemingly impossible in the industrial buying process). Interviews with one individual involved in the purchasing process led to interviews with other individuals involved in the process, which led to the identification and subsequent interviews with still others. This expanding interview process eventually exhausted itself when all the individuals within a firm who had a part in the purchasing process were identified and interviewed.

Thus, membership in the buying center required participation in the communication network concerning the specific purchase being investigated. This definition of the buying center is more quantifiable than previous attempts because it readily adapts to digraph analysis developed in the communications and sociology disciplines. A limitation of this approach, however, exists in that it is plausible for individuals to have an effect on the purchase decision without having been involved in the communication network. An example might be the CEO who has instilled his/her values throughout the organization, with the effect that those involved in the purchase decision act based on their perceptions of what the CEO wants—without any participation by the CEO in the buying decision process. This type of influence, however, should be captured in the independent measures of formalization and centralization.

A total of 241 interviews were conducted. It was not always possible to interview everyone that had been involved in each purchase. It did prove possible to interview enough organizational members connected with each purchase decision to get a highly detailed description of how each decision evolved. A minimum of two individuals were interviewed in each purchase decision, a procedure suggested by Wind (1978a). In addition, the protocols of various organizational members showed a high degree of consistency, indicating some validity for the observations. In a few cases, an individual identified as having been involved could not recall his or her involvement. This was resolved in each case by carefully reconstructing the purchasing process and describing the role and communication that individual had been reported to have had. The individual in each case then remembered his/her involvement and was able to discuss his/her role and communication concerning the purchase.

One capital equipment and one industrial service purchase were investigated from each firm. In no way were the selections of the particular purchase items random, but rather, they were unsystematic in the sense that the primary contact person was asked to choose a recent equipment or service (or both, in the rare case the individual was involved in both) decision for our analysis. All of these purchases had been completed within the past six months and the majority within the past two months. Some purchases of capital equipment and services had been made within the past week. The time that it took to complete the entire buying process from first recognized need to the final purchase conclusion varied to a considerable extent. The shortest time to complete a capital equipment purchase was one week. The longest was two years. Service purchase time periods ranged from two weeks to over several years (a special situation). The mean time periods were 27 weeks for capital equipment and 20 weeks for services.

Table 3 Regression analysis of buying center dimensions

| | Organizational structural variables | | | | | Purchase situation attributes | | | | | | |
| | | Complexity formalization | | Centralization (ORGPRCH) | | Importance complexity | | Novelty (NEWNESS) | | Purchase class | | |
Buying center dimension	Size (SALES) beta weight (t)	(DIVSUB) beta weight (t)	(WRITTEN) beta weight (t)	(combi-nation) beta weight (t)	(central-ized) beta weight (t)	(IMPORT) beta weight (t)	(TIME) beta weight (t)	(straight rebuy) beta weight (t)	(modi-fied) beta weight (t)	(PURCLS) (service) beta weight (t)	R^2	F (10,49)
Extensivity	.17 (1.24)	−.05 (0.11)	.20 (3.22)[a]	−.07 (0.36)	−.14 (1.21)	.36 (8.69)[a]	.26 (4.77)[a]	−.18 (1.10)	−.08 (0.27)	−.16 (2.09)[b]	.41	5.14[a]
Lateral involvement	.09 (0.28)	−.03 (0.04)	.33 (7.99)[a]	−.14 (1.09)	−.19 (1.91)	.25 (3.55)[a]	.17 (1.68)	−.43 (4.99)[a]	−.29 (2.49)[b]	−.03 (0.05)	.31	3.62[a]
Vertical involvement	−.09 (0.31)	.25 (2.77)[a]	.05 (0.17)	.16 (1.57)	.18 (1.97)	.32 (6.43)[a]	.33 (7.29)[a]	.02 (0.02)	−.01 (0.00)	−.25 (4.47)[a]	.38	4.55[a]
Connect-edness	−.20 (1.22)	.18 (1.15)	−.44 (12.04)[a]	.13 (0.82)	.27 (3.41)[a]	−.11 (0.58)	−.15 (1.26)	.16 (0.58)	.21 (1.23)	.07 (0.31)	.22	2.70[b]
Purchasing manager's centrality	−.24 (1.35)	.23 (1.39)	.17 (1.45)	−.11 (0.41)	−.16 (0.92)	−.07 (0.24)	−.12 (0.63)	−.27 (1.37)	−.03 (0.03)	.01 (0.00)	−.04	.76

[a] $p \leq .01$
[b] $p \leq .05$.

RESULTS

Table 3 shows the results of regression analyses run with the buying center dimensions as criterion variables and the organizational structure measures and purchase situation attributes as predictor variables. Dummy variables were used for organizational centralization, purchase situation novelty, and purchase class (equipment or service). Three levels of organizational centralization were analyzed via the regression analyses. Dummy variables were used to indicate companies whose purchasing function was either totally or partially centralized. The null state represented companies with completely decentralized purchasing. Dummy variables were also used to analyze the effects of the purchase situation's novelty on buying center dimensions. The Robinson et al. (1967) typology of new task, modified rebuy, and straight rebuy was used to indicate the novelty of the purchase

situation. New task situations represented the null state with modified and straight rebuy situations receiving dummy variable weights. The purchase class (equipment or service) also received dummy variable regression treatment. Purchases of capital equipment represented the null state and service purchases received dummy weights. One company was dropped from the regression analysis because it would not release its annual sales data. Thus the regression is based on 60 purchase situations.

Of the five regression equations, four were statistically significant at the $p \leq .05$ level or better. The regression equation concerned with the centrality of the purchasing manager in the buying center communication network indicated that neither organizational structural variables nor purchase situation attributes had a significant effect on the purchasing managers' involvement. The purchasing managers' centrality did, however, vary to a great extent across the situations sampled. In purchases of both capital equipment and industrial services, the degree of centrality of the purchasing manager varied from zero (not even involved) to 100% (communicating to and receiving communications from all other individuals involved). Table 3 shows the most central person(s) in each of the 31 purchase situations.

Extensivity

The number of participants in the buying center communication network was significantly affected by both organizational structural variables and purchase situation attributes. The degree of organizational information had a positive effect on this dimension of the buying center. The more formalized the organization, the greater the extensivity of the buying center. The purchase class, importance, and complexity of the purchase situation also affected the buying center's extensivity. Services had less people involved in the buying center than did capital equipment purchases. The importance and complexity of a purchase both had a positive effect on the total number of individuals involved in the buying process. These two purchase situation attributes had the largest effect of all the independent variables examined in this study.

Lateral Involvement

The lateral involvement dimension of the buying center was also affected by organizational structural variables and purchase situation attributes. The formalization of the organization increased the lateral involvement of the buying center. The importance and novelty of the purchase situation also affected the lateral involvement of the buying center. The more important a purchase was perceived to be, the greater the number of departments and divisions involved in the buying process. The more novel a purchase situation, the greater the lateral involvement in the buying center. This was indicated by the negative beta weights for the dummy variables, indicating straight and modified rebuy situations. Both had lower involvement laterally than the new task situation, which was the base line in the regression.

Vertical Involvement

The vertical involvement dimension is most heavily influenced by purchase situation attributes. However, the complexity of the organization had a statistically significant positive effect on this aspect of the buying center as well. Purchase situation attributes that affect the vertical involvement in the buying center are the purchase class, importance, and complexity of the situation. The vertical involvement for service purchases was lower than for capital equipment. Both important and complex purchase situation increased the degree of vertical involvement in the buying center, as expected. The complexity of the situation had the greatest effect on vertical involvement.

Connectedness

Purchase situation attributes did not seem to affect the connectedness of the buying center communication network. The degree of organizational formalization had a very strong effect on the buying center's connectedness. The greater the amount of written communication concerning the purchase, the less the connectedness of the buying center. This relationship was further investigated by examining each purchase situation closely. It was discovered that in companies where the amount of written communication was a high percentage of the total communications, a purchase requisition procedure was used. This procedure usually resulted in a written communications flowing from one member to another with little verbal contact between members, thus reducing the amount of contact between all members. The amount of connectedness was also affected by the organization's centralization. The more centralized an organization, the greater the connectedness of the buying center.

Other Aspects

The size of the company did not affect any of the dimension of the buying center. Every other organizational structural variable or purchase situation attribute affected at least one dimension of the buying center. The two variables that, overall, most seemed to shape buying center were the degree of organizational formalization and the importance of the purchase situation. Each of these variables was significantly related to three of the five buying center dimensions.

With the new task, modified rebuy, straight rebuy purchase typology was found to affect the lateral involvement in the buying center, but not the extensivity. It appears that in new task situations higher levels of departmental and divisional representation occur, but this does not necessarily lead to greater numbers of people involved in the buying process.

There were some differences between the two purchase classes of capital equipment and industrial services. Services tended to have less extensive buying centers with lower vertical involvement as predicted.

The lack of any significant relationships between the purchasing manager's centrality and the other variables is discouraging. Understanding this aspect of the buying center could make an important contribution to industrial marketing.

CONCLUSIONS AND IMPLICATIONS

Finally, one of the most useful outcomes of this research, we believe, is contained in the sort of diagram outlined in Figure 1. This systems picture of a buying center seems to present sales managers, purchasing agents, and would-be purchase champions alike with numerous opportunities to increase their understanding of, and hence influence on, buying deliberations. This type of diagram can be constructed by sales or marketing managers for any specific purchase decision in a customer firm. By starting with the question of who first identified the need for the product or service, and then continuing to ask a series of questions, the entire buying decision communication network can be developed. Each dimension has implications for marketing and/or purchasing management.

It is important to stress that the work reported here must be thought of as exploratory, in the sense that the number of companies sampled is small, the measures rough, and the fledgling systems perspective element somewhat inelegant. However, the research does represent a first step toward modeling and measuring a dynamic system with relational variables. Future research, using this approach, could do well to consider how personal and organizational factors affect interaction patterns in the buying center. Do certain organizational designs result in different interaction patterns than others? Do certain kinds of personalities engage in different interaction patterns? These are issues for future examination.

REFERENCES

Anyon, G. J. (1963), *Managing an Integrated Purchasing Process,* New York: Holt, Rinehart, and Winston.

Bales, Robert F. (1950), *Interaction Process Analysis: A Method for the Study of Small Groups,* Cambridge, MA: Addison-Wesley Press.

Bonoma, T. V., R. Bagozzi, and G. Zaltman (1978), "The Dyadic Paradigm with Specific Application to Industrial Marketing," in *Organizational Buying Behavior,* T. Bonoma and G. Zaltman, eds., Chicago: American Marketing Association, 49–67.

———, and Wesley J. Johnston (1978), "The Social Psychology of Industrial Buying and Selling," *Industrial Marketing Management,* 7 (November), 62–84.

———, Gerald Zaltman, and Wesley J. Johnston (1977), *Industrial Buying Behavior,* Cambridge, MA: Marketing Science Institute.

Brand, G. T. (1972), *The Industrial Buying Decision,* New York: Wiley.

Buckner, H. (1967). *How British Industry Buys,* London: Hutchinson.

Calder, Bobby J. (1976) "Structural Role Analysis of Organizational Buying: A Preliminary Investigation," in *Consumer and Industrial Buying Behavior,* J. Sheth, A. Woodside, and P. Bennett, eds., New York: North-Holland, 193–200.

Choffray, J. M. (1977), "A Methodology for Investigating the Nature of the Industrial Adoption Process and the Differences in Perceptions and Evaluation Criteria Among Decision Participants," unpublished Ph.D. Dissertation.

———, and G. Lillien (1978), "Assessing Response to

Industrial Marketing Strategy," *Journal of Marketing,* 42 (April), 20–31.

Corey, E. R. (1978), *Procurement Management: Strategy, Organization, and Decision-Making,* Boston, MA: CBI, Inc.

Cyert, R. M., H. A. Simon, and D. B. Trow (1956), "Observation of a Business Decision," *Journal of Business,* 29 (October), 237–248.

———, and K. R. MacCrimmon (1968), "Organizations," in *The Handbook of Social Psychology,* 2nd ed., G. Lindsey and E. Aronson, eds., 2, 568–611.

———, and J. G. March (1963), *A Behavioral Theory of the Firm,* Englewood Cliffs, NJ: Prentice Hall.

Downs, George W., Jr. and Lawrence W. Mohr (1972), "Conceptual Issues in the Study of Innovation," *Administrative Science Quarterly,* 17 (June), 163–177.

Fortin, P. A. and J. R. B. Ritchie (1980), "Influence Structure in Organizational Buying Behavior," *Journal of Business Research,* 8 (March), 1–23.

Grashof, J. F. and G. P. Thomas (1976), "Industrial Buying Center Responsibilites: Self Versus Other Member Evaluations of Importance," *Proceedings,* Chicago: American Marketing Association, 344–349.

Gronhaug, K. (1975), "Autonomous vs. Joint Decisions in Organizational Buying," *Industrial Marketing Management,* 4 (October). 265–271.

——— (1977), "Exploring A Complex Organizational Buying Decision," *Industrial Marketing Management,* 6 (November), 439–44.

———, and T. V. Bonoma (1980), "Industrial-Organizational Buying: A Derived Demand Perspective," in *Theoretical Developments in Marketing,* C. Lamb and P. Dunne, eds., Chicago: American Marketing Association, 224–228.

Hillier, T. J. (1975), "Decision-Making in the Corporate Industrial Buying Process," *Industrial Marketing Management,* 4 (June), 99–106.

Johnston, Wesley, J. (1979), "Communication Networks and Influence Patterns in Industrial Buying Behavior," unpublished Ph. D. Dissertation, University of Pittsburgh.

———, and Thomas V. Bonoma (1981), "Purchases of Capital Equipment and Industrial Services: Buying Center Composition and Task Accomplishment," *Industrial Marketing Management,* in press.

Kelly, J. Patrick (1974), "Functions Performed in Industrial Purchasing Decisions with Implications for Marketing Strategy," *Journal of Business Research,* 2 (October), 420–434.

Martilla, John A. (1971), "Word-of-Mouth Communication in the Industrial Adoption Process," *Journal of Marketing Research,* 8 (May), 173–178.

McMillen, James R. (1973), "Role Differentiation in Industrial Buying Decisions," *AMA Proceedings,* Chicago: American Marketing Association, 207–211.

Nicosia, Francesco and Yoram Wind (1977), "Behavioral Models of Organization Buying Processes," in *Behavioral Models for Market Analysis: Foundations of Marketing Action,* F. Nicosia and Y. Wind, eds., Hinsdale, IL: Dryden Press, 96–120.

Patchen, Martin (1974), "The Locus and Basis of Influence in Organizational Decisions," *Organizational Behavior and Human Performance,* 11 (April), 195–211.

Pettigrew, Andrew M. (1975), "The Industrial Purchasing Decision as a Political Process," *European Journal of Marketing,* 9 (March), 4–19.

Robinson, P. J., C. W. Farris, and Y. Wind (1967), *Industrial Buying and Creative Marketing,* Boston, MA: Allyn and Bacon.

Schroder, H., M. Driver, and S. Streufert (1966), *Human Information Processing.* New York: Holt, Rinehart and Winston.

Scientific American (1969), *How Industry Buys 1970,* New York: *Scientific American.*

Shaw, Marvin E. (1976), *Group Dynamics: The Psychology of Small Group Behavior,* 2nd edition, New York: McGraw Hill.

Silk, Alvin J. and M. U. Kalwani (1979), "Measuring Influence in Organizational Purchase Decisions," working paper, Massachusetts Institute of Technology, 1077–79.

Spekman, Robert E. (1978). "A Macro-Sociological Examination of the Industrial Buying Center: Promise or Problems?," in *Research Frontiers in Marketing: Dialogues and Directions,* Subhash C. Jain, ed., Chicago: American Marketing Association, 111–115.

———, and Louis W. Stern (1979), "Environmental Uncertainty and Buying Group Structure: An Empirical Investigation," *Journal of Marketing,* 43 (Spring), 54–64.

Strauss, George (1962), "Tactics of Lateral Relationship: The Purchasing Agent," *Administrative Science Quarterly,* 7 (September), 161–186.

Weigand, Robert E. (1968), "Why Studying the Purchasing Agent is Not Enough," *Journal of Marketing,* 32 (January), 41–45.

Wind, Yoram (1978a), "Organizational Buying Center:

A Research Agenda," in *Organizational Buying Behavior*, G. Zaltman and T. V. Bonoma, eds., Chicago: American Marketing Association.

_____ (1978b), "The Boundaries of Buying Decision Centers," *Journal of Purchasing and Materials Management*, 14 (Summer), 23–29.

_____ (1978c), "Organizational Buying Behavior," in *Review of Marketing 1978*, G. Zaltman and T. Bonoma, eds., Chicago: American Marketing Association.

Zaltman, G., R. Duncan, and J. Holbek (1973), *Innovations and Organizations*, New York: John Wiley and Sons.

SUBLIMINAL ADVERTISING: WHAT YOU SEE IS WHAT YOU GET

TIMOTHY E. MOORE

Source: Timothy E. Moore, "Subliminal Advertising: What You See Is What You Get," *Journal of Marketing,* Vol. 46, Spring, 1982, pp. 38–47. Adapted from *Journal of Marketing,* published by the American Marketing Association.

In September 1957 some unwitting theatre audiences in New Jersey were invited to "drink Coca-Cola" and "eat popcorn" in briefly presented messages that were superimposed on the movie in progress. Exposure times were so short that viewers were unaware of any message. The marketing firm responsible reported a dramatic increase in Coke and popcorn sales, although they provided no documentation of these alleged effects. Public reaction was, nevertheless, immediate and widespread:

> ". . . the most alarming and outrageous discovery since Mr. Gatling invented his gun." (*Nation,* 1957 p. 206)

> ". . . take this invention and everything connected with it and attach it to the center of the next nuclear explosive scheduled for testing." (Cousins 1957, p. 20)

Opponents were indignant that unforgiveable psychological manipulations would be visited upon innocent and unknowing consumers. Minds had been "broken and entered" according to the *New Yorker* (1957, p. 33). There was much talk of *Brave New World* and *1984.* But even while laws were being drafted prohibiting the use of subliminal advertising on television, Hollywood was incorporating the idea into two new movies, and a Seattle radio station started broadcasting 'subaudible" messages such as "TV's a bore." The potential importance of the topic has not escaped those in marketing (Hawkins 1970, Kelly 1979, Saegert 1979); however, all lament the dearth of empirical research.

There are at least three identifiable means of subliminal stimulation for which strong behavioral effects have been claimed. The first of these involves very briefly presented visual stimuli. Presentation is usually by means of a tachistoscope, a device for carefully controlling the exposure duration of a visual stimulus. Directives or instructions are flashed so quickly that the viewer is unaware of their presence. Such stimulation purportedly registers subconsciously and allegedly affects subsequent behavior. This method of stimulus presentation has been used frequently by investigators interested in subliminal perception, although their purposes have usually been quite different. As a result, a body of research literature exists that bears on the claims being made for some kinds of subliminal advertising. Some examples from this literature will be described and some studies analyzed in detail. It should be emphasized that stimulation below the level of conscious awareness *can* be shown to have measurable effects upon some aspects of behavior. The point at issue is whether these effects are sufficient to warrant the conclusion that goal-directed behavior can be manipulated by such stimulation.

Another means by which behavior control is attempted is through the use of accelerated speech in low volume auditory messages. Here too, the claim is that while the message may be unintelligible and unnoticed at a conscious level, it is nevertheless processed subconsciously and imparts direction to the receiver's behavior.

The third procedure consists of embedding or hiding sexual imagery (or sometimes words) in pictorial advertisements. These are concealed in such a way that they are not available to conscious perusal. They have, however, a subconscious effect or so it is argued.

The effects attributed to these procedures may consist of either (1) general, nonspecific, affective consequences that are assumed to have some positive but unspecified persuasive influence, or (2) a highly specific, direct impact upon some particular motive or behavior. In what follows, the evidence and arguments put forth in defense of the effectiveness of these procedures will be reviewed and critiqued.

SUBLIMINAL PERCEPTION

Measurable responses of one kind or another can sometimes be shown to be contingent upon stimulation that the perceiver is unaware of.

The Threshold Concept

Today, the notion that people can respond to stimuli without being able to report on their existence is accepted and well documented (Bevan 1964a, 1964b; Dixon 1971; Erdelyi 1974). Taken literally, subliminal means "below threshold." However,

there exists no absolute cut-off point for stimulus intensity below which stimulation is imperceptible and above which it is always detected. When stimuli of varying intensities are presented over several trials, the minimum signal strength that is always detected is much higher than the one that is almost never detected. If some absolute threshold existed, then there ought to be a determinable stimulus intensity above which the receiver always responds and below which there is no response. Instead, a particular stimulus is sometimes detected and sometimes goes unnoticed. As a result, an individual's perceptual threshold is usually defined as that stimulus value that is correctly detected 50% of the time. The threshold, or limen, is, therefore, a statistical abstraction.

For a given individual, this threshold may vary from day to day or from minute to minute. Moreover, thresholds differ rather widely between individuals. Many studies of subliminal perception are flawed because the investigators assumed that some specific exposure duration or stimulus intensity automatically guaranteed that the stimulus would be sufficiently below threshold that its presence would be undetected for all the experimental subjects on all the trials. Often this assumption is unwarranted. Stimuli below the statistical limen (which itself fluctuates) may be noticed as much as 49% of the time. As a result, studies that make little or no effort to determine a threshold for individual subjects are at risk because stimuli are presented that are effectively *supra*liminal for some subjects on some trials. The results may thus be due to the effects of weak (but not subliminal) stimulation.

Obviously the notion of a perceptual limen is of limited usefulness. For present purposes we may use the term subliminal perception to refer to the following situations (Dixon 1971, p. 12):

(a) The subject responds to stimulation the energy or duration of which falls below that at which he *ever* reported awareness of the stimulus in some previous threshold determination

(b) He responds to a stimulus of which he pleads total unawareness.

(c) He reports that he is being stimulated but denies any awareness of what the stimulus was.

Some Illustrations of Subliminal Perception

There is ample evidence that weak stimuli that are not reportable *can* be demonstrated to influence behavior. Many studies have shown that taboo or emotionally loaded words have higher recognition thresholds than do neutral words. That is, it takes a longer exposure duration for *whore* to be identified than for *shore*. At first this may appear illogical. How can something taboo be defended against unless it is first recognized as being taboo? The paradox is resolved if it is assumed that "perception" is by no means a discrete experiential event that is automatically determined by some particular stimulus pattern. Rather, perception is treated as a multiprocess chain of events that begins with stimulus input and terminates (subjectively) with conscious recognition of an object or event. However, not all input is subjected to the same sequence of mental processing. Stimuli are selectively filtered, transformed and attended to according to a variety of factors that are independent of the particular input. These include memory, expectations, attention, affect and other variables. Perception then, as we conventionally use the term, represents ". . . the conscious terminus of a sequence of nonconscious prior processes" (Erdelyi 1974). Conscious recognition need not be and often is not the end point for many sorts of input. Some stimuli may initiate mental activity of one sort or another without being available to conscious reflection or report. This is what is typically meant by the term subliminal perception. In the case of taboo items, some kind of defensive selectivity operates to bias the processing of emotionally charged input—such selectivity having its impact *prior* to a conscious recognition of the input.

Recently Zajonc (1980) has reviewed evidence from several studies showing that under some circumstances, unattended stimuli can be processed to a degree that is sufficient to elicit a subsequent affective reaction (i.e., like/dislike) *without* their being recognized as having been previously encountered. "Affective reactions can occur without extensive perceptual cognitive encoding. Reliable affective discriminations (like/dislike ratings) can be made in the total absence of recognition memo-

ry (old-new judgments)" (Zajonc 1980, p. 151). While unattended stimuli are not necessarily subliminal, one study purports to show that affect can be influenced by stimuli that *are* truly subliminal (Kunst-Wilson and Zajonc 1980). That some behavioral processes may be influenced by stimuli whose presence is not consciously noticeable by the receiver is not at issue here. The preceding examples testify to the validity of subliminal perception as a phenomenon. The important question is critical because what must be posited in order to support such a proposition is not merely *an effect*, but specific, (relatively) powerful and enduring effects on the buying preferences of the public.

SUBLIMINAL ADVERTISING

Could subliminally presented stimuli have a marketing application? Can advertising effectiveness be enhanced through subliminal stimulation? Before reviewing the few laboratory studies that have addressed this question directly, it will be useful to consider what sorts of subliminal influences would be necessary in order to obtain some marketing relevance. At a minimum, we might hypothesize that a subliminal stimulus produces (or increases) some positive affective reaction to that stimulus. Whether or not such an affective response, if obtained, could have any relevant motivating influence is another question. It is probably safe to assume that positive affect would not do any harm and could conceivably influence a product's attractiveness. A much stronger prediction for subliminal effects would be one that hypothesizes some direct behavioral consequence (i.e., purchasing). Since the former prediction does not *necessarily* entail any interesting marketing implications, and the latter prediction clearly does, these hypotheses will be referred to as weak and strong claims respectively.

Practical Difficulties

Regardless of which claim is under investigation, there are some profound if not insurmountable operational constraints associated with presenting subliminal stimuli in a typical marketing context. One problem has to do with individual differences in threshold. There is no particular stimulus intensity or duration that can guarantee subliminality for all viewers. In order to preclude detection by those with relatively low thresholds, the stimulus would have to be so weak that it would not reach viewers with higher thresholds at all. Lack of control over position and distance from the screen would further complicate matters. Finally, without elaborate precautions, supraliminal material (i.e., the film or commercial in progress) would almost certainly wash out any potential effects of a subliminal stimulus. In order to duplicate the results of laboratory studies that have shown subliminal effects, it is crucial to duplicate the conditions under which the effects were obtained. From a practical standpoint, this is virtually impossible.

Does the relevant research indicate that some positive affect could become associated with a particular product through the use of subliminally presented stimuli? The evidence is not strong. The Kunst-Wilson and Zajonc (1980) study referred to earlier used irregular, randomly constructed octagons as stimuli. The stimuli themselves were first presented at one-milisecond durations and filtered so that recognition was at chance level. Subjects were instructed to pay close attention to the screen, even if nothing was distinguishable. The same stimuli were subsequently presented for one-second intervals, paired with new stimuli. Subjects' recognition of old versus new stimuli was reported to be at chance; however, the old stimuli were judged to be preferable to the new ones 60% of the time. The effect was subtle but statistically reliable ($p < .01$, 2-tail). Two points about the Kunst-Wilson and Zajonc study are worth emphasizing.

First, the stimuli themselves, consisting of (relatively) meaningless geometric shapes, were subjected to subliminal exposure levels; this exposure seems to have had a subsequent effect upon preference. Second, the experimental subjects were actively attending to the stimuli throughout the subliminal viewing condition; during this time, no other stimulation was present that could distract attention or mask the subliminal stimuli.

Could this procedure be utilized in an advertising context? It is possible that a display's attractiveness could be subliminally enhanced by having that same display exposed for subliminal durations pri-

or to its supraliminal presentation. Whether the magnitude of the resultant effect could have any practical importance is not known. Moreover, it is not obvious how the subliminal exposure could be accomplished. Superimposing the subliminal display on top of supraliminal material is not a good bet:

". . . Ongoing supraliminal stimulation to which attention may be directed almost certainly will swamp any effect by a simultaneous stimulus below the awareness threshold . . . at a peripheral level, lateral inhibition and contour suppressing mechanisms could well block any neural transmission from the weaker of two stimulus arrays . . . a similar effect of restricted channel capacity would almost certainly operate centrally as well. The potential effects of one stimulus may be completely negated by the presence of another" (Dixon 1971, p. 175–76).

Splicing or somehow integrating the subliminal stimulus into ongoing supraliminal material (even if technologically possible) is not too promising either, because unless a sufficient blank interval is included before and after the insert, supraliminal material will mask the subliminal stimulus (Kahneman 1968). If such intervals are provided, the viewer will most probably be aware of an interruption, even though the stimulus itself may not be detectable. At least 100 milliseconds of "clean" background on either side of the target stimulus would be necessary to preclude a masking effect. As a result, subjects could infer the presence of a stimulus. If complete unobtrusiveness is a priority, the stimulus and surrounding interval would have to be carefully located at naturally occurring breaks or cut points. Even then, completely disguising the fact of stimulation may not be possible.

Evidence Involving the Weak Claim

In addition to Kunst-Wilson and Zajonc (1980), two other studies report subliminal effects relevant to the weak claim. Byrne (1959) flashed the word "beef" for successive five millisecond intervals during a sixteen-minute movie. Experimental and control subjects did not differ in their verbal references to beef, as measured by word association tests. Nor did experimental subjects report a higher preference for beef sandwiches, when given a list of five alternatives. Experimental subjects did, however, rate themselves as hungrier than control subjects. This difference held up when ratings were co-varied with hours of food deprivation. Byrne offered no explanation for this finding. It is not obvious why the word "beef" should induce hunger particularly when it failed to influence semantic associates. Moreover, the method of presentation involved superimposing the stimulus on the movie. For reasons outlined earlier, such a procedure is likely to interfere with rather than enhance any potential subliminal affects.

In a similar study, Hawkins (1970) flashed the word "coke" for 2.7 millisecond-intervals during the presentation of other supraliminal material. Subjective thirst ratings were higher for the "coke" group than for a control group that received a subliminal nonsense syllable. Hawkins concludes that "a simple subliminal stimulus can serve to arouse a basic drive such as thirst." (p. 324). As Saegert (1979) has pointed out, "Hawkin's results may simply be a Type I error, especially in view of the fact that other tries have been made" (p. 55). The fact that Hawkins performed five independent 1-tail statistical tests where one analysis would have sufficed lends support to Saegert's position. There are methodological short-comings in both of these studies. Even if the results are taken at face value, their relevance to advertising is minimal.

Evidence Involving the Strong Claim

The strong claim for subliminal advertising posits specific behavioral consequences as a result of a subliminal directive. A study by Zuckerman (1960) requiring student nurses to write stories describing the contents of a series of pictures that were projected onto a screen in front of them is pertinent to this issue. Unknown to the subjects, the instructions "write more" and "don't write" were tachistoscopically superimposed on the pictures at successive points during the presentations. A control group was treated in a similar fashion but received blank slides in place of those containing the subliminal directives.

The study was composed of three successive conditions: (1) baseline, during which no sublimi-

nal messages were presented, (2) "write more," during which subjects in the experimental group received a "write more" instruction for .02 seconds, concurrently with the picture they were asked to describe, and (3) "don't write," during which the experimental subjects received a "don't write" directive, again superimposed for .02 seconds on the picture being projected. During each condition, pictures were presented for 10 trials each. After each trial, subjects wrote a description of what they had seen. Zuckerman found that nurses in the experimental group wrote more during condition 2 ("write more") than they had during baseline. Furthermore, he noted a slight drop in output between condition 3 ("don't write") and condition 2, and interpreted this as evidence that the subliminal instructions were effective.

Unfortunately, there is a strong possibility that these results were due to a methodological artifact which psychologists call a "ceiling effect." This occurs when performance reaches an asymptote and cannot be further improved upon. The slight drop that Zuckerman observed may not have been a real decrease in performance but rather, a leveling off. This interpretation is supported by a comparison of the performances of experimental and control subjects. For some reason the students in the experimental group were enthusiastic writers. They wrote much more during baseline than did the controls. They wrote still more during condition 2 ("write more"), and the controls increased their output as well. By condition 3 the experimental subjects may have reached asymptote. They were all "written out," and a slight drop was observed in the number of words written.

Because of time constraints (and possibly writer's cramp), experimental subjects may already have been writing as much as could reasonably be expected by the end of condition 2. The slight drop during condition 3 may be due to statistical artifact. When variability is possible in only one direction (in this case down), a slight decrease in performance is predictable. Controls were still increasing their output during condition 3 and by the end, their output had barely surpassed that of the experimental subjects' performance during baseline. When differences between groups are large prior to any experimental manipulation, it is risky to attribute some subsequently observed differences to that manipulation. In this study, the preexisting difference between experimental and control subjects was as great or greater than any other subsequently observed difference between or within groups. Zuckerman has little to say by way of explaining the finding, but submits that "the subject's operant behavior is supposedly brought under control by suggestive cues of which he is not aware" (p. 404). This is not an explanation but rather a description of the outcome couched in operant terminology.

Dixon (1971), commenting on Zuckerman's results, speculates that "it may be impossible to resist instructions which are not consciously experienced" (p. 177). Again, this is more an assertion than an explanation, but it does reflect an apparently prevalent (although not articulated) notion that instructions, directives and/or slogans are intrinsically compelling. When the instruction is delivered supraliminally the receiver can counter-argue or derogate the source, thereby diminishing the stimulus' influence. However, if the instruction is presented subliminally, the recipient is unaware of its presence and is consequently unable to counter-argue.

Perhaps the single most important lesson to be learned from cognitive psychology in the last decade is that the meaning of a stimulus does not reside in the stimulus itself. Meaning is constructed by the receiver in active, complex and often specialized ways. With respect to advertising the selectivity of attention and the active control over subsequent processing of the input means that stimulation is not a sufficient condition for any response at all, let alone some particular response. We are constantly subjected to a barrage of external and internal stimuli, of which only a fraction acquire phenomenal representation. Some neural activity is no doubt provoked by stimuli that are not consciously processed. But to attribute to a subliminal stimulus a strong influence, which it cannot be shown to have when supraliminal, is not justified by any theoretical rationale. For this reason it is appropriate to insist on especially clear well-replicated empirical evidence before accepting such a proposition. To the author's knowledge, Zuckerman's (1960) finding has *not* been replicated, and the study itself is vulnerable to an important methodological criticism.

SUMMARY

On the basis of what little data are available, one could tentatively conclude that subliminal presentation of a stimulus may produce a positive affective response to that stimulus (Kunst-Wilson and Zajonc 1980). This positive affective response was obtained with subjects who were attending only to the subliminal stimuli. Whether this finding could be utilized successfully in a marketing context remains to be seen. Apart from the question of the magnitude of the effect, not to mention its validity (Birnbaum 1981, Mellers 1981), there are some practical difficulties associated with achieving a real-world application.

The evidence that subliminal directives can exert any control over behavior is much less compelling (Zuckerman 1960), although there has been ample opportunity for replication. Moreover, this strong claim for subliminal influence is not accompanied by a coherent explanatory rationale. Previous reviews of the strong claim have reached similar conclusions.

Empirical documentation has remained elusive: "all things considered . . . secret attempts to manipulate people's minds have yielded results as subliminal as the stimuli used" (McConnell 1977, p. 231).

REFERENCES

Bevan, W. (1964a), "Subliminal Stimulation: A Pervasive Problem for Psychology," *Psychological Bulletin*, 61 (no. 2), 89–99.

———— (1964b), "Contemporary Problems in Adaptation Level Theory," *Psychological Bulletin*, 61 (no. 3), 161–187.

Birnbaum, M. (1981), "Thinking and Feeling: A Skeptical Review," *American Psychologist,* 36 (no. 1), 99–101.

Broadbent, D. E. (1958), *Perception and Communication,* New York: Pergamon.

———— (1973), *In Defence of Empirical Psychology,* London: Camelot Press.

Byrne, D. (1959), "The Effect of a Subliminal Food Stimulus on Verbal Responses," *Journal of Applied Psychology,* 43 (no. 4), 249–251.

Carr, T. and V. Bacharach (1976), "Perceptual Tuning and Conscious Attention," *Cognition,* 4 (no. 3), 281–302.

Comstock, G., S. Chaffer, N. Katzman, M. McCombe and D. Roberts (1978), *Television and Human Behavior,* New York: Columbia University Press.

Cousins, N. (1957), "Smudging the Subconscious," *Saturday Review,* 40 (October 5).

Dixon, N. F. (1971), *Subliminal Perception: The Nature of a Controversy,* London:McGraw Hill.

———— (1981), *Preconscious Processing.* London: Wiley.

Erdelyi, M. H. (1974), "A New Look at the New Look: Perceptual Defense and Vigilance," *Psychological Review,* 81 (no. 1), 1–25.

Eriksen, C. W. and H. J. Johnson (1964), "Storage and Decay Characteristics of Nonattended Auditory Stimuli," *Journal of Experimental Psychology,* 68 (no. 1), 28–36.

Foulke, E. and I. G. Sticht (1969), "Review of Research on the Intelligibility and Comprehension of Accelerated Speech," *Psychological Bulletin,* 72 (no. 1), 50–62.

Hawkins, D. (1970), "The Effects of Subliminal Stimulation on Drive Level and Brand Preference," *Journal of Marketing Research,* 8 (August), 322–26.

Hochberg, J. (1978), *Perception,* 2nd ed., Englewood Cliffs, NJ: Prentice-Hall.

Kahneman, D. (1968), "Method, Findings and Theory in Studies of Visual Masking," *Psychological Bulletin,* 70 (no. 6), 404–425.

———— (1973), *Attention and Effort,* Englewood Cliffs, NJ: Prentice-Hall.

Kelly, J. S. (1979), "Subliminal Embeds in Print Advertsiting: A Challenge to Advertising Ethics," *Journal of Advertising,* 8 (no. 3), 20–24.

Key, W. B. (1973), *Subliminal Seduction,* Englewood Cliffs, NJ: Signet.

———— (1976), *Media Sexploitation,* Englewood Cliffs, NJ: Prentice-Hall.

———— (1980), *The Clamplate Orgy,* Englewood Cilffs, NJ: Prentice-Hall.

Kunst-Wilson, W. and R. Zajonc (1980), "Affective Discrimination of Stimuli That Cannot Be Recognized," *Science,* 207 (no. 1), 557–558.

Liberman, A. M., F. S. Cooper, D. P. Shankweiler and M. Studdert-Kennedy (1967), "Perception of the Speech Code," *Psychological Review,* 74 (no. 6), 431–461.

Licklider, J. and G. Miller (1951), "The Perception of Speech," in S. Stevens, ed., *Handbook of Experimental Psychology,* New York: Wiley.

McCauley, C., C. Parmelee, R. Sperber and T. Carr (1980), "Early Extraction of Meaning From Pictures and Its Relation to Conscious Identification," *Journal of Experimental Psychology: Human Perception and Performance,* 6 (no. 2), 265–76.

McConnell, J. V. (1977), *Understanding Human Behavior,* 2nd ed., New York: Holt, Rinehart & Winston.

Mellers, B. (1981), "Feeling More Than Thinking," *American Psychologist,* 36 (no. 7), 802–803.

Moray, N. (1969), *Attention: Selective Processes in Vision and Hearing,* London: Hutchinson Ltd.

Nation (1957), "Diddling the Subconscious: Subliminal Advertising," 185 (October 5), 206.

New Yorker (1957), 33 (September 21), 33.

Peterson, L. R. and S. Kroener (1964), "Dichotic Stimulation and Retention," *Journal of Experimental Psychology,* 68 (no. 2), 125–130.

Poe, A. (1976), "Active Women in Ads," *Journal of Communication,* 26 (no. 4), 185–92.

Rush, F. (1980), "Child Pornography," in *Take Back the Night: Women on Pornography.* L. Lederer, ed., New York. Morrow.

Saegert, J. (1979), "Another Look at Subliminal Perception," *Journal of Advertising Research,* 19 (no. 1), 55–57.

Schulman, M. (1981), "The Great Conspiracy," *Journal of Communications,* 31 (no. 2), 209.

Shevrin, H. and S. Dickman (1980), "The Psychological Unconscious: A Necessary Assumption for All Psychological Theory?" *American Psychologist,* 35, 421–34.

Time (1979), 114 (September 10), 63.

Toronto Star (1978) (October 23), c1.

Treisman, A. M. and G. Geffen (1967), "Selective Attention: Perception or Response?" *Quarterly Journal of Experimental Psychology,* 19 (no. 1), 1–17.

Walstedt, J. J., F. Geis and V. Brown (1980), "Influence of Television Commercials on Women's Self-Confidence and Independent Judgment," *Journal of Personality and Social Psychology,* 38 (no. 2), 203–210.

Washington Post (1979) (May 27), c4.

Zajonc, R. B. (1980), "Feeling and Thinking: Preferences Need No Inferences," *American Psychologist*, 35 (no. 2), 151–175.

Zuckerman, M. (1960), "The Effects of Subliminal and Supraliminal Suggestions on Verbal Productivity," *Journal of Abnormal and Social Personality*, 60 (no. 3), 404–11.

SECTION VI

LEARNING AND INFORMATION PROCESSING

Each section of this reader discusses a particular influence on consumer behavior. Yet unless some kind of information about a particular product or service reaches and is processed by the consumer, none of these influences can have an effect. Information processing is the sequence of mental activities that a person goes through in becoming aware of and either remembering or forgetting some information. The information that is processed may or may not correspond to the message that was intended. Thus, information processing is the end result of the communication process.

The information that is processed in a consumer setting can be of several types. Marketers provide some information through advertisements. Additional information can be found in a store on product labels. Some information may be obtained from friends or acquaintances who have tried the product. Other information is available in government pamphlets and consumer magazines. These latter sources may even encourage consumers to actively seek and compare information available from any of the above sources. Finally, legislation may be enacted that requires that certain information be available.

Yet all of this information must be processed in some way by consumers for it to affect the choices they make. Before we can suggest that providing additional information will improve consumers' satisfaction with the choices they make, we must understand how and when information processing and learning occur. The four articles in this section provide a base for this understanding.

"BEHAVIORAL EVIDENCE OF THE EFFECTS OF TELEVISED FOOD MESSAGES ON CHILDREN"

A controversial area that is currently being debated is the issue of the effect television has on children. The Gorn and Goldberg paper presents some new evidence that television advertising can and does influence a child's behavior toward a product.

It should be noted that this study is in the form of an experiment. The variable manipulated (independent variable) was the type of commercial shown to the children. The variable observed (dependent variable) was the child's choice of beverage and snack food. There was control for extraneous factors by the experimental design so that the effect was produced by the experimental stimulus, not other factors. The factors controlled for were the children's eating habits and their television viewing.

Gorn and Goldberg measured the behavioral aspects of children. Another approach used could have been a survey asking children of their awareness, beliefs, and attitudes concerning advertising of snack foods. How would these results have differed from those obtained?

This article does not concern itself with the actual information processing of the children. How did they process the information from the ads and arrive at their decisions? How important is it to know the actual processes?

Further research could be done extending this study to other age groups. Robertson and Rossiter (see Section 10) found that younger children (first graders) did not attribute persuasive intent to advertising and were thus more persuasible by trusting and liking ads and wanting all products they see advertised. The children in the Gorn and Goldberg study were at this "persuasible" stage.

While reading this article, consider the following questions:

- What recommendations would you make to a candy manufacturer with regard to future television advertising?
- What recommendations would you make to a legislative group establishing guidelines for advertising on Saturday morning children's programming if their goal is to ensure children are not unduly persuaded into wanting products?
- What suggestions would you make to the producer of a public service announcement to ensure that the educational messages of the program reach the children and are remembered and used by them?

"DEVELOPMENTAL RECOGNITION OF CONSUMPTION SYMBOLISM"

People can communicate information about themselves through their consumption choices. The Belk, Bahn, and Mayer article attempts to determine the *degree* of consumption symbolism used by various age groups of children while making inferences about others based upon observations of others' consumption behavior. This article does not address, however, the question of *how* children acquire attitudes about the social significance of goods.

A child's consumer learning is believed to be a dual process that is based on two models: a cognitive development model and a social learning model. According to Piaget, a cognitive development theorist, a child proceeds through four developmental stages in which qualitatively different cognitive structures are developed that enable the child to perceive and cope with the environment (see Section 10, Article 29). A second approach known as the social learning approach emphasizes sources of influence called "socialization agents" that transmit norms, attitudes, motivation, and behaviors to the learner. Socialization takes place during a child's interaction with these agents. The socialization agents investigated in this study are media, family, school, and peers. One must also ask, however, what other sources of information should be considered as influential to the development of expressive consumption.

An important contribution to Belk, Bahn, and Mayer paper makes is its recognition of two important concepts: nonverbal communication through consumption and the self-concept.

Nonverbal communications are expressive behaviors that are unintentional. We assume the person did not intend or choose the behaviors consciously in an attempt to manipulate us.

It is hypothesized that people have a self-concept or image of themselves. People use various processes to verify or confirm this self-concept. This self-verification can be supported and reinforced by various clues given by the person. The choice of products can be a clue of the self-concept given by a consumer to maintain it. The person tries to be consistent in his/her behavior to maintain the self-image.

Notice that this study only considers the symbol of status in its investigation of consumption symbolism. As stated in this paper, while conspicuous consumption and status messages are part of this study, other consumption messages may be encoded for any purchase selection that has social value. The reader may wish to consider which other judgments could be studied.

Though the design of this experiment is simple, it leads us to many interesting implications. Not only do children go through processes of change in their inferences about others based on their product choices, but adults also go through the process of continuous change. What does this mean to a producer of a current fad item? How do current trends influence the consumer in his/her inferences? Which categories of products and services are more inclined to be recognized for their symbolic value? How should these be marketed to the public?

This study considers only a few dimensions (size, style, age, cost) of two products (automobiles and houses). How could this study be expanded to include more relevant properties of other products?

Finally, Belk, Bahn, and Mayer conclude that developmental trends are the major reason for the different levels of consumption stereotyping. What are some alternative explanations for the developmental differences in the degrees of the consumption stereotyping?

"THE INFLUENCE OF COGNITIVE PERSONALITY TRAITS AND DEMOGRAPHICS ON CONSUMER INFORMATION ACQUISITION"

The Schaninger and Sciglimpaglia article addresses the influence that personality and demographics have on the amount of information a consumer will seek. This study employs the use of the information display-board. Because consumers are not accurate in reporting their search for information related to making a decision and because it is impractical to follow consumers and observe their information gathering techniques, survey methods and observation methods are not always efficient or effective. Thus, consumer behavior researchers often rely on the information display-board technique. This technique studies external search behavior in a laboratory setting. Consumers are presented with a matrix of product information. Brands are displayed across the top of the matrix; dimensions are displayed down the sides. Each cell in the matrix contains cards that hold information about the brand on that dimension. Respondents are asked to act as if they were shopping for one brand. They can seek as much information as they feel they need, in any order they see fit. The researcher records the information selected and the order in which it was selected.

One drawback of the use of the information display-board is that it does not consider the information already stored in memory prior to the experiment. There are two types of searches for information—internal search and external search. Internal search is the searching of a person's own memory for information related to the product. External search is the deliberate search for information from sources other than memory. The Schaninger and Sciglimpaglia article is only concerned with external search.

The artificiality created by the laboratory setting of the information display-board denies the reality of the costs associated with external search. If consumers in attempting to make a product decision actively seek additional information about the various products and attributes, they will be expending time, effort, and money to gather this information. However, the information display-board technique is not concerned with this cost attributed to the information. Remember, however, that there are also benefits derived from an information search, namely, a better choice and personal satisfaction.

In reading this paper, the reader should consider how a marketer would segment the market given that the findings from this study are true. Also, how would product information be presented to the target market in the best possible way?

"THE EXPERIENTIAL ASPECTS OF CONSUMPTION: CONSUMER FANTASIES, FEELINGS, AND FUN"

It was once believed that the consumer was a logical thinker: rational, capable, and inclined toward problem solving. This consumer was reduced to a simple model of information processing. Holbrook and Hirschman take this model one step further by including the dynamic aspects of a consumer's behavior. The experiential model that is added to the information-processing model gives the consumer "humanness" by putting emotions, feelings, and experience back into consumer behavior.

A few definitions will be helpful in understanding the experiential model:

Affect - a person's feelings or emotional state.

Cognition - any knowledge, opinion, or belief.

Esthetic - having to do with beauty, as opposed to usefulness.

Experiential - based on or coming from experience.

Hedonic - characterized by or related to pleasure.

Phenomenological - something that the mind or the senses directly take note of.

Semantic - having to do with meaning.

Symbolism - attaching meaning to products that goes beyond the fundamental aspects of the product.

Syntactic - having to do with structure.

Variety seeking - the changing of brands, product classes, or activities or the searching for information about these brands, products, or activities in the pursuit of variety for variety's sake in order to fulfill a need to be different.

While reading this article, it would be interesting to compare its ideas with those of Belk, Bahn, and Mayer in regard to a child's development of the experiential aspects of consumption.

The supplementing of the information-processing model with the experiential view appears to combine the best of both worlds. Under what circumstances might a consumer focus on the conventional model and when might a consumer focus on the experiential model? Are some products more inclined to be experiential? Try to relate frequently purchased grocery store items to this idea of the pursuit of fantasies, feelings, and fun.

Finally, one can ask if consumers ever make "rational decisions." What is the definition of a rational choice?

BEHAVIORAL EVIDENCE OF THE EFFECTS OF TELEVISED FOOD MESSAGES ON CHILDREN

GERALD J. GORN
AND
MARVIN E. GOLDBERG

Source: Gerald J. Gorn and Marvin E. Goldberg, "Behavioral Evidence of the Effects of Televised Food Messages on Children," *Journal of Consumer Research*, Vol. 9, September, 1982, 200–205. Reprinted with permission.

The effects of television advertising on children have been the subject of considerable research for well over a decade. The substantial body of literature that has accumulated is effectively summarized in a number of recent reviews (Adler et al. 1980; Atkin 1980; Goldberg and Gorn forthcoming). Given that the preponderance of children's television advertising is for snack and breakfast foods (other than at Christmas time), particular attention has been paid to the effects of televised food advertising on children. In a recent review of nine experimental studies of the impact of televised food messages on children's nutritional attitudes, beliefs, and behaviors, Scammon and Christopher (1981, p. 35) concluded that:

> exposure to commercials for sugared products leads to greater consumption of sugared products, greater preference for sugared foods—even unadvertised sugared foods, and lower nutrition knowledge. Exposure to commercials for healthy foods (or non-sugared foods) did not always lead to increased consumption of healthy foods, but did appear to dampen any increased consumption of sugared food.

Not all judgments have been equally unequivocal:

> In general, because the currently existing research appears to be in a state of controversy, it would be very useful if more empirical research on the relationship between children's exposure to advertising for sugared products and children's nutritional attitudes, food preferences and consumption patterns could be done (Federal Trade Commission, 1981, p. 55).

The present study represents an effort to assess the causal link between exposure to varying types of televised food messages and the nature of children's actual food selection and consumption. Two recent experiments focusing on this question have yielded equivocal results.

Fox et al. (1980) tested 47 four- and five-year-olds who watched a 12-minute television program with three 30-second commercials (inserted twice) for (1) low nutrition foods, (2) high nutrition foods, or (3) toys (control). One week prior to and immediately after the treatment, subjects were asked to taste food from a tray of 12 foods, eat as much of the foods as they wished, and state their preferences for the foods. No significant between-group differences were found with regard to the amount of food consumed, although a pre-post difference was noted within the low nutrition group, where subjects increased their consumption of sugared food.

Galst (1979) structured an experiment using 65 three- to six-year-olds, where two independent variables were of critical concern: the nature of exposure to televised messages for foods (highly sugared or healthy), and the presence or absence of adult comments related to the wisdom of eating healthy as opposed to highly sugared foods. For four weeks, children in each of the four treatment conditions viewed two brief cartoons with 4.5 minutes of commercials daily. Each day, following the television exposure, the children made snack selections from a table displaying a large variety of sugared and nonsugared foods. The results of this food selection test revealed an interaction but no main effects. Subjects who saw commercials for nonsugared foods and public service announcements (PSAs) *followed* by adult comments chose significantly fewer sugared snacks.

METHOD

Both the single-exposure setting of the Fox et al. (1980) study and the lack of control over extraexperimental factors (children's at-home eating and television viewing) in the Galst (1979) study seem likely to contribute to the relatively weak results of these two studies. The present study attempted to increase the power and sensitivity of similar experimental treatments by (1) structuring a high degree of control over each child's extraexperimental eating and television viewing behavior by using a children's summer camp setting, and (2) employing a longitudinal design in which children were exposed to 14 consecutive days of television messages and in which measurement focused on the last seven days of the study to allow for a building of the treatment effect.

The camp in question was a low-income camp in the province of Quebec, about an hour's drive from Montreal. The children came to the camp for two-week sessions. Officials at the camp agreed to have the children view a half-hour videotaped cartoon program each afternoon during their "quiet hour." This immediately preceded their snack period, which was the setting for the main dependent measures.

A critical element in the study design was the camp's agreement to offer no fruit or candy to the children other than that offered experimentally as part of the afternoon snack. In fact, because the camp could not afford it, they typically served no fresh fruit. . . . Furthermore, no television was available to the children other than the half-hour per day that was the critical part of the experimental treatment.

· · ·

In the spring, children enrolling in the camp were randomly assigned to different two-week sessions. The camp was structured into 12 cabins of six "juniors" (five- to six-year-olds) and 12 cabins of six "seniors" (seven- to eight-year-olds). In each 14-day session, two experimental treatments were administered. Six cabins at each of the two age levels were randomly assigned to one treatment or another. Thus 72 children were assigned to each of two treatments during each of the two sessions (total $n = 288$).

The television programs were typical half-hour cartoons taped off-air from Saturday morning television. The children viewed a different 30-minute show on each of the 14 days. The experimental conditions were defined as a function of the nature of the 30-second messages introduced during the program. There were 4.5 minutes of these messages during each half-hour program. Four conditions were created.

1. *Candy commercials:* typical Saturday morning 30-second commercials for sweets (candy bars such as Hersheys, Mounds, Almond Joy, Kit Kat, Three Musketeers, and other highly sugared foods, including Kool Aid, M & M's, Lifesavers, Crackerjacks, and so on).

2. *No commercial messages:* control programs only; no messages at all.

3. *Fruit commercials:* 30-second messages for oranges, orange juice, apples, grapes, and so on; commercials for yogurt were also included in this condition.

4. *Public service announcements* (PSAs): 30-second messages on the value of moderating one's intake of sugar and eating a balanced variety of foods each day.

At the camp, the candy commercial condition and the fruit commercial condition were administered during the first two-week session. The PSA and no-message conditions were administered during the second such session.

Description of Televised Messages

In an effort to characterize and compare the public service announcements, fruit commercials, and candy commercials, four messages of each type were randomly selected and shown to a convenience sample of 45 undergraduate management students. The messages were shown twice, with half the students exposed to the messages in reverse order. Students were asked to evaluate each message on a five-point scale with regard to five different dimensions:

1. Extremely boring (1) . . . Extremely interesting (5).
2. Extremely amateurish/rough (1) . . . Extremely professional/polished (5).
3. Makes one basic point (1) . . . Covers a number of points (5).
4. Emphasizes a teaching strategy (1) . . . Emphasizes an entertainment strategy (5).

5. Emphasizes emotions (1) . . . Emphasizes ideas (5).

On each dimension, each "judge's" score was summed for the four public service announcements, the four fruit commercials, and the four candy commercials; means are presented in Table 1. . . . A three-group (PSAs, fruit commercials, and candy commercials), one-way analysis of variance was performed on each of the four dimensions, with post hoc Newman-Keuls tests performed where appropriate. Summarizing the significant differences ($p < 0.05$) the following profile emerges for each set of messages.

In contrasting entertainment and teaching strategies, candy commercials were seen as emphasizing entertainment, PSAs were seen as stressing teaching, and the fruit commercials were judged to be in between. The candy commercials were viewed as emphasizing emotions relative to the PSA and fruit commercials' emphasis on ideas. Both the candy and the fruit messages were seen as significantly more "professional/polished" than the more "amateurish/rough" PSAs. The fruit commercials were perceived as focusing on one specific point in comparison to several points for the candy commercials and PSAs. Fruit commercials were viewed as significantly more interesting than the PSAs, with the candy commercials falling in between but not differing significantly from either one.

Table 1 Mean scores describing televised messages used in the study[a]

Scales describing TV messages		Candy commercials	Fruit commercials	PSAs
Extremely boring (1)	. . . . Extremely interesting (5)	3.6[b,c]	3.8[b]	3.4[c]
Extremely amateurish/rough (1)	. . . . Extremely professional/polished (5)	3.8[b]	3.8[b]	3.3[c]
Makes one basic point (1)	. . . . Covers a number of points (5)	1.9[c]	1.5[b]	2.1[c]
Emphasizes a teaching strategy (1)	. . . . Emphasizes an entertainment strategy (5)	4.0[b]	2.8[c]	1.6[d]
Emphasizes emotions (1)	. . . . Emphasizes ideas (5)	2.9[b]	3.4[c]	3.6[c]

[a]In each row, means with different superscripts (i.e., b, c, and/or d) are significantly different from one another (Neuman-Keuls post hoc tests, $p < 0.05$).

Experimental Procedures

Each afternoon, the counselors led the children in each bunk to their designated television viewing room in either the first or last half of their "quiet period." After viewing the program with appropriate food messages, the children went to another part of the room, where snack choices were made available to them. The choices consisted of (1) orange juice or Kool Aid, and (2) two of four food choices, which typically consisted of two fruits and two candy bars. The children were asked to select a small glass of one of the beverages and two of the four snack foods. During the measurement period, their choices were recorded inconspicuously by an assistant who stood off to the side of the food table.

. . .

Identical food choices were offered on each given day across each two-week session. In each session, the children were offered bananas, apples, oranges, grapes, and raisins four times each, and peaches, pears, plums, and yogurt twice each. Candies such as Hersheys, Almond Joy, Three Musketeers, and Crackerjacks were offered twice each. Orange juice and Kool Aid were offered every day.

During the first two-week session—i.e., in the fruit and the candy commercial conditions—a commercial for a particular fruit or candy was embedded in the television program each day that item was offered to the children. Moreover, that commercial—or a similar one, where more than one commercial was available—was shown on each of the three days prior to offering the item as a snack choice. Thus when a peach was offered, it had been preceded by four exposures to a peach commercial—one on each of four successive days. One orange juice and one Kool Aid commercial were shown each day to either the fruit or the candy commercial groups. There were four versions of each of these commercials, which were rotated.

In the PSA condition, over 50 messages were repeated in four-day cycles—i.e., with 4.5 minutes of messages each day, each message was repeated either three or four times over the 14-day session.

. . .

On the final day of camp, the older children were asked a limited set of questions regarding their attitudes towards snack foods. In particular, a five-point scale was provided in which one pole (1) consisted of a sketch of 10 or so candies with the words "all candy" and the other pole (5) consisted of a sketch of 10 or so fruits and the words "all fruit." The middle point was labeled "half candy/half fruit" with an appropriate sketch. Points on either side of the midpoint were labeled "mostly fruit" or "mostly candy" with appropriate sketches. The children were then asked to circle one number on the scale in response to:

1. The experimenter (*name*) wanted me to eat . . .
2. The doctor at the camp would like me to eat . . .
3. The camp should buy . . . for the new kids who are coming to camp next week.
4. The camp should buy Kool Aid (1) . . . orange juice (5) for the new kids coming to camp next week.

HYPOTHESES

It was hypothesized that relative to the candy commercial condition, the fruit commercials would be most effective in persuading children to shift at least some of their choices away from candy and toward fruit, while the public service announcements would be second most effective in persuading children to select fruit over candy. The fruit messages were seen by adult judges as equally interesting and professional as the candy commercials and as more entertaining than the PSAs.

The group that was exposed to no messages in the course of the television program was thus a group for whom normal levels of precamp exposure to televised candy commercials were terminated for the relatively brief two-week camp session. It was hypothesized that this strategy would not be as effective in stimulating fruit choices and minimizing candy choices as active exposure to PSAs or fruit commercials would be. Yet it was anticipated that even this temporary withdrawal of candy commercials might make the candy less salient/appealing to the children and succeed in reducing the amount of candy they selected.

With regard to the main (projective) attitudinal measure—"What should the camp get for the kids next session? Mostly candy (1) . . . Mostly fruit (5)"—the same order of response was hypothesized. . . .

With regard to the beverage selections, it was hypothesized that because of their exposure to commercials for orange juice or Kool Aid, children in the fruit commercial condition would be most positive toward orange juice, while those in the candy commercial condition would be most positive toward Kool Aid. No mention was made in any of the PSAs as to what children should *drink*. Thus it was hypothesized that children viewing the PSAs—much like the children viewing no messages at all—would fall between the other two groups in their choice of orange juice or Kool Aid. . . .

RESULTS

A two-way nonrepeated measures ANOVA (age × condition) was used to analyze each of the dependent measures.

Expectations of the children. There were no significant between-group differences with regard to the question used to assess demand characteristics ("Experimenter (*name*) wanted me to eat all candy (1) . . . all fruit (5)"; $F(3,126) = 1.1, p > 0.05$). The mean scores indicated that children generally felt the experimenter wanted them to eat "mostly fruit" $\bar{x} = 3.9$). The same was true when the children were asked to respond to "The camp doctor would like me to eat. . . ." No significant differences were noted on this measure, while the average for each group was close to the pole "all fruit" ($F(3,126) = 1.16, p > 0.05$). It seems apparent that all children "know" the foods they "ought" to eat, regardless of the television to which they are exposed. Demand characteristics per se do not appear to have played a role in their actual choice selections. The key question is whether televised messages can activate this general level of nutritional awareness to account for real behavioral change on the part of the children.

Beverage choices. There was a treatment effect for the drinks the children chose ($F(3,280) = 4.18, p < 0.01$). A Newman-Keuls test revealed that children in the fruit condition (exposed to orange juice commercials) selected the most orange juice (45 percent). Those in the candy commercial condition (containing Kool Aid commercials) selected the least orange juice (25 percent, $p < 0.05$). As predicted, those in the no message (35 percent) and PSA (40 percent) conditions (in which there was no discussion of beverages) fell in between the two extremes and were not significantly different from the candy commercial group.

Snack food choices. A significant treatment effect was noted for the proportion of fruit picked ($F(3,280) = 5.32, p < 0.001$). A Newman-Keuls test revealed that those in the candy commercial condition picked significantly less fruit (25 percent) than did those in the other three groups, which were not significantly different from one another (see Table 2).

Attitude. No treatment effect was noted among the older children in response to the question regarding the type of snacks the camp should provide during the next session ($F(3,126) = 1.66, p > 0.05$). The overall tendency was in the direction of somewhat more candy than fruit ($\bar{x} = 3.71$), but this did not differ significantly between conditions. Similarly, there was no significant treatment effect with regard to what beverages the camp should provide for the children in the next session

Table 2 Proportion of fruit and orange juice selected in each condition

Condition	Orange juice	Fruit
Fruit commercials	.45	.36
PSAs	.40	.35
No message	.35	.33
Candy commercials	.25	.25

($F(3,126) = 1.87$, $p > 0.05$). The children may have differentiated themselves from the "kids next session," in which case the effort to have them project their own preferences may have failed. Alternatively, it may be that the specific and immediate daily choice of the snacks was a more sensitive type of dependent measure than these delayed and generalized paper-and-pencil measures.

DISCUSSION

Children's beverage and snack food choices were significantly affected by exposure to different televised food messages over a two-week period. Children who viewed the typical Saturday morning set of candy/Kool Aid commercials picked the most candy/Kool Aid and the least fruit/orange juice.

For beverages, a 20 percent difference (45 percent versus 25 percent) developed over the two-week period between those exposed to the orange juice and Kool Aid commercials. More generally, the order of response was as predicted for the beverage choices, with children in the no-message and PSA conditions falling between the other two conditions. . . .

For the snack food selections, the candy commercials were effective in encouraging the children to choose candy over fruit. Unexpectedly, the no-message condition was as effective as the fruit commercials or PSAs in encouraging the children to pick fruit. One reason why the candy commercials were able to generate significantly different results from the no-message condition—while the fruit commercials or PSAs were not—may be the children's ready familiarity with the candy commercials. Most of these commercials were familiar (and appealing) enough that the children readily sang along with the jingles. Viewing the candy commercials made these products, which were already familiar to the children, even more so. The alternative messages—the fruit commercials and PSAs—were largely unfamiliar and probably would have required a much longer exposure period to make an equivalent impression. One way this relative "deficit" was treated was by repeating a given fruit commercial once a day for four days before the fruit was offered to the children. The PSAs were

repeated with about the same frequency. In addition, we waited a week before assessing the effects of the televised messages. Even so, four repetitions and seven days are hardly a match for the years of daily exposure to the typical candy commercials that were reinforced in the candy commercial condition.

Orange juice commercials were the only commercials in the fruit commerical condition that appeared to influence children's choices significantly. It may be that the children were already familiar with these commercials, or the 14 days of exposure for the orange juice commercials may have been more effective than the less frequent repetition of commercials for the other fruits. While a number of studies have questioned the effectiveness of commercial repetition with children (e.g., Goldberg and Gorn 1974; Gorn and Goldberg 1977), these studies have assessed the issue within the context of a single half-hour television program. It is likely that a single commercial exposure can make a product salient in the minds of the viewer for a half-hour and needs no repetition. However, across a two-week period, daily exposure is probably useful in maintaining the product's salience.

A number of networks and local stations have been persuaded to introduce occasional public service announcements emphasizing a balanced diet. This study suggests that these messages must be aired frequently and continuously if they are to be effective. An occasional PSA or fruit commercial aired against a barrage of candy messages is not likely to change children's snack behavior.

Further, as professional or as interesting as the fruit commercials or PSAs were, they were still viewed by the adult judges as lacking in emotional appeal for young children. Great strides have been taken to make more recent nutritional messages less pedantic (e.g., avoiding discussion of the four food groups), but less attention has been paid to the feeling or emotional side so effectively utilized in advertising. As persuasive nutritional messages directed at children are developed, it would be wise to consider this emotional dimension carefully.

This study confirms once again that by and large, children at a very young age know what they *should* eat (e.g., Goldberg, Corn, and Gibson

1980; Roberts, Gibson, and Bachen, 1979). Children in all conditions indicated that they knew the camp doctor wanted them to eat fruit as opposed to candy. Whether they *acted* upon this awareness and actually chose more fruit seemed to be a function of whether or not they had been exposed to commercials for candy. Viewing these commercials daily appears to have ensured the salience of the candies with their considerable stimulus appeal.

Finally, it should be noted that institutions other than television are critical in this regard. The type of food available in home pantries and refrigerators and in school cafeterias and vending machines does much to attract children to various foods. Eliminating televised candy messages directed to children can do only so much, as long as the corner convenience store with its array of candy remains as attractive as ever to children.

REFERENCES

Adler, R. P., S. Ward, G. S. Lesser, L. K. Merringoff, T. S. Robertson, and J. R. Rossiter (1980), *The Effects of Television Advertising on Children: Review and Recommendation,* Lexington, MA: Lexington Books.

Atkin, C. K. (1980), "Effects of Television Advertising on Children," in *Children and the Faces of Television,* eds. E. L. Palmer and A. Dorr, New York: Academic Press, 287–305.

Federal Trade Commission (1981), *FTC Final Staff Report and Recommendation in the Matter of Children's Advertising,* 43, Washington D.C.

Fox, Daniel, Jeffrey Balfour, JoAnn Dahlkoetter, Robert W. McLellan, and J. Scott Hickey (1980), "How Television Commercials Affect Children's Attitudes and Eating Behavior," paper presented at American Psychological Association, Montreal.

Galst, Joann P. (1979), "Young Children's Snack Choices: Is Television an Influential Factor?" paper presented at American Psychological Association, New York.

Goldberg, M. and Gerald J. Gorn (forthcoming), "Researching the Effects of TV Advertising on Children: A Methodological Critique," in *Learning From Television: Psychological and Educational Research,* ed. M. Howe, London: Academic Press, in press.

———, Gerald J. Gorn, and Wendy Gibson (1978), "TV Messages for Snack and Breakfast Foods: Do They Influence Children's Preferences?" *Journal of Consumer Research,* 5(September), 73–81.

Gorn, Gerald J. and Marvin E. Goldberg (1977), "The Impact of Television Advertising on Children from Low Income Families," *Journal of Consumer Research,* 4(September), 86–88.

Roberts, Donald F., Wendy Gibson, and Christine Bachen (1979), "The Impact of Animated Public Service Announcements on Children's Responses to Questions About Health and Safety," technical report submitted to ABC Television Inc. by the Institute for Communications Research, Stanford University, Stanford, CA.

Scammon, Debra L. and Carole L. Christopher (1981), "Nutrition Education with Children via Television: A Review," *Journal of Advertising,* 10(2), 26–36.

DEVELOPMENTAL RECOGNITION OF CONSUMPTION SYMBOLISM

RUSSELL W. BELK
KENNETH D. BAHN
ROBERT N. MAYER

Perhaps one of the strongest and most culturally universal phenomena inspired by consumer behavior is the tendency to make inferences about others based on their choices of consumption objects. This phenomenon has certain potentially negative consequences in that it may involve prejudicial stereotyping and superficial interpersonal response criteria. On the other hand, this tendency is also a part of the processes that allow us to communicate nonverbally and to achieve the satisfaction of self-expression through consumption. . . .

For children as well as for adults, the major sources of information about the "language" of expressive consumption are media, family, schools, and peers. Because institutions have some discretion in teaching children the language of consumption symbols, it is important to study the developmental attainment of consumption symbolism among children. This was Ward's point in observing that "one needs to understand how children acquire attitudes about the 'social significance' of goods, or more precisely, how people learn to perceive that the acquisition of some kinds of products or brands of goods can be instrumental to successful social role enactment" (1974, p. 3).

The present paper addresses this problem through a cross-sectional investigation of the development of consumption stereotypes involving selected automobiles and houses. Children and adolescents were examined in four age groups, from 4 through 14 years old. Inferences about the owners of the same consumption stimuli were measured among college students and among older adults to provide bases of comparison. These data are examined for developmental trends, with some further attention to the effects of gender and social class.

PRIOR RESEARCH

Consumption Encoding

A focus on the decoding of consumption cues presumes that there is meaning present in the consumption patterns of others. If people have no intent to communicate by encoding messages about self through their consumption selections,

Source: Russell W. Belk, Kenneth D. Bahn, and Robert N. Mayer, "Developmental Recognition of Consumption Symbolism," *Journal of Consumer Research,* Vol. 9, June, 1982, 4–17. Reprinted with permission.

there is less reason to examine the effects of these selections on impressions formed by observers. However, evidence suggests that people do express themselves through consumption.

It appears that people see their possessions as a part of or an extension of themselves (Secord 1968). In a study in which Prelinger (1959) asked subjects to sort 160 concepts representing eight conceptual categories into groups representing "self" and "non-self," the 20 items representing possessions and productions were placed predominantly in the "self" category. The only conceptual categories judged to be even more clearly "self" were body parts, psychological/intraorganismic processes, and personal identifying characteristics and attributes.

Examining the relationship between self and consumption through the congruence of self-images and images of owned or desired products has revealed a number of product categories in which there is significant image congruence. These include the following:

1. *Automobiles* (Birdwell 1968; French and Glaschner 1971; Green, Maheshwari, and Rao 1969; Grubb and Hupp 1968; Grubb and Stern 1971; Hughes and Guerrero 1971; Hughes and Naert 1970; Jacobson and Kossoff 1963; Maheshwari 1974; Munson, 1973; Munson and Spivey 1980; Ross 1971; Sirgy 1980).
2. *Health, grooming, and cleaning products* (Belch and Landon 1977; Delozier and Tillman 1972; Dolich 1969; French and Glaschner 1971; Gentry, Doering, and o'Brien 1978; Landon 1974).
3. *Beer* (Belch and Landon 1977; Dolich 1969; Gentry, Doering, and O'Brien 1978; Landon 1974).
4. *Leisure products and activities* (Belch and Landon 1977; Gentry, Doering, and O'Brien 1978; Landon 1974; Munson 1973; Munson and Spivey 1980).
5. *Clothing and accessories* (French and Glaschner 1971; Gentry, Doering and O'Brien 1978; Munson 1973).
6. *Retail store patronage* (Bellenger, Steinberg, and Stanton 1976; Dornoff and Tat-

ham 1972; Mason and Mayer 1970; Stern, Bush, and Hair 1977).
7. *Food products* (Belch and Landon 1977; Landon 1974).
8. *Cigarettes* (Dolich 1969; Gentry, Doering, and O'Brien 1978).
9. *Home appliances* (French and Glaschner 1971; Landon 1974).
10. *Magazines* (Ross 1971; Sirgy 1980).
11. *Home and home furnishings* (French and Glaschner 1971; Landon 1974).

In some of these studies, the consumption images that were compared to self-images were for the product category as a whole (e.g., beer), while in other studies, brand image data were employed (e.g., *Ladies Home Journal*). In both types of studies, it appears that individuals do prefer products with images more similar to their images of themselves.

. . .

. . . However, while conspicuous consumption and status messages are a part of the present view of consumption symbolism, consumption messages may be encoded for any purchase selection of which others may become aware, and the intended message may involve any aspect of self-concept. . . . Thus, there is a long history of evidence and observation establishing the fact that we attempt to encode messages about ourselves through at least some of our consumption selections. The evidence is not strong enough to conclude that symbolic considerations are the main determinants of these selections, but such messages about self at least appear to be an important consideration in a variety of consumption choices.

Consumption Decoding

Although there is consistent evidence that we also utilize the consumption cues of others in forming impressions of these people,[1] the ability of consumption objects to clearly communicate status messages has been challenged in recent years.

---

[1]For a more critical review of this literature, see Wackman (1973) and Holman (1981b).

Noting the decline in material scarcity in post-industrial societies, Blumberg (1974, 1980) argued that status symbols are rapidly disappearing in the face of abundance. A similar conclusion that status symbols will disappear is based on a nearly opposite premise—i.e., that key material resources are dwindling, and that as this happens, people will adopt similar lifestyles that are devoid of status symbols (Elgin and Mitchell 1977; Grønhaug and Ogaard forthcoming; Inglehart 1977; Leonard-Barton and Rogers 1980; Sharma 1981; Valaskakis et al. 1979).

. . .

. . . The possibility remains that status symbols have declined in significance or at least have changed (*U.S. News and World Report* 1979, 1981) since the era when Riesman and Roseborough (1955) described the "standard package" of goods and services to which all but a few among middle class Americans aspired.

Whether or not consumption communicates status as clearly as was once the case, it is clear that there are still a number of inferences about people which are affected by the goods and services that they presumably have selected. The most heavily researched of these cues is clothing. It has been found to affect reactions to people in a number of ways.[2] . . .

. . .

Products and services that affect personal appearance are far from being the only consumption decisions that are perceived as conveying information about a person. Choice of alcoholic beverages and recreational drugs are two other areas of consumption found to affect person perception (Belk 1980; Woodside 1972; Woodside, Bearden, and Ronkainen 1977). Starting with Haire's (1950) classic study of the differences in images of regular and instant coffee users, a number of studies have given new meaning to the phrase, "you are what you eat," by finding systematic effects of food and

restaurant choices on impression formation (Anderson 1978; Belk 1978; Hill 1968; Holbrook and Hughes 1978; Orpen and Chase 1976; Reid and Buchanan 1979; Sadalla and Burroughs 1981; Sommers 1964; Webster and Von Pechman 1970; Westfall, Boyd, and Campbell 1957).

. . . A number of studies show distinctive attributions are made to the owners of different types of automobiles (Belk, Mayer, and Bahn, forthcoming; Doob and Gross 1968; Green and Wind 1973; Grubb and Hupp 1968; King and King 1980a, 1980b; Munson and Spivey 1981; Wells et al. 1957). . . . Make and model as well as age and condition of automobile differ among different types of owners (Rainwater 1974). . . .

Housing and home furnishings have also been found to affect person perception. While Felson (1978) investigated differences in perceptions of people living in different suburbs, smaller neighborhood units as well as cues concerning size, location, condition, and cost of housing seem more telling (Coleman and Rainwater 1978; Katona 1964; Rainwater 1974).

. . .

. . . Belk (1981) used associational and experimental methodologies to attempt to isolate the product and service category characteristics that tend to make such an item a useful cue in person perception. The properties found to be most influential in determining stimulus usefulness to inferences about personality and social class were cost, decision involvement, uniqueness of choice, variety of choices, and noticeability. Based upon these factors—and the additional considerations of desiring stimulus objects that are familiar to children and are able to be visually presented without the interfering stimuli of persons—automobiles and houses were selected for investigation in the present study.

Children's Perceptions of Consumption Symbolism

While something is known about recognition of consumption symbolism among adults and about children's perceptions of people based on noncon-

---

[2]There have been over three dozen studies of clothing symbolism. See Holman (1980, 1981b) for critical review of this work.

sumption cues such as facial features and occupation (e.g., Dubin and Dubin 1965; Feldman and Ruble 1981; Guttentag and Longfellow 1978; Livesley and Bromley 1973; Peevers and Secord 1973; Rhine, Hill, and Wandruff 1967; Secord and Peevers 1974; Simmons and Rosenberg 1971; Yarrow and Campbell 1963), little research exists on children's recognition of consumption symbolism. The research that *does* exist is confined to status recognition studies by Jahoda (1959) in England, and by Estvan (Estvan 1952, 1958, 1965, 1966; Estvan and Estvan 1959) in the United States. In these studies, children were shown line drawings depicting composites of people and consumption objects, such as homes, furniture, and clothing. The children were then asked to perform matching tasks, such as placing differently dressed people or people displaying different emotions in the status-congruent settings; in the Estvan studies, they were also asked to tell a story about the pictures. Development of status symbol recognition was measured primarily as the ability of the 3- to 12-year-old children (6- to 9-year-old in the Jahoda study) to accurately perceive the status differentials implied by the composite of consumption objects and people in the drawings. (Because the stimuli were composites of people and various consumption objects, it is not possible to isolate those cues most responsible for the status inferences). Both studies found some ability to recognize status cues by the youngest children and a general increase in this ability with age. . . .

. . .

Hypotheses

Little in the way of a theoretical perspective was offered in the studies of children's perceptions of status symbols, but there are some theoretical perspectives which suggest that these status perception findings may generalize to inferences about other dimensions of person perception. Piaget (1926, 1928) concluded that preschool children do not commonly think about how people differ, but he did not hold that they are incapable of making such observations. Piaget (1954, 1969) later concluded that while children younger than 4 or 5

years of age have notions of cause and effect, only older children begin to make inferences about others based upon their actions. It is also consistent with Piaget's theory that, as children develop from preoperational intelligence (from about 2 to 7 years old) to concrete operational intelligence (about 7 to 11) and thence to formal operational intelligence, their judgments of others mature from simple and concrete to more complex and abstract. Watts (1944) and Ginsburg and Opper (1969) offer similar predictions based on the development of language in children; they also present some evidence that preschool children commonly characterize others as simply "good" or "bad," with refinements occurring after this age. . . .

From any of these perspectives, we may hypothesize that the tendency for children to draw inferences based on others' consumption increases with age. It is less clear when this tendency becomes developed, and whether consumption-based stereotyping eventually declines with the perception of more complex determinants of consumption. Applying the present automobile and house stimuli to adults, the authors (Belk, Mayer, and Bahn, forthcoming) have previously reported greater stereotyping among college students than among older adults (over 28 and not in college). Based on this finding and the preceding argument, it was hypothesized that the extent of consumption-based stereotyping would increase with age, but only through college. However, as Guttentag and Longfellow (1978) point out, the fact that a person perception is clear and consistent among a group of children does not guarantee that the *nature* of their perceptions are the same as those of adults. Accordingly, the hypothesis regarding the nature of consumption stereotypes was that the similarity of each age group's perceptions to those of the older adults would be greater with each increment in age.

The Belk et al. study (forthcoming) with adults also revealed that males drew significantly stronger person inferences for automobiles and houses than did females. This was opposite to the majority of previous findings involving both nonconsumption cues (Hall 1978) and consumption cues (Belk

1978; Hamid 1972). This apparent contradiction was interpreted as being due to the fact that the automobiles and houses used in the present study are more within the domain of the traditional male sex role, while the apparel and fashion goods used in the prior studies are more within the domain of the traditional female sex role. Since sex role socialization has been found to have effects on children as young as 20 months (Fein et al. 1975), the present study also hypothesized that males would make stronger automobile and house-based person inferences than females. In addition to finding that adult males made stronger consumption-based inferences in general than adult females made, the Belk et al. study (forthcoming) found that this tendency was especially pronounced for judgments concerning the success (or status) of the stimulus person. . . .

Some previous research and theorizing (Estvan 1952, 1965; Jahoda 1959; Davis and Moore 1945; Simmons and Rosenberg 1971) suggests that members of higher social classes should make stronger status inferences than members of lower social classes. This was not true of the adults discussed in the previous study (Belk, Mayer, and Bahn, forthcoming), but lower social class subjects did ascribe ownership of the higher status houses and automobiles to luck, while the higher social class adults saw the same consumption profiles as representing the kinds of persons they aspired to be. . . . It was hypothesized that higher and lower social class subjects would not differ in the extent of their consumption-based stereotyping and that lower social classes would be more likely to view higher status automobile and house owners as lucky, while higher social classes would be more likely to view them as people to be emulated.

METHODOLOGY

Selection of Consumption Objects

To test the main hypothesis concerning developmental recognition of consumption symbolism and the secondary hypotheses concerning gender and social class effects, automobiles and houses were chosen as the consumption categories of interest. . . . In order to select specific consumption objects, automobiles and houses were sought that were common enough to be within the subjects' range of experience and distinctive enough to evoke potentially distinct consumer images. No prior knowledge existed about what features of automobiles and houses would ensure distinct consumer images, but some of the prior literature on determinants of social status (Coleman and Rainwater 1978; Rainwater 1974) suggests that age, cost, size, and style are among these factors. However, in order to manipulate these features through selections of existing automobiles and houses, it must be recognized that certain of these features covary. For houses, style and age as well as size and cost are not independent, so that only two dimensions could be manipulated. For automobiles, age (condition) and cost (current value) tend to covary. Taken with size and style, this resulted in three independent dimensions. Besides seeking automobiles and houses that varied in these dimensions, an attempt was made to hold other attributes of these objects (e.g., color) constant.

All stimuli were presented in the form of paired comparisons. In addition to isolating desired manipulations of stimulus properties, the paired comparison format allowed a task that could be performed by preschoolers as well as adults. This task was to assign person descriptions to the owner of one of the two objects in the pair.

There were four automobiles selected to fit the research design:

1. A blue 1981 Chevrolet Chevette two-door sedan.
2. A blue 1981 Chevrolet Caprice two-door coupe.
3. A blue 1981 Chevrolet Camaro two-door coupe.
4. A blue 1971 Chevrolet Camaro two-door coupe.

. . . They were then presented to the subjects in three pairs:

1. The first and second cars, differing in size.[3]
2. The second and third cars, differing in style.[4]

---

[3] There was also some difference in price (the Caprice being more expensive), which was unavoidable with brand held constant.

[4] The Camaro was intended to be sportier.

3. The third and fourth cars, differing in age and cost.[5]

The design called for three houses. Those selected were:

1. A large white Bauhaus style contemporary house.
2. A large white Colonial style traditional house.
3. A small white Colonial style traditional house.
   . . . The houses were presented in two pairs:
1. The first and second houses, differing in style and age.
2. The second and third houses, differing in size and cost.

. . .

Samples

To examine the emerging recognition of consumption symbolism, four grade levels were sampled: preschool, second grade, sixth grade, and eighth grade. In addition, to provide bases of comparison, college students as well as adults over 28 years of age and not attending college were sampled. The sample sizes, mean ages, and proportions of females in these six samples are shown in Table 1.

. . .

Administration Procedures and Instrument

Administration of stimuli took three slightly different forms. The most common method, used for second grade through college subjects, was to show two slides representing the pairs of stimuli and then verbally ask each question printed in subjects' questionnaire booklets. This was done for one class at a time except in the eighth grade, where large group administration was possible. . . .

The second method of administration, used with preschool children, was to present the stimuli as photographs and ask questions in personal interviews. . . .

The third method of administration, used with the adult sample, involved self-administered questionnaire booklets with approximately 5-by-7-inch

Table 1 Characteristics of samples

Sample	Size	Characteristic Mean age	Percent female
Preschool	81	4.9	41.8
2nd grade	152	7.7	48.7
6th grade	199	11.7	51.3
8th grade	292	13.7	48.3
College	170	20.6	53.4
Adult	62	40.4	62.9
Total	956	14.5 years	51.9%

black and white photographic reproductions of the stimuli. Since color did not differ with the set of houses or within the set of automobiles, the effect of lack of color on the paired judgments task was deemed to be minimal.

The criterion measures of consumption symbolism took the form of the question, "Which of these two cars/houses is most likely to be owned by a man who is _____?" Drawing on the literature regarding children's person-perception with non-consumption cues (little standardization was found) and on small-scale pretests with preschoolers (the sternest test of the measures), a set of 12 person attributes was selected to represent an array of demographic, personality, emotional, and interpersonal inference dimensions:

1. "a grandfather"
2. "someone who has a lot of friends"[6]
3. "a doctor"
4. "someone I would like to visit"[7]
5. "happy"
6. "has a lot of money"
7. "smart"
8. "a mailman"
9. "has a lot of new things"
10. "the kind of person I would like to be"
11. "mean"[8]
12. "lucky to live the way they do"

---

[5]"Cost" refers to *current* value; "age" entails differences in condition.

[6]"Friendly" in adult sample.
[7]". . . to meet" in college sample.
[8]"Bossy" in adult sample.

The structure of these stereotype dimensions is considered in the results.

RESULTS

Developmental Differences in Strengths of Consumption Stereotypes

To assess the strength of consumption-based stereotypes within each sample, indices were constructed to measure the sum (over all attributions) of the absolute differences between the percent of a sample selecting one member of a stimulus pair and the reciprocal percent selecting the other member of the pair. For instance, the absolute difference between the 89 percent of the sixth grade sample who said the Caprice owner "is a grandfather" and the 11 percent who chose the Chevette owner instead is 78 percent. Table 2 presents these results averaged over the 12 attributes for each sample.

One clear finding was that, in total, the preschoolers sampled were only able to provide random judgments based on the pairs of automobile and house stimuli presented. None of their aggregate judgments showed an absolute difference between two members of a pair that is statistically greater than zero. By second grade, however, all of the five stimulus comparisons showed that, in the aggregate, consistent stereotypes had emerged. The 30 percent average difference among second graders suggests an average 65 percent/35 percent split in attributions to a pair of objects. That is, nearly ⅔ make the same judgment on the average. All other age groups also showed significant aggregate stereotypes over all five stimulus pairs.

Each of the second-grade average absolute differences is greater than the corresponding average for preschoolers. Similarly, as described previously (Belk, Mayer, and Bahn, forthcoming), each of the adult group's average absolute differences is significantly lower than the corresponding difference among the college group. Thus it appears that general consumption-based stereotyping follows a curvilinear pattern, emerging sometime between preschool and second grade and tending to decline after college age. . . .

An examination of average stereotype strengths by attribute but over all stimulus pairs shows only three characteristics for which stereotype strength is not greatest among the college group. These are: "a grandfather," "someone who has a lot of friends," and "someone I would like to visit." The average absolute differences in the first two stereotype dimensions are greatest among sixth gra-

Table 2 Average absolute differences by sample in proportions of subjects making attributions to different members of each stimulus pair

Product category and stimulus pair	Subject group					
	Preschool	2nd grade	6th grade	8th grade	College	Adult
Automobiles						
Small vs. large	19.5%[a]	29.0%	38.5%	45.0%	55.5%	43.8%
New (costly) vs. old (less costly)	10.3[a]	28.7	63.0	56.3	63.0	41.2
Nonsporty vs. sporty	14.3[a]	28.5	23.3	28.5	44.1	31.5
Houses						
New (contemporary) vs. old (traditional)	10.3[a]	43.7%	63.0%	59.0%	57.7%	54.4%
Large (costly) vs. small (less costly)	3.2[a]	20.2	36.8	28.5	60.2%	11.8%

[a]Not significantly different from zero; all others significantly different at $p < 0.01$ via z-test.

ders, while the third dimension has the clearest stereotypes among eighth graders. This may suggest that age and sociability inferences based on consumption cues are strongest during adolescence, while the other judgments that are generally more indicative of status and success are made more clearly in college. This interpretation is supported by the fact that the most strongly stereotyped dimension among college students was "has a lot of money." This was not the case for any other group. All other groups stereotyped "a grandfather" most strongly, except the adult group, which most strongly stereotyped "a doctor." In addition, the two most weakly stereotyped dimensions for the college students were the sociability dimensions of "someone who has a lot of friends" and "someone I would like to visit." This was not true of any other group. The second through eighth grade groups all stereotyped the "happy" and "smart" dimensions least strongly.

As hypothesized, males tended to form stronger stereotypes than females based on these consumption objects. As discussed previously for college students and adults (Belk, Mayer, and Bahn, forthcoming), the average absolute difference in male attributions was 53.8 percent, versus 46.4 percent for females. Among the preschool through eighth grade groups, the corresponding figures were 40.6 percent for males versus 35.1 percent for females.[9] The same is true, though to no greater degree, for the status-related cues: "doctor," "money," "mailman," "new things," and "lucky to live the way they do." . . .

While it had been expected that there would be no significant difference between the extent of consumption stereotyping by upper and lower social classes, the average difference in attributions by higher social class subjects (40.5 percent) was significantly greater than the average difference by lower social class subjects (33.1 percent), when data from the preschool through eighth grade groups are considered. The hypothesis that higher

social class subjects would tend to ascribe ownership of higher status objects to ability and effort and that lower social class subjects would attribute these patterns to luck was not supported. Apparently, this distinction does not emerge until adulthood (Belk, Mayer, and Bahn, forthcoming).

Similarities in Inference Patterns

Another question that can be raised about the development of consumption symbolism is which ones of the six age groups show the greatest similarities in the overall patterns of their attributions. In addition, the similarity of responses between males and females and between lower and higher social class subjects might be examined. Table 3 presents Pearson product moment correlation coefficients measuring these similarities. The correlations are based on the 60 pairs of observations. Each observation represents the aggregate proportion of a group choosing a fixed (but arbitrary) member of each stimulus pair in response to one of the 12 attribution questions for one of the five stimulus pairs.

Again, the nonsystematic nature of responses by the preschool group emerges. Their responses are not significantly correlated with those of any other group. . . .

Between the age groups after preschool, the strongest correlations are between adjacent groups. . . . The bottom row of correlation coefficients shows an increasing similarity to adult consumption stereotypes as grade level progresses from preschool through college. With adults as the standard, there appears to be a monotonic development of consumption symbolism with age.

Developmental Differences in the Nature of Consumption Stereotypes

Thus far, the data presented have considered differences in the strength of consumption-based stereotypes and similarities between the overall profiles of these inferences. But the *nature* of the stereotypes formed and the developmental differences in specific aspects of these stereotypes have not yet been addressed. Table 4 summarizes the overall stereotypes that emerged from presentation of the five stimulus pairs and the age-specific

---

[9]Without the preschool sample, these numbers increase to 45.4 percent and 37.4 percent. These proportions are significantly different via a z-test at alpha = 0.05. Retaining the preschool responses requires an α of 0.10 for significance.

Table 3 Correlations between average proportions of subjects making attributions to a particular member of each stimulus pair[a]

High vs. low social class[b]	Males vs. females	Group	Preschool	Group 2nd grade	6th grade	8th grade	College	Adult
.17	.28	Preschool	—					
.77	.76	2nd grade	.00	—				
.90	.92	6th grade	.04	.88	—			
.96	.94	8th grade	.08	.86	.97	—		
—	.91	College	.07	.51	.69	.76	—	
.91	.93	Adult	.01	.65	.79	.82	.86	—

[a]Each correlation is based on the 60 observations consisting of 12 attributes for 5 stimulus pairs; a minimum correlation of ± .25 is needed to conclude that the relationship is different from zero with an alpha level of .05 (a minimum of .325 is needed with an alpha level of .01).
[b]Defined by school choice for preschool through 8th grade; by median split on Hollingshead two-factor index of social class (Hollingshead and Redlich, 1958; median = 32.5, mean = 34.2 on 11 to 77 scale) for adults; no social class split was attempted among college students.

differences in these stereotypes. Since few of the preschool attributions varied from a random 50–50 split, these findings are drawn from the other age groups.

The greatest consensus in these consumption-based stereotypes emerged from the stimulus pairs manipulating size and cost. The style manipulations were perceived somewhat more uniquely by the different age groups. One set of items that showed related responses was the group of traits involving "success" or status. Those owning the larger, newer, and less sporty consumption objects were consistently judged to be higher in these traits. An interesting covariate of these judgments involves the trait designated "mean." While attributions of this trait were unrelated to attributions of success among the preschoolers through eighth grade groups, meanness tended to be assigned with success inferences by college students and adults.[10] This may suggest that by adulthood, a cynical attitude has emerged that one must be mean in order to succeed.

[10]This was confirmed by cluster analyses within grade for each stimulus pair except the automobile pair varying in size (Chevette vs. Caprice). In preschool through eighth grade groups, meanness tended to cluster with another group of items instead of with success items.

Another interesting developmental trend that distinguishes college students and adults from the younger subject groups involves judgments of which owners of differently styled consumption objects respondents would like to be like. For the two comparisons involving style differences, college students and adults preferred to be like the less sporty car owner and the more traditional house owner, while younger respondents preferred the sportier car and more contemporary house. Superficially, this seems to reflect a shift toward more conservative tastes with age, but a deeper explanation may be suggested by the fact that these conservative choices were also perceived, across all groups, to be indicants of greater success. It may be that concern with *demonstrating* status to others comes to dominate other consumption message interests sometime after the eighth grade and that this concern then continues. There is some prior evidence of increases in status concern with age (Cunningham, Anderson, and Murphy, 1974). This shift to preferring the higher status objects may occur even earlier for the first pair of cars, where eighth graders also showed such a preference. In spite of the fact that the small car owner was perceived as smarter, happier, and friendlier, all but the two youngest groups preferred the large car.

Table 4 Summary of overall and age-specific stereotypes for five pairs of consumption stimuli

Stimulus pair	Overall stereotype	Age-specific differences
Automobiles I. Size: Chevette vs. Caprice	1. The grandfather drives the large car (Caprice). 2. The small car (Chevette) owner is happier and has more friends. 3. The owner of the large car is more successful ("doctor," "money," "new things," "lucky," *not* a "mailman"). 4. The large car owner is mean.	1. Second and sixth graders would like to be like the Chevette owner; others would like to be like the Caprice owner. 2. All except college students see the small car owner as smarter.
II. Style: Camaro vs. Caprice	1. The grandfather drives the less sporty car (Caprice). 2. The owner of the less sporty car is generally judged to be more successful (more likely to be a "doctor," have "money" and be "lucky," but no more likely to have "new things" or *not* be a "mailman"). 3. Stereotypes were weaker for this stimulus pair than for other stimulus pairs.	1. Adults and college students would like to be like the Caprice owner; others would like to be like the Camaro owner. 2. All except college students see the sporty car owner as happier, with more friends, and more desirable to visit. 3. All except adults see the owner of the less sporty car as more mean.
III. Age/cost: 1981 vs. 1971 Camaro	1. The grandfather drives the older car. 2. Subjects would rather be like the new car owner. 3. The owner of the newer car is more succesful ("doctor," "money," "new things," "lucky," *not* a "mailman"). 4. The new car owner is smarter.	1. All except adults see the new car owner as happier, with more friends, and more desirable to visit. 2. All except college students and adults see the old car owner as more mean.
Houses IV. Style/age: New Bauhaus vs. old traditional	1. The grandfather lives in the traditional house. 2. The owner of the new house is more successful ("doctor," "money," "new things," "lucky," *not* a "mailman"). 3. The owner of the new house is smarter.	1. All except college students and adults would like to be like the new house owner. 2. All except college students and adults see the new house owner as happier, with more friends, and more desirable to visit. 3. College students, adults, and sixth graders see the new house owner as more mean.
V. Size/cost: small traditional vs. large traditional	1. The grandfather lives in the small house. 2. Subjects would rather be like the large house owner. 3. The large house owner is seen as happier, with more friends, and more desirable to visit. 4. The large house owner is seen as more successful ("doctor," "money," "new things," "lucky," *not* a "mailman").	1. Success stereotypes are most extreme among college students and adults. 2. All except college students and adults see the owner of the small house as more mean.

CONCLUSIONS

While caution is warranted in generalizing these findings, given the single city in which samples were obtained and the consideration of only five consumption objects, some clear patterns emerge from the present findings. The ability to recognize the social implications of consumption choices is minimal among preschoolers, significant by second grade, and almost fully developed by sixth grade. Although college students show the greatest degree of consumption stereotyping, it is not yet clear how much of this is due to age and how much is due to other factors distinguishing college students from the rest of the population. In either case, the stereotypes among older adults are weaker than among younger age groups. It is perhaps an encouraging sign that consumption stereotyping decreases in adulthood, but the ability to recognize consumption symbolism is still quite pronounced at this point. The possibility that the adult perceptions may be more *veridical* is suggested by the fact that the perceptions of all other groups grow increasingly more like those of adults with increasing age.

The hypothesis that males would be more sensitive to these consumption cues than females was supported, but the hypothesis that the extent of consumption stereotyping would not differ by social class was rejected. Unlike the prior findings with the adult sample (Belk, Mayer, and Bahn, forthcoming), higher social class children drew stronger consumption-based inferences than lower social class children. . . .

Further developmental differences were found in the more detailed examinations of the nature of the consumption stereotypes. Although the hypothesis that higher social class subjects would show greater aspirations to be like the owners of higher status objects was not supported, this tendency did appear in comparing older and younger subjects. The shift toward more conservative (higher status) tastes with age was interpreted as being due to increasing status consciousness. The other major developmental difference in the nature of consumption stereotypes is also susceptible to such an explanation. The fact that "meanness" in-ferences were positively associated with success inferences only among older subject groups was interpreted as reflecting—whether rightly or wrongly and whether as cause or effect—a late developing belief that successful people are mean.

Taken as a whole, these findings indicate that consumption symbolism recognition develops during grade school. Since a substantial portion of this consumption language is attained by second grade,[11] efforts to affect symbol vocabulary and usage must be undertaken early. More detailed work is needed to understand the role of various socializing forces on the development of consumption symbolism. Further work also is needed to learn more about the role of consumption symbolism in interpersonal relations, career aspirations, and personal consumption behavior. Our further research is pursuing these questions, as well as the issue of whether the present findings may be affected by using more child-directed consumption objects, such as toys and games.

With changing affluence, evolving sex roles, and altering life styles, learning more about the dynamics of consumption symbolism is increasingly important. It is time that consumer research shows a greater interest in investigating consumption symbolism in adults as well as children.

REFERENCES

Anderson, James C. (1978), "The Validity of Haire's Shopping List Projective Technique," *Journal of Marketing Research*, 15:644–9.

Belch, George E. and Landon, E. Laird, Jr. (1977), "Discriminant Validity of a Product-Anchored Self-Concept Measure," *Journal of Marketing Research*, 14:252–6.

Belk, Russel W. (1978), "Assessing the Effects of Visible Consumption on Impression Formation," in *Advances in Consumer Research*, Vol. 5, ed. H. Keith Hunt, Ann Arbor: Association for Consumer Research, pp. 39–47.

——— (1980), "Effects of Consistency of Visible Consumption Patterns on Impression Formation," in *Advances in Consumer Research*, Vol. 7, ed. Jerry Ol-

[11]Samples were taken late in the school year, as reflected by the mean ages shown in Table 1.

son, Ann Arbor: Association for Consumer Research, pp. 365–71.

—— (1981), "Determinants of Consumption Cue Utilization in Impression Formation: An Associational Derivation and an Experimental Verification," in *Advances in Consumer Research,* Vol. 8, ed. Kent B. Monroe, Ann Arbor: Association for Consumer Research, pp. 170–5.

——, Mayer, Robert, and Bahn, Kenneth (forthcoming), "The Eye of the Beholder: Individual Differences in Perceptions of Consumption Symbolism," in *Advances in Consumer Research,* Vol. 9, ed. Andrew Mitchell, Ann Arbor: Association for Consumer Research.

Bellenger, Danny, Steinbery, E., and Stanton, William W., (1976), "The Congruence of Store Image and Self Image," *Journal of Retailing,* 52:17–32.

Bem, Sandra L. (1974), "The Measurement of Psychological Androgeny," *Journal of Consulting and Clinical Psychology,* 42:155–62.

Birdwell, Al E. (1968), "A Study of the Influence of Image Congruence on Consumer Choice," *Journal of Business,* 41 (January): 76–88.

Blumberg, Paul (1974), "The Decline and Fall of the Status Symbol: Some Thoughts on Status in a Post-Industrial Society," *Social Problems,* 21 (April): 490–8.

—— (1980), *Inequality in An Age of Decline,* New York: Oxford University Press.

Coleman, Richard P. and Rainwater, Lee (1978), *Social Standing in America: New Dimensions of Class,* New York: Basic Books.

Cunningham, William H., Anderson, W. Thomas, Jr., and Murphy, John H. (1974), "Status Consciousness vs. State Position: Marketing Implications," *Journal of Business Research,* 2: 147–56.

Davis, Kingsley and Moore, W. E. (1945), "Some Principles of Stratification," *American Sociological Review,* 10: 242–5.

Delozier, M. Wayne and Tillman, R. (1972), "Self Image Concepts—Can They Be Used to Design Marketing Programs?" *Southern Journal of Business,* 7: 9–15.

Dolich, Ira J. (1969), "Congruence Relationships Between Self Images and Product Brands," *Journal of Marketing Research,* 6 (February): 80–4.

Doob, Anthony N. and Gross, Alan E. (1968), "Status of Frustrator as an Inhibitor of Horn-Honking Responses," *Journal of Social Psychology,* 76: 213– 218.

Dornoff, R. J. and Tatham, R. L. (1972), "Congruence Between Personal Image and Store Image," *Journal of the Market Research Society,* 14: 45–52.

Dubin, Robert and Dubin, Elisabeth R. (1965), "Children's Social Perceptions: A Review of Research," *Child Development,* 36:809–38.

Elgin, Duane S. and Mitchell, Arnold (1977), "Voluntary Simplicity: Lifestyle of the Future?" *The Futurist,* 11: 200–9.

Estvan, Frank J. (1965), "The Relationship of Nursery School Children's Social Perception to Sex, Race, Social Status, and Age," *Journal of Genetic Psychology,* 107: 295–308.

—— (1952), "The Relationship of Social Status, Intelligence and Sex of Ten and Eleven Year Old Children to an Awareness of Poverty," *Genetic Psychology Monographs,* 46: 3–60.

—— (1966), "Stability of Nursery School Children's Social Perception," *Journal of Experimental Education,* 34: 48–54.

—— (1958), "Studies on Social Perception: Methodology," *Journal of Genetic Psychology,* 92: 215–46.

Estvan, Frank J. and Estvan, Elizabeth W. (1959), *The Child's World: His Social Perception,* New York: G. P. Putnam's Sons.

Fein, Greta, Johnson, David, Kosson, Nancy, Stork, Linda, and Wasserman, Lisa (1975), "Sex Stereotypes and Preferences in the Toy Choices of 20-month-old Boys and Girls," *Developmental Psychology,* 11: 527–528.

Feldman, Nina S. and Ruble, Diane N. (1981), "The Developmental of Person Perception: Cognitive and Social Factors," in *Developmental Social Psychology,* eds. Sharon S. Brehm, Saul M. Kassin, and Frederick X. Gibbons, New York: Oxford University Press, pp. 191–206.

Felson, Marcus (1976), "The Differentiation of Material Life Styles: 1925 to 1966," *Social Indicators Research,* 3: 397–421.

—— (1978), "Invidious Distinctions Among Cars, Clothes, and Suburbs," *Public Opinion Quarterly,* 42 (Spring): 49–58.

French, W. A. and Glaschner, A. B. (1971), "Levels of Actualization as Matched Against Life Style Evaluation of Products," *Combined Proceedings of the American Marketing Association,* Chicago: American Marketing Association, pp. 358–62.

Gentry, James, Doering, Mildred, and O'Brien, Terrence V. (1978), "Masculinity and Femininity Factors in Product Perception and Self-Image," *Advances in Consumer Research,* Vol. 5, ed. H. Keith Hunt, Ann Arbor: Association for Consumer Research, pp. 326–32.

Ginsburg, Herbert and Opper, Sylvia (1969), *Piaget's Theory of Intellectual Development,* Englewood Cliffs, NJ: Prentice-Hall,Inc.

Grønhaug, Kjell and Ogaard, Torvald, Jr. (forthcoming), "Exploring Success and Failure in Intended Changes of Life Style," in *Advances in Consumer Research,* Vol. 9, ed. Andrew Mitchell, Ann Arbor: Association for Consumer Research.

Green, Paul E., Maheshwari, Arun, and Rao, Vithala R. (1969), "Self-Concept and Brand Preference: An Empirical Application of Multidimensional Scaling," *Journal of the Market Research Society,* 11 (October): 343–60.

—— and Wind, Yoram (1973), *Multiattribute Decisions in Marketing: A Measurement Approach,* Hinsdale, IL: The Dryden Press.

Grubb, Edward L. and Hupp, Gregg (1968), "Perception of Self, Generalized Stereotypes, and Brand Selection," *Journal of Marketing Research,* 5 (February): 58–63.

—— and Stern, Bruce L. (1971), "Self-Concept and Significant Others," *Journal of Marketing Research,* 8: 382–5.

Guttentag, Maria and Longfellow, Cynthia (1978), "Children's Social Attributions: Development and Change," in *Nebraska Symposium of Motivation 1977,* Vol. 25.

Haire, Mason (1950), "Projective Techniques in Marketing Research," *Journal of Marketing,* 14: 649–56.

Hall, Judith (1978), "Gender Effects in Decoding Nonverbal Cues," *Psychological Bulletin,* 845–57.

Hamid, Paul N. (1972), "Some Effects of Dress Cues on Observational Accuracy, A Perceptual Estimate and Impression Formulation," *Journal of Social Psychology,* 86: 279–89.

Hill, Conrad R. (1968), "Haire's Classic Instant Coffee Study—18 Years Later," *Journalism Quarterly,* 45 (August): 466–72.

Holbrook, Moris B. and Hughes, Neville C. (1978), "Product Images: How Structured Rating Scales Facilitate Using a Projective Technique in Hypothesis Testing," *The Journal of Psychology,* 100: 323–8.

Holman, Rebecca M. (1980), "Clothing as Communication: An Empirical Investigation," in *Advances in Consumer Research,* Vol. 7, ed. Jerry C. Olson, Ann Arbor: Association for Consumer Research, pp. 372–7.

—— (1981a), "Apparel as Communication," in *Symbolic Consumer Behavior,* eds. Elizabeth C. Hirschman and Morris B. Holbrook, Ann Arbor: Association for Consumer Research, pp. 7–15.

—— (1981b), "Product Use as Communication: A Fresh Appraisal of a Venerable Topic," in *Review of Marketing,* eds. Ben M. Enis and Kenneth J. Roering, pp. 250–272.

Hughes, G. David and Naert, P. A. (1970), "A Computer Controlled Experiment in Consumer Behavior," *Journal of Business,* 43: 354–72.

—— and Guerrero, Jose L. (1971), "Automobile Self-Congruity Models Reexamined," *Journal of Marketing Research,* 8: 125–7.

Inglehart, Ronald (1977), *The Silent Revolution: Changing Values and Political Styles Among Western Publics,* Princeton, NJ: Princeton University Press.

Jacobson, Eugene and Kossoff, Jerome (1963), "Self-Percept and Consumer Attitudes Toward Small Cars," *Journal of Applied Psychology,* 47: 272–245.

Jahoda, Gustav (1959), "Development of the Perception of Social Differences in Children from 6 to 10," *British Journal of Psychology,* 50: 159–75.

King, Algin B. and King, Joyce P. (1980a), "Does the Consumer Still Perceive the Automobile as a Status Symbol under Current Changing Market Conditions: A Behavioral Analysis," Paper presented at the Midwest American Institute for Decision Sciences Conference, April, 1980, Dayton, OH.

—— (1980b), "The Ranking of Automobiles as Status Symbols: A Comparative Analysis of Consumer Perceptions Based on Five Elected Socio-Economic Variables," Paper presented at the Midwest American Institute for Decision Sciences Conference, April, 1980, Dayton, OH.

Landon, E. Laird, Jr. (1974), "Self Concept and Consumer Purchase Intentions," *Journal of Consumer Research,* 1 (September): 44–51.

Leonard-Barton, Dorothy and Rogers, Everett M. (1980), "Voluntary Simplicity," in *Advances in Consumer Research,* Vol. 7, ed. Jerry C. Olson, Ann Arbor: Association for Consumer Research, pp. 28–34.

Livesley, W. J. and Bromley, D. B. (1973), *Person Perception in Childhood and Adolescence,* London: John Wiley & Sons, Ltd.

Maheshwari, Arun K. (1974), "Self-Product Image Congruence: A Micro-Level Analysis," Unpublished Ph.D. dissertation, University of Pennsylvania, Philadelphia, PA.

Mason, Joseph B. and Mayer, Morris L. (1970), "The Problem of the Self-Concept in Store Image Studies," *Journal of Marketing,* 34: 67–9.

Munson, J. Michael (1973), "A Typological Investigation of Self-Concept Congruity and Brand Preferences: Toward a Predictive Model," Unpublished Ph.D. dissertation, University of Illinois.

Munson, J. Michael and Spivey, W. Austin (1980), "Assessing Self-Concept," in *Advances in Consumer Research*, Vol. 7, ed. Jerry C. Olson, Ann Arbor: Association for Consumer Research.

Orpen, Christopher and Chase, Anthony (1976), "A Shopping List Experiment of the Images of Prepared and Non-Prepared Foods," *Journal of Social Psychology*, 98: 145–6.

Peevers, Barbara H. and Secord, Paul F. (1973), "Developmental Changes in Attribution of Descriptive Concepts to Persons," *Journal of Personality and Social Psychology*, 27: 120–28.

Piaget, Jean (1926), *The Language and Thoughts of the Child*, New York: Harcourt Brace and Co.

_____ (1928), *Judgment and Reasoning in the Child*, New York: Harcourt Brace and Co.

_____ (1954), *The Construction of Reality in the Child*, New York: Basic Books.

_____ (1969), *The Child's Conception of the World*, Totowa, NJ: Littlefield Adams.

Prelinger, Ernst (1959), "Extension and Structure of the Self," *Journal of Psychology*, 47: 13–23.

Rainwater, Lee (1974), *What Money Buys: Inequality and the Social Meanings of Income*, New York: Basic Books.

Reid, Leonard N. and Buchanan, Lauranne (1979), "A Shopping List Experiment of the Impact of Advertising on Brand Images," *Journal of Advertising*, 8 (Spring): 26–8.

Riesman, David and Roseborough, Howard (1955), "Careers and Consumer Behavior," in *Consumer Behavior*, Vol. 3, ed. Lincoln H. Clark, New York: NYU Press.

Ross, Ivan (1971), "Self-Concept and Brand Preference," *Journal of Business*, 44 (January): 38–50.

Sadalla, Edward and Burroughs, Jeffrey (1981), "Profiles in Eating: Sexy Vegetarians and Other Diet-based Social Stereotypes," *Psychology Today*, October: 51–7.

Secord, Paul F. (1968), "Consistency Theory and Self-Referent Behavior," in *Theories of Cognitive Consistency: A Sourcebook*, eds. Robert P. Abelson et al., Chicago: Rand McNally & Co., pp. 349–354.

Secord, Paul F. and Peevers, Barbara H. (1974), "The Development and Attribution of Person Concepts," in *Understanding Other Persons*, ed. Theodore Mischel, Oxford: Blackwell, Basil, and Mott.

Semon, Robert (1979), "On Felson's 'Inviduous Distinctions,'" *Public Opinion Quarterly*, 43: 119–20.

Sharma, Avraham (1981), "Coping with Stagflation: Voluntary Simplicity," *Journal of Marketing*, 45: 120–34.

Simmons, Roberta G. and Rosenberg, Morris (1971), "Functions of Children's Perceptions of the Stratification System," *American Sociological Review*, 36 (April): 235–49.

Sirgy, M. Joseph (1980), "Self-Concept in Relation to Product Preference and Purchase Intention," in *Developments in Marketing Science*, Vol. 3, ed. V. V. Bellur, Marquette, MI: Academy of Marketing Science.

Sommers, Montrose S. (1964), "Product Symbolism and the Perception of Social Strata, in *Toward Scientific Marketing*, ed. Stephen A. Greyser, pp. 200–16.

Stern, Bruce L., Bush, Ronald F., and Hair, Joseph F. Jr. (1977), "The Self-Image/Store Image Matching Process: An Empirical Test," *Journal of Business*, 50: 63–9.

U.S. News and World Report (1979), "Status Symbols: U.S. Swings Back to Basics," November 26, pp. 70–71.

_____ (1981), "Flaunting Wealth: It's Back in Style," September 21, 61–64.

Valaskakis, Kimon, et al. (1979), *The Conserver Society: A Workable Alternative for the Future*, New York: Harper and Row.

Wackman, Daniel B. (1973), "Theories in Interpersonal Perception," in *Consumer Behavior: Theoretical Sources*, eds. Scott Ward and Thomas Robertson, Englewood Cliffs, NJ: Prentice-Hall, Inc., pp. 200–229.

Ward, Scott (1974), "Consumer Socialization," *Journal of Consumer Research*, 1(2): 1–15.

Watts, A. F. (1944), *The Language and Mental Development of Children*, London: Harrap and Company.

Webster, Frederick E., Jr. and Von Pechmann, Frederick (1970), "A Replication of the 'Shopping List' Study," *Journal of Marketing*, 34 (April): 61–77.

Wells, William D., Andriuli, Frank J., Goi, Fedele J., and Seader, Stuart (1957), "An Adjective Check List for the Study of 'Product Personality,'" *Journal of Applied Psychology*, 41: 317–19.

Westfall, Robert L., Boyd, Harper W., and Campbell, Donald T. (1957), "The Use of Structural Techniques in Motivation Research," *Journal of Marketing*, 22:134–9.

Woodside, Arch G. (1972), "A Shopping List Experiment of Beer Images," *Journal of Applied Psychology,* 56 (December): 512–13.

———, Bearden, William O., and Ronkainen, Ikeda (1977), "Images on Serving Marijuana, Alcoholic Beverages, and Soft Drinks," *The Journal of Psychology,* 96: 11–14.

Yarrow, Marian R. and Campbell, John D. (1963), "Person Perception in Children," *Merrill-Palmer Quarterly,* 9: 57–72.

THE INFLUENCE OF COGNITIVE PERSONALITY TRAITS AND DEMOGRAPHICS ON CONSUMER INFORMATION ACQUISITION

**CHARLES M. SCHANINGER
AND
DONALD SCIGLIMPAGLIA**

Source: Charles M. Schaninger and Donald Sciglimpaglia, "The Influence of Cognitive Personality Traits and Demographics on Consumer Information Acquisition," *Journal of Consumer Research,* Vol. 8, September, 1981, 208–216. Reprinted with permission.

In the past few years, a number of studies have utilized information-display-board approaches to examine consumer information acquisition and processing. . . . Most of these studies focused on nondurable goods, such as cereal, toothpastes, margarines, and headache remedies. Although the specific issues and measures in those studies vary, three principal types of criteria were used—*depth of search* (number of cues, attributes or alternatives examined, and decision time); *information content* (specific types of information drawn); and *sequence of search* (classification typology schemes based on within-brand or within-attribute transitions).

PRODUCT/TASK INFLUENCES ON INFORMATION ACQUISITION

Capon and Burke (1977) examined differences in information-search typologies and search-depth criteria (the total number of cues drawn and number of dimensions examined) for three durable goods (microwave ovens, toaster ovens, and steam irons). Housewives in that study tended to draw considerably more cues for the durable goods tested than did housewives for nondurable goods tested in previous research. Housewives also tended to draw more cues for the riskier microwave decision, although they did not examine more attributes. The number of information dimensions (attributes) examined was also found to be directly related to the number of dimensions available. Thus, the nature of the product types examined, the relative degree of risk involved, and structural aspects of the information-acquisition task have been shown to influence depth of information acquisition.

Individual Difference Trait Influences

A number of authors have suggested that two different classes of individual difference traits should influence information processing and acquisition: demographic/socioeconomic factors and congitive personality traits. However, few specific hypotheses have been generated and empirically tested for either class, and no studies to date have examined linkages between such variables and information-display-board criteria. This study attempts to review pertinent literature, and then to empirically test a set of hypotheses relating demographic and cognitive personality variables to depth of search criteria.

DEMOGRAPHICS AND INFORMATION ACQUISITION

Age and Family Life Cycle

Phillips and Sternthal (1977), in reviewing the existing literature on age differences and information processing, concluded that older consumers are likely to process less information than younger consumers, for two major reasons. First, older consumers are less capable of processing large amounts of information. Second, due to greater market experience, older consumers are more capable of distinguishing between relevant and irrelevant information for familiar products. As older consumers are more likely to have stored product information for familiar brands, they are also likely to use a more restricted set of alternatives in these instances. However, younger consumers may exhibit opposite tendencies. Engel, Kollat, and Blackwell (1973) cite a study by Katona and Mueller that concluded that the greatest amount of information search is likely for individuals under 35 years of age.

Socioeconomic Variables

Previous research has not clearly established a relationship between socioeconomic factors and information processing. Although not dealing directly with information acquisition or utilization, Engle, Kollat, and Blackwell (1973) state that extended decision making is more likely for individuals of higher education, middle income, and white collar occupations. Although contradictory evidence exists (Fry and Siller 1970), Engel, Blackwell, and Kollat (1978) concluded that highest social class consumers engage in less search than average, suggesting a curvilinear relationship. . . . Engel, Blackwell, and Kollat (1978) and Robertson (1970) also concluded that lower social class consumers shop less and tend to depend more on word-of-mouth communications. These findings suggest that lower-status households engage in less search for information. Although conflicting results have been reported on middle- and upper-status households, information search appears to increase with social class, education, and income.

The emerging literature on working wives (Douglas 1976a; 1976b; Schaninger and Allen 1980; Strober and Weinberg 1977) suggests that, compared to their nonworking counterparts, working wives may engage in less information search, spend less time shopping, and visit fewer stores. Lower-status working wives also tend to use more instant products.

COGNITIVE PERSONALITY TRAITS AND INFORMATION PROCESSING

Much of the existing literature on cognitive personality and information processing is conceptual rather than empirical. By and large, this literature suggests that cognitive personality traits should influence information search and utilization. Perceived risk theory (Cox 1967a), the Howard and Sheth (1969) model, and the Engel, Blackwell, and Kollat (1978) model all suggest individual cognitive differences in search and processing behavior, as well as in tolerance for discrepant information and for perceived risk.

To date, no empirical research has been reported that directly relates cognitive personality to information processing. A review of the consumer behavior literature that examined cognitive personality revealed six traits as most likely to be related to individual differences in information processing—tolerance for ambiguity, rigidity, cognitive style, need for cognitive clarity, self-esteem, and trait anxiety. . . .

Tolerance for Ambiguity

Budner (1962) defined tolerance for ambiguity as the tendency to perceive ambiguous or inconsistent situations as desirable, and intolerance for ambiguity as the tendency to perceive or interpret ambiguous situations as threatening or undesirable. Those most tolerant of ambiguity should enjoy making more difficult and complex decisions, particularly when ambiguous or discrepant information is present.

Budner classifies three types of situations as ambiguous: a completely new situation with no familiar cues; a complex situation in which a great number of cues are to be taken into account; and a contradictory situation in which incongruous information exists for different elements (choice criteria) of a given alternative or in which the evaluation of alternatives varies with different criteria. These three types of situations are characterized as novelty, complexity, and insolubility.

The concept of tolerance for ambiguity has been linked to information processing and to new product acceptance. Bettman (1971), in developing a theoretical model of information processing, incorporated tolerance for ambiguity as an influence on both information search and information processing behavior. Individuals more tolerant of ambiguity should search for more information and should process rather than reject discrepant information. . . . Mazis and Sweeney (1973) found that tolerance for ambiguity was positively related to trying new product entries for what they termed "homogeneous" products, but not for "heterogeneous" products.[1] They stated that consumers tend to utilize more objective information, rather than subjective or stored information, in the evaluation and purchase of heterogeneous (or durable) products.

• • •

In an information-acquisition task, behavioral reactions that would indicate the presence of threat for intolerant individuals would be repression and denial of discrepant information or avoidance of potentially discrepant information, unfamiliar attributes or brands, or of other information that increases either the complexity or incongruity of in-

[1]Homogeneous products were defined as low-cost convenience items that consumers evaluate using subjective (taste, flavor, aroma) experientially based criteria. Heterogeneous product classes, on the other hand, were defined as goods (durables for the most part) that differed from each other on such objective information as physical product features or posted prices.

formation. We would expect such relationships to be strongest in situations characterized by high degrees of novelty, complexity, and/or insolubility, that is, for an innovative product class characterized by a large number of unfamiliar attributes and alternatives and by incongruous information. A familiar product class with a few salient objective attributes should be least likely to evidence such reactions among intolerant individuals.

Rigidity

Rokeach (1960) and Budner (1962) view rigidity as related to intolerance for ambiguity, but regard it as a more general influence, not as much affected by such situational factors as novelty, complexity, or insolubility. Rokeach found that rigid individuals are more likely to approach life in a fixed or set manner. Rigidity was found to be negatively related to acceptance of information, particularly for new or discrepant information, and negatively related to the ability to structure information in problem solving. . . .

Cognitive Style and Need for Cognitive Clarity

Cox (1967b) examined two cognitive personality traits in his research on information utilization for new product decisions—cognitive style and need for cognitive clarity. Cognitive style measures an individual's tendency to react to uncertain or inconsistent information by simplifying (avoiding or rejecting incongruous information) rather than clarifying (seeking new information for clarification). Simplifiers tended to resist changing their product preferences following additional information. . . .

Cox regarded the need for cognitive clarity scale as measuring need for cognitive certainty. The actual items tend to measure the need to immediately resolve, rather than postpone the resolution of, uncertainty. Individuals high in need for cognitive clarity (certainty) were more likely to incorporate new information and to change their prior product evaluations. Thus, such individuals should also access more information, particularly for unfamiliar product-class decisions.

Self-Esteem and Trait Anxiety

A number of perceived-risk studies have found self-esteem to be positively related to confidence in ability to evaluate alternatives and make purchase decisions (Cox 1967a). Self-esteem has also been shown to be negatively correlated with various anxiety scales. It has been demonstrated that anxiety is positively related to perceived risk and negatively related to confidence (Schaninger 1976). . . . Bariff and Lusk (1977) suggest that anxiety, like tolerance for ambiguity, relates to the stress level at which individuals can effectively function in decision-making tasks.

These findings suggest that high anxiety and low self-esteem individuals should regard complex or unfamiliar purchase decisions as more threatening, and should be less capable of handling (acquiring) information for such tasks.

Relationships Among Cognitive Personality Traits

Previous research indicates many of these cognitive personality traits to be interrelated. Schaninger (1976) found self-esteem and anxiety to be negatively correlated. The similarity between the scales for tolerance for ambiguity and cognitive style suggest a strong (negative) relationship between these two variables. . . . If need for cognitive clarity does measure need for certainty, it should be positively related to tolerance for ambiguity and self-esteem, and (slightly) negatively related to cognitive style, rigidity, and trait anxiety. Budner (1962) also suggests that rigidity should be negatively correlated with tolerance for ambiguity, and should demonstrate a comparable pattern of intercorrelations with the other measures.

HYPOTHESES

Based on this literature review, the following sets of hypotheses were generated:

Product Task Differences Hypotheses

H(PT)1: Consumers will process more information and examine more attributes and alternatives for durable (heterogeneous) than for convenience (homogeneous) products, due to larger between-brand differences, greater complexity, and higher perceived risk.

H(PT)2: For convenience (homogeneous) products, the number of attributes and alternatives examined will be directly related to the number of attributes available.

Demographic Hypotheses

H(D)1: Older (or later life cycle) consumers will process less information and examine fewer attributes and alternatives.

H(D)2: Lower socioeconomic status (education, occupation, income) consumers will process less information and examine fewer attributes and alternatives compared to middle- or upper-status consumers.

H(D)3: Working wives, particularly of the lower-status, will process less information and examine fewer cues and fewer alternatives than nonworking wives (especially for instant homogeneous products).

H(D)4: Because nonhomeowners are typically younger and in earlier life-cycle stages, they will process more information and examine more attributes and alternatives than homeowners.

Cognitive Personality Hypotheses

H(CP)1: Tolerance for ambiguity will be positively related to the number of cues, attributes, and alternatives examined.

H(CP)2: Among homogeneous products, the prior relationships will be strongest for an innovative product task with a large number of attributes (high on Budner's dimensions of novelty and complexity), and weakest for a familiar product with a small number of attributes (low on novelty and complexity, high on stored information).

H(CP)3: The prior relationships [H(CP)1] will

also be strong for a durable (hetero-geneous) product class characterized by a large number of salient attributes and large between-brand differences, reflecting high complexity and insolubility.

H(CP)4: The relationship of tolerance for ambiguity with number of attributes examined will be weaker than that with number of alternatives examined for homogeneous products, due to the tendency to utilize subjective stored information (taste, aroma) rather than objective package information.

H(CP)5: Cognitive style (simplifier) will be negatively related to number of cues, attributes, and alternatives examined in a manner consistent with H(CP)2 through H(CP)4.

H(CP6: Trait anxiety will be negatively related and self-esteem will be positively related to number of cues, attributes, and alternatives examined in a manner consistent with hypotheses H(CP)2 through H(CP)4.

H(CP)7: Rigidity will be negatively related to number of cues, attributes, and alternatives examined.

H(CP)8: Need for cognitive clarity (certainty) will be positively related to number of cues attributes, and alternatives examined.

METHOD

The experiment devised to test these hypotheses consisted of a battery of questionnaire measures followed by four information display board (IDB) shopping tasks designed to vary with regard to degree of novelty, complexity, and insolubility. The experiment was specifically designed to include both homogeneous (convenience good) tasks and a heterogeneous (durable good) task. The four product classes chosen were instant coffees, nondairy coffee creamers, instant lemonades, and electric clothes dryers.

Information Display Board Tasks

Table 1 presents a summary of the product-task characteristics for the four IDB tasks utilized in this study. Instant coffee was chosen to represent a noninnovative, familiar, frequently purchased homogeneous shopping good, low in structural complexity (few available package/shelf information attributes). Coffee creamers were chosen to represent a less frequently purchased and less familiar (hence, moderate novelty) homogeneous convenience good, high in structural complexity (many attributes). Instant lemonades, more recently introduced to the market, were chosen to represent a homogeneous convenience product, higher in novelty and in structural complexity. Dryers were chosen to represent a high-cost, infrequently purchased, high-risk durable good with large interbrand differences.

. . . Actual package information and price attributes were included for both store and national brand alternatives for the three low-cost convenience goods. For dryers, feature possession, capacity, and price attributes were utilized. Attributes were ordered alphabetically as rows in the matrix, and alternatives were labeled by brand name, with different sizes on the same brand name randomly ordered as columns. . . .

Questionnaire Measures

The questionnaire contained demographic measures, seven-point semantic differential type ratings for various product classes (confidence in choosing among brands, perceived decision complexity, degree of danger/risk present, and the degree of perceived interbrand differences), and the six cognitive personality trait measures discussed previously. Demographic information included age of husband and of wife, occupation of household head, wife's occupation, life-cycle stage, dwelling type, home ownership status, and combined family income.

The six cognitive personality scales administered were:

- Cognitive Style, as used by Cox (1967b), to measure the tendency to resolve uncertainty or cognitive unclarity by simplifying (avoiding discrepant information) or by clarifying (seek-

Table 1 Characteristics of product categories included

Product category	Product type	Number of alternatives	Number of attributes	Total cues	Structural complexity	Novelty	Insolubility	Inter-purchase interval
Dryers	Durable good	13	10	130	High[a]	Moderate	High	Long
Instant coffee	Convenience good	14	6	84	Low	Low	Low	Short
Coffee creamer	Convenience good	14	14	196	High	Moderate	Moderate/low	Moderate
Instant lemonade mix	Convenience good	13	16	208	High	High	Moderate/low	?

[a]Dryers were given a high rating because most of the ten product-feature attributes were likely to be salient, whereas a smaller percentage of the homogeneous products' attributes were likely to be salient.

ing additional information to clarify understanding);

- Spielberger's Trait Anxiety measure (Spielberger 1972; Spielberger, Gorusch, and Lushene 1970);
- Need for Cognitive Clarity, as used by Cox (1967b) to measure the need for certainty;
- Budner's (1962) measure of Intolerance for Ambiguity (with loadings reversed to measure tolerance for ambiguity);
- the Short Form of the Janis test for Self-Esteem, as reported in Cox (1967a); and
- the Gough-Sanford Rigidity scale as used by Rokeach (1960).

The Sample

One hundred twenty housewives were recruited from church-affiliated social groups in a midsized midwestern city. . . . The sample was slightly skewed toward higher socioeconomic categories (as was the community) and toward older age categories. Twenty-four percent reported combined family income (in June 1976) of $23,000 or more, with 27 percent at $10,000 or less. On husband's occupation, 33 percent were managerial-professional, 21 percent lower-status white collar, 36 percent blue collar, and 11 percent retired. Twenty-nine percent of the housewives had college degrees, and 37 percent had high-school degrees or

less. Seventy-six percent did not work; 11 percent worked at blue-collar or sales-clerical jobs, and 13 percent at white-collar jobs. Ninety-two percent were homeowners. Ten percent were below 30, and 20 percent above 60 years of age. Eighteen percent were newly married couples or younger couples with a child under six; 34 percent fell into empty-nest working, empty-nest retired, or solitary survivor family life-cycle categories.

RESULTS

Product-Task Differences

Three depth-of-search criteria (number of cues drawn, number of attributes, and number of alternatives examined) were compared across the four product categories (Table 2). Subjects examined the greatest number of alternatives and cues for dryers, followed by instant lemonades, creamers, and instant coffees, supporting Hypotheses (PT)1 and 2. No significant difference in number of alternatives examined was observed, probably because the number of alternatives available in the experiment did not vary appreciably.

Mean ratings and *F*-tests for each product on confidence, perceived complexity, perceived danger/risk, and perceived interbrand differences are presented as a manipulation check. Dryers, as expected, were perceived as the most complex deci-

Table 2 Means and *F* values for information-acquisition criteria and product-specific psychological variables

Criterion variable	Coffee	Creamers	Lemonades	Dryers	F value
Total cues examined	9.66	13.84	15.11	20.42	19.92[c]
Attributes examined	3.12	4.70	6.77	6.77	56.05[c]
Alternatives examined	4.35	5.06	4.96	4.62	0.47
Confidence[a,b]	3.00	4.51	3.54	2.96	10.94[c]
Complexity[a]	2.63	2.78	2.40	4.21	20.53[c]
Danger/risk[a]	2.05	2.11	1.94	4.36	51.06[c]
Perceived differences[a]	3.65	2.59	2.29	4.56	42.45[c]
Percent never buying product	16%	50%	41%	18%	—
Percent buying in last month	38%	12%	29%	—	—

[a]Seven-point scales (e.g., 1 = not very complex, 7 = very complex).
[b]Reverse coded, low score represents high confidence.
[c]$p < 0.001$.

sion, as highest in interbrand differences, and as having the highest degree of danger/risk. The high mean confidence rating for dryers probably reflects the use of unambiguous objective search criteria. Surprisingly, subjects perceived less confidence, greater complexity, and greater danger/risk toward creamers than toward instant lemonades. This is consistent with the percentage of subjects who never purchased these two products, and with the percentage of those who bought these products within the last month. . . . Instant coffees, as expected, showed a higher degree of confidence and evidence of more recent purchase than the other two convenience beverage items.

Demographics and Cognitive Personality

To examine the relationships between demographics and cognitive personality traits with depth-of-search criteria, bivariate product correlations and MANOVAs were employed. These bivariate correlations provided linear tests of the hypothesized relationships. MANOVAs were run by breaking the sample into quartiles for all demographic and cognitive personality variables except family life cycle (three groups) and home ownership (two groups), and testing for between-group differences on all 12 depth-of-search criteria. The MANOVAs were employed to determine whether or not nonlinear relationships between demo-

graphics and cognitive personality traits existed. With a few minor noted exceptions, the relationships examined proved to be linear.

Three sets of canonical correlation analyses were also employed to examine multivariate relationships between (respectively) demographics, cognitive personality traits, and the combination of both demographics and cognitive personality traits as predictors of the 12 depth-of-search criteria. Because the bivariate correlations and multivariate canonical loadings provided comparable results, only the canonical results are presented (see Table 3).

SUMMARY AND CONCLUSIONS

Depth-of-information search criteria in information display board tasks were significantly related to product/task structure, as well as to individual differences in demographics and in cognitive personality traits, as hypothesized.

Housewives examined more cues and more attributes for durables than for convenience goods, and for product tasks that presented more available attributes. Number of alternatives examined was not significantly different across the four tasks chosen, probably because the four tasks did not substantially differ in number of alternatives available.

Table 3 Canonical analyses: loadings and tests of significance for demographic and cognitive personality measures with depth-of-search criteria

Variable	Demographic predictors		Cognitive personality predictors	Combined predictor set		
	First variate	Second variate	First variate	First variate	Second variate	Third variate
Demographic predictors						
Wife's age	−.374	−.145		.456	−.080	−.058
Wife's education	.760	−.082		−.558	−.466	−.259
Husband's occupation	−.049	−.387		.003	−.180	.507
Wife's occupation	−.209	−.588		.348	−.439	.192
Family income	.002	−.277		−.023	−.132	.295
Home ownership	−.756	.235		.496	.531	.138
Family life cycle	−.370	.336		.352	.269	−.363
Cognitive personality predictors						
Cognitive style (simplifier)			−.640	.411	−.166	−.337
Trait anxiety			−.232	.148	.231	−.277
Need for cognitive clarity			−.128	.114	−.038	.078
Tolerance for ambiguity			.944	−.659	.180	.407
Self-esteem			.298	−.277	−.289	.204
Rigidity			−.106	.080	−.015	−.025
Depth-of-search criteria						
Coffee cues	.311	−.037	.262	−.336	−.084	.035
Coffee attributes	−.232	.305	−.515	.224	.011	−.608
Coffee alternatives	.686	−.031	.611	−.744	−.195	.053
Creamer cues	.254	.178	.565	−.550	.237	.220
Creamer attributes	.049	−.013	.055	−.053	−.062	−.010
Creamer alternatives	.462	.119	.489	−.623	.012	.031
Lemonade cues	.480	−.055	.532	−.618	−.066	.293
Lemonade attributes	.146	−.161	−.091	−.026	−.249	.054
Lemonade alternatives	.731	.095	.653	−.812	−.115	−.027
Dryer cues	.440	.216	.687	−.656	.244	.169
Dryer attributes	.323	.067	.347	−.410	.057	.061
Dryer alternatives	.466	.506	.456	−.600	.298	−.213
Eigenvalue	.408	.324	.333	.510	.363	.298
Canonical R	.638	.569	.577	.714	.602	.546
Veldman's Chi square	44.228[d]	33.029[c]	34.387[c]	58.132[d]	36.132[b]	28.834[a]
Degrees of freedom	18	16	17	24	22	20

[a] $p < 0.10$.
[b] $p < 0.05$.
[c] $p < 0.01$.
[d] $p < 0.001$.

Number of cues and number of alternatives examined were consistently and significantly related to individual differences in demographics and cognitive personality. Housewives who were younger, earlier in the family life cycle, more educated, of higher social class, and nonhomeowners examined more cues and alternatives for all four decisions. They also tended to examine more attributes for dryers, but fewer for instant coffees.

As hypothesized, those more tolerant of ambiguity, having clarifier cognitive styles, and higher self-esteem examined more cues and alternatives for all four decisions. They examined more attributes only for the highly complex and insoluble dryer task. Furthermore, these relationships were stronger for the more complex and novel instant lemonade task than for the less complex and more familiar instant coffee task, as hypothesized.

Canonical correlation analyses revealed that trait anxiety may act as a moderator variable with other cognitive personality traits, and demonstrated the existence of complex nonlinear and interactive relationships between wife's occupation and other predictors. The two working-wife profiles that emerged (lower status, older homeowners and higher status, earlier family life cycle nonhomeowners) were consistent with the dual-career/dual-income distinction in the sociology literature. These canonical analyses shed greater insight into the role of demographics and cognitive personality structure as they interact with each other to produce different patterns of information search.

Future research with information display board data might focus on how demographics and cognitive personality variables influence sequence of search criteria or search-sequence typologies, such as those developed by Bettman and Jacoby (1976) or Jacoby et al. (1976). Future research on cognitive personality structure might also focus on survey studies such as that by Claxton, Fry, and Portis (1974), which examined prepurchase information-seeking patterns, and utilized a wide variety of shopping and information search criteria for durables. Other forms of experimental shopping studies under more realistic simulated store settings could utilize observation and postinterviews to examine willingness to try new products, as well as depth-of-search criteria (number of alternatives examined, specific information considered, etc.) for convenience goods. Administration of pen-and-paper demographic and cognitive personality questionnaires after the experimental session would not only verify the findings of this study, but would extend them to other criteria in less artificial settings.

REFERENCES

Bariff, M. L., and Lusk, E. J. (1977), "Cognitive Personality Tests for the Design of Management Information Systems," *Management Science,* 23, 820–9.

Bartos, R. (1977), "The Moving Target: The Impact of Women's Employment on Consumer Behavior," *Journal of Marketing,* 41, 31–7.

Bettman, James R. (1971), "The Structure of Consumer Choice Processes," *Journal of Marketing Research,* 8, 465–71.

———, and Jacoby, Jacob (1976), "Patterns of Processing in Consumer Information Acquisition," in *Advances in Consumer Research,* Vol. 3, ed. B. B. Anderson, Cincinnati: Association for Consumer Research, pp. 315–20.

———, and Kakkar, Pradeep (1977), "Effects of Information Presentation Format on Consumer Information Acquisition Strategies," *Journal of Consumer Research,* 3, 233–40.

Budner, Stanley (1962), "Intolerance of Ambiguity as a Personality Variable," *Journal of Personality,* 30, 29–50.

Capon, Noel, and Burke, Marion (1977), "Information Seeking in Consumer Durable Purchases," in *Contemporary Marketing Thought, 1977 Educator's Proceedings,* eds. Barnett A. Greenberg and Danny N. Bellenger, Chicago: American Marketing Association, pp. 110–15.

Claxton, John, Fry, Joseph N., and Portis, Bernard (1974), "A Taxonomy of Prepurchase Information Gathering Patterns," *Journal of Consumer Research,* 1 (December), 35–42.

Cox, Donald F. (1967a), "Synthesis—Perceived Risk and Information Handling," in *Risk Taking and Information Handling in Consumer Behavior,* ed. D. F. Cox, Boston: Harvard University Press, pp. 603–39.

——— (1967b), "The Influence of Cognitive Needs and Styles on Information Handling in Making Product Evaluations," in *Risk Taking and Information Han-*

dling in Consumer Behavior, ed. D. F. Cox, Boston: Harvard University Press, pp. 370–92.

Douglas, Susan P. (1976a), "Cross-national Comparisons and Consumer Stereotypes: A Case Study of Working and Nonworking Wives in the U.S. and France," *Journal of Consumer Research,* 3, 12–20.

———— (1976b), "Working Wife vs. Non-Working Wife Families: A Basis for Segmenting Grocery Markets?" in *Advances in Consumer Research,* Vol. 3, ed. B. B. Anderson, Cincinnati: Association for Consumer Research, pp. 191–8.

————, Kollat, D. T., and Blackwell, R. D. (1973), *Consumer Behavior,* 2nd edn. New York: Holt, Rinehart, & Winston.

Fry, Joseph N., and Siller, Frederick H. (1970), "A Comparison of Housewife Decision Making in Two Social Classes," *Journal of Marketing Research,* 7, 333–7.

Jacoby, J., Chestnut, Robert W., Weigl, Karl C., and Fisher, William A. (1976), "Pre-Purchase Information Acquisition: Description of a Process Methodology, Research Paradigm, and Pilot Investigation, in *Advances in Consumer Research* Vol. 3, ed. B. B. Anderson, Cincinnati: Association for Consumer Research, pp. 306–14.

Phillips, Lynn, W., and Sternthal, Brian (1977), "Age Differences in Information Processing: A Perspective on the Aged Consumer," *Journal of Marketing Research,* 14, 243–9.

Rapoport R., and Rapoport R. (1971), "Further Considerations on the Dual Career Family," *Human Relations,* 24, 519–33.

Robertson, Thomas S. (1970), *Consumer Behavior,* Glenview, IL: Scott-Foresman and Co., p. 124.

Rokeach, Milton (1960), *The Open and Closed Mind,* New York: Basic Books, Inc.

Schaninger, Charles M. (1976), "Perceived Risk and Personality," *Journal of Consumer Research,* 3, 95–100.

————, and Allen, Chris (1980), "Dual Career, Dual Income, and Non-Working Wife Families: Perspectives and Research Directions," in *Marketing in the 80's,* ed. Richard P. Bagozzi et al., Chicago: American Marketing Association, pp. 93–5.

Spielberger, C. D. (ed.) (1972), *Anxiety: Current Trends in Theory and Research,* Vols. 1 and 2, New York: Academic Press.

————, Gorusch, D. L., and Lushene, R. E. (1970), *Manual for the State-Trait Anxiety Inventory,* Palo Alto, CA: Consulting Psychologists Press.

Strober, Myra H., and Weinberg, Charles B. (1977), "Working Wives and Major Family Expenditures," *Journal of Consumer Research,* 4, 141–7.

THE EXPERIENTIAL ASPECTS OF CONSUMPTION: CONSUMER FANTASIES, FEELINGS, AND FUN

MORRIS B. HOLBROOK
AND
ELIZABETH C. HIRSCHMAN

Source: Morris B. Holbrook and Elizabeth C. Hirschman, "The Experiential Aspects of Consumption: Consumer Fantasies, Feelings, and Fun," *Journal of Consumer Research,* Vol. 9, September, 1982, 132–140. Reprinted with permission.

In its brief history, the study of consumer behavior has evolved from an early emphasis on rational choice (microeconomics and classical decision theory) to a focus on apparently irrational buying needs (some motivation research) to the use of logical flow models of bounded rationality (e.g., Howard and Sheth 1969). The latter approach has deepened into what is often called the "information processing model" (Bettman 1979). The information processing model regards the consumer as a logical thinker who solves problems to make purchasing decisions. The information processing perspective has become so ubiquitous in consumer research that, like fish in water, many researchers may be relatively unaware of its pervasiveness.

Recently, however, researchers have begun to question the hegemony of the information processing perspective on the grounds that it may neglect important consumption phenomena (e.g., Olshavsky and Granbois 1979; Sheth 1979). Ignored phenomena include various playful leisure activities, sensory pleasures, daydreams, esthetic enjoyment, and emotional responses. Consumption has begun to be seen as involving a steady flow of fantasies, feelings, and fun encompassed by what we call the "experiential view." This experiential perspective is phenomenological in spirit and regards consumption as a primarily subjective state of consciousness with a variety of symbolic meanings, hedonic responses, and esthetic criteria. Recognition of these important aspects of consumption is strengthened by contrasting the information processing and experiential views.

CONTRASTING VIEWS OF CONSUMER BEHAVIOR

Our bases for contrasting the information processing and experiential views appear in Figure 1. This diagram is not all-inclusive. It simply represents some key variables typically considered in logical flow models of consumer behavior. In brief, various environmental and consumer inputs (products, resources) are processed by an intervening response system (cognition-affect-behavior) that generates output consequences which, when appraised against criteria, result in a learning feed-

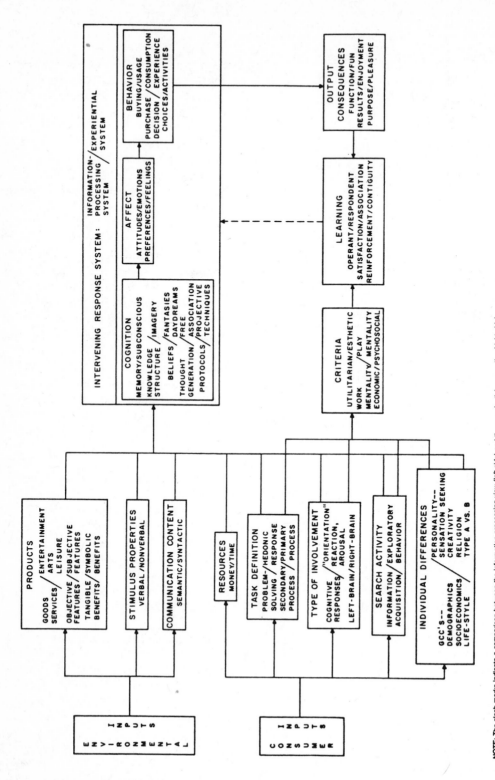

Figure 1 Contrasts between the information processing and experiential views of consumer behavior.

back loop. Individual differences, search activity, type of involvement, and task definition affect the criteria by which output consequences are evaluated.

Though Figure 1 neglects some variables that have interested consumer researchers,[1] it reflects the general viewpoint embodied by most popular consumer behavior models. Moreover, the diagram facilitates the intended comparison between approaches by distinguishing between the phenomena of primary interest to the information processing perspective (left side of slash marks) and those of central concern to the experiential view (right side of slash marks). In the following sections, we discuss these distinctions as they pertain to (1) environmental inputs, (2) consumer inputs, (3) intervening responses, and (4) output consequences, criteria, and learning effects.

ENVIRONMENTAL INPUTS

Products

Much consumer research has focused on the tangible benefits of conventional goods and services (soft drinks, toothpaste, automobiles) that perform utilitarian functions based on relatively objective features (calories, flouride, miles per gallon). By contrast, the experiential perspective explores the symbolic meanings of more subjective characteristics (cheerfulness, sociability, elegance).

All products—no matter how mundane—may carry a symbolic meaning (Levy 1959, 1980). In some cases, the symbolic role is especially rich and salient: for example, entertainment, the arts, and leisure activities encompass symbolic aspects of consumption behavior that make them particularly fertile ground for research . . . . The growth of research on leisure, entertainment, and the arts reflects a shift of attention toward the experiential side of the distinctions shown in the figure.

[1]For example, the Figure omits the effects of general economic conditions and related expectations, some elements of the marketing mix (e.g., channels of distribution), social influence through reference groups, perceived risk and other conflict-related phenomena, joint decision making in households, and considerations of economic externalities or social welfare.

Methodologically, this shift promotes certain advantages. One benefit stems from the tendency for leisure, entertainment, and arts products to prompt high levels of interest and involvement among their target markets. The growing body of work in these areas suggests that respondents can typically provide meaningful data on perceptions and preferences across a broad array of relevant objects or activities. Hence, applications of multivariate methods may be more valid with this type of product than with some low-involvement consumer nondurables, such as detergents or canned peas, for which consumers may be unable to make valid perceptual or affective distinctions among more than a few different brands. For this reason, many of our available statistical procedures—especially those directed toward intraindividual analysis across brands—may actually be more appropriate within the context of experiential consumption than for the frequently purchased nondurables to which they have typically been applied.

Stimulus Properties

Traditional consumer research paradigms have concentrated on product attributes that lend themselves to verbal descriptions. Both conjoint analysis and multiattribute models, for example, have relied heavily on designs that make use of verbal stimuli. However, many products project important nonverbal cues that must be seen, heard, tasted, felt, or smelled to be appreciated properly. . . . Accordingly, the experiential perspective supports a more energetic investigation of multisensory psychophysical relationships in consumer behavior.

Turning one's attention from primarily verbal to nonverbal sensory cues requires a very different mode of presenting experimental stimulus objects. While verbal descriptions have often sufficed in conventional research on consumer preferences, an experiential outlook must involve subjects in consumption-like experiences based on real—or at least realistic—product samples.

Communication Content

Content analyses of communication in consumer research have more often focused on drawing inferences about the source of a message than on explaining its effects (Kassarjian 1977). When the latter perspective has been considered, it has generally involved an information processing orientation toward the study of consumer responses to the semantic aspects of communication content (Shimp and Preston 1981). Focusing on effects attributable to the syntactic aspects of message content—that is, their structure and style—is more germane to the experiential perspective.

In other disciplines, message syntax has often been found to exert a direct effect on hedonic response. This concept is central, for example, to the so-called "Wundt curve" and its relationship to collative stimulus properties such as uncertainty or complexity (Berlyne 1971). . . .

Work on syntactic structure in consumer research is less well developed. However, Taylor's (1953) "Cloze" technique has been used to measure subjective verbal uncertainty in English prose (Wallendorf, Zinkhan, and Zinkhan 1981) and advertising copy (Zinkhan and Martin 1981).

CONSUMER INPUTS

Resources
In examining the resources that a consumer brings to the exchange transaction, conventional research has generally focused on monetary income constraints and the effects of prices. In more recent economic analysis, this money-oriented focus has been expanded to acknowledge the fundamental role played by the consumer's allocation of time resources to the "household production function" (Becker 1976). In this view, households both produce and consume "commodities" that combine inputs of goods and time to maximize overall utility, subject to resource constraints.

. . .

Task Definition
In making assumptions concerning the consumer's task definition, the information processing and experiential perspectives envision different kinds of consumption behavior. The information processing view conjures up an image of the consumer as a problem solver engaged in the goal-directed activities of searching for information, retrieving memory cues, weighing evidence, and arriving at carefully considered judgmental evaluations. Freud called such mental activities "secondary process" thinking. It is "secondary" in the sense that it reflects the way our mental processes function as a result of socialization (Hilgard 1962).

By contrast, the experiential view emphasizes the importance of primary process thinking in accord with the pleasure principle. Primary process thinking involves a task definition oriented toward hedonic response and is "primary" in the sense that it hearkens back to the way a baby pursues immediate pleasure or gratification (Hilgard 1962). This type of consumption seeks fun, amusement, fantasy, arousal, sensory stimulation, and enjoyment. . . .

Regarding consumption as a primary process directed toward the hedonic pursuit of pleasure raises certain methodological issues. These include: (1) the need to develop better measures of hedonic response—especially valid and operational definitions of what constitutes "pleasure"; (2) the fact that hedonic responses are likely to be unusually susceptible to fluctuations across situations, thereby posing problems of reliability and validity; and (3) the difficulty of using available indices of chronic hedonic energy, such as sensation seeking, in the context of explaining acute, volatile, sensory-emotive phenomena. The experiential view performs a useful role by insistently calling attention to these conceptual and methodological problems.

Type of Involvement
We focus here not on the degree of involvement (low versus high), but rather on its type (engagement of cognitive responses versus orientation reaction involving arousal). Krugman's (1965) early definition of involvement emphasized the tendency to make personal connections between one's own life and the stimulus, explicitly excluding components such as attention, interest, or excitement. This early view has proven most congenial to information processing proponents, who define involvement in terms of personal relevance or multi-

plicity of cognitive responses (Leavitt, Greenwald, and Obermiller 1981). Attention, interest, excitement, and so forth bear more directly on the experiential view by emphasizing degree of activation or arousal, with consequent implications for the availability of psychobiological indices (Kroeber-Riel 1979). . . .

Further, any argument that involvement is primarily a left-brain phenomenon refers implicitly to cognitive responses associated with analytic, logical, problem-oriented cerebration (Hansen 1981). If one referred instead to "involvement" in the sense of the orientation reflex, its arousal component might be more closely associated with right-brain phenomena related to emotion.

. . .

Search Activity

The nature of the associated search activity is closely tied to involvement issues. Here, proponents of the information processing perspective adopt various strategies for the study of information acquisition. Those inclined toward laboratory methods have developed ingenious techniques to study how cues are acquired (Russo 1978). Meanwhile, survey researchers have investigated the general characteristics of information seekers at the cross-cultural level (Thorelli, Becker, and Engledow 1975).

By contrast, an experiential view of search activity might draw more heavily from the work by psychologists on exploratory behavior (Berlyne 1960). For example, Howard and Sheth (1969) consider stimulus ambiguity, working through arousal, as a determinant of specific exploration via what they call "overt search." . . .

Diversive exploration via the entertainment and arts media appears to be a context well suited to the extension of Berlyne's (1960) work on exploratory behavior. Indeed, toward the end of his career, Berlyne (1971) devoted increased attention to the experimental study of esthetics, focusing particularly on a proposed nonmonotonic relationship between stimulus complexity and hedonic value. Aspects of his approach may be usefully applied to an investigation of the consumption experience. . . .

Individual Differences

For some time, consumer researchers' interest in individual differences has focused on general customer characteristics such as demographics, socioeconomic status, and psychographics. The relatively poor performance of personality measures in predicting consumer behavior has encouraged their gradual abandonment in favor of the subcategory of psychographics known as life style variables. . . .

The investigation of experiential consumption appears to offer considerable scope for the revival of personality and allied variables, such as subculture, though the specific dimensions investigated will almost certainly differ from those of interest to the information processing view. Some experientially relevant personality constructs include:

- *Sensation seeking* (Zuckerman 1979), a variable likely to affect a consumer's tendency to enjoy more complex entertainment, to be fashion conscious, to prefer spicy and crunchy foods, to play games, and to use drugs
- *Creativity* and related variables tied to variety-, novelty-, or arousal-seeking (Raju 1980)
- *Religious world view* (Hirschman 1982), a dimension that affects daydreaming as well as other forms of sensation and pleasure seeking
- *Type A versus Type B personality* (Friedman and Rosenman 1974), a dimension closely linked with perceived pressure and therefore likely to affect the way one allocates psychotemporal expenditures among work and leisure activities

. . .

INTERVENING RESPONSE SYSTEM

Cognition

Due to its cognitively oriented perspective, the information processing approach has focused on memory and related phenomena: the consumer's cognitive apparatus is viewed as a complex knowledge structure embodying intricately interwoven subsystems of beliefs referred to as "memory schemas" or "semantic networks" (Olson 1980). Such knowledge structures include what Freudians call "manifest" content—those ideas that are accessible to introspection and therefore form the substance of conscious thought patterns.

By contrast, the experiential perspective focuses on cognitive processes that are more subconscious and private in nature. Interest centers on consumption-related flights of fancy involving pictorial imagery (Richardson 1969), fantasies (Klinger 1971), and daydreams (Singer 1966). Such material often masks embarrassing or socially sensitive ideas and perceptions. This "latent" content does not appear in overt verbal reports, either because it has been repressed or because its anxiety-provoking nature encourages disguise at a subconscious level.

. . .

Affect

It might be argued that, in the area of affect, the conventional information processing approach has been studying experiential consumption all along. After all, the traditional expectancy value models ($\Sigma E \cdot V$) conform in spirit to Bentham's felicific calculus. Fundamentally, however, the information processing perspective emphasizes only one aspect of hedonic response—namely, like or dislike of a particular brand (attitude) or its rank relative to other brands (preference). This attitudinal component represents only a tiny subset of the emotions and feelings of interest to the experiential view.

The full gamut of relevant emotions includes such diverse feelings as love, hate, fear, joy, boredom, anxiety, pride, anger, disgust, sadness, sympathy, lust, ecstasy, greed, guilt, elation, shame, and awe. This sphere of human experience has long been neglected by psychologists, who are just beginning to expand early work on arousal in order to develop systematic and coherent models of emotion (Plutchik 1980).

. . .

Behavior

At the behavioral level, traditional consumer research has focused almost exclusively on the choice process that generates purchase decisions culminating in actual buying behavior. Thus, brand purchase is typically viewed as the most important behavioral outcome of the information processing model.

A quarter of a century ago, however, Alderson (1957) drew a sharp distinction between buying and consuming. This contrast was further elaborated in Boyd and Levy's (1963) discussion of the consumption system with its emphasis on brand-usage behavior. By focusing on the configuration of activities involved in consumption, this viewpoint calls attention to the experiences with a product that one gains by actually consuming it.

. . . Given the operation of the pleasure principle in multisensory gratification, exciting fantasies, and cathected emotions, one's purchase decision is obviously only a small component in the constellation of events involved in the overall consumption experience.

In exploring the nature of that overall experience, the approach envisioned here departs from the traditional positivist focus on directly observable buying behavior and devotes increased attention to the mental events surrounding the act of consumption. The investigation of these mental events requires a willingness to deal with the purely subjective aspects of consciousness. This exploration of consumption as conscious experience must be rigorous and scientific, but the methodology should include introspective reports, rather than relying exclusively on overt behavioral measures. The necessary methodological shift thus leads toward a more phenomenological approach—i.e., "a free commentary on whatever cognitive material the subject is aware of" (Hilgard 1980).[2]

A recent state-of-the-art review of theory, method, and application in the study of conscious experience has been provided by Singer (1981/1982). Comparable approaches in conventional consumer research would include problem-solving

---

[2]The recently accumulating studies on the stream of consciousness serve also to introduce the new introspectionism. In this light, consider the avowed objective of the new journal entitled *Imagination, Cognition and Personality:* "An important purpose of this journal is to provide an inter-disciplinary forum for those interested in the scientific study of the stream of consciousness, directly relevant to theory, research, and application" (Pope and Singer 1981/1982, p. 2).

protocols, thought-generation techniques, and similar ideation-reporting procedures. It remains for the experiential perspective to extend this cognitively oriented work toward the investigation of *all* aspects of the consumption experience. In such a phenomenological approach, experience is "acknowledged as a part of the psychological universe and addressed as an object of study" (Koch 1964, p. 34):

> The phenomenologist . . . accepts, as the subject-matter of his inquiry, all data of experience . . . . Colors and sounds are data; so are impressions of distance and duration; so are feelings of attraction and repulsion; so are yearnings and fears, ecstasies and disillusionments; . . . . These are data, given in experience, to be accepted as such and wondered about (MacLeod 1964, p. 51).

MacLeod's statement comes close to encapsulating our central theme—namely, that the conventional approach to consumer research addresses only a small fraction of the phenomenological data that compose the entire experience of consumption. Investigation of the remaining components of the consumption experience should serve as one key target of future methodological developments in consumer research.

One qualitative approach, advocated by Levy, "accepts introspection as data" and involves the use of personal narratives: "A protocol in which a consumer tells the story of how the product is consumed can be examined for how the consumer interprets the consumption experience" (1981, p. 50). Such relativly unstructured procedures may be usefully complemented by more structured quantitative methods.[3] . . .

viewed in terms of the product's useful function. The criteria for evaluating the success of a purchasing decision are therefore primarily utilitarian in nature—as, when judging a "craft," one asks how well it serves its intended purpose or performs its proper function (Becker 1978). The operative logic behind this criterion reflects a work mentality in which objects attain value primarily by virtue of the economic benefits they provide.

By contrast, in the experiential view, the consequences of consumption appear in the fun that a consumer derives from a product—the enjoyment that it offers and the resulting feeling of pleasure that it evokes (Klinger 1971, p. 18). In this generally neglected perspective, the criteria for successful consumption are essentially esthetic in nature and hinge on an appreciation of the product for its own sake, apart from any utilitarian function that it may or may not perform (McGregor 1974). This is analogous to the appreciation of a work of "art" (versus a "craft") as a thing in itself, without regard to its functional utility (Becker 1978). In making such appraisals, one conforms to a play mentality (Huizinga 1970) wherein perceived benefits are primarily psychosocial and "episodes designated as playful are assumed to be free from any immediate purpose" (Lancy 1980, p. 474): "Play is disinterested, selfsufficient, an interlude from work. It brings no material gain" (Stephenson 1967, pp. 192–193).[4]

As indicated in Figure 1, the relative salience of evaluative criteria is assumed to depend in part on the individual's task definition, type of involvement, search activity, and personality. . . .

OUTPUT CONSEQUENCES, CRITERIA, AND LEARNING

Output Consequences and Criteria

From the information processing perspective, the consequences of consumer choice typically are

---

[3]Levy (1981) views his analysis as "structural." The distinction between "structured" and "unstructured" methods pursued here refers to the type of data-collection procedure.

[4]Note that, in no sense, do we imply that the esthetic criteria involved in the play mentality are irrational or maladaptive. Indeed, as Becker's (1976) work has made clear, rational economic models can be built to account for playful activities—not to mention child bearing, marriage, and other forms of behavior generally viewed as psychosocial or non-purposive in origin. We merely wish to indicate that, in our current state of knowledge, the psychodynamics of enjoyment and fun are perhaps less well understood than are the more technological and physiological relationships that underlie the conventional utilitarian approach to customer value (cf. Becker 1976, pp. 13–14.

Learning

Ever since Howard and others included a feedback loop via brand satisfaction in the early models of buyer behavior (Howard and Sheth 1969), it has been clear that learning effects exert a strong impact on future components of the intervening response system (shown by a dotted feedback line in Figure 1). The traditional view of learning in consumer behavior has been based on operant conditioning or instrumental learning, where satisfaction with the purchase serves to reinforce future behavioral responses in the form of repeat purchases.

But Howard and Sheth (1969) also recognized a second learning principle, contiguity, which depends on the frequency with which neural events have been paired in experience. The resulting patterns of association, which Osgood (1957) called "associative hierarchies," exhibit a form of respondent conditioning. When extended to the experiential perspective, this contiguity principle suggests that sensations, imagery, feelings, pleasures, and other symbolic or hedonic components which are frequently paired together in experience tend to become mutually evocative, so that "fantasy, dreams, and certain forms of play can similarly be construed as respondent sequences" (Klinger 1971, p. 35). This argument implies that—though satisfaction certainly constitutes one important experiential component—the stream of associations that occur during consumption (imagery, daydreams, emotions) may be equally important experiential aspects of consumer behavior.

CONCLUSION

Much buyer behavior can be explained usefully by the prevailing information processing perspective. Conventional research, however, has neglected an important portion of the consumption experience. Thus our understanding of leisure activities, consumer esthetics, symbolic meanings, variety seeking, hedonic response, psychotemporal resources, daydreaming, creativity, emotions, play, and artistic endeavors may benefit from a broadened view.

Abandoning the information processing approach is undesirable, but supplementing and enriching it with an admixture of the experiential perspective could be extremely fruitful. Such an expansion of consumer research will raise vital but previously neglected issues concerning (1) the role of esthetic products, (2) multisensory aspects of product enjoyment, (3) the syntactic dimensions of communication, (4) time budgeting in the pursuit of pleasure, (5) product-related fantasies and imagery, (6) feelings arising from consumption, and (7) the role of play in providing enjoyment and fun. This is the point of asking questions concerning the nature of experiential consumption—questions such as:

- "Which painting is the most beautiful?"
- "Which tastes better, chocolate or strawberry?"
- "What makes Beethoven great?"
- "How much do you watch television?"
- "What do you see when you turn out the lights?"
- "What makes you happy?"
- "How did you spend your vacation?"

In sum, the purpose of this paper has been neither to advocate a "new" theory of consumer behavior nor to reject the "old" approach, but rather to argue for an enlarged view that avoids any adherence to the "-isms" or "-ologies" that so often constrict scientific inquiry. One cannot reduce the explanation of human behavior to any narrowly circumscribed and simplistic model, whether that model be behavioristic or psychoanalytic, ethological or anthropomorphic, cognitive or motivational: the behavior of people in general and of consumers in particular is the fascinating and endlessly complex result of a multifaceted interaction between organism and environment. In this dynamic process, neither problem-directed nor experiential components can safely be ignored. By focusing single-mindedly on the consumer as information processor, recent consumer research has tended to neglect the equally important experiential aspects of consumption, thereby limiting our understanding of consumer behavior. Future research should work toward redressing this imbalance by broadening our area of study to include some consideration of consumer fantasies, feelings, and fun.

REFERENCES

Alderson, Wroe (1957), *Marketing Behavior and Executive Action,* Homewood, IL: Richard D. Irwin.

Becker, Gary S. (1976), *The Economic Approach to Human Behavior,* Chicago: University of Chicago Press.

Becker, Howard S. (1978), "Arts and Crafts," *American Journal of Sociology,* 83 (4), 862–889.

Berlyne, Daniel E. (1960), *Conflict, Arousal, and Curiosity,* New York: McGraw-Hill.

———— (1971), *Aesthetics and Psychobiology,* New York: Appleton-Century-Crofts.

Bettman, James R. (1979), *An Information Processing Theory of Consumer Choice,* Reading, MA: Addison-Wesley.

Boyd, Harper W., Jr. and Sidney J. Levy (1963), "New Dimensions in Consumer Analysis," *Harvard Business Review,* 41 (November-December), 129–140.

Friedman, Meyer and Ray H. Rosenman (1974), *Type A: Your Behavior and Your Heart,* New York: Knopf.

Hansen, Flemming (1981), "Hemispherical Lateralization: Implications for Understanding Consumer Behavior," *Journal of Consumer Research,* 8 (June), 23–36.

Hilgard, Ernest R. (1962), "Impulsive Versus Realistic Thinking: An Examination of the Distinction Between Primary and Secondary Processes in Thought," *Psychological Bulletin,* 59 (6), 477–488.

———— (1980), "Consciousness in Contemporary Psychology," *Annual Review of Psychology,* 31, 1–26.

Hirschman, Elizabeth C. (1982), "Religious Affiliation and Consumption Processes: An Initial Paradigm," forthcoming in *Research in Marketing.*

Howard, John A. and Jagdish N. Sheth (1969), *The Theory of Buyer Behavior,* New York: John Wiley.

Kassarjian, Harold H. (1977), "Content Analysis in Consumer Research," *Journal of Consumer Research,* 4 (June), 8–18.

Klinger, Eric (1971), *Structure and Functions of Fantasy,* New York: Wiley-Interscience.

Koch, Sigmund (1964), "Psychology and Emerging Conceptions of Knowledge as Unitary," in *Behaviorism and Phenomenology,* ed. T. W. Wann, Chicago: University of Chicago Press, 1–45.

Kroeber-Riel, Werner (1979), "Activation Research: Psychobiological Approaches in Consumer Research," *Journal of Consumer Research,* 5(March), 240–250.

Krugman, Herbert E. (1965), "The Impact of Television Advertising: Learning Without Involvement," *Public Opinion Quarterly,* 29(Fall), 349–356.

Lancy, David F. (1980), "Play in Species Adaptation," *Annual Review of Anthropology,* 9, 471–495.

Leavitt, Clark, Anthony G. Greenwald, and Carl Obermiller (1981), "What Is Low Involvement Low IN?" in *Advances in Consumer Research,* Vol. 8, ed. Kent B. Monroe, Ann Arbor, MI: Association for Consumer Research, 15–19.

Levy, Sidney J. (1959), "Symbols for Sale," *Harvard Business Review,* 37(July-August), 117–124.

———— (1980), "The Symbolic Analysis of Companies, Brands, and Customers," Albert Wesley Frey Lecture, Graduate School of Business, University of Pittsburgh, PA.

———— (1981), "Interpreting Consumer Mythology: A Structural Approach to Consumer Behavior," *Journal of Marketing,* 45(Summer), 49–61.

MacLeod, R. B. (1964), "Phenomenology: A Challenge to Experimental Psychology," in *Behaviorism and Phenomenology,* ed. T. W. Wann, Chicago: University of Chicago Press, 47–78.

McGregor, Robert (1974), "Art and the Aesthetic," *Journal of Aesthetics and Art Criticism,* 32(Summer), 549–559.

Olshavsky, Richard W. and Donald H. Granbois (1979), "Consumer Decision Making—Fact or Fiction?" *Journal of Consumer Research,* 6(September), 93–100.

Olson, Jerry C. (1980), "Encoding Processes: Levels of Processing and Existing Knowledge Structures," in *Advances in Consumer Research,* Vol. 7, ed. Jerry Olson, Ann Arbor, MI: Association for Consumer Research, 154–160.

Osgood, Charles E. (1957), "Motivational Dynamics of Language Behavior," in *Nebraska Symposium on Motivation,* ed. Marshall R. Jones, Lincoln: University of Nebraska Press, 348–424.

Plutchik, Robert (1980), *Emotion: A Psychoevolutionary Synthesis,* New York: Harper & Row.

Pope, Kenneth S. and Jerome L. Singer (1981/1982), "Imagination, Cognition, and Personality: Personal Experience, Scientific Research, and Clinical Application," *Imagination, Cognition and Personality,* 1(1), 1–4.

Raju, P. S. (1980), "Optimum Stimulation Level: Its Relationship to Personality, Demographics, and Exploratory Behavior," *Journal of Consumer Research,* 7(December), 272–282.

Richardson, Alan (1969), *Mental Imagery,* New York: Springer.

Russo, J. Edward (1978), "Eye Fixations Can Save the World: A Critical Evaluation and a Comparison Between Eye Fixations and Other Information Processing Methodologies," in *Advances in Consumer Research,* Vol. 5, ed. H. Keith Hunt, Ann Arbor, MI: Association for Consumer Research, 561–570.

Sheth, Jagdish N. (1979), "The Surpluses and Shortages in Consumer Behavior Theory and Research," *Journal of the Academy of Marketing Science,* 7(4), 414–427.

Shimp, Terence A. and Ivan L. Preston (1981), "Deceptive and Nondeceptive Consequences of Evaluative Advertising," *Journal of Marketing,* 45(Winter), 22–32.

Singer, Jerome L. (1966), *Daydreaming: An Introduction to the Experimental Study of Inner Experience,* New York: Random House.

——— (1981/1982), "Towards the Scientific Study of Imagination," *Imagination, Cognition and Personality,* 1(1), 5–28.

Taylor, Wilson L. (1953), "Cloze Procedure: A New Tool for Measuring Readability," *Journalism Quarterly,* 30(Fall), 415–433.

Thorelli, Hans B., Helmut Becker, and Jack Engledow (1975), *The Information Seekers,* Cambridge, MA: Ballinger.

Wallendorf, Melanie, George Zinkhan, and Lydia Zinkhan (1981), "Cognitive Complexity and Aesthetic Preference," in *Symbolic Consumer Behavior,* ed. Elizabeth C. Hirschman and Morris B. Holbrook, Ann Arbor, MI: Association for Consumer Research, 52–59.

Zinkhan, George M. and Claude R. Martin, Jr. (1981), "Two Copy Testing Techniques: The Cloze Procedure and the Cognitive Complexity Test," working paper, Graduate School of Business, University of Michigan.

Zuckerman, Marvin (1979), *Sensation Seeking: Beyond the Optimal Level of Arousal,* Hillsdale, NJ: Lawrence Erlbaum.

SECTION VII

NEEDS AND MOTIVATION IN CONSUMER BEHAVIOR

Any effort to understand consumer behavior must consider consumer needs and motivations. In many instances consumer needs and motivations are the fuel for the buying process. Needs might be thought of as discrepancies consumers experience between an actual and a desired state of being. The larger this discrepancy, the greater the likelihood of a behavior such as making a purchase to reduce or satisfy the felt need. Commonly discussed needs are needs for social contact and belonging, identity, power, satisfaction, security, sex, sleep, and stimulation. The force that leads a person to act in a particular way in response to a need is called motivation. Motivations may assume a variety of forms. They can be physiological or social, internal or external to the consumer, conscious or unconscious, and instinctual or learned.

There are several different perspectives about needs and motivations. A classical construct of needs frequently used in the consumer behavior literature is Abraham Maslow's hierarchy of needs. Maslow suggested that needs are arranged in a hierarchy. As needs lower in the hierarchy are satisfied, people shift to higher-order needs. Maslow's ordering or hierarchy is presented below:

1. Physiological needs.
2. Safety needs.
3. The need for belonging.
4. The need for esteem.
5. The need for self-actualization.

Maslow has suggested that the proportion of our needs that are unsatisfied increases as one moves from physiological needs to self-actualization needs. In a developed society consumers may thus display more motivation for satisfying needs for esteem and self-actualization. This suggests that marketplace motivations among consumers may be more sociological and psychological than physiological, and more learned than instinctual. Consumers experiencing a strong need for belonging may follow a consumption pattern that is approved of by the group or set of people they want to be accepted by. This consumption pattern may be more extravagant or lavish than is actually necessary for the consumer's physical well-being. The motivation in this case is the force that caused the consumer to satisfy the need for belonging through lavish consumption rather than through an alternative action. Needs, then, can tell us what it is that consumers are satisfying, while motivations can explain the particular way in which these needs are satisfied. For example, our extravagant consumers seeking approval could have joined a monastic order or, more plausibly, become active as volunteers in a number of charitable or community service groups.

"A MOTIVATIONAL MODEL OF INFORMATION PROCESSING INTENSITY"

In the past several years, many government regulations have been passed that require the disclosure of certain types of information to consumers. In addition, due to the ever-increasing number of new products that are introduced, commercial messages about products are so widespread as to practically bombard consumers with product information. Yet, in the face of this information explosion, it appears that consumers pay attention to and use only a very small proportion of those bits of information with which they have contact.

Information-processing models describe what people do with information once they have decided to use it. Yet these models leave open to question how the selective choices of which information to use are made. The Burnkrant article uses the concept of motivation to describe this selective processing.

As with many other behaviors, the processing of information can be seen as a motivated behavior. Consumers use information when they are motivated to do so. But what does it mean to be motivated to do something? This question is the subject of the Burnkrant article.

Burnkrant describes a general model of motivation and then shows how it can be used in the specific case of information-processing behavior. This general model states that motivation is the multiplicative product of three components: need, value, and belief. With respect to information-processing behavior, need refers to the need for information to reduce uncertainty to a desired level. The value of the information resides in its ability to meet the desired goal (e.g., reducing uncertainty). The final component is one's belief that a particular piece of information will satisfy the need.

Since consumers use so few of the bits of product information that they encounter, it can be concluded that this is due to a low motivation to process the information. But what is the source of the low motivation to process the information? It may be that different components (i.e., need, value, belief) are responsible for low usage of different types of information. Which component(s) is (are) probably responsible for low motivation to process much of the information contained in commercial messages? For the information that is required by law to be disclosed, for instance, on product packages? What could 'be done in each of these cases to bring about higher rates of usage of the information provided?

"WHY SPIRITS SALES ARE SLIPPING A BIT"

The strategic implications of changes in consumer needs and motivation for marketing management are clearly illustrated in recent marketing mix decisions in the liquor industry. The liquor industry's primary target, drinkers from 25 to 44 years of age, have shown an alarming penchant for a wider variety of beverages of all kinds, including fruit juices and bottled water, and for lighter and sweeter flavors, including cordials and brandies.

Liquor industry marketers have responded with modifications of product positioning, pricing, and promotion in order to adapt to changes in consumer needs as well as to competitive threats. The outstanding example of such successful strategic marketing is Bailey's Irish Cream, which now leads the competition in a new and expanding liqueur segment.

A MOTIVATIONAL MODEL OF INFORMATION PROCESSING INTENSITY

ROBERT E. BURNKRANT

Source: Robert E. Burnkrant, "A Motivational Model of Information Processing Intensity," *Journal of Consumer Research,* Vol. 3, June, 1976, pp. 21–30. Reprinted with permission.

Information processing theorizing has sought to specify the mechanism by which information is taken in and interpreted (e.g., Newell, Shaw, and Simon, 1958; Reitman, 1965; Norman, 1968). This work has generally assumed a level of motivation sufficient to move the person into an information processing cognitive state. As such, it appears to minimize the motivational and information selection issues in order to grapple with how and what occurs during or as a function of information processing.

The motivational model presented here treats information processing as another act of behavior and, hence, ties information processing to more general work on motivated behavior. It focuses on the issue of approach/avoidance of information and the implications of this approach/avoidance for attitude change. It seeks to account for the intensity of this cognitive behavior and specify the implications of this intensity for attitude change.

The model of information processing intensity to be presented here will be developed directly from theory and research in motivation. The following section presents aspects of this theory and research. It will provide the theoretical basis for the information processing model to be developed in the subsequent section. The final section of the paper will treat evidence supporting the information processing model and consider implications of the model for future research.

Motivation may be regarded as a complex integrative process which accounts for all those contemporaneous influences which determine the action, vigor and persistence of behavior (Atkinson, 1964).

The emergence of expectancy × value theory is perhaps best identified with the work of two researchers—Edward Tolman and Kurt Lewin. While both psychologists developed specific theories with many striking similarities, Tolman's work, following his behaviorist orientation, is more precisely and operationally defined than is Lewin's (Atkinson, 1964). We shall follow Tolman's theorizing for the basic framework of the model turning to later formulations and more recent evidence for further elaboration.

Three types of mediating variables may be identified as representing the distinguishing aspects of Tolman's theory. Tolman has identified these constructs in their general form as need, belief, and value (e.g., Tolman, 1951).[1] The level of these constructs at a point in time is said to determine the magnitude of a performance tendency which immediately precedes and is directly related to overt performance (Tolman, 1951; Atkinson, 1964). Tolman viewed the strength of the tendency to obtain a particular type of food, for example, as being directly related to performance in obtaining that type of food (i.e., the time required to reach the food in the goal box of a maze). The same principles employed to develop a tendency to obtain a particular type of food could be applied to develop a tendency to process a particular type of message. The strength of this tendency would then be directly related to the intensity of the processing engaged in with respect to that message.

Need or Motive

According to Tolman (1951), the total set of needs which, for the organism, are active at a given point in time comprise his need system. Each need within the need system is seen as a readiness to approach a class of goal objects believed to be instrumental in the satisfaction of that need and to avoid other classes of objects believed to be irrelevant or detrimental to the satisfaction of that need.[2]

Tolman operationally defined need as "the propensity of an individual to perform a characteristic type of consummatory response" (1949, p. 362). The response is defined in terms of the goal which satisfies it. To take a classic example, the need for food may be defined in terms of the propensity for eating. This observed readiness of the organism to approach and consume food objects and to avoid nonfood objects provides a basis for inferring that the organism has an aroused need for food.

[1]Tolman distinguishes between the general form of these constructs and their specific representations which he labels need-push, expectancy and valence, respectively (e.g., Tolman, 1951).

[2]The one exception to the directive nature of needs is a general need which Tolman calls the "libido need." This libido need is seen as a general multiplier of all the specific needs acting at a given point in time and is said to vary across individuals and over time within individuals (Tolman, 1951).

An activated need or motive (whether for food or for information) is said to call up a belief-value matrix within the organism (e.g., Tolman, 1951). This belief-value matrix is a representation of that part of the individual's cognitive structure which is believed to be relevant to the satisfaction of the aroused need. More specifically, the matrix is said to contain images of those objects which the individual has learned, through past experience, are relevant to his satisfaction of the aroused need.

Value

Associated with each object in the matrix is a value, "that is, goodness or badness deposited on the various cells of the matrix" (Tolman, 1951, p. 293). For instance, if a person is hungry, "given types of food are represented as having different degrees of positive values insofar as they are 'believed' to lead on successfully to hunger gratification and away from hunger deprivation" (Tolman, 1951, p. 293). Similarly, if a person has an aroused need for information, given types of informational stimuli would be "represented as having different degrees of positive values insofar as they are 'believed' to lead on successfully" to the satisfaction of the need for information.

The readiness for a specific type of object from among a class of objects is treated as a function of not only the degree of need arousal for an object of that general class but also the value of the specific type of object within that class as a satisfier of the aroused need.

Belief or Expectancy

A complete representation of a model capable of accounting for behavior requires, in addition to need and valued objects, a construct representative of the associative link between the performance of a behavior with respect to those objects and the satisfaction of the need. This link is provided by what Tolman calls "means-end beliefs" (Tolman, 1951) or "means-end readiness" (Tolman, 1932).

A means-end belief, therefore, may be said to account for the expectation that performing a particular behavior with respect to a particular object will lead to goal attainment. For instance, it may be said to account for the expectation that processing a particular informational stimulus will lead to the attainment of information relevant to that which is needed. The strength of this belief may be operationalized in terms of the probability that an individual would assign to the occurrence of the association (Tolman, 1959; Hilgard and Bower, 1966).

MOTIVATION TO PROCESS INFORMATION

As a general theory of motivation, the previously discussed framework is applicable to the determination of the tendency to perform any specific behavior. Since cognitively processing information may be viewed as a behavior, the strength of the tendency to perform this behavior should be determinable through the appropriate application of this model.

Need for Information

The strength of the tendency to process information may be viewed, therefore, as being determined by three constructs. The first construct to be considered is the relevant need confronting the individual and directing his behavior. In order to determine the appropriate need, it is necessary to infer the goal toward which the behavior is being directed (Tolman, 1951; MacCorquodale and Meehl, 1954; Schroder, Driver, and Streufert, 1967). The goal toward which the organism strives on a particular occasion may be inferred from an assessment of the organism's behavior on that occasion.

All behavior directed at seeking out and processing information seems to have one characteristic in common: that the acquisition and processing of the information leads to a change in uncertainty. Furthermore, it appears that after some amount of uncertainty change takes place, the individual ceases to perform behavior directed at further changing his uncertainty (e.g., Berlyne, 1960; Berlyne, 1965).

We may postulate that an individual processes information to satisfy a need for uncertainty change. The need for uncertainty change may be viewed as a psychological state of readiness for informational stimuli or a class of informational stimuli. It may be more concise, however, to refer to the need simply as the need for information.

Expectancy

The remaining constructs comprising the tendency to process a particular stimulus display are specifiable in terms of the goal identified as motivating the organism. As noted earlier, the construct expectancy accounts for the cognitive association between the performance of a particular response (i.e., processing a particular message) and the expected consequence in terms of goal attainment. Its strength is accounted for in terms of likelihood or probability. Therefore, the expectancy appropriate to the tendency to process a particular message is the cognitive association between processing that particular message and the attainment of information relevant to that which is needed. If the association is perceived as being very likely or very probable, the expectancy would be considered to be strong.

Value

The value construct represents the object-specific (message-specific) aspect of incentive to act. As such, it is meant to account for the value of the particular message as a source of information relevant to that which is needed. It is measured in terms of the goodness or badness of the given message as a source of the type of information needed. If the message is perceived as being a very good source of the type of information needed, its value would be considered to be very high.

Model of Information Processing

It is suggested here that the need for information combines multiplicatively with the appropriate expectancy and value to yield a tendency to process a particular message. The proposed motivational model of information processing, therefore, may be represented as follows:

$$M \times E \times V = B_{TP} \cong B_p$$

where:

1. M is the need for information on some topic.

2. E is the expectancy that processing a particular stimulus display will lead to exposure to information relevant to M.
3. V is the value of the particular stimulus display as a source of information relevant to M.
4. B_{TP} is the behavioral tendency to process the stimulus display.
5. B_p is the processing behavior.

TESTABLE IMPLICATIONS OF THE MODEL

The tendency to process a message should be directly related to the intensity of the processing behavior engaged in with respect to that message.

An increase in any one or more of the constructs making up the tendency to process a message, leaving all else constant, will produce an increase in the tendency to process that message. Therefore, one may infer a manipulation of the tendency to process a message from evidence supporting the manipulation of the constructs which comprise this tendency. The attainment of a direct relationship between each of the constructs which comprise the tendency and belief change would provide support for the contention that message processing intensity is a determinant of belief change.

The functional form by which motive, expectancy and value combine to yield a tendency to process the message was specified as being multiplicative. Therefore, the manipulation in a factorial design of the constructs comprising the tendency to process the message and the subsequent measurement of belief change would be expected to yield significantly positive two- and three-way interaction effects. These effects should be concentrated in the bilinear and trilinear components of the model, respectively (Anderson, 1970; Shanteau and Anderson, 1972). That is, only the bilinear and trilinear components of the interactions should be significant, all residual interaction effects should be nonsignificant.

Empirical research could be designed to test the separate and interactive effects of the constructs represented in the model. The research would employ a message which is logically believable and of sufficient duration to permit variation in comprehension. The attainment of the effects suggested here would provide support for the proposed model as a determinant of belief change.

SUPPORT FOR THE MODEL

Prior and Indirect Evidence

We shall turn now to a consideration of research, which although directed at other issues, may be interpreted as providing findings consistent with the proposed tendency to process information as a determinant of information processing intensity and belief change.

Perhaps the clearest indicant of the tendency to process a message (at least insofar as it relates to message exposure) is provided by research on selective exposure to information. The research paradigm typically employed in this area manipulates both subjects' commitment to a course of action and the usefulness of information on some topic (e.g., Canon, 1964; Freedman, 1965; Lowe and Steiner, 1968; Brock, Albert, and Becker, 1970). Subjects are then either given the opportunity to process or state their desire for a number of alternative messages (or message titles). The messages generally vary in terms of their supportiveness and in terms of their information providing (or uncertainty resolving) qualities. The typical finding is that messages likely to provide information beneficial in coping with an impending task or lending greater clarity to an uncertain situation are preferred to those which are unlikely to provide such information. This preference for the former type of message is frequently obtained even when it deviates from the subject's own past behavior.

Sears and Freedman (1965) exposed subjects to summaries of a trial and then presented to one group a message which they identified as providing new information. They presented to a second group a message which they identified as providing old information. In fact, both groups were presented with the same message. They found that more opinion change occurred in the group which was told they would be exposed to new information than occurred in the group told they would be exposed to old information ($p < 0.05$). This greater effectiveness of expected new information held regardless of whether it was consonant or dissonant with the subjects' initial votes. It occurred even though the groups did not differ significantly with regard to their elapsed reading time. The finding is particularly germane to the position taken here that, given the need for information, the expected value of the message should determine not only the message to which a subject will attend but also the amount of opinion change resulting from exposure to that message.

It has been suggested in reviews of the selective exposure literature that the message will be preferred which is perceived as having most utility (e.g., Sears and Freedman, 1967; McGuire, 1968; Sears, 1968). However, treatments employed in this research suggest the operation of a more complex motivational construct (such as the tendency to process the message) as a mediator of exposure and subsequent belief change. Utility in this context seems to include a manipulated state of need for information as well as learned associations with and evaluations of the alternative message types available. If an individual is about to refute the arguments of the opposition on some issue (e.g., Canon, 1964; Freedman, 1965), he would be likely to have an aroused need for information on that topic. Similarly, messages which are believed to provide new information would be likely to be more highly valued than messages believed to provide old information. These factors should lead to more intense information processing and, given logically believable messages, greater belief change.

CONCLUSION

The model presented here represents an attempt to conceptualize the determinants of information-processing intensity in terms of more basic motivational theory. The substantiation of the link between message processing and theories of behavior should enhance the present understanding of the communication process by providing a theoretical framework within which message processing intensity and belief change may be jointly accounted for.

If its role as a mediator of belief change is verified, this theoretical model has the potential of pulling together and making more meaningful many of the seemingly discrepant and isolated findings in the communications literature.

If research supports the validity of the model, its use by practitioners offers the potential of improving the effectiveness of their communication efforts. This may be accomplished by directing attention toward the variables which the model suggests are determinants of processing intensity and belief change. For instance, it follows from the motivational model that communications will be most effective if they reach the target audience when the audience's *need* for that type of information is aroused. Hence, programs may be inaugurated with the objective of enhancing the level of this arousal, for example, by making the recipient's lack of information about a decision more salient. Greater effort could also be made to reach the intended audience at the time when they would most likely be in this aroused state (i.e., when in the process of making the decision).

REFERENCES

Anderson, Norman H. (1970), "Functional Measurement and Psychophysical Judgment," *Psychological Review*, 77, 153–70.

Atkinson, J. W. (1964), *An Introduction to Motivation*, New York: Van Nostrand Reinhold.

Berlyne, D. E. (1960), *Conflict, Arousal and Curiosity*, New York: McGraw-Hill.

Berlyne, D. E. (1965), *Structure and Direction in Thinking*, New York: John Wiley and Sons.

Bolles, R. C. (1972), "Reinforcement, Expectancy and Learning," *Psychological Review*, 79, 394–409.

Brock, R. C.; Albert, S. M.; and Becker, L. A. (1970), "Familiarity, Utility and Supportiveness as Determinants of Information Receptivity," *Journal of Personality and Social Psychology*, 14, 292–301.

Canon, L. R. (1964), "Self-Confidence and Selective Exposure to Information," in *Conflict, Decision and Dissonance*, L. Festinger, ed., Stanford, Calif.: Stanford University Press.

Freedman, J. L. (1965), "Confidence, Utility, and Selective Exposure: A Partial Replication," *Journal of Personality and Social Psychology,* 2, 778–80.

Hilgard, E. R., and Bower, G. H. (1966), *Theories of Learning,* (3rd ed.) New York: Appleton-Century-Crofts.

Lowe, R. H., and Steiner, I. D. (1968), "Some Effects of Reversibility and Consequences of Decisions on Post-Decision Information Preferences," *Journal of Personality and Social Psychology,* 8, 172–79.

MacCorquodale, K., and Meehl, P. E. (1954), "Edward C. Tolman," in W. K. Estes, L. Koch, L. MacCorquodale, P. E. Meehl, C. G. Mueller, R., W. N. Schoenfeld, and W. S. Verplanck, eds., *Modern Learning Theory,* New York: Appleton-Century-Crofts.

McGuire, W. J. (1968), "Selective Exposure: A Summing UP," in R. P. Abelson, E. Aronson, W. J. McGuire, T. N. Newcomb, M. J. Rosenberg, and P. H. Tannenbaum, eds., *Theories of Cognitive Consistency: A Sourcebook,* Chicago: Rand McNally.

Newell, A., Shaw, J. C., and Simon, H. A. (1958), "Elements of a Theory of Human Problem-Solving," *Psychological Review,* 65, 151–66.

Norman, D. A. (1968), "Toward a Theory of Memory and Attention," *Psychological Review,* 75, 522–36.

Reitman, W. R. (1965), *Cognition and Thought,* New York: John Wiley and Sons.

Schroder, H. M., Driver, M. J., and Streufert, S., (1967), *Human Information Processing,* New York: Holt, Rinehart and Winston.

Sears, D. O. (1968), "The Paradox of DeFacto Selective Exposure Without Preferences for Supportive Information," in R. P. Abelson, E. Aronson, W. J. McGuire, T. N. Newcomb, M. J. Rosenberg, and P. H. Tannenbaum, eds., *Theories of Cognitive Consistency: A Sourcebook,* Chicago: Rand McNally.

Sears, D. O., and Freedman, J. L. (1965), "Effects of Expected Familiarity with Arguments Upon Opinion Change and Selective Exposure," *Journal of Personality and Social Psychology,* 2, 420–26.

Sears, D. O., and Freedman, J. L. (1967), "Selective Exposure to Information: A Critical Review," *Public Opinion Quarterly,* 31, 194–213.

Shanteau, J., and Anderson, N. H. (1972), "Integration Theory Applied to Judgments of the Value of Information," *Journal of Experimental Psychology,* 92, 266–75.

Tolman, E. C. (1932), *Purposive Behavior in Animals and Man,* New York: Century.

Tolman, E. C. (1949), "The Nature and Functioning of Wants, *Psychological Review,* 56, 357–69.

Tolman, E. C. (1951), "A Psychological Model," in T. Parsons and E. A. Shils, eds., *Toward a General Theory of Action,* Cambridge, Mass.: Harvard University Press.

Tolman, E. C. (1959), "Principles of Purposive Behavior," in S. Koch, ed., *Psychology: A Study of Science,* New York: McGraw-Hill.

WHY SPIRITS SALES ARE SLIPPING A BIT

During 1981, liquor sales posted their first decline since 1957, as consumption of distilled spirits in the U.S. slipped 0.13%. This dip, following 1980's slight 1% uptick, reinforces liquor's image as a slow-growth business and has liquor executives scrambling to grab larger shares of their market. "There is a very hostile environment out there," observes John Powers, senior vice-president for alcoholic beverages at Heublein, Inc. "The consumer's disposable income is squeezed, making him more value conscious." Adds Alvin Ferro, president of Paddington Corp., which markets J&B Scotch: "Every beverage marketer is competing for gullets today. And wine and Perrier are formidable competitors. If someone orders a $2.50 Perrier with lunch, it's not likely he'll follow it with a $5 Scotch drink."

Indeed, *Business Week's* annual scoreboard of brands retailing more than 500,000 cases reveals an industry caught by indecision. Liquor executives seem unable to entice, or even hang on to, their prime customers: drinkers aged 25 to 44, who are fickle consumers. Not only is this group choosing a wider array of drinks, running the gamut of wine, juices, beer, soft drinks, and bottled water, but it also is constantly sampling new items that are light and sweet or possess a cachet, such as cordials and brandy.

Bourbon's decline. Glummest of all are marketers in the brown-goods sector, particularly those in bourbon and blends, whose share is steadily dropping. Scotch marketers managed to arrest that category's decline last year through copious production and advertising efforts. But Canadian products, which previously had seen increased sales, thanks to a perceived "lighter" taste than U.S. whiskey, showed a slight decrease.

While the total nonwhiskey area strengthened its grip on the market to a 52.1% share, vodka's momentum, beginning to slow last year, appears to have run out of steam. The consumer shift to rum, a flavorful but still mixable drink, has accelerated. Bacardi Corp. easily held on to its crown as the top-selling brand, and the company has buttressed its hold on the rum category by positioning its Castillo brand as a lower-priced alternative to the leader. Castillo posted a 23% gain.

The consumer inclination to shun products in the midprice range is forcing marketers to reappraise their product positioning. "I would hate to be a middle brand," comments Ferro. "As long as you're cheapest or the best, you have a reason for being." Taking his own advice, Ferro says he is trying to lift J&B out of the lagging category with a new $15 million image-building ad campaign "and make it *sui generis*."

Import magic. In fact, some of the best performers this year were brands that exploited the market's price polarization. Walter M. Haimann, president of Seagram Distillers, credits Crown Royal's steady increase to glossy packaging and advertising that omits the word Canadian and simply says import—a word that has worked its magic for several other premium brands, also.

Generally, liquor marketers are breaking little new ground in their struggle to vitalize a stagnant market. Ad budgets for premium products are being fattened; efforts to reposition slipping franchises are keeping Madison Avenue busy; couponing and contexts are emerging as prime sales tools, and the shelf space battle intensifies.

Buckingham Corp., which raised its marketing budget 50% to $15 million in 1981 to launch a new campaign for its faltering Cutty Sark brand, has seen some encouraging results. The flagship brand, which recorded a 12.7% loss in 1980, recouped enough to register a 2.4% gain last year. Still, says Brian W. Dunn, senior vice-president for marketing, "We're cutting up a shrinking pie. The category will continue to decline, and competition will only intensify." To keep its progress smooth, Buckingham will increase its budget to $18 million this year, and where legal, undertake a large-scale couponing effort.

Pricing has become a touchy issue. In a slow-growth market, all companies aim to wring the most profit possible out of their brands to make up for lagging volume. But tampering can backfire. For instance, 18 months ago, Heublein raised the tag on Smirnoff vodka 4.7% and saw the brand tumble. "It was like the sinking of the Maine," says Powers. "We're correcting that mistake."

While most liquor marketers merely bemoan the market's lethargy, a few are sensing new opportunities. The public's adventurous appetite for more varied drinks has propelled brandies, cognacs, and specialties to new popularity. Super-premium brandies rose a dramatic 17% last year but were bested by E & J Gallo, which scored a smashing 60% gain for its low-priced product and landed in the sales derby for the first time. Gallo's success "cut into everyone else's share of the domestic market," says Melvin Chernev, president of Fromm & Sichel Inc., which distributes Christian Bros. brandy. Gallo, he says, "merchandises brandy as if it were wine."

However, the most astonishing results in 1981 can be credited to Bailey's Irish Cream, a liqueur that in two years has spawned numerous imitators and launched a new product category. Bailey's, a 34-proof whiskey base drink blended with fresh cream, was developed in Ireland by Gilbey's, a

How U.S. drinkers' tastes changed in a decade

Category	1981*	1980	1971
	Percent		
Bourbon	13.5%	13.9%	21.7%
Scotch	12.9	12.9	13.6
Canadian	12.4	12.5	9.5
Blends	8.8	8.9	18.5
Other	0.3	0.3	0.3
Total whiskey	**47.9%**	**48.5%**	**63.6%**
Vodka	19.1	19.0	13.3
Gin	9.6	9.5	9.8
Cordials	7.9	7.8	4.9
Rum	7.6	7.1	3.2
Brandy	4.2	4.1	3.7
Other	3.7	4.0	1.5
Total nonwhiskey	**52.1%**	**51.5%**	**36.4%**
Total consumption (millions of gal.)	**448.8**	**449.4**	**382.5**

*Estimated
Data: Clark Gavin Associates Inc.

How the leading liquor brands fared in 1981

Rank	Brand	Sales (thousands of cases) 1981	1980	Percent change	Marketer	Type
1	Bacardi	7,750	7,600	2.0%	Bacardi	Rum
2	Smirnoff	6,000	6,100	−1.5	Heublein	Vodka
3	Seagram's 7 Crown	5,675	5,800	−2.2	Seagram	Blend
4	Seagram's V.O.	3,675	3,800	−3.6	Seagram	Canadian
5	Canadian Club	3,450	3,600	−3.8	Walker	Canadian
6	Jack Daniel's	3,250	2,800*	16.7	Brown-Forman	Tennessee
7	Jim Beam	3,075	2,950	4.0	Beam	Bourbon
8	Canadian Mist	2,850	2,650*	7.8	Brown-Forman	Canadian
9	Popov	2,775	3,000	−7.6	Heublein	Vodka
10	Seagram's Gin	2,700	2,500	8.0	Seagram	Gin
11	Gordon's Gin	2,550	2,600	−2.3	Renfield	Gin
12	Dewars	2,400	2,350	2.2	Schenley	Scotch
12	Windsor Supreme	2,400	2,400	—	National	Canadian
14	J&B	2,175	2,325	−6.5	Paddington	Scotch
15	Gilbey's Gin	2,100	2,100	—	National	Gin
16	Gordon's Vodka	1,900	1,850	2.6	Renfield	Vodka
16	Black Velvet	1,900	1,875	1.8	Heublein	Canadian
18	Cutty Sark	1,775	1,725	2.4	Buckingham	Scotch
19	Christian Bros.	1,700	1,625	5.0	Fromm & Sichel	Brandy
20	Kamchatka	1,650	1,650	—	National	Vodka
21	Early Times	1,600	1,650*	−3.7	Brown-Forman	Bourbon
22	Johnnie Walker Red	1,575	1,550	1.7	Somerset	Scotch
23	Beefeater	1,550	1,600	−3.1	Kobrand	Gin
24	Kahlua	1,500	1,400	7.1	Walker	Specialty
25	Kessler	1,450	1,500	−3.2	Seagram	Blend
26	Ancient Age	1,425	1,575	−9.5	Schenley	Bourbon
27	Gilbey's Vodka	1,375	1,350	1.9	National	Vodka
27	Ten High	1,375	1,525	−9.4	Walker	Bourbon
29	Calvert Extra	1,225	1,300	−6.2	Seagram	Blend
30	Fleischmann's Gin	1,200	1,225	−2.8	Fleischmann	Gin
31	Southern Comfort	1,150	1,175*	−2.9	Brown-Forman	Specialty
31	Wolfschmidt	1,025	975	6.0	Seagram	Vodka
31	Chivas Regal	1,025	1,050	−2.3	Seagram	Scotch
31	Lord Calvert Canadian	1,025	1,050	−2.3	Seagram	Canadian
35	Crown Royal	900	775	15.0	Seagram	Canadian
35	Old Grand-Dad	900	950	−6.3	National	Bourbon
37	Imperial	875	1,000	−12.8	Walker	Blend
38	Castillo	850	700	23.0	Bacardi	Rum
38	Tanqueray	850	825	2.4	Somerset	Gin
38	Fleischmann's Pref.	850	950	−11.0	Fleischmann	Blend
41	Old Smuggler	800	650	23.1	Walker	Scotch
41	Old Crow	800	875	−7.6	National	Bourbon
43	Skol	775	575	33.0	Medley	Vodka
43	Jose Cuervo	775	700	11.2	Heublein	Tequila
43	MacNaughton's	775	800	−4.4	Schenley	Canadian
46	E&J	750	475	60.0	Gallo	Brandy
46	Ronrico	750	775	−4.2	Seagram	Rum
46	Old Charter	750	800	−5.2	Schenley	Bourbon
49	Schenley's Vodka	725	825	−11.2	Schenley	Vodka
50	Crown Russe	700	700	—	Seagram	Vodka
50	Amaretto Di Saronno	700	725	−3.2	Glenmore	Specialty
52	Canadian Ltd.	675	600	12.9	Fleischmann	Canadian
52	Fleischmann's Vodka	675	675	—	Fleischmann	Vodka
54	Relska	625	675	−6.7	Heublein	Vodka
55	Johnnie Walker Black	600	575	5.0	Somerset	Scotch
56	Passport	575	525	10.5	Seagram	Scotch
56	Old Forester	575	650*	−12.3	Brown-Forman	Bourbon
58	Wild Turkey	550	500	9.5	Austin, Nichols	Bourbon
58	Nikolai	550	575	−4.4	Seagram	Vodka
60	Bailey's	525	225	132.0	Paddington	Specialty
60	Hennessy	525	425	23.5	Schieffelin	Cognac
60	Inver House	525	550	−3.8	Wile	Scotch
63	Barton's	500	325	53.0	Barton	Vodka
63	Evan Williams	500	425	17.6	Heaven Hill	Bourbon
63	Old Taylor	500	550	−9.1	National	Bourbon
63	Mr. Boston Vodka	500	550	−10.0	Glenmore	Vodka
63	Hiram Walker Vodka	500	575	−13.0	Walker	Vodka

*Revised figure

Data: BW survey and estimates of retail sales, rounded to nearest 25,000 mixed cases, based on data by Clark Gavin Associates Inc.

subsidiary of International Distillers & Vintners, and imported into the U.S. in 1979.

A tenfold leap.   From selling 50,000 cases the first year, Bailey's sold 525,000 cases in 1981. "We've got a tiger by the tail," exults Paddington's Ferro, its U.S. distributor. "We just don't know how high up is. We've only hit about a third of the drinking public." To satisfy demand, production facilities in Ireland are being boosted from a 2.5 million-case capacity to 8.5 million cases by 1983.

Ferro predicts sales of "nearly a million cases this year." To ensure that it is not a pie-in-the-sky target, Paddington will put $8 million behind the brand, which it claims appeals to all consumer segments—provided they are well-heeled. Bailey's is an expensive product, retailing anywhere from $12 to $17 a bottle. "At that price, it's hardly a fad," says Ferro, disputing one criticism of the drink. To further enhance its upscale image and home in on the gift-giving market, Bailey's is packaged in a fancy gold foil box year-round, and its ample ad dollars are spent in magazines that deliver a high-income public. Paddington positions Bailey's as a stand-alone drink, a mixer, or a cooking aid. The consumer seems to be finding a lot of uses for the product: Research indicates the bottle is finished within 48 hours of its opening.

'Riding a wave.'   This sort of popularity has hardly gone unnoticed. There are now about 19 similar products trying to exploit the cream market. Most observers expect a shake-out to occur in the next two to three years. "Because of need and greed, everybody felt they had to be in this category," says Marvin Shanken, the publisher of several wine and spirits newsletters. "But they're riding a wave created by Bailey's, and when it recedes, there will probably just be three left."

At the moment, there are several brands in contention for the place and show spots behind Bailey's. These include Renfield Importers' Carolans, which quickly followed Bailey's into the market; Fleishmann's Dunphy's, a made-in-the-U.S. product; W. A. Taylor's Venetian Creme, which uses Italian brandy as its base; "21" Brand's Emmett's, which is pursuing a low-price strategy; and Waterford Cream, from Buckingham, which is spending $2 million tying its image to that of the famed Irish crystal manufacturer.

Observers believe Emmett's has the inside track to emerge a strong No. 2 because of its strategy to deliver taste parity at a lower cost. "We had to come up with a brand that would move the consumer and the retailer," says Kenneth W. Bray, marketing director at "21" Brands Inc., "so we priced it $4 to $5 less a bottle than Bailey's."

As the U.S. consumer's palate becomes more quixotic, all sorts of products are likely to prosper. Industry-watcher Shanken believes that it is the smaller, specialized beverages that will flourish. "Items like single-malt Scotches, imported vodkas, and cordials and liqueurs will grow 10% to 20% a year, while the mass market languishes," he predicts. "The game now is the consumer's desire to discover new tastes—everybody's looking for brands they can associate with themselves, rather than those that have mass appeal."

SECTION VIII

PERSONALITY AND CONSUMER BEHAVIOR

Personality is not only something that we often speak of in our everyday lives, but it is also a topic of interest to consumer researchers. Many researchers have tried to determine the relationship between a consumer's personality and that person's consumer behavior. That is, since personality reflects consistent responses to the world, it was believed that personality traits could account for consistent consumer behaviors across product types. For example, if a person is extremely concerned about other people's reactions to what he or she does, then we could hypothesize that the person would actively seek the advice of others before purchasing new items and would respond favorably to advertising appeals based on social approval.

Researchers have tried to discover if in fact people purchase items that reflect their personalities and consider these purchases in ways consistent with their personalities. However, we could also make a case for the possibility that consumers may purchase items that reflect their *desired* personalities rather than their actual personalities. Or, people may purchase certain items that serve as stimuli for developing a personality that is consistent with the item. Thus, a very daring and popular young man may purchase a sports car. This would fit his personality. On the other hand, a rather shy, quiet young man may purchase the same type of car with the hope that others will think of him as more daring and popular.

What is the relationship between consumer behavior and personality? This question is addressed in the three articles in this section.

"PERSONALITY AND CONSUMER BEHAVIOR: ONE MORE TIME"

There are so many studies of the relationship between personality and consumer behavior that it is almost unthinkable to try to count them all. Even more difficult would be an attempt to review the findings of even a substantial portion of these studies. Yet this is exactly what is done in the following article. In spite of the cumbersome nature of the task, this article does an excellent job of reviewing extant studies by placing similar work together into categories that describe different approaches.

The article reviews almost 80 studies of the relationship between various personality concepts and consumer behavior. Readers can easily become swamped if they try to remember the results of each of these studies. Instead, the point of the article is to give a general idea of the strength of personality as a predictor of consumer behavior.

Actually this article, as indicated by its title, is one of two articles written by Kassarjian on the topic of the effect of personality on consumer behavior. The first article, written by Kassarjian, was published in 1971; the second article, which appears here, written by Kassarjian and Sheffet, was published in 1975.

The first article states that the results of the 100 studies reviewed in the article are "equivocal." That is, some studies find a relationship between some personality concepts and some behaviors of consumers, whereas other studies find no relationship between the two. The problem is that no one seems to know why these differing results were obtained. In the first article, Kassarjian discusses *why* the results are equivocal. Kassarjian states that it should almost be expected, given the nature of the studies, that results would often seem inconsistent with each other. Concerns are raised about the frequency with which psychological testing forms are altered by consumer researchers, the lack of tests specifically designed for consumer rather than clinical or medical settings, and the lack of guiding hypotheses or theories.

The second article was written about five years later and reviews developments since the publication of the first article. This article is reprinted here. Again, many studies are reviewed. Sadly, there is almost no change in the way in which most of these studies were conducted. They are laden with many of the problems described in the first article. As is evident from the article, there is substantial contribution to the breadth of knowledge since so many studies were published, but they produced no change in the depth of knowledge about the relationship between personality and consumer behavior. Kassarjian and Sheffet offer several suggestions about how to improve the quality of personality research done with regard to consumer behavior.

Probably the most useful way to read this article is to take notes while reading. We suggest using list form with three major headings:

1. Approaches to the study of personality in consumer behavior.
2. Why results are equivocal (i.e., problems with extant research).
3. Suggestions for improving personality research in consumer behavior.

Using these headings will help the reader focus on the broader issues and not become swamped with the results and findings of the many studies of the relationship between personality and consumer behavior.

"OPTIMUM STIMULATION LEVEL: ITS RELATIONSHIP TO PERSONALITY, DEMOGRAPHICS, AND EXPLORATORY BEHAVIOR"

A personality characteristic that has gained increasing attention among consumer researchers is optimum stimulation level. According to the theory, every individual strives to maintain an optimum level of arousal. If arousal level falls below the optimum threshold, the individual becomes bored and seeks stimulation. Above the optimum level the individual experiences anxiety and tries to reduce stimulation. Although OSL was originally conceived as a characteristic dependent on situational arousal conditions, it now appears that an arousal seeking tendency may be a more general personality characteristic operating at a relatively stable level within individuals.

Raju's paper suggests that optimum level of arousal (or the arousal seeking tendency) has a positive relationship with selected personality traits, demographic variables, and general exploratory tendencies. Consistent with his hypotheses Raju finds that individuals who sought arousal experiences were also (1) able to tolerate ambiguous situations, (2) not rigid, (3) young, (4) higher in income and education, (5) prone to take higher risks, (6) eager to buy or know about new products or services, (7) likely to shop around, (8) likely to switch brands, and (9) likely to be communicative to friends about purchases. Raju's results suggest some general differences between high OSL and low OSL individuals on their consumer activities. The two groups may look for very different things in products, show different interest in exploring the market and learning about new products in general, and differ in their brand loyalty tendencies. Underlying these behaviors are individual differences in exploratory behavior, risk taking, and curiosity.

Note that the Arousal Seeking Tendency Scale is highly reliable, in contrast to other personality inventories. Also note that the results tend to be quite strong and generalizable, although they refer to self-reported assessments rather than to overt behaviors. The reader may want to try to identify some of the marketing implications of high and low OSL other than those presented by Raju. In addition, it is possible to evaluate this theory based on the criticisms made in the Kassarjian article.

"IDENTIFYING THE ENVIRONMENTALLY RESPONSIBLE CONSUMER: THE ROLE OF INTERNAL-EXTERNAL CONTROL OF REINFORCEMENTS"

Another personality characteristic of interest is Rotter's external control dimension. According to Rotter, individuals high on internal control believe that their actions determine their fate. In other words, they see themselves as controlling whether they will succeed or fail in a given situation. At the opposite extreme are those individuals high on external control. Central in their belief structure is the idea that future rewards or punishments come from some source outside the self (an external agent or chance).

In his article Tucker hypothesizes that some relationship exists between locus of control and a consumer's environmental responsibility. Namely, those high on internal control should have actions that demonstrate their environmental awareness; they believe their actions will make a difference. On the other hand, those high on external control should feel overwhelmed at the monumental task of cleaning the environment—feel it is out of their control—and thus show no effort at being environmentally conscious.

Tucker employs an interesting seminaturalistic study to test these hypotheses. Housewives shopping at a local shopping center were given the choice of Pepsi from either bottles or cans. They were also allowed to choose a free box of detergent. Environmentally aware consumers should choose soda from bottles and detergent with low phosphate content. Besides these behavioral measures of environmental awareness, attitudinal assessments of the central construct were also gathered.

As predicted, environmentally aware individuals were high on internal locus of control. They also tended to have higher scores on a measure of social responsibility and social class. Furthermore, locus of control most clearly differentiated the environmentally aware from those less environmentally aware in a discriminant analysis. One of the important aspects of Tucker's study is the use of both behavioral and attitudinal variables to assess environmental awareness. Second, the study was conducted in a seminaturalistic setting—a shopping center.

Environmental concern has recently been linked with the consumer movement. To better understand the variables involved in consumer activism, marketers may do well to profile the environmentally aware consumer. To the extent that marketing efforts utilized show consumers' power in influencing environmental awareness, these findings offer great value. Furthermore, marketers may appeal to environmentally conscious individuals by demonstrating how their product can enhance (or at least not deteriorate) environmental conditions.

PERSONALITY AND CONSUMER BEHAVIOR: ONE MORE TIME

**HAROLD H. KASSARJIAN
AND
MARY JANE SHEFFET**

Source: Harold H. Kassarjian and Mary Jane Sheffet, "Personality and Consumer Behavior: One More Time," *AMA 1975 Combined Proceedings,* Series No. 37, pp. 197–201. Reprinted with permission.

By late 1969 some one hundred studies were available in the marketing literature relating personality variables to consumer behavior. A review of these studies (Jacoby, 1971; Kassarjian, 1971; and Wells and Beard, 1973) can be summarized by the single word, "equivocal." The purpose of this paper is to enumerate what has happened to the field in the ensuing half decade. The previous quarter century had produced some one hundred studies. The outpouring of recent research has accumulated an additional one hundred studies in the last five years, not including working papers, privately distributed pre-prints and unpublished proprietary studies.

No major obvious changes have been discernible although some new fads in researchable variables have emerged. For example, one no longer finds the topic of motivation research from a psychoanalytic point of view in the literature. The only true attempt to use a projective technique to be found in the published literature is a replication of the classic Mason Haire Shopping List study by Webster and Von Pechman (1970) which interestingly, yielded significantly different results from the original paper. Instant coffee users are no longer perceived as psychologically different from drip grind users.

The use of the traditionally available paper and pencil psychological inventories is still quite popular. Donnelly and Ivancevich (1974) in turn found a weak but positive relationship between inner other-direction and innovator characteristics. Perry (1973) tied in anxiety, the Eysenck variables, and heredity to product choice concluding that consumption was genetically influenced. He claimed that this genetic relationship has application to primary demand but not product choice.

Rokeach's dogmatism as a variable appeared in some half a dozen studies (Anderson and Cunningham, 1972; Blake, Perloff, and Zenhausern, 1973; Darden and Reynolds, 1972; Joyce, 1972; Michman, 1971; and Peters and Ford, 1972) correlating the variable to risk, innovation and adoption, generally with weak but significant results. Open-mindedness seems to be positively related to risk taking and willingness to innovate.

Several new instruments appeared for the first time in consumer type studies. Morris and Cundiff

(1971) and Vavra and Winn (1971) turned their attention to anxiety and the Taylor Manifest Anxiety Scale, and Hawkins (1972) used the State-Trait Anxiety Inventory. The mixed results generally indicate that low anxiety is related to acceptance of more threatening material such as males' acceptance of feminine products. Peters and Ford (1972) used the California Test of Personality and could find no personality difference between women who buy and do not buy from door-to-door salesmen.

The most widely used instrument new to consumer behavior is the Jackson Personality Research Form. Wilson, et al., (1971) correlated these scores with segmentation variables, Fry (1971) and Ahmed (1972) with cigarette smoking, Kinnear and Taylor (1972; 1974) with ecological products, Worthing, et al., (1973) with a variety of consumer products, and Matthews, et al., (1971) with perceived risk.

Self-confidence had been heavily examined prior to 1969. Its fascination to researchers has not diminished. Studies by Bither and Wright (1973), Barach (1969; 1972) and Ostlund (1969; 1971; 1972) have since appeared. Work in self-concept continues to appear in some eleven studies (American Market Research Bureau, 1972; Dolich and Shilling, 1971; French and Flaschner, 1971; Green, Maheshwari and Rao, 1969; Grubb and Stern, 1971; Hughes and Guerrero, 1971; Joyce, 1972; Landon, 1974; Martin, 1973; Mason and Mayer, 1970; and Ross, 1971) in the struggle to explain purchase behavior by measuring the ideal self and actual self concept.

Perhaps the most dramatic change in the field has been the influence of studies using life style, AIO, or psychographics as they are alternatively termed. These factor analyzed scales have been applied to media exposure (King and Tigert, 1971; and Michaels, 1972), credit card usage (Plummer, 1971b), advertising (Plummer, 1971a), creativity (Winter and Russell, 1973), opinion leadership and innovation (Tigert and Arnold, 1971), and market segmentation (Bushman, 1971; Hustad and Pessemier, 1971a; 1971b; and Ziff, 1971). Discussion articles of the methodology (Reynolds and Darden, 1972; Wells, 1972; Wind, 1971; and

Ziff, 1972) as well as reliability and validity studies (Bruno and Pessemier, 1972; and Tigert, 1969) are now available among many others. No topic in our memory has produced as many unpublished papers, university working papers, and private preprints as has life style research. Interestingly, the impact has not been as great as the sheer weight of publications might suggest, although psychographics certainly has become a buzz word in industry.

On overview, the conclusions from published research studies over the past five years remain quite similar to those drawn in 1969. The additional studies have generally made little contribution to the depth of our knowledge, although its breadth has certainly been expanded. The correlation or relationship between personality test scores and consumer behavior variables such as product choice, media exposure, innovation, segmentation, etc., are weak at best and thus of little value in prediction. The reasons for such poor predictions have been discussed by Jacoby (1971), Wells and Beard (1973) and Kassarjian (1971), and all agree that personality is a critical variable in the explanation of the purchasing process. The critical question is why do we insist on considering personality, by itself, a salient variable when the data are at best equivocal?

Nakanishi, in a most insightful paper (1972) presented at the 1972 meetings of the Association for Consumer Research, has suggested that the low explanatory power of personality characteristics may have stemmed, in part, from naive conceptualizations of the relationship between personality and consumer behavior often held by researchers in the field. It is obvious that simple linear statistics such as variance analysis, chi square and t-tests are insufficient. For example, canonical correlations have been used by Sparks and Tucker (1971), Bither and Dolich (1972), Alpert (1971) and Darden and Reynolds (1974) with more complex results and somewhat more variance statistically explained. Unfortunately, this adding of additional variables still involves a static view of the consumer. Personality is perhaps better conceived of as a dynamic concept which is not constant over a variety of situations. Rather, personality is a consistency in the manner the individual adjusts to change over time and over situations. Nakanishi writes it is perhaps "more correct to conceive of personality as a moderator variable whose function is to moderate the effects of environmental change in the individual's behavior. This dynamic concept of personality has not been taken seriously in personality research."

Nakanishi seems to be suggesting that what we need is data somewhat analogous to a combination of cross-sectional and times series analysis. The studies conducted to date are of the cross-sectional variety correlating test inventory variables with consumption variables over subjects. And yet, as Wells (1973) points out, a single personality trait may lead to a variety of behaviors. For instance compulsiveness can lead to extremely orderly behavior or expulsive disorderly behavior depending on the situation. On the other hand, several personality traits may lead to a single response, again depending on the situation. Correlating a single trait with a single behavior is bound to be frustrating.

Hence, according to Nakanishi, the relevant variables include personality traits, response and behavior patterns, moderator variables, situations and individuals. Furthermore, for some of these variables it is essential that measurements be taken over time. That is, as we sample individuals, traits and responses, we should also take samplings of situations over time.

If one can generalize from Nakanishi, the low explanatory power of each of these variables stems from naive conceptualizations of the relationships between the variable and the actions of the consumer in the marketplace.

Trained as we have been by psychoanalytic logic, simplistic beliefs emerging from stimulus-response psychology, and basic Aristotelian modes of thought, we insist on retaining the belief that, "The stimulus possesses an adhesion with certain reactions" (Lewin, 1935). This adhesion is regarded as the cause of the event, and somehow, there are mechanically rigid connections or associations between a stimulus and a response. The purchase of canned peas is somehow related to a specific personality variable, a specific type of perceived risk, or to a set of attributions. The belief is that once the mathematical relationship of this mechanically rigid connection is uncovered, the variance will be accounted for and a statistical error term will no longer exist. Hence, if the Edwards schedule does not account for the variance, perhaps the Jackson Inventory will, and if not, there are still Fishbein attitude models, reference groups, and measures of the level of involvement upon which to fall back.

The conception that the individual must be perceived as a dynamic whole has not yet been internalized by the modern-day consumer researcher. We ought not to be concerned with rigid connections, but rather with temporally extended whole individuals. In short, further traditional research attempting to connect the purchase of canned peas with a personality variable using cross-sectional data is bound to fail. What is missing are the interaction effects of that personality variable with other personality characteristics as well as the interaction effects accounted for by needs, motives, moods, memories, attitudes, beliefs, opinions, perceptions, values, etc. in addition to the situation or field. As Tucker (1967) has already suggested, our theories must begin with the study of the whole individual in a purchase act, at a point in time. In short, every specific instance of behavior must be viewed as the result of the interaction and integration of a variety of influences or forces impinging upon the person. The description of behavior cannot concentrate exclusively on one or another of the variables involved. Only after the analysis examines the situation as a whole is it possible to turn to the specific elements and the interactions among the elements (Kassarjian, 1973). Unfortunately a simple methodology for research of this sort has not yet emerged. We do not necessarily advocate a return to the extensive study of a single individual such as the psychoanalytic methodology employed by Freud, or the environmental probability of Egon Brunswick. But, greater awareness of views espoused by Tolman, Freud, Brunswick, Lewin, and other great minds in the social sciences and philosophy might help point out the location of the light at the end of the tunnel.

Only when we can explain the behavior of a

single individual in a variety of situations over time can we grasp the idea that there are, in fact, interactions between personality, attitudes, perceived risk, and the psychological field or situation. Once the concept of an interaction effect has been internalized, we can turn from an examination of the whole to analyses of the parts. The proper question then would be, "All other things being equal, what is the relationship between a specific personality variable and a specific act?" The problem with the literature as it exists today is that "all other things are not equal" and yet we continue to express dismay, surprise, or pleasure that personality measures, or attitude measures, or what have you, only account for 5% of the variance. As has already been expressed (Kassarjian, 1971), "What is amazing is not that there are many studies that show no correlation between consumer behavior and personality but rather that there are any studies at all with positive results. That 5% or 10% or any portion of the variance can be accounted for by personality variables (taken out of context and studied independently of other cognitive or physical variables) . . . is most remarkable, indeed!"

REFERENCES

Ahmed, S. A. (October, 1972), "Prediction of Cigarette Consumption Level with Personality and Socioeconomic Variables," *Journal of Applied Psychology,* 56, 437–38.

Alpert, Mark I. (1971), "A Canonical Analysis of Personality and the Determinants of Automobile Choice," *Combined Proceedings,* American Marketing Association, 312–16.

_____ (February, 1972), "Personality and the Determinants of Product Choice," *Journal of Marketing Research,* 5, 89–92.

American Market Research Bureau (May, 1972), "Measuring Self-Concept," unpublished working paper.

_____ (1971), *Attitude Research Reaches New Heights,* Chicago: American Marketing Association.

Anderson, W. T., and Cunningham, William H. (February, 1972), "Gauging Foreign Product Promotion," *Journal of Advertising Research,* 12, 29–44.

Barach, Jeffrey A. (1969), "Self-Confidence, Risk Handling, and Mass Communications," *Proceedings,* Fall

Conference, American Marketing Association, 323–29.

_____ (1972), "Self Confidence and Four Types of Persuasive Situations," *Combined Proceedings,* American Marketing Association, 418–22.

Bither, Stewart W., and Dolich, Ira J. (1972), "Personality as a Determinant Factor in Store Choice," *Proceedings,* Association for Consumer Research, 9–19.

_____, and Wright, Peter L. (May, 1973), "The Self Confidence-Advertising Response Relationship: A Function of Situational Distraction," *Journal of Marketing Research,* 10, 146–52.

Blake, Brian, Perloff, Robert, and Heslin, Richard (November, 1970), "Dogmatism and Acceptance of New Products," *Journal of Marketing Research,* 7, 483–86.

Blake, Brian, Perloff, Robert, Zenhausern, Robert, and Heslin, Richard (October 1973), "The Effect of Intolerance of Ambiguity Upon Product Perceptions," *Journal of Applied Psychology,* 58, 239–243.

Bruno, Albert V., and Pessemier, Edgar A. (1972), "An Empirical Investigation of the Validity of Selected Attitude and Activity Measures," *Proceedings,* Association for Consumer Research, 456–73.

Bushman, F. Anthony (1971), "Market Segmentation Via Attitudes and Life Style," *Combined Proceedings,* American Marketing Association, 594–99.

Cohen, Joel B., and Golden, Ellen (February, 1972), "Informational Social Influence and Product Evaluation," *Journal of Applied Psychology,* 50, 54–59.

Darden, William R, and Reynolds, Fred D. (August, 1972), "Predicting Opinion Leadership for Men's Apparel Fashions," *Journal of Marketing Research,* 9, 324–28.

_____ (February, 1974), "Backward Profiling of Male Innovators," *Journal of Marketing Research,* 11, 79–85.

Dolich, Ira J., and Shilling, Ned (January, 1971), "A Critical Evaluation of 'The Problem of Self-Concept in Store Image Studies,'" *Journal of Marketing,* 35, 71–73.

Donnelly, James H., Jr., and Ivancevich, John M. (August, 1974), "A Methodology for Identifying Innovator Characteristics of New Brand Purchasers," *Journal of Marketing Research,* 11, 331–34.

French, Warren A., and Flaschner, Alan B. (1971), "Levels of Actualization as Matched against Life Style Evaluation of Products," *Combined Proceedings,* American Marketing Association, 358–62.

Fry, Joseph N. (August, 1971), "Personality Variables

and Cigarette Brand Choice," *Journal of Marketing Research*, 8, 298–304.

Gardner, David M. (1972), "An Exploratory Investigation of Achievement Motivation Effects on Consumer Behavior," *Proceedings*, Association for Consumer Research, 20–33.

Green, Paul E., Maheshwari, Arun, and Rao, V. R. (1969), "Self Concept and Brand Preference: An Empirical Application of Multidimensional Scaling," *Journal of the Marketing Research Society*, 11, 343–60.

Greeno, Daniel W., Sommers, Montrose S., and Kernan, Jerome B. (February, 1973), "Personality and Implicit Behavior Patterns," *Journal of Marketing Research*, 10, 63–69.

Grubb, Edward L., and Stern, Bruce L. (August, 1971), "Self-Concept and Significant Other," *Journal of Marketing Research*, 8, 382–85.

Hawkins, Del I. (July, 1972), "Reported Cognitive Dissonance and Anxiety: Some Additional Findings," *Journal of Marketing*, 36, 63–66.

Horton, Raymond L. (August, 1974), "The Edwards Personal Preference Schedule and Consumer Personality Research," *Journal of Marketing Research*, 11, 333–37.

Hughes, G. David, and Guerrero, Jose L. (February, 1971), "Automobile Self-Congruity Models Reexamined," *Journal of Marketing Research*, 8, 125–27.

———, Juhasz, Joseph B., and Contino, Bruno (October, 1973), "The Influence of Personality on the Bargaining Process," *Journal of Business*, The University of Chicago, 46, 593–603.

Hustad, Thomas P., and Pessemier, Edgar A. (1971a), "Industry's Use of Life Style Analysis: Segmenting Consumer Markets with Activity and Attitude Measures," *Combined Proceedings*, American Marketing Association, 296–301.

——— (1971b), "Segmenting Consumer Markets with Activity and Attitude Measures," unpublished working paper, Purdue University.

Jacoby, Jacob (1971), "Multiple-Indicant Approach for Studying New Product Adopters," *Journal of Applied Psychology*, 55, 384–88.

Joyce, Timothy (1972), "Personality Classification of Consumers," unpublished paper presented at 1972 Annual Meetings, American Psychological Association.

Kassarjian, Harold H. (November, 1971), "Personality and Consumer Behavior: A Review," *Journal of Marketing Research*, 8, 409–18.

——— (1973), "Field Theory in Consumer Behavior,"

in Scott Ward and Thomas S. Robertson, eds, *Consumer Behavior: Theoretical Sources*, Englewood Cliffs, N.J.: Prentice-Hall, Inc. 118–40.

Kegerreis, Robert J., and Engel, James F. (1969), "The Innovative Consumer: Characteristics of the Earliest Adopters of a New Automotive Service," *Proceedings*, American Marketing Association, 357–61.

King, Charles W., and Tigert, Douglas J., eds. (1971), *Attitude Research Reaches New Heights*, Chicago: American Marketing Association.

Kinnear, Thomas C., Taylor, James R., and Ahmed, Sadrudin A. (1972), "Socioeconomic and Personality Characteristics as They Relate to Ecologically Constructive Purchasing Behavior," *Proceedings*, Association for Consumer Research, 34–60.

———, (April, 1974), "Ecologically Concerned Consumers: Who Are They?," *Journal of Marketing*, 38, 20–24.

Landon, E. Laird, Jr. (1972), "A Sex-Role Explanation of Purchase Intention Differences of Consumers Who are High and Low in Need Achievement," *Proceedings*, Association for Consumer Research, 1–8.

——— (September, 1974), "Self Concept, Ideal Self Concept, and Consumer Purchase Intentions," *Journal of Consumer Research*, 1, 44–51.

Lewin, Kurt (1935), *A Dynamic Theory of Personality*, New York: McGraw-Hill, 43–65.

Martin, Warren S. (1973), *Personality and Product Symbolism*, Austin, Texas: Bureau of Business Research, Graduate School of Business, University of Texas.

Mason, Joseph Barry, and Mayer, Morris L. (April, 1970), "The Problem of the Self-Concept in Store Image Studies," *Journal of Marketing*, 34, 67–69.

Mathews, H. Lee, Slocum, John W. Jr., and Woodside, Arch G. (1971), "Perceived Risk, Individual Differences, and Shopping Orientations," *Proceedings*, Association for Consumer Research, 299–306.

Michaels, Peter W. (1972), "Life Style and Magazine Exposure," *Combined Proceedings*, American Marketing Association, 324–31.

Michman, Ronald D. (1971), "Market Segmentation Strategies: Pitfalls and Potentials," *Combined Proceedings*, American Marketing Association, 322–26.

Morris, George P., and Cundiff, Edward W. (August, 1971), "Acceptance by Males of Feminine Products," *Journal of Marketing Research*, 8, 372–374.

Nakanishi, Massao (1972), "Personality and Consumer Behavior: Extentions," *Proceedings*, Association for Consumer Research, 61–65.

Nicely, Roy E. (1972), "E, I-O and CAD Correlations,"

unpublished working paper, Virginia Polytechnic Institute and State University, 1972.

Ostlund, Lyman E. (1969), "The Role of Product Perceptions in Innovative Behavior," *Proceedings,* Fall Conference, American Marketing Association, 259–66.

———— (1971), "The Interaction of Self Confidence Variables in the Context of Innovative Behavior," *Proceedings,* Association for Consumer Research, 351–57.

———— (April, 1972), "Identifying Early Buyers," *Journal of Advertising Research,* 12, 25–30.

Perry, Arnon (November, 1973), "Heredity, Personality Traits, Product Attitude and Product Consumption— An Exploratory Study," *Journal of Marketing Research,* 10, 376–79.

Peters, William H., and Ford, Neil M. (January, 1972), "A Profile of Urban Inhome Shoppers: The Other Half," *Journal of Marketing,* 36, 62–64.

Peterson, Robert A. (June, 1972), "Psychographics and Media Exposure," *Journal of Advertising Research,* 12, 17–20.

Plummer, Joseph T. (1971a), "Life Style and Advertising: Case Studies," *Combined Proceedings,* American Marketing Association, 290–95.

———— (April 1971b), "Life Style Patterns and Commercial Bank Credit Card Usage," *Journal of Marketing,* 35, 35–41.

Reynolds, Fred D., and Darden, William R. (1972), "An Operational Construction of Life Style," *Proceedings,* Association for Consumer Research, 475–89.

Ross, Ivan (January, 1971), "Self Concept and Brand Preference," *The Journal of Business,* The University of Chicago, 44, 38–50.

Sparks, David L., and Tucker, W. T. (February, 1971), "A Multivariate Analysis of Personality and Product Use," *Journal of Marketing Research,* 8, 67–70.

Tigert, Douglas J. (1969), "Psychographics: A Test-Retest Reliability Analysis," *Proceedings,* Fall Conference, American Marketing Association, 310–15.

————, and Arnold, Stephen, J. (1971), "Profiling Self-Designated Opinion Leaders and Self-Designated Innovators Through Life and Style Research," *Proceedings,* Association for Consumer Research, 425–45.

Tucker, William T. (1967), *Foundations of a Theory of Consumer Behavior,* New York: Holt, Rinehart and Winston, Inc.

Vavra, Terry G., and Winn, Paul R. (1971), "Fear Appeals in Advertising: An Investigation of the Influence of Order, Anxiety and Involvement," *Combined Proceedings,* American Marketing Association, 444–49.

Webster, Frederick E. Jr., and Von Pechmann, Frederick (April, 1970), "A Replication of the 'Shopping List' Study," *Journal of Marketing,* 34, 61–63.

Wells, William D. (1972), "Seven Questions About Lifestyle and Psychographics," *Combined Proceedings,* American Marketing Association, 462–65.

————, and Beard, Arthur D. (1973), "Personality and Consumer Behavior," in Scott Ward and Thomas S. Robertson, eds., *Consumer Behavior: Theoretical Sources,* Englewood Cliffs, N.J.: Prentice-Hall, 141–99.

Wilson, David T., Mathews, H. Lee, and Sweeney, Timothy W. (1971), "Industrial Buyer Segmentation: A Psychographic Approach," *Combined Proceedings,* American Marketing Association, 327–31.

Wind, Jerry (1971), "Life Style Analysis: A New Approach," *Combined Proceedings,* American Marketing Association, 302–5.

Winter, Edward, and Russell, John T. (1973), "Psychographics and Creativity," *Journal of Advertising,* 2, 32–35.

Wiseman, Frederick (April, 1971), "A Segmentation Analysis on Automobile Buyers During the New Model Year Transition Period," *Journal of Marketing,* 35, 42–49.

Worthing, Parker M., Venkatesan, M., and Smith, Steve, "A Modified Approach to the Exploration of Personality and Product Use," *Combined Proceedings,* American Marketing Association, 363–67.

———— (April, 1973), "Personality and Product Use Revisited: An Exploration with the Personality Research Form," *Journal of Applied Psychology,* 57, 179–83.

Ziff, Ruth (April, 1971), "Psychographics for Market Segmentation," *Journal of Advertising Research,* 11, 3–9.

———— (1972), "Closing the Consumer-Advertising Gap Through Psychographics," *Combined Proceedings,* American Marketing Association, 457–61.

OPTIMUM STIMULATION LEVEL: ITS RELATIONSHIP TO PERSONALITY, DEMOGRAPHICS AND EXPLORATORY BEHAVIOR

P. S. RAJU

Source: P. S. Raju, "Optimum Stimulation Level: Its Relationship to Personality, Demographics, and Exploratory Behavior," *Journal of Consumer Research,* Vol. 7, December, 1980, 272–282. Reprinted with permission.

Optimum stimulation level (OSL) is a property that characterizes an individual in terms of his general response to environmental stimuli. The concept was introduced almost simultaneously in the psychology literature by Hebb (1955) and Leuba (1955). They argued that every organism most prefers a certain level of stimulation, which may be termed "optimum stimulation." When the environmental stimulation (which is determined by properties such as novelty, ambiguity, complexity, etc.) is below optimum, an individual will attempt to increase stimulation; when it is above optimum s/he will strive to reduce it.

The magnitude of OSL, therefore, leads to attempts to adjust stimulation from the environment. Such behavior, aimed at modifying stimulation from the environment, can be termed "exploratory behavior." According to Berlyne (1960), exploratory responses "afford access to environmental information that was not previously available. They do so by intensifying or clarifying stimulation from objects that are already represented in the stimulus field, and thus reducing uncertainty about the properties of these objects" (p. 79). Exploratory behavior is a major topic of research in the psychology literature, and several theories of exploratory behavior have been proposed (Berlyne 1960; Driver and Streufert 1965; Fiske and Maddi 1961; Fowler 1965).

Recently, exploratory behavior has received considerable attention in consumer behavior research. Venkatesan (1973) and Raju (1977) reviewed several existing theories from a consumer behavior perspective. Howard and Sheth (1969) used Berlyne's theory to postulate the nature of the relationship between stimulus ambiguity and attention. Sawyer (1977) and Faison (177) have suggested applications of exploratory behavior concepts to advertising repetition and message content, respectively. Recent developments in activation research applied to advertising and consumer behavior also bear close similarity to research on OSL (Kroeber-Riel 1979). As Raju and Venkatesan (1980) suggest, exploratory behavior and underlying constructs, such as OSL, are useful in (1) studying the response to stimulus characteristics such as novelty and complexity, (2) studying

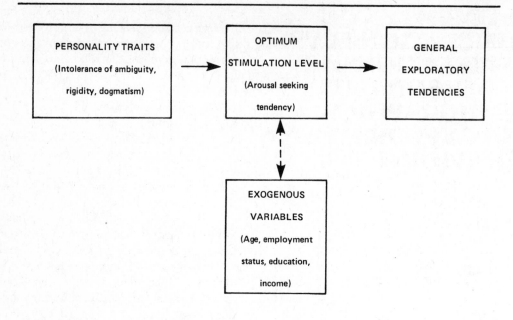

NOTE: The dotted arrow indicates that the exogenous variables are not directly part of psychological explanations of exploratory behavior, but are expected to be useful for consumer research.

Figure 1 Framework of relationships.

the information-search behavior of consumers, (3) studying the effects of stimulus (e.g., advertising) repetition, and (4) studying individual differences in exploratory behavior.

The focus of this paper is on OSL and its relationships with other constructs. More specifically, relationships are examined involving OSL and:

- Selected personality traits.
- Selected demographic variables.
- General exploratory tendencies in the consumer context.

Figure 1 illustrates these relationships. The literature suggests that OSL is a key factor in determining the degree of exploratory tendencies of an individual across many situations. In general, individuals with high OSLs will be more likely to explore new stimuli and situations because of a higher need for environmental stimulation. Individuals with low OSLs, on the other hand, are likely to feel more comfortable with familiar situations and stimuli, and withdraw from new or unusual ones. It has also

been suggested that OSL is a function of more basic personality traits.

BACKGROUND

Three personality traits relevant for consumer behavior are included in the present investigation. The traits are intolerance of ambiguity, rigidity, and dogmatism. Intolerance of ambiguity refers to the general ability of a person to handle uncertainty. Higher levels of this trait mean greater discomfort in the face of uncertainty. Rigidity is the general reluctance to try new responses over time. The third trait, dogmatism, is the extent to which a person can react to relevant information on its own merits, unencumbered by irrelevant factors in the situation. Less dogmatic people are generally more open-minded (Rokeach 1960).

There are no available empirical studies linking these traits directly to OSL. However, the following findings can guide us in hypothesizing the nature of the relationships:

1. Intolerant persons are expected to engage less in exploratory behavior (Berlyne 1960). They also perceive atypical products as "newer" than do people who can tolerate ambiguity, and are more reluctant to buy such products (Blake, Perloff, Zenhausern, and Heslin 1973).

2. Ridigity has been found to correlate negatively with risk-taking behavior (Kogan and Wallach 1964; Schaninger 1976). Rigidity has also been found to correlate negatively with innovativeness in a sample of farmers (Robertson 1971).

3. Highly dogmatic people are generally less receptive to new or unfamiliar stimuli, such as new styles of music (Mikol 1960) and new products (Coney 1972; Jacoby 1971).

. . .

. . . . Only two recent studies have investigated OSL in relation to consumer behavior. Grossbart, Mittelstaedt, and Devere (1976) found stimulation needs to be related to consumers' acceptance of recycled urban facilities, because these facilities offered shopping experiences different from the typical shopping situation.

Mittelstaedt, Grossbart, Curtis, and Devere (1976) hypothesized that those with higher OSLs are likely to exhibit a greater awareness of and a greater tendency to evaluate, symbolically accept, try, and adopt new products and retail facilities. Most of their hypotheses were supported. In addition, their study showed high OSL people to have a significantly shorter decision time from awareness to trial of new products. They attribute this result to the fact that high OSL people and low OSL people behave differently with respect to trial; the former use trial experience to make the adoption decision, whereas the latter first symbolically evaluate the alternative and try it only if it is acceptable. High OSL people, therefore, proceed faster to the trial stage and take a greater risk that the product will be acceptable.

These findings suggest that OSL is positively cor-related with various exploratory tendencies in the consumer context, such as adopting new products, switching brands, and seeking information out of curiosity. Optimum stimulation level is also likely to correlate positively with risk-taking behavior in consumers.

HYPOTHESES

This background literature indicates that much of the evidence pertaining to the relationships outlined in the Figure is of an indirect nature. This paper empirically examines these relationships. The following hypotheses are tested:

H1: Optimum stimulation level will have significant negative correlations with the personality traits of intolerance of ambiguity, rigidity, and dogmatism.

H2: Optimum stimulation level will correlate significantly and positively with income and education.

H3: Optimum stimulation level will have significant positive correlations with exploratory tendencies in the consumer context.

The rest of the paper describes two studies conducted to test these hypotheses. Study 1 examines the relationship between OSL and personality, and Study 2 examines the relationship between OSL and demographic variables, as well as exploratory tendencies in the consumer context. . . .

OPERATIONALIZATION OF OSL

. . .

After a review of the available scales, the Arousal Seeking Tendency scale was selected for operationalizing OSL in the two studies discussed here. This scale has 40 items scored on nine-point Likert scales ranging from "very strong disagreement" (-4) to "very strong agreement" $(+4)$. There are an equal number of positively worded and negatively worded items. The total score of the items, after appropriate scale reversals, indicates the optimum stimulation level of the respondent. This scale was chosen because of certain advantages it possesses. First, being a more recent instrument, it incorporates several of the best items of the previous scales. Second, a rigorous sequential factor analytic method was used to select the best items from an initial pool of 312 items. Third, it has fewer items than most other measures and is, therefore, easier to administer. Fourth, the scale incorporates preference for arousal caused by five major factors: arousal from change, arousal from unusual stimuli, arousal from risk, arousal from sensuality, and arousal from new environments. As all of these sources of arousal are encountered in purchase and consumption contexts, the scale seems more appropriate for use in the examination of consumer behavior.

A few additional points regarding the scale are worth mentioning. Although Mehrabian and Russell (1974) call the measure "Arousal Seeking Tendency," it is clear from their book that they are in fact measuring what other researchers have called optimum stimulation level. The following statement illustrates this: "An individual's preference for an environment is closely related to his preferred arousal level; some people characteristically prefer calm settings whereas others actively seek to increase their arousal by selecting novel, complex, or unpredictable settings" (p. 30). . . .

The Arousal Seeking Tendency scale has also been demonstrated to have high reliability and validity. The Kuder-Richardson reliability was found to be 0.87 and the test-retest reliability was 0.88, with a period of four to seven weeks between test and retest. The validity of the scale has been established by correlating it with other constructs, such as anxiety and extroversion.[1]

STUDY 1: OSL AND PERSONALITY TRAITS

Method

. . . The respondents comprised convenience samples of 107 homemakers and 185 students. As relationships between constructs, and not general-ization to specific populations, were of interest, convenience samples were judged to be appropriate. The data were collected by questionnaire during the spring of 1975. The homemaker sample was obtained from local women's clubs in the area, which were paid one dollar per response to encourage member participation. Because it was difficult to obtain a substantive time slot during club meetings, respondents were allowed to take the questionnaire home and return it in postage-paid envelopes within the next few days. To improve internal validity, it was emphasized that the respondents should answer the questionnaire carefully by themselves. The student sample was comprised of juniors and seniors from undergraduate business administration classes.

Optimum stimulation level was measured using the Arousal Seeking Tendency scale. The instruments used to measure the personality traits were:[2]

- *Intolerance of ambiguity.* Two separate instruments were used to measure this trait.
  1. Budner's scale (1962): Budner defines intolerance of ambiguity as "the tendency to perceive ambiguous situations as sources of threat" (p. 29). The scale has 16 items, with eight items positively worded and eight items negatively worded. Novel, complex, and insoluble situations are used to characterize ambiguity. Response to each item is measured on a seven-point scale ranging from "strongly disagree" to "strongly agree."
  2. Martin and Westie's scale (1959): This scale operationalizes intolerance of ambiguity as the tendency to perceive dimensionalized stimuli as absolutely dichotomous, to seek unambiguous solutions to complex problems and to demonstrate rigid, categorical thinking. It has eight items; responses are measured using five-point Likert scales ranging from "strongly disagree" to "strongly agree."

---

[1]The Arousal Seeking Tendency scale is reproduced in the Appendix.

[2]These scales were obtained from the collection of measures of social and psychological attitudes compiled by Robinson and Shaver (1973). Further details, including the reliability and validity of the scales, are available in this source.

- *Rigidity* (Wesley 1953). Wesley defines rigidity as "the tendency to persist in responses that may previously have been suitable in some situation or other, but that no longer appear adequate to achieve current goals or to solve current problems" (p. 129). The scale has 41 items requiring a "true" or "false" response to each item.
- *Dogmatism* (Rokeach 1956, Form E). This scale measures the openness or closedness of belief systems. It has 50 items, each measured on a six-point agree-disagree scale with the zero point excluded.

As the questionnaire also included other parts that are not relevant here, it was not possible to administer all the personality scales and the Arousal Seeking Tendency scale to each respondent. The homemaker and student samples were, therefore, divided into three groups of approximately equal size. The Arousal Seeking Tencency scale was administered to all three groups. In addition, Group 1 responded only to the intolerance of ambiguity scales of Budner and Martin and Westie, Group 2 responded only to Wesley's rigidity scale, and Group 3 responded only to Rokeach's dogmatism scale. . . .

Results

Correlations of OSL with personality traits are shown in Table 1. Hypothesis 1 was generally supported. Only the correlation between OSL and dogmatism for the student sample was in the wrong direction, but this correlation was not statistically significant. Intolerance of ambiguity (Budner's scale) and rigidity showed significant correlations with OSL; intolerance of ambiguity (Martin and Westie's scale) and dogmatism did not. The fact that the two intolerance of ambiguity scales showed very different correlations with OSL might seem inconsistent, but from the descriptions of the scales provided earlier it is evident that they operationalize the construct very differently. They also differ in the nature of items they comprise. As the Budner scale incorporates ambiguity from novel, complex, and insoluble situations, it is understandably closer to the OSL construct. The tendency to perceive stimuli in a limited number of

Table 1   Correlations of OSL with personality traits

Trait	Homemakers[a]	Students[a]
Intolerance of ambiguity (Budner 1962)	−.60[b] (38)	−.55[b] (69)
Intolerance of ambiguity (Martin and Westie 1959)	−.23 (38)	−.19 (69)
Rigidity (Wesley 1953)	−.43[b] (39)	−.45[b] (51)
Dogmatism (Rokeach 1956)	−.25 (30)	.09 (65)

[a]Sample sizes are given in parentheses.
[b]Significant at the 0.05 level; one-tailed test.

categories, as Martin and Westie operationalize intolerance of ambiguity, seems to bear little relationship to OSL. From the nature of items included in the scales, it appears that the Budner scale measures *response* to ambiguous stimuli, whereas the Martin and Westie Scale measures *perception* of ambiguous stimuli. This suggests that OSL is correlated with the ability to confront ambiguous stimuli and respond to them, but not the ability to perceive ambiguities in stimuli.

The negative correlation of OSL with rigidity shows that those with higher OSLs are less bound by past experiences and are willing to experiment with new response patterns. On the other hand, the insignificant correlation with dogmatism indicates that those with high and low OSL are equally open-minded or close-minded.

From Table 1, the following conclusions can, therefore, be drawn regarding the characteristics of those with high and low OSLs:

- Those with higher OSLs can respond better to ambiguities in the environment. When these people are faced with new or unusual stimuli or situations, such as new brands or retail environments, they are more likely to face them than to withdraw from them.
- Those with high and low OSLs are similar in the perception of ambiguities in stimuli.
- Those with high OSLs are less rigid in their

response patterns; they are more likely to seek change or variety.

- Those with high OSLs are not more open-minded than those with low OSLs. Thus, those with low OSLs are less receptive to new stimuli or situations, not because they are unwilling to accept a different viewpoint, but because of other reasons, such as risk avoidance.

Table 1 also shows a high degree of similarity in the correlations for the homemaker and the student samples. This supports the geneal expectation that basic psychological relationships should be independent of the population tested.

STUDY 2: OSL, DEMOGRAPHICS AND EXPLORATORY BEHAVIOR

Method

A questionnaire containing the Arousal Seeking Tendency scale, demographic measures, and a measure of general exploratory tendencies in the consumer context was administered to convenience samples of 336 homemakers and 105 students in the spring of 1975. As in Study 1, the homemaker sample was obtained through local women's clubs, and the student sample was obtained from mostly junior and senior level undergraduate classes.

Information on age, education, employment status, and annual household income was obtained for the homemaker sample. The demographic analysis was not done for the student sample because of the high homogeneity on the demographic variables for this sample. The variables were operationalized as follows:

Age.   Actual age of respondent.

Employment status. Full-time employment (1), part-time employment (2), unemployed (3).

Education. Eight categories ranging from "some grade school" (1) to "master's or doctorate degree" (8).

Annual household income.   Twelve categories, ranging from "under $3,000" (1) to "over $40,000" (12).

To measure general exploratory tendencies, a life-style type instrument was designed: . . . The 60 best items were chosen separately for the homemaker and student samples.

These 60 items were combined with the Arousal Seeking Tendency scale and included in the main questionnaires administered to the 336 homemakers and 105 students. As in Study 1, the items were presented in random order and the responses were measured on seven-point agree-disagree scales. Of the 60 items on exploratory behavior that were used for each sample, 39 were common to both samples. These 39 items were presumed to offer the best general representation of exploratory tendencies in the consumer context for the following reasons: (1) they are not affected by social desirability considerations as indicated by the low correlations with the Crowne and Marlowe scale; (2) they capture the essence of exploratory behavior as indicated by the high item-total correlations; and (3) they are generalizable to the homemaker and student populations, which are of interest to marketers. Attention is, therefore, confined to the analyses using these items.

Results

Table 2 shows the intercorrelations among the demographic variables as well as their correlations with OSL. Age, employment status, and education had significant correlations with OSL, whereas income did not. Hypothesis 2 is, therefore, partially

Table 2   Intercorrelations among demographic variables and correlations with OSL

Variable	Age	Employment status	Education	Household income
Age	1.000			
Employment status	.455[a]	1.000		
Education	−.076	−.079	1.000	
Household income	−.068	−.042	.233[a]	1.000
Arousal seeking tendency	−.365[a]	−.269[a]	.118[a]	.006

[a]Significant at the 0.05 level; two-tailed test.

confirmed. Although the correlations are not large, they suggest that relatively younger, educated, and employed people are higher in OSL. Because there was a significant correlation between age and employment status, a stepwise regression analysis (Nie, Hull, Jenkins, Steinbrenner, and Bent 1975) was also performed to examine the relationships between these three variables and OSL . . . Age was by far the more important of the two variables accounting for 13.3 percent of the total variance. . . .

. . . Most of the correlations between OSL and the exploratory behavior items are statistically significant at the 0.05 level in the expected directions. Hypothesis 3 is, thus, generally supported. There is also a considerable degree of similarity in the correlations for homemakers and students. Items 3, 11, 12, 13, 18, 19, 25, 28, 37, 38, and 39 have relatively higher correlations with OSL. This suggests a profile for a person with a high OSL as:

> one who is not afraid of taking risks or trying new or unusual products/services, is eager to find out about new products/services and takes the initiative in trying them, seeks variety or change in repetitive purchases, and likes introducing new products and brands to others.

The correlation of OSL with the total of all 39 exploratory behavior items was 0.53 for the homemaker sample and 0.51 for the student sample, both significant at the 0.05 level. About 25 to 28 percent of the variance in consumers' exploratory behavior is thus explained by OSL.

In order to gain more insight into the relationship between OSL and exploratory behavior, the 39 items were grouped into seven different response categories, and the category totals were then correlated with OSL. The seven categories were:

1. *Repetitive behavior proneness:* the tendency to stick with the same response over time.
2. *Innovativeness:* eagerness to buy or know about new products/services.
3. *Risk taking:* a preference for taking risks or being adventurous.
4. *Exploration through shopping:* a preference for shopping and investigating brands.
5. *Interpersonal communication:* communicating with friends about purchases.

Table 3 Correlation coefficients of OSL with exploratory behavior categories

Category	Homemakers	Students
1. Repetitive behavior proneness	.425	.356
2. Innovativeness	.465	.507
3. Risk taking	.546	.622
4. Exploration through shopping	.256	.218
5. Interpersonal communication	.274	.261
6. Brand switching	.438	.394
7. Information seeking	.278	.224

NOTE: All correlations were significant at the 0.01 level; two-tailed test. A two-tailed test was used because hypotheses were not stated with respect to specific categories.

6. *Brand switching:* switching brands primarily for change or variety.
7. *Information seeking:* interest in knowing about various products and brands mainly out of curiosity.

The 39 items were classified into these categories based on the wording of the items and inter-item correlations. This method of categorization, although to an extent subjective, facilitated the formation of response categories of particular interest to consumer researchers and usage of the same categorization for the two samples.[3]

Table 3 presents the correlations of OSL with the item totals for the seven categories (after appropriate scale reversals to bring all items in the same direction). All correlations were significant at the 0.05 level. The highest correlations were found for innovativeness and risk taking. Brand switching and repetitive behavior proneness had the next

[3]It was decided not to use methods like principal components analysis or factor analysis because such techniques would group items together solely on the basis of inter-item correlations. Thus, even though it is apparent from the wording of two items that they represent distinct aspects of exploration, such as information seeking and innovativeness, they might end up in the same category because they happen to be correlated. However, principal components analysis was performed for both samples and used as an aid in the subjective classification procedure.

highest correlations with OSL. Information seeking, exploration through shopping, and interpersonal communications had the lowest correlations.

The results . . . are in conformity with Hypothesis 3, and suggest that people who have higher OSLs are generally more likely to manifest exploratory behaviors in the consumer behavior context. The exploratory tendencies are most likely to be manifested as risk taking and innovativeness, somewhat likely to be manifested as brand switching and changing response patterns over time, and least likely to be manifested through shopping activities, interpersonal communications, and information seeking. Further, homemakers and students seem to be quite similar in the satisfaction of their stimulation needs in the purchase and consumption context.

IMPLICATIONS

The results show that those with high OSLs are somewhat different in their response patterns; they feel less threatened by ambiguous stimuli and are more likely to respond rather than withdraw from such stimuli. Also, they are less rigid in their response patterns. However, there seems to be no difference in openmindedness or tendency to perceptually categorize stimuli. From these results it appears that those with high OSLs and low OSLs are cognitively similar, but behaviorally different.

The linkage between OSL and demographic variables should make it easier to identify segments with high and low OSLs. Younger, educated, and employed people seem to have higher OSLs. An interesting extension of this research would be to examine whether OSL changes along with life-cycle stages, and if it has any relevance for changes in decision-making patterns or purchasing behavior occurring within stages.

Relationships between OSL and exploratory tendencies show that certain types of behavior are more closely related to stimulation needs. The results suggest that those with high OSLs and low OSLs differ most with respect to risk taking and innovativeness, differ somewhat in brand switching and repetitive behavior proneness, and differ the least in exploration involving information seeking, shopping, and interpersonal communications. A priori, the basic motivations underlying these exploratory responses seem to be *risk taking, variety seeking,* and *curiosity.* For example, innovativeness may be primarily motivated by risk taking; brand switching and repetitive behavior proneness by variety seeking; and information processing, interpersonal communication, and shopping, by curiosity. If this is the case, the results suggest that stimulation needs are satisfied most by risk taking, followed by variety seeking and curiosity, in that order.

It is also worth examining, in future research, why the risk-taking-related responses, e.g., innovativeness, correlate better with OSL than the curiosity-related responses, e.g., information seeking. It is possible that curiosity-related responses are manifested to an almost equal degree by those with high OSLs and low OSLs, but for very different reasons. For example, those with high OSLs may seek information because of a genuine desire to explore something unfamiliar, whereas those with low OSLs may seek information to reduce the risk of trying an unfamiliar product.

. . .

For a marketer, the results are significant in several ways. In the case of new product offerings, benefits should be considered not merely in terms of functional features, but also in psychological terms, such as the risk, novelty, or variety that the product offers. It is also desirable to place different promotional emphases for different segments. For the high OSL segment, such as a market comprised primarily of younger people, it may not be worthwhile to reduce perceived risk. Such a segment may actually prefer to take risks. On the other hand, greater emphasis on the novelty of the brand and how it differs from other brands may be beneficial. For the low OSL segment, such as older or retired homemakers, the emphasis should be on reducing the perceived risk or ambiguity of the brand. It might also help to offer a deal or premium to encourage them to try the brand. Finally, the high OSL segment and the low OSL segment may be very different in terms of the evaluative criteria they use and in the decision process.

REFERENCES

Berlyne, D. E. (1960), *Conflict, Arousal, and Curiosity,* New York: McGraw-Hill.

Blake, Brian, Perloff, Robert, and Heslin, Richard (1970), "Dogmatism and Acceptance of New Products," *Journal of Marketing Research,* 3, 483–6.

———, Perloff, Robert, Zenhausern, Robert, and Heslin, Richard (1973), "The Effect of Intolerance of Ambiguity upon Product Perceptions," *Journal of Applied Psychology,* 58, 239–43.

Budner, Stanley (1962), "Intolerance of Ambiguity as a Personality Variable," *Journal of Personality,* 30, 29–50.

Coney, Kenneth (1972). "Dogmatism and Innovation: A Replication," *Journal of Marketing Research,* 9, 453–4.

Driver, Michael J., and Streufert, Siegfried (1965), "The 'General Incongruity Adaptation Level' (GIAL) Hypothesis: An Analysis and Integration of Cognitive Approaches to Motivation," working paper No. 114, Institute for Research in the Behavioral, Economic, and Management Sciences, Purdue University, Layayette, IN.

Faison, Edmund W. J. (1977), "The Neglected Variety Drive: A Useful Concept for Consumer Behavior," *The Journal of Consumer Research,* 4, 172–5.

Fiske, Donald W., and Maddi, Salvatore R. (1961), *Functions of Varied Experience,* Homewood, IL: The Dorsey Press.

Fowler, Harry (1965), *Curiosity and Exploratory Behavior,* New York: Macmillan Publishing Co. Inc.

Grossbart, Sanford L., Mittelstaedt, Robert A., and Devere, Stephen P. (1976), "Consumer Stimulation Needs and Innovative Shopping Behavior: The Case of Recycled Urban Places," in *Advances in Consumer Research,* Vol. 3, ed. Beverlee B. Anderson, Chicago, IL: Association for Consumer Research, pp. 30–5.

Hebb, D. O. (1955), "Drives and the C.N.S. (Central Nervous System)," *Psychological Review,* 62, 243–54.

Howard, John A., and Sheth, Jagdish N. (1969), *The Theory of Buyer Behavior,* New York: John Wiley & Sons.

Jacoby, Jacob (1971), "Personality and Innovation Proneness," *Journal of Marketing Research,* 8, 244–7.

Kogan, Nathan, and Wallach, Michael A. (1964), *Risk Taking: A Study in Cognition and Personality,* New York: Holt, Rinehart, and Winston.

Kroeber-Riel, Werner (1979), "Activation Research: Psychobiological Approaches in Consumer Behavior," *The Journal of Consumer Research,* 5, 240–50.

Leuba, Clarence (1955), "Toward Some Integration of Learning Theories: The Concept of Optimal Stimulation," *Psychological Reports,* 1, 27–33.

Martin, J. G., and Westie, F. R. (1959), "The Tolerant Personality," *American Sociological Review,* 24, 521–8.

Mehrabian, Albert, and Russell, James A. (1974), *An Approach to Environmental Psychology,* Cambridge, MA: MIT Press.

Mikol, Bernard (1960), "Enjoyment of New Musical Systems," in *The Open and Closed Mind,* ed. M. B. Rokeach, New York: Basic Books, Inc.

Mittelstaedt, Robert A., Grossbart, Sanford L., Curtis, William W., and Devere, Stephen P. (1976), "Optimum Stimulation Level and the Adoption Decision Process." *The Journal of Consumer Research,* 3, 84–94.

Raju, P. S. (1977), "Theoretical Perspectives on Exploratory Behavior: A Review and Examination of Their Relevance for Consumer Research," paper #67, Working Series in Marketing Research, the Pennsylvania State University Park, PA.

Rokeach, Milton (1956), "Political and Religious Dogmatism: An Alternative to the Authoritarian Personality, *Psychological Monographs,* 70, 18, 1–43.

——— (1960), *The Open and Closed Mind,* New York: Basic Books.

Saywer, Alan G. (1977), "Repetition and Affect: Recent Empirical and Theoretical Developments," in *Consumer and Industrial Buying Behavior,* eds. A. G. Woodside, J. N. Sheth, and P. D. Bennett, New York: Elsevier North-Holland, Inc., pp. 229–42.

Schaninger, Charles M. (1976), "Perceived Risk and Personality," *The Journal of Consumer Research,* 3, 95–100.

Venkatesan, M. (1973), "Cognitive Consistency and Novelty Seeking," in *Consumer Behavior: Theoretical Sources,* eds. S. Ward and T. S. Robertson, Englewood Cliffs, NJ: Prentice-Hall, pp. 354–84.

Wesley, Elizabeth (1953), "Perseverative Behavior In a Concept Formation Task As a Function of Manifest Anxiety and Rigidity," *Journal of Abnormal and Social Psychology,* 48, 129–34.

IDENTIFYING THE ENVIRONMENTALLY RESPONSIBLE CONSUMER: THE ROLE OF INTERNAL-EXTERNAL CONTROL OF REINFORCEMENTS

LEWIS R. TUCKER, JR.

Source: Lewis R. Tucker, Jr., "Identifying the Environmentally Responsible Consumer: The Role of Internal-External Control of Reinforcements," Journal of Consumer Affairs, 14, Winter, 1980, 326–340. Reprinted with permission.

Given the relationship of environmental concern to the consumer movement, the profiling of environmentally concerned consumers could contribute to a better understanding of the dynamics of consumer activism. Consequently, research interest in systematic identification of consumerist population segments is increasing [10, 18, 28], with considerable effort devoted to establishing profiles of environmentally responsible individuals [1, 7, 8, 11, 12, 13, 15, 16, 22, 23, 29]. In these studies, environmental responsibility has been operationalized through a variety of attitudinal and behavioral measures, ranging from stated concerns about pollution to participation in a community recycling program.

This investigation builds upon and extends existing research efforts through its development of the construct of internal and external control of reinforcements [24] as a correlate of environmental concern. Internal-external control of reinforcements refers to an individual's perception of rewards as being contingent on uncontrollable forces (external control) or directly attributable to personal action (internal control).

The objective of this research was to explore the relationship between the construct of internal and external control and multiple attitudinal and behavioral measures of environmental responsibility. A multivariate dependent variable is utilized to address the validity issue inherent in the measurement of the environmental responsibility phenomenon. The control variables used include social responsibility [2, 3], social class [5, 7, 8, 11, 15, 16], age [12, 15, 16, 21, 23] and income [12, 15, 17, 21, 23, 27, 29]. These control variables have been used in other studies of environmental concern or have been found to be associated with the internal-external control phenomenon.

ENVIRONMENTAL RESPONSIBILITY AND INTERNAL-EXTERNAL CONTROL OF REINFORCEMENTS

The effectiveness of directing communications to segments already predisposed to them indicates the usefulness of developing a profile of the environmentally conscious consumer [1, 15, 19, 23,

29]. Research on environmental concern has utilized a number of variables in attempts to profile individuals exhibiting these predispositions. Significant differences along several social psychological and demographic dimensions have been observed. Of particular interest here are the relatively consistent findings observed on personal competence and alienation [1, 3, 24] and powerlessness [15]. Webster [29] summarizes the results for these descriptor variables in the development of his Social Involvement Model. The Social Involvement Model suggests that beyond being informed on environmental problems, socially concerned consumers perceive themselves as active, socially involved and not alienated. Although other components of Social Involvement Model were not empirically supported, Webster [29, p. 193] found that individuals who scored high on an ecologically oriented index measuring environmental attitudes and intentions and who participated in a free recycling program were "willing to exercise initiative (Dominance) based on a conviction that their own actions can make a difference (Consumer Effectiveness)." Interestingly, Novic and Sandman [21] found the more informed individuals were on environmental issues the less likely they were to prefer personal as opposed to societal solutions to these problems. Their interpretation was that the heavy reader experienced a "syndrome of well informed futility that resulted in knowing about environmental problems but being too overwhelmed to personally do anything about them."

Thus, it appears that different measures of an individual's perceived ability to influence the outcome of events are consistent predictors of environmental responsibility. . . .

In order to test how valuable the internal-external control variable could be, it was necessary to develop a means of operationalizing environmental responsibility. Greater validity (i.e. minimization of response bias) was sought by combining nine environmentally oriented attitudinal and behavioral variables. The selected dichotomous and continuous measures ranged from the in-store selection of environmentally correct products to attitudinal statements regarding the seriousness of environmental problems. The relationship between

internal-external control trait orientations and environmental responsibility was specified through the following hypothesis: Individuals exhibiting more positive environmentally responsible attitudes and behaviors will be classified as more internal as opposed to external control oriented. The methodology used to operationalize this hypothesis is discussed next.

METHODOLOGY

Data Collection

The data for this study were obtained in a multiple subject format, day long session, in the community room of a central Pennsylvania shopping center. Specifically, the subjects consisted of females, from the State College, Pennsylvania area. This community is comprised of approximately 50,000 residents. Subjects were solicited through local newspaper advertisements, the community announcement services of a local radio and television station and with signs posted throughout the mall. Potential subjects were prescreened at the data collection point to determine if they were regularly involved in household shopping. Participants were allowed to come in and be processed at any time during the hours the mall center was open.

Time and financial constraints precluded recruiting study participants using a strictly random selection technique. However, given the nature of the selection process and the number of participants, it is felt that the respondents are approximately representative of the population from which they were drawn. Use of a nonprobability sample does not appear to be a serious limitation, since the study is concerned with the examination of theoretical relationships rather than generalizing the attitudes and behavior of the sample group to a larger and more diverse population. The data collection efforts resulted in 139 usable questionnaires.

The actual data collection was undertaken as a two-stage process. The first stage involved self-administered questionnaires containing the personality and attitude scales and the demographic and self-report behavior items. The second stage was concerned with recording behavioral observations.

Upon completion of the questionnaire, the respondent was requested to take her forms to a processing station. Here she was asked to indicate (from a list of available detergent brands) her choice as a free gift. This form also contained an explanation of the chance drawing for a $100 savings bond. Respondents were informed that the brand selection form (coupon) they had just completed would serve as a lottery ticket in a chance drawing, only after redemption at the nearby supermarket. The importance of redeeming the coupon at the mall's supermarket that day was strongly stressed. The questionnaire was assigned a number and the subject signed for and was given her monetary compensation and the free coupon. Subjects then proceeded to another station where they were asked to select one six-pack of 12-ounce Pepsi-Cola in returnable bottles or in cans. The subject was given her choice and also a written request not to discuss the nature of the study with other prospective participants. A brief reminder on the importance of redeeming the coupon for eligibility in the savings bond drawing was also included.

The respondent could obtain a free box of detergent by presenting both the detergent selected and the coupon to the cashier at the participating supermarket's check-out station. The cashiers were instructed to have the respondent sign the coupon and then mark the brand actually selected from a list printed on the coupon.

Environmental Responsibility Measures

Observed behavioral measures consisted of two product selection decisions. First, subjects were observed as they selected, as a gift, either a six-pack of Pepsi-Cola 12-ounce cans or a six-pack of 12-ounce Pepsi-Cola returnable bottles. The returnable bottles were categorized on an *a priori* basis as the environmentally responsible alternative. The second measure was based on the subjects' in-store selection of a giant size box of laundry detergent when redeeming the coupon they had been given. The phosphate content of the selected brand indicated the extent to which subject behavior was environmentally responsible.

Three self-report behavioral measures were also

incorporated into the investigation. Self-report purchase behavior of soft drinks and detergents was obtained from subject's completion of a detailed shopping list containing a number of extraneous questions included to disguise the purposes of the study. The test items were the returnable bottles and phosphate content of the reported purchases of detergents. A highly valid measure for detergent phosphates was available through cross-referencing reported phosphate attributes with the actual phosphate content of the subject's specified preferred brand. The third self-report measure was a statement of intended selection for the detergent brand to be redeemed with the coupon which was completed. The phosphate level for the stated brand was also recorded. All observed and self-report behavior variables were dichotomously scored.

Attitude measurements were obtained using five continuous centigrade thermometer scales [4]. Responses on this scale to an item or set of items can be scored from 0 to 100. First, subjects were asked to assess the perceived importance of 15 determinant attributes for soft drinks, detergents, and toilet paper on three separate scales. The test items were "returnable bottles" for soft drinks and "low phosphate" for detergents. The toilet paper alternative was included for disguise purposes. Secondly, subjects indicated their assessments of the seriousness of seven contemporary social problems, including the "environmental pollution" test item. Finally, a fifth thermometer scale specifically measured two items addressing the degree of personal concern about environmental pollution as well as the perceived concern of others.

Internal-External Control and Control Variable Measures

The internal-external control of reinforcements scale [24] is a 29 item forced choice scale including five dummy items which are not scored. For example, subjects were asked to indicate which of two statements (e.g., "Many of the unhappy things in people's lives are partly due to bad luck" versus "People's misfortunes result from the mistakes they make") they were most in agreement with.

Scores were calculated by assigning the value of one to each external choice and summing over the 24 test items. The reported test retest-reliability results on the instrument has ranged from .49 to .83 [24].

The Social Responsibility Scale [2] is a 22 statement 5-point Likert-type instrument designed to measure an individual's prosocial orientation or willingness to positively affect the welfare of others. Subject feelings about each statement (e.g., "Every person should give some of his time for the good of the community") were summed over all items to provide an individual's social responsibility score. Internal reliability results obtained for this item indicate that all 22 items had correlations of .45 or greater with the scale as a whole [2].

Social class was determined using the Hollingshead Two-Factor Index of Social Position [14] which was derived by assigning weighted values to occupation and education levels and adding the two together. Age and income measures were derived form subject responses to age and income class intervals.

. . .

ANALYSIS

The analysis involved classifying subjects as high or low in environmental responsibility and evaluating the two groups in terms of differences in their characteristics and discriminant analysis results. . . .

. . .

The relationship between environmental responsibility and internal-external control and the control variables of social responsibility, social class, age, and income variables was evaluated in two ways: (a) tests of mean differences and (b) discriminant analysis.

First, differences between the two groups on the internal-external (I-E) control measure and the four control variables were investigated using t tests. From Table 1 it can be seen that the mean difference on I-E control scores between the high and low environmental responsibility groups was significant and in the predicted direction . . . More specifically, the hypothesis that individuals who exhibit responsible attitudes and behaviors perceive themselves as being more in control of their life

Table 1 Mean values of personal characteristics measures for high and low environmental responsibility groups

	Mean score on measure			
Personal characteristic	*High environmental responsibility group (n = 45)*	*Low environmental responsibility group (n = 94)*	*Mean difference*	*t statistic*
Internal-external control[1]	8.62	11.41	2.79	4.10***
Social responsibility[2]	92.64	90.70	1.94	1.85*
Social class[3]	30.93	36.35	5.42	2.16**
Age	5.33	5.21	.12	.27
Income	6.06	5.71	.35	.78

HOTELLING T^2 = 15.31; F = 4.22***
(5,133)

[1]Possible range 0 to 24 with score representing the total number of responses in the external direction.
[2]Possible range 22 to 110 with higher scores representing a greater social responsibility orientation.
[3]Possible range 11 to 77 with lower scores representing higher social class standing.

*Statistically significant at the .06 level.
**Statistically significant at the .03 level.
***Statistically significant at the .01 level.

experience as indicated by lower I-E control scores has been supported.

The results in Table 1 also indicate that mean differences on the control variables, with the exception of age, were in the expected direction and thus consistent with previous research. The differences between the two groups were significant for both social responsibility and social class. That is, the high environmental responsibility group as measured by the SR Scale displayed a greater propensity to positively affect the welfare of others than did its low environmental responsibility counterpart. A negative mean difference on the Hollingshead Index of Social Position also indicates that the members of the high environmental responsibility group were typically of a higher social class standing.

Although the mean income for high environmental responsibility group was higher as expected, the mean difference was not significant. Similarly, the difference on the age variable was not significant. This finding was not consistent with the results of previous studies that suggest environmentally responsible individuals tend to be younger.

. . .

To determine how effective the independent variables were in predicting environmental responsibility, a discriminant model was constructed. The objective of discriminant analysis is "to classify objects by a set of independent variables, into one or more mutually exclusive and exhaustive categories" [20]. . . .

. . .

. . . Internal-external control was the most powerful predictor (i.e., first variable entered into the discriminant function and largest F-value) followed by social class, social responsibility, age and income.

CONCLUSION

The inclusion in this research design of actual homemaker subjects and multiple unobtrusive, as well as obtrusive dependent measures was done to increase the external validity of the findings. A number of implications for consumer affairs professionals, marketing managers, consumer activists and government officials can be derived from the findings. From the marketing concept or customer orientation perspective the most significant implication for consumer affairs executives and marketers is that identified environmentally responsible markets may be substantial enough to warrant the development of specific environmentally oriented consumer affairs or marketing programs. For example, the marketing manager could use the results in creating appeals that emphasize the direct favorable impact an individual's purchase of a given low pollution product can have on the environment. Social class and income information can be used in the selection of media vehicles and distribution outlets. Consumer affairs decision makers providing consumer information in the form of publicity releases, brochures, films, etc., on environmentally responsible behavior (e.g., recycling) can use these results both to identify target audience and as a basis for developing perceived effectiveness appeals.

A marketing approach could also be used by public policy-makers and consumer activists attempting to engender ideological, financial and other forms of support. For example, the identification of and communication with environmentally responsible citizens can provide officials with valuable insights into reactions to public policy issues. In addition, the results can be used in identifying supporters for environmental protection proposals. Finally, consumer concern groups such as the Sierra Club or the Wildlife Federation can use the results to more effectively target membership or solicitation campaigns.

REFERENCES

1. Anderson, W. T., and W. H. Cunningham, "The Socially Conscious Consumer," *Journal of Marketing,* Vol. 36 (July, 1972), pp. 23–31.
2. Berkowitz, L., and L. Daniels, "Responsibility and Dependency," *Journal of Abnormal and Social Psychology,* Vol. 66 (1963), pp. 429–36.
3. Berkowitz, L., and K. G. Lutterman, "The Tradi-

tional Socially Responsible Personality," *Public Opinion Quarterly,* Vol. 32 (1968), pp. 169–85.

4. Bilkey, W. J., "A Psychological Approach to Consumer Behavior Analysis," *Journal of Marketing,* Vol. 18 (July, 1965), pp. 18–25.

5. Buttel, F. H. and W. L. Flinn, "The Structure of Support for the Environmental Movement," *Rural Sociology,* Vol. 39 (September, 1974), pp. 56–69.

6. Dixon, W. J., *BMD: Biomedical Computer Programs,* Berkeley: University of California Press, 1973.

7. Dunlap, Riley E., "Impact of Political Orientation on Environmental Attitudes and Actions," *Environment and Behavior,* Vol. 7 (December, 1975), pp. 428–54.

8. Dunlap, R. E. and R. B. Heffernan, "Outdoor Recreation and Environmental Concern: An Empirical Examination," *Rural Sociology,* Vol. 40 (Spring, 1975), pp. 18–30.

9. Gore, P. and J. B. Rotter, "A Personality Correlate of Social Action," *Journal of Personality,* Vol. 31 (1963), pp. 58–64.

10. Grikscheit, G. M. and K. L. Granzin, "Who Are the Consumerists," *Journal of Business Research,* Vol. 3 (January, 1975), pp. 1–12.

11. Harry, J. R. Gale and J. Hendee, "Conservation: An Upper-Middle Class Social Movement," *Journal of Leisure Research,* Vol. 3 (1969), pp. 246–54.

12. Hendee, J. C., W. R. Catton, Jr., L. D. Marlow, and C. F. Brockman, "Wilderness Users in the Pacific Northwest—Their Characteristics, Values and Management Preferences," USDA Forest Service Research Paper PNW-61, Portland, Oregon, 1968.

13. Heberlein, T. A. and J. S. Black, "The Land Ethic in Action: Personal Norms, Beliefs and the Purchase of Lead-Free Gasoline," paper presented at The Annual Meeting of The Rural Sociology Society, Montreal, 1974.

14. Hollingshead, A. B. and F. C. Redlich, *Social Class and Mental Illness,* New York: John Wiley, 1958.

15. Kinnear, T., J. R. Taylor, and S. Ahmed, "Ecologically Concerned Consumers: Who Are They?" *Journal of Marketing,* Vol. 38 (April, 1973), pp. 2–24.

16. Koenig, D. J., "Additional Research on Environmental Activism," *Environment and Behavior,* Vol. 7 (December, 1975), pp. 472–85.

17. Kotler, P., "What Consumerism Means for Mar-

keters," *Harvard Business Review,* Vol. 50 (May-June, 1972), pp. 48–57.

18. Liefeld, J. P., F. H. C. Edgecombe, and L. Wolfe, "Demographic Characteristics of Canadian Consumer Complainers," *Journal of Consumer Affairs,* Vol. 9 (Summer, 1975), pp. 73–80.

19. Mildarsky, E., "Some Antecedents of Aiding Under Stress," *Proceedings of the 76th Annual Convention of the American Psychological Association,* Vol. 3 (1968), pp. 385–86.

20. Morrison, D. J., "On the Interpretation of Discriminant Analysis," *Journal of Marketing Research,* Vol. 11 (May, 1969), pp. 156–63.

21. Novic, K. and P. M. Sandman, "How Use of Mass Media Affects Views on Solutions to Environmental Problems," *Journalism Quarterly,* Vol. 51 (1974), pp. 622–40.

22. Overall, J. E. and C. J. Klett, *Applied Multivariate Analysis* (New York: McGraw-Hill, 1972).

23. Peters, W. H., "Who Cooperates In Voluntary Recycling Efforts?" *American Marketing Association Combined Conference Proceedings,* AMA: Chicago, Spring & Fall, 1973, pp. 505–08.

24. Rotter, J. B., "Generalized Expectancies for Internal Versus External Control of Reinforcements," *Psychological Monographs,* Vol. 80 (1966) (1, Whole No. 609).

25. Shimkunas, A. and R. G. Kime, "Personality Correlates of Student Commitment to Social Action," *Journal of Personality Assessment,* Vol. 35 (1972), pp. 561–68.

26. Strickland, B., "The Prediction of Social Action From a Dimension of Internal-External Control," *Journal of Social Psychology,* Vol. 66 (1965), pp. 353–58.

27. Tognacci, L. N., R. H. Weigel, M. F. Wideen, and D. T. A. Vernon, "Environmental Quality: How Universal is Public Concern," *Environment and Behavior,* Vol. 4 (1972). pp. 73–86.

28. Warland, R. H., R. O. Herrmann, and J. Willits, "Dissatisfied Consumers: Who Gets Upset and Who Takes Action," *The Journal of Consumer Affairs,* Vol. 9 (Winter, 1975), pp. 148–63.

29. Webster, F., Jr., "Determining the Characteristics of Socially Conscious Consumers," *Journal of Consumer Research,* Vol. 2 (December, 1975), pp. 188–96.

SECTION IX

ATTITUDES AND CONSUMER BEHAVIOR

Attitudes are learned predispositions to respond to some object in a consistent way. The response may be favorable or unfavorable. These learned predispositions are important because they influence intentions to behave in various ways. These intentions in turn influence behavior. However, the causal linkages among attitudes, intentions, and behavior are not unfailing. Many factors may prevent attitudes from being expressed in stated intentions or in behavior. A consumer may have a favorable attitude toward a retail outlet but never really intend to shop there because it is a very expensive store. The consumer may develop an intention to visit that store when it is conducting a sale but may be ill or without adequate transportation on the day of the sale. The factors that may prevent consumers from converting their attitudes into intentions and buying behavior are very numerous and frequent. Hence it is not surprising that researchers in marketing and other contexts have found that attitudes have a very low correlation with behavior.

Nevertheless, there are many reasons for studying consumer attitudes. Several are noted below.

1. Attitudes are sometimes expressed in behavior.
2. The attitudes of consumers may affect their openness to information about products and services.
3. The attitudes of opinion leaders are important even when they are nonbuyers since they may influence the attitudes of people who are able to buy. Attitudes of parents may influence the socialization of their children, for example.
4. The certainty of attitudes appears to affect their impact on behavior. Thus, knowing what degree of certainty consumers possess about

their attitudes can suggest to the marketer whether those attitudes may be relied on in promotional efforts.

5. The certainty of attitudes is a clue about the importance the marketer should place on variables other than attitudes. These other variables may be consumers' abilities to behave in certain ways and the role of other people.

6. Studying consumer attitudes may provide clues to opportunities for developing new products and for improving present products by uncovering product attributes consumers do not like.

7. The study of attitudes, especially of how attitudes change, may help evaluate the impact of advertising, particularly advertising directed to creating awareness of a new or forthcoming product.

The literature on consumer attitudes is very large. Most textbooks devote at least one entire chapter to this topic. The four articles selected in this section are representative of some of the more frequently appearing issues or topics related to attitudes.

"DO ATTITUDE CHANGES PRECEDE BEHAVIOR CHANGE?"

The role of attitudes in affecting behavior has received much academic as well as everyday attention. We can all think of a time when we heard a teacher tell a misbehaving youth, "I don't like your attitude!" We understand this to mean that the teacher didn't like the youth's behavior, and that the teacher thought that a change in the youth's attitude would produce a change in the youth's behavior.

In many cases, it does appear that attitude changes produce behavior changes. For instance, potential voters who are originally indifferent about a campaign may develop positive attitudes toward one candidate. It is expected then that these voters will cast their ballots for the candidate. Similarly, many advertising campaigns are designed with the goal of improving the attitude consumers have toward the product. The idea is that this improved attitude will lead to increased sales.

In their article Pinson and Roberto point out, however, that just because attitudes precede behavior in some cases does not mean that this is always the case. For example, a friend may encourage a person to try a new food that is being served. When the person asks what the food is, the friend may say, "Don't worry about that—just try it!" What the friend is actually saying is, "Don't try to label the item so you can connect previously formed attitudes with it. Consume it and then form an attitude toward it." The friend is supporting a sequence that is different from the sequence usually proposed in stages of adoption. The proposed sequence is trial (limited behavior); then attitude formation; then complete awareness. This final stage occurs when the friend finally tells the person what the food is.

Attribution theorists (see Section 10) are very interested in attitude changes that follow behavioral changes. For instance, in self-attributions the foot-in-the-door technique relies on attitude changes that follow behavioral changes. In this situation, a person who initially agrees to do some task will later agree to do a much larger task that would not be accepted if it were not for the initial small request. The process that occurs between the two behaviors is a change in attitude. The sequence is outlined below:

1. Person is asked to do a small task;
2. Person agrees (behavior$_1$).
3. Person asks, "Why did I do that?";
4. Person explains the action, "I must believe that this is a worthwhile activity" (attitude change).
5. Person is asked to do a larger related task;
6. Person agrees (behavior$_2$).

This frequently studied and frequently used phenomenon is based on the fact that attitude change can either precede or follow behavioral change.

Pinson and Roberto make one other key point. They mention a problem that is encountered in comparing different studies of the attitude-behavior link. Many of these studies use the same terminology (e.g., attitude, behavioral intention, behavior), but very different measurement techniques. This makes it seem that the various studies are referring to the same thing, when in fact they are not. Therefore, in reading articles on the effect of attitudes on consumer behavior, one must always check to see how the concepts have been measured.

"AN INVESTIGATION OF SITUATIONAL VARIATION IN BRAND CHOICE BEHAVIOR AND ATTITUDE"

It seems reasonable to assume that attitudes and actual purchase behavior may be affected by the particular situation in which the consumer finds him/herself. A consumer with plenty of time on the weekend after payday, for example, is likely to view a product in an entirely different light than when he or she is running out of money late the next week and is busy at work. The changed situation and the different viewpoint are likely to translate into different buying patterns. Several studies do exist that show empirically that preferences for product types vary across situations.

The marketing manager, however, may be more interested in how demand for a specific brand within a single product type changes as situations change. Miller and Ginter investigate how situations affect perception of brands and buying behavior within a specific product type. They establish a number of points:

- Purchase levels for brands vary with situations.
- The importance consumers attach to attributes of the product vary with situations.
- Perceptions of specific brands vary with situations.
- By considering the impact of situations on perceptions and attribute importance, predictions of brand choice can be improved.

These findings show that the marketing manager should be able to consider the competitive advantage of his or her product within a situational context. If the aggregate market is divided into the various situations consumers consider important, one can better study a product's relative advantages or weaknesses. Results may show, to use the authors' example, that consumers consider convenience to be more important for weekday lunch than in other situations. The manager can then examine whether consumers perceive convenience to be one of the product's major attributes. If they do not, the manager should be able to improve the competitive position by improving the perceived convenience of the brand in this situation.

"AFFECTIVE AND COGNITIVE FACTORS IN PREFERENCES"

Preferences and the formation of preferences by consumers have been the topic of much research in marketing and psychology. Traditional approaches to preferences have tended to view them as combined utilities. The consumer considers all of the product's features, decides how much he or she likes each feature, and determines how important each one is to him/her. Research has then focused on isolating the relevant attributes and discovering how the weights were assigned in summing up all attributes. The underlying assumption is that preference formation is essentially cognitive; that is, consumers form preferences toward a product because they have evaluated the product in some way.

This is not necessarily so, assert Zajonc and Markus. They point to the example of very highly spiced national foods in many cultures. Preferences for such spices are not formed by cognitive evaluation; in fact, initial aversions must often be overcome and the preference can only be developed by repeated exposure. In generalizing this observation, Zajonc and Markus therefore propose that preferences are precognitive rather than postcognitive. That is, affective responses, including preferences, may in many circumstances be independent of cognition and actually precede it.

The authors discuss a number of studies from the field of psychology that support their contention that repeated exposure can lead to preference, even if the subject is not aware of the exposure or cannot recall it. Preference has formed without cognition. Furthermore, cognition may follow preference formation and be used to justify it. In otherwords, the subjects preferred stimuli to which they had previously been exposed, even if they were unaware that they had been exposed. But when asked why they preferred the stimuli, they then formed evaluations based on the features of the stimuli. This was done to justify the preexisting preference.

Upon establishing that affect may indeed be separate from and precede cognition, it becomes necessary to examine affect more closely. Preferences that are not formed by cognitive means are not likely to be changed by appeals to reason. Thus, marketers need to gain a better understanding of affect. The remainder of the article discusses the manner in which precognitive affect can be viewed.

DO ATTITUDE CHANGES PRECEDE BEHAVIOR CHANGE?

**CHRISTIAN PINSON
AND
EDUARDO L. ROBERTO**

Source: Christian Pinson and Eduardo L. Roberto, "Do Attitude Changes Precede Behavior Change?" *Journal of Advertising Research*, Vol. 4, August, 1973, pp. 33–38. Reprinted with permission.

The question of whether attitude change comes before or after behavior change has been a raging controversy for many years in consumer behavior research and in the social sciences, and the subject has served as a central theme in three consecutive attitude research conferences of the American Marketing Association.

Studies linking attitude and behavior change have not gone any further than those by social psychologists in clarifying the real connection between the two variables. There is a group of consumer behaviorists who maintain that a necessary connection between attitude change and behavior change exists, or, more specifically, that behavior change must be somehow generated by an attitude change. Contesting this view is another group which holds the position that an attitude change is not necessary for behavior to change. Those who favor this position suggest that the only attitude change often observed comes from an antecedent behavior change.

The following article presents an analysis of some of the theoretical and empirical arguments exchanged by these two groups. In this analysis, the propositions developed are that: (1) the theoretical basis of the controversy suffers from the fallacy of division, and (2) that the empirical arguments exchanged are obscured by terminological and methodological ambiguities, failure to take account of third factors, and the unbounded nature of the proposition empirically tested.

The belief that attitude change and behavior change are strongly related is intuitively accepted as obvious on the basis of indirect evidence from many studies showing high correlations between measures of attitudes and behavior (Bauer, 1966).

The major issue here concerns the presumption that, in a logical sense, there cannot be behavior change without attitude change. As Robertson (1971) more specifically states: "It is difficult to conceive of a change in behavior occurring without some prior change within the organism." Supporters of this view allow only one exception—the case of "coercion." For example, Roper (1966) found that ". . . some attitude change must precede behavioral change barring the circumstances of coercion. Some internal change must precede a new external act assuming that that act is voluntary.'' Fothergill (1968) takes the same stand: ''The natural feeling of those in the advertising business that attitude changes must precede changes in behavior must be tautologically true unless, for example, people buy things which, at least at the time of purchase, they dislike.'' There is the problem here of deciding what situations should be defined as coercive, but more importantly the logical basis of these statements must be questioned.

THE FALLACY OF DIVISION

Some interesting insights are gained by representing the preceding reasoning in the following syllogistic arguments: Some internal change must precede a new external act; attitude change is an internal change and behavior change is a new external act; therefore, some attitude change must precede behavior change.

While the premise is reasonable, the conclusion is not because the argument is logically fallacious.

The invalid argument involved here is what logicians call the ''fallacy of division.'' This is found in the faulty transition from the premise that something holds true for some whole to the conclusion that the same holds true for a part of that whole (Mackie, 1967). In the present context of the attitude/behavior debate, this transition is readily seen. While it may be true that some internal change must precede a new external act, it does not necessarily follow that some attitude change must precede a behavior change, even if attitude change is a form of internal change and even if behavior change is also a form of an external act.

The real question is that of identifying the internal change. There are many plausible forms of internal changes that one can elect as possible explanatory variables. Is it, for example, a motivational variable, an opinion variable, or some other psychological factor? All too readily internal change is interpreted to be attitude change without seriously considering and screening the plausibility of these alternative internal variables.

Some may counter argue that there is not, in fact, a fallacy of division. It may be contended that the concept of attitude is broad enough to encom-

pass any internal change. This position is best stated by Robertson (1971): ''The concept of attitude as originally introduced into psychology was so broad as to refer to any intervening state of the organism that preceded and presumably accounted for a change in behavior.''

The above understanding of the concept of attitude cannot be challenged on logical or theoretical grounds. After all, any definition of attitude is valid in a theoretical context. What is at stake, however, is the soundness of the controversy. If attitude is conceived as subsuming all hypothetical mediators, then there is no reason for dispute since the argument that there cannot be behavior change without attitude change is then true by definition. This holds even in the case of coercion. The conception of attitude as the set of behavior mediators must be opposed not on theoretical or logical grounds but on practical ones.

EMPIRICAL ARGUMENTS

For a proper, empirically grounded evaluation of the controversy, it is important to have studies dealing directly with the relationship between changes rather than between levels. Studies of change constitute the relevant evidence in the controversy.

In the consumer behavior literature, there is no shortage of studies dealing with the relationship between levels of attitude and behavior, although several do exist.

Achenbaum (1968) presented data derived from a three-wave study of 4,000 women regarding their purchase behavior and attitudes toward 19 brands of packaged products. His conclusion was:

> If attitudes shift upward among non-users from June to September, the likelihood of their becoming users from September to December increases. . . . As attitudes from June to September dropped . . . the chances of a non-user becoming a user dropped too. . . . . The situation is much the same among users. (Thus) . . . there is a direct relationship—a predictive one if you wish—between attitude changes and purchase behavior.

Assael and Day (1968) reported finding support

for the proposition that "changes in attitudes are more closely related to subsequent behavior change, than are changes in awareness (and) that attitude change precedes rather than follows a behavioral change." Support came from the results of their analysis of time series data using a set of regression equations. The data came from Bristol-Myers' 14-month survey of brand attitude, awarenesss, and reported usage of deodorants and analgesics, and the Nestle Company's two-and-a-half year survey on the same variables for instant coffee.

Challenging the results of the foregoing studies are researchers who are skeptical about the empirical connection between attitude change and behavior change. The studies of Appel (1966) and Atkin (1962) represent this opposing view.

Appel reported an advertising experiment where attitude change supposedly was found not to precede a change in sales. His analysis concluded that, "The relationship between attitude and behavior is not nearly so simple as has been assumed." Atkin came to a similar interpretation after analyzing the results of a study on store patronage. He found that attitudes toward various stores changed only after shoppers bought there.

In his review of attitude research in England, Fothergill (1968) stated, "Changes in the attitude variables follow changes in the usage variable." In support of this proposition, he invoked evidence from data collected from some 250,000 interviews conducted by the British Market Research Bureau, Ltd. over a five-year period (Bird and Ehrenberg, 1965; 1966).

Conflicting interpretations in the studies just reviewed prompt a closer look. Doing so reveals that major sources of disagreement of results are in the variations of terminological usages and in the measurement techniques. Achenbaum, for example, measured attitude toward a brand as the position that a person takes on a five-point rating scale from excellent to poor. Assael and Day indicated that the Bristol-Myers survey measured brand attitudes by respondent agreement with a series of statements derived from advertising themes and product characteristics, while the Nestle survey derived measures of attitudes from statements based on the

relative perception of each brand. Fothergill considered "intentions to buy" and "top of the mind awareness" of a product as measures of generalized attitude.

This kind of situation is, of course, not peculiar. Use of terms with associated alternative meanings pervades the whole of social sciences. The confusing use of ambiguous terms in attitude research has even been noted by some attitude researchers themselves. For instance, Crespi (1966) comments:

> One difficulty is the inconsistencies in the use of terminology and of techniques of measurement. These inconsistencies can easily lead to a situation in which people think they are talking about the same thing when they are not, so that they think their findings are in conflict when they are merely different.

The different definitions of attitude can always be justified on the grounds that they merely represent what is judged by each investigator to be the most useful measure of the concept for his purposes. After all, an attitude is a hypothetical construct. By definition, it can have no true expression nor a valid measure. However, it must be realized that the ambiguity of the concept of attitude greatly reduces the possibility of a given proposition's confirmation or refutation. As a consequence, the consumer behavior studies reviewed are semantically inconsistent, thereby obstructing the possibility of reaching an agreement among different observers on the meaning of the empirical evidence they obtain.

RIVAL HYPOTHESES

It is also worthwhile noting that an observed absence or presence of a relationship between an attitude change and a behavior change does not necessarily mean that the two variables are unrelated or truly related. The way attitude change and behavior change co-vary may, in the first place, be highly contextual as suggested by Campbell (1963), McGuire (1969), and Wicker (1969).

Moreover, several intervening variables exist which may have a suppressing or multiplier effect on the empirical connection between attitude change and behavior change. First, the threats to internal and external validity developed by Campbell and Stanley (1963) constitute a set of potential factors that can affect the degree of empirically discernible relationships between attitude and behavior change. A partial treatment of this in the marketing context is found in Lipstein (1968).

A second factor is the degree to which the consumer perceives the connection between his attitude change and the possiblity of changing his future behavior. Researchers mistakenly may assume the existence of a linkage when in fact, insofar as the consumer is concerned, there are no such ties.

A third factor is the cost of behaving relative to the cost of the act at an earlier point in time, or relative to those of other alternative forms of behaving. Krugman (1965), for example, suggested that when the individual is highly involved with an object the precedence of attitude over behavior holds. When there is low involvement, behavior precedes attitude change.

Lipstein cited "the degree of economic risk which the consumer incurs in buying a product" and "the degree of anxiety surrounding a product category" as being the important cost contingencies. He went on to say that "Attitude change does in fact precede purchase in the case of big ticket items."

From the attitude consistency school comes a fourth factor: the degree of interrelationships among different attitudes that may individually influence the same behavior. A fifth factor is the presence or absence of opportunities to perform the behavior expected. Howard and Sheth (1969) discussed this factor under the name of "inhibitory factors" and included under its rubric such variables as time pressure, lack of availability, financial constraint, and momentary price change.

Finally, a sixth factor resides in the time gap between the attitude change and the expected behavior change. The foregoing intervening factors will have a higher probability of exerting their influence as this time gap increases. As Day (1972) explained, "There is a strong likelihood that unforeseen circumstances may intervene between the attitude measurement and the actual behavior."

The implication is clear. The important question is not whether attitude precedes behavior change but rather under what conditions does attitude change precede behavior change.

EMPIRICAL TESTING

A closer look at the studies reviewed indicates still another source of ambiguity in the current controversy. Explicating this source requires reference back to the studies that have sought to test the proposition that attitude change precedes behavior change.

Logicians call this an unbounded universal general proposition. This means that all types of attitude and behavior change that have taken place in the past, are taking place at present, and will occur in the future. What is crucial to note is that, from a philosophy of science viewpoint, this proposition can never be confirmed because of its high level of spatial and temporal universality. However, a single negative instance could suffice to falsify it. This means that the proposition is refutable but unconfirmable.

In order to be refutable and confirmable, the proposition should be bounded. This means that instead of working with the proposition "attitude change precedes behavior change," we should work with its more restricted form of "all cases in x universe are such that attitude change precedes behavior change." As a research requirement, this may be attained by working with and paying more attention to singular cases under varying contexts.

REFERENCES

Achenbaum, Alvin A. (1968), "Relevant Measures of Consumer Attitudes," cited in J. Fothergill, "Do Attitudes Change Before Behavior?" *Proceedings of ESOMAR Congress,* Opatija, 875–900.

Appel, V. (1966), "Attitude Change: Another Dubious Method for Measuring Advertising Effectiveness," in Lee Adler and Irving Crespi, eds., *Attitude Research at Sea,* Chicago: American Marketing Association, 141–52.

Assael, H., and Day, George (1968), "Attitudes and

Awareness as Predictors of Market Share," *Journal of Advertising Research,* Vol. 8, No. 4, 3–10.

Atkin, K. (1962), "Advertising and Store Patronage," *Journal of Advertising Research,* Vol. 2, No. 4, 18–23.

Bauer, Raymond (1966), "Attitudes, Verbal Behavior and Other Behavior," in Lee Adler and Irving Crespi, eds., *Attitude Research at Sea,* Chicago: American Marketing Association, 3–14.

Bird, M., and Ehrenberg, A. S. C. (1965), "Intentions-to-Buy and Claimed Brand Usages," a paper presented at the 9th ESOMAR-WAPOR Congress.

_____ (1966), "Non-Awareness and Non-Usage," a paper presented at the ESOMAR Seminar, Deauville.

Campbell, Donald T. (1963), "Social Attitudes and Other Acquired Behavioral Dispositions," in S. Koch, ed., *Psychology: A Study of a Science,* Vol. 6, New York: McGraw-Hill, 94–172.

_____, and Stanley, J. C. (1963), "Experimental and Quasi-Experimental Designs for Research in Teaching," in N. L. Gage, ed., *Handbook of Research on Teaching,* Chicago: Rand McNally, 171–246.

Crespi, Irving (1966), "The Challenge to Attitude Research," in Lee Adler and Irving Crespi, eds., *Attitude Research at Sea,* Chicago: American Marketing Association, 187–89.

Day, George (1972), "Theories of Attitude Structure and Change," in Scott Ward and T. Robertson, eds., *Consumer Behavior: Theoretical Sources,* Englewood Cliffs, N.J.: Prentice-Hall.

Fothergill, Jack (1968), "Do Attitudes Change Before Behavior?" *Proceedings of the ESOMAR Congress,* Opatija, 875–900.

Howard, John A., and Sheth, Jagdish N. (1969), *The Theory of Buyer Behavior,* New York: John Wiley and Sons.

Krugman, Herbert (Fall, 1965), "The Impact of Television Advertising: Learning without Involvement," *Public Opinion Quarterly,* Vol. 30, 583–96.

Lipstein, Benjamin (1968), "Anxiety, Risk, and Uncertainty in Advertising Effectiveness Measurements," in Lee Adler and Irving Crespi, eds., *Attitude Research on the Rocks,* Chicago: American Marketing Association, pp. 11–27.

Mackie, J. L. (1967), "Fallacies," in Paul Edwards, ed., *The Encyclopedia of Philosophy,* New York: Macmillan Co., 172–73.

McGuire, W. J. (1969), "The Nature of Attitude and Attitude Change," in G. Lindzey and E. Aronson, eds., *The Handbook of Social Psychology,* 2nd ed., Reading, Mass.: Addison-Wesley, 136–314.

Mueller, E. (1967), "Effects of Consumer Attitudes on Purchases," *The American Economic Review,* Vol. 47, 946–65.

Robertson, Thomas S. (1971), *Innovative Behavior and Communication,* New York: Holt, Rinehart and Winston, 66–67.

Roper, Burns (1966), "The Importance of Attitudes, the Difficulty of Measurement," in J. S. Wright and J. Goldstucker, eds., *New Ideas for Successful Marketing,* Chicago: American Marketing Association.

Wicker, Allan, (1969), "Attitudes versus Actions: The Relationship of Verbal and Overt Behavioral Responses to Attitude Objects," *The Journal of Social Issues,* Vol. 25, 41–78.

AN INVESTIGATION OF SITUATIONAL VARIATION IN BRAND CHOICE BEHAVIOR AND ATTITUDE

**KENNETH E. MILLER
AND
JAMES L. GINTER**

Source: Kenneth E. Miller and James L. Ginter, "An Investigation of Situational Variation in Brand Choice Behavior and Attitude," *Journal of Marketing Research*, Vol. 16, February, 1979, pp. 111–123. Reprinted from *Journal of Marketing Research*, published by the American Marketing Association.

Recent marketing literature contains reports of several studies in which the affective component of consumer attitudes is modeled on the basis of product attributes and the resultant measure used to predict preference or behavior. One of the reasons for the popularity of this approach to the study of consumer behavior is the diagnostic value which the attribute-based model holds for the marketing manager. Explicit consideration of situation-related variables that are specific to the consumer's decision-making context may reduce the unexplained variance and increase the managerial value of the research for product positioning decisions.

Researchers recently have considered only broad product categories in investigating the situational variation of preference for product types (Belk, 1974; Sandell, 1968). The emphasis has been placed on the situational variation of primary demand for the product types. The marketing manager, however, typically is concerned with the secondary demand for his brand as it competes with other brands of the same product type. Marketing strategies for specific brands are related to their relative strengths and weaknesses. The concept of situation becomes managerially important if these relative strengths and weaknesses differ by situation, i.e., if the effect of situation is not the same for all brands. In addition to the greater managerial importance of studying the situational variation in purchase of brands rather than general product classes, the use of brands provides a more conservative test of the influence of situations. For example, it is less impressive to show that a person's choice of dining out in an expensive restaurant rather than in a fast food franchise is related to the nature of the eating occasion than to show that choice of one fast food franchise over another is related to eating occasion.

The research reported here is designed to assess whether situation-specific measures improve the measured relationship between attitude and behavior (consistent with suggestions by Wicker, 1969). Specifically, the authors extend previous research by: (1) using competing brands in a narrowly defined product category, and (2) considering self-reports of behavior rather than preference, thus allowing examination of situational attitude-behavior congruence.

BACKGROUND

Situational variation of stated preference for specific product types within a general product class has been established empirically. Belk (1974), for example, found that 19.7% of the variance in preference for snack products (e.g., potato chips, popcorn, cookies, fruit, ice cream) and 34.3% of the variance in preference for meat products (e.g., hot dogs, steak, chicken, hamburgers, fish) were explained by main effects of situation and the interaction of situation with other variables. The appeal of the concept of situational variance in consumer behavior has led to a discussion of adequate and generalizable methods of defining and measuring situations (Belk, 1974; Lutz and Kakkar, 1975).

Belk (1974) defines situation as "all those factors particular to a time and place of observation which do not follow from a knowledge of personal (intra-individual) and stimulus (choice alternative) attributes, and which have a demonstrable and systematic effect on current behavior." This definition separates the influences of the person, the situation, and the stimulus object (brand) on consumer behavior. It therefore establishes situation as external to the individual's psychological nature. Though other researchers (Lutz and Kakkar, 1975) have argued that situation should be defined psychologically in terms of how the individual transforms the situational input to behavioral output, the primary managerial value of the concept appears to lie in its generalizability. Situation may interact with individual characteristics to determine response, but a greater benefit can be derived from objective specification of commonly occurring situations. Such specification allows for their description, isolation, and control in relation to the consumers' actual responses toward the brands. The advantage, in managerial terms, is that situations are identified across individuals, and brand-related decisions specific to these situations can be made.

No previously reported research has examined the situational variation of measures of attitude toward specific brands. This research focuses on the issue of managerial relevance in that the situational variation of importances, perceptions, and self-reported behavior is examined. The relationship between situation-specific attitudes and situation-specific brand choice behavior also is investigated.

The research issues were examined through testing of the following hypotheses.

H1: Purchase levels of specific brands vary differentially across situations.

H2: Attribute importances vary differentially across situations.

H3: Perceptions of specific brands vary differentially across situations.

H4: Situation-specific measurement of attribute importances and perceptions improves prediction of brand choice over general (nonsituational) measurement.

METHOD

Selection of Product and Attributes

The product category of fast food restaurants was chosen for analysis. This product category was narrowed to include primarily those fast food restaurants oriented toward hamburgers. Inclusion of different types of products could have led to emphasis on differences between brands selling different types of products and masking of differences between brands selling the same type of product. This definition of the product category also seemed consistent with that which would be used by one of the brand managers in identifying the closest competitors. The following eight fast food restaurants were used in the study.

Arby's
Borden Burger
Burger Chef
Burger King
Hungry Herman's
McDonald's
Wendy's
White Castle

Seven of the eight brands specialize in hamburgers, and Arby's offers roast beef sandwiches. Hungry Herman's is a local operation with only one location, and Borden Burger is a local chain with more locations in the city than any other brand at the time of the study. The other brands have broad regional or national distribution.

According to preliminary investigation, these brands were frequently used by much of the local population and permitted consideration of a series of choices. The use of a set of choices provided a richer measure of behavior than a single choice because the effects of factors unique to any one choice were reduced. Moreover, each choice in this setting could be affected by the situational context. The selection of the fast food market also made brand-specific analysis possible. Preliminary investigation indicated that this local market had some degree of benefit segmentation. White Castle, for example, was perceived to be lowest in price, whereas Wendy's was seen as offering a higher quality product at a higher price, and Borden Burger was seen to have a wide variety of menu and to be very convenient. The fact that different brands were perceived as being most favorable on different attributes would tend to reduce "halo" effects, whereby the preferred brand is seen as the best on all attributes.

Six group interviews of six to eight persons were conducted to determine the criteria on which consumers differentiate fast food restaurants and decide which restaurant(s) to frequent. The following attributes were elicited.

Speed of service.
Variety of menu.
Popularity with children.
Cleanliness.
Convenience.
Taste of food.
Price.

Selection of Situations

The external definition of situation was used in this study because of its managerial advantage, and situation was operationalized as different eating occasions. The eating occasions were chosen on the basis of two criteria: (1) they should be encountered frequently by customers so that an adequate number of observations could be obtained for each situation, and (2) they should be perceived by respondents as clearly different so that variation between them could be measured.

Table 1   Proportion of respondents who frequented fast food restaurants in each situation

Situation	Percentage
Lunch on a weekday	79.2
Snack during a shopping trip	70.4
Evening meal when rushed for time	55.0
Evening meal with the family when not rushed for time	47.7

Group interviews resulted in selection of the following four eating occasions.

Lunch on a weekday.
Snack during a shopping trip.
Evening meal when rushed for time.
Evening meal with the family when not rushed for time.

The proportion of respondents indicating that they frequented fast food restaurants in each of the situations is shown in Table 1. These findings suggest that the eating occasions selected met the criteria established for the study.

Data Collection

Data were collected over a three-month period from a mail panel residing in Columbus, Ohio, by a five-wave questionnaire. The panel was constructed by a solicitation letter to a random sample of 2,800 residents whose names appeared in the Columbus telephone directory. A total of 950 fast food users initially agreed to participate in the study. Introductory instructions for each questionnaire specified that the same household member was to respond each time, and demographic checks were made to assure the consistency of respondents. Compensation for completing all five questionnaires consisted of five dollars and a small gift.

The number of usable responses from each of the five questionnaire waves is shown in Table 2. Demographic features and initial attitudes of respondents who dropped out of the study were compared with those of respondents who completed all five questionnaires. The two groups were different ($\alpha = .05$) on only three of 96 explanatory

Table 2   Number of usable responses

Questionnaire wave	Number of responses[a]
1	742
2	622
3	502
4	487
5	440

[a]Original mailing 950.

variables considered. Tests also were conducted to ascertain whether participation in the study influenced attitudes or behavior. Five days after the mailing of the fourth questionnaire, a similarly generated independent sample received the same questionnaire (76 fast food users returned the questionnaire in usable form). Comparison of these responses with those from wave four of the panel showed that the panel members were more familiar with some of the brands. The increased familiarity may have been caused by the study's use of some fast food restaurants which were not very well known (e.g., Hungry Herman's). Attitudinal differences between the groups were minor (near the level of chance), and behavioral differences were nonexistent. Also, situational usage frequency was not significantly different. Respondents were asked to identify the objectives of the research project on the fifth questionnaire, and six individuals were excluded from further analysis because of their insight.

Attitude Measures

A primary concern in the managerial setting is the relative positions of competitive brands in a single product category. Therefore, attitude toward each brand is expressed in this study as a function of attribute importance and the perceived performance of the brand on each of the attributes.

Attribute importances and perceptions on one attribute (convenience) were measured within eating occasion scenarios. The situational measurement of perception on convenience only was based on the notion that the relevance of eating occasion may not be the same for perceptions on

all attributes. Beliefs on some attributes may be tied directly to the brand and invariant across situations, and beliefs on other attributes may be related to the eating occasion for which the brand is considered. Belk (December 1975) also made the distinction between characteristics which are "lasting and general" features and those which are specific to "time and place." Perceptions of convenience of the brands were expected to vary across the eating occasions, because differences in the respondents' general locations for different occasions could have caused differences in the relative perceived proximity of the alternative fast food establishments. Because perceptions on the other attributes were not expected to vary across the eating occasions considered and questionnaire length was an important consideration, these perceptions were not measured within the situational contexts.

The situational measures of brand choice behavior, attribute importances, and perceived convenience were used in testing for the existence of situational variation of these constructs. Attribute importances and perceptions (on all attributes) also were measured without reference to eating occasion. These nonsituational measures and their situational counterparts were compared in terms of their ability to predict brand choice.

ANALYSIS AND RESULTS

Situational Variation of Behavior (H1)

Reported brand choice was the dependent variable in the predictive phase of the study, and its variation across eating occasions was tested. Each respondent's reported choice data over the 12 weeks of the study were used in the analysis (respondents who did not purchase any of the brands on any of the eating occasions were eliminated). The data for each respondent consisted of an eight brand by four eating occasion matrix of number of purchases. The cell means are shown in Table 3.

Significance of differences in the purchase frequencies across brands and situations was tested by a two-way analysis of variance (see Table 4). The main effects of brands and situations were significant. In addition, the interaction term was significant, thus indicating that the effect of situation on

Table 3 Mean numbers of purchases during the study (n = *391*)

Brand	Sit. A Lunch on a weekday (mkt. share)	Sit. B Evening meal when rushed for time (mkt. share)	Sit. C Evening meal with family when not rushed for time (mkt. share)	Sit. D Snack during a shopping trip (mkt. share)
1. Arby's	.24[a] (4.8)	.11 (5.4)	.06 (3.7)	.05 (4.2)
2. Borden Burger	.91 (18.4)	.39 (19.1)	.17 (10.4)	.16 (13.3)
3. Burger Chef	.46 (9.3)	.11 (5.4)	.09 (5.5)	.05 (4.2)
4. Burger King	.69 (13.9)	.32 (15.7)	.20 (12.3)	.17 (14.2)
5. Hungry Herman's	.17 (3.4)	.03 (1.5)	.03 (1.8)	.01 (0.8)
6. McDonald's	1.40 (28.3)	.68 (33.3)	.62 (38.0)	.43 (35.8)
7. Wendy's	.65 (13.1)	.28 (13.7)	.36 (22.1)	.16 (13.3)
8. White Castle	.43 (8.7)	.12 (5.9)	.10 (6.1)	.17 (14.2)

[a]The 391 respondents averaged .24 purchases of Arby's on the eating occasion "lunch on a weekday," and this figure represents 4.8% market share in this situation.

purchase frequencies was different for different brands (H1 was supported). The existence of situational variance of individual brands was examined by analysis of simple main effects of situation at each brand (see Kirk, 1968). These texts showed that purchase levels of six of the brands varied significantly across situations and that the purchase levels of Arby's and Hungry Herman's did not.

The significant interaction term also can be viewed as showing that differences among brands varied by situation. Analysis of simple main effects of brand at situation led to sums of squares indicating that brands were most different on the eating occasion "lunch on a weekday" and least on "snack during a shopping trip." Table 4 notes that the analysis of both sets of simple main effects is somewhat redundant, as each partitions the in-

teraction term. Both sets of analyses are reported, however, because the importance of the research question may depend on one's perspective.

Situational Variation of Attribute Importance (H2)

If the use of situation-specific attribute importances is to improve predictive power of the attitude measure, the values of these measures must show situational differences. The existence of situational variation in attribute importance was tested on data collected from the first questionnaire, on which the number of respondents was greatest. Each respondent had indicated the eating occasions on which he/she used the product and the importance of the attributes for each of these eating occasions. The data for each respondent potentially consisted

Table 4 ANOVA of brand choice

Source	d.f.	s.s.	F
Brands	7	568.95	44.55[a]
at sit. A	(7)	431.81	33.89[a]
at sit. B	(7)	123.66	9.71[a]
at sit. C	(7)	105.85	8.31[a]
at sit. D	(7)	45.45	3.57[b]
Brands × subjects	2730	4980.58	
Situations	3	426.26	49.94[a]
at br. 1	(3)	9.03	1.06
at br. 2	(3)	145.57	17.09[a]
at br. 3	(3)	41.90	4.92[b]
at br. 4	(3)	68.28	8.01[a]
at br. 5	(3)	6.66	.78
at br. 6	(3)	214.08	25.13[a]
at br. 7	(3)	50.51	5.93[b]
at br. 8	(3)	28.19	3.31[c]
Situations × subjects	1170	3328.65	
Brands × situations	21	137.97	4.50[a]
Brands × situations × subjects	8190	11970.38	
Subjects	390	1140.17	
Total	12511	22552.96	

[a]$p < .001$.
[b]$p < .01$.
[c]$p < .05$.
The Geisser-Greenhouse (1958) correction for use of the *F* distribution in multivariate analysis was used in all tests of significance.

of a seven attribute by four eating occasion matrix of attribute importances. Table 5 shows the mean attribute importances within each eating occasion. The means of the nonsituational responses, which were used in the general form of the multiattribute model, also are shown. The significance of situational differences in attribute importances was tested by a two-factor repeated measurements analysis of variance design. The use of this analytical design limited the analysis to only those individuals who had reported using the product on all of the eating occasions and who provided complete data

$(n = 111)$. The attribute "popularity with children" was eliminated from this analysis because it was relevant only for respondents with children, and its inclusion in the analytical design would have further reduced the number of responses analyzed. A one-way analysis of variance with repeated measures of importance of "popularity with children" showed that it varied significantly across the four eating occasions.

The results of the two-way analysis of variance are shown in Table 6. The main effects of attributes and situations and their interaction were significant in this analysis. The significant interaction term indicates that the difference in importance on various eating occasions was not the same for all attributes and therefore supports H2. The differential effect of situations on attribute importances raises the question of where this influence was strongest. That is, which attributes varied most across situations, and were there attributes whose importance was constant across situations? These questions were investigated by analysis of simple main effects of situation at attribute. The sums of squares indicated that importance of "speed of service" was most different across the situations and that importance of "taste of food," "cleanliness," and "price" did not vary with situation.[1] Another way of viewing the significant interaction term is that differences among attribute importance ratings varied by situation. This view leads to the question of which stiuations showed greater (or less) difference in importance among attributes. The analysis of simple main effects of attribute at situation showed that attribute importances were most different for "evening meal when rushed for time" and least for "snack during a shopping trip," although attribute importances were significantly different within each of the eating occasions. As in the analysis of purchase level, the investigation of both

[1]The effect of the reduced sample size, due to the requirement of complete data for all four eating occasions, on these results was examined by testing equality of importance of each attribute in all possible pairs of eating occasions. This step allowed use of data from all respondents who had frequented fast food restaurants in the two situations compared. Results supported findings shown in Table 6.

Table 5 Mean attribute importances (n = 111)

Attribute	Nonsituational	Lunch on a weekday (sit. A)	Evening meal when rushed for time (sit. B)	Evening meal with family when not rushed for time (sit. C)	Snack during a shopping trip (sit. D)
1. Taste of food	4.76[a]	4.64	4.60	4.72	4.48
2. Cleanliness	4.54	4.32	4.31	4.41	4.35
3. Convenience	3.47	4.32	4.32	3.40	4.23
4. Price	3.64	3.92	3.84	3.83	3.89
5. Speed of service	3.65	4.45	4.45	3.05	3.98
6. Variety of menu	2.83	2.70	2.62	3.43	2.79
7. Popularity with children (n = 62)	2.28	1.95	2.69	3.21	2.58

[a]Importances were measured on a scale from 1 = very unimportant to 6 = very important.

Table 6 ANOVA for attribute importance

Source	d.f.	s.s.	F
Attributes	5	774.42	64.68[a]
at sit. A	(5)	275.90	23.09[a]
at sit. B	(5)	297.89	24.93[a]
at sit. C	(5)	232.42	19.45[a]
at sit. D	(5)	206.29	17.26[a]
Attributes × subjects	550	1317.08	
Situations	3	24.83	12.89[a]
at att. 1	(3)	3.41	1.78
at att. 2	(3)	.75	.39
at att. 3	(3)	66.38	34.57[a]
at att. 4	(3)	.62	.32
at att. 5	(3)	146.16	76.13[a]
at att. 6	(3)	45.59	23.74[a]
Situations × subjects	330	212.00	
Attributes × situations	15	238.08	29.06[a]
Attributes × situations × subjects	1650	901.09	
Subjects	110	896.28	
Total	2663	4363.78	

One-way ANOVA for attribute 7 (n = 62)

Situations	3	49.65	13.40[a]
Situations × subjects	183	226.92	

[a]p < .001.

sets of simple main effects is somewhat redundant as each involves partitioning of the interaction term. Results of both sets of analyses are presented, however, because of the different questions they address.

Situational Variation of Belief (H3)

Convenience was the only attribute on which perception was measured in a situational format. Responses of individuals who had indicated use of fast food establishments on all four eating occasions and who had provided a complete set of data on perceived convenience were considered (n = 120). As in the previous analysis, this limitation of the sample was necessary for the repeated measures design. The data for each respondent consisted of an eight brands by four eating occasions matrix of perceived convenience. Mean situational and nonsituational perceptions of convenience from the first questionnaire are shown in Table 7.

The results of the two-factor repeated measurements analysis of variance are shown in Table 8. Main effects of situations and brands and their interaction were significant. The significance of the interaction term indicates that perceptions of the individual brands varied differentially across the situations and therefore supports H3. As in the previous analyses, this finding raises the question of the location of the situational influence. Analysis of

Table 7 Mean convenience perceptions (n = *120)*

Brand	Nonsituational	Lunch on a weekday (sit. A)	Evening meal when rushed for time (sit. B)	Evening meal with family when not rushed for time (sit. C)	Snack during a shopping trip (sit. D)
1. Arby's	2.50[a]	1.56	2.09	2.26	2.49
2. Borden Burger	3.64	3.00	3.64	3.67	3.43
3. Burger Chef	2.81	2.04	2.71	2.87	2.53
4. Burger King	2.99	2.89	3.34	3.49	3.64
5. Hungry Herman's	.88	1.24	.69	.74	.87
6. McDonald's	3.75	3.29	3.82	3.82	3.72
7. Wendy's	2.80	2.63	2.74	2.94	2.83
8. White Castle	2.65	2.27	2.18	2.35	2.18

[a]Perceptions of convenience were measured on a scale from 1 = out of the way to 6 = close to where I am.

simple main effects of situation at brand showed that perceived convenience of Arby's was most different across situations and that perceived convenience of Wendy's and White Castle did not vary by situation.[2] The interaction term also can be interpreted as showing that differences in perceived convenience among brands varied across situations. Analysis of simple main effects of brand at situation showed that perceived convenience was most different in the situations "evening meal when rushed for time" and "evening meal with family when not rushed for time" and least in "lunch on a weekday," although perceived convenience of the brands was significantly different on each of the eating occasions.

The results of the analyses indicate that, as hypothesized, purchases of specific brands, attribute importances, and perceived convenience varied across the four eating occasions. The ability of situational measurement of attitude to improve prediction of subsequent behavior over that obtained from nonsituational measurement was examined by the following analysis.

Table 8 ANOVA for perceived convenience

Source	d.f.	s.s.	F
Brands	7	2752.33	66.48[a]
at sit. A	(7)	436.39	10.55[a]
at sit. B	(7)	869.83	21.03[a]
at sit. C	(7)	843.18	20.38[a]
at sit. D	(7)	739.20	17.87[a]
Brands × subjects	833	4926.48	
Situations	3	92.44	11.16[a]
at br. 1	(3)	56.64	6.84[a]
at br. 2	(3)	34.75	4.20[b]
at br. 3	(3)	46.01	5.56[a]
at br. 4	(3)	37.83	4.57[b]
at br. 5	(3)	22.22	2.69[c]
at br. 6	(3)	22.98	2.78[c]
at br. 7	(3)	5.95	.75
at br. 8	(3)	2.34	.28
Situations × subjects	357	985.87	
Brands × situations	21	136.26	
Brands × situations × subjects	2499	2790.42	
Subjects	119	2474.17	
Total	3839	14157.97	

[2]The effect of the reduced sample size was examined in the same manner as for the attribute importance analysis. Results shown in Table 8 were supported.

[a]$p < .001$.
[b]$p < .01$.
[c]$p < .05$.

Prediction of Behavior (H4)

Self-reported behavior within situations was predicted with two forms of the multiattribute model. In the first form, attribute importances and perceptions were measured without situational scenario.

$$A_j = \sum_{i=1}^{n} V_i B_{ij}$$

where:

A_j = attitude toward brand j,
V_i = affective importance of attribute i,
B_{ij} = perceived amount of attribute i contained by brand j, and
n = number of attributes considered.

This operationalization is consistent with previous managerial applications of the model, and this form is referred to as the "general" form, or "model G." The predictive power of model G provides a basis for comparison of the performance of the situation-specific multiattribute model.

In the second form of the model, attribute importances and perceptions of one attribute (convenience) were measured within eating occasion scenarios. Perceptions on the other six attributes were measured without reference to eating occasion. This model form is referred to as the "situational" model, or "model S," and can be shown as:

$$A_{js} = \sum_{i=1}^{n} V_{is} B_{ijs}$$

where:

A_{js} = attitude toward brand j in situation s,
V_{is} = importance of attribute i in situation s,
B_{ijs} = perceived amount of attribute i contained by brand j, in situation s.
n = number of attributes considered,
s = situation ($s = 1, 2, \ldots, p$), and
p = number of situations considered.

Respondents had indicated number of purchases of each brand within each eating occasion. Brand chosen within each eating occasion was predicted with model S by using attribute importance and convenience perception data specific to that eating occasion.

The predictive ability of the two forms of the model was compared within each situation to test the hypothesized superiority of model S. For each model form, the attitude data from each questionnaire were used to predict the brand purchased during the subsequent three-week period. The dependent measure in this analysis was the brand (or brands) purchased within the situation during each three-week period. Through this procedure every purchase made by the individual during a three-week period was predicted to be that brand with the most favorable attitude score from the immediately preceding questionnaire. Distribution of purchases across more than one brand during one of the three-week periods lowered the predictive accuracy. The measure of performance of each model was the cumulative proportion of correct predictions during the 12-week course of the study. Predictions were made separately for each of the 440 individuals completing the study who frequented fast food restaurants during the course of the study.

The model forms were compared in each situation by subtracting model G's percentage correct from that of model S for each person. The means and standard deviations of the differences were used to test the hypothesis that model S led to greater predictive accuracy. The results of the comparisons shown in Table 9 indicate that model S led to a significantly greater proportion of correct predictions in three of the four situations. Therefore, H4 was supported for "lunch on a weekday," "evening meal when rushed for time," and "evening meal with family when not rushed for time" and was rejected for "snack during a shopping trip." A possible explanation for the unique finding with respect to "snack during a shopping trip" can be developed from Tables 5 and 7. The attribute importances and perceptions of convenience within this situation appear to be generally closer to the nonsituational values than are the corresponding measures within other situations.

Table 9 Accuracy of prediction of behavior

Situation	n^a	Mean proportion correct		Mean difference (s.d.).	Z
		Model G	Model S		
Lunch on a weekday	210	.305	.413	.108 (.023)	4.65[b]
Evening meal when rushed for time	159	.386	.440	.054 (.017)	3.05[b]
Evening meal with family when not rushed for time	128	.459	.495	.036 (.021)	1.69[b]
Snack during a shopping trip	94	.316	.347	.031 (.034)	.92

[a]Sample size is number of respondents who purchased on each occasion during the course of the study.
[b]$p < .05$.

DISCUSSION AND MANAGERIAL IMPLICATIONS

The tests of situational variation of the attitude and choice measures and comparison of the two model forms led to the following findings for the fast food market.

1. Mean number of purchases varied over the four eating occasions for six of the eight brands.
2. Perceived importance of four of the seven restaurant attributes varied across eating occasions. The significant interaction between attribute and situation indicated that situational differences in importance were not the same for all attributes.
3. Perceived convenience of the restaurants varied according to situational scenario presented. The interaction between situation and brand indicated that situational differences in perceived convenience were not the same for all brands.
4. The use of situation-specific measures of attribute importance and perceived convenience increased the predictive power of the multiattribute model significantly for three of the four eating occasions.

The first three findings are clearly not independent of each other. The results showed situational variation in purchase level, attribute importance, and perceptions, but many attribute-based models assume linkages among these constructs. Lutz and Kakkar (1976), for example, provide a conceptual framework for the ways in which situations may affect attitudes and behavior. These linkages among the constructs lead to the managerial usefulness of situational analysis. The existence of situational variation of behavior in a closely competitive product category was established. The situational advantages (or deficiencies) of those brands exhibiting situational variation can be assessed through measurement of situation-specific attribute importances and perceptions. Consideration of competitive position within situational context, rather than in the general setting, may lead to greater diagnostic precision and, therefore, to additional information for decision making. Wendy's, for example, has a higher mean proportion of purchases for "evening meal with the family when not rushed for time" than for other situations (Table 3). Table 5 shows that speed of service is relatively less important for that situation than for the others. A check of mean perceptions of speed of service indicated that Wendy's was perceived to be about average on that attribute. Management of this brand may be able to increase sales in other situations by increasing speed of service (if necessary) and/or promoting that characteristic.

The variation of attribute importances across situations may have implications for promotional strategy. For example, Table 3 shows that the number of purchases on the eating occasion "lunch on a weekday" was higher than on the other eating occasions ($p<.01$), and Table 5 shows that "convenience" was relatively important in that situation. Yet analysis of Table 7 shows that four brands were perceived as less convenient for "lunch on a weekday" than for any other eating occasion. Managers of these brands may be able to increase lunchtime sales by improving the perceived convenience of their brands for "lunch on a weekday." If a product characteristic is much more important in one situation than in others, it may be beneficial to promote that characteristic in a situational context. The alternative strategy of promoting a product characteristic without reference to situation requires the consumer to associate the message with the setting in which it is important and may be less effective. Because the same consumer may purchase the product in several situations and may have different concerns in each of these situations, a potential strategy is to develop a *set* of situation-specific messages. Each consumer then would be exposed to a set of promotions which would focus on product characteristics most applicable to specific contexts in which the product is purchased.

Many of the managerial implications were developed from the analyses of simple main effects of situation within the other variables. The alternative investigations of the interaction terms, analyses of simple main effects of variables within situation, may be of greater interest to the consumer researcher and of less interest to the brand manager. These results show that differences in purchase level among brands, differences in importance among attributes, and differences in perceived convenience among brands varied by situation. Although these differences were statistically signifi-

cant in each case, those eating occasions on which the differences were greater or less were identified.

CONCLUSIONS

The results of the model comparison were consistent with the previously cited proposals for situation-specific measurement of attitude and behavior. Both the significance of the relative predictive power of the situational model and its absolute level of predictive accuracy (49.5% in the best situation) support its use. The procedure of predicting subsequent actual brand choice enhances the credibility of these figures.

The findings of this study support the argument that explicit consideration of situational contexts may contribute to the understanding of consumer behavior. In addition, the use of brands in this study demonstrates that situational influence is not restricted to grossly different product types. As the discussion indicates, the added understanding of influences of behavior can be very helpful to a marketing manager. Use of nonsituational models is equivalent to the aggregation over contexts, and differences among situations then contribute to the unexplained variance of the measures.

One possible avenue of future research is the investigation of the relationship between nonsituational measures and situational measures. A weighted composite of situational measures (perhaps by frequency with which the situations are encountered) may reflect general attitudes and behavior. This approach would be especially relevant to product categories in which one purchase is used in several situations (e.g., durable goods).

REFERENCES

Belk, Russell W. "An Exploratory Assessment of Situational Effects in Buyer Behavior," *Journal of Marketing Research,* 11 (May 1974), 156–63.

———. "Situational Variables and Consumer Behavior," *Journal of Consumer Research,* 2 (December 1975), 157–64.

Geisser, Seymour and Samuel W. Greenhouse. "An Extension of Box's Results on the Use of the *F* Distribution in Multivariate Analysis," *Annals of Mathematical Statistics*, 29 (1958), 885–9.

Kirk, Roger E. *Experimental Design: Procedures for the Behavioral Sciences,* Belmont, California: Brooks/ Cole, 1968, 263–6.

Lutz, Richard J. and Pradeep Kakkar, "The Psychological Situation as a Determinant of Consumer Behavior," *Proceedings,* Vol. II, Association for Consumer Research, 1975, 439–53.

_____ and _____. "Situational Influence in Interpersonal Persuasion," *Proceedings,* Vol. III, Association for Consumer Research, 1976, 370–8.

Sandell, Rolf G. "Effects of Attitudinal and Situational Factors on Reported Choice Behavior," *Journal of Marketing Research,* 5 (November 1968), 405–8.

Wicker, Allan W. "Attitudes Versus Actions: The Relationship of Verbal and Overt Behavioral Responses to Attitude Objects," *Journal of Social Issues,* 25 (1969), 41–78.

AFFECTIVE AND COGNITIVE FACTORS IN PREFERENCES

**ROBERT B. ZAJONC
AND
HAZEL MARKUS**

Source: Robert B. Zajonc and Hazel Markus, "Affective and Cognitive Factors in Preferences," *Journal of Consumer Research*, Vol. 9, September, 1982, pp. 123–131. Reprinted with permission.

One of the clearest manifestations of the puzzling interplay of cognitive and affective influences is found in food preferences. All collectivities—be they ethnic groups, tribes, or nations—have a favorite food, which often carries a symbolic and ceremonial significance. This food is an important element of ethnic identity, and there are rigid standards about its proper taste and preparation. Any group member who dislikes it or rejects it on grounds other than health is treated as a deviant whose ethnic loyalty—and perhaps mental health— should be seriously questioned. Yet for each of these collectivities, there is another one somewhere in the world that finds this food entirely inedible, if not repulsive. Dog meat is a delicacy in some parts of East Asia, but few Americans would find it appetizing. The same can be said of snakes, birds' nests, chocolate-covered cockroaches, fish eyes, veal pancreas, and rams' testicles. Most Americans like corn, but in various countries corn has been thought suitable only for pigs. Consider martinis, for example: the first martini we taste as children is an abominable experience and we wonder what on earth could prompt adults to ingest such a vile substance.

Some foods are so pungent that a considerable period of habituation is required to neutralize the fiery effects and severe irritation of the oral mucosa. Chili pepper, which is an indispensable food ingredient in Mexico, is a case in point. Chili pepper is the major flavoring of food in a Zapotec village extensively studied by Rozin and Schiller (1980). The inhabitants of that village have chili pepper with every meal—at least three times a day—and they start eating chili at age five. All nonsweet food receives chili flavoring. When forced to do without chili, the villagers miss it and complain. There is other research indicating this remarkable tenacity of food habits. In all instances, the fanciers of these pungent foods must have started with a strong aversion that gradually became transformed into a strong preference, sometimes verging on addiction.

PREFERENCES: TRADITIONAL AND ALTERNATIVE VIEWS

These examples dramatize two questions that are basic in social psychology and of some importance in consumer research as well: how preferences are acquired and how they are modified. Mexican children are not born with a craving for chili pepper: it is clearly an acquired taste. But to say that it is an acquired taste is a serious understatement, because one acquires a taste for chili pepper only after overcoming a powerful innate aversion. The initial reaction is far from neutrality or indifference. If it is possible to change an innate aversion to something like chili pepper, then it should be possible to change almost any attitude and any preference. How is this accomplished? Clearly, people do not acquire a craving for chili pepper by being told about its nutritive properties. One cannot tell people that chili pepper contains vitamins A and C and expect an instant, insatiable craving for chili pepper. Because the aversive reaction that invariably occurs on initial encounters with pungent food represents powerful negative affect, Mexican mothers in the Zapotec village studied by Rozin and Schiller (1980) start feeding children unseasoned versions of various foods and add chili pepper very gradually. At the same time, a great deal of social support comes from the surroundings—all the neighbors and relatives eat seasoned food—and eating seasoned food seems to be a mark of growing up. Thus, becoming fond of the pungent flavoring involves overcoming strong negative affect by other significant affective factors, such as parental reinforcement, social conformity pressures, identification with the group, machismo, and so on.

Of course, many attitudes can be formed without these affective supports, by means of cognitive factors alone—for example, when a person is given some persuasive communication. If some authority such as *Consumer Reports* prints a very favorable evaluation of an otherwise unknown and unused product—say a newly patented corkscrew—some segment of the population will become favorably disposed to it. Thus, the antecedents of preferences may involve cognitive *and* affective components in a variety of combinations. In some cases the cognitive component may be dominant, in some the cognitive and affective factors may interact with each other, and in other cases the affective factors may be dominant and primary.

Preferences are themselves primarily *affectively based behavioral phenomena.* A preference for X over Y is a tendency of the organism to approach X more often and more vigorously than Y. Approach, in turn, which is manifested in the attainment and maintenance of proximity, is a tendency controlled mainly by affective processes. The prototype of such an approach tendency is seen in imprinting in animals. Thus, a presocial bird that is repeatedly presented with a conspicuous object soon after hatching shows a strong preference for that object by remaining close to it over extended periods of time (Bateson 1966). Approach tendency among humans may be evidenced in a variety of other ways, such as making favorable comments, buying a product, proselytizing, contributing money, giving blood, or giving life.

Most of the literature on development and change of preferences has a cognitive emphasis. In this paper, however, we shall stress affective factors. In doing so, we mean neither to negate cognitive influences in preferences, nor to minimize their importance. Cognitive influences are quite important. We shall only argue that, in themselves, they do not always tell the whole story.

Preferences as Combined Utilities
Preferences occupy a very important position in social psychology. They must be considered and examined in attitude research, in impression formation, in decision making, in experimental aesthetics, and in many other fields. All these fields share a theoretical paradigm in which preferences are conceptualized as the subjective counterparts of object utilities and values. In the confines of the preference paradigm, if X is preferred to Y, it is because X has greater utility or value than Y. In turn, preferences and utilities are understood by decomposing the overall utilities and values into their more elementary components, each of which has utility of its own. According to this traditional view, if we wish to know why a given individual prefers one brand of cigarettes to another, we need only know how much he likes each of its features and how important these features are in contributing to the overall evaluation. We may examine such features as tar content, length, taste, smell, price, and so forth.

The contemporary analysis of preferences begins with this formulation and takes it as a given. The only questions that remain are how the elementary attributes can be isolated, how their utilities can be discovered, and how these utilities combine. Thus one major school of thought in this area takes it for granted that the preference of X over Y can be fully explicated by the weighted preferences for the components and features of X and Y.

The second, equally important assumption of this research is that these component utilities attach themselves to the very same features that allow the subject to detect X and Y, to discriminate between X and Y, to recognize X and Y, and to categorize X and Y. In other words, the analysis of preferences is simply the analysis of cognitive representations of the features of objects, with the addition that these descriptive representations now have some affect attached to them in the form of utilities. In fact, in some cases, utility is conceived of as a property of an object—a property that is not essentially different from other properties, such as hue, shape, age, or function. There are no a priori grounds for distinguishing between utilities and other features of objects in analyzing preferences; as such, the strictly cognitive analysis of preferences represents a parsimonious approach to the problem. It follows that, in attempts to change a given preference, it is first necessary to identify the features of the object and, once these features have been identified, to try to influence the person's evaluation of these features.

Preferences as Cognitive Constructs

It should be quite obvious that in the study of preferences, we cannot hope to write models that focus on object attributes alone. Could we explain, on the basis of even the most exacting and painstaking analysis of the attributes of chili pepper and of its component utilities, why millions of people crave this spice?

A preference for an object can be radically changed with experience while its properties remain constant. This means that object properties do not contain the complete information on object utilities. Hence a complete analysis of preference dynamics and antecedents must involve an *interaction* between object properties and the history of the individual's experience with the alternatives among which the choice is made.

The approach to the study of preferences and decision making that relies exclusively on object properties has been prevalent for almost a century and progress has been shamefully slow. We are quite far from a successful prediction of object utilities on the basis of their features. Even in the case of successful choice models, it is not clear that an accurate fit of a decision model describing choice as a function of weighted attribute utilities can always be taken as evidence of its validity. For example, the fit need not show that the subject made his choice by "computing" (consciously or unconsciously) the component utilities as specified by the model. In many cases, the information offered by the subject about the attributes of the object and about their utilities may well represent his justification for rather than the basis of his choice. Assuming that individuals strive to supply consistent justifications for their choice behavior, weighted linear models in themselves might not be able to distinguish between the ratings of attributes that *justify* the choice and the ratings that *determine* the choice. Only experimental manipulations of attributes could reveal their contributions to the choice. Models that are successful in describing these types of experimental situations are quite rare and, for the most part, deal with choices among trivial alternatives.

It is, therefore, not a folly to question these basic assumptions about preferences. The assumption questioned here is that affect, such as that contained in preferences, is necessarily *postcognitive,* which implies that a feeling of a preference is generated *upon* the encoding of the specific properties of the object, *after* the evaluation of their utilities, and *after* the computation of the individual component utilities into a joint product that represents the overall preference.

In contrast to this traditional view, under some circumstances, affective responses, including preference judgments, may be fairly independent of cognition.

Role of Cognitive Factors in Preferences

According to the traditional approach, affect in preferences attaches itself to cognitive representations of the properties and attributes of the object: before you can like something, you must know what it is. If you say that you like John because John is intelligent, rich, and generous, you must have discovered—*before* making up your mind about liking John—that he is indeed intelligent, rich and generous. It follows that the judgments of John's attractiveness should be predictable from the judgments of John's intelligence, wealth, and generosity. They should also be more reliable, more consistent, they should be made more rapidly, and the individual should have more confidence in these judgments.

In contrast, consider the possibility that the judgment and choice process can be quite the opposite. Under some circumstances, affect or preference comes as the first experience. The congnitions that have generally been taken to be the very basis of this preference can actually occur afterwards—perhaps as justification. Note that we are not suggesting that affect contained in preferences always comes as the first experience. The cognitions that er, we are stating that there are many circumstances in which the affective reaction *precedes* the very cognitive appraisal on which the affective reaction is presumed to be based.

Acquiring Preferences Through Exposures

We have carried out a number of studies in our laboratory to investigate the relationship between some primitive affective and cognitive factors. The paradigm studied was that of the so-called "exposure effect." This effect, in the form of the enhancement of positive affect toward a given object, arises merely as a result of repeated stimulus exposure. When objects are presented to the individual on repeated occasions, the mere exposure is capable of making the individual's attitude toward these objects more positive. A great deal of research has confirmed these results—both in humans as well as in animals—and there is little doubt today about its validity. However, we have never been sure why exposure has these positive effects. The traditional theories explained liking for familiar objects as depending on subjective factors and, in particular, on the subjective feelings of recognition.

The exposure effect is indeed a remarkable psychological phenomenon. It is a basic process in preference and attitude formation and change. It ranges from very trivial to very serious manifestations. On the one hand, a mild preference for nonsense syllables can be established in just a few exposures. On the other hand, similar exposures can produce a powerful attachment such as we find in imprinting, where the removal of an object (as innocuous as a rotating cube) to which the animal has become attached by virtue of previous exposures causes an enormous distress.

The phenomenon of exposure is very easy to demonstrate. It occurs in a variety of contexts and can be produced by a number of *sufficient* conditions that are quite well known and understood. But no one has discovered whether there are *necessary* conditions for its occurrence or what they are. It is possible that there are no necessary conditions for the exposure effect, but only sufficient ones. Because the exposure effect represents a very basic process that has considerable adaptive significance, it may well be that nature has provided several different but substitutable conditions assuring that, in one way or another, the organism will develop preferences for objects with which it has repeated experience.

The results of our experiments on the exposure effect revealed that recognition—which, according to the traditional view, was thought to be the basic necessary condition for its occurrence—was in fact not necessary. Recognition was found to be a factor that *could* influence affective ratings of the stimuli, but it was not at all a necessary factor. Stimuli that had been presented previously but that the person did not recognize as having seen before were liked more than objectively new stimuli that the person also thought were new. Several experiments using a variety of stimulus materials were performed: all show the same pattern of results. These experiments generally consist of two sessions. During the first session, stimuli such as nonsense paralogs, photographs of faces, or Chinese ideographs are presented, usually in varied frequencies. During the second session, the subjects judge the stimuli either for familiarity or for liking, or in some experiments, for both. Thus, for example, Matlin (1971) found that objectively old stimuli were liked more than objectively new stimuli, regardless of the subject's impression of their familiarity.

In another study, Kunst-Wilson and Zajonc (1980) presented visual stimuli—high contrast polygons—at viewing conditions that resulted in chance recognition. Exposure parameters, such as duration and level of illumination, were established to bring the subjects to no better than chance recognition. The polygons were exposed a number of times each, under the conditions observing the established parameter values. During the second session, the subject was shown pairs of stimuli, now under perfectly optimal viewing conditions. In each pair, one item was on old stimulus, shown during the exposure series, and the other was a similar, new stimulus, never previously exposed. Subjects were asked which of the two polygons was new and which was old, and which of the two they preferred. These results showed no recognition above chance. However, this was not the case with liking judgments. Subjects liked the old stimuli more than the new ones, even though they were unable to recognize them.

Inadvertently, this study repeated one carried out a quarter of a century ago and published under the suggestive title, "A Methodological Study of Cigarette Brand Discrimination" (Littman and Manning 1954). These authors asked smokers of *Camels, Chesterfields,* and *Lucky Strikes* to taste camouflaged *Camels, Chesterfields,* and *Lucky Strikes* and to answer two questions: (1) which cigarette they were tasting, and (2) how much they liked each sample cigarette. In Littman and Manning's study, as in Kunst-Wilson and Zajonc's, the subjects given the blind cigarette test were unable to discriminate the cigarettes reliably: they did not know whether they were smoking their own brand or another one. However, when asked about preference among the three camouflaged sample cigarettes, they thought that their own brand tasted best, even though they could not at the time tell which of the three samples *was* their own brand.

These experiments tell us something about preferences and about their relative independence of cognitive factors—even of quite primitive cognitive factors, such as recognition memory. There are many other considerations that would lead us to believe that, in general, affect is partially indepen-

dent of cognition and that preferences are as well. Even when a preference has been developed out of cognitive material (say you learned to like something because of some favorable information), the preference may eventually become functionally autonomous and lose its original cognitive justification.

In part, the dissociation of a preference from its origins is suggested by the fact that, when asked about the reasons for preferring one stimulus to another, participants in exposure studies never mention familiarity, subjective recognition, or frequency of exposure. Instead, they point to stimulus features. In experiments with Chinese ideographs, the subjects often mentioned the form of a particular ideograph that seemed quite pleasing to them. In experiments with photographs of faces, it was generally a particular feature (nice eyes, fine hair) or the overall appearance ("he looks kind") that was given as the reason for liking. In experiments with nonsense paralogs, the subjects often said that they liked the frequently presented paralog because it "reminded them of something good" or because "it sounded nice."

According to our theoretical argument, cognitive participation is not necessary for the occurrence of an affective reaction. Mandler (1982) holds to the view that a cognitive process *always* precedes evaluative judgments. Lazarus (1981), too, sees affect as requiring cognitive participation. Certainly, evaluative judgments necessarily involve cognition, especially when they are communicated to the experimenter. The subject must somehow "look inside" for the affective reaction that has arisen in him/her and report this reaction to the experimenter. Clearly, the subject processes a good deal of information in the course of this event. The crucial question is whether the original affective reactions themselves, on which overt evaluative judgments are presumably based, must also contain cognitive components. Given the current state of knowledge and research technology, no empirical test can be made that would rule out such participation entirely and categorically. To date, we have no empirical means to decide in favor of one view or the other, so they must be considered primarily on theoretical and heuristic grounds. Some affective reactions may *appear* not to have been preceded by cognitive input, when in fact some form of covert cognitive processes may have accompanied them. For example, when the routines become highly automated, the resulting information processing becomes covert, rapid, and contracted. The possibility cannot be ruled out that this automated, covert form of cognition—a form, however, that cannot be demonstrated as having occurred—is essentially implicated in affective reactions.

Note that the primacy of affective reactions and their independence of prior cognitive process require only one demonstration. We need to find only one experimental situation where affect can be shown to have occurred without an antecedent cognitive process and the matter will be settled. In part, of course, the question of the participation of cognitive functions in affective reations is a matter of definition. There may not have been cognitive processes involved in the experiments by Kunst-Wilson and Zajonc (1980) or in the one by Littman and Manning (1954), but we cannot be sure. If by "cognition" we mean a nonsensory process that transforms sensory input and produces or recruits representations, then the question of cognitive participation in affect is reduced to the presence of representational processes. A sensory process must have taken place in the experiment by Kunst-Wilson and Zajonc; was there also a transformation of the sensory input into a representational form, or was the sensory process itself, in unadulterated form, sufficient for an affective discrimination? The possibility of direct sensory-motor links has been demonstrated in animals for various, even complex affect-triggered behavior, such as escape. Such links also exist in human beings (Goodale 1982). Were the stimuli in Kunst-Wilson and Zajonc's experiment represented by the subjects as cognitions? Even if they were, were these representations *necessary* for the generation of differential affective reactions to familiar and unfamiliar stimuli?

Affective and Cognitive Factors in Attitudes

It is entirely plausible that there are significant differences in attitudes and preferences depending on their basis of origin. Preferences acquired in infan-

cy and childhood are formed primarily on affective basis. A taste for chili pepper is acquired through habituation, familiarization, and positive reinforcement from the social surroundings, not by means of persuasive information. On the other hand, some later preferences—say for certain makes of cars or food processors—have as their basis a rich cognitive structure. To change an attitude that has evolved primarily from affective sources and so has considerable extracognitive supports, may require methods different from those needed to change an attitude based on cognition: it may require an attack on the affective basis of the preference.

Of course, psychotherapy is one such method, in that it seeks to attack an affective predisposition that has pathological consequences. We are not suggesting psychotherapeutic methods in the advertising and marketing of commercial products (although there is a great deal to be learned from these methods, since many product preferences and loyalties have a near-pathological character). If preferences are to be changed, both the affective and the cognitive elements must be carefully examined, because in the end, it is the affective element that must be altered. This appears to be quite well understood in psychotherapy and in advertising, although it is not always understood at a systematic level. For example, it is very clear that affect is recruited to help out in various forms of advertising: you are shown a soft drink *and* a smile, a brand of whiskey *and* sex, a new automobile model *and* excitement. It is the same in psychotherapy when transference is exploited for gaining an affective support in dealing with an affective disturbance.

Preference and Attitude Development and Change

What is the interplay between affective and cognitive factors in the course of preference development? By the time the child develops an extensive knowledge structure about chili peppers—i.e., before he learns to discriminate among them, identify various subtle features, and discover all their uses—his preference for them may well be completely established. In this case, it is unlikely that affect would become attached to the *specific* features of chili peppers that the child discovers after his preference is formed, although he may nevertheless learn to describe and express his preference in terms of these features. Appeals to the features of chili peppers in describing one's preferences may be simply justifications that overlay the affective aspects of the preference but do not reflect the affective *representation* of the object. Efforts to change attitudes in which the affective components have been fully developed before the cognitive elements became articulated are likely to meet with failure. An effective method would have to take direct aim at the affective component and bring in affective consequences—an idea that appears to be implicitly understood in brainwashing (Lifton 1956). It may be that attitudes that have a firm emotional basis, developed prior to cognitive elaboration, can be changed only by methods that have a direct emotional influence on the one hand, and that bypass cognitive components on the other.

Other attitudes may have quite a different natural history of acquisition and development. In the example of the new corkscrew mentioned previously, the affective component and the cognitive component of the attitude may develop very much in tandem; in fact, most of the cognitive elements may become consolidated before one's preference is fully developed. In this case, these cognitions may form an important basis for the preference and thus figure significantly in its formation. The process of preference acquisition may start with an initial overall affective reaction to the corkscrew arising out of a previously developed knowledge structure—i.e., after the person has learned a great deal about the infallibility of the corkscrew's performance, its durability, its low cost, and all its other advantages over other corkscrew designs. It is this knowledge structure that is the original source of positive feelings and the major basis of preference formation (which, as previously noted, is not the case in the acquisition of preference for chili pepper). Thus it is likely that, in the case of the corkscrew, particular preferences will attach themselves to particular features of the corkscrew, so that the affective and the cognitive components will be more closely intertwined than in the case of chili pepper. Hence an attempt to change preferences by cognitive methods would be more effective than

in the case of chili pepper, because in the case of the corkscrew, it is the cognitions that "carry" the affect.

It is possible to change preference by cognitive means alone only in the early stages of preference formation, because even when a preference has been built up from cognitions, its affect may become partly or fully autonomous and independent of the cognitive elements that were originally its basis. With the passage of time and due to habitual contact with and use of the corkscrew, one tends to forget its particular advantages because contact and comparison with other designs is precluded. One tends to pay little attention to the fact that the corkscrew works well, how little it cost, and that it has lasted all these years. One begins to like it simply by virtue of repeated exposure. The impact of this type of separation of affective basis of preference from its original cognitive support can be easily appreciated when one is asked why he likes an old friend. Such a question is often followed by a long pause, as one tries to retrieve the original cognitive supports for the attitude. The current attachment and affection are held in place by reciprocal "good feeling" (surely a diffuse and nondescript state) and by habitual patterns of positive interaction. As friendship grows, relatively little attention is paid to the particular features of the friend. The original bases no longer provide support for the affection and do not form a part of the attitude complex.

REPRESENTATION OF AFFECT

Once we acknowledge the possibility of a separation of affect from cognition, it becomes necessary to establish, conceptually and empirically, how affect is represented and, for the purposes of this paper, how preferences are represented. Traditionally, preferences and decisions have been analyzed in a heavily cognitive context, so psychologists are used to thinking that preferences "sit" somewhere in the mental space—as representations—and that they are, therefore, like any other representations. Is this always the case, and is it the case for all forms of preference? In the final analysis, preferences are *behavioral* phenomena. A preference is a behavioral tendency that exhibits itself not so much in what the individual thinks or says about the object, but how s/he acts toward it. Does s/he take it, does s/he approach it, does s/he buy it, does s/he marry it? The study of attitudes, aesthetics, decision making, and consumer preferences must take as its basic aim the prediction of what is taken, approached, bought, and married.

Somatic Representations of Preferences

We wish to consider quite literally the proposition that preferences are, above all, behavioral tendencies. In the early days of attitude research, attitude was perceived as a motor disposition. One spoke of an approach attitude as "leaning toward" an object, and of an avoidance attitude as "moving away" from an object.

Not only preferences but all affect has a significant motor component. The expression of emotion occurs above all at the motor level, although, of course, the visceral, glandular, cardiovascular, and autonomic systems are very much involved as well.

Thus far, the study of preferences and of the ways whereby they are established and modified has relied primarily on cognitive methods. For the most part, social psychologists have tried to see what information could be given to a person so that s/he would become fond of some item. They asked how should this information be imparted and, for best results, who should do it. Needless to say, the method of attitude change by means of persuasion has not met with a great deal of success.

The study of preferences involves knowledge about the interaction between affect and cognition. This interaction has been studied in a number of other areas of psychology as well, such as perceptual defense, cognitive dissonance, and social comparison. Typically, it has been studied at the subjective level—i.e., at the level of higher mental processes. For example, in the analysis of the effects of mood on learning and remembering word lists, mood is conceptualized in terms of associative structures (Bower 1981). Mood has nodes in memory, just like any other cognitive representation. These nodes, which are parts of the associative structures that represent the mood state, are said to

make contact with the nodes of the associative structure that represent the word lists. The effect of mood on the retention of the words in the list takes place by virtue of the contact between the two associative structures.

Another very reasonable possibility exists: the motor component of affect, which is primarily the expressive aspect of emotion, can also serve *representational* and *mnestic* functions—i.e., behavioral correlates of affect can be considered as much a representation of the affective state as the higher mental structures. After all, what is a representation? What is recalled when we recall affect? A representation is nothing more than some event within the organism that *stands for* some other event, whether outside of the organism in the environment, or inside the organism itself. There need not be a one-to-one correspondence between the two events: such a correspondence does not exist in language, for example. Nor need there be an isomorphism between the two events, because there is hardly any isomorphism assumed for *any* form of representation. It suffices that the correspondence be repeatable, that on some occasion the same internal event arises in representing its referent, that it is possible to combine it with some other events that are representations, and that structures of representations could be formed. If this is the case, then any class of events—subjective, muscular, visceral, cardiovascular, glandular, hormonal, or neural—could very well serve representational functions.

Thus, it is quite reasonable to say that when a person "stores" affect, what he "stores" (among other things) are motor tendencies and other somatic manifestations. He also stores subjective and cognitive features of affect, which neither substitute for nor preclude the presence of other forms of representation. Note that we do not mean to involve the subjective representations of the attitudinal motor correlates. We assume that the motor output itself can serve significant representational and mnestic functions, without the participation of the subjective processes and without kinesthetic feedback or the proprioceptive cues that constitute a basis for the subjective process.

The motor features of affect that serve representational functions and the motor features that may be recalled when the person recalls an affective experience need not occur with the same intensity as they did on the original occasion. When a person recalls an incident that enraged him, his fists may not be quite as clenched and he may not need to scream as loudly as he did at the time. But the same muscles may well be involved at lower amplitudes. If electromyographic measures were taken, low amplitude impulses would be revealed in the same muscles that were involved in the original expression of the person's rage. The growing sophistication in electromyography today allows us to do many complicated procedures that were previously not possible. Subtle levels of impulses coming from multiple sites can be recorded, integrated, and compared with previous ones obtained under similar or different conditions (Cacioppo and Petty 1981).

Attitudes and preferences have a significant motor component that can be a postural tendency or some other somatic form. The behavioral correlates that are involved in taking and ingesting a chili pepper are quite numerous and involve a variety of motor components, glandular organs, and the alimentary and gastrointestinal systems, for example. These somatic components of preference may become quite independent of the original cognitions that were at one time responsible for establishing these preferences. The behavior pattern is not easy to change. The behavioral correlates involved in eating chili peppers have a stability of their own and are hard to overcome by persuasion. It follows that while preferences have cognitive correlates, they may become functionally autonomous of these cognitive correlates and persist merely by virtue of the behavioral tendencies that have become their expressions. Once they are autonomous, behavioral tendencies that represent attitudes and preferences are hard to change, particularly if only cognitive means are to be employed. A simple communication is seldom sufficient to change a well-established behavioral habit. Methods are needed that can reach habitual behavior and motor output. What these specific methods are may well be a question for skill learning, behavior

modification, and human factors theory—areas that have not heretofore been thought of as parts of attitude theory. We know little about these processes as methods of attitude change, but we will have to consider them in the future.

There are a few good examples of what may be done, such as Wells and Petty's (1981) attempt to change attitudes by a simple and ingenious behavioral method. The ostensible purpose of the experiment was to evaluate the quality of headphones. Subjects were told that since headphones are now used by joggers, runners, and bikers, it was important to study how well they work when the listener is moving. They were given a set of headphones to put on and listened to a variety of auditory samples. Some were pieces of music; others were bits of verbal material including an editorial about tuition. One group of subjects was instructed to listen to these auditory samples while shaking their heads from left to right. Another group listened to the same pieces while nodding their heads up and down. These movements were ostensibly presented to the subjects as motions that simulate the motions people make while jogging and biking.

Afterwards, all subjects judged the quality of the headphones and were asked various questions about the material they heard. They were asked how much they liked the music and whether the music came through the headphones without distortion. Attitude questions relating to the editorial presented over the headphones were also asked: the subjects were asked what they thought about the editorial and whether they agreed or disagreed with it.

The results were quite clear. The attitudes were more positive among the subjects who nodded their heads than among those who shook their heads from left to right. The very act of appropriately engaging the motor system apparently was sufficient to influence the subjects' attitudes. The effects were quite strong—stronger, in fact, than they would have been had Wells and Petty tried to change these attitudes by simple persuasion.

In general, we should not be terribly surprised that it is so difficult to change attitudes and preferences by cognitive methods. These methods do not reach the motor system and other somatic representational systems of the organism. They only deal with one representational system—the one that exists in the form of associative structures, images, and other subjective states. Since attitudes contain such a substantial affective component, they are likely to have multiple representations—and somatic representations are probably among the more significant ones. We should—and can—take a closer look at them—a much closer look, at any rate, than we can take at associative structures, cognitive organizations, nodes, or scripts, which are hard to see. Muscles are out there in the open to be seen, measured, and manipulated.

Motor Basis of Preferences and Attitude Change

In general—as was the case with affect and cognition—the somatic representations of a person's affect toward a given object can gain autonomy from his knowledge structure about that object. For example, a rich and stable pattern of habitual sensorimotor correlates emerges in relation to chili pepper. There are powerful sensory inputs: gustatory, olfactory, gastrointestinal, and visual. Particular motor responses of the lips, tongue, and esophagus are acquired and attached to the sensory input. A fixed sequence of eating the various courses of meals develops as a strong habit. The reactions of others—especially of the uninitiated—to the chili pepper are quickly recognized and readily interpreted. This rich configuration of sensorisomatic reactions, organized around the chili pepper, forms an integral part of the preference. It can be much more significant than its cognitive counterpart because it participates quite intimately in the *expression of the preference*, i.e., in the consumption of the substance.

With respect to the new corkscrew design, the motor representations of the affect and of the preference are more diffuse and emerge later in the course of preference development. These representational motor correlates are probably associated with actions such as reaching into the drawer to take out the corkscrew (a motion representing a positive *inclination* toward it); they may also occur in association with a particular twist of the wrist when inserting the corkscrew into a cork, or they may be parts of the pulling motion. All these muscular responses may have parameters that *represent* the person's affective predisposition to the corkscrew. Reaching for the corkscrew, taking it out, and screwing it in may all have a "good feeling." Therefore, a change of preference for a corkscrew would have to be accomplished by attention to these motor correlates, since they are so firmly fixed within the structure of the preference.

CONCLUSIONS

An open field for research emerges from the view of affect and cognition presented here. A number of research problems can be readily formulated and explored. In our laboratory, we are now engaged in the study of the interaction of affect and cognition at a more general level. We are looking at the motor system more closely and trying to see what it can tell us about information processing and about how information processing is influenced by emotion. It is not unlikely that this approach may have a number of useful consequences for basic consumer research.

REFERENCES

Bateson, Patrick P. G. (1966). "The Characteristics and Context of Imprinting." *Biological Review,* 41, 183–220.

Bower, Gordon H. (1981), "Mood and Memory," *American Psychologist,* 36, 129–148.

Cacioppo, John T. and Richard E. Petty (1981), "Electromyograms as Measures of Extent and Affectivity of Information Processing," *American Psychologist,* 36, 441–456.

Goodale, M. A. (1982), "Vision as a Sensorimotor System," in *A Behavioral Approach to Brain Research,* ed. T. E. Robinson, New York: Oxford University Press.

Kunst-Wilson, William R. and Robert B. Zajonc (1980), "Affective Discrimination of Stimuli That Cannot Be Recognized," *Science,* 207, 557–558.

Lazarus, Richard S. (1981), "A Cognitivist's Reply to Zajonc on Emotion and Cognition," *American Psychologist, 36,* 222–223.

Lifton, Robert J. (1956), " 'Thought Reform' of Western Civilians in Chinese Communist Prisons," *Psychiatry, 19,* 173–195.

Littman, Richard A. and Horace M. Manning (1954), "A Methodological Study of Cigarette Brand Discrimination," *Journal of Applied Psychology, 38,* 185–190.

Mandler, George (1982), "The Structure of Value: Accounting for Taste," in *Cognition and Affect,* eds. S. Fiske and M. Clarke, New York: Academic Press.

Matlin, Margaret W. (1971), "Response Competition, Recognition, and Affect," *Journal of Personality and Social Psychology, 19,* 295–300.

Rozin, Paul and Deborah Schiller (1980), "The Nature and Acquisition of a Preference for Chili Pepper by Humans," *Motivation and Emotion, 4,* 77–101.

SECTION X

ATTRIBUTION PROCESSES IN CONSUMER BEHAVIOR

How does a consumer's perception of the persuasive intent of commercials influence that consumer in his or her belief of the message of the commercial, attitude toward the product, and purchase intent? To whom do consumers attribute their dissatisfaction with a product and does this influence the action that is taken? To what extent does a person's belief of the cause of a national dilemma influence his/her opinion of the remedy that is needed?

These questions address various inferences or attributions a consumer can make about the causes of events related to consumption. The field of psychology that is concerned with determining how people perceive the causes of events in their everyday lives is called attribution. Understanding the processes whereby attributions are made is central to understanding consumer behavior. Attribution theorists see people as actively trying to understand their world by forming explanations for events and behavior that they encounter. People are seen as everyday scientists who try to understand *why* certain events took place. They attribute meanings and conditions to objects and events.

In order to understand attribution theory fully, one must put aside the notion that there exists an objective reality. Attribution theorists deal only with people's perceptions and explanations of their experiences. To exist in any form for people, the world must be internalized, perceived, and experienced, which necessarily means that individual understanding and explanation will be created.

The attribution process can be applied to marketing problems by defining the *antecedent* of the attribution (the information sought to assess causation), the *content* of the attribution (the cause attributed such as ability or luck), and the *consequences* of the attribution (lack of trust in a product or increase in source credibility).

There is not just one theory of attribution, but a number of different approaches. The classic theories of attribution will be discussed briefly.

Fritz Heider, the father of attribution theory, proposed that people perceive behavior as being caused and that the causal locus can be either in the stimulus person or in the environment. Heider's theory states that every action is the result of these two factors—personal forces and environmental forces. In analyzing the causes of another person's behavior, the perceiver attempts to determine the relative strengths of these two factors.

Like scientists, people have developed systematic methods for determining the causes of events by attempting to find sufficient and necessary reasons for the occurrence of a particular behavior. Kelley's theory perceives people as basing causal attributions on the covariance of cause and effect. Four types of information may be used in seeking covariance between causes and observed effects:

1. *Distinctiveness* of the object, person, or event. For example, if your experience with the product appears to be unique to that product, then you will attribute your satisfaction to that product and develop loyalty to that product.

2. *Consensus* of people. For example, if there is a high consensus about the product, consumers tend to make attributions to the product. If there is a low consensus among people, consumers tend to make attributions to situational variables rather than to product characteristics. Knowing how others have reacted to a product will help people determine whether their reactions are due to the product itself or due to unusual circumstances surrounding its consumption.

3. *Consistency over time.* For example, the more consistent a consumer's experience with the product at different times, the more the consumer will attribute satisfaction to the product itself.

4. *Consistency over modality.* For example, the more consistent a consumer's experience with a product in different situations, the more certain the consumer will be that his or her satisfaction or dissatisfaction is due to the product itself.

For a person to be certain that his/her reaction to something is due to the object itself, the product must show consistency across these four criteria.

Jones and Davis have proposed a theory concerning how a person makes dispositional inferences in regard to another's observed behavior. The theory focuses on how an observer determines whether an action is representative of the underlying disposition of the actor or not. A correspondent inference is made when a person's behavior corresponds to this disposition. Whether a correspondent inference is made is affected by an action's social desirability. If it is socially desirable behavior, nothing can be inferred; if it is not socially desirable behavior, a correspondent inference can be made. The drawing of a correspondent inference is also affected by the number of noncommon effects present. If some effects are unique to an action, it can be a source of information about an actor's disposition.

An extension of the correspondent inference theory is suggested by Jones and McGillis, which brings the idea of expectation to attribution theory. People can develop target-based expectancies, which are based on past knowledge of the actor, and category-based expectancies, which are based on knowledge of an actor's membership in a group (stereotype). There will be higher correspondence when behavior departs from target and category expectancies.

People feel uncomfortable with the notion that events are random or accidental. That is why they prefer to believe that most events have understandable causes. Attribution provides structure to experiences by allowing people to organize their conceptions of the world around assumptions about causality.

The two articles in this section discuss different attempts to study how consumers' attributions are related to their behavior. Each discusses consumer attributions in a different context.

"CHILDREN AND COMMERCIAL PERSUASION: AN ATTRIBUTION THEORY ANALYSIS"

Attribution theory can be applied to consumer behavior in the area of mass communication because consumers attribute intentions to advertisers. This is demonstrated in the study by Robertson and Rossiter, which examines attributions made by children about advertisers' intentions. This study can also lead to a better understanding of the consumer socialization process.

Consumer socialization has been defined as the "processes by which young people acquire skills, knowledge, and attitudes relevant to their functioning as consumers in the marketplace" (Ward, 1980). But what are the processes by which children learn to become consumers? How do children develop attitudes in their perceptions of advertisements?

It has been hypothesized by marketing scholars that the consumer socialization process is based on the cognitive development model posited by Jean Piaget, a Swiss psychologist. Piaget believed a child's reasoning processes are qualitatively different from those of adults—not just less developed. Children are not just miniature adults; they lack the cognitive ability that mature individuals possess. Instead, children progress through various stages of conceptual learning, each of which is a necessary precondition for progression to the next. There are four stages of cognitive development through which the child progresses in perceiving and dealing with the environment at the different ages (see chart).

Piaget's developmental stages have important implications for the Robertson and Rossiter paper. Children can only make attributions of intent if they have the cognitive ability to do so. According to Piaget, younger children do not have the ability to make these attributions. As children mature and pass through these developmental stages, they are then able to attribute persuasive intentions to advertisers. This idea is tested by Robertson and Rossiter.

Stage	Age	Characteristics
I. Sensorimotor period	Birth to 2 years	• Intelligence based on overt action • Object permanence (an object continues to exist even when no longer seen) • Differentiates self from environment
II. Preoperational period	2 to 7 years	• Develops ability to use symbols to represent parts of the environment through the use of language • Egocentric (can't take viewpoint of another) • Classifies objects by a single salient feature • Representation (constructs a simple mental scheme in the absence of the objects or events the scheme deals with) • Insight learning (mental solving of simple problems) • Inability to coordinate thoughts into integrated concepts (complex thinking)
III. Concrete operations	7 to 11 years	Able to use: • Reversibility • Classification (organizing objects into hierarchies of classes) • Seriation (organizing objects into ordered series) • Conservation (object maintains identity despite visible transformation) • System of operations (scheme that is internalized and transformed)
IV. Formal operations	11 to 15 years	• Abstract thinking and conceptualization • Hypothesis testing

There are several important reasons for studying the effects of persuasion on the child. Public policymakers can determine the extent of external influences on the child and formulate public policy accordingly. Marketers are interested in improving their communication campaigns directed at children. Knowledge of the persuasiveness of ads to children and their reception of the ads can increase the efficiency of the advertisements. Researchers are interested in child development theory and its relationship to consumer socialization.

Robertson and Rossiter attempt to determine what factors mediate the persuasive impact of TV commercials on children. This study identifies two types of attributions children can make about the apparent purpose of advertisements: persuasive intent and assistive intent. The study demonstrates the centrality of these attributions in determining the child's degree of responsiveness to TV advertising. The data are based on personal interviews with the children concerning their understanding of and reaction to commercials. The strong age-dependency of the persuasive intent attribution suggests that it is a fundamental cognitive learning process.

A limitation of the study—that the subjects are all boys from a Catholic school in the Philadelphia area—makes the generalizability of the findings questionable. Also, as the child matures, communication skills could substantially improve making comparison of different age levels difficult. The differences obtained in the results could be due to increased verbal ability versus the hypothesized cognitive stages.

It should be noted that this is a cross-sectional rather than a longitudinal study. That is, students from the first, third, and fifth grades were interviewed at one point in time rather than interviewing the same students when they were in each of these grades. In a cross-sectional study only correlational conclusions can be drawn. We cannot conclude that increases in age cause increases in the likelihood of attributions of persuasive intent solely from this study. But by combining information from Piaget's longitudinal studies with Robertson and Rossiter's findings, the conclusion that age is a causal factor can be supported.

"PREFERRED SOLUTIONS TO THE ENERGY CRISIS AS A FUNCTION OF CAUSAL ATTRIBUTIONS"

Belk, Painter, and Semenik posit the hypothesis that those accepting personal responsibility for the energy crisis favor and report adopting the personal solution of voluntary energy conservation, and those making attributions to nonpersonal causes (OPEC, oil companies, U.S. government) are more likely to favor nonpersonal solutions.

This article can be compared to other research which has been done on consumer dissatisfaction. Both involve negative events to which one can make attributions to causes and thus make assessments of blame. There are some major differences, however. The energy problem is shared by all of society, whereas dissatisfaction with a product is usually an individual problem. The two implications of this are:

1. Personal attributions are more socially acceptable for socially shared problems.
2. The solution involving voluntary conservation action must be shared to be effective. This presents the free-rider problem, which suggests an alternative hypothesis: Those who attribute the energy crisis to attitudes or behaviors of individuals may nevertheless prefer the less personal solution of mandatory conservation.

While reading this article, one should question what is meant by preference. The paper deals with *preferred* responses to the energy crisis. Is there a difference between what a person prefers and what a person will comply with?

Also, concerning the ranking of the preference of solutions, do subjects answer not with their preferences, but with the answer they believe is most viable and would be most successful? For example, those who blame OPEC support mandatory conservation; perhaps they see no justification in demanding a solution by the causal agent OPEC.

Belk, Painter, and Semenik imply that by educating the public on the cause of the energy dilemma, enough public support can be generated to support the appropriate solution.

The reader should consider the implications the hypothesis of Belk et al. has to other social problems. If causal attributions are related to preferred solutions, what kinds of solutions are seen for the problems of inflation, recession, other shortages, littering, pollution, and war?

CHILDREN AND COMMERCIAL PERSUASION: AN ATTRIBUTION THEORY ANALYSIS

**THOMAS S. ROBERTSON
AND
JOHN R. ROSSITER**

Source: Thomas S. Robertson and John R. Rossiter, "Children and Commercial Persuasion: An Attribution Theory Analysis," *Journal of Consumer Research,* Vol. 1, June, 1974, pp. 13–20. Reprinted with permission.

This study was prompted by the question of the extent to which children are capable of understanding the purposes of television commercials and the effects of such understanding on attitudes and purchase requests. In conceptualizing these problems into a research structure, it appeared that attribution theory would provide the most relevant and meaningful theoretical perspective.

Attribution theory concerns the processes by which individuals interpret events in their subjective environment. It is a theory of perception which takes the point of view of the lay observer, as he sorts and interprets incoming information and infers causality, rather than the analytic framework of the scientific observer (Heider, 1958). As such, attribution theory has been termed a "naive psychology." Its value is its focus on *subjectively operative causal processes*—the "real" factors from the actor's vantage point—which determine his perception, thought, and action.

The central idea of attribution theory is that an individual is motivated "to attain a cognitive mastery of the causal structure of his environment" (Kelley, 1967, p. 193). The individual attempts to make sense out of his environment by the attribution of causal relationships. This process of causal attribution, according to Piaget (1970), begins at a very young age and much of the child's subsequent development is toward a more sophisticated and discriminating sense of causality.

THE RESEARCH PROBLEM

The present study, then, investigates a particular class of causal perceptions—children's attributions about the intent of television commercials. Essentially, we are dealing with the child's inferences as to what the communicator intends. In order to attribute a motive of intent, the child must first presumably be capable of: discerning commercials as discrete from regular programming, recognizing a sponsor as the source of the commercial message, and perceiving the idea of an intended audience for the message. Furthermore, it would appear that full comprehension of the purposive intent of commercials would be evidenced by the child's ability in: understanding the symbolic nature of product, character and contextual representation in commercials and discriminating, by example, between products as advertised and products as experienced.

In the pilot study for this research project, open-ended interviews revealed that children exhibited two basic forms of attributional intent—"assistive" and "persuasive"—and that these were not necessarily independent. A child might see only assistive intent (for example, "commercials tell you about things") or only persuasive intent (for example, "commercials try to make you buy things"), or some combination of both. . . .

The case in which the child simultaneously attributes assistive and persuasive intent to commercials is interesting. Extant attribution theory, in fact, offers contrary predictions as to the relative weight of "positive" and "negative" factors when jointly perceived. Kelley (1971, p. 12) suggests that positive or "facilitative" factors will outweigh negative or "inhibitory" factors, whereas Kanouse and Hanson (1971, p. 56) suggest the opposite—that negative factors will be dominant. The assistive-persuasive intent dichotomy allows us to test these alternative predictions.

Hypotheses

The primary concern is what attributions (as to commercial intent) children hold and what factors account for these attributions. We are further concerned with the ramifications of these attributions in attitudinal and response tendency outcomes.

Hypothesis 1: Developmental Factors Related to Intent. Ability to perceive intent in commercials (either assistive or persuasive) will be positively associated with (a) the child's age, (b) the presence of older siblings, (c) the educational level of his parents, (d) the child's level of interaction with his parents, and (e) the child's peer integration.

Prior research on the devlopment of children's attributions toward television advertising has focused primarily on age as the explanatory variable. More recently, however, Ward and Wackman (1974) have used Piagetian concepts in an attempt to explain age-related differences in children's reactions to commercials. In general the existing research indicates tht the older the child, then the greater his awareness, understanding, and discernment of television commercials. It should be noted that age, as such, is a surrogate for both level of cognitive development and cumulative level of exposure to television advertising. It is assumed that some minimum level of exposure to commercials is a prerequisite in the development of valid attributions. In the absence of longitudinal research, of course, it is extremely difficult to sort out developmental and experiential factors in age-related effects.

The initial hypothesis, therefore, also takes into account the child's level of social support, postulating that development of the concepts of assistive or persuasive intent will be fostered by the presence of older siblings, higher levels of parental education, higher levels of interaction with parents, and higher levels of peer integration. Because the child is informationally dependent upon other people—parents, peers, and siblings in particular—in their relative absence he will be slower to develop a valid attributional set (Kelley, 1967; Festinger, 1954).

Hypothesis 2: Cognitive Factors Which Would Logically Precede Attribution of Intent. Ability to recognize assistive or persuasive intent in television commercials is dependent upon the child's making a number of prior cognitive distinctions: (a) discrimination between programming and commercials; (b) recognition of an external source; (c) perception of an intended audience; (d) awareness of the symbolic nature of commercials; and (e) experience of discrepancies between the product as advertised and the actual product.

These factors would logically appear to precede the development of valid attributions of commercial intent. Given the cross-sectional nature of the research, however, we are not truly testing a development process but rather examining the incidence of these cognitive distinctions by age level and the relationship to intent. Operationalization of these cognitive factors is shown in Table 1 (variables 3–7).

Attribution of intent must, by necessity, be preceded by discrimination as to what a commercial is. A pilot study by Blatt, Spencer and Ward (1971) suggests that discrimination between commercials and programming may be absent in some children, even by first grade.

Increasing perceptual ability logically requires

Table 1 Measurement components

Variables	Code values	Questionnaire items
Attributions		
1. Assistive Intent	1— No assistive intent perceived 2— Recognition of assistive intent	
2. Persuasive Intent	1— No persuasive intent perceived 2— Recognition of persuasive intent	
Antecedents		
3. Discrimination Between Programs and Commercials	1— No discrimination 2— No confusion but discreteness not explicit 3— Explicit discrimination	Variables 1 to 7 were assessed independently based on responses to the following questions:
4. Recognition of Source	1— No source perceived 2— Ambiguous source reference 3— Clear source reference	What is a television commercial? Why are commercials shown on television?
5. Perception of Audience	1— No audience perceived 2— Personal audience 3— Peer audience 4— General audience 5— Segmented audience	What do commercials try to get you to do?
6. Awareness of Symbolic Nature of Commercials	1— No symbol-reference distinction 2— Implicit distinction 3— Explicit perception of representational techniques	
7. Perception of Discrepancy Between Message and Product	1— No discrepancy experienced 2— Discrepancy experienced	
Consequences		
8. Trust in Commercials	1— Disbelieves all commercials 2— Believes some only or disbelieves some 3— Believes all commercials	Do you believe what television commercials tell you?
9. Liking of Commercials	1— Dislikes all commercials 2— Likes some only or dislikes some 3— Likes all commercials	Do you like television commercials?
10. Consumption Motivation	1— Wants some peer-oriented products 2— Wants all peer-oriented products, with some limitations, e.g., price 3— Wants all advertised products	Do you want every toy or game that you see advertised on television?

that the child be able to recognize the existence of an "other" whose perspective he may be able to adopt (Mead, 1934). Flavell (1970) notes that "perspective," or alternative source perception, is only partly accomplished in early school years and that children at Piaget's pre-operational stage have difficulty in "taking the role of another." The development of attribution as to the assistive or persuasive intent of commercials would seem to proceed, in part, as a function of external source perception.

Perception of an implied audience as the target of the advertiser's message would seem to be a further attributional prerequisite. We might posit that the child advances from a lack of audience perception to the egocentric view that all commercials are directed at him. Later he realizes that commercials are directed to his peers as well as himself and later still he realizes that commercials are directed to a general audience. Finally, the child recognizes that commercials are directed at specific segments of the general audience, of which he may not always be a part.

As regards perception of symbolic representation, we again posit a developing sequence. The child initially shows no recognition of the symbolic nature of commercials. He then proceeds to an implicit recognition of the distinction between images and reality without clear articulation of the representation devices used to enhance the presentation of the product. Lastly, the child becomes aware of the symbolic devices used in many commercials, for example, idealized settings for product display or dramatized character emotions.

Personal experience of discrepancies between products as advertised and products in actuality is the final variable hypothesized to precede attribution of intent in commercials. This variable is operationally dichotomized because the child either has or has not experienced specific commercial-product discrepancies.

Hypothesis 3: Consequences of Perceived Intent. Given that an attribution of intent is made, assistive intent attribution will be positively related, and persuasive intent negatively related, to: (a) belief and trust in television commercials, (b) liking of commercials, and (c) consumption motivation, that is, desire for the advertised products. As a corollary: persuasive intent will

outweigh assistive intent in cases where both attributions are made.

The present hypothesis differs from the first hypothesis in that it considers not just the emergence of attributions, per se, but the "directionality" of their consequences. Our expectation is that recognition of the persuasive purpose of commercials will reduce thier influence on the child, while recognition of assistive intent will increase their influence.

These would seem to be logical predictions. Although the available research evidence is indirect, it indicates that as children grow older they exhibit more cynical attitudes toward commercials, and make fewer consumption requests (Ward, 1972; Wells, 1965). In the present research we are postulating that attribution of intent is an important mediating factor in this process.

Furthermore, previous research has tended to conceptualize persuasiveness as though it were part of a perceptual continuum which ranges from the favorable perceptions of young children to the cynical outlook of older children. Our pilot study indicated, however, that children can hold dual perceptions, just as adults recognize both the informative functions of advertising and the inherent selling motives (Bauer and Greyser, 1968; Bower, 1973).

In the dual attribution situation, our prediction is that persuasive intent attribution will outweigh assistive intent attribution in determining commercial believability, liking, and consumption motivation (Kanouse and Hanson, 1971).

RESEARCH DESIGN

Sample
Respondents for this study were 289 primary school boys in three grades, ranging from upper-lower to upper-middle social class. The grades represented are first, third, and fifth. The sample was selected from five schools within the Philadelphia area Catholic school system in which we interviewed the entire set of boys at each grade level, or, in the case of one large school, the entire set of boys within one class at each grade level. . . .

. . .

Table 2 Overview of results by grade level[a]

Variables	First grade	Third grade	Fifth grade
Attributions			
Assistive Intent	51.7%	68.3%	55.3%
Persuasive Intent	52.7	87.1	99.0
Antecedents[b]			
Discrimination Between Programming and Commercials	73.5	90.1	100.0
Recognition of Source	48.2	81.2	94.7
Perception of Audience	50.0	73.7	88.3
Awareness of Symbolic Nature of Commercials	43.2	71.3	93.7
Perception of Discrepancies Between Message and Product	12.5	48.0	78.7
Consequences			
Trusts All Commercials	64.8	30.4	7.4
Likes All Commercials	68.5	55.9	25.3
Wants All Products Advertised	53.3	26.7	6.4

[a]Percentages are based on minimum response rates of 85 first graders, 95 third graders, and 94 fifth graders. Total sample size varied from 276 to 289 due to deletion of responses that did not attain modal agreement in coding.
[b]Percentages for antecedent variables are based on minimum levels of concept acquisition (see Table 1).

Measurement

The measurement components are exhibited in Table 1 for those variables for which judgment was necessary in coding. For those variables not exhibited, such as age and presence of older siblings, standard closed-end measures were used. Parent-child interaction was based on frequency for a sequence of interaction events, as reported by the child, and peer integration was based on the child's designation by other students in the sample as a "best friend."

An obvious issue when interviewing children is whether results are affected by children's differential abilities to articulate. This is a point worthy of elaboration since the measurement components (Table 1) are open-ended and could differentially favor children with superior verbal facility. The child was, however, given ample opportunity to express his ideas and, in fact, interviews with first graders took significantly longer to complete than interviews with fifth graders—an average of 30 minutes versus 20 minutes.

Analysis

Two statistical procedures were employed to test the three main hypotheses. Because the dependent variables involved discrete categorical measurement, nonparametric tests were indicated. The separate effects of the independent variables were examined by computing the relevant Kendall bivariate correlation coefficients (τ).[1] The combined operation of independent variables within each hypothesis set was assessed by performing stepwise multivariate discriminant analyses.

RESULTS

An overview of results is proivded in Table 2 indicating the data patterns by grade level for the main research variables. These results show clear developmental trends toward increasingly sophisticated

[1]Kendall's tau coefficient is usually preferred to Spearman's when a relatively large proportion of tied ranks is involved, as with the present data.

cognitions and less positive attitudinal structures. The single exception to the grade-related pattern is assistive intent attribution which reaches a maximum among third graders.

Hypothesis 1: Developmental Factors

Children's attribution of persuasive intent to commercials is very much related to age and parental education. That is, those children who see commercials as designed to induce purchases are older and have parents of higher educational levels than those children who do not perceive persuasive intent (Table 3). The child's interaction level with his parents, the presence or absence of older siblings, and his level of peer integration are all unrelated to his ability to perceive persuasive intent. The discriminant equation based on this hypothesis shows age to be the most significant factor. . . .

In comparison, the only factor associated with the child's holding assistive intent attributions is the absence of older siblings; that is, the child who sees advertising as designed to assist tends to be the oldest or only child in the home.

It is interesting that age correlates so well with perception of persuasive intent yet is unrelated to assistive intent. Apparently, attribution of assistive intent is not inconsistent with a concurrent attribution of persuasive intent. Persuasive intent, as would clearly be surmised, is a higher order of at-

tributional sophistication and is dependent upon maturational development and, by implication, cumulative exposure to television commercials.

· · ·

Hypothesis 2: Cognitive Factors Likely to Precede Attribution of Intent

Focusing on the attribution of *persuasive intent*, the hypothesized results are borne out uniformly by the correlation data at a .001 level of significance (one-tailed test) and the discriminant function correctly classifies 73 percent of the cases (Table 4). This suggests that those children who are capable of recognizing commercials as persuasive messages meet a set of (hypothesized) antecedent criteria: (1) they can distinguish commercials from programming; (2) they recognize the existence of an external source or commercial sponsor; (3) they perceive the idea of an intended audience; (4) they are aware of the symbolic nature of commercials; and (5) they cite instances of negative discrepancies where the product did not meet their expectations based on the commercial message.

Analysis of the results for *assistive intent* (Table 4) indicates that only two of the hypothesized variables achieve significant correlations. Bivariate relationships indicate that assistive intent attribution is predicated only on the ability to understand basic source and receiver concepts. The discriminant

Table 3 Developmental factors related to intent (hypothesis #1): Kendall τ correlations and discriminant weights

Developmental factors	Assistive intent		Persuasive intent	
	Kendall τ	Discriminant weights	Kendall τ	Discriminant weights
Age	.05	.27	.41[a]	.94
Parental Education	.03	.40	.19[a]	.32
Parent-Child Interaction	.04	.74	.02	.08
Presence of Older Siblings	−.13[a]	−1.02	−.06	−.30
Peer Integration	.03	.23	.02	.09
Percentage Correctly Classified (vs. 50% Chance Level)		59%		75%
Significance of F Value		NS		.01

[a]Correlation significant at .001 level.

Table 4 Cognitive factors likely to precede attribution of intent (hypothesis #2): Kendall τ correlations and discriminant weights

Cognitive antecedent factors	Assistive intent		Persuasive intent	
	Kendall τ	Discriminant weights	Kendall τ	Discriminant weights
• Discrimination Between Program and Commercials	.04	*	.18[a]	−.21
• Recognition of Source	.10[b]	.21	.42[a]	−.06
• Perception of Audience	.16[a]	−.62	.37[a]	.58
• Awareness of Symbolic Nature of Commercials	.06	−.75	.45[a]	1.23
• Perception of Negative Discrepancies Between Message and Product	.01	1.15	.43[a]	−.81
Percentage Correctly Classified (vs. 50% Chance Level)		61%		73%
Significance of F Value		.01		.01

[a]Correlation significant at .001 level.
[b]Correlation significant at .01 level.
*Variable did not pass tolerance level for inclusion.

function, furthermore, is fairly weak, correctly classifying only 61 percent of the cases, versus a chance level of 50 percent.

Hypothesis 3: Consequences of Intent

In this hypothesis we are looking at the effects of children's attributions of commercial intent on their levels of trust, liking, and consumption motivation. Thus, the two intent measures are now used as the independent variables in examining impact upon attitude structures. From Table 5 some rather interesting results emerge, consistent with this hypothesis.

First of all, the correlational results indicate that children holding assistive intent attributions tend to trust commercials more, whereas children seeing persuasive intent place less trust in them. Similarly, if a child sees commercials as assistive, he tends to like them, while persuasive attribution connotes dislike.

Finally, ability to recognize either type of intent has negative consequences for consumption moti-

vation. In the case of assistive intent this is contrary to our predicted direction, although the effect of assistive attribution on motivation is near zero (−.05). However, a highly significant (p < .001) relationship holds, as predicted, between persuasive intent recognition and diminished desire for advertised products.

Moreover, when both types of intent are considered *in combination*, persuasive intent is clearly the dominantly weighted factor. This is evidenced by the discriminant functions in Table 5 which combine assistive intent and persuasive intent as predictors of trust, liking and consumption motivation. Persuasive intent carries at least seven times the weight of assistive intent according to the standardized coefficients. This result is consistent with Kanouse and Hanson's (1971) general hypothesis that individuals will weigh negative factors more heavily than positive factors in evaluative situations.

In sum, the data suggest that the development of persuasive intent attribution, regardless of "offset-

Table 5   Consequences of intent (hypothesis #3): Kendall τ correlations and discriminant weights

	Trust in commercials		Liking of commercials		Consumption motivation	
Intent	Kendall τ	Discriminant weights	Kendall τ	Discriminant weights	Kendall τ	Discriminant weights
Assistive Intent	.16[a]	.13	.08[c]	.01	−.05	.07
Persuasive Intent	−.16[a]	−1.00	−.12[a]	1.00	−.32[a]	−.99
Percentage Correctly Classified (vs. 33% Chance Level)	58%		38%		49%	
Significance of F Value	.01		.05		.01	

[a]Correlation significant at .001 level.
[b]Correlation significant at .01 level.
[c]Correlation significant at .05 level.

ting" assistive attribution, acts as a cognitive defense for the child against persuasion. . . . Cognitive defense is reflected in a more skeptical, less accepting reception of television commercials, and, in particular, in less intention to respond to the advertising message. Persuasive intent attribution is almost universally operative by fifth grade.

Nevertheless, possible limitations of the present research should be indicated. The study does not examine sex differences since the sample was limited to boys. It is possible that girls may have somewhat different processes of attributional development. Furthermore, the study was confined to children within the Catholic school system. This control was imposed after a pilot study, conducted by Rossiter at a public Philadelphia school representing a mix of religions, found that differential beliefs and gift-giving practices associated with Christmas and Chanukah tended to complicate interview content and measurement.

Finally, our analysis centers on television commercials as a generalized concept. Children's ability to recognize persuasive intent in commercials should not be taken as implying immunity to all commercials; clearly, individual commercials may be highly persuasive for children, just as for adults. Attribution of persuasive intent merely signifies that

the child has acquired the general capability to recognize commercial persuasion.

CONCLUSIONS

Our conclusions can be stated as a series of tentative propositions.

Proposition 1.   Although children are capable of perceiving both the informative and the persuasive characteristics of commercials, recognition of persuasive intent is the main determinant of the child's attitudinal response set to television advertising.

Proposition 2.   Although attribution of persuasive intent can be advanced in homes with high parental education ("enriched environment"), it is primarily age-dependent. Age, as a variable, reflects not only maturational factors but also cumulative experience with commercial messages.

Proposition 3.   The development of persuasive intent attributions acts as a cognitive defense to persuasion. The child who is able to discern persuasive intent is less influenced by advertising in that he is less trusting, likes commercials less, and tends to make fewer consumption requests.

Proposition 4. Alternatively, younger children who lack persuasive intent attributions are more persuasible.

Proposition 5. The cognitive antecedents to attribution of persuasive intent are program-message discrimination, sponsor perception, audience perception, awareness of symbolic representation, and awareness of possible message-product discrepancies.

IMPLICATIONS

The logical social policy question emerging from this research is whether younger children are deserving of some form of special protection from the effects of advertising. This might seem to be a natural conclusion since first graders appear to be quite persuasible; roughly two-thirds of them indicate that they trust all commercials and like all commercials and roughly one-half claim to want all products that they see advertised. Alternatively, it can be indicated that these percentages decline dramatically among third and fifth graders and the argument can be advanced that exposure to advertising is a necessary prerequisite for the development of cognitive defenses against advertising's persuasive effects.

REFERENCES

Bauer, R. A., and Greyser, S. A. (1968), *Advertising in America*, Boston, Mass.: Division of Research, Harvard Business School.

Blatt, J., Spencer, L., and Ward, S. (1971), "A Cognitive Development Study of Children's Reactions to Television Advertising," in *Effects of Television Advertising on Children and Adolescents*, Cambridge, Mass.: Marketing Science Institute.

Festinger, L. (May, 1954), "A Theory of Social Comparison Processes," *Human Relations, 7,* 404–17.

Flavell, J. H. (1970), "Concept Development," in P. H. Mussen, *Carmichael's Manual of Child Psychology,* 3rd ed., Vol. 1, New York: John Wiley and Sons.

Heider, F. (1958), *The Psychology of Interpersonal Relations,* New York: John Wiley and Sons.

Kanouse, D. E., and Hanson, L. R. (1971), "Negativity in Evaluations," in E. E. Jones, et al., eds., *Attribution: Perceiving the Causes of Behavior,* Morristown, N.J.: General Learning Press.

Kelley, H. H. (1971), "Attribution in Social Interaction," in E. E. Jones, et al., eds., *Attribution: Perceiving the Causes of Behavior,* Morristown, N.J.: General Learning Press.

Kelley, H. H. (1967), "Attribution Theory in Social Psychology," in D. Levine, ed., *Nebraska Symposium on Motivation,* Lincoln: University of Nebraska Press.

Mead, G. H. (1934), *Mind, Self and Society,* C. W. Morris, ed., Chicago: University of Chicago Press.

Piaget, J. (1970), "Piaget's Theory," in P. H. Mussen, *Carmichael's Manual of Child Psychology,* 3rd ed., Vol. 1, New York: John Wiley and Sons.

Ward, S., and Wackman, D. B. (1974), "Children's Information Processing of Television Advertising," in G. Kline and P. Clark, eds., *New Models for Communication Research,* Beverly Hills, Calif.: Sage Publishing, 81–119.

PREFERRED SOLUTIONS TO THE ENERGY CRISIS AS A FUNCTION OF CAUSAL ATTRIBUTIONS

RUSSEL BELK
JOHN PAINTER
RICHARD SEMENIK

Since the 1973-74 OPEC oil embargo on North America and the subsequent shortages and price increases that eventually convinced most consumers of a worldwide shortage of petroleum fuels, numerous studies have measured consumer perceptions of why such a shortage exists. . . . The four major perceived causes are (in descending order of blame):

- The governments of large oil-importing countries have mismanaged fuel policies.
- Oil companies have created an artificial shortage.
- The public, or certain segments of it, is squandering finite energy resources.
- The actions of oil producing and exporting countries (OPEC) have created the shortage. . . .

There have also been a number of studies of preferred solutions to the energy shortage. In general, voluntary conservation tends to receive the most support, followed by some form of government intervention. . . . However, little previous research has specifically considered the relationship between consumer perceptions of the causes of the energy crisis and preferences for solutions to the energy crisis.

As inquisitive beings, we seek to know and understand the events that shape our lives. If we can explain the causes of these events, we can learn to anticipate them or even affect their occurence. In addition, we can learn to formulate a more appropriate response when we understand why something has happened. Depending on the particular cause an individual uses to explain present energy shortages, an energy *crisis* may or may not be perceived, future shortages may or may not be perceived to be likely to occur, and a variety of reactions may or may not be perceived to be appropriate to remedy or accommodate energy shortages. Furthermore, depending on whether the individual accepts any personal responsibility for the energy shortage, there may be varying degrees of guilt present to motivate certain reactions.

An especially relevant implication of a person's choice of an explanation is that it may well affect willingness to engage in energy conservation behaviors and to support various other programs of

Source: Russell Belk, John Painter, and Richard Semenik, "Preferred Solutions to the Energy Crisis as a Function of Causal Attributions," *Journal of Consumer Research*, vol. 8, December, 1981, pp. 306–312. Reprinted with permission.

energy policy. If it can be shown that attributions of the causes of energy shortages are systematically related to preferences for various responses, then the task of generating public support for a specific *response* to energy shortages may be reduced to educating the public about the *causes* of the shortage. This article provides evidence that perceptions of the causes of energy shortages *are* related to preferred responses, examines the nature of this relationship, and discusses implications for public policy.

HYPOTHESES AND RATIONALE

The most directly relevant previous research is a study by Hummel, Levitt, and Loomis (1978) of Colorado residents' attitudes toward energy and the environment. They found that those who blamed environmentalists for the energy crisis tended to be less receptive to proposals for cleaner air and energy conservation, but more receptive to proposals to reduce energy shortages at the expense of the environment. They also found that those who blamed individual consumers for the energy crisis favored proposals for cleaner air and mandatory energy conservation efforts. Although the authors did not offer a generalized explanation of their findings, these patterns may be interpreted to suggest the following two hypotheses:

H1: Those who attribute a shared problem such as energy shortages to a personal cause, rather than to a nonpersonal cause, are more likely than others to prefer personal actions toward solving the problem.

H2: Those who attribute a shared problem such as energy shortages to a nonpersonal cause, rather than to a personal cause, are more likely than others to prefer nonpersonal actions toward solving the problem.

Both nonpersonal causes and actions are viewed as those largely outside of the control of the perceiver, and personal causes and actions are construed as those over which the perceiver has some direct control. In terms of the list of causal attributions for the energy crisis discussed earlier, governments, oil companies, and OPEC are considered to be nonpersonal, and the public is considered to be a personal cause. Among the potential actions that can be taken to alleviate energy problems, conservation (especially voluntary conservation) is taken to be the most personal solution.

. . .

Henion and Kinnear (1976) demonstrate that consumers believe more strongly in ecological activism if they generally display an "internal locus of control" (a belief in personal responsibility for their lives) rather than an "external locus of control" (a belief that chance or powerful others control their lives). . . . A series of energy-specific studies summarized by Murray et al. (1974) . . . support the view that those who believe in the ability of individuals to solve the energy shortage are more likely than others to report reduced consumption of gasoline and electricity. . . .

. . .

The studies of consumer dissatisfaction and complaining behavior by Valle and her associates (Krishnan and Valle 1979; Valle and Wallendorf 1977; Valle and Koeske 1977) also provide support for the present hypotheses. They find that consumers are more likely to voice complaints when an unsatisfactory purchase is attributed to a retailer or manufacturer than when it is attributed to poor shopping or improper product use by the purchaser. As complaining implies seeking a nonpersonal solution to consumption problems, and was found to be more likely when a nonpersonal (retailer or manufacturer) cause was inferred, these findings are also consistent with the present hypotheses.

. . .

Finally, indirect support for the present hypotheses may be gleaned from the attribution-theory literature. Selected findings in this literature suggest an alignment of personal attributions with expectations of personally caused future success at a task. For instance, Phares (1957) found that subjects who were told their success at a task was due to their skill (a personal cause) had higher expectations of future successes than those subjects who were told their success was due to chance (a nonpersonal cause). Conversely, the "learned help-lessness" literature within attribution theory . . . demonstrates that those who are made to perceive aversive outcomes as being caused by external (nonpersonal) factors, see little point in trying to affect a personal solution, and resign themselves to the aversive situation.

Also, research concerning the "just world hypothesis" (Lerner and Miller 1978) strongly suggests that we believe that the guilty should pay. This in turn suggests that if we see ourselves as being responsible for the energy crisis we should expect to "pay" for it, but if we blame a specific nonpersonal cause, that causal agent should be expected to solve the problem. . . .

METHOD

Two studies were conducted to test the hypotheses. The studies were parallel except the first concentrated on responses to the gasoline shortage, while the second also obtained reports of home-heating fuel-conservation attitudes and behaviors.

The first study employed personal interviews with 253 heads of households who traveled over 140 miles by automobile each month. The study was conducted during a period of rapidly escalating gasoline prices and spot shortages during the spring and summer of 1979. The second study interviewed 359 heads of households during the winter and spring of 1980, and employed the additional criteria that respondents must have had the responsibility of paying their heating bills and the ability to control their home thermostat settings. . . . Respondents were asked about mileage traveled to and from place of employment, automobiles owned and their gasoline consumption, previous automobiles owned, and changes in gasoline consumed and local bus usage in the past five years, as well as reasons for the changes. . . . Where there were multiple potential motives for such actions, the question stipulated that the behaviors were intended to save fuel or reduce fuel bills. These questions were followed by several questions concerning beliefs in the existence of the energy crisis, a ranking of preferences for three

solutions (voluntary conservation, government enforced conservation, and government pressure on oil companies), a forced judgment of the most important cause of fuel shortages [the general public, foreign oil producers (OPEC), our government, or oil companies], and endorsements of a series of specific solutions that had been proposed to combat energy shortages. . . .

The second study interview format differed primarily by adding questions related to home heating energy conservation activities, such as daytime and nighttime thermostat settings. In this study, the conservation data were combined into additive indices (one for gasoline conservation and one for home heating-fuel conservation) by adding one point for each of the "positive actions" and subtracting one point for each of the "negative actions" as shown in Exhibit 1.

Exhibit 1 Variables used in assignments of conserver status

Positive actions	Negative actions
A. Gasoline conservation	
Moved to decrease travel	Move that increased travel
Purchased more fuel-efficient automobile	Purchased less fuel-efficient automobile
Started car-pooling	Stopped car pooling
Use the bus more	Use the bus less
Drive less	Drive more
Car gets more than 24 mpg	Use the bus less than once a week
B. Home heat conservation	
Moved to smaller home to save fuel	Moved to larger home
Moved to more fuel-efficient home	Moved to less fuel-efficient home
Installed more insulation	Higher thermostat setting
Installed storm windows/doors	At home more
Installed automatic set-back thermostats	Day and night thermostat settings equal
At home less	Day or night thermostat 70° or more

Table 1 Percentage endorsing (as best) three energy-shortage solutions by attributions: study 1

| | Solution | | | | |
Attributed cause	Voluntary conservation	Government-enforced conservation	Government pressure on oil companies	Total	Base
The general public	74.5%	25.5%	0.0%	100.0%	51
Foreign oil producers (OPEC)	46.8	19.4	33.8	100.0	77
Our government	60.8	9.8	29.4	100.0	51
Oil companies	38.2	8.9	52.9	100.0	68
Overall	53.0	15.8	31.2	100.0	247
Average for non-public (nonpersonal) causal attributions	47.5	13.2	39.3	100.0	196

NOTE: $\chi^2 = 41.8$ (6 d.f.), $p < 0.0001$.

RESULTS

Study 1
The first study examined the relationship between attribution of the fuel shortage to four possible causes and preferences among a set of general "solutions," as well as among a set of more specific "solutions," Table 1 shows the proportions of those attributing the energy shortage to each of the four causes that advocated each of three general solutions as best. . . .

Clearly, these results support the hypotheses. Those who attributed the energy shortage to a personal cause were more likely to favor the personal solutions than those who attributed the energy shortage to nonpersonal causes; and those who attributed the energy shortage to nonpersonal causes were more likely to favor the least personal solution (pressure on oil companies) than those who made personal attributions.

Further insight into the effects of personal versus nonpersonal attributions may be seen in Table 2, which compares the proportions of each attribution group that endorse each of nine more *specific* "solutions." Here, the most personal solutions

may be viewed as those that are most likely to necessitate change in respondent behavior; these are the first five solutions in Table 2.

· · ·

Study 2
Besides adding home heating conservation to gasoline conservation and examining reported behaviors in addition to attitudinal preferences, the second study hoped to distinguish between the attribution of the energy shortage to "the general public in the U.S." and the more specific personal attribution to "me and people like me." However, the fact that only 11 of 359 respondents gave the latter attribution as the most important cause of the energy shortage precludes the use of this category in the statistical analyses.[1]

Table 3 parallels Table 1 from the first study, both in format and findings. Here again, those making personal attributions were most likely to

[1]The category is still reported in Table 3 for the speculative insights it offers, but the statistical analyses are based on merging the two personal attribution categories.

Table 2   Percentage endorsing (as acceptable) nine energy shortage solutions by attributions: study 1

	Attributed cause				
Solution	The general public	Foreign oil producers	Our government	Oil companies	Average for all nonpublic (nonpersonal) causal attributions
Gas stations closing certain days	56.9%	55.1%	45.3%	47.8%	50.2%
High prices to reduce demand	29.4	15.4	20.8	18.8	18.0
Gasoline rationing	52.9	33.3	37.7	42.2	37.5
Restricting driving to no more than 6 days per week	37.3	30.8	28.3	30.4	30.0
Better enforced 55 mile-per-hour speed limits	90.2	89.7	64.2	75.4	78.0
Improved public transportation	80.4	87.2	84.9	81.2	84.5
Stricter limits on new car mileage	68.6	80.8	73.6	78.3	78.0
Development of other fuels	90.2	87.2	86.3	91.3	88.4
No action at all	0.0	1.3	3.8	1.4	2.0
Base	51	78	53	69	200

Table 3   Percentage endorsing (as best) four energy shortage solutions by attributions: study 2

	Solution					
Attributed cause	Voluntary conservation	Government enforced conservation	Government pressure on oil companies	No action	Total	Base
The general public	76.1%	17.9%	3.0%	3.0%	100.0%	67
Foreign oil producers (OPEC)*	62.5	18.8	17.2	1.5	100.0	64
Me and people like me	81.8	9.1	0.0	9.1	100.0	11
Our government*	55.0	12.6	20.7	11.7	100.0	111
Oil companies*	40.6	11.3	45.3	2.8	100.0	106
Overall	56.3	14.2	23.4	6.1	100.0	359
Average for nonpersonal attributions(*)	51.3	13.5	29.2	6.0	100.0	281

NOTE: $\chi^2 = 59.8$ (based on collapsing "the general public" and "me and people like me"; 9 d.f.), $p \leq 0.0001$.

favor voluntary conservation as the best solution, and those making nonpersonal attributions were most likely to favor nonpersonal solutions to the energy shortage. The alternate hypothesis that those blaming the general public would be more likely to prefer mandatory conservation over voluntary conservation does not receive support in either study. . . .

Exhibit 2 shows the results of the analyses of variance on the two conservation indices, with causal attributions as the independent variables. Both patterns of mean conservation scores show that those making personal attributions (to "the general public" or "me") reported engaging in the greatest amount of conservation, but the results for gasoline conservation are not statistically significant.

Exhibit 2 Mean scores on gasoline and heating conservation indices as a function of attributed cause of energy shortage

Attributed cause	Sample size	Group mean[a]
A. Gasoline		
1. The general public or me	77	.90
2. Foreign oil producers (OPEC)	64	.69
3. Our government	111	.60
4. Oil companies	106	.70
Nonpersonal (Groups 2, 3, and 4)	281	.66
B. Heating fuel		
1. The general public or me	77	.38
2. Foreign oil producers (OPEC)	64	.09
3. Our government	111	−.20
4. Oil companies	106	−.05
Nonpersonal (Groups 2, 3, and 4)	281	−.08

[a]Higher scores indicate greater reported gasoline conservation (A) or greater reported heating fuel conservation (B).
NOTE: $F = 1.376$, $p < 0.25$ (A); $F = 2.877$, $p < 0.05$, group 1 differs from groups 3 and 4 via Duncan's multiple range test, with $p < 0.05$ (B).

DISCUSSION

Both the first and second studies support the basic hypotheses that attributions of nonpersonal causes for the energy shortage call for nonpersonal solutions, and that attributions of personal causes call for personal solutions. This may be seen most clearly in the fact that those blaming the general public preferred conservation solutions, whereas those blaming oil companies preferred government actions against these firms.

· · ·

The most immediate public policy implication is that the failure of most consumers to see themselves and the general public as the major source of the energy problem is likely to be a substantial deterrent to energy conservation. For those 25 to 30 percent in the present studies who blame oil companies for the energy shortage, a majority favor government pressure on these companies to improve supplies and reduce prices and profits. If the associations found between attributed blame and preferred solutions are truly causal, then in order to gain more support for voluntary conservation, nonpersonal perceptions of the causes of the energy shortage must be superseded by recognititon that public consumption patterns are mostly to blame.

Government officials and oil company executives should also have an interest in shifting perceptions of blame from themselves to the public in order to reduce pressures on them to bring about a solution. Although more research is needed to understand how such attributions form and change, public opinion seems to be slowly changing from nonpersonal to personal attributions for the energy shortage (Farhar et al., 1979). Presuming that this is a shift toward more *veridical* perceptions, efforts at education may be designed to reinforce and accelerate such a change. In addition, direct efforts to encourage conservation could provide the persuasive rationale that public conservation is the answer because public consumption is the cause of the shortage.

· · ·

REFERENCES

Farhar, Barbara C., Wells, Patricia, Unseld, Charles T., and Burns, Barbara A. (1979), *Public Opinion About Energy: A Literature Review,* Golden, CO: Solar Energy Research Institute.

Henion, Karl E. II, and Kinnear, Thomas C. (1976), "The Ecologically Concerned Consumer and Locus of Control," in *Ecological Marketing,* eds. Karl E. Henion II and Thomas C. Kinnear, Chicago: American Marketing Association, pp. 131–44.

Krishnan, S., and Valle, Valerie A. (1979), "Dissatisfaction Attributions and Consumer Complaint Behavior," in *Advances in Consumer Research,* Vol. 6, ed. William Wilkie, Ann Arbor, MI: Association for Consumer Research, pp. 445–9.

Lerner, M. J., and Miller, Donald T. (1978), "Just World Research and the Attribution Process: Looking Back and Ahead," *Psychological Bulletin,* 85, 1030–51.

Murray, James R., Minor, Michael J., Bradburn, Norman M., Cotterman, Robert F., Frankel, Martin, and Pisarski, Alan E. (1974), "Evolution of Public Response to the Energy Crisis," *Science,* 19, 257–63.

Phares, E. J. (1957), "Expectancy Changes in Skill and Chance Situations," *Journal of Abnormal and Social Psychology,* 54, 339–42.

Valle, Valerie, and Koeske, Randi (1977), "Elderly Consumer Problems: Actions, Sources of Information, and Attributions of Blame," in *Proceedings of the Division 23 Program, 85th Annual Convention of the American Psychological Association,* ed. Clark Leavitt, Columbus, OH: American Psychological Association, pp. 7–8.

———, and Wallendorf, Melanie (1977), "Consumer Attributions of the Cause of Their Product Satisfaction and Dissatisfaction," in *Consumer Satisfaction, Dissatisfaction and Complaining Behavior,* ed. Ralph L. Day, Bloomington, IN: Indiana University, pp. 26–30.

SECTION XI

INNOVATIONS AND CONSUMER BEHAVIOR

The processes whereby new ideas, products, and services are purchased by individuals and organizations have fascination for consumer researchers and are important to marketers. We will refer to ideas, products, and services that consumers perceive to be new as *innovations*. In the literature on innovations, buyers are referred to as *adopters*. Five categories of adopters are usually identified. The first category is called *innovators*. Innovators are consumers who are among the first 10 percent of a population to adopt an innovation. The second category are the *early adopters*, approximately the next 15 percent to adopt after the innovators. The third and fourth categories are the *early* and *late majority* groups, respectively. The early and late majority each represent about 30 percent of the total population. The fifth and last group to adopt an innovation, if ever, are called *laggards*. Laggards represent approximately 15 percent of the population. Note that the term *laggard* has a pejorative connotation. It implies there is something wrong with a person who does not adopt an innovation until almost everyone else has.

Considerable research exists about the characteristics of the different adopter (or buyer) categories. Some studies have found innovators and early adopters to be younger and to have higher levels of formal education than other adopter categories. Innovative firms have been found to be larger than many other firms in their industries and to send employees to professional meetings more often than less innovative firms. Various research studies are not always in agreement about the traits of the different adopter categories. For this reason studies about consumer behavior involving innovations should be used more as a source of clues and less as a guideline as to what a specific group of consumers will do with regard to a very specific innovation.

Research findings about the nature of innovative organizations are somewhat more consistent. Innovative organizations are more clearly aware of their needs and spend more staff time trying to understand them. In addition there is usually a strong consensus among members of an innovative organization that action should be taken in response to a need. Members of an innovative organization are less likely to feel threatened by an innovation than members of a much less innovative organization. There is also a greater potential for change in innovative firms or agencies. Potential for change refers to the capacity of an organization to accept and implement change. This capacity may consist of financial ability and the presence of individuals who have the ability to use the innovation appropriately. There is also evidence that members of innovative organizations usually believe they have substantial control over the change process. They feel that to a considerable degree they can influence the selection and implementation of the innovation. Members of less innovative organizations feel they have less authority.

The papers included in this section collectively address many of the issues and research findings in the literature on consumer innovativeness.

"INNOVATIVENESS, NOVELTY SEEKING, AND CONSUMER CREATIVITY"

Innovativeness has received extensive attention in consumer behavior research, and it is a very important concept. Without innovativeness, or openness to change, new products would find great difficulty in gaining acceptance. Several other concepts, however, may be equally relevant to consumer behavior, but have not received equal attention by marketers. Hirschman organizes innovativeness, novelty seeking, and creativity into a theoretical framework.

Novelty seeking refers to the desire to seek out or acquire novel information. On one level, it is nearly the same as innovativeness: the desire to seek out new and different information is very similar to the willingness to adopt new products. However, gaining new information (on a new product, for example) is very different from actually trying the product. (Hirschman sorts out these distinctions.) She also incorporates creativity, including the ability to solve consumption problems, into the model, and comes up with a number of propositions regarding innovative behavior.

Role accumulation is another concept that must be addressed in the article, because the various roles which the consumer performs in society will affect the manner in which the consumer shows innovativeness, novelty seeking, and creativity. All of these concepts must, of course, be operationalized in order to test the model, and Hirschman points out a number of approaches to measuring the concepts.

While this model has not been tested as a whole, a number of the individual components have been verified empirically. Therefore, while noting that an empirical test of the model as a whole is still needed, one can nevertheless point out some of the implications if the model does hold. It would be useful for marketers to learn more about the consumers who progress through the various stages of the model; i.e., persons who never gain awareness of new products, persons who do become informed but do not purchase it, and those who do adopt the product. What characteristics are important in considering the divergent behaviors? The concept of role accumulation may provide a partial answer, and creativity may further contribute to explaining differences. At the very least, Hirschman has pointed the way toward some important research questions in consumer behavior.

"ORGANIZATIONAL PSYCHOGRAPHICS AND INNOVATIVENESS"

In the field of consumer research, demographic characteristics have not usually been particularly good predictors of consumer buying behavior. Similarly, variables such as Standard Industrial Classification, size, or location have not allowed any better results in predicting organizational buying behavior. Robertson and Wind attempt to improve upon the understanding of organizational buying behavior by utilizing organizational psychographics to help explain organizational innovativeness. They note that in consumer research psychographics are sometimes rather sloppily applied, and are careful to develop guidelines for the use of organizational psychographic concepts.

Based on previous work, Robertson and Wind select six dimensions for their psychographic model. They test the relationship between organizational innovativeness and direction (clarity of goals), decision centrality, openness of communication, achievement motivation, resistance to change, and conflict. (It is a useful exercise to study how the concepts are operationalized in a particular context, in this case a hospital.) An organizational demographics model has also been developed, because the aim of the authors' psychographic model is to improve prediction by adding the psychographic concepts to the demographic model.

Results of the test show that the addition of organizational psychographics does improve the model somewhat. The addition of yet another concept, consensus, further improves the explanation of variance. However, even the full model, which incorporates demographics, psychographics, and consensus, remains fairly weak. Marketers should probably conclude that an understanding of organizational psychographics will improve knowledge of organizational buying behavior, but that many other factors must still be considered.

"PROFILES OF SIGNATURE GOODS CONSUMERS AND AVOIDERS"

Many consumers may buy products such as designer jeans because of the status attached to them, rather than for the purely utilitarian value. Marketers of signature goods (products that carry external brand marks) certainly depend upon consumers who attach symbolic value to the product. Nevertheless, very little data is available on the characteristics of consumers who adopt signature goods, or for that matter, on characteristics of those who avoid such products. Marketers of signature goods therefore have a very incomplete view of their target market.

Jolson, Anderson, and Leber contribute to the understanding of adoption or rejection of such products by identifying characteristics of consumers relevant to signature goods and defining segments. They find in their survey of patrons of fashion stores that about 9 percent of the respondents are prone to adopt signature goods, while about 13 percent avoid them. The remainder are more or less indifferent. (The reader may wish to relate this to the brief discussion of innovators and laggards in the introductory remarks at the beginning of this section.) After identifying these segments, the authors analyze how the characteristics of the two extreme groups differ from the general population of the survey.

These findings are of immediate practical use to marketers, who can better define segments and target their consumers. However, the authors note that this is only the first step. Understanding of the causes of signature goods proneness or avoidance is still very vague, and therefore researchers cannot yet predict future consumer behavior relative to such products. Will the current popularity of signature goods lead to increasing sales? Or will the abundance of such goods serve to lower their status and lead to decreased demand? To answer these and similar questions, better understanding of the causes of consumer behavior in this sphere is needed.

INNOVATIVENESS, NOVELTY SEEKING, AND CONSUMER CREATIVITY

ELIZABETH C. HIRSCHMAN

A conceptual framework is presented of the interrelationships among three constructs relevant to the behavior of consumers—innovativeness, novelty seeking, and creativity. These concepts are organized into a theoretical framework that integrates existing paradigms, consolidates previously independent constructs, and generates hypotheses for research.

The first of these behavioral constructs, *innovativeness,* has been the subject of lengthy and extensive investigations in several areas of behavioral science, and has received great attention by consumer researchers. By way of contrast, *novelty-seeking* behavior has been investigated to some extent within the innovation-diffusion context, yet has received relatively greater attention by psychologists and other behavioral scientists not directly involved with consumer behavior. *Creativity* has been primarily an object of study by trait psychologists, who have concentrated their efforts on investigating creativity in its most extreme manifestations as characterized by outstanding artistic or scientific achievement. Investigations of creativity have not focused on its potential applicability to everyday consumption activities.

INNOVATIVENESS

Few concepts in the behavioral sciences have as much immediate relevance to consumer behavior as innovativeness. The propensities of consumers to adopt novel products, whether they are ideas, goods, or services, can play an important role in theories of brand loyalty, decision making, preference, and communication. If there were no such characteristic as innovativeness, consumer behavior would consist of a series of routinized buying responses to a static set of products. It is the inherent willingness of a consuming population to innovate that gives the marketplace its dynamic nature. On an individual basis, *every* consumer is, to some extent, an innovator; all of us over the course of our lives adopt some objects or ideas that are new in our perception.

Innovativeness has undergone two major conceptualizations. The first is captured in the statement by Rogers and Shoemaker (1971, p. 27) that

Source: Elizabeth C. Hirschman, "Innovativeness, Novelty Seeking, and Consumer Creativity," *Journal of Consumer Research,* Vol. 7, December, 1980, pp. 283–295. Reprinted with permission.

innovativeness is "the degree to which an individual is relatively earlier in adopting an innovation than other members of his social system." However, as Midgley and Dowling (1978, p. 230) observe, "This is essentially an operational definition since it is couched directly in terms of measurement of innovativeness, viz., the time taken for an individual to adopt." It is also hindered, as those authors point out, by potential measurement error in determining when an innovation was introduced into the social system.

A conceptual strength of the Rogers and Shoemaker (1971) definition, however, is its dependence on the notion that an innovation is "an idea, practice, or object *perceived as new* by the individual," (p. 19). Although there may be large variations in the perceptions of product "newness" among consumers, which confound measuring their roles as innovators, it will be argued that this diversity of perceived novelty is closely tied to the cognitive origins of innovativeness.

The second major conceptualization of innovativeness was constructed in a recent article by Midgley and Dowling (1978) who, after an extensive literature review, expressed the notion that innovativeness was "the degree to which an individual is receptive to new ideas and makes innovation decisions independently of the communicated experience of others" (p. 236). These writers viewed innovativeness as a personality construct possessed to a greater or lesser degree by all individuals. It is believed to be a continuous variable normally distributed within a population of consumers and generalizable across products. Midgley and Dowling put forward no explanations of the causes generating innovativeness, nor did they discuss why some individuals exhibited more innovativeness than others.

Causes of Innovativeness

Although innovativeness has generated a vast amount of empirical research, its origins and causes remain obscure. Despite the search for demographic and sociopsychological correlates for this construct, few attempts have been made to chart the development of innovativeness within an individual over time.

One explanation for the lack of causal investigation is that innovativeness may have been assumed constant for each individual; that each consumer is "born with" a certain allotment of innovativeness and this personality trait remains invariant over his/her life course. However, given the fact that innovativeness has been found highly correlated with such variables as educational attainment, occupational status, and urbanization (Rogers and Shoemaker 1971), it would seem more plausible that it is not a genetic constant, but rather socially influenced.

NOVELTY SEEKING

The basic notion underlying the construct of novelty seeking appears to be that through some internal drive or motivating force the individual is activated to seek out novel information.

It is useful to divide novelty seeking into two components—inherent novelty seeking and actualized novelty seeking. Inherent novelty seeking is viewed as the desire of the individual to seek out novel stimuli; actualized novelty seeking represents the actual behavior by the individual to acquire novel stimuli.

Potential Sources of Novelty Seeking

Flavell (1977) notes that at a very early age human infants already are engaged in novelty seeking. When presented with two visual stimuli of equal intensity, one familiar and one novel, the infant will select the novel stimulus. Thus, novelty seeking would seem to represent an innate search for information. However, even if novelty seeking is innate, it is logical to assume that it serves some constructive purpose to the individual.

One straightforward explanation is that novelty seeking serves as a means of self-preservation. The individual may find it useful to create a "bank" of potentially useful knowledge. Because the future is unknowable and unexpected, consumption problems are almost inevitable; the consumer may wisely decide to seek information that is not "useful" now, but may assume great importance in the future. It stands to reason that the consumer who has sought and stored more data is likely to be better equipped for novel problem circumstances. The data that are stored may include (1) vicarious "adoption" of unfamiliar product concepts, (2) the vicarious "experiencing" of unfamiliar consumption situations, (3) the actual adoption of novel products, (4) and personal exposure to novel consumption situations.

A second, complementary, explanation for novelty seeking is that it functions to improve problem-solving skills. That is, the consumer may seek information pertaining to presently adopted products and consumption situations in an effort to improve his/her performance. This rationale for novelty seeking could also lead the consumer to both seek information about and to the actual adoption of new products.

As an example, magazine readership is likely to be due, at least in part, to novelty-seeking behavior. One feature that makes magazines valuable to the consumer is that every issue contains novel information. In a genuine sense, a magazine subscription represents a commitment by the consumer to acquire novel data.

RELATING INNOVATIVENESS AND NOVELTY SEEKING

In their discussion of innovativeness, Midgley and Dowling (1978) distinguished between generalized or inherent innovativeness and actualized innovativeness. The notion of actualized innovativeness is consistent with innovativeness as conceptualized by Rogers and Shoemaker (1971), in that it deals with product adoption (measurable behavior) rather than willingness to adopt (predispositions to act in a certain way).

Reexamination of these definitions reveals that they are closely related to the constructs of inherent and actualized novelty seeking. The desire to seek out the new and different (i.e., inherent novelty seeking) is conceptually indistinguishable from the willingness to adopt new products (i.e., inherent innovativeness). Especially when one defines products in their broad sense, it becomes apparent that new products may constitute new information in the form of ideas (e.g., from magazines), services (e.g., education courses), and tangible goods (e.g.,

apparel, automobiles). Thus, a consumer who expresses a willingness to adopt a new product is necessarily also expressing a desire for novel information.

However, actualized novelty seeking and actualized innovativeness are not the same phenomenon. Actualized novelty seeking refers to the initiation of behaviors intended to acquire new information: whereas actualized innovativeness refers to the actual acquisition of new information. Thus, actualized novelty seeking may be represented by purchasing a ticket to a movie or buying a newspaper. The individual is undertaking this action in an attempt to obtain novel information; however, upon viewing the movie or reading the newspaper, s/he may discover that no new information was forthcoming. Thus, although the attempt was made (actualized novelty seeking), the desired objective was not achieved (actualized innovativeness).

ADOPTIVE AND VICARIOUS INNOVATIVENESS

To develop this idea further, let us make a subtle distinction between two components of actualized innovativeness. The component termed *adoptive innovativeness* refers to the actual adoption of a new product, and the component termed *vicarious innovativeness* refers to the acquisition of information regarding a new product. Through vicarious innovativeness the individual can, in essence, adopt the product concept without adopting the product itself. S/he can enter novel information into memory and have it available for consumption decision making, but avoid the expense and risk inherent in adopting the actual product. Further s/he can similarly enlarge his/her knowledge of consumption situations through the vicarious experiencing of novel consumption situations. For example, s/he may read about how to fix a flat tire or how to cope with being "bumped" from an airplane, rather than acquiring this knowledge by personal experience.

Thus inherent novelty seeking can be used in place of inherent innovativeness and is posited to lead to two forms of actualized innovativeness:

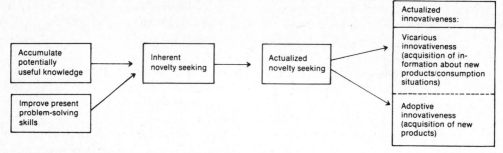

Figure 1 Novelty seeking and actualized innovativeness.

adoptive innovativeness and vicarious innovativeness. Both vicarious and adoptive innovativeness may result from the successful implementation of actualized novelty seeking, as illustrated in Figure 1.

CREATIVITY

The conceptual perspective of creativity used here is that of the ability to engage in what Guilford (1965) terms *productive thinking*—the capacity to generate novel cognitive content. Creativity is required for problem solving: as Guilford states: "Problem solving is creative" (p. 8). To solve a problem, the consumer must create some novel cognitive content. The extent of creativity will depend on both the nature of the problem confronted and the capability of the individual.

Consumer Creativity
Consumer creativity may be defined as the problem-solving capability possessed by the individual that may be applied toward solving consumption-related problems (Hirschman 1980). In line with this reasoning, this component of creativity could be an important factor in the individual's ability to deal effectively with the consumption environment.

The effects of cognitive development on creativity are directly linked to consumer behavior in that consumers must learn to comprehend[1] two key

sets of concepts: products and consumption situations. This is especially true of consumers in modern societies. The more modern the society, the more the individual's role as a consumer grows in complexity; thus, more creativity will be required for successful performance as a consumer.

The creativity of consumers is posited to result from two related cognitive sources: (1) the density of the product-relevant interconcept network possessed by the individual and (2) the repertoire of consumption situations that s/he has mentally retained (Hirschman 1979).

Interconcept Networks
Throughout life, the consumer acquires knowledge about products and their attributes. This information is retained mentally as categories of product concepts with associated attributes. Concurrent with the acquisition of product concepts is the establishment of a network of interconcept linkages that consists of dimensions relating one product concept to another according to the correlative pattern of their attributes. These dimensions reflect the similarity or dissimilarity of interconcept characteristics.

It stands to reason that the more diversified the consumption experiences an individual has had, the more product concepts s/he will have acquired, and the more attributes s/he will have associated with each concept, either from vicarious or actual experience. Thus, more experienced consumers will have a more highly developed interconcept network than the less experienced. Interconcept network density represents the number of dimensions the consumer has available for comparing

[1]Comprehension in this sense connotes the notion of *verstehen*, that is, to understand and be capable of interpreting.

alternative product concepts. It is one important cognitive source of consumer creativity, because the more dimensions one has available for comparing alternatives, the closer congruence can be attained between problem criteria and the attributes of potential solutions.

Scripts

A second component of consumer creativity springs from the same factors as the first, but may be represented differently in the individual's mind; this component is termed a script or episodic schema. These are described by Simon (1979, p. 377) as follows: "The nodes (mental storage areas) of episodic schema represent a system of temporally and causally related events . . . (for example) the schema associated with 'restaurant' could be a script describing the typical sequence of events that occurs when one enters a restaurant." In essence, then, these scripts or episodic schema may represent a repertoire of consumption situations that the consumer has stored and may manipulate mentally.

The importance of scripts to consumer creativity derives from the fact that the individual may use them to mentally recall how s/he solved prior consumption problems (e.g., solution criteria, decision strategies), and may apply this knowledge to solve similar problems. Further, the individual may mentally rearrange parts of various scripts into new configurations to represent a novel consumption situation s/he is facing or expects to encounter. Therefore, the notion of scripts may provide a deeper and expanded theoretical framework for the construct of situation.

Scripts, like concepts, are acquired through exposure to environmental stimulation. As with product concepts, the more diversified the consumption experiences of the consumer, the larger and more varied will become the mental repertoire of consumption situations.

One important distinction between interconcept networks and scripts is that the former are static and propositional in nature, whereas the latter are dynamic and experiential. In other words, interconcept networks deal with the facts the consumer has acquired about a product concept. For example, s/he may "know" that a Honda Civic has a 40 mpg energy rating or that a Holdiay Inn room costs $50 per night. Such knowledge does not have to be acquired through actual experience with the product. It can be obtained, for example, from advertising, friends, a product rating service, and so forth.

In contrast, the repertoire of consumption situations that the individual has stored in memory represents the scripts resulting from various consumption experiences. Whereas, they may contain some factual information (e.g., "I remember I paid $50 per night at the Holiday Inn in Atlanta, Georgia"), they are most useful because they allow the individual to recall the temporal and spatial series of actions realted to a given act of consumption.

For example, scripts may permit the individual to reconstruct the physical movements necessary to solve a consumption problem, alert him/her to certain verbal or visual cues that may be important (e.g., "The last time I was in a restaurant like *this,* and the waiter said *that,* then . . ."), and develop a set of strategic actions.

Source of Creativity

By combining interconcept networks and scripts, the individual is provided with the essential elements for consumer creativity. That is, to solve a consumption problem one must mentally represent the situational context (either actual or hypothetical) and isolate the criteria that are required to satisfactorily "solve" the problem, This may be accomplished by calling up a stored script or by combining portions of several scripts to mentally recreate the problem environment. Once the necessary solution criteria have been identified, the individual may search along various interconcept network linkages for product concepts that possess the set of attributes appropriate for solving the problem.

Thus, consumer creativity is believed to be a function of the density of the consumer's interconcept network and his/her mental repertoire of consumption situations. Together they provide the two essential components of problem solving: (1) the ability to mentally represent the problem context, isolate solution criteria, and identify decision strategies, and (2) the ability to evoke potential product solutions that possess the required attributes.

CONSUMER CREATIVITY AND ACTUALIZED INNOVATIVENESS

Consumer creativity is related to actualized innovativeness in a way distinct from that of novelty seeking. To discuss this relationship, a series of deductive propositions is put forward, and a third component of actualized innovativeness is specified—*use innovativeness*. The basic idea underlying use innovativeness is that the consumer acts in an innovative fashion when s/he uses a previously adopted product to solve a novel consumption problem. In other words, when the consumer uses a product that s/he already possesses to solve a problem that has not been previously encountered, s/he is displaying use innovativeness. Before developing these notions, however, a brief review of research relating to consumer perceptions of product innovations is pertinent.

Perceptions of Innovations

The variance that has been observed in the adoption and diffusion of new products may be due in part to consumers' perceptions of these products. Various classification schemes involving product attributes have been proposed to account for the observed differences in diffusion rates. However, the Rogers and Shoemaker (1971) typology, adopted by most consumer researchers, proposes five characteristics found to have general relevance:[2]

- *Relative advantage.* The degree to which an innovation is perceived superior to the one it will replace or compete against (positively related to adoptability).
- *Compatibility.* The extent to which the new product is consistent with existing values and the past experience of the adopter (positively related to adoptability).

- *Complexity.* The degree to which the innovation is difficult to understand or to use (negatively related to adoptability).
- *Trialability (or divisibility).* The degree to which an innovation may be tried by consumers on a limited basis (positively related to adoptability).
- *Observability (or communicability).* The extent to which an innovation is visible to others (positively related to adoptability).

Exploring the relative efficacy of product-related and adopter-related variables in predicting actualized innovativeness, Ostlund (1974) was able to correctly classify innovators 79 percent of the time using only the five product perceptual variables. This value increased only to 80 percent when 13 personal characteristic variables were included.[3] In a second study (Ostlund 1974), the perceived product attributes correctly classified 77 percent of the eventual innovators; whereas a rate of 79 percent was obtained by including personal characteristic variables in the discriminant function.[4] Taylor (1977), following Ostlund, found a significant, positive relationship between usage of a product class and time of adoption. This suggests that prior knowledge of the product class may lead to greater ability to detect superior new products in that class and, hence, contribute to the probability that they will be adopted.

Combining this empirical evidence with the factors believed to underlie consumer creativity leads to the following propositions:

P1: The probability that a novel product[5] will be adopted is inversely related to the amount of cognitive effort that must be expended by a consumer to comprehend it as a concept.[6]

---

[2]For confirmation of the direction of these relationships with adoptability in empirical studies, see Schiffman and Kanuk (1978). pp. 405–7.

[3]The figures are for unaided recall; they were lower for aided recall.

[4]Of the personal characteristic variables, only venturesomeness and socioeconomic status were found to have any significant statistical relationship (positive) to innovativeness.

[5]A novel product is one unfamiliar to the consumer; it is perceived to be an innovation.

[6]Comprehend means to understand how the product will be able to function and to interpret its potential utility.

P2: Comprehension of the novel product as a concept will, generally, precede actual adoption of the product.[7]

P3: The fewer attributes the novel product possesses in common with presently conceptualized products, the more cognitive effort must be expended to comprehend it as a concept.

P4: By definition, the more creative the consumer, the more product concepts have been comprehended (either vicariously or through actual adoption). Thus, the greater the likelihood that the creative consumer will be able to detect common attributes, between conceptually comprehended products and the novel product.

P5: The more creative the consumer, the less cognitive effort must be expended to comprehend any novel product as a concept, *ceteris paribus*.

P6: From Proposition 5 it follows that the more creative the consumer, the better equipped s/he is to evaluate the similarities and differences among previously adopted products and unfamiliar products.

P7: The enhanced ability the creative consumer possesses to perceive analogies and differences among new and familiar products, coupled with his/her greater ability to mentally manipulate a consumption problem environment, increases the competence with which alternative products are evaluated and the probability of the superior product being selected.

These propositions suggest that the highly creative consumer is better able to decide whether to adopt a novel product to solve an existing consumption problem. If s/he compares the novel product to the product now used and perceives that the innovation is superior, the new product will be adopted. Thus, high levels of consumer creativity do not necessarily lead to increased new product adoption, but rather to more competent new product evaluation. If the new product is judged potentially superior to the presently used product, it is adopted (adoptive innovativeness). If it is not judged potentially superior, it is not adopted, *ceteris paribus*.

Following this same line of reasoning, it is also probable that high levels of consumer creativity will lead to increased incidence of use innovativeness. Let us assume that the consumer is faced with a novel consumption problem, rather than a novel product. To solve this new problem the consumer can undertake one of two courses of action. First, s/he can adopt a new product that is perceived to be better for solving the new problem. This, of course, is adoptive innovativeness. A second viable course of action is to use a presently adopted product to solve the new consumption problem. This is use innovativeness.

The highly creative consumer will be more adept at both types of actualized innovativeness. S/he should be better able to construct an appropriate mental representation of the problem situation, and, by sorting through his/her extensive set of familiar product concepts (adopted either actually or vicariously), choose the one that will "best" solve the problem. If the product concept decided on is one which has been previously adopted, then it will be utilized, i.e., use innovativeness. If the chosen product concept has been adopted only in a vicarious sense, then actual adoption will ensue, i.e., adoptive innovativeness.

ROLE ACCUMULATION

Role accumulation refers to the number of nonoverlapping roles the individual is performing. It would appear logical to assume that when the individual adopts a new role whose responsibilities are not redundant with roles currently played, a new set of consumption problems will often be encountered. This will be especially true if the role is highly specialized, requiring perhaps special training or instruments for proper performance.

---

[7]Exceptions include receipt of the product as a gift, emergency purchases, externally required adoption (e.g., "to enter this contest, you must purchase this product"), and the like.

For example, a woman who is a wife and mother obtains a job as a management trainee. To perform her new role, she will likely undertake a variety of innovative actions. Some products presently owned can be successfully reapplied to new uses required by the new role. For instance, the dress suit that was used only for special occasions may now be worn to work. Other products, for example, a briefcase, may be adopted for the first time, although the woman is likely to already have vicarious knowledge of them. Once on the job, she may face a fresh set of completely unfamiliar product concepts or consumption situations that can be adopted vicariously or in actuality. Thus, acquiring a new role may generate all three types of innovativeness—vicarious, adoptive, and use.

Causes of Role Accumulation

At least two types of agents may initiate role accumulation. First, there are a variety of life-cycle-related factors that may provide external impetus for the accumulation of new roles. For example, as the individual matures, certain roles are acquired due to socialization or social expectations. The individual is required to attend primary and secondary schools for a certain number of years; after graduation s/he often is expected to attend college and/or to acquire a job for self-sufficiency. S/he also may experience social pressure to marry and produce children. With each of these additional, socially-induced roles, s/he confronts novel consumption situations and must adopt new products or use present ones in novel ways. Thus, one likely source of role accumulation, and hence actualized

innovativeness, is external pressure through the process of socialization.

A second probable source of role accumulation is internal inducement. Many roles acquired by an individual may be due to one's desire for novel experiences, to seek self-fulfillment, or to express his/her talents. Regardless of the source, however, role accumulation precipitates actualized innovativeness, as outlined in Figure 2.

CONSTRUCT OPERATIONALIZATION

To implement the theoretical framework suggested here, a set of operational measures is necessary. To this end, some suggestions for possible empirical measures are advanced for consumer creativity, role accumulation, inherent novelty seeking, actualized novelty seeking, vicarious innovativeness, adoptive innovativeness, and use innovativeness.

Consumer Creativity

Because consumer creativity is posited to consist of two components—interconcept network density and repertoire of consumption situations—it is essential to measure each component as a separate entity, and then to combine them into an overall measure of creativity.

Interconcept network density.   Interconcept network density refers to the number of linkages existing among concepts based on the perceived intercorrelations of their respective attribute sets.

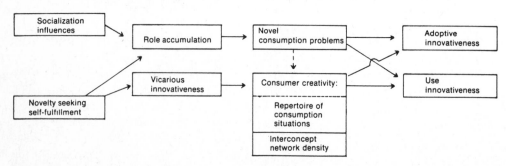

Figure 2   Model of role accumulation and innovativeness.

The more concepts the individual has acquired and the more attributes s/he has associated with each concept, the more dense the interconcept network is likely to become. To obtain an empirical measure of interconcept network density, the following operational procedure is suggested.

First, provide the subject with a diversified list of products representative of various domains of consumption, e.g., apparel, transportation, food, entertainment. Products within each domain will be arranged in a paired comparison format. Second, the individual will be asked to list as many similar and dissimilar attributes as s/he can for each pair. The rationale for measuring both similarity and dissimilarity dimensions across product pairs is that these represent the consumer's ability to generalize across and discriminate among product concepts. Third, compute the average number of similar and dissimilar product-pair linkages named by the respondent within each domain, and sum across all domains. If one desires to tap interconcept network density for only one domain of consumption, e.g., food products, the same method may be employed, but the product list would include only food items.

Situational repertoire. Measuring situational repertoire is more problematic, as less empirical research and theoretical effort have been expended in this area. Until firmer foundation has been laid, a more narrowly focused strategy seems desirable. One approach would consist of using focus groups of consumers with varied levels of experience in a given consumption domain to generate typologies of problem situations. It is anticipated that one of two general forms of typology will emerge from this process, which will dictate the operationalization of situational repertoire.

One form that the typology may take is that of a simple additive structure. This form implies that as the consumer gains incremental experiences in a given domain of consumption, s/he simply adds additional scripts to situational repertoire. No reorganization of existing scripts occurs as a result of learning about new situations. Thus, if a consumer had experienced situations A, B, and C, and then learned about situations D and E, his/her situa-

tional repertoire would simply be incremented by these latter two scripts. Hence,

$$A, B, C + D, E = A, B, C, D, E.$$

If this form of typology for situational repertoire emerges from the focus groups,[8] then the construct may be defined straightforwardly as the sum of all situations identified by a subject in a given domain of consumption, summed across all consumption domains. Similarly, a measure of situational repertoire within a given domain is the number of different situations identified by the consumer within that domain.

A second form of situational repertoire typology that may emerge from the focus groups is one which is integrative. This form of typology would result from the cognitive reorganization of situational scripts as increased experience was obtained. That is, experiencing a novel consumption situation might result not only in its being added to situational repertoire, but also to the reformation of scripts already existing in repertoire. Under this set of conditions, if situations A, B, and C were already in repertoire and novel situations D and E were encountered, their addition to the repertoire may result in a typology consisting of W, X, Y, and Z. That is, the absolute number of scripts may be reduced (or enlarged) and their identifying characteristics altered. Hence,

$$A, B, C + D, E = W, X, Y, Z.$$

A useful approach to measurement under this set of conditions would be to first construct profiles of the situational repertoire used by consumers having low, moderate, and high levels of experience in various domains of consumption. A given consumer could then be classified by the proximity of his/her repertoire to a "high", "moderate", or "low" level profile for each domain. Although some cognitive reorganization is known to occur in cognitive structure as a result of increased experience, it is not yet documented that similar reorga-

---

[8]Indication that this is the appropriate form would be the focus group finding that highly experienced consumers named all situations given by less experienced consumers plus several additional ones.

nization effects occur for scripts. Thus, the simpler additive model may prove valid.

The concept of role accumulation has been recently introduced to consumer behavior theory largely through the efforts of Wallendorf (Hirschman and Wallendorf, 1979; Wallendorf, 1979; Zaltman and Wallendorf, 1979). The concept refers to the number of nonoverlapping roles being performed by an individual that require substantively different activities to properly perform them.

To operationalize the concept, two measures are required—the number of different roles performed by the individual and the relative degree of overlap among these roles. The first aspect may be operationalized by asking the individual to what formal and informal groups s/he belongs and in what social activities s/he participates. These can be compared for duplicate reporting, and adjusted accordingly. The degree of overlap among the various roles the individual performs can be measured by asking him/her to report the requirements for each role, and then comparing these across the role set. The underlying assumption is that the more similar or homogeneous the role set as measured by overlap of role requirements, the less incremental consumption knowledge the individual will need to perform each one. Conversely, the more heterogeneous the role set, the more consumption knowledge will be required.

Inherent Novelty Seeking

Inherent novelty seeking may be measured by scales constructed of items asking the individuals how willing s/he is to seek information that is new and different. A combination of generalized/abstract questions and specific/concrete questions pertinent to several consumption domains may be most appropriate for adequately assessing inherent novelty seeking. For example, generalized items may include such questions as, "How willing are you to seek out novel information?" or "Do you search for the new and different?" More specific items could include such questions as, "How willing are you to try new fashions" or "Do you look for new foods to eat?", which cover a broad spectrum of consumption domains.

This approach to measuring inherent novelty seeking would generate both a composite set of domain-specific scores, which should correlate highly with the individual's score on general items. Further, the use of a battery of domain-specific questions could help in locating consumption areas in which the consumer is especially high/low in novelty seeking. Consumers could be compared not only as to their overall novelty-seeking scores, but also as to the similarity between their domain-specific profiles for novelty seeking.

Actualized Novelty Seeking

Actualized novelty seeking may be measured by asking the individual what sources s/he consults to obtain novel information. Thus, measures such as newspaper and magazine subscriptions, book purchases, movie attendance, and inquiries to other individuals may be used to form indices that would tap actualized novelty seeking. Note that it is the acquisition or purchase of the medium (or questioning another person) that is viewed as constituting actualized novelty seeking, not the actual consumption of novel information.

An approach somewhat analogous to that described for inherent novelty seeking may be used to develop an operational taxonomy for actualized novelty seeking. This would require the *a priori* classification of various information media into general and consumption domain-specific groups. The individual consumer could then be assigned a set of scores for actualized novelty seeking based on how many media vehicles s/he used, and into which categories they fell. Some information sources, e.g., *Time* magazine, would fall into the general information category, whereas others, e.g., *Tennis* magazine, would be classified in a specific consumption domain. Composite scores could be developed by summing across specific domains and combining with the general category. Further, individual profiles of domain-specific information exposure could also be calculated.

Vicarious Innovativeness

This concept may be measured by asking the individual what new products and consumption situations s/he has learned about within a given time frame, but not actually adopted or experienced. An important aspect of investigating vicarious innovativeness in this way is that the individual may also be asked to report the source(s) from which s/he learned of the novel product or consumption situation. This will aid in tracing the diffusion of novel information.

Second, the individual may be questioned concerning the level and accuracy of knowledge s/he has acquired about the novel stimulus. This may have implications for marketers and other social change agents who are concerned with developing accurate perceptions of the innovation prior to adoption.

The operational measure of vicarious innovativeness, thus, should have at least three components: (1) the absolute number of innovations (i.e., new products and novel consumption situations) learned about within a given time frame, (2) the level of knowledge about each innovation, and (3) the relative accuracy of the knowledge about each innovation. As a key linkage between vicarious innovativeness and actualized innovativeness is the cognitive ability of the consumer to compare novel with presently possessed alternatives, it is clear that evaluative competence will depend not only on the volume of information possessed, but also upon its quality, i.e., accuracy.

A consumer who has vicariously acquired a good deal of inaccurate information on an innovation may be less able to properly evaluate its utility than a consumer who has acquired less, but more accurate, information regarding its attributes. Hence, if research conducted using the vicarious innovativeness construct is to have value for studies of consumer satisfaction/dissatisfaction, for example, not only the volume but quality of vicariously acquired information concerning innovations must be measured.

Adoptive Innovativeness

This concept may be perhaps most appropriately measured by asking the individual what products s/he has purchased (or otherwise adopted) within a certain time frame, and to report the degree of novelty s/he perceives the product to have compared with other products presently adopted. All products acquired by an individual within the time frame are to be included and arrayed along a continuum of novelty, as perceived by the individual. This method of operationalizing adoptive innovativeness appropriately refocuses the attention of consumer researchers away from their perceptions and definitions of what constitutes a product innovation and toward what the consumer perceives and defines as a product innovation. A further useful extension of this measurement approach is to ask the individual how much product knowledge s/he possessed (through vicarious innovativeness) prior to adopting the new product, and how accurate that knowledge proved to be subsequent to adoption.

Use Innovativeness

To measure use innovativeness, the individual can be asked a set of questions such as, "Have you encountered any new consumption problems lately that you solved by using a product you already had?" and then asking the consumer to describe the new use to which the product was put. A complementary approach to operationalizing this construct would be to ask, "Have you used any product(s) you own in a new or unusual way?" and following up by asking him/her to describe the conditions that prompted this instance of use innovativeness. Both these question types could be accompanied by complementary inquiries concerning the degree of novelty perceived by the consumer to characterize the new use.

Thus, use innovativeness also has two components: (1) the number of instances in which new uses occurred, and (2) the degree of novelty characterizing each new use.

CONCLUSIONS, IMPLICATIONS, AND APPLICATIONS

The implications of this conceptual framework for consumer research can perhaps best be illustrated through an example. Let us consider how the framework might be applied to studying the adoption process for a "home" computer. Several companies, notably Apple, have been marketing small computers that, in pricing and programming structure, are amendable to adoption by individual consumers. From both a behavioral theory and marketing strategy perspective, it may be useful to study the factors influencing adoption of such a complex and versatile innovation.

First, it would be anticipated that individuals having high levels of inherent novelty seeking would be influenced by this characteristic to monitor a wide range of media (e.g., magazines, television programming, newspapers) through which they may be exposed to information regarding home computers. That is, strong tendencies toward inherent novelty seeking should lead to high levels of actualized novelty seeking and, hence, to the potential for exposure to information regarding the home computer innovation. Further, if actualized novelty seeking were especially high in a consumption domain such as computer technology, then the probability for exposure is even greater.

The level and domain-specific pattern of actualized novelty seeking will determine the likelihood of vicarious adoption of the home-computer innovation concept. However, to adopt the innovation in a vicarious sense, the consumer must not only be exposed to information, but must cognitively acquire knowledge of the computer and its attributes. It is at the vicarious adoption stage that research can first be applied in a meaningful fashion to innovation adopters and nonadopters. Although they have not yet "acted," consumers who have gained knowledge of the home computer innovation do differ in an important way from those who do not have this knowledge, for it is from the "pool" of vicarious adopters that actual adopters will later be drawn. Hence, research on the characteristics of vicarious adopters could be useful for the formulation of strategies designed to transform vicarious knowledge into product purchase.

Those persons who, after learning about the home-computer innovation (i.e., vicarious adopters), purchase it are exhibiting actualized innovativeness. Actual adopters will likely constitute only a subset of vicarious adopters. Therefore, in conducting research on innovation adoption, it may be useful to incorporate at least three "nested" populations into the design: (1) persons who never gain awareness, (2) persons who gain awareness (i.e., adopt vicariously), but who do not adopt, and (3) persons who adopt both vicariously and actually. The absolute and relative size of all three groups will have a great deal of impact on the diffusion of the innovation.

One issue that this example raises is that of the factors that may influence the translation of vicarious into actualized innovativeness. One useful variable to consider here is role accumulation. Persons who have accumulated roles that necessitate or would benefit from the acquisition of a home computer can be expected to have a higher than average likelihood of purchasing one. It is interesting to note that in many consumer research studies of innovativeness, the need of the individual for a product to perform his/her role(s) has rarely been taken into account. Thus, although a potent reason an individual may choose to adopt a home computer is because s/he needs it for role performance, rarely has this factor ever been explicitly included in the research. The notion of role accumulation would seem to be one effective way of accomplishing this.

A second factor that may influence the translation of vicarious innovativeness into actualized innovativeness is consumer creativity. This construct can affect the decision to adopt in two ways. First, the denser the interconcept network possessed by the consumer, the better able s/he should be to comprehend the functioning of the innovation. This will, of course, be moderated by the domain-specific networks characterizing the individual. In the case of the home-computer innovation, an individual with a dense network, especially in technology-related domains, may be able to generate several realistic comparisons between the home computer and several alternative products. S/he may reason, for example, that the home computer could be used to replace a calculator, a series of filing cabinets, and a checkbook.

Also, the highly creative consumer may have a well-developed repertoire of consumption problems the home computer could be used to solve. S/he could mentally construct alternative performance environments for the computer innovation and, based on its utility in "solving" these cognitively generated problems, decide whether actual purchase was desirable. Thus, high levels of consumer creativity do not necessarily increase the probability that a home computer will be adopted, but do ensure that the innovation will be given appropriate consideration.

To complete our example, let us assume that due to role requirements and creative perceptions of product performance, the consumer purchases the home computer. One useful avenue of research may be to test the congruence between anticipated and actual performance of the innovation. That is, how accurate was the consumer's mental construction of the home computer's functioning? The answer could contribute a great deal to our understanding of consumer satisfaction and dissatisfaction.

A second potentially valuable area of investigation would be instances of use innovativeness regarding the home computer. A versatile and complex innovation such as this readily lends itself to use innovativeness. Without experience, it is unlikely that the adopter could a priori envision the variety of uses to which the home computer could be put. Once it is adopted and its capabilities have become more familiar to the consumer, it probably will be applied to several problem situations not viewed as relevant at the outset. One may hypothesize that the more inherent flexibility possessed by a product, the greater the incidence of use innovativeness.

Although this example is hypothetical, it illustrates the variety of research applications suggested by this framework. It is a structure that, in its present form, can unite constructs such as novelty seeking, new product adoption, and the acquisition of additional roles that previously were often examined in isolation. Extended beyond the linkages developed here, additional aspects of consumer behavior, such as reactions of satisfaction and dissatisfaction, may also be incorporated.

REFERENCES

Flavell, John H. (1977), *Cognitive Development*, Englewood Cliffs, NJ: Prentice-Hall, Inc.

Guilford, James P. (1965), "Intellectual Factors in Productive Thinking," in *Productive Thinking in Education*, Washington, DC: National Education Association, pp. 5–20.

Hirschman, Elizabeth C. (1980), "Consumer Creativity: Nature, Measurement and Application," *Proceedings, Second Annual National Conference on Marketing Theory*, Chicago, IL: American Marketing Association, forthcoming.

———— (1979), "Some Cognitive Notions Concerning Perception and Preference," working paper, Graduate School of Business, New York University.

————, and Wallendorf, Melanie (1979), "Correlations Among Three Indicators of Stimulus Variation," in *Advances in Consumer Research*, (Vol. 6), ed. William I. Wilkie, Ann Arbor, MI: Association for Consumer Research.

Midgley, David F., and Dowling, Grahame R. (1978), "Innovativeness: The Concept and Its Measurement," *Journal of Consumer Research*, 4, 229–42.

Ostlund, Lyman E. (1974), "Perceived Innovation Attributes as Predictors of Innovativeness," *Journal of Consumer Research*, 1, 23–9.

Rogers, Everett M., and Shoemaker, Floyd F. (1971), *Communication of Innovations*, New York: The Free Press.

Schiffman, Leon G., and Kanuk, Leslie L. (1978), *Consumer Behavior*, Englewood Cliffs, NJ: Prentice-Hall, Inc.

Simon, Herbert A. (1979), "Information Processing Models of Cognition," in *Annual Review of Psychology*, eds. Mark R. Rosenzweig and Lyman W. Porter, Palo Alto, CA: Annual Reviews, Inc. pp. 363–96.

Taylor, John W. (1977), "A Striking Characteristic of Innovators," *Journal of Marketing Research*, 14, 104–7.

Wallendorf, Melanie (1979), *Role Accumulation and the Diffusion of Innovations*, unpublished doctoral dissertation, Graduate School of Business, University of Pittsburgh.

Zaltman, Gerald, and Wallendorf, Melanie (1979), *Consumer Behavior*, New York: John Wiley & Sons, Inc.

ORGANIZATIONAL PSYCHOGRAPHICS AND INNOVATIVENESS

**THOMAS S. ROBERTSON
AND
YORAM WIND**

Source: Thomas S. Robertson and Yoram Wind, "Organizational Psychographics and Innovativeness," *Journal of Consumer Research,* Vol. 7, June, 1980, pp. 24–31. Reprinted with permission.

Most commonly, organizational buying behavior has been explained using organizational "demographic" characteristics. Variables such as Standard Industrial Classification (SIC) codes, size, geographic location, and other demographic characteristics have been found, not unlike their consumer counterparts, to be relatively poor predictors of organizational buying behavior (Webster and Wind 1972).

In household consumer behavior, the low predictive ability of demographic characteristics has led to the development of psychographics (Wells 1974) as an alternative set of explanatory factors. A similar development for organizational buying behavior has been missing.

The objectives of this paper are to offer some initial conceptual guidance and empirical results toward the development of organizational psychographic models. The paper starts with a brief discussion of the concept of organizational psychographics, proposes a model of organizational psychographics as it relates to innovativeness, and discusses the results of an empirical test of the model, which seeks to explain hospital adoption of medical innovations. The paper concludes with a brief discussion of the interrelationship between consumer and organizational psychographics.

THE CONCEPT OF ORGANIZATIONAL PSYCHOGRAPHICS

In its broadest context, the concept of consumer psychographics has been defined by Wells (1975) as a quantitative research tool intended to place consumers on psychological—as distinguished from demographic—dimensions (p. 197). This all-encompassing definition accurately reflects the current practice of psychographic research, which has included diverse categories of variables, such as Activities, Interests, and Opinions (often denoted as an AIO battery), personality traits, lifestyle measures, and attitude measures.

A similarly broad definition might be appropriate for organizational psychographics. Yet, given that organizational psychographics is just emerging, it might be possible to avoid three major problems associated with research on consumer psychographics:

- The use of the psychographics construct as a catchall for psychological explanations of behavior.
- The fairly arbitrary, or, at least, nonconceptual, selection of psychographic variables.
- The diversity of operational definitions, which are often of questionable reliability.

The goal of this paper is to develop a conceptual model of organizational psychographics appropriate to classes of organizational buying behavior. Logically, the conceptual model should guide the selection of dimensions and their operational definitions. Particular attention is given to the question of reliability.

In developing an organizational psychographic model, four major guidelines should be considered:

1. Different models might be required for the explanation of different behaviors. In general, it is necessary to consider at least three psychographic models, appropriate to each of the three major types of buying situations—*new task,* defined in terms of high information requirements; *modified rebuy,* defined as moderate information requirements; and *straight rebuy,* defined as minimal information requirements.

2. The psychographic model should be based on current relevant theories and findings of organizational behavior.

3. Regardless of the breadth of the psychographic definition, comprehensive explanation of organizational buying behavior requires the examination of the relationship between psychographics and other possible determinants of behavior, such as demographic characteristics. Operationally, one should, therefore, examine the incremental explanatory power of psychographics rather than viewing psychographics as a sufficient determinant of behavior.

4. Given that most organizational buying decisions involve more than a single individual [note the buying center concept (Wind 1977)], data on organizational psycho-

graphics should be collected from a number of members of the buying center, and the congruency among them incorporated as an explicit dimension of organizational psychographics.

A MODEL OF PSYCHOGRAPHICS TO EXPLAIN INNOVATIVENESS

The proposed model of organizational psychographics is designed to help explain the degree of organizational innovativeness—the "new task" case of buying decisions. It relies heavily on the constructs of organizational climate (Joyce 1979; Lyon and Ivancevich 1974; Tagiuri 1967) and the presence of specific hypotheses (based on extensions of previous findings and theories) on the possible relationship between organizational climate variables and organizational innovativeness.

The model is not intended as a comprehensive description of organizational climate (psychographics), but rather as a parsimonious description of the key organizational psychographic variables that conceptually can be linked to organizational innovativeness, and that have been found highly reliable in previous organizational behavior studies.

Given these criteria, the proposed organizational psychographic model is based on six dimensions:

- *Direction*—the clarity of an organization's objectives and priorities. It is hypothesized that the higher the perceived clarity of direction, the greater the organizational innovativeness.
- *Decision centrality*—the level of centralization in organizational decision making. It is hypothesized that the higher the perceived decision centrality, the greater the innovativeness.
- *Openness of communication*—openness to communicate is a surrogate for the affective orientation of the organization's participants. It is hypothesized that the higher the perceived openness of communication, the greater the organizational innovativeness.
- *Achievement motivation*—the degree to which the organization attempts to excel. It is hypothesized that the higher the perceived

achievement motivation, the greater the innovativeness.

- *Resistance to change*—the extent to which the organization is perceived to resist change. It is hypothesized that the higher the resistance to change, the lower the organizational innovativeness.
- *Conflict*—the pattern of agreement or disagreement in decision making about new technology among members of the buying center. It is hypothesized that the higher the conflict, the lower the organizational innovativeness.

Four sets of factor analyses were conducted on a split-run basis for the 28 specified attitude items.

These included separate runs for the administrators, chief radiologists, staff radiologists, and all respondents. Results indicated that there were no significant differences among the three designated groups, nor between the split runs of each group. Therefore, Exhibit 1 reports the resulting factors (dimensions of organizational psychographics) for the total sample only.

These variables and resulting factors meet the first two requirements for the organizational psychographic model specified previously, that is, selection of variables appropriate to the category of behavior investigated and based on organizational behavior theory. The third requirement (examination of psychographics as only one determinant of

Exhibit 1   Factor loadings and questionnaire items*

Variable	Factor loadings	Variable	Factor loadings
Achievement motivation		The hospital administration has created too much administrative bureaucracy that interferes with acquiring needed new medical technology	.77
This hospital is among the most innovative in this section of the country	.80		
This hospital has a real drive to be number one in this section of the country	.72	The hospital administration and the radiology staff are frequently at odds about what new equipment is needed	.66
This hospital's *radiology department* is among the most innovative in this section of the country	.71	Eigenvalue 3.09	
This hospital likes to tackle challenging cases and new medical problems	.58	Decision centrality	
This hospital is constantly concerned with improvement and new achievement	.57	All important decisions here are made jointly by senior and junior physicians	−.75
This is a status quo hospital	−.52	Even a young physician here has a voice in deciding what new equipment to acquire	−.74
Eigenvalue 3.50			
Conflict		A physician has to be very senior here before he has the opportunity to make any important decisions about new equipment and technology	.67
The hospital administration here has too much control over decisions as to what new radiology equipment is needed	.80	Decision making about new equipment and technology is highly centralized here	.49
The hospital administration here is too involved with decisions about new technology without having the necessary medical expertise	.80	Eigenvalue 2.15	

(continued)

Exhibit 1 *(Continued)*

Variable	Factor loadings	Variable	Factor loadings
Direction		Resistance to change	
The priorities of this hospital are not well defined	−.82	This hospital's *radiology department* would be among the *last* to try a novel procedure, *even if it appeared promising*	.71
This hospital has well defined objectives	.80		
The direction and mission of this hospital are vague and poorly specified	−.79	Meaningful change and innovation in the *radiology department* are stifled because of too many vested interests	.65
There is considerable disagreement as to the future directions that this hospital should take	−.66	This hospital would be among the *last* to try a novel procedure even if it appeared promising	.50
Eigenvalue 3.45		Meaningful change and innovation in this hospital are stifled because of too many vested interests	.50
Communication openness		Eigenvalue 1.87	
Physicians here know each other very well	.82		
There are many close relationships among physicians at this hospital	.80		
An extremely open and friendly atmosphere exists among the physicians at this hospital	.73		
Physicians here tend to be cool and aloof towards each other	−.57		
Eigenvalue 2.66			

[a]The administrator and radiologist item wordings were identical for all factors except the conflict factor. The four conflict items were from reverse perspectives. The items in this exhibit are for the radiologist.

behavior) was satisfied by adding six organizational "demographic" characteristics to our model. Multiple participants in the adoption decision were also included to satisfy the fourth requirement, that the model focus on the buying center and not on individual respondents.

The analysis, therefore, is based on three sets of independent variables—organizational psychographics, organizational demographics, and a set of consensus measures between the radiologist and administrator. The consensus measures were operationally defined as the set of correlations between the two respondents on the items comprising each psychographic factor. The broadly defined demographic variables were selected based on previous work by Mahajan and Schoeman

(1977) and Rapoport (1976) involving hospital adoption of technology; namely:

• *Size of hospital*—defined in terms of number of beds. It is hypothesized, in line with the results of the Mahajan/Schoeman and Rapoport studies, that size will not be related to innovativeness. Number of beds may, in fact, be a surrogate variable for patient (many beds) versus professional (few beds) orientation. Also, the sample selection process, which matched the CT-scanner adopter and nonadopter groups by size, severely limits our ability to test this hypothesis.

• *Budget.* Unlike bed count we expect a positive relationship between budget and innovativeness. Budget more fully encompasses the broader mission of the hospital and, based on our data, is only somewhat correlated with number of beds ($r = 0.21$).

- *Percent occupancy.* This variable should relate positively to innovativeness given the generation of internal funds to finance new equipment. However, it has also been argued that hospitals with high occupancy rates tend to invest in beds rather than sophisticated facilities (Ginsburg 1972). Indeed, our data show a significant positive relationship between number of beds and occupancy rate ($r = 0.36$).
- *Teaching versus nonteaching.* Because of their educational and research responsibilities, we expect teaching hospitals to be more innovative.
- *Prestige*—defined in terms of number of special accreditations (e.g., cancer unit, cardiac unit). We hypothesize that prestige is positively related to innovativeness (Coleman, Katz, and Menzel 1966).
- *Size of community.* Major metropolitan versus secondary metropolitan or tertiary communities. It is expected that the larger the community, the more likely a hospital is to innovate.

The analysis of the adoption of medical innovations (new task) takes into account, therefore, three sets of variable types and consists of 18 specific variables: (1) six organizational demographic variables, (2) six psychographic variables, and (3) six consensus measures between the radiologist and administrator members of the buying center.

TESTING THE MODEL

The organizational psychographic model was tested in a national study of hospital adoption of new medical instruments for the radiology department. The research design was based on a mail survey with multiple respondents in each of 209 hospitals. For each hospital we sought responses from the administrator, the chief radiologist, and at least one staff radiologist.

The sample encompassed two sets of hospitals: (1) all hospitals (excluding specialty care hospitals, such as psychiatric) that had adopted a CT-scanner[1] as of the date of the study and (2) a sample of nonadopter hospitals, matched on number of beds and region of the country. In total, questionnaires were mailed to 610 hospitals. This resulted in 209 complete data sets that encompassed both the administrative and radiology viewpoints at a particular hospital, allowing analysis of organizational psychographics from both perspectives within the buying center.

Comparison of our sample with the universe of hospitals indicates a close approximation to the population distribution, as follows:

- Number of beds—sample mean = 528, σ = 246 versus population mean = 491, σ = 391.
- Budget level—sample mean = \$30.8 million, σ = \$18.6 million versus population mean = \$28.8 million, σ = \$24.4 million.
- Occupancy rate—sample mean = 78.7 percent, σ = 80.1 percent versus population mean = 81.6 percent, σ = 50.1 percent.

The analysis is designed to assess the incremental contribution of organizational psychographics to the explanation of organizational innovativeness—the number of medical innovations adopted by the hospital. A series of multiple regression analyses served as the primary analytic tool. The dependent variable was the number of innovations adopted. This was based on a reported list of seven radiology innovations—ultrasound, head CT-scanners, body CT-scanners, nuclear imaging, thermography, mammography, and arteriography. These seven items were identified in the pilot study by radiology expert judges as the most recent radiology innovations.

RESULTS

Multiple regression analyses were conducted to assess the relationship of the three sets of explanatory variables to hospital innovativeness, and were cross-validated using a holdout sample. The cross-validated results suggested highly stable regression

---

[1]A CT-scanner is a three-dimensional computerized X-ray machine costing approximately \$500,000.

equations, and, therefore, for presentation purposes, the results are for the total sample. Only minimal collinearity existed; inspection of the correlation matrix indicated that the predictor variables were not highly correlated.[2]

Three sets of regression analyses were run:

1. Demographic characteristics alone.
2. Demographic plus psychographic characteristics. This stage of the analysis involved two sets of runs, both including the demographic characteristics of the hospitals, plus (a) the factor scores of the organizational psychographics as rated by the administrator and (b) the factor scores as rated by the chief radiologist.
3. The same two runs as in the second set but, in addition, each run also included a measure of the degree of consensus between the administrator and radiologist in evaluation of the organizational psychographic characteristics.

The results of these multiple regression analyses (Table 1) suggest that the inclusion of organizational psychographic characteristics improves the predictive efficacy of organizational innovativeness. The R^2 increases from 0.19 for demographic characteristics alone to 0.27 for demographic characteristics plus the organizational psychographic data as obtained from the administrator, or to 0.24 when the data are obtained from the chief radiologist.

This increase in explained variance by adding psychographics is fairly moderate and not dissimilar to the results obtained in the household consumer literature. Nevertheless, it is the incremental gain in explanatory power that is of interest. Further improvement in predictive ability is achieved when the degree of consensus (as measured by the correlation between administrators and chief radiologists on the items comprising the psychographic factors) is added explicitly to the model. The consensus variables improve the R^2 to 0.37 for the administrator equation and 0.33 for the radiologist equation.

[2]Average $r = 0.12$ with a standard deviation of 0.11; only 11 of 153 correlations (7 percent) were above $r = 0.30$.

The value of explicitly adding consensus measures has not previously received much attention in the literature. The general procedure has been to use only one participant's responses or an average of several participant responses rather than the degree of consensus represented. In the present case, a regression equation using the average of administrator and radiologist scores on the psychographic variables indicated minimal improvement in R^2 over either the individual administrator or individual radiologist equations. Hence, this average measure does not improve R^2, whereas the consensus measure does improve it significantly. This would seem to be because averaging conceals the true difference between responses, whereas the consensus measure (the correlation coefficient between the two respondents) takes the difference explicitly into account.

Examination of the Specific Variables and Hypotheses

Demographic variables. The strongest variable to enter the demographic-only equation, as indicated by the standardized regression coefficients, is budget (positively related to innovativeness), followed by size of community (negative), prestige rating (positive), occupancy rate (negative), teaching hospital (positive), and size of hospital (essentially no relationship). The negative relationship between size of community and innovativeness is counter to our hypothesis, which may suggest the effects of government Health System Agency planning boards in limiting duplicate medical technology within major cities. The negative relationship between percent occupancy and innovativeness is also counter to our hypothesis, and favors the argument of Ginsburg (1972) that high occupancy hospitals invest in beds rather than new technology.

Psychographic variables. Adding the psychographic variables to the demographics improves the explained variance by more than 25 percent. With respect to the specific relationships between

Table 1 The contribution of demographic, psychographic, and consensus variables in explaining organizational innovativeness

Explanatory variables	Demographics only	Demographics and psychographics		Demographics, psychographics, and consensus	
		Administrator	Radiologist	Administrator	Radiologist
Demographics					
Size (number of beds)	.03	−.01	.06	.00	.05
Budget	.29[a]	.16	.22[a]	.09	.12
Occupancy rate	−.10	−.09	−.11	−.11	−.09
Teaching/nonteaching	.08	.06	.12	.08	.05
Prestige rating	.13	.17[a]	.10	.19[a]	.18[a]
Size of community	−.20[a]	−.20[a]	−.18[a]	−.14	−.16
Psychographics					
Achievement motivation		.07	.12	.02	.02
Clarity of direction		.17[a]	.03	.21[a]	.04
Level of conflict		−.12	.08	−.15	.08
Communication openness		−.13	−.12	−.14	−.16
Decision centrality		.09	−.06	.09	−.13
Change resistance		−.17[a]	−.12	−.15	−.18
Consensus					
Achievement consensus				.07	−.06
Direction consensus				−.21[a]	−.21[a]
Conflict consensus				.17[a]	.17
Communication consensus					
Centrality consensus				−.04	−.17
Change resistance consensus				.14	.20[a]
R^2	.19	.27	.24	.37	.33
Improvement in R^2		+.08[b]	+.05[b]	+.10[c]	+.09[c]

[a]Significant variables at the 0.05 level.
[b]Due to adding psychographic variables.
[c]Due to adding consensus measures.

the psychographic variables and innovativeness, some support is shown for the hypothesized relationships, but this depends on whether the administrator or radiologist equation is examined. In brief (based on the demographics plus psychographics equations):

1. Minor support is provided for the expected positive relationships between achievement motivation and clarity of direction with innovativeness.

2. Conflict is negatively related to innovativeness for administrators, but positively related for radiologists.

3. In contrast, decision centrality is positively related to innovativeness for administrators, but negatively related for radiologists.

4. Change resistance is negatively related to innovativeness, as expected.
5. Communication openness is surprisingly negatively related to innovativeness, suggesting perhaps that "friendly" environments do not foster innovative behavior.

Consensus variables. These variables assess level of agreement by means of the correlation between radiologists' and administrators' responses to the various items comprising each factor. The relationships between consensus and innovativeness are as follows:

1. Innovativeness is related positively (for both the administrator and radiologist equations) with the following variables: consensus on the level of conflict between the administrative and radiology departments of the hospital; consensus on the level of communication openness in the hospital; and consensus on the level of resistance to change in the hospital.
2. Innovativeness is related negatively (for both the administrator and radiologist) with the following variables: consensus on the clarity of the hospital's direction; consensus on the decision centrality within the hospital.
3. A mixed pattern is shown between consensus and innovativeness between the administrator and the radiologist on the achievement motivation factor.

These findings indicate a tenuous pattern of relationships, reflecting the lack of theoretical development of the effects of interpersonal relations on organizational behavior. The consensus measures do add appreciably to our ability to explain the variance in innovativeness among hospitals, suggesting the value of further research in this area.

Discussion

Psychographics can improve our ability to predict organizational innovativeness. For the most part, organizational innovativeness is a relatively untapped field of research. Most diffusion research has focused on individuals—whether consumers, farmers, or physicians. Organizational innovativeness, with a few exceptions, such as Zaltman, Duncan, and Holbek (1973), has followed in the industrial diffusion tradition of Mansfield (1968) and has focused almost exclusively on organizational demographic variables. In general, however, psychographics should be viewed as complementary to demographics in predicting behavior. The R^2 increases when psychographic variables are added, but as in household consumer research, the improvement in explained variance is moderate.

The value of a buying center model is also demonstrated based on the higher explained variance for models explicitly including measures of consensus among members of the buying center. Given that most organizational buying is multiperson in nature, it is incumbent on researchers to design studies that incorporate a number of members of the buying team. As indicated, the best model for predicting innovativeness in this research is one that includes organizational demographic variables, organizational psychographic variables as perceived by the administrators, and a consensus measure for the organizational psychographic variables between the administrator and the radiologist, It would seem to follow that, given the frequent multiperson buying unit in households, consumer research on psychographics might also encompass a buying center model.

Predictive ability could be improved using multiple responses within the household unit together with consensus measures. In fact, the organizational psychographics approach utilized here can be applied with minor modifications to the household unit, as in previous research (Ferber and Lee 1974), and consensus measures can be similarly developed. The generalizability of the present concept in terms of the variables used will have to be further tested. As indicated, these variables were selected to explain decisons on innovative technology. Other variables may be more appropriate to different types of behavior, such as the straight rebuy or modified rebuy situations. Further research may also improve predictive ability by developing a model that incorporates the *degree* of influence of various participants in tbe buying center.

REFERENCES

Coleman, James S., Katz, Elihu, and Menzel, Herbert (1966), *Medical Innovation: A Diffusion Study,* Indianapolis: Bobbs-Merrill Publishing Co.

Ferber, Robert, and Lee, Lucy Chao (1974), "Husband-Wife Influence in Family Purchasing Behavior," *Journal of Consumer Research,* 1, 43–50.

Ginsburg, Paul B. (1972), "Resource Allocation in the Hospital Industry," *Social Security Bulletin,* 35, 20–30.

Joyce, William (1979), "Climates in Organizations," in *Organizational Behavior,* ed. Steven Kerr, Columbus, OH: Grid, Inc.

Lyon, Herbert L., and Ivancevich, John M. (1974), "An Exploratory Investigation of Organizational Climate and Job Satisfaction in a Hospital," *Academy of Management Journal,* 17, 635–47.

Mahajan, Vijay, and Schoeman, Milton E. G. (1977), "The Use of Computers in Hospitals: An Analysis of Adopters and Nonadopters," *Interfaces,* 7, 95–107.

Mansfield, Edwin (1968), *Industrial Research and Technological Innovation,* New York: W. W. Norton & Co., Inc.

Rapoport, John (1976), "Diffusion of Technological Innovation in Hospitals: A Case Study of Nuclear Medicine," working paper, National Technical Information Service, U.S. Department of Commerce, Springfield, VA.

Tagiuri, Renato (1967), "The Concept of Organizational Climate," in *The Human Organization,* ed. Rensis Likert, New York: McGraw-Hill., pp. 9–32.

Webster, Frederick E. Jr., and Wind, Yoram (1972), *Organizational Buying Behavior,* Englewood Cliffs, NJ: Prentice-Hall, Inc.

Wells, William, ed. (1974), *Life Style and Psychographics,* Chicago: American Marketing Association.

_____ (1975), "Psychographics: A Critical Review," *Journal of Marketing Research,* 12, 196–213.

Wind, Yoram (1977), "Organizational Buying Center: A Research Agenda," in *Organizational Buying Behavior,* eds. Thomas V. Bonoma and Gerald Zaltman, Chicago: American Marketing Association.

Zaltman, Gerald, Duncan, Robert, and Holbek, Jonny (1973), *Innovations and Organizations,* New York: Wiley-Interscience.

PROFILES OF SIGNATURE GOODS CONSUMERS AND AVOIDERS

MARVIN A. JOLSON
ROLPH E. ANDERSON
NANCY J. LEBER

Source: Marvin A. Jolson, Rolph E. Anderson, and Nancy J. Leber, "Profiles of Signature Goods Consumers and Avoiders," *Journal of Retailing,* Vol. 57(4), Winter, 1981, pp. 19–38. Reprinted with permission.

Not so long ago, labels were put only on the inside of garments and other products to identify the manufacturer or retail outlet. But times have changed and an epidemic of "signature goods" has broken out. A signature good carries an external brand mark such as a symbol, logo, or name that has the purpose of endowing the product with high perceived quality and affiliation with a famous designer in order to create the basis for status and price differentiation. Many people are willing or even eager to flaunt the Lacoste "alligator," the Ralph Lauren "polo-player," the Calvin Klein name-plate, or the familiar Louis Vuitton or Gucci logo on their sleeves, breast pockets, derrières, luggage, or handbags.

Names such as Yves Saint Laurent, Pierre Cardin, Emilio Pucci, Calvin Klein, Diane von Furstenberg, and Bill Blass appear on items from women's dresses and sweaters, jeans, handbags, and scarves to men's shirts, belts, shoes, and sportswear. In less than 12 years, 37-year-old Calvin Klein has developed 11 licensees, producing a full range of men's, women's, and children's apparel and accessories surpassing $400 million in 1980 retail sales. During the same year, signature jeans sales by major designers are estimated at $800 million to $900 million, while counterfeit versions of these products may account for an additional $85 million in retail sales. Although the explosive growth in status jeans sales has reached a plateau in the New York area, sales continue to grow in most other regions. For example, major department store and specialty shop executives in California report fall 1980 sales that are more than 10 percent higher than sales in the same 1979 season (*Women's Wear Daily*).

As representatives of designers, producers, and end users of signature goods, retailers are expected to serve as channel gatekeepers, opinion leaders, and change agents. These roles call for the retail organization to control and regulate the flow of signature goods from manufacturer to consumer; to keep potential consumers and suppliers abreast of what is currently fashionable, available, and acceptable; and to influence customer attitudes and purchasing behavior (Hirschman and Stampfl 1980). The effective performance of these functions demands that retailers be constantly aware of consumer-demand characteristics, available and potential signature products, and merchandising and promotional methods that will coordinate the supply of and demand for these products.

There are few signs that resellers or producers of designer goods have conducted formalized empirical studies to explain the signature "craze" or to identify the market segments for these products. An early step in the research process is understanding consumer acceptance and rejection of currently available signature items. Accordingly, the purpose of this study is to identify and contrast signature goods buyers and avoiders in terms of demographic, personality, sociographic, and price-sensitivity dimensions. Owing to the lack of previous research in this specific area, we shall relate our findings to the several relevant conceptual frameworks that describe the behavior of consumers who are confronted with products that have symbolic values.

RESEARCH DESIGN

Sample

Fashion-goods awareness and consumption experience have been found to be positively correlated with the consumer's socioeconomic status, which, in turn, is ordinarily measured by the family's annual income, occupational status, and self-designated or perceived social class position (King 1964). Accordingly, in an effort to create a sample of subjects in middle and high socioeconomic strata, a judgment sample-selection method was used in three major eastern cities to recruit respondents who subscribed to fashion-related magazines, and/or were on mailing lists of or were private credit card customers of recognized fashion specialty stores. Respondents provided an appropriate range of demographic backgrounds as well as a diversity of personality types, life-styles, and sociographic orientations. In comparison with the United States population, our sample was somewhat upscale in terms of income and education but intuitively representative of our universe of interest.

A self-administered questionnaire was designed, pretested, and hand-delivered to the homes or of-

fices of individuals who were notified that the purpose of the research was to study the effectiveness of print advertisements of men's and women's clothing by department stores and leading specialty stores. Questionnaires were completed by 600 of the 712 people who were contacted. The researchers felt that full disclosure of the study's true purpose would have introduced considerable bias, since many people may be reluctant to admit that they direct their behavior to achieve social recognition.

The Signature Goods Continuum

Section I of the questionnaire asked respondents to view simulated color advertisements of two versions of six fashion clothing items, and then to state their degree of preference for one version of each product on a 5-point scale that included a neutral point. The two versions of each product were almost identical; however, one version included a prominent external designer's signature or symbol while the other did not. Products for males in the sample were shirts, sweaters, socks, robes, neckties, and belts. Females were exposed to sweaters, jeans, shawls, handbags, gloves, and socks. Prices were visibly shown on both versions of all products.

Scale scores ranged from +5 (strong preference for signature good) to +1 (strong preference for nonsignature good); a neutral response was scored as +3. Out of a possible 30 points, respondents who scored 24 or more points were considered to be signature goods prone (SGP), since their minimum average score per product item was 4, that is, supportive of signature goods. Persons with scores of 12 points or less were placed in a signature goods avoidance (SGA) category, since their maximum average score per product item was 2, in other words, supportive of nonsignature goods. The remaining respondents were considered to be neither supportive of nor in opposition to signature goods, that is, indifferent (SGI).

To determine the possible influence of price differentials, each respondent was randomly assigned one of three price combinations for the six products. In one version, prices were identical for signature and nonsignature goods. In a second set, signature goods were priced 15 percent higher, and in the third set, they were 25 percent higher.

Interpersonal Orientations

In Section II of the instrument, Cohen's (1967) 35-item Likert-type device was used to measure respondents' compliant, aggressive, and detached (CAD) interpersonal orientations based on Horney's tripartite paradigm. CAD scores were obtained by adding individual responses for each of the three sets of questions and then using these scores as independent variables for identifying those who exhibit signature goods proneness and avoidance. Although Noerager (1979) and others posed some possible limitations of the CAD approach, there is considerable evidence of the usefulness of this model in studying consumer behavior within a personality-related context (Cohen 1967, Kernan 1971, Nicely 1972, Cohen and Golden 1972, Schlacter, Fisk, and Phee 1980).

In the present study, Cronbach's (1946) coefficient alpha was used to assess the internal consistency of the CAD instrument. The reliability coefficients for the three personality dimensions were: compliant (.879), aggressive (.823), and detached (.772).

Life-Style and Demographic and Socioeconomic Variables

Section III consisted of 31 questions designed to uncover respondents' life-styles, e.g., hobbies, leisure activities, social functions, and other interests. These emerged following factor analysis of numerous variables developed through a current literature review and focus-group interviews. Veblen's (1899) hypothesis of economic consumption is supportive of the notion that many of the above variables are effective predictors of the strong emulative influences that motivate the choice of conspicuous goods. Finally, Section IV identified the sex, age, race, marital status, religion, education, and income of respondents.

Analysis

Of the 554 usable questionnaires, 48 respondents (9 percent) were SGPs, 71 subjects (13 percent) were SGAs, and 435 (78 percent) were SGIs. Mar-

keters who seek to cultivate the SGP market segment envision the marketplace as consisting of two distinct segments, those who are signature goods prone (SGPs) and those who are not (SGAs + SGIs). Conversely, those who perceive signature goods avoidance as a distinct market opportunity divide the market into avoiders (SGAs) and all others (SGPs + SGIs). In each case, the marketer attempts to profile the consumer in the *extreme group* to which he or she wishes to appeal.

Accordingly, separate two-group, step-wise discriminant analyses were performed for (1) SGPs versus all other respondents and (2) SGAs versus all others, in order to determine which interpersonal orientations, life-style variables, or demographic characteristics predicted either position. Univariate analysis of variance was then employed to compare the profile of subjects in each extreme group with that of the corresponding remaining subjects in each case.

When groups are unequal in size, prior probabilities will bias the discriminant analysis classification procedure in favor of the largest group. One of several approaches suggested by Morrison (1969) was used to minimize this bias. The 48 members of the SGP group were matched versus three random samples of 48 each from the 506 remaining "all other" respondents. After performing discriminant analyses comparing each of these three "all other" samples with the same SGP group, the average number correctly classified was computed. Then, this same procedure was followed to compare the SGA group with three samples of 71 each from the 483 remaining "all other" respondents.

FINDINGS

Discriminant Analysis Results: Signature-Goods Proneness

The jackknifed classification matrix shown in Table 1 correctly identified 87.5 percent of all others (AOs). This validation process uses all the information in the sample data while providing an unbiased estimation of the error rates (Crask and Perreault 1977).

Only the eight variables shown in the stepwise discriminant analysis summary (Table 2) were

Table 1 Jackknifed classification matrix

	Prone group versus all others	Predicted groups[a]	
Tendency toward signature goods	Actual groups	Number	Percentage correct
Proneness (SGP)	48	43	89.6
All others (SGA + SGI)	48[b]	41	85.4
Totals	96	84	87.5

	Avoidance group versus all others	Predicted groups[a]	
Tendency away from signature goods	Actual groups	Number	Percentage correct
Avoidance (SGA)	71	55	77.5
All others (SGP + SGI)	71[b]	57	80.3
Totals	142	112	78.9

[a]t-tests significant at .01 level.
[b]Based on three random samples of this size.

needed to achieve this prediction accuracy. For each predictor variable, the table shows its order of entry into the function and its standardized discriminant function coefficient. Intercorrelation of predictor variables was not a serious problem, as the highest pairwise correlation was below .50. A chi-square value of 56.91 ($df = 8$) reveals that the group centroids are significantly different—beyond the 0.0000 level.

An individual's aggressive personality score was found to be the most effective variable in discriminating between SGP consumers and all others. The overwhelming importance of this variable is indicated by (1) first entry into the discriminant function, (2) the size of its F-value, and (3) the size of its standardized coefficient, which exceeds that of all other variables. When the discriminant analysis results are viewed in concert with the group mean differences shown in Table 3, it is possible to compare the profile of consumers who are prone to

purchase signature goods with that of all other respondents.

Profile of Signature-Goods Prone Consumers

Only three demographic characteristics proved to be significant in identifying signature goods advocates. In contrast with other fashion-conscious individuals, the SGP person is more likely to be female than male and at a higher level of formal education. Additionally, blacks are more likely to be members of the SGP segment.

Out of a maximum of 90 points on the *aggressive personality* dimension of the CAD model, the

Table 2 Prone group versus all others: stepwise discriminant analysis results

Variable entered[a]	F-value to enter/remove[b]	Standardized discriminant function coefficients[c]
Aggressive personality score	20.31	0.843
Gourmet dining enthusiast	12.16	0.612
Dancing enthusiast	5.47	0.359
Observer of crime drama on TV	8.86	0.539
Sex (male)	6.20	−0.419
Camera/photography enthusiast	5.19	0.352
Reader of general magazines	3.87	−0.313
Race (white)	2.07	0.187

[a]In order of inclusion in discriminant solution.
[b]$p < .01$.
[c]$\chi^2 = 56.91$; $df = 8$; $p < .0000$. Note that standardized discriminant function coefficients indicate the relative importance of a variable in differentiating between groups. Although multicollinearity can sometimes cause the coefficients to be misleading, this does not seem to be a problem here since correlations between discriminant function variables were all below .50.

Table 3 Characteristics differentiating signature-goods prone (SGP) respondents from all others (AO): test of group means

Variables[a]	SGP	AO	F
Aggressive person-ality score[b]	52.42	43.87	22.12[c]
Gourmet dining enthusiast	1.60	2.32	18.40[c]
Country club member	2.35	2.80	12.46[c]
Camera/photography enthusiast	2.09	2.55	10.55[c]
Observer of weight control	1.76	2.13	6.76[c]
Travel enthusiast	1.47	1.62	6.67[c]
Observer of talk shows on TV	1.85	2.18	6.49[c]
Education[b]	3.56	3.25	5.82[d]
Dancing enthusiast	1.91	2.25	5.45[d]
Theater/concert goer	1.93	2.20	4.37[d]
Observer of crime dramas on TV	1.98	2.22	4.22[d]
Participant in garden-ing activities	2.19	2.26	4.20[d]
Consumer of intox-icating beverages	1.96	2.16	4.13[d]
Sex (male)[e]	.44	.56	3.69[d]
Race (white)[e]	.77	.86	3.46[d]
Reader of general magazines	1.93	2.18	3.09[f]
FM radio or sound system enthusiast	1.95	1.80	2.94[f]
Participant in tennis or other sports	1.62	1.71	2.01[f]

[a]Lower mean scores indicate increased participation in activities or higher levels of variables. (Exceptions are indicated by b and e).
[b]Higher mean scores indicate greater presence of attribute.
[c]$p < .01$.
[d]$p < .05$.
[e]Measured on a dichotomous 1/0 basis, so that mean scores indicate the percentage of respondents possessing that characteristic.
[f]$p < .10$.

mean score of SGPs is significantly greater than those of subjects who are either indifferent to or opposed to signature good purchases.

Finally, the psychographic variables lead to the conclusion that signature-goods prone individuals are significantly more active than other consumers in social activities (theater and concerts, country clubs, dancing, traveling, alcoholic beverage consumption, gourmet dining) and participation in sports (tennis, skiing). SGPs are also more active FM radio or sound-system listeners and watchers of television talk shows and crime dramas, and are more concerned about weight control than other respondents. On the other hand, SGPs tend to be significantly less active readers of general magazines and less involved in gardening activities.

Discriminant Analysis Results: Signature Goods Avoidance

As shown in Table 1, the jackknifed classification matrix correctly predicted 78.9 percent of the sample, 77.5 percent of the SGAs, and 80.3 percent of AOs. This level of accuracy was achieved with the nine variables of the stepwise discriminant analysis summary in Table 4. The chi-square value of 51.87 ($df = 9$) indicates that group centroids are significantly different beyond the 0.0000 level. Again, intercorrelation of predictor variables was not a problem, as the highest pairwise correlation was 0.39. When the discriminant analysis results are combined with the group mean differences provided in Table 5, a profile emerges of consumers who prefer to avoid the purchase of signature goods.

Profiles of Signature Goods Avoiders

Three demographic characteristics significantly differentiate between SGAs and other fashion goods consumers (AOs). The SGA person is much more likely to be male, white, and older than AOs. Further, SGAs tend to possess significantly less aggressive personalities. Finally, the psychographic variables indicate that SGAs are less active than AOs in dancing, country club membership, attending movies, consuming alcoholic beverages, watching crime dramas on television, or enjoying FM radio and sound systems. On the other hand, SGAs are

Table 4 Avoidance group versus all others: stepwise discriminant analysis results

Variable entered[a]	F-value to enter/remove[b]	Standardized discriminant function coefficients[c]
Country club member	12.35	−0.626
Sex (male)	11.38	0.612
Aggressive personality score	7.14	−0.402
Dancing enthusiast	5.86	−0.414
FM radio or sound system enthusiast	5.09	−0.385
Visitor to major shopping centers	5.77	0.438
Observer of crime dramas on TV	5.51	−0.400
Race (white)	2.43	0.266
Participant in gardening activities	2.10	0.247

[a]In order of inclusion in discriminant solution.
[b]$p < .01$.
[c]$\chi^2 = 51.87$, df $= 9$; $p < .0000$. Note that standardized discriminant function coefficients indicate the relative importance of a variable in differentiating between groups. Although multicollinearity can sometimes cause the coefficients to be misleading, this does not seem to be a problem here since correlations between discriminant function variables were all below .40.

Table 5 Characteristics differentiating signature goods avoider (SGA) respondents from all others (AO): test of group means

Variables[a]	SGA	AO	F
Observer of crime dramas on TV	2.35	2.13	5.28[b]
Country club member	2.77	2.55	5.27[c]
Aggressive personality score[d]	44.74	48.59	5.22[c]
Race (white)[e]	.93	.82	5.10[c]
Age[d]	3.23	2.81	4.77[f]
Movie goer	2.00	1.86	3.93[c]
Sex (male)[e]	.58	.50	3.39[f]
Visitor to major shopping centers	1.62	1.81	3.35[f]
Consumer of intoxicating beverages	2.23	2.04	3.23[f]
Price[d]	110.65	113.91	3.10[f]
Participant in gardening activities	2.23	2.42	2.76[f]
FM radio or sound system enthusiast	2.51	2.23	2.45[f]
Reader of general magazines	1.66	1.74	2.03[f]

[a]Lower mean scores indicate increased participation in activities or higher levels of variables. (Exceptions are indicated by d and e).
[b]$p < .01$.
[c]$p < .05$.
[d]Higher mean scores indicate greater presence of attribute.
[e]Measured on a dichotomous 1/0 basis, so that mean scores indicate the percentage of respondents possessing that characteristic.
[f]$p < .10$.

much more likely to read general magazines (e.g., *Reader's Digest, Time, Newsweek)*, visit major shopping centers, and participate in gardening.

Impact of Price

The relative price of a signature good compared with its nonsignature counterpart had no significant influence upon the proportion of consumers who are inclined toward signature goods purchases. In fact, in the current sample, the proportion of SGPs

was found to be an increasing function of the price differential. Thus, the results suggest that a sizable proportion of signature-goods prone individuals would be willing to pay as much as a 25 percent premium for a designer's signature on a garment or accessory.

On the other hand, price plays an important role in identifying SGAs, for they are significantly less willing than other subjects to pay premium prices for clothing. As expected, a sizable proportion of the signature goods avoiders will select an unsigned product over one with a signature even if both are priced identically.

DISCUSSION

The results of the study suggest that significant differences exist between consumers who exhibit signature goods proneness and fashion-conscious individuals who are strongly opposed to such personal purchases. Clearly, the propensity for a consumer to purchase signature goods is an increasing function of that individual's aggressiveness. These findings run parallel to those of Cohen (1967), who found that aggressive people select name-brand products as indicators of social status and reinforcement of their self-concept. Moreover, an inspection of Table 3 suggests that one's aggressive response to others might be reflected in a wide range of life-style activities and certain demographic dimensions.

Aggressive Orientation

An explanation of the construct of aggression within Horney's interpersonal CAD model will help to relate our findings to the literature base offered at the outset of this paper. According to Joel Cohen (1967, p. 271):

> Aggressive-oriented people want to excel, to achieve success, prestige, and admiration. Other people are seen as competitors. Aggressive people strive to be superior strategists, to control their emotions, and to bring their fears under control. . . . The aggressive person . . . needs people to confirm his self-image, to bolster what may well be uncertain confidence in his competitive talents. He will go out of his way to be noticed, if such notice brings admiration.

Demographic Variables

The high visibility of females in the SGP profile may be related to their rapidly changing social and economic status. Since 1950, the number of working women has more than doubled, for reasons beyond financial gain. Lazer and Smallwood (1977) observe that women want to fulfill their roles as employees, wives, mothers, and homemakers in a manner that permits them to realize themselves, to establish a valid sense of identity and self-esteem, and to inject glamour, excitement, challenge, and rewards in their lives.

The consciousness of the black consumer in the SGP segment is also a reflection of an aggressive orientation toward purchase decisions. Blacks value power, prestige, and status because of their long deprivation (Barnett 1978). The possession and display of signature goods may serve to reinforce a desired self-concept. Barnett (1978) identified two major segments of black consumers—those who strive for material goods and the social values of whites, and those who live more for the moment and forsake the societal values that have been set by whites. His findings lead us to believe that signature goods marketers can best reach the "strivers" in the black community by integrated promotional programs that appeal to both blacks and whites.

Psychographic Variables

The SGP individual's membership in a country club or attendance at theaters, concerts, and gourmet restaurants correlates well with an aggressive orientation, since these activities help one to be noticed and admired. Aggressiveness in terms of the desire to compete, win, excel, or support a winner is manifested by the SGP's enthusiasm for tennis, skiing, and horse racing.

Similarly, aggressive people may perceive crime dramas on TV as strategic struggles between "cops and robbers." Interest in travel and in variety and talk shows on television may indicate a need to gain up-to-date reference-group information and support in the form of exposure to performers, artists, authorities, and a wide array of cultures. Drinking and dancing are forms of exhibitionism that may be predictive of other conspicuous behavior; such as displaying the Givenchy, Cardin, or Vuitton symbol.

The most unlikely buyer of signature goods has been found to be an older, white male who prefers solitary activities such as reading and gardening. Because this person is less oriented toward strong interpersonal relationships and competition, he may repel accepted roles of behavior and tradition.

Owing to a desire to feel distinct from other people, he is likely to shun wearing items that display someone else's name or symbol. His visits to shopping centers may serve as major forms of diversion, recreation, or physical activity. Finally, the SGA may possess a unique capability of relating product inspections to ultimate functional suitability. Thus, his prepurchase anxieties may be relieved more from shopping center comparisons than from designer identification or established brands or outlets (Jolson and Proia 1976).

Additional Observations

Why is it that signature-goods proneness is not correlated with income and other socioeconomic variables, while some social-class-related life-style variables are effective discriminators? One answer may be rooted in the hypothesis that "the accumulation of product symbols and the accumulation of money are often in opposition" (Warner and Lunt 1950). Many high-income people have little concern for upward social mobility and are accumulators of wealth in the form of cash, household possessions, and other assets. Others, regardless of income brackets, think of themselves as poor relative to their status aspirations and are accordingly supportive of conspicuous activities and expenditures.

LIMITATIONS AND CONCLUSIONS

The results of this study indicate that a person's sex, race, level of education, aggressiveness of personality, and propensity to engage in interpersonal relationships are significant predictors of his or her propensity to favor the purchase of garments and accessories with prestigious external brand marks.

Surely our analysis of signature-goods buying preferences fails to include all the predictor variables that are worthy of exploration. Probably the most serious shortcoming is the artificiality introduced by our use of self-reported buying preferences as a surrogate for actual purchases. Despite these shortcomings, we believe that this study will serve as a springboard to encourage future researchers to seek powerful, managerially actiona-

ble correlates of signature goods purchasing behavior.

Given the findings, several recommended areas for future research become apparent:

- Are SGPs seeking support for their self-concept as they now perceive themselves, or are they seeking responses from members of society that will promote the attainment of a more ideal self?
- How inelastic is the demand for signature goods? The answer could be determined by extending the experimental price differential well beyond the 25 percent used in this study.
- What are the underlying causes of signature avoidance behavior? Are they related to the consumer's personality, patterns of taste, measures of social mobility, tendencies to reject conspicuous expenditures and symbolism, or other factors?
- What does the future hold for signature goods? Are signature-goods proneness and avoidance growing or diminishing?

REFERENCES

Barnett, Arthur D. (1978), "Black-White Consumer Differences in a Market Study," *Proceedings of the Southern Marketing Association* (November), 359–362.

Cohen, Joel B. (1967), "An Interpersonal Orientation to the Study of Consumer Behavior," *Journal of Marketing Research,* 4 (August), 270–277.

———, and Ellen Golden (1972), "Informational Social Influence and Product Evaluation," *Journal of Applied Psychology,* 50 (February), 54–59.

Crask, Melvin R., and William D. Perreault, Jr. (1977), "Validation of Discriminant Analysis in Marketing Research," *Journal of Marketing Research,* 14 (February), 60–68.

Cronbach, L. J. (1946), "Response Sets and Test Validity," *Educational and Psychological Measurement,* 10, 475–494.

Hirschman, Elizabeth C., and Ronald W. Stampfl (1980), "Roles of Retailing in the Diffusion of Popular Culture: Microperspectives," *Journal of Retailing,* 56 (Spring), 16–36.

Horney, Karen (1937), *The Neurotic Personality of Our Time,* New York: W. W. Norton & Company.

_____ (1939), *New Ways in Psychoanalysis,* New York: W. W. Norton & Company.

_____ (1945), *Our Inner Conflicts,* New York: W. W. Norton & Company.

_____ (1950), *Neurosis and Human Growth,* New York: W. W. Norton & Company. .

Jolson, Marvin A., and Stephen L. Proia (1976), "Classificaton of Consumer Goods—A Subjective Measure?" *Proceedings of the American Marketing Association* (August), 71–75.

Kernan, Jerome B. (1971), "The CAD Instrument in Behavioral Diagnoses," *Proceedings of the Association for Consumer Research,* 307–312.

King, Charles W. (9164), "Fashion Adoption: A Rebuttal to the 'Trickle Down' Theory," in Stephen A. Greyser (ed.), *Toward Scientific Marketing,* Chicago: American Marketing Association, 108–125.

Lazer, William, and John E. Smallwood (1977), "The Changing Demographics of Women," *Journal of Marketing,* 41 (July), 14–22.

Morrison, Donald G. (1969), "On the Interpretation of Discriminant Analysis," *Journal of Marketing Research,* 6 (May), 156–163.

Nicely, Roy E. (1972), "E, I-O and CAD Correlations," unpublished working paper, Virginia Polytechnic Institute.

Noerager, Jon P. (1979), "An Assessment of CAD—A Personality Instrument Developed Specifically for Marketing Research," *Journal of Marketing Research,* 16 (February), 53–59.

Schlacter, John, Ray Fisk, and John Phee (1980), "Personality and Its Measurement: A Replication Study Using C.A.D.," in *Proceedings of the Southern Marketing Association* (November), 204–206.

Veblen, Thorstein (1899), *The Theory of the Leisure Class,* New York: The Macmillan Company.

Warner, W. Lloyd, and Paul Lunt (1950), *The Social Life of a Modern Community,* New Haven, Conn.: Yale University Press.

Women's Wear Daily (1980), "Sales of Status Jeans Plummenting in New York," (November 10), pp. 3, 8; "Unzipping the Bogus-Jeans Trade." (December 2), 1, 16.

SECTION XII

INVOLVEMENT AND CONSUMER BEHAVIOR

There have been many noteworthy models of consumer behavior conceived over the last decade:
- Fishbein's attitude model
- Multi-attribute models
- Attribution theory
- Cognitive-Dissonance theory
- Perceptual and preference mapping
- Personality research
- Consumer satisfaction dissatisfaction research

Underlying each of these models is the assumption that the consumer through deliberate information processing and complex decision making carefully chooses the product. True, when large monetary outlays are involved and/or there is a social or psychological commitment to the product, the consumer may behave as the models predict. However, there are a large number of products that do not hold a high level of involvement for the consumer.

Involvement can be defined as a general level of interest in the product. Involvement theory had its beginnings in social psychology. It was conceptualized as a variable that influenced attitude change resulting from exposure to persuasive communication. Sherif and Hovland (1961) stated that "involvement in one's position on an issue is one of the most significant factors creating resistance to persuasion."

Involvement entered the consumer behavior field with Howard and Sheth's notion in 1969 that it is the construct that connects a consumer to a product class in terms of importance of purchase. It is the psychological, social, or economic stake a consumer has in a product. Several other consumer behavior theorists have proposed definitions of involvement. Wright (1975) argued that if a product was not involving, a consumer would tend to satisfice rather than optimize in his/her decision. Robertson (1976) believed low involvement was low commitment, commitment being defined as the strength of the individual's belief system with regard to the product or brand. Tyebjee (1979b) used response time to measure a consumer's information activity to determine the degree of involvement. Assael (1980) hypothesized that a highly involved consumer would be an information seeker, actively searching for information from alternative sources.

Involvement has played a key role in the communication models. The hierarchy of communication effects model formulated by Lavidge and Steiner in 1961 posited that there is a three stage process through which the viewer progresses in his or her response to a communication message. The stages of this model are: first cognition (learning), then affect (development of attitudes), and finally conation (action). This learning hierarchy occurs when the audience is involved in the topic of the communication. A second model, the low involvement model, proposed by Krugman reorders the stages: cognition, conation, affect. In this model, a consumer first learns about the brand, then buys the brand, and then after use develops attitudes about the brand. This appears to be an efficient way for brand evaluation of low cost items, to try them before establishing attitudes about them.

The two articles in this section discuss involvement and how it pertains to consumer behavior. While reading these articles, it is important for the reader to develop a personal definition of involvement and then to try to assess its importance in consumer behavior.

"FAMILIARITY AND ITS IMPACT ON CONSUMER DECISION BIASES AND HEURISTICS"

Throughout this book we have been concerned with how a consumer chooses a product from among several competing products. But what exactly is a choice? Webster defines choice as a preference, which implies that the person to choose is looking for the best thing. Hansen (1972) indicates that there are three criteria of choice: (1) there must be two or more alternatives; (2) the alternatives must arouse conflict; and (3) cognitive processes aimed at reducing conflict must occur.

Scientists know relatively little about how the mind works, but it is known that the mind has limited information-processing capability. It has been shown that cognitive simplification is used for a choice that requires mental capacity that exceeds one's capabilities. The decision maker in trying to make decisions in a complex environment attempts to simplify the situation. Sometimes a decision maker restricts his/her intake of information to only certain data. This possibly distorts the situation because of the subjectivity of the judgment. Biases result from the heuristics or decision rules that are applied to reduce the complexity of the task to an acceptable level of complexity.

Heuristics then are fairly simple procedures, rules, or tricks used to reduce the mental effort that is needed to integrate information in making a consumption decision.

Park and Lessig examine several heuristics used by consumers at different levels of familiarity: perceptual category breadth, the use of functional and nonfunctional product dimensions, the decision time, and the confidence in the choice. What other heuristics might have been measured other than the ones used in this study? Are there other important decision rules that should have been considered?

Familiarity was operationalized as a subjective familiarity that was standardized using the same familiarity assessment criteria for everyone. The study could have used a completely subjective measure of familiarity by asking the subjects to define their own perspective of familiarity. The question could have been posed, "How much do you believe you know about microwave ovens?" Or the study could have taken the completely objective approach and tested the participants on their knowledge of microwaves. Each of these approaches could possibly result in different conclusions. The reader should consider how Park and Lessig define familiarity and whether their definition is consistent with their measurement technique.

It is hypothesized by Park and Lessig that the three groups of respondents differ not only in their familiarity with the product class, but also in their involvement with the product class. Is the degree of familiarity correlated with the degree of involvement? What implications does this have?

"HOW TO SOLVE PROBLEMS THAT DON'T MATTER: SOME HEURISTICS FOR UNINVOLVED THINKING"

Contemporary psychologists have proposed that what is encoded, or stored in memory, is determined by a guiding schema or knowledge framework that selects and actively modifies experience in order to arrive at a coherent, unified, expectation-confirming, and knowledge-consistent representation of an experience. Schema refers to the general knowledge structure a person possesses about a particular domain. It allows for the encoding, storage, and retrieval of information related to that domain.

There are several forms of schema. Frames (Minsky, 1975) and scripts (Shank and Abelson, 1977) refer to schema that contain specific information about the structure of a familiar event. It is this knowledge that tells a person what to expect in a particular situation and the order in which events should occur. Frames and scripts are stereotyped event sequences. People's knowledge of routine activities such as eating in a restaurant or visiting a dentist are believed to be organized in a schematic nature of mental representations of these events.

Schemata have important implications to marketers. How a consumer purchases in a supermarket and how a viewer perceives an advertisement could each be defined in the form of a schema.

Knowledge structures enable the perceiver to go beyond the information given. Schematic representations of objects, events, and actors permit one to process and interpret new experiences quickly.

The Deighton article discusses schema in the context of low involvement advertising and its influence on inference. Low involvement advertising is defined in this paper as advertising of products that are not of keen interest to the consumer.

Keep in mind that this paper proposes a theory that at this time has no empirical evidence to support it. Before beginning, quickly examine Figure 1, (p. 363) which summarizes the main points that will be made in the article. Advertising attempts to influence the viewer, while the viewer is making inferences in a low involvement state, in three ways:

1. An advertisement dictates which schema people will apply.
2. The ad's theme will fit neatly into this readily available schema.
3. Consumers by their nature tend to look for confirming evidence in their everyday experiences to coincide with the ad's message.

The assimilation to a schema is discussed in some detail. This idea was first proposed by Piaget, who believed that adaptation is based upon organization. There are two processes that move a person toward equilibrium: assimilation and accommodation. Assimilation is the process of applying established patterns of behavior to a new object or event. You make external reality fit your point of view. Accommodation is the process of creating a new schema when existing categories are not appropriate for certain incoming stimuli. This conflict is present throughout life and is instrumental in the development of cognitive structure. Deighton proposes that the viewer will use assimilation while making inferences. Does a person ever create new schema (accommodation) in regard to television ads?

Langer's theory of mindlessness states that people basically don't think at all. A large portion of thinking is on automatic pilot. A very few minimal cues can generate a script, which is defined as a set of behaviors that follow one another in a well-learned way. How does this idea relate to Deighton's theory of uninvolved thinking?

Under what circumstances would casual diagnostic inferences not be made for advertising? What factors need to be taken into account?

FAMILIARITY AND ITS IMPACT ON CONSUMER DECISION BIASES AND HEURISTICS

C. WHAN PARK
AND
V. PARKER LESSIG

Source: C. Whan Park and V. Parker Lessig, "Familiarity and Its Impact on Consumer Decision Biases and Heuristics," *Journal of Consumer Research,* Vol. 8, September, 1981, 223–230. Reprinted with permission.

Two major approaches are available for operationalizing and measuring product familiarity. One is to measure product familiarity in terms of *how much a person knows about the product;* the other is to measure familiarity in terms of *how much a person thinks s/he knows about the product.* According to the former, product familiarity may be examined with respect to the knowledge structure of an individual's long-term memory (LTM). According to the latter, product familiarity is based on the person's self-report of how much s/he knows about the product (Lichtenstein and Fischhoff 1977). The former approach (amount of knowledge) contributes to understanding the impact of memory contents on the decision maker's evaluation and choice decisions; the latter (self-assessed familiarity) provides information about decision makers' (DM) systematic biases and heuristics in choice evaluations and decisions.

The objective of the present study is to examine, in a descriptive framework, decision (evaluation) biases and heuristics of consumers at different levels of familiarity, with specific attention to the impact on such information-processing heuristics as (1) perceptual category breadth, (2) use of functional and nonfunctional product dimensions, (3) decision time, and (4) confidence in choice.

Construct of Product Familiarity

The conceptualization of product familiarity in this study follows the DM's *subjective familiarity assessment* at three different levels. However, different individuals may employ different criteria in assessing familiarity, thus making comparisons across subjects difficult. This assessment is, therefore, made using a common base defined in terms of the subject's perceived knowledge of those dimensions important in the evaluation of the product.

. . . In order to maximize the difference in self-assessed familiarity levels among subjects, the following three prior behavioral considerations were specified: (a) microwave oven information search experience; (b) microwave oven usage experience; and (c) microwave oven ownership status. A subject with no information-search experience, no product-usage experience, and nonownership was defined to have low familiarity (LF). A subject defined to have a moderate level of familiarity (MF) met conditions (a) and/or (b), but not (c). A subject classified as having high familiarity (HF) had search experience, usage experience, and was a microwave oven owner. . . .

When familiarity is defined subjectively, controlling prior behavioral activities, it is treated as a "state" variable, and two points should be noted. First, the three familiarity groups are expected to differ in their information about the product, their subjective judgment of cue selection and processing (i.e., confidence in choosing and processing product attributes for a choice decision task), and their organization of product information in long-term memory. Second, due to differences in prior behavioral activities (prior interest in the product class), differences among the three groups may be expected in their motivational involvement with the experimental task.

THEORY

Perceptual Category Breadth
In the present study, it is proposed that a decision maker's level of product familiarity affects her perceptual category breadth. According to Bruner (1957), perceptual category breadth refers to a DM's viewing the various levels of a given dimension, e.g., size, as belonging to different categories, e.g., small, medium, large. A dimension whose levels are assigned to few categories, i.e., where there is very little discrimination, is said to have broad category breadth, i.e., each category covers a large range of the dimension's levels (Bruner and Tajfel 1961; Pinson 1978).

Two factors are considered in examining category breadth—a cognitive capability and a psychological desire to differentiate among dimensional categories. In this study, category breadth assumes that the DM has both the cognitive ability to differentiate among dimensional categories and utility differences across these categories. A DM at LF (low familiarity) is expected to exhibit broad category breadth with respect to the functional product dimensions evaluated. The greater the number of categories created for the classification of a dimension's levels, i.e., the narrower the category

breadth, the more difficult is the assignment of utility, because more classes exist that require evaluation. With only indirect information or experience (based on other product usage) to draw upon and with the absence of a well-established dimensional salience hierarchy, the assignment of utility to a large number of categories would be a difficult and frustrating task. One way of reducing frustration and cognitive burden would be to broaden a dimension's categories, i.e., reduce the number of perceptual categories on that dimension.

The DM at MF (moderate familiarity) has relevant and needed product information from previous usage experience and/or from information material provided to them. However, this DM has rather fragmented information about the meaning of dimensions and their salience hierarchy. Although this information is less than desired, it does aid in the DM's *constructive process* of a choice decision, thus reducing the degree of complexity involved. The MF DM is, therefore, capable of processing greater amounts of, and more complex, information (Park and Lessig 1977). To facilitate the development of this complex processing, the MF DM is expected to have narrower category breadth, i.e., more categories.

The HF DM is also expected to have a narrower category breadth than the DM at LF. Based on previous purchase decision making and on usage experience, the HF DM has developed a relatively complex and rigidly fixed utility for different levels of the various dimensions and their associated salience. This information, which is contained in long-term memory, is well defined and effectively retrieved for a specific choice decision task (Bettman 1979). Category breadth for the HF DM is not expected to differ from that of the MF DM. . . .

Reliance on Price and Brand Name Information
It is proposed that confidence in the utilization of brand name and price information is a function of the DM's familiarity level. Based upon previous discussion, it would seem that a DM at LF would find it less difficult and be more confident to extrapolate a product's utility from familiar concepts, such as the nonfunctional dimensions of price and

brand name, than from unfamiliar product functional dimensions. . . .

The DM at HF is also expected to have high confidence in usage of brand name and price in the choice decision. Due to her previous purchase experience and knowledge about the brand that she owns, brand name and its price are expected to be placed very high on a dimensional salience hierarchy with high confidence. Due to her knowledge, the DM at MF is not expected to find it as difficult or as ambiguous to rely on the functional attributes as is the LF DM. Nor is the MF DM expected to have biases toward these dimensions that are as strong as those expressed by the HF DM. Given this and her ability to form utility through information on functional dimensions, the DM at MF would not feel as confident as LF and HF decision makers in evaluating choice options through the use of brand name and price information. The DM at MF is thus expected to have a higher confidence in functional dimensions than in price and brand-name dimensions.

Decision Time

The time required to make a decision is an important process-tracing measure (Hansen 1972). A number of investigators have described the consumer's decision task as consisting of two general stages (Howard and Sheth 1969; Park 1978; Payne 1976). In the first stage (choice reduction), the consumer reduces the number of available alternatives to a smaller set consisting of those options considered to be acceptable. In the second stage (choice selection), the consumer decides which alternative among those in the acceptable set is best. In the present study, decision time is hypothesized to be a function of both the level of the consumer's product familiarity and the stage of the decision process. Specifically, in the choice reduction stage, the DM at MF is expected to require more time than either LF or HF decision makers.

This expectation is in line with Pollary's (1970) and Kiesler's (1966) findings on the nonmonotonic relationship between decision time and the difficulty of the choice task. According to Pollary and Kiesler, decision time is expected to increase as difficulty increases until the choice becomes quite difficult, at which point decision time decreases. That is, due to her relatively simple information processing strategy, the DM at LF should need less time to evaluate alternatives than MF DM whose decision making process is much more involved. On the other hand, the HF DM can achieve information search and processing efficiency due to her high level of familiarity (Sheth and Venkatesan, 1968). This should result in the HFDM requiring less decision time than the DM at MF.

Decision time at the choice selection stage is expected to exhibit a different pattern due to changed perception of the task's difficulty. Specifically, during the choice reduction stage, the LF DM greatly simplified her choice task. This simplification now makes choice less difficult than at the reduction stage. The DM now feels motivated to select the brand that will give her the greatest utility. This motivation is expected to lead her to a careful and perhaps timeconsuming examination of additional information, due to lack of familiarity. Furthermore, when the remaining alternatives are barely discriminable on those dimensions upon which she heavily relied in the choice reduction state, the DM may be forced to consider additional information for which she is not an efficient information processor. On the other hand, the thoroughness of the choice reduction activities of the MF DM is likely to make her task simpler at the choice selection stage, although she is a careful information processor. This implies that the decision-making time difference between a DM at LF and a DM at MF would not be significant at the choice selection stage.

The HF DM is very efficient in processing information due to her well-established cognitive structure relating to decision alternatives. Therefore, she is expected to need a shorter decision time in her selection than is required by LF and MF decision makers.

Choice Confidence

The degree of confidence that the DM places on the appropriateness of the ultimate choice is viewed as being related to the DM's familiarity. The LF DM is expected to feel less confident than the MF DM, who has relevant knowledge for the decision-making task. The HF DM is also expected to have higher confidence in the choice than the MF DM, due to the HF DM's greater product usage experience and ownership. The confidence of the DM in her choice is thus hypothesized to increase monotonically with the level of her familiarity, for both the choice reduction stage and the choice selection stage.

HYPOTHESES

Based on the previous section, the following hypotheses are proposed:

H1: The perceptual category breadth on functional dimensions of the DM at a low level of familiarity is broader than that of DMs at either a moderate or a high level of familiarity.

H2: There is a significant difference between a DM at a moderate level of familiarity and DMs at either a low or a high familiarity level with respect to the processing and utilization of the nonfunctional dimensions of brand name and price. Specifically:

H2a: A DM at a moderate level of familiarity feels less confident in relying on price and brand name than DMs at either a low or a high level of familiarity.

H2b: A DM at a low level of familiarity feels more confident in relying on the nonfunctional dimensions of price and brand name than in relying on functional dimensions.

H2c: A DM at a moderate level of familiarity feels less confident in relying on the nonfunctional dimensions of price and brand name than in relying on functional dimensions.

H2d: A DM at a high level of familiarity feels as confident in relying on the nonfunctional dimensions of price and brand name as in relying on functional dimensions.

H3a: In reducing the alternatives to a smaller set of acceptable options, the decision time of a DM at a moderate level of familiarity is greater than that of DMs at either low or high levels of familiarity.

H3b: In selecting the best alternative in the acceptable set, the decision time of DMs at either low or moderate levels of familiarity is greater than that of a DM at a high level of familiarity.

H4: The DM at low familiarity feels less confident than moderate familiarity DMs, and the DM at a moderate familiarity level feels less confident than the DM at high familiarity. This holds for both the choice reduction and the choice selection stages.

SUBJECTS

Data were obtained from 99 women living in a midwestern college community. Each subject was contacted by telephone and asked whether she had ever searched for information about microwave ovens, had ever used a microwave oven, and currently owned a microwave oven. The responses were used to assign the subject to one of three familiarity groups . . .

These three conditions were chosen to maximally discriminate among familiarity groups. . . .

. . .

EXPERIMENTAL TASK AND DATA

At the beginning of the interview, the subject indicated, through a five-point scale (ranging from "very familiar" coded as 5, to "unfamiliar" coded as 1), her opinion on which microwave oven features would be important in making a choice: The subject was then presented a matrix that described 15 models of microwave ovens in terms of ten dimensions: brand, price, type of microwave distribution, number of cooking levels, expanded scale timer, temperature setting, browner, microwave leakage, safety start, and usable oven capacity. Most of the descriptions accurately portrayed models available at the time. . . .

The subject examined the product description matrix and identified the options acceptable to her.

She then indicated on a seven-point scale (extremely difficult to extremely easy) the difficulty of this choice reduction task. She also indicated, on a five-point scale (extremely confident to not confident at all), her confidence in the selections made with respect to her perceived certainty that the alternative(s) chosen will enhance her overall satisfaction. The options just identified as being acceptable were then reevaluated to determine which would be her first choice. The perceived difficulty of this choice selection task was also measured. The subject verbalized her thoughts (which were tape recorded) while performing both the choice reduction and the choice selection tasks; the time (rounded to the nearest minute) required to complete each task was also noted.

Also, for each of the ten microwave oven dimensions, the subject indicated on a seven-point scale her confidence that reliance on the dimension would enhance the satisfaction that she received from the oven chosen. Finally, for each dimension, she indicated (using an 11-point scale) the satisfaction she would receive from each of the dimension's levels, e.g., for the dimension "browner," the satisfaction associated with having and with not having a browner.

FINDINGS

Verbal Protocol Examination
Sixty-two of the tape-recorded protocols were transcribed and divided into coded phrases; these 62 contained 24, 15, and 23 subjects from the LF, MF, and HF groups, respectively. Two coders then independently examined each protocol statement to determine which product dimensions the subject had used in her choice task. . . . The coders decided that the attribute was used for processing when examined in any of the following ways: attribute comparison process (e.g., attribute evaluation across brands), within-brand process (e.g., examining the attributes of a particular brand), and use of prior knowledge for evaluating attributes. . . .

Perceptual Category Breadth
The subject's satisfaction associated with each of the dimension's levels was used to measure per-

ceptual category breadth—the number of different satisfaction scale values that the subject assigned to the dimension's levels. The fewer the number of satisfaction categories used, the broader the breadth (Clayton and Jackson 1961). As the eight functional dimensions examined in this study differ in number of levels, the measure of breadth was standardized by dividing the number of categories assigned to a dimension by the number of levels of that dimension.

. . . A subject's standardized breadth scores on these dimensions were then averaged to measure her total category breadth. Using ANOVA, these scores (for the 62 protocol subjects) were then compared across the three familiarity groups. The mean values for the LF, MF, and HF groups were 0.66, 0.76, and 0.76, respectively (the smaller the value, the *broader* the breadth). As expected (Hypothesis 1), a significant difference does not exist between the MF and HF groups. It should also be noted that although not significant ($p < 0.16$), the directional differences between LF category breadth and that of MF and HF are as expected.

Reliance on Price and Brand Name
Hypotheses 2 through 2d are concerned with the difference of confidence in price and brand name among the three familiarity groups. These hypotheses were tested using responses to how confident a subject was in relying on the particular dimension in maximizing her overall satisfaction. . . . For brand the average confidence scores were 5.38, 4.79, and 5.85 for the LF, MF, and HF groups, respectively (7 = very confident, 1 = not confident at all). The LF, MF, and HF group averages for price were 5.19, 5.10, and 5.89, respectively. The DM at MF shows less confidence than DMs at either low or high familiarity levels in relying on brand-name information. This observation is consistent with Hypothesis 2a. Also, as expected, when confidence in the usage of price information is examined, the DM at MF shows significantly less confidence than the DM at HF ($p < 0.05$); on the other hand, no significant difference is noted between the MF and the LF decision makers. These observations are inconsistent with Hypothesis 2a. Perhaps the LF subjects do not perceive price as being

as useful an index of quality as is brand name (Park and Winter 1979).

An examination of the confidence scores for brand name and for price, as compared to those for the functional dimensions, reveals that the LF DM places higher confidence on the nonfunctional dimensions (5.36 average score for brand name and price) than on the functional dimensions (4.59 average for the eight functional dimensions). This contrast is statistically significant ($p < 0.003$) and supports Hypothesis 2b. On the other hand, the MF DM placed less confidence in her usage of price and brand name (mean score of 4.87) than on her usage of any of the functional dimensions (average score is 5.43); this difference is also significant ($p < 0.02$) and supports Hypothesis 2c. Finally, the HF DM appears to place as much confidence on price and brand name (average of 5.86) as on usage of the functional dimensions (average of 5.88).

· · ·

Decision Time

Hypothesis 3a states that in the choice-reduction decision stage, the MF DM would require a significantly longer time to complete the task than DMs at either LF or HF. An ANOVA on the decision times for subjects in the three familiarity groups supports this hypothesis at the 0.01 level; the mean decision times were 6.70, 9.38, and 7.72 for subjects in the LF, MF, and HF groups, respectively.

Hypothesis 3b, on the other hand, states that LF and MF decision makers will require significantly more time than the HF DM in the choice selection decision stage. To test Hypothesis 3b, an adjustment in the data base was made to nullify (or standardize) the effect that differing numbers of choice options would have on decision time comparisons across familiarity groups. As a result of this standardization, when ANOVA (Duncan's Multiple Range test) is used to compare the subsets on the basis of decision time, differences in decision time are a reflection of familiarity and not the number of options evaluated. The mean decision time for the LF, MF, and HF subsets were 2.43, 2.14, and 1.04, respectively ($p < 0.08$). Duncan's Multiple Range test showed the differences between the low and the high familiarity subsets and between the mod-

erate and the high familiarity subsets to be marginally significant ($p < 0.10$). No significant difference was found between the low and the moderate familiarity subsets. These findings marginally support Hypothesis 3b.

These findings are further supported by an examination of the perceived difficulty of the decision task. ANOVA across the three familiarity groups on the perceived difficulty of the decision task at the choice reduction stage showed that the LF DM perceived the task to be more difficult than did MF and HF decision makers ($p < 0.002$). Because of her perceived task difficulty, the LF DM is expected to greatly simplify her decision task, reducing the decision time from that which would be expected from looking at perceived task difficulty only.

However, ANOVA showed no significant difference among the three groups in the level of task difficulty.

Confidence in Decision

Hypothesis 4 states that a DM's confidence in her choice decision increases monotonically with her level of familiarity in each of the two choice tasks. Subject responses on confidence in the decision were analyzed through Duncan's Multiple Range test; the findings partially support the hypothesis.

Specifically, confidence increases monotonically with the level of familiarity. At the choice reduction stage, the monotonic increases in confidence between the LF and the MF groups and between the LF and the HF groups are both significant at the 0.05 level; no significant difference was noted between the MF and the HF groups. The monotonic increases in confidence with familiarity is also noted at the choice selection stage with the difference between the low and the high familiarity groups also significant at the 0.05 level. No significant difference, however, is noted between the low and the moderate familiarity groups. This suggests that the LF group is perhaps more confident than they should be, and the MF group is less confident than they should be.

Unlike subjects in other familiarity groups, the LF subjects expressed greater confidence in their choice reduction decision than in their decision at the choice selection stage. Although this difference is not significant at the 0.05 level, it seems to support the implications of previous discussion on the LF DM's choice processes at the two different choice tasks, i.e., more elaborate processing at the choice selection stage led the LF group to think that they chose the right brand no matter how low their perceived level of knowledge.

DISCUSSION

The decision biases and heuristics revealed by the three groups of subjects may be close approximations of those used by consumers at different stages of familiarity. . . .

These generalizations should, however, be made with some caution. Specifically, the present study and the study by Bettman and Park (1980), using the same design and subjects, were not able to address motivational differences among the three groups of subjects in terms of the degree of their prior interest in microwaves and the impact of this interest on the study's findings. These questions are important in view of the recent findings about the state-of-mind effect on utility formation and choice decision (Wright and Kriewall 1980).

It is highly likely that differences among the three groups exist in the subjects' enduring involvement (Rothshild and Houston 1980) or prior interest in the product. The LF subjects would have a lower prior interest in the product than the MF group who had some prior product-usage experience and relevant product-attribute information; the MF interest may have been heightened through receiving relevant information material. Similarly, the MF subjects would have a lower interest in the product than HF subjects who have actually purchased the product.

Did differences in enduring involvement (prior interest) affect the situational involvement (involvement with the experimental task)? A concern of particular interest could relate to the LF subjects. Could their low interest in the experimental task have affected the results (i.e., "I am not interested in microwave ovens, thus I'm not really interested in this 'choose a microwave oven' task."). Several of the study's findings do not appear to support this possible bias. If the LF subjects had little involve-

ment in the experimental task, they might simply have given up, using significantly fewer attributes and requiring a substantially shorter decision time than subjects in the MF and HF groups. However, comparison of the number of dimensions used in the choice-reduction stage revealed no significant difference among the three groups; the average number of dimensions used by the LF, MF, and HF subjects were 5.58, 6.60, and 6.04, respectively. Similarly, at the choice-selection stage, no significant difference among the groups was noted; at this stage the average number of dimensions used were 2.71, 2.58, and 2.68 for the LF, MF, and HF groups, respectively. Also, careful examination of the protocols revealed that most of the subjects in the LF groups tried to infer the meaning of various product attributes based on experience with other products, and lamented their lack of knowledge about microwave ovens (Bettman and Park 1980).

Decision-time comparisons among the three groups also do not appear to support the notion of a bias among the LF subjects. Although there was a significant difference in decision time at the choice-reduction stage between the LF and MF subjects, and between the MF and HF subjects, there was no significant difference between subjects in the LF and the HF groups. Furthermore, at the choice-selection stage, the LF group required the longest time to make a decision, whereas the HF subjects required the least. If the level of prior interest had influenced the subjects' decision during the experimental task, the reverse decision time order would have been expected. It should also be noted that the MF subject's motivation with the task could have been higher than that of the LF and HF subjects. It could be argued that this motivation rather than the subject's perceived knowledge systematically influenced the findings of this study and the Bettman and Park (1980) paper, which revealed more extensive processing by MF than by LF or HF subjects. However, an examination of the category breadth, decision time, and confidence analyses shows no evidence of a systematic bias.

Finally, given that there is no commonly accepted (or even proposed) conceptual definition of product familiarity, the results of this study should be interpreted in accordance with how the level of familiarity was operationalized. If, for example, the level of the DM's familiarity is defined differently, e.g., in terms of the amount of knowledge in long-term memory, a different set of research questions may be raised. To illustrate, investigation is needed into the information-acquisition process of decision makers at different familiarity levels. Particular attention needs to be placed on the cognitive processes that are initiated during exposure to communication stimuli and to the content and organization of the information acquired after exposure (Edell and Mitchell 1978; Mitchell 1980). Decision makers at different familiarity levels may reveal differences in encoding strategies for which category breadth is only a part. The decision makers may also differ in their abilities (and modes) to retrieve this information at a later point in time.

REFERENCES

Bennett, Peter D., and Harrell, Gilbert D. (1975), "The Role of Confidence in Understanding and Predicting Buyers' Attitudes and Purchase Intentions," *Journal of Consumer Research,* 2, 110–7.

Bettman, James R. (1979), *An Information Processing Theory of Consumer Choice,* Reading, MA: Addison-Wesley Publishing Co.

———, and Park, C. Whan (1980), "Effects of Prior Knowledge and Experience on Consumer Decision Processes: A Protocol Analysis," *Journal of Consumer Research,* 7, 234–48.

Bruner, Jerome S. (1957), "On Perceptual Readiness," *Psychological Review,* 64, 123–52.

———, and Tajfel, Henri (1961), "Cognitive Risk and Environment Change," *Journal of Abnormal and Social Psychology,* 62, 231–41.

Clayton, M. A., and Jackson, D. N. (1961), "Equivalence Range, Acquiescence and Overgeneralization," *Educational and Psychological Measurement,* 21, 371–82.

Edell, Julie A., and Mitchell, Andrew A. (1978), "An Information Processing Approach to Cognitive Response," in *Research Frontiers in Marketing: Dialogues and Directions,* ed. S. C. Jain, Chicago: American Marketing Association, pp. 178–83.

Hansen, Flemming (1972), *Consumer Choice Behavior: A Cognitive Theory,* New York: The Free Press.

Howard, J. A., and Sheth, Jagdish A. (1969), *The Theory of Buyer Behavior,* New York: John Wiley & Sons.

Kiesler, Charles A. (1966), "Conflict and Number of Choice Alternatives," *Psychological Reports,* 18, 603–10.

Lichtenstein, Sarah, and Fishhoff, Baruch (1977), "Do Those Who Know More Also Know More about How Much They Know?" *Organizational Behavior and Human Performance,* 20, 159–83.

Mitchell, Andrew A. (1980), "Cognitive Process Initiated by Exposure to Advertising," in *Information Processing Research in Advertising,* ed. Richard Harris, Hillsdale, N.J.: Lawrence Erlbaum Associates.

Park, C. Whan (1978), "A Conflict Resolution Choice Model," *Journal of Consumer Research,* 5, 124–37.

———, and Lessig, V. Parker (1977), "Judgmental Rules and Stages of the Familiarity Curve: Promotional Implications," *Journal of Advertising,* 6, 10–6.

———, and Winter, Frederick W. (1979), "Product Quality Judgment: Information Processing Approach," *Journal of the Market Research Society,* 21, 211–7.

Payne, J. W. (1976), "Task Complexity and Contingent Processing in Decision Making: An Information Search and Protocol Analysis," *Organizational Behavior and Human Performance,* 16, 366–87.

Pinson, Christian (1978), "Consumer Cognitive Styles," in *Marketing: Neue Ergebnisse aus Forschung und Praxis,* ed. E. Topritzhofer, Dusseldorf, Germany: Westdeutscher, Verlag.

Pollay, Richard W. (1970), "A Model of Decision Times in Difficult Decision Situations," *Psychological Review,* 77, 274–81.

Rothschild, Michael L., and Houston, Michael J. (1980), "Individual Differences in Voting Behavior: Further Investigations of Involvement," in *Advances in Consumer Research,* Vol. 7, ed. Jerry C. Olson, San Francisco: Association for Consumer Research.

Sheth, Jagdish N., and Venkatesan M. (1968), "Risk-Reduction Processes in Repetitive Consumer Behavior," *Journal of Marketing Research,* 5, 307–10.

Wright, Peter, and Kriewall, Mary Ann (1980), "State-of-Mind Effect on the Accuracy With Which Utility Functions Predict Marketplace Choice," *Journal of Marketing Research,* 17, 277–93.

HOW TO SOLVE PROBLEMS THAT DON'T MATTER: SOME HEURISTICS FOR UNINVOLVED THINKING

JOHN DEIGHTON

Source: John Deighton, "How To Solve Problems That Don't Matter: Some Heuristics for Uninvolved Thinking." *Advances in Consumer Research,* Vol. 10, 1983, 314–319. Published by the Association for Consumer Research.

ABSTRACT

What are the cognitive consequences of low involvement? A set of heuristics are identified which are hypothesized to be used in inferences on topics that do not matter. How might advertising influence this kind of inference? Three occasions are identified in the context of a model of heuristic-driven inquiry.

INTRODUCTION

. . .

In the long history of the involvement concept, the thrust of empirical work has been to contrast the consequences of high and low involvement. Zeigarnik (1932) for example found less recall of interrupted tasks that were involving than those that were not. . . . Ray (1973) proposed alternative hierarchies of response to persuasion for uninvolved and involved audiences. Thus the field has amassed a reasonably large body of research which treats involvement as a dichotomous or, at least, bipolar variable that mediates in a variety of contexts.

By contrast, little research has been done with the concept of low involvement as a state variable, tracing its antecedents and consequences. This focus holds, perhaps, more potential interest for marketing management than does work which simply articulates the high/low involvement distinction. Marketing, more than most disciplines, is concerned with the ordinary, the unimportant and the inconsequential in human behavior. Progress in understanding the structure of uninvolved thinking bears directly on some fundamental marketing concerns. One such concern is the problem of accounting for advertising's influence on consumers who have no active interest in the topic of the advertising.

This paper's focus is not the high/low involvement distinction, but rather the low involvement state. It is concerned with the cognitive consequences of low involvement. It proposes that inference under low involvement can be described by a limited number of well-defined heuristics which, while often yielding reasonably valid outcomes, are sometimes vulnerable to significant and predictable biases.

In particular, this paper hypothesizes a set of heuristics claimed to guide the uninvolved consumers' diagnostic inferences under the influence of advertising.

CASUAL DIAGNOSTIC INFERENCE

I use inference to refer to the kind of thinking that moves from beliefs to revised expectations in response to evidence. Inference includes reasoning as a special case, but embraces also those modes of thinking that are not accessible to introspection. Diagnostic or inductive inference is distinguished from deduction or fantasy by its use of evidence from sources exogenous to the inferor. Casual diagnostic inference is the thinking that accompanies the revision of expectations that have no important consequences for the thinker.

Hammond (1978) has drawn attention to the range of modes of inquiry that people use. He classified by the degree to which manipulation of variables is possible, identifying six strategies from formal experimentation through quasi-experimentation to unaided inquiry. Our domain is this latter end, where "interdependent variables must be disentangled sheerly by cognitive activity, that is, by reaching a judgment about what the results of disentanglement might be" (Hammond 1978). Brehmer (1980) has also noted the fact that, in the environment of everyday life, learning is complicated by multicollinearity. He observes that the reason we often do not learn from experience is that experience often gives us very little to learn from. The world seldom presents itself to us in the form of an experimental design, so that a given outcome will support many hypotheses.

These citations suggest an image of the consumer as a naive scientist, and suggest that the high and low involvement modes of inquiry may be represented by good and poor scientific practice. At one extreme the cognitive processes are those of the rigorous scientist: conceptualize, hypothesize, test by disconfirmation and hold beliefs tentatively and with consciousness of the evidence that supports them. The other extreme will be called sche-

matic inquiry. The schematic thinker classifies by stereotypes, invokes interpretive schemas, makes schema-consistent inferences and then acts on them. Beliefs are supported by recall of the schema, not the evidence, that supports them. . . . The contribution of this paper is to suggest that the short cuts of the naive scientist are points at which advertising operates.

Before the nature of that operation is set out, it is necessary to define what is meant by a naive theory or schema.

THE CONCEPT OF A SCHEMA

The audience for mundane advertising is seldom on the brink of buying. A model of advertising's effect therefore requires a view of how "ordinary" knowledge accumulates and is stored for later use. The schema theory of knowledge has some desirable properties in that regard.

The notion of a schema is long-established. It can be traced to Head (1920) and Piaget (1926), but its contemporary use is most compatible with Bartlett's (1932). Bartlett needed to explain the errors that occur in the recall of prose and drawings. He proposed that recall is reconstructive and quite inventive, drawing on a schema, "an active organization of past reactions, or of past experiences, which must always be supposed to be operating in any well-adapted organic response."

. . .

My use of the term owes most to Rummelhart and Ortony (1977) and Tesser (1978). In this view a schema is like an informal, unarticulated theory of the nature of events, objects or situations in the world. Information at the most concrete, perceptual level is organized into higher-order structures that form a hierarchy of schemata. Understanding, then, is finding a schema that fits the stimulus to be understood, and then using it to predict.

Schematic thinking begins with the adoption of a schema. The schema guides search and directs attention to certain features of the stimulus. It interprets ambiguous features. It directs the reconstruction of the stimulus in memory. It inserts default options in inference. The benefit of schematic thinking is that it makes the environment readily comprehensible and predictable. The cost is the risk of erroneous interpretation, inaccurate expectations and inflexible modes of response.

. . .

What, then, is the relevance of a schema to low involvement thinking? One answer lies in consumers' misapplication of schemata. As the next section of this paper will show, an interesting case occurs when an uninvolving choice is resolved by the use of a schema from some more involving domain.

ADVERTISING'S INFLUENCE ON INFERENCE

The central thesis of this paper is that low-involvement advertising—that which seeks to influence the outcomes of decisions of small consequence—does not work by offering compelling argument. Rather it channels inference in self-serving directions.

Effective advertising is sensitive to the heuristics that abound in everyday casual inference. It influences the path of thinking so that the consumer reaches a desired understanding with no sense that inquiry was exogenously directed.

Advertising's opportunities to influence the path

of inference can be recognized at three points (see Figure 1):

1. Advertising first may determine which interpretive schema is invoked to comprehend the problem that the consumer is addressing (the adoption phase).
2. Next advertising may relate a self-serving proposition or hypothesis to the adopted belief structure or schema (the assimilation phase).
3. Finally the induced expectations may be tested against experience, a process which is vulnerable to a predisposition to confirm (the confirmation phase).

The discussion that follows will expand on these three elements of advertising-directed inquiry.

1. Adoption of a Schema

I shall begin with an illustration of the capacity of choice among schemata to exert a persuasion–like influence on decisions, reported by Gilovich (1981). One of his experiments required students of political science to decide, on the facts given in a fictional scenario, whether the USA should intervene to defend a hypothetical small country against agression from a large neighbor. Two conditions of the scenario were used. In one, terms and phrases evocative of Vietnam were used, while the other used terms more associated with Munich.

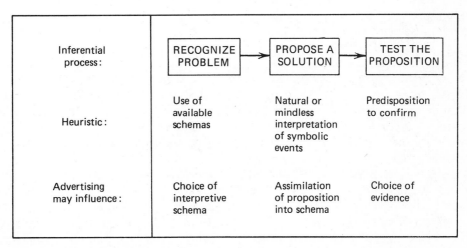

Figure 1 Advertising's influence on the path of inference under low involvement.

The manipulations were confined to trivial details, quite irrelevant to the question posed. For example in one scenario minorities were fleeing in boxcars, and in the other they used small boats. Respondents who read the Munich manipulation favored intervention significantly more often than those who read the Vietnam manipulation. Respondents denied subsequently that the allusions to past events had influenced at all their appraisal of the facts in the cases they had reviewed.

Similarly irrelevant but schema-evoking information influenced judgments in a study by Langer and Abelson (1974). They had professional therapist subjects listen to a recording of two men talking. One group was told the discussion was a job interview and another was told it was a psychiatric intake interview. The latter group judged the incidence of pathology in the interviewed person's conversation to be significantly higher than the former.

. . .

In . . . [these] studies, the subjects made inferences that depended on information other than that contained in the data. The direction of that 'going beyond the information given' (Bruner, Goodnow and Austin's (1959) definition of cognition) was set by inducing the subjects to choose one schema rather than another. Once chosen, the schemata filled several roles: they supplied default values for questions not answered in the data, they interpreted ambiguities and they directed attention within the data. These studies suggest that choice of the schema within which to make an inference is central to the outcome of thinking.

In going beyond the information in a problem to reach a solution, there is some interesting evidence that mere transient availability in memory of one or another schema is sufficient to secure its use. While this idea is not directly supported in the work of Tversky and Kahneman (1973), it is tested in some subsequent studies. Higgins, Rholes and Jones (1977) influenced subjects' interpretation of a personality profile by manipulating subjects' prior exposure to adjectives in an ostensibly unrelated memory test. Hornstein, Lakind, Frankel and Manne (1975) influenced behavior in a prisoner's

dilemma game by manipulating the content of a simulated radio program overheard before the game was played.

I am asserting that advertising does what the experimenters did in the studies just cited. It offers schemata within which consumers may pursue inquiry, for example, to predict future product performance or to diagnose the causes of past performance. Effective advertising determines the questions that are posed, even before it seeks to influence the answers that are found.

2. Assimilation to a Schema

What has been proposed thus far might be stated colloquially as 'advertising reminds the audience of what it believes'. Virginia Slims advertising reminds smokers that they believe smoking by women is liberating: Now cigarettes remind them about the hazards to health.

The advertiser, however, goes further. He chooses a schema so as to lend plausibility to a proposition which the advertiser seeks to establish either as the product of the consumer's inquiry or as a crucial intermediate conclusion. The proposition's face validity is inferred from its assimilation to the schema, just as an hypothesis is plausible if it can be deduced from a well-founded theory.

Consider how the idea that Michelob is a premium beer emerges from an advertisement in which four young men set it up as the prize in a game of tennis ("would four friends really go at it this hard just for a beer?"). To the extent that a viewer of the commercial comes to treat Michelob as a premium beer, he behaves as if the incident really happened. If a jury found an accused guilty because the prosecutor had him act out the crime, one would be surprised. Why should the manufacturers of Michelob expect this vignette to be more persuasive?

The explanation offered here is that assimilation in schematic thought is a less rigorous process than deduction in scientific thought. In particular, it fails to preserve the distinction between natural and symbolic events (Worth and Gross 1974). A symbolic event, in this conceptualization, is one whose meaning is inferred with full recognition of an intention to communicate. A natural event has meaning attributed to it without allowing for communicative intent. With the advertiser's motive discounted, Michelob's claim to be premium beer depends on inference from the "fact" that the beer served as a prize in a game, not on attribution of the advertiser's motive in simulating the event.

Is there evidence to support the idea that communication may be processed as a natural and not symbolic event? Langer (1978) argues that a good deal of social interaction is mindless. The mindless actor "interacts with the environment in a passive reactive fashion and fails to ask questions about the environment, fails to reconsider preformed categories and fails to seek new distinctions among stimuli" (Langer and Imber 1980).

. . .

. . . Langer, Blank and Chanowitz (1978) suggest that mindless behavior may be directed by well-learned scripts. If scripts are intended as a subset of schemata, (c.f. Abelson 1981), then this research provides the concepts for a model of the assimilation of advertising. Mindlessness is likely to be a relatively frequent condition for reception of advertising when the topics are banal, the consequences of choice are trivial, and the audience has no urgent use for the communication at the time it is received. In attributing meaning to the communication, its communicative intent will be disregarded. The advertised hypothesis will take its place within the schema suggested by the advertising without the critical thought that accompanies mindfulness. Virginia Slims will be understood as an appurtenance of liberation, without having supported the claim by any method other than "vivid" (Taylor and Thompson 1982) assertion.

3. Confirmation

The influence of advertising would be slight if it induced expectations that were not supported by experience. There is strong evidence, however, that naive inquiry is biased toward fulfilment of expectations. Two factors in particular favor this result: a bias toward confirmation and an insensitivity to covariance.

The confirmatory bias hypothesis claims that the naive investigator has a predisposition to confirm rather than to disconfirm: that evidence supporting an expectation increases the subjective probability of the expectation's truth by more than equal evidence contradicting the expectation will diminish it.

Strong evidence for this claim comes from Lord, Ross and Lepper (1979). Subjects previously classed as strongly for or against capital punishment were shown two contradictory studies on the topic. Belief in their positions was strengthened by the confirming study, but little affected by the disconfirming study. The effect was that mixed evidence, far from reducing confidence in opinions, polarized them.

. . .

For illustration, consider advertising which asserts that a cigarette's recessed filter tip eliminates the taste of tar. A confirmation test might be to ask whether the cigarette does taste of tar. If the smoker set out to disconfirm, he might rather ask whether other brands with the same tar level taste more of tar. Confirmatory tests foster an unjustifiably strong belief in the contribution of a recessed filter tip to eliminating the taste of tar.

One reason for the tendency for confirming diagnosis is given by Einhorn and Hogarth (1978): consumers in general will limit trial to those products they expect to do well. When they do so, provided that there is any correlation at all between the hypothesized cue and the outcome, they increase the proportion of successful outcomes above that which random trial would yield.

The second characteristic likely to impede naive inquiry is insensitivity to covariance. Beliefs depend on judgments about variance: causal statements imply covariation between causes and effects. Descriptive statements imply covariation among attributes, or low variance in repeated measures of one attribute. Whereas the attribution literature suggests in the main that people perform analysis of variance well, there is another research stream that points to predictable and substantial biases.

The basic work on the ability of subjects to recognize covariation was done by Smedslund (1963), Jenkins and Ward (1965) and Ward and Jenkins (1965) for 2×2 tables. The conclusion was that subjects measure covariation by counting joint occurrence of positive instances of an outcome and a cue. Thus what is perceived as covariation may be statistical independence or worse.

This kind of performance would be poor if there were no ambiguity in nature—if truth were manifest as it is in a paired associate learning test (c.f. Brehmer 1980). The situation is worse, however. We do not know what cues to attend to: we infer them. The consumer, armed with a seriously flawed sense of covariation, must decide not only whether great checkups really are related to Crest's kind of flouride, but whether flouride is the cue to use at all. Not only will the consumer tend to fail to make appropriate diagnoses but, more seriously, he will fail to recognize that inferences ostensibly drawn from experience actually derive from schema-induced expectations. Exogenously-induced persuasion will feel like learning from experience.

CONCLUSION

Barthes (1972), making a distinction similar to that in Worth and Gross (1974), observes that "what allows the reader to consume myth innocently is that he does not see it as a semiological system but as an inductive one."

This paper has attempted to elaborate that point into a perspective on the process of influence by advertising under low involvement. In this view, advertising first invokes a particular set of our beliefs (adoption), next relates an hypothesis to the adopted belief structure (assimilation) and finally (confirmation) depends on habits of inference to lead us to decide that what was plausible is in fact truth.

REFERENCES

Abelson, Robert P. (1981), "Psychological Status of The Script Concept," *American Psychologist,* 36, 715–729.

Barthes, Roland (1972), *Mythologies,* London: Jonathan Cape.

Bartlett, Frederick C. (1932), *Remembering: A Study in Experimental and Social Psychology,* Cambridge: Cambridge University Press.

Einhorn, Hillel, and Hogarth, Robin (1978), "Confidence in Judgment: Persistence of the Illusion of Validity," *Psychological Review,* 85, 395–416.

Gilovich, Thomas (1981), "Seeing the Past in the Present: The Effect of Association to Familiar Events on Judgments and Decisions," *Journal of Personality and Social Psychology,* 40, 797–808.

Hammond, Kenneth R. (1978), "Toward Increasing Competence of Thought in Public Policy Formation," in *Judgment and Decision in Public Policy Formation,* ed. K. R. Hammond, Denver: Westview.

Head, Henry (1920), *Studies in Neurology,* London: Frowde.

Higgins, E. Tory, Rholes, W. S., and Jones, C. R. (1977), "Category Accessibility and Impression Formation," *Journal of Experimental Social Psychology,* 13, 141–154.

Hornstein, H. A., LaKind, E., Frankel, G., and Manne, S. (1975), "Effects of Knowledge About Remote Social Events on Prosocial Behavior, Social Conception and Mood," *Journal of Personality and Social Psychology,* 32, 1038–1046.

Jenkins, Herbert M., and Ward, William C. (1965), "Judgments of Contingency Between Responses and Outcomes," *Psychological Monographs* 79, Whole No. 594.

Langer, Ellen (1978), "Rethinking the Role of Thought in Social Interaction," in eds. John Harvey, William Ickes, and Robert Kidd, *New Directions in Attribution Research,* Hillside, N.J.: Lawrence Erlbaum Associates.

Langer, Ellen J., and Abelson, Robert P. (1974), "A Patient by any Other Name . . . : Clinician Group Difference in Labelling Bias," *Journal of Consulting and Clinical Psychology,* 42, 4–9.

Langer, Ellen, Blank, Arthur, and Chanowitz, Benzion (1978), "The Mindlessness of Ostensibly Thoughtful Action: The Role of "Placebic" Information in Interpersonal Interaction," *Journal of Personality and Social Psychology,* 36, 635–642.

Langer, Ellen, and Imber, Lois (1980), "Role of Mindlessness in the Perception of Deviance," *Journal of Personality and Social Psychology,* 38, 360–367.

Lord, Charles, Ross, Lee, and Lepper, Mark (1979), "Biased Assimilation and Attitude Polarisation: The Effects of Prior Theories on Subsequently Considered Evidence," *Journal of Personality and Social Psychology,* 37, 2098–2109.

Piaget, Jean (1926), *The Lanugage and Thought of the Child,* London: Routledge and Kegan Paul.

Ray, Michael L. (1973), "Marketing Communications and the Hierarchy of Effects," in *New Models for Mass Communication Research Volume II,* ed. Peter Clarke, Beverly Hills: Sage.

Smedslund, Jan (1963), "The Concept of Correlation In Adults," *Scandanavian Journal of Psychology,* 4, 165–171.

Taylor, Shelley E., and Thompson, Suzanne C. (1982), "Stalking the Elusive 'Vividness' Effect," *Psychological Review,* 89, 155–181.

Tesser, Abraham (1978), "Self-Generated Attitudes Change," *Experimental Social Psychology,* Leonard Berkowitz, ed., 11, 289–325.

Tversky, Amos, and Kahneman, Daniel (1973), "Availability: A Heuristic for Judging Frequency and Probability," *Cognitive Psychology,* 5, 207–232.

Ward, William C., and Jenkins, Herbert M. (1965). "The Display of Information and The Judgment of Contingency," *Canadian Journal of Psychology,* 19, 231–241.

Worth, Sol, and Gross, Larry (1974), "Symbolic Strategies," *Journal of Communication,* 4, 27–39.

Wyer, Robert S. (1974), *Cognitive Organization and Change: An Information Processing Approach,* Potomac: Erlbaum.

Zeigarnik, B. (1932), "On Finished and Unfinished Tasks," in *A Source Book on Gestalt Psychology,* ed. W. D. Ellis, New York: Humanities Press.

SECTION XIII

SENSORY EXPERIENCES AND CONSUMER BEHAVIOR

Consumers receive information about the world through their senses. The first experience with a product or a store is based upon stimuli received and processed by the senses. Marketers would therefore like to know something about the way people receive, transform, and organize information that the senses pick. How, for example, does the sensory environment of a store (colors, shapes, smells, lights, music, etc.) affect the shopper's senses and ultimately his or her behavior?

Although the receptors and channels are different for each sense, the processing is similar in concept and consists essentially of six steps: stimulus generation, stimulus reception, stimulus transformation, electrical transmission, information processing, and stimulus interpretation. Research has shown, however, that different parts of the brain may process qualitatively different kinds of information. The left hemisphere is responsible for cognitive activity based upon verbal or symbolic representation. It dominates people's abilities to use logic. The right hemisphere processes visual and auditory information and allows people to respond intuitively.

To see one example of how information concerning sensory experiences can aid marketers, simply consider the following proposition:

- Impulse buying may be the result of a choice based on visual information about a product rather than on written information about the product.

In other words, depending upon the product objectives, advertising may be designed in many cases to appeal to one hemisphere of the brain rather than the other. Examining the field of sensory processing can therefore often prove very useful to marketers.

"ACTIVATION RESEARCH: PSYCHOBIOLOGICAL APPROACHES IN CONSUMER RESEARCH"

Psychobiology is a science that examines the relationship between behavior and physiological processes of the nervous system, particularly processes of the brain. An important field within psychobiology focuses on activation, which may be described as arousal, inner tension, or alertness. Activation provides energy to an organism and thus is responsible for psychological and motor activity. Much activation research has addressed issues directly relevant to the study of consumer behavior.

Kroeber-Riel introduces the theory and measurement of activation. Theory states that increasing activation will lead to improved psychological response. He examines this hypothesis in the context of response to consumer advertising. Advertisements that can stimulate greater activation should result in quicker and more accurate acquisition and storage of information contained in the ad.

The findings of this research show that higher activation leads to greater recall. (Also of interest is the discussion of elements one can include in ads to stimulate higher activation.) The author cautions, however, that one must be careful to insure that the information that the consumer processes is actually the information that the marketer wished to convey. With proper care, marketers can apply these findings not only to advertising but also in such areas as product labels or packaging.

"USING BACKGROUND MUSIC TO AFFECT THE BEHAVIOR OF SUPERMARKET SHOPPERS"

Nearly everyone can recall having shopped at one time or another in a store that provided background music. It has generally been assumed that such music encourages some desired behavior in employees and/or customers. Store managers may hope, for example, that the proper music will encourage buying. However, Milliman points out that much research examining music in such situations is actually measuring attitudes or beliefs. Since it has been well established that the relationship between attitudes and behavior is weak, managers should not rely upon these studies if they are interested primarily in the impact of music on behavior. Other studies that do look directly at behavior may not have controlled variables other than music, so that they are not reliable.

Only a few studies in fact tell the manager anything about how music can affect behavior, so Milliman has designed research that will yield such information. He examines three hypotheses: that fast tempo, slow tempo, or no music will significantly affect:

- The pace of in-store traffic flow.
- The daily gross sales volume.
- The customer's awareness of background music.

The results indicate that the different tempos of music (including no music) produced no significant differences in awareness of the music (or lack of it). The experiment did clearly show, however, that the different music treatments affect the traffic pace and the sales volume. These results are immediately relevant to managers interested in the effects of music on shopping behavior.

ACTIVATION RESEARCH: PSYCHO-BIOLOGICAL APPROACHES IN CONSUMER RESEARCH

WERNER KROEBER-RIEL

Source: Werner Kroeber-Riel, "Activation Research: Psycho-biological Approaches in Consumer Research," *Journal of Consumer Research,* Vol. 5, March, 1979, pp. 240–250. Reprinted with permission.

Psychobiology is an interdisciplinary branch of research incorporating the findings of biology, physiology (neurophysiology, in particular), and psychology. It has also been termed neuropsychology and psychophysiology. In simplified terms, psychobiology can be described as a science concerned with the relationship between behavior and the physiological processes of the nervous system—in particular, those taking place in the brain.

Psychobiological explanations are generally based on the findings of experiments in which brain activity is taken as the independent variable and behavior as the dependent variable: sometimes this is reversed. Brain activity is manipulated by physical intervention (brain lesions) or by external stimulation. Usually the following processes are taken as dependent variables: learning, activation and attention, emotion and motivation, sleeping and dreaming, as well as the interacting effects between these processes. Both the independent variables (brain activity) and the dependent variables (behavior) are usually measured by physiological indices.

Typical questions posed by researchers in psychobiology include:

- How are stimuli aimed at a person's receptors converted into inner signals, transported along nerve pathways, and processed in the central nervous system?
- Why do these stimuli create emotions?
- How are physiological processes, conscious experiencing, and behavior linked together during emotional processes?

In answering questions of this kind, psychobiology has made it clear that psychological processes originate from physiological ones, and that behavior evolves according to biological laws. This is what Thompson (1975, p. 7) is alluding to when he tersely states, "Man is an animal. This simple fact is all too often ignored in psychology." Yet, "Man is a unique animal—an obvious fact all too often ignored in biology."

This also implies certain fundamental insights for consumer research. For example, to a large extent the consumer responds automatically, according to biologically determined patterns of behavior.[1] Almost like an animal, s/he can be manipulated by classical conditioning. In short, there are biological limits imposed on "consumer sovereignty"—on the person's deliberate and conscious control of his/her behavior. In consumer research there is a tendency to overlook this fact, for the following reasons:

1. The "cognitive revolution" in psychology (McGuire 1976, p. 314) has given priority to investigations into cognitive processes; that is, into the processing of information. Yet in the field of consumer research, psychobiological knowledge has not advanced as far as it has in the study of human drives (emotions, motivations).

2. Ideological barriers stand in the way. Considering the enthusiasm with which proponents of consumerism are trying to make consumer sovereignty a reality, mention of natural (biological) limits to this sovereignty can only be embarrassing. [Who wants to have the (easily acquired) reputation of denying the consumer's sovereignty?]

3. Psychobiological research demands many years of experience, entailing considerable expenditure for laboratory equipment.

4. In consumer research there are preconceived notions against the application of psychobiological methods, because in market research psychobiological measurements are often interpreted incorrectly, as discussed in a later section.

In this paper we outline the significance and applicability of psychobiological findings and methodology for consumer research, drawing upon activation research carried out at the Institut für Konsum- und Verhaltensforschung (Institute for Consumer and Behavioral Research) at the University of the Saarland, Germany.

ACTIVATION RESEARCH: A PSYCHOBIOLOGICAL APPROACH

Theoretical Basis

Activation, like cognition, is a basic variable of human behavior. It can also be described as arousal, inner tension, or alertness. Activation provides the organism with energy and is responsible for the psychological and motor activity of the organism. In neurophysiological theories, the way in which activation comes about and its effects are described as the result of physiological processes in the central nervous system.

Activation is provoked by stimulating a subcortical unit known as the reticular activation system (RAS). The RAS consists of the *formatio reticularis,* and is located, roughly speaking, in the brain stem. The limbic system, closely interrelated to the reticular system, also takes part in this activation process.

Excitement is triggered in the RAS by impulses directly evoked from external stimuli (arriving at the *formatio reticularis* via collateral connections) or from other areas of the central nervous system. For example, the sight of a product can activate the RAS in the same way as might a thought process. The arousal, first released in the RAS, travels to other functional units of the brain, alerting them to take a stand-by position. Figuratively speaking, the RAS awakens the other cortical units, spurring them to activity. By this chain of reactions, the RAS becomes a chief regulator of central nervous system activities.

In addition, the RAS is linked to the cerebral cortex in a variety of ways, and can therefore alert the upper areas of the brain.[2] It is in these upper cerebral areas that the processing of information takes place (perception, thought, memory). Physiological investigations have proven that processes

[1] In this connection, one should think above all of automatic responses in the affective and cognitive domain. See, for example, the remarks of Staats and Staats (1957) and Staats (1968) on the classical conditioning of emotional dispositions, or those by Shiffrin and Schneider (1977) on automatic information processing. Reference to activation by means of "manipulative" stimuli and the influence of activation on cognitive performance can also be classified among the responses that occur automatically.

[2] Actually, it would be more accurate to call it the ARAS (ascending reticular activation system). This is the term used for that part of the RAS that works in cooperation with the cortex.

of arousal in the RAS have the effect of increasing the overall cortical processing of information.[3]

As a result of directly provoking arousal processes in the RAS, there is an increase in the processing of information. The relationships between arousal processes in the RAS and information processing in the cortex are expressed by the ∩-hypothesis (the inverted ∪-hypothesis): moving from low activation to an optimum activation level, an individual's performance increases. Beyond the optimum level, however, increasing activation leads to lower performance scores. (By performance we are referring to any psychological or motor performance of the individual.)

This ∩-hypothesis, however, is little more than a highly obvious assumption. Transferring the ∩-hypothesis to the realm of consumer behavior in communication and decision making leads to a host of important questions that have received little attention in previous research. It is still, for example, an open question whether there are situations in which the strength of arousal is so great that cognitive performance is substantially impeded. For example this might be the case for the consumer who is suffering under the burden of very strong conflicts or is under stress, such as severe time pressure.

In operationalizing the ∩-hypothesis, it is important to distinguish between two forms of activation:

1. Long-lasting, tonic level of activation.
2. Briefer, phasic activation.

In the course of daily rhythm, tonic activation fluctuates between mild arousal (e.g., during sleep or boredom) and very intense arousal (e.g., during a fit of rage). The level rises and falls slowly, and is governed primarily by the individual's emotional and motivational state. When, for example, Hebb (1972, p. 199) talks of the ∩-hypothesis as the "relation of the effectiveness with which stimuli guide behavior to the level of arousal," or when

Krech and Crutchfield (1974) describe the ∩-hypothesis as the relationship between "degree of motivation and problem-solving efficiency," they are referring to tonic activation.

The individual's level of activation stimulates his/her entire performance: a rise in tonic activation encourages the processing of information in general, affecting the processing of any stimulus. We leave open the question of the validity of the ∩-hypothesis for tonic activation, because in the following remarks we intend to limit our observations to phasic activation.

At a given level of activation there are also brief periods (usually a matter of seconds) when activation again fluctuates. These short-term variations have been called phasic activation—changes in excitement that determine an individual's performance in processing single stimuli. Phasic activation is thus a short-term fluctuation in activation. It appears in attention responses and in orienting responses, and serves to sensitize the organism to the pick-up and processing of stimuli. It remains unclear to what extent the ∩-hypothesis also holds true for phasic activation, because a distinction between tonic and phasic activation is seldom made in presentations that deal with the ∩-hypothesis. Schönpflug (1968) explicitly relates the ∩-hypothesis to tonic and phasic activation, but is skeptical regarding the ∩-hypothesis as it relates to the interconnections between phasic activation and information retention.

In light of the lack of empirical findings on the destructive effects of very strong phasic activation on performance, and in view of the fact that an extremely strong phasic activation is unlikely in consumer behavior, we formulate the following basic hypothesis:

BH: The higher the phasic activation triggered by a specific stimulus, the more efficient will be the processing of the information mediated by this stimulus.

Operational Bases

Apart from examining the human brain through surgery for brain injuries, etc., direct (micro-) observation of brain activity (cellular activity) is not

---

[3]The physiologically present and measurable strength of activation (arousal) directly influences cortical activity. The interconnection between activation and cognitive performance (efficiency), described in a later section, takes place independent of the subjective (qualitative) interpretation of activation, in Schachter's sense (1975).

feasible. We are, therefore, dependent on indices obtainable without injury to the brain, which shed light on brain activity and on related psychological processes. The indices can be measured on three levels:

- Physiological-organic.
- Reported subjective experiences.
- Observed behavior.

Physiological methods seem to be the most valid in determining activation, because physiological responses are universal; that is, they always occur when the organism is aroused or when there is a change in the level of activation. This is not true for directly observable motor activities. For example, a person reading a book shows no external signs of his constantly changing activation responses to particularly exciting passages. Neither do subjective experiences verbally expressed by the individual sufficiently reflect variations in activation. We do know, though, that physiological methods are the most accurate in detecting slight (yet still influential for behavior) changes in activation that are not subjectively perceived at all.

If we use verbal methods to measure activation or processes of arousal in the brain, we are only making a needless detour. We will be measuring the perception of responses in the nervous system, when the responses themselves can be measured directly. Besides, verbal statements are tremendously influenced by cognitive processes. Often the subject being interviewed is neither able nor willing to divulge his/her excitement when, for example, his/her self-esteem is at stake. A psychophysiological investigation carried out by Kroeber-Riel, Barg, and Bernhard (1975) into the stimulating effect of political slogans demonstrated that although the subjects claimed to be highly moved by noble political ideals (such as justice and equal opportunity), physiological measurements and data yielded by experiments suggested that in reality they were stirred only to a slight extent by such ideals. Summarizing these and other arguments discussed in the literature on measuring activation, Schönpflug (1969) maintains that physiological indices are a sensitive and valid measurement of activation levels and changes.

The physiological indices can be divided into the following areas: (1) electrophysiological, (2) blood circulation, respiration, and energy expenditure, and (3) biochemical. Electrophysiological indices are the most revealing; they reflect bioelectric processes. Sensors (electrodes) are attached to a person's skin, which receive bioelectric body impulses. These signals are then converted, usually after being amplified, into digital values. An instrument called a polygraph records analogous values in the form of curves. Figure 1 shows part of one of these curves with the parameters used for the analysis.

The electrophysiological indices reflect either responses of the central nervous system (central indices) or those of the peripheral nervous system (peripheral indices). Responses in the central and peripheral nervous systems constitute an integrated system, so that peripheral responses, too, are able to shed light on the processes in the central nervous system.

The electroencephalogram (EEG) is a central index, which measures rhythmic fluctuations of the electric potential in the brain. It is probably the most versatile and sensitive procedure for detecting arousal, but involves expensive laboratory apparatus, as activation research (in contrast to the medical use of the EEG) requires complex data analysis by means of computer.

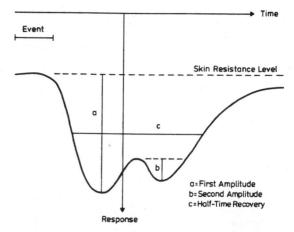

Figure 1 Polygraph curve with parameters of computation.

An example of a peripheral index is the electrodermal response (EDR), most commonly termed galvanic skin response (GSR) or skin resistance reaction (SRR). This index reflects changes in the electric resistance of the skin associated with activation processes. Extensive tests of the validity and reliability of the EDR have yielded satisfactory results. At the present time, the EDR is the most frequently applied activation index.

The activation rates cited in this paper were detected by measuring the EDR. A small electric current of constant intensity is sent into the skin through electrodes attached to the palmar side of the fingers. The changes in voltage observed between the electrodes indicate the amplitude of skin resistance, and are plotted in Figure 1. Each curve shows, first, the level of activation (the level prior to a phasic fluctuation) and second, the phasic fluctuation itself. The latter is termed the "response segment" of the curve and is rated by means of various parameters (e.g., amplitude, half-time recovery). We use amplitudes as the basis for digital ratings—either the amplitude of the first response or the sum of all the amplitudes released by one stimulus. The measurement of EDR is based on:

1. Amplitude of an EDR to a corresponding stimulus.
2. Skin resistance level before stimulus presentation.

These two scores are related to each other to eliminate individual differences due to different initial resistance levels that influence the range of the EDR. We call this relation RELAMP (RELative AMPlitude). The logarithm of RELAMP tends to produce a normal distribution, necessary for a parametric statistical test (Craig and Wood 1971, Fletcher 1971).

EMPIRICAL WORK

The experimental research at our Institute served primarily to test the preceding hypothesis. Activation is taken as the independent variable, the consumer's performance (that is, his/her processing of information) as the dependent variable.

Variables

Independent variable. A person can be aroused by exposure to certain stimuli in the same way that s/he is stimulated by "drugs" (such as coffee, adrenalin, etc.). The stimuli most likely to have an impact are those that evoke innate reactions. These function to a large extent automatically. Color and erotic appeal are examples of this type of stimulus (Berlyne 1960). By exposing a subject to them, the independent variable, activation, can be manipulated systematically.

In the investigations reported here, advertisements were used as arousing stimuli. By planning the advertising copy and illustration accordingly, activation was evoked in exact dosages. In preliminary experiments, stimulating material was selected so that the variance between individuals would be relatively low. The success of manipulating the independent variable was determined by measuring the evoked changes in activation by means of the EDR (represented by RELAMP scores).

Dependent variable. A consumer's overall processing of information may be seen as his total performance. We can divide this performance into parts. Thus, partial performances would be his pick-up, processing, and storing of the information (as well as even smaller partial performances, such as short- and long-term storage). Each of these separate, partial performances is, in its own way, determined by activation. Activation influences the *level* of the performance, not its *content*. The dependent variable, performance, has thus also been termed "behavioral efficiency."

When we say that, based on our hypotheses, activation will result in "better" perception, this means that perception will be quicker, or more accurate, always regardless of *what* is perceived. This is an important stipulation for application purposes: increased activation does not necessarily imply more effective manipulation of the consumer. As an example, suppose that the message projected by an advertisement does not fulfill its purpose; that is, the advertisement evokes cognitive processes that work counter to the advertising aim. Activation will still promote the processing of a message, even though it counteracts the original intention of the advertiser.

In the experiments reported here, two elements of information processing were singled out as dependent variables:

- Pick-up of information.
- Storage of information.

The theoretical background for our conception of these information processes is provided by the so-called "multi-store"-memory system, described by Lindsay and Norman (1977, with more references to literature). The pick-up of information is defined as the transfer of a sensory input into the short-term memory (STM) for further processing. Information acquisition can be operationalized by measuring eye movement: recording the eye-movement patterns during exposure to advertisements shows which elements of the advertisement the eyes are fixed upon. Only these elements are picked up and transferred to the STM for further processing.

Fixations can thus be used as indices for the pick-up of information. In our projects the BIO-METRICS Eye-Movement Monitor was used, which functions according to the cornea reflex method.

Long-term storage of information can be determined in various ways by recall and recognition tests. For our purposes, we administered recall tests approximately 20 minutes and 24 hours after the information had been received. As no significant differences were noticed between the relative scores obtained in these two recall tests (recall scores at a certain degree of arousal in comparison to the scores of another degree), we shall refer here to the 20-minute recall data.

Experimental research into activation demands particularly accurate control of the artifacts that, in addition to being independent variables, can also influence activation. These factors may be related to the particular person being tested (his/her introversion/extraversion), the stimulus material (subject's interest in the advertised product, the sequence in which the stimuli are exposed), or the situation (time of day, temperature of the room). A large number of possible artifacts (also affecting the dependent variable, the consumer's performance) must be eliminated or controlled.

Experimental Findings

In an investigation by Witt (1977), the 60 students who served as subjects were shown advertisements on a projection screen for a standardized duration of six seconds. Each advertisement was of similar design, with the same slogan, brand names, copy, and kind of illustration. By modifying the illustration (illustrated person wearing less, thus achieving more erotic stimulus), mild and intense arousal was created. Four advertisements, each in one mild and one intense version, were projected—totalling eight advertisements. The subject's eye movement was recorded during each exposure.

A manipulation check demonstrated that three of the more intense versions (with the erotic illustration) had stimulated considerably higher activation than their milder counterparts ($p \leq 0.01$). Only Advertisement 2 did not produce significant differences between the two versions. The reason for this was a technical defect in Advertisement 2 (poor quality of the picture).

The frequency of eye fixation serves as a dependent variable. This frequency was determined separately for the pictorial elements that evoked the activation, and for the textual elements. The figures in Table 1 refer to frequency of fixations on the arousing pictorial elements of the advertisement, and indicate the subject's pick-up of information. Even if we include Advertisement 2 in our computations, we still conclude that higher activation increases the frequency of fixations, from an average of 3.9 to 5.5.

These findings substantiate the preceding hypothesis (BH): stronger activation will promote the pick-up of information. Here the question arises whether activation really is the independent variable in the relationship between activation and the frequency of fixations. This is presumed to be true because according to psychobiological findings the activation potential of a stimulus determines the viewer's orientation reaction and consequently eye behavior. The activation called forth by the pic-

Table 1 Activation and acquisition of information from an advertisement illustration

| Advertisement | Frequency of fixation | | Level of significance (t-test) | df^a |
	A-version	B-version		
1 A/B	3.0	6.0	.01	58
2 A/B	4.6	4.3	—	58
3 A/B	3.4	6.0	.01	58
4 A/B	4.7	5.7	.05	58
Average 1–4	3.9	5.5	.01	238

Source: Witt (1977, p. 85).
$^a df$ = discriminant function.
NOTE: The figures indicate the frequency of fixations for illustrations with low activation potential (A-version) and with high activation potential (B-version). Each version was presented to 30 subjects.

torial elements of the advertisement had no influence on the fixation of the textual elements. There was approximately the same fixation frequency on the text in all of the ads. Thus, the activation effect was not transferred to the entire ad. This finding will be examined in greater detail later in a comparison with the results of the next experiment.

Another finding yielded by Witt's testing of recall corroborates the empirically supported hypothesis (Loftus 1972, Tversky 1974, Bernhard 1978): the more frequently a person fixes his/her eyes upon a stimulus, the better s/he will recall it. Elements of the advertisement upon which a person fixes his/her eyes more frequently are thus recalled better. The correlations between these two variables, however, are not particularly high, ranging from 0.3 to 0.4. A closer relationship exists between the duration of fixation and recall of the advertisement elements.

Barg (1977) concerned himself exclusively with the relationship between activation and recall, using advertisements similar to those just described. He examined the impact of an advertisement, modifying its illustration so that he could distinguish between these different degrees of activation. The activation was ascertained in the pre-

liminary experiment by means of verbal judgments. The ads were classified in terms of "weak," "average," and "strong" activation. The EDR measurements showed that the differences between the activating ability of Ads 1 and 2 were substantially less than the differences between Ads 2 and 3 (Table 2).

A total of 84 male students participated in the study. After exposure to the advertisements, there was a measurement of the short retention, followed by a change of room and a subsequent interview. After the interview, and at least 20 minutes after the presentation of the material, the long retention was measured by means of a structured recall. This recall measurement was checked once again after an interval of 24 hours, and no significant deviations were found. For purposes of recall, the subjects were presented with sheets that indicated the schematic structure of the ads, and were asked to fill in the elements they recalled. A point score was then tabulated for these elements, and is presented in Table 2 both for the activating pictorial elements and the ad as a whole.

Among the controlled variables were age (no significant correlation, corresponding to the findings of Mundy-Castle and McKiever 1953), extraversion (no significant correlation, corresponding to the findings of Perry 1971; for diverse results, see Eysenck 1977), and the influence of the time of day (no significant correlation; but note that the relativized phasic activation, not the tonic activa-

Table 2 Activation and recall for three illustrated advertisements

Item	1 (Weak activation)	2	3 (Strong activation)	Significance level (F test)
Activation score	0.95	1.05	1.38	.01
Recall score A Pictorial elements	1.22	1.39	2.48	.01
Recall score B All elements	4.28	4.49	6.77	.01

Source: Barg (1977).

tion, was measured). A large number of additional interfering variables were eliminated by keeping them constant (Barg 1977).

The findings conform with the hypothesis: higher activation leads to higher recall values. A smaller increase in recall values also corresponds to the smaller difference in activation between Ads 1 and 2. The increase in the recall values is related to the activating pictorial elements and to the text, and thus to the entire ad. The findings also lend support to a number of psychological studies in which, however, much simpler stimuli were used (see Eysenck 1976).

There is a discrepancy between the findings of Barg and Witt. In both instances, the activating advertisement elements (Element A-illustration of the ads) were processed better. The processing of the remaining ad elements (Element B-slogan, brand name) was, on the other hand, not promoted by higher activation in the experiment by Witt. This is in keeping with our basic hypothesis, which states that the activation elicited by a stimulus only benefits the processing of *this* stimulus.

Nonetheless, under certain conditions the activation provoked by Element A may promote the processing of the information contained in Element B. Witt (1977, p. 116) was the first to formulate this condition in a more precise manner: if the content of one activating element is coordinated or integrated into another (non-activating) element, the activating effect of the first element will enhance the processing of information contained in the second. In other words, when the elements are integrated and one element has the potential to stimulate more activation, the entire advertisement will be better retained. This condition was not present in Witt's experiment, but was fulfilled in Barg's experiment (Barg 1977, p. 139). As a result, the higher activation there, which was evoked by the pictorial elements, also stimulated recall of the textual elements, and thus benefited the entire ad.

Practical Implications

These experimental findings have important implications for advertising. Advertisements that fail to arouse will have no effect, as the information conveyed by the advertisement will not be pro-

cessed efficiently. The more advertising arouses, the more prepared the target audience is to respond, i.e., to pick up, process, and store the information presented.

Strong activation stimulates processing of information transmitted independent of whether this information is effective or not in terms of the advertising goal. In other words, activation is a necessary condition for advertising impact, but it is by no means a sufficient condition. Activation contributes only if the advertising message is processed in such a manner as to guide the decision process of the consumer in the desired direction. It is not sufficient to evaluate simply the activating effectiveness to determine the impact of an advertisement. In addition, the cognitive effects must always be examined and rated. The arousal potential of an advertisement, however, should be seen in terms of both tonic and phasic activation.

If the advertisement succeeds in provoking a lasting increase in the consumer's level of activation, that is, a rise in his tonic activation, this will affect overall performance in processing information. An increase in tonic activation level then promotes the processing of all stimuli, regardless of which elements created the increase. This type of tonic change in activation level will be brought about most successfully if longlasting emotional or motivational tensions are evoked by strong stimuli.

If the advertisement arouses only short-term, phasic activation, the effect will usually be limited to stimuli that provoked the phasic activation. Because it is difficult to predict with any certainty the influence of an advertisement on the consumer's activation *level*, the easiest way to increase its impact is to expose the most important information (key informative elements) in an arousing form. In this way, the key elements will evoke phasic activation. Berlyne (1960) deals with the properties that a stimulus must possess to evoke phasic activation and to spur on the processing of information. In this connection, it should be noted that extremely pronounced and striking stimuli can have cognitive side-effects that reduce the acceptance of the advertising (Peterson and Kerin 1977).

Illustrations are particularly useful in arousing the consumer. For this reason, it is advantageous to communicate the message as much as possible through pictures. If this is not possible, and if pictures are used only to stir an initial arousal, the less arousing areas of the copy will only be processed more efficiently if the activating (pictorial) and non-activating (copy) elements are integrated with each other, by either content or some other association. Deliberately aimed arousal and stimulation can be dispensed with if the consumers are already aroused and thus more receptive toward what is being solicited. This would apply when the consumers are actively seeking information.

BENEFITS OF ACTIVATION RESEARCH FOR CONSUMER RESEARCH

First, we inquire about the value of the findings presented here for psychophysiological activation research. Our hypotheses distinguish between tonic and phasic activation. Such a distinction has important consequences: tonic activation reflects a general disposition, while phasic activation reflects a disposition that is specifically stimulus-related. Nevertheless, this distinction is not made consistently enough in the literature. Investigations into the influence of activation on cognitive performance are sometimes related to both tonic activation (e.g., stimulated by white noise) and phasic activation (e.g., stimulated by emotional words) without further differentiation. Moreover, our investigations deviate from lines of basic psychophysiological research in so far as we make use of more complex stimulus material (printed advertisements). Our findings should be viewed as a further contribution to the study of the still controversial interconnections between activation and information processing (in its broadest sense).

Next, we consider the value of activation research for consumer research. Activation research can be regarded as a veritable paradigm of psychobiological research, which is concerned with gaining insight into intervening variables of consumer behavior by using biological responses, such as the EDR or eye movement. The systematic transference of this area of research to the field of consumer research satisfies the desideratum expressed by Ferber that there must be "interdisciplinary re-

search in consumer behavior" (Ferber 1977, p. 189).

With the aid of the concept of activation, it is possible to reduce a number of very different problems in consumer research to a common denominator. The fact that more strongly aroused and alert consumers react "better" involves a broad range of different situations and circumstances: for example, the stimulating effect exerted by store windows on the consumer's search for information and information pick-up, the influence of the activating potential of packaging or product design on perception, the effects of conflicts or other arousal states on decision behavior, etc.

Since activation expresses the intensity of affective processes, psychobiological activation measurements can be used to measure the strength of emotions, motives, and attitudes. These can replace other less valid methods. The measuring and explanation of emotional and motivational behavior according to psychobiological guidelines, e.g., as Buck (1976) advocates, is a modern alternative to classical motivation research. This might help to overcome the stagnation in which motivation research now finds itself due to the psychoanalytical approach of Dichter (1964) and to its present, one-sided cognitive way of looking at problems.

It should be borne in mind that the advertising studies reported here encompass only one area of the practical application for activation research. We are interested in other applications as well: thus, Trommsdorff (1978) was able to conclude that arousing labels tempt the consumer to reach for the product more often. In each instance, it is a matter of arousing the consumer by deliberately stimulating him in doses, thus increasing the chances for information to be communicated more efficiently.

The insights of activation research are also noteworthy from the point of view of consumer policy. The consumer often reacts to activating stimuli automatically, without being able to control his behavior. Activation, then, is a means of manipulation from which the consumer is not able to escape. Kroeber-Riel (1977a,b) discusses the consequent implications for consumer policy.

Nevertheless the question arises whether psychobiological research is nothing but an "exotic orchid" of research—whether its applicability and significance are severely limited. In answering this question, a distinction should be made between the use of psychobiological measuring methods and the theoretical knowledge gained by these methods.

It is indeed true that psychobiological measurements are costly and awkward, requiring expensive equipment and expertise. For the most part the researcher is dependent on a laboratory as well as on people's willingness to come to the laboratory—limitations that prevent wide use of these measuring methods. The fact remains, however, that psychobiological measurements are in many cases considerably more valid than other methods, and are thus indispensable for scientific research. This is particularly so when measuring psychological processes that the subject is not conscious of or cannot easily verbalize. (These processes cannot be ignored just because they are difficult to measure.) Moreover, psychobiological methods of measurement have practical implications: they can help validate simplified and more economic methods, such as verbal measurements of attention, which would create a basis for the use of more simplified measurements.

On the theoretical aspect—the limited applicability of psychobiological methods does not mean that the knowledge gained thereby must be put to only limited use. Thus, the most direct and valid measure of pick-up (acquisition) of information is to record eye movements. Undoubtedly, this is a costly psychobiological method and hardly suitable for wide use. By recording eye movements, relationships between activation and information acquisition, or relationships between acquisition and recall of information, can be determined, as shown earlier. These relationships are highly significant for explaining and influencing consumer behavior. The same holds true for the theoretical findings gained by EDR measurements on the relationship between activation (arousal, strength of emotion) and human information processing. Apart from these considerations, psychobiological research can contribute greatly to broadening and substantiating psychological research.

To look into the future, we are beginning a series of experiments using a thermo-vision-system: we assume that the thermographs of a human face, which are obtained by using infrared detectors, can be used to record changes in the level of activation. As it is possible to make thermographs by thermo-vision at a distance—unobserved by the subjects—the possibility exists for a new *nonreactive* method of measuring activation. Using this technique, we hope to be able to measure the strenth of affect in field situations, i.e., during collective decision processes or during conflict behavior at the cash register.

REFERENCES

Barg, Claus-Dieter (1977), "Measurement and Effects of Psychological Activation Through Advertising", Ph.D. dissertation, University of the Saarland, Germany (in German).

Berhard, Ulrich (1978), "Exposure to Advertising: Eye Movement and Memory", Ph.D. dissertation, University of the Saarland, Germany (in German).

Berlyne, Daniel E. (1960), *Conflict, Arousal and Curiosity,* New York: McGraw-Hill.

Buck, Ross (1976), *Human Motivation and Emotion,* New York: John Wiley & Sons.

Craig, Kenneth D., and Wood, Keith (1971), "Autonomic Components of Observers' Responses to Pictures of Homicide Victims and Nude Females," *Journal of Experimental Research in Personality,* 5, 304–9.

Dichter, Ernest (1964), *Handbook of Consumer Motivations,* New York: McGraw-Hill.

Eysenck, Michael W. (1976), "Arousal, Learning, and Memory," *Psychological Bulletin,* 83, 389–404.

———— (1977), *Human Memory: Theory, Research and Individual Differences,* Elmsford, NY: Pergamon Press.

Ferber, Robert (1977), "Can Consumer Research be Interdisciplinary?" *Journal of Consumer Research,* 4, 189–92.

Fletcher, James E. (1971), "The Orienting Response as an Index of Mass Communication Effect", *Psychophysiology,* 8, 699–703.

Hebb, Donald O. (1972), *Textbook of Psychology,* 3rd ed. Philadelphia: Saunders.

Krech, David, and Crutchfield, Richard S. (1974), *Elements of Psychology,* New York: Knopf.

Kroeber-Riel, Werner (1977a), "Goals of Consumer Policy," *Der Arbeitnehmer,* 5, 221–9 (in German).

―――― (1977b), "Criticism and New Conceptions of Consumer Policy—a Behavioral Approach," *Die Betriebswirtschaft,* 37, 89–103 (in German).

―――― , Barg, Claus-Dieter, and Bernhard, Ulrich (1975), "The Stimulus Intensity of Political Slogans," paper of the Institute of Consumer and Behavioral Research, University of the Saarland, Germany, Vol. 29 (in German).

Lindsay, Peter H., and Norman, Donald A. (1977), *Human Information Processing,* 2nd ed., New York: Academic Press.

Loftus, Geoffrey R. (1972), "Eye Fixations and Recognition Memory for Pictures," *Cognitive Psychology,* 3, 525–51.

McGuire, William J. (1976), "Some Internal Psychological Factors Influencing Consumer Choice," *Journal of Consumer Research,* 2, 302–19.

Mundy-Castle, A. C., and McKiever, B. L. (1953), "The Psycho-physiological Significance of the Galvanic Skin Response," *Journal of Experimental Psychology,* 46, 15–24.

Perry, John W., Jr. (1971), "Arousal and Memory: Psycho-physiological and Personality Factors", Ph.D. dissertation, University of Texas.

Peterson, Robert A., and Kerin, Roger A. (1977), "The Female Role in Advertisements: Some Experimental Evidence," *Journal of Marketing,* October, 59–64.

Schachter, Stanley (1975), "Cognition and Peripheralist-Centralist Controversies in Motivation and Emotion," in *Handbook of Psychobiology,* eds. Michael S. Gazzaniga and Colin Blakemore, New York: Academic Press.

Schönpflug, Wolfgang (1968), "Memory and Generalized Psychophysiological Activation," *Zeitschrift für erziehungswissenschaftliche Forschung,* 2, 195–221 (in German).

―――― (1969), *Methodology of Research into Activation,* Bern: Huber-Verlag (in German).

Shiffrin, Richard M., and Schneider, Walter (1977), "Controlled and Automatic Human Information Processing: II. Perceptual Learning, Automatic Attending, and a General Theory", *Psychological Review,* 84, 127–91.

Staats, Carolyn K., and Staats, Arthur W. (1957), "Meaning Established by Classical Conditioning", *Journal of Experimental Psychology,* 54, 74–80.

Thompson, Richard F. (1975), *Introduction to Physiological Psychology,* New York: Harper and Row.

Trommsdorff, Volker (1978), Attitudes Towards New Brands—Study on Validity of Experimental Methods for the Pretest of New Products, Saarbrücken (in preparation).

Tversky, Barbara (1974), "Eye Fixations in Prediction of Recognition and Recall," *Memory and Cognition,* 2, 275–8.

Witt, Dieter (1977), "Emotional Advertising: The Relationship Between Eye-Movement Patterns and Memory—Empriical Study With the Eye-Movement Monitor," Ph.D. dissertation, University of Saarland, Germany (in German).

USING BACKGROUND MUSIC TO AFFECT THE BEHAVIOR OF SUPERMARKET SHOPPERS

RONALD E. MILLIMAN

Source: Ronald E. Milliman, "Using Background Music To Affect the Behavior of Supermarket Shoppers," *Journal of Marketing,* Vol. 46, Summer, 1982, pp. 86–91. Adapted from the *Journal of Marketing,* published by the American Marketing Association.

Although music is generally thought of as an entertainment medium, it can also be used to achieve other objectives. In particular, music is employed in the background of production facilities, offices and retail stores to produce certain desired attitudes and behaviors among employees and/or customers. For example, background music is thought to improve store image, make employees happier, reduce employee turnover and stimulate customer purchasing.

Despite the widespread use of music in the marketplace, research documenting the effects of music is limited, and the results of existing research are inconclusive regarding its effects on consumer behavior. This is unfortunate because music is an atmospheric variable readily controlled by management. Past decisions to use background music in the marketplace have generally been based more on intuition or folklore rather than on strong empirical results. Much of the existing literature is more directly concerned with the effects of music on attitudes rather than behavior. In many instances attitude measurements were taken, then generalizations were made about behavior. However, as very aptly pointed out by Wicker (1971) and Fishbein and Ajzen (1975), attitude measures and actual behavior often show only a weak relationship.

THE STUDY

This study examines the possible link between the use of programmed background music and behavior, specifically, in-store shopping behavior. A type of latin square experimental design with controls was used to investigate the effects of three treatment variations on the in-store shopping behavior of supermarket customers. These treatments were: (1) no music, (2) slow tempo music, and (3) fast tempo music. These music tempo variations were chosen as experimental treatments because of a claim made in the sales literature of a nationally known marketer of programmed background music systems that music tempo, among several other factors, could be varied to affect human behavior. When contacted, the firm refused to produce research data in support of its claim. Therefore, tempo was selected as the independent variable for this research to find out whether, in fact, a link existed between music tempo and human behavior.

HYPOTHESES

For reader convenience, the following *three* hypotheses are stated in positive form. The experimental treatments of no music, slow tempo music and fast tempo music will significantly affect (1) the pace of in-store traffic flow of supermarket shoppers, (2) the daily gross sales volume purchased by supermarket customers, and (3) the number of supermarket shoppers expressing an awareness of the background music after they have left the store.

RESEARCH DESIGN

This study was conducted in a medium-size store operated by a large, nationally known chain of supermarkets. The store is located in a southwestern U.S. city with a population of approximately 150,000. The store's patrons are predominantly middle-class Anglo-Saxons. Additionally, the store had been in existence at its current location for several years and had a reasonably stable core market.

The study covered a nine-week period starting on January 28 and ending on March 31, 1980. The timing was very important, as it made it possible to fit nine weeks nicely between two holidays—New Year's and Easter—in such a way as to maximize experimental controls and minimize the effects of holiday shopping on the research results.

It should also be pointed out that to minimize the influence of various exogenous factors and maximize experimental controls, the normal level and timing of advertising was placed during these nine weeks. In addition, all other variables such as in-store promotions, point-of-purchase displays, store layout and all atmospheric conditions were kept as constant as possible.

Independent Variable

The independent variable of this research consisted of three background music treatments. To be more precise, multiple comparisons were made among the treatments of no music (designated M_0), slow tempo music (designated M_1), and fast tempo music (designated M_2). It became imperative to develop an operational definition for the music variables slow tempo and fast tempo; that is, how slow is *slow* and how fast is *fast?* To answer this a sample was selected at random from the trading area of the supermarket. Subjects were chosen to reflect the age, sex and other relevant socioeconomic characteristics of the store's customers. Each subject was asked to listen to several instrumental musical arrangements and to classify them as slow, fast or somewhere in between. A total of 95% of the subjects classified musical selections with a tempo of 72 beats per minute or fewer as slow. Selections with a tempo of 94 beats per minute or more were classified as fast. Thus, the range from 73 to 94 beats per minute was considered between fast and slow, although this category was not directly a part of this study. Therefore, based on these findings, slow tempo music was defined as having a tempo of 72 beats per minute or fewer, an average of 60 and a standard deviation of 6. Fast tempo music was defined as having 94 beats per minute or more, an average of 108 and a standard deviation of 7. However, perceptions of slow and fast may vary across geographic regions or demographic parameters and, therefore, the reader must be cautioned against generalizing these findings too far beyond the scope of this study.

It should also be pointed out that only instrumental selections were employed in this experiment. It was believed that using exclusively instrumental pieces would allow for greater control over the music variable, as no concern had to be given to female versus male vocalist, popular versus less popular artists, etc.

After defining the operational parameters of the independent variable, the rest of the experimental design was developed for the in-store tests. A replicated, random block experimental design was employed. That is, the experimental treatments, M_0, M_1 and M_2, were randomly assigned to each day of the week, with each treatment-day combination having three replications over the nine-week test period. A random number table was used to determine which treatment would be selected to begin the rotation schedule. Thus, since zero was the first eligible number appearing in the table and two was the next selectable number, the rotation schedule became M_0, M_2, then M_1. Hence, with the study beginning on a Sunday, M_0-Sunday was the first treatment-day combination, M_2-Monday was the second, and M_1-Tuesday was the third. M_0 recurred on Wednesday and so forth.

M_1 and M_2 each consisted of 40 different instrumental musical selections. The order of presentation for the different pieces was randomly assigned. In addition, the music selected tended to accentuate the rhythm or cadence enough so that while not dominant, it was easily discerned. Further, as a result of the findings of previously cited research (Smith and Curnow 1966), the volume of the music was maintained at a constant level throughout the nine-week experimental period. To make this procedure more precise, a decibel meter was used. The music's volume level was set to be perceived as soft background music, though clearly audible from all parts of the store. Each experimental treatment was run through its entire assigned day (from store opening to store closing) without intermission. Finally the PA system over which the music was played was also used for in-store announcements. However, it was assumed that because these announcements were infrequent, random and across all treatments, they would not significantly affect the results of this study.

Dependent Variables

The first dependent variable for which data was needed was the pace of in-store traffic flow. To obtain this information, shoppers were observed as they passed between designated points in the supermarket. The time it took each customer to pass between these locations was recorded in seconds. These measurements were restricted to one day of the week, in the evening, and for one hour because of the limitations placed upon the researchers by the store's management. In compliance with these extremely tight limitations, Wednesday was randomly selected, and all pace of in-store traffic flow measurements were made on this day. Further, to minimize any possibility of arousing management's

anxiety, the pace of the first five customers moving between these designated points from 7:00 p.m. to 8:00 p.m. was recorded. Hence, because every treatment-day combination was replicated three times over the nine-week experimental period, each of the music variables, M_0, M_1 and M_2 was tested over three different Wednesdays. These data were then collected and tested in an attempt to determine whether the tempo of the music had any effect on the pace of in-store traffic flow.

The second dependent variable was daily gross sales. This information was obtained by simply adding all of the cash register totals for each day and recording these amounts with the appropriate treatment. Subsequently, these data were tested to determine whether variations in gross sales receipts could be attributed to the experimental treatments.

To gather data for the third dependent variable, music awareness, customers were randomly selected outside the supermarket as they were leaving. Each subject was asked, "Do you recall music playing in the supermarket while you were shopping?" The subjects were given the response choices of (1) yes, (2) not sure or (3) no. The interviews were conducted on two randomly chosen days of each treatment. Thus, a total of 36 customers were interviewed for each of the six days.

To test hypotheses 1 and 2 pertaining to the pace of in-store traffic flow and daily gross sales, respectively, the analysis of variance statistical procedure was used for the overall test of significance. This technique was selected because it best met the requirements of the data and was readily available for computer processing. When justified, more in-depth analysis was made using the t-test. In the case of hypothesis 3, music awareness, the chi-square procedure was more appropriate for the type of data collected. Although the 0.05 level of significance was the acceptance criterion for all statistical tests, absolute probabilities are reported for all findings.

RESULTS OF THE STUDY

Pace of In-Store Traffic Flow

The overall analysis of variance test indicated a highly significant difference or differences somewhere among the three treatments ($F = 4.85$, 2/42 df, $p = .01$). The t-test was used to determine which pair or pairs of treatments produced the significant results. As shown in Table 1, it was found that:

- There was no significant difference between treatments M_0 and M_1 ($p = 0.22$).
- There was no significant difference between treatments M_0 and M_2 ($p = 0.08$).
- There was, however, a clearly significant difference betweeen treatments M_1 and M_2 ($p = 0.004$).

The results of these tests indicate that the pace of in-store traffic flow was significantly slower with the slow tempo music (M_1 mean $= 127.53$ seconds) than for the faster tempo music (M_2 mean $= 108.93$ seconds). Additionally, it is interesting to note the slower tempo of M_1 stimulated an even slower pace than no music (a mean of 127.53 sec-

onds for M_1 compared to a mean of 119.86 for M_0), although this difference was not considered statistically significant. In what appears to be a similar pattern, no music at all resulted in a slower traffic flow than that of the fast tempo music (M_0 mean $= 119.86$ seconds compared to $M_2 = 108.93$ seconds), although this difference was not considered statistically significant because it fell just short of the level of significance accepted in this research (0.05). However, in the final analysis, hypothesis 1 was accepted; that is, based upon these findings, there is sufficient evidence to conclude that the tempo of in-store background music can significantly affect the pace of the in-store traffic flow of supermarket customers.

Sales Volume

Here, too, when the three independent variables were examined together with the analysis of variance procedure, a significant difference was found ($F = 3.21$, 2/60 df, $p = .05$). Thus, a more in-depth investigation of the relevant data was appropriate (see Table 1). The t-test showed that:

- There was no statistically significant difference in sales volume between treatments M_0 and M_1 ($p = 0.27$).
- There was no significant difference between treatments M_0 and M_2 ($p = 0.17$).
- There was a highly significant difference in sales volume between treatments M_1 and M_2 ($p = 0.02$).

The higher sales volumes were consistently associated with the slower tempo musical selections while in contrast, the lower sales figures were consistently associated with the faster tempo music (M_1 mean $= \$16,740.23$ compared with M_2 mean $= \$12,112.85$). This difference is significant, and these findings follow quite logically from the in-store traffic flow results. That is, as customers move more slowly through the store, they tend to buy more. Conversely, as customers move more quickly through the store, they tend to purchase less. Nevertheless, there is sufficient evidence to accept hypothesis 2 and conclude that the daily gross sales volume purchased by supermarket customers can be significantly influenced by the tempo of the in-store background music.

Table 1 Summary of t-tests results for pace of in-store traffic flow and sales volume

Dependent variable	Groups	df	t value	Prob.
Pace	No music with slow tempo music	28	−1.25	0.222
	No music with fast tempo music	28	1.82	0.079
	Slow tempo music with fast tempo music	28	3.18	0.004
Sales volume	No music with slow tempo music	40	−1.12	0.271
	No music with fast tempo music	40	1.41	0.165
	Slow tempo music with fast tempo music	40	2.53	0.016

Table 2   The effects of music tempo upon the awareness of in-store music

Response choice	No music			Slow tempo music			Fast tempo music			$\Sigma\chi^2$
	N	%	χ^2	N	%	χ^2	N	%	χ^2	
Yes	21	9.72	.375	25	11.57	.042	27	12.50	.375	0.792
Not sure	24	11.11	0	24	11.11	0	25	12.50	.042	.042
No	27	12.50	.375	23	10.65	.042	20	9.26	.667	1.084
Total χ^2										1.918

$p < .95$, not significant.

Awareness of In-Store Background Music

The chi-square statistic was used to test whether there was any significant difference in the level of music awareness among the three independent variable treatment groups because the data for this dependent variable were expressed as frequencies. However, the analysis failed to reveal any significant variations in the subjects' responses ($p = 0.97$, $df = 8$, $\chi^2 = 1.92$, see Table 2). Therefore, in accordance with accepted research and statistical procedures, there was no further manipulation of the data beyond the overall chi-square test, and hypothesis 3 was rejected as stated. That is, the subjects in one treatment group were found to be no more or less likely to recall the music than subjects in another group. Additionally, it should be noted that there were no statistically significant differences in the number of subjects selecting each response choice, although more said "not sure" than either of the other two choices. Thus, subjects were something less than totally conscious of the music while shopping, but it cannot be said that they were completely unaware of it. Rather, the music may have been in the background of the shoppers' perceptual fields. Nothing definite, however, can be stated about the customer's exact level of music awareness while shopping. It does point to the possibility of subconscious motivational effects on in-store shopping behavior.

CONCLUSION

The reader must be cautioned against generalizing these findings too far beyond the scope of this study. The results may not apply to all supermarkets, nor to any other market situation. There is a need for more research in this area, not just concerning the effects of music on behavior but also in the whole area of "atmospherics."

This study along with others like it, can help marketing managers interested in influencing the behavior of consumers. The tempo of instrumental background music can significantly influence both the pace of in-store traffic flow and the daily gross sales volume purchased by customers, at least in some situations. In this study the average gross sales increased from $12,112.35 for the fast tempo music to $16,740.23 for the slow tempo music. This is an average increase of $4,627.39 per day, or a 38.2% increase in sales volume.

The exact figures are not important, as they pertain only to this research situation. However, what these findings say is important: It is possible to influence behavior with music, but this influence can either contribute to the process of achieving business objectives or interfere with it. Thus, it would appear that Grayston was correct in saying that the music chosen and its intended objectives must be matched.

Certainly, in some retailing situations the objective may be to slow customer movement, keeping people in the store for as long as possible in an attempt to encourage them to purchase more. However, in other situations, the objective may be the opposite, that is, to move customers along as a way of increasing sales volume. A restaurant, for instance, will most likely want to speed people up, especially during lunch, when the objective is to maximize the "number of seats turned" in a very short period of time, normally about two hours or less. Playing slow tempo music in a restaurant might result in fewer seats turned and lower profit, although it could encourage return visits if customers preferred a relaxed luncheon atmosphere. Again, the point is that the music chosen must match the objectives of the business and the specific market situation.

Finally, this study raises as many questions as it answers. It appears that the effect of music on behavior is at a relatively low level of awareness; thus, a more accurate determination of the precise level of awareness needs to be made. In addition this study raises the issue of what influence, if any, does background music have upon the employees of a business? Does such an effect exist? Is it important? There could even be an "interaction effect" between the employees' behavior and the customers'

behavior. A definite need exists for more research in this area.

REFERENCES

Fishbein, Martin, and Icek Ajzen (1975), *Belief, Attitude, Intention, and Behavior: An Introduction to Theory and Research,* Manila, Philippines: Addison-Wesley.

Grayston, D. (1974), "Music While You Work," *Industrial Management,* 4 (June), 38–39.

Smith, Patricia Cane, and Ross Curnow (1966), "Arousal Hypotheses and The Effects of Music on Purchasing Behavior," *Journal of Applied Psychology,* 50 (no. 3), 255–256.

Wicker, A. W. (1971), "An Examination of the Other Variables' Explanation of Attitude-Behavior Inconsistency," *Journal of Personality and Social Psychology,* 19 (July), 18–30.

SECTION XIV

CONSUMER PROTECTION

Consumerism is a national social movement that is concerned with five basic consumer rights. Each of these rights is sometimes violated as consumers enter into transactions with for-profit and not-for-profit organizations. The five rights are:

1. *The right to safety.* This involves protection against physically harmful goods and services.
2. *The right to be informed.* Consumers should be provided with relevant information that is easily understood and easily obtained. They should not be deliberately misled or confused.
3. *The right to choose.* Consumers should not be forced to purchase in a monopolistic situation. Consumers have the right to benefit from the advantages accruing to them from a competitive market.
4. *The right to be heard.* Consumer interests should be represented in the development of corporate marketing policy, in the development of policy by not-for-profit agencies such as hospitals, and in the development of government policy.
5. *The right to high quality.* Consumers have the right not simply to an absence of physical harm and deception, but also to the best array of products and services provided in the best manner possible, given reasonable constraints organizations face if they are to survive and to continue to serve the consumer.

There are several issues relating to consumer protection and the various parties involved with or affected by consumer protection issues. One issue focuses on which groups should legitimately be involved in buyer-seller relationships and how they should be involved. Should trade associations, community action groups, states' attorney generals, and the Federal Trade Commission be involved? If so, how should any one of these groups be involved? A second issue concerns the criteria for evaluating consumers' opinions of an organization's marketing practices, including product offerings. Are consumers' perceptions inherently better or worse or much different than those of the legal staff of a government agency? A third issue addresses product information. What type of information should be provided? By whom? Just how much information is it fair to require a vendor to make available (in some way)? An important issue is whether or not regulatory efforts may fail or even backfire. Can a regulation create a false sense of protection among the consumers? May the implementation be conducted in a way that actually contradicts the intention of the regulations?

Different assumptions are often made about the nature of consumer problems. This leads to different types of regulatory actions or practices. One set of assumptions emphasizes consumer characteristics as a cause of difficulty. That is, some consumers experience problems because they lack the educational ability to process product information. A response to this problem entails providing special counseling services to consumers and consumer education programs. Another common assumption is that many consumers, especially those who are elderly, poor, and immobile, do not have any real choice. They must rely on mail order catalogs and stores that provide home delivery. The remedial action implied by this assumption is that mail order firms, door-to-door salespeople, and others who are used frequently by disadvantaged groups should be regulated carefully. Another assumption is that consumers have problems with particular kinds of merchants who may be found in any location and in any type of business establishment. Since these merchants cannot be readily located or identified, it becomes necessary to regulate the kind of practices they commonly use.

As might be expected, the entire issue of consumerism is fraught with conflict. The parties involved—government, business, consumer advocacy groups, and consumers—differ considerably in terms of what they perceive the problems to be and what they see as appropriate solutions. Moreover, there are very different perspectives among the various parties about the effectiveness of different approaches and different legislation and regulations. The reader should keep this in mind when reading the papers selected for this section.

"CORRECTIVE ADVERTISING AND AFFIRMATIVE DISCLOSURE STATEMENTS: THEIR POTENTIAL FOR CONFUSING AND MISLEADING THE CONSUMER"

Remedial messages using "plain English" may not always be understood. If the meaning contained in a remedial message is not comprehended, then the purpose behind the corrective action is defeated. First, why are corrective advertising and affirmative disclosure statements necessary? In the case discussed in the Jacoby, Nelson and Hoyer article, the Federal Trade Commission (FTC) does not believe that there is enough empirical proof to substantiate the claims made by Bufferin and Excedrin. The FTC felt it necessary to inform consumers that while some proof exists, the degree of evidence is insufficient.

The reasoning behind the FTC's concern is to protect the consumer. Only correct and proven information can be presented to the consumer. If the information is incorrect, misleading, or deceptive, then corrective advertising may be ordered. If the consumer is to be protected, he or she must understand the corrective message; otherwise the first, incorrect message will remain in the mind of the viewer.

This article is an excellent example of the relevancy of understanding information processing. A brief review by the reader of Section 6 on Learning and Information Processing would be helpful at this point. This case applies the findings presented about information processing to a real life situation.

In the article, the measurement criterion used to determine understanding of the message was very rigid. In order for an answer to be considered correct, the person had to check the correct statement(s) and only the correct statement(s). One can question how comprehensible the advertising message need be. Is it sufficient for the majority of viewers to understand the general message or is it necessary for the viewer to comprehend the exact message the sender wishes to convey? What are the costs involved in achieving near perfect comprehension and what are the benefits?

Finally, what implications do this article's findings have for the creation of an advertisement?

"PUBLIC POLICY AND CONSUMER INFORMATION: IMPACT OF THE NEW ENERGY LABELS"

Consumers are continually bombarded with an abundance of detailed product information. The consumer movement has led to many changes and additions to legislation. In particular, many industries are now required by law to disclose various kinds of product information to consumers. Some policymakers argue that it is not important whether the consumer uses the information; their main concern is that the information be made available to the consumer.

The McNeill and Wilkie article takes the opposite perspective. These authors are concerned with the consumer's use of information. This study investigates the use of energy consumption labels that are required under a federal energy labeling program. The authors discuss the effect alternative formats of this information presentation might have on the consumer. Given the weak and conflicting results of the study, what interpretation can be made of the results and what conclusions can be drawn?

There is a limit to the amount of information that a person can process. How does the addition of yet another feature (energy use) affect consumers? Is there any reason why information on energy consumption might differ from the processing of information concerning other features (size, style, price, etc.)?

The three elements of consumerism were previously stated as consumer protection, consumer education, and consumer information. This study demonstrates the complementary and interdependent nature of each of these elements. What does the energy labeling program contribute to each of these three elements?

CORRECTIVE ADVERTISING AND AFFIRMATIVE DISCLOSURE STATEMENTS: THEIR POTENTIAL FOR CONFUSING AND MISLEADING THE CONSUMER

JACOB JACOBY
MARGARET C. NELSON
AND
WAYNE D. HOYER

Source: Jacob Jacoby, Margaret C. Nelson, and Wayne D. Hoyer, "Corrective Advertising and Affirmative Disclosure Statements: Their Potential for Confusing and Misleading the Consumer," *Journal of Marketing,* Vol. 46, Winter, 1982, 61–72. Adapted from the *Journal of Marketing,* published by the American Marketing Association.

The topics of deceptive and misleading advertising have witnessed increasing regulatory and academic interest over the past decade (e.g. Cohen 1974; Gardner 1975; Jacoby, Hoyer, and Sheluga 1980, Chapter 2; Jacoby and Small 1975; Russo, Metcalf, and Stephens 1981). The remedies that can be employed in the event an ad is judged deceptive or misleading have also stimulated considerable discussion. Two of the more controversial remedies are corrective advertising and affirmative disclosure. The objective of corrective advertising is to change or correct purportedly erroneous beliefs, while the objective of affirmative disclosure is to instill new beliefs.

. . .

Awareness, beliefs, attitudes, and intentions are the dependent variables most often used to assess communication impact and are usually major components in most accepted conceptualizations of the communication process (e.g., Engel, Blackwell, and Kollat 1978; Lavidge and Steiner 1961; McGuire 1976). Consideration of these models reveals that, in each case, comprehension is assumed to precede belief formation and change. It is only after information has been comprehended that one can reasonably expect it to influence beliefs, attitudes, intentions, and behavior. Hence, both regulator efforts to mandate remedial statements and previous researcher efforts to assess the impact of such statements necessarily rest on a critical, but as yet unverified assumption, namely, that the logically prior step of comprehension has been accomplished.

Further, comprehension of a remedial message does not guarantee that said understanding will necessarily be accurate. ". . . there is often quite a variation between the actual content of a message and the content as it is perceived and retained by the consumer" (Engel et al. 1978, p. 25). . . .

In other words, remedial statements may be at least as confusing and misleading as the advertising they are designed to counteract. This investigation tested this possibility using the actual language proposed by the FTC for implementation in a case now under judicial consideration. This case is described below and is followed by the conceptual framework which underlies the rationale employed in the present investigation.

BACKGROUND OF THE CASE

The case revolves around two familiar analgesic products, Bufferin and Excedrin. The FTC contends that Bufferin advertising claimed that Bufferin is a faster pain reliever and gentler to the stomach than plain aspirin. Similarly, the FTC asserted that advertising claimed Excedrin is a more effective pain reliever than plain aspirin. According to the FTC staff, while some evidence to substantiate these claims does exist, the degree of empirical proof available to support these claims is not as conclusive as the FTC staff believes it should be. The FTC staff wanted consumers to know that while some proof is available to show that the claims may be true, the degree of proof is insufficient according to some authorities. The rejoinder made by Bristol-Myers is that while there is no irrefutable and incontrovertible proof positive to support these claims, the proof that is available does meet commonly accepted standards for such evidence.

Expecting that the FTC Administrative Law Judge hearing the case would rule in his favor, the complaint counsel sent the judge a letter containing the following two sets of remedial statements, one for each product, and proposed that one statement in each set be mandated for inclusion in future advertising (Fisherow 1979, pp. 1–2).

"For inclusion in Excedrin advertising, the disclosure that:

1. Excedrin has not been proven to be a more effective pain reliever than aspirin; or,
2. It is not known whether Excedrin is a more effective pain reliever than aspirin; or,
3. There is a real question whether Excedrin is a more effective pain reliever than aspirin.

"For inclusion in Bufferin advertising, the disclosure that:

4. Bufferin has not been proven to be a faster pain reliever or gentler to the stomach than aspirin; or,
5. It is not known whether Bufferin is a faster pain reliever or gentler to the stomach than aspirin; or,

6. There is a real question whether Bufferin is a faster pain reliever or gentler to the stomach than aspirin."

Serving as an expert witness, the senior author expressed the belief that a substantial number of consumers would either be confused as to the intended meaning or would extract some nonintended meaning from the proposed remedial statements. The investigations described below represent an empirical attempt to confirm (or disconfirm) this belief. If supported, the findings would suggest that, regardless of their well-intentioned nature, corrective advertising and affirmative disclosure statements are capable of misleading consumers, just as are the advertising claims they are designed to counteract. Further, such findings would also suggest that, just like the advertising they are designed to counteract, such statements need to be empirically evaluated before being mandated and implemented.

THE CONCEPTUAL FRAMEWORK

Consider the process whereby human beings extract meaning from the communications they receive. When a source deliberately engages in communication, he/she does so because there is some thought or feeling that he/she wishes the other party (i.e., the receiver) to understand. Unfortunately, the thought that exists in the mind of a source cannot be directly transposed into the mind of a receiver. For the source to communicate a thought (i.e., evoke the intended meaning in the mind of the receiver), he/she must convert it into some externally denotable form (e.g., the spoken word, written words, some visible gesture) and convey this to the receiver. In turn, the receiver must then decode or interpret this overt expression and extract meaning from it—hopefully, the same meaning intended by the source.

$\cdots$

Hypotheses

Evidence suggests that comprehension is made more difficult as the number of concepts increases and finite memory resources are expended to maintain information in active memory for processing (cf. Kaplan 1974, Rumelhart 1977, Wanner and Maratsos 1974). Considering the proposed remedial statements, the set for Bufferin is seen to be more complex than their Excedrin counterparts. That is, when the words that are common to the pairs of corresponding statements are deleted, the statements for Bufferin are left with two concepts (namely, "faster" and "gentler"), whereas those for Excedrin are left with only one (namely, "effective"). Accordingly, it is predicted that:

H1: The three statements for Excedrin will be associated with higher rates of correct comprehension than will the three counterpart statements for Bufferin.

Second, considerable research (e.g., Clark and Chase 1972; Just and Carpenter 1971; Trabasso 1972; Trabasso, Rollins, and Shaughnessy 1971) has demonstrated that sentences containing negation are semantically more complex and, therefore, more difficult to comprehend. Statements 1, 2, 4 and 5 are couched in negative terms, whereas statements 3 and 6 are stated in the affirmative. Accordingly:

H2: The third statement in each set (namely, "There is a real question . . .") will be correctly comprehended at higher rates than the other two remedial statements proposed for that brand.

Combining hypotheses 1 and 2 leads to another prediction.

H3. Statement 3 will be better comprehended than Statement 6.

To summarize, both the implementation of remedial advertising messages and previous research on the impact of such messages have implicitly assumed accurate message comprehension on the part of the public. This assumption remains unverified and warrants empirical testing. The present study provides such a test. Despite the considerable amount of thought and well-intentioned effort underlying the development of these messages, it is possible that remedial statements may generate as much miscomprehension as the advertising messages they are designed to counteract.

METHOD

Samples

Three qualitatively different samples were employed. The first consisted of 92 undergraduates enrolled in a consumer psychology course at Purdue University during spring 1979. Since these individuals were all between 18 and 22 years of age, mostly unmarried, and possessed a comparable amount of formal education, efforts were directed toward obtaining more representative groups of adults. The second sample, obtained in the fall of 1979, consisted of 281 members of social and fraternal organizations in Lafayette, Indiana. . . . Sample 2 was 46% male, 53% married, and contained almost equal numbers of respondents distributed in 10-year age brackets ranging from 20 and below to 60 and above. In terms of highest grade of formal education, 4% had less than a high school diploma, 17% had a high school diploma, 36% had some college, and 43% reported having a college degree or better. The third sample consisted of 78 black adults living in two small south suburban Chicago communities and were obtained via door-to-door canvassing during the last 10 days of 1979. Sample 3 was 37% male, 47% married, 13% were age 20 or below, 49% were 21–30, 15% were 31–40, and 22% were 41–50. In terms of highest grade of formal education, 9% had less than a high school diploma, 21% had a high school diploma, 53% had some college, and 16% had a college degree or better. In all, a total of 451 respondents were employed. . . .

Instruments

Closed-ended assessment. The primary means for assessing (mis)comprehension was a close-ended questionnaire. A set of eight derived meanings was generated for each of the six proposed remedial statements. For each such set, one (or two in the case of Excedrin) of the derivations was judged roughly equivalent in meaning to the corrective statement under consideration; the other six (or seven) derivations were judged to be incorrect. . . .

Each of the remedial statements, followed by its set of derivations, constituted a separate page in a questionnaire. The instructions requested that the subjects read the statement typed at the top of each page, then check as many or as few of the interpretations as they felt accurately paraphrased the meaning which they had derived. These pages were randomized across statements and respondents.

In addition to the set of eight derivations, each page contained two additional response options. These were: "None of the choices presented above reflect the meaning I get from this statement," and "I am uncertain as to what the statement actually means and, therefore, cannot check any of the above meanings as being correct or incorrect." A sample page of the instrument is provided in the Appendix.

To understand the scoring system employed, one needs to consider what may occur at the point of message reception. Either the recipient will be unable to make any sense out of the message, in which case we have noncommunication, or the person will be able to extract at least some meaning (communication). In the latter instance, the extracted meaning may be correct, incorrect, or confused. . . . This set of comprehension/miscomprehension responses can be outlined as follows:

I. Noncommunication   (no meaning extracted)
II. Communication (some meaning extracted)
   A. Accurate (extracting only Meaning Structure 1)
   B. Inaccurate
     1. Accepting an incorrect meaning structure.
     2. Rejecting a correct meaning structure (option 9 on the questionnaire).
   C. Confused
     1. Accepting both Meaning Structure 1 and some other meaning structure.
     2. Being uncertain as to what the meaning is (option 10 on the questionnaire).

Thus, for any given page, an individual's response was scored correct if he/she checked the one accurate derivation in the case of Bufferin, or checked one or both accurate derivations in the case of Excedrin, *and* marked *no* other response options. An answer was scored incorrect if the individual checked any of the inaccurate derivations on the page and failed to check an accurate response, or if the individual marked the response option "None of the choices. . . ." A response was scored "confused" either if the individual marked a correct derivation as well as one or more incorrect derivations or if this individual marked the response option "I am uncertain. . . ."

. . .

Open-ended   assessment. The   greater amount of time available with the first sample permitted an open-ended assessment as well. This was done to provide some idea of convergent validity. Using the first two pages of the questionnaire, this assessment preceded the closed-ended assessment. One of the six proposed remedial statements appeared at the top of each of these pages and was followed by the instruction, "Please explain what the author of this statement is trying to say, using words other than those used here. That is, what does the statement mean or imply to you?" Each subject received one Excedrin statement and one of the two remaining wordings for Bufferin. Thus, statement 1 was always paired with 5 or 6, statement 2 with 4 or 6, and statement 3 with 4 or 5. The order of the open-ended questions was also counterbalanced across subjects.

RESULTS

Closed-Ended Assessment
Table 1 summarizes the results obtained with the closed-ended assessment for each of the samples. As can be seen from these data, extracting either an incorrect or confused meaning was much more prevalent than extracting the intended meaning. Except for statement 3 (with its weighted mean correct comprehension score of 43%), all of the other five statements had correct comprehension scores ranging ± 5% from 20%. Not surprisingly (in terms of the rationale underlying hypothesis 1), the dominant reaction to the three Excedrin statements was one of confusion, whereas the dominant reaction to the three Bufferin statements was

Table 1 Proportion of respondents who extracted accurate, inaccurate, and confused meanings from the proposed remedial statements

| | Remedial statements | | | | | | | |
| | Excedrin | | | | Bufferin | | | |
	1	2	3	Overall mean	4	5	6	Overall mean
Accurate								
Sample 1	.21	.23	.46		.13	.15	.33	
Sample 2	.25	.17	.40		.17	.13	.25	
Sample 3	.19	.15	.48		.15	.23	.23	
Weighted mean	.23	.18	.43	.28	.16	.15	.26	.19
Inaccurate								
Sample 1	.26	.20	.06		.33	.33	.33	
Sample 2	.32	.40	.13		.56	.52	.41	
Sample 3	.35	.33	.20		.58	.46	.35	
Weighted mean	.31	.35	.13	.26	.52	.47	.39	.46
Confused								
Sample 1	.53	.57	.48		.54	.52	.35	
Sample 2	.43	.43	.47		.27	.35	.33	
Sample 3	.46	.52	.32		.27	.31	.42	
Weighted mean	.46	.47	.44	.46	.32	.38	.35	.35

Sample 1 = 92 Purdue University undergraduates.
Sample 2 = 281 post-college age adults residing in Lafayette, Indiana.
Sample 3 = 78 black adults residing in south suburban Chicago.
Total N = 451

to extract an incorrect meaning. Also, college students seemed no better (or worse) at extracting the correct meaning than did more heterogeneously composed samples of adults (samples 2 and 3). As Table 2 indicates, most inaccuracy was due to accepting an incorrect meaning rather than rejecting a correct meaning. Similarly, all confusion was due to accepting both a correct and incorrect meaning, not to being confused about the meanings of the eight derivations.

Hypothesis 1. While the data in Table 1 suggest that the Excedrin statements were more correctly comprehended than their Bufferin counterparts (H1)—an average of 28% vs. 19%—there is really no practical difference. . . . Hence, H1 is not

confirmed when an adjustment for guessing is factored in.

Hypothesis 2. The hypothesis that positively worded statements would be better understood than negatively worded ones (H2) was strongly confirmed in all three samples. . . . For Excedrin, the mean percentage for statements 1 and 2 was 20.5% compared to 43% for statement 3. The corresponding means for the Bufferin statements were 15.5% and 26% respectively. . . . Were one forced to make a choice from among the three statements proposed, the "There is a real question . . ." version seems best, as it was most often correctly understood and least often incorrectly understood for both Excedrin and Bufferin. Still,

Table 2 Patterns of inaccurate and confused interpretations for the six proposed corrective statements (sample 1 responses)

	Statements					
	1	2	3	4	5	6
Response categories[a]						
A. Accurate	21	23	46	13	15	33
B. Inaccurate						
1.	21	18	4	26	30	21
2.	5	2	2	7	3	12
Total %	26	20	6	33	33	33
C. Confused						
1.	53	57	48	54	52	35
2.	0	0	0	0	0	0
Total %	53	57	48	54	52	35

[a]See definitions of response categories provided in text under the section entitled "Closed-Ended Instrument."

fewer than half the respondents were able to derive the correct meaning even from this version.

Hypothesis 3. This hypothesis stated that relatively simple positively worded statements would be better understood than relatively complex ones. Indeed, the Excedrin version (statement 3) was better understood overall than its Bufferin counterpart (statement 6)—43% vs. 26% (see Table 1). Again, however, this finding needs to be tempered by an adjustment for guessing. . . . The difference between the proportions accurate on statement 3 ($p_2 = .46$) vs. statement 6 ($p_1 = .32$) is significant at the .01 level; the difference is no longer significant when the 10% advantage for guessing is removed from Statement 3. Thus, it cannot be concluded that hypothesis 3 has been supported.

Open-Ended Assessment

. . .

The statements differed considerably in terms of the number of correct and incorrect interpretations they seemed to evoke. The total numbers of correct interpretations for statements 1 through 6 were

4, 21, 23, 10, 14, and 19, respectively. The numbers of incorrect interpretations were 24, 7, 3, 15, 9, and 2. Thus, the wording of statements 3 and 6 seemed to elicit the largest number of correct interpretations (a combined total of 42) and the smallest number of incorrect interpretations (a combined total of 5). On the other hand, the wording represented by statements 1 and 4 elicited the smallest number of correct interpretations (a total of 14) and the greatest number of incorrect ones (a total of 39). The wording represented by statements 2 and 5 fell in between in terms of both frequency of correct (total 35) and incorrect interpretations (total 16). The data from the open-ended assessment support all three hypotheses: The three Excedrin statements elicited greater correct comprehension than their Bufferin counterparts; the third statement in each set was associated with better comprehension then either of the other two; and statement 3 was better comprehended than statement 6. Thus, the corrections for guessing employed in relation to the closed-ended assessment may have overestimated the extent of such guessing and understated the support for H1 and H3.

DISCUSSION

Relying on prior information processing theory and research (cf. Lindsay and Norman 1977, Rumelhart 1977), the present investigation outlined a procedure that could be used, in lieu of full-blown and expensive field tests, to evaluate whether such proposed messages were being comprehended as intended. The principal objective was to examine the question, Are corrective advertising or affirmative disclosure statements subject to being miscomprehended, just as are the advertising messages they are designed to remedy? From the data obtained, the answer would appear to be a resounding "yes." Despite the considerable amount of thought and well-intentioned effort that went into their development, the six remedial statements proposed by the FTC for inclusion in Bufferin and Excedrin advertising appear to be more often associated with confused or incorrect comprehension than with correct comprehension. The fact that this finding was obtained with three very heterogeneous samples—including an adult sample that was above average in terms of reported education and family income (sample 2)—provides a measure of confidence in the results.

The difficulty involved in accurately communicating meaning is often underestimated, and regulators would seem to be no exception in this regard. As Rumelhart (1977, p. 102) notes: "Of all the complex tasks the human information system carries out, perhaps the most sophisticated is language processing. . . . Only when we stop and analyze the intricate reasoning that appears to underlie even the simplest cases of language comprehension can we begin to appreciate the complexity of the language understanding process."

. . . The fact that high levels of miscomprehension were found for remedial statements generated and proposed by well-intentioned staff members of the FTC suggests caution in being quick to blame an advertiser when some consumers miscomprehend the message. Indeed, some amount of miscomprehension is likely to occur regardless of whether the communication is an ad, a TV program, news, a speech, an educational program, etc. (Jacoby, Hoyer, and Sheluga 1980). Hence, requiring that advertising reach a zero-level base of miscomprehension appears totally unreasonable.

It could be argued, of course, that the relatively high rates of confusion obtained (that is, extracting the correct meaning along with some additional, but incorrect meaning) should not be of major concern since they suggest that at least some of the correct meaning was being received. However, consider Cohen's (1974, p. 9) description of the criteria, used by the FTC to arrive at a finding of deception in advertising:

> On the basis of FTC cases and court interpretations, an advertisement will be considered false, misleading, or deceptive when the following [applies:] . . . An advertisement that is capable of two meanings, one of which is false, is misleading.

One might therefore reasonably ask, should not the same criteria apply to remedial statements as well?

The conclusions offered above need to be tempered by the limitations of the present investigation. Principal among these is the fact that our procedure involved a one-time forced-exposure. A legitimate question is, would miscomprehension and confusion decrease (and comprehension, therefore, increase) given the repeated exposures that typically occur under real world conditions? At the very least, our findings need to be replicated using realistic field tests.

A second problem stems from the reliance placed on paper and pencil instruments to present remedial statements designed primarily for presentation over broadcast media. This problem is probably not as severe as might be thought, however, since research indicates that information presented via the print mode is better comprehended than when the same information is conveyed via audio or audiovideo media (Chaiken and Eagly 1976; Jacoby, Hoyer, and Zimmer 1981). If anything, such findings suggest that the present results may overestimate the degree of accurate comprehension that might occur with a single exposure, real world televised presentation.

The present findings are also limited by the fact that no baseline data (collected under conditions comparable to the present study) are yet available for the set of advertisements in question. Conducting such research would require that some knowledgeable party (representing either Bristol-Myers and/or the advertising agency that developed the specific ads in question) specify exactly what it was that was being communicated, as was done with the remedial statements in the present investigation. Without such comparison research, one cannot say whether the remedial messages are more, less, or as greatly miscomprehended as are the messages they were designed to remedy. One can only say that the set of six remedial statements prepared by the FTC, using what it considered plain English, may not be all that clear to large segments of the population.

It also needs to be noted that for purposes of simplification, we have written as if the communication of Meaning Structure 1 is an all-or-none-phenomenon; i.e., regardless of how many other meanings the receiver does or does not extract, he/she either does or does not comprehend Meaning Structure 1. Although this simplistic fiction was employed throughout, miscommunication, in the form of "misinterpretation and misunderstanding [will usually] vary from subtle nuances of meaning to a complete distortion of the intended message" (Harris and Monaco 1978, p. 2). Future research needs to address such subtleties.

. . .

Perhaps the most important implication of the present investigation is that, just as is the case for advertising proper, the likely impact of remedial statements needs to be thoroughly assessed and evaluated before such statements are inserted in advertising. Regulatory agencies need to recognize that the language of the remedial statements which they devise may be equally (and in some cases, perhaps even *more*) confusing to the consumer than the advertising messages they are designed to correct. In other words, it cannot be safely assumed that language decided upon in good faith and with the consumer's best interests at heart will be sufficient for accomplishing its objective. There is no substitute for empirically assessing the perceived meanings of corrective advertising or affirmative disclosure statements before such remedial statements are mandated for use in advertising.

APPENDIX

Assessment Instrument

. . .

"EXCEDRIN HAS NOT BEEN PROVEN TO BE A MORE EFFECTIVE PAIN RELIEVER THAN ASPIRIN."

Possible Derivations

☐ 1. Excedrin *is* a more effective pain reliever than aspirin.

☐ 2. Excedrin *is not* a more effective pain reliever than aspirin.

☐ 3. Excedrin *is neither a more nor less* effective pain reliever than aspirin.

☐ 4. Excedrin *is a less* effective pain reliever than aspirin.

☐ 5. Excedrin *may be* more effective than aspirin, but *no proof whatsoever* exists for this statement.

☒ 6. Excedrin *may be* more effective than aspirin, but *no conclusive proof* exists for this statement.

☐ 7. Excedrin *may be* more effective than aspirin, but no studies have yet been done which would show this to be true.

☒ 8. Excedrin *may be* more effective than aspirin, but there is at present *insufficient evidence* to show that this is true.

☐ 9. None of the derived meanings presented above (1 through 8) reflect the meaning I derive from this statement.

☐ 10. I am uncertain as to what the statement actually means and, therefore, cannot check any of the above as being either an accurate or inaccurate derivation from that statement.

Note: Interpretations scored as "correct" are indicated by an asterisk.

REFERENCES

Chaiken, S., and A. H. Eagly (1976), "Communication Modality as a Determinant of Message Persuasiveness and Message Comprehensibility," *Journal of Personality and Social Psychology,* 34 (October), 605–614.

Clark, H. H., and W. G. Chase (1972), "On the Process of Comparing Sentences Against Pictures," *Cognitive Psychology,* 3 (July), 472–515.

Cohen, D. (1974), "The Concept of Unfairness As It Relates to Advertising Legislation," *Journal of Marketing,* 38 (July), 8–13.

Engel, J. F., R. D. Blackwell, and D. T. Kollat (1978), *Consumer Behavior,* 3rd ed., Hinsdale, IL: The Dryden Press.

Fisherow, W. B. (1979), "FTC Complaint Counsel's Statement Concerning Corrective Advertising for Excedrin and Bufferin." In the matter of Bristol-Myers Company, Ted Bates and Company, Inc., and Young and Rubicam, Inc. Docket No. 8917, Federal Trade Commission.

Gardner, D. M. (1975), "Deception in Advertising: A Conceptual Approach," *Journal of Marketing,* 39 (January), 40–46.

Harris, R. J., and G. E. Monaco (1978), "Psychology of Pragmatic Implication: Information Processing Between the Lines," *Journal of Experimental Psychology: General,* 107 (January), 1–22.

Hoyer, W. D., J. Jacoby, and M. C. Nelson (1982), "A Model for the Development, Evaluation and Implementation of Remedial Advertising Statements," in *1982 Proceedings: Southwestern Marketing Conference,* ed. R. P. Leoe. Southwestern Marketing Association.

Jacoby, J., W. D. Hoyer, and D. A. Sheluga (1980), *The Miscomprehension of Televised Communication,* New York: American Association of Advertising Agencies.

———, M. C. Nelson, W. D. Hoyer, and H. G. Gueutal (1981), "Probing the Locus of Causation in the Miscomprehension of Remedial Advertising Statements," New York University, Graduate School of Business Administration, working paper.

——— and C. S. Small (1975), "The FDA Approach To Defining Misleading Advertising," *Journal of Marketing,* 39 (April), 65–68.

Just, M., and P. Carpenter (1971), "Comprehension of Negation with Quantification," *Journal of Verbal Learning and Verbal Behavior,* 10 (June), 244–253.

Kaplan, R. M. (1974), "Transient Processing Load in Relative Clauses, unpublished Ph.D. dissertation, Harvard University.

Lavidge, R. J., and G. A. Steiner (1961), "A Model of Predictive Measurements of Advertising Effectiveness," *Journal of Marketing,* 25 (October), 59–62.

Lindsay, P. H., and D. A. Norman (1977), *Human Information Processing: An Introduction to Psychology,* 2nd ed., New York: Academic Press.

McGuire, W. J. (1976), "Internal Psychological Factors Influencing Consumer Choice," *Journal of Consumer Research,* 2 (April), 302–319.

Rumelhart, D. E. (1977), *Introduction to Human Information Processing,* New York: John Wiley and Sons.

Trabasso, T. (1972), "Mental Operations in Language Comprehension," in *Language Comprehension and the Acquisition of Knowledge,* eds. R. O. Freedle and J. B. Carroll, Washington, DC: Winston.

———, H. Rollins, and E. Shaughnessy (1971), "Storage and Verification Stages in Processing Concepts," *Cognitive Psychology,* 2 (March), 239–289.

Wanner, E., and M. M. Maratsos (1974), "On Understanding Relative Clauses," unpublished manuscript, Harvard University, Department of Psychology and Social Relations.

PUBLIC POLICY AND CONSUMER INFORMATION: IMPACT OF THE NEW ENERGY LABELS

DENNIS L. MCNEILL
AND
WILLIAM L. WILKIE

Source: Dennis L. McNeill and William L. Wilkie, "Public Policy and Consumer Information: Impact of the New Energy Labels," *Journal of Consumer Research*, vol. 6, June, 1979, 1–11. Reprinted with permission.

The term "Consumer Information Environment" is emerging as a key concept for research in public policy, marketing, and consumer research. While the term originally suggested an objective assessment of informational stimuli in the marketplace (Wilkie 1973), recent emphasis has shifted to the dynamics of public policy information programs, and the attendant need for consumer research to provide both evidence and guidance for these programs. . . .

The present study addresses a new federally mandated program under which marketers must present the energy consumption of each model of home appliance on an attached label. The research was done with the program as a focus and with the research tradition in marketing as guidance. In addition, the research was conducted at such a time in the policy process as to lead, rather than lag behind, the policy effort (Wilkie and Gardner 1974).

THE PUBLIC POLICY PROGRAM

The energy labeling program was conceived as part of a larger national effort to attack the energy crisis. Its focus is at the consumer level, unlike most major energy initiatives. It is, moreover, aimed at one-time behavior—the purchase of a major appliance—rather than repetitive consumption settings.

Most consumer programs have been geared to these repetitive behaviors: consumers have been asked to slow down, turn down, commute together, and generally to adjust their energy consumption on a daily basis. However, in most cases consumer behavior has gradually returned to pre-crisis norms.

In light of the overall problem of the shortage of energy, what is really needed is a more fundamental change in energy-use patterns. This change—given that the consumer in his or her car and in his or her home uses one-third of the total energy in the United States (Millstein 1977)—could be better structured to obtain consumer response on a continuing basis. Purchase of energy-efficient products provides such continuing structure and, when achieved through increased availability of relevant information, does so with a minimum of interference in marketer and consumer freedoms. The energy labeling program is intended to provide this information at the point of sale.

Voluntary Labeling Program (1973–1975)

The current energy labeling program was preceded by an effort housed in the Department of Commerce's National Bureau of Standards. This program received the cooperation of manufacturers, and early signs indicated some success with air conditioner labels, the program's first product. . . .

Energy Policy and Conservation Act (1975–Present)

In December 1975, the Congress passed the Energy Policy and Conservation Act (EPCA). Among other major goals, the EPCA attempts to improve efficiency of major home appliances through required energy labels.[1] Responsibility for the communication decisions on the energy labels was assigned to two agencies. The Federal Trade Commission (FTC) was given responsibility for establishing the exact format of the labels. The EPCA suggested that the format portray the dollars per year of energy consumption by each product, together with a comparative range of energy use for similar products. The FTC then contracted for a study to determine which format might be most effective (Response Analysis 1977).

Meanwhile, the Department of Energy (DOE) was given responsibility for a consumer education (persuasion) program to increase the importance of energy information in consumer decisions. This activity is intended to complement the energy labeling program. Thus, while the goal of the labeling program is clearly to reduce energy consumption, the labels themselves are not expected to totally serve both motivational and informational roles.[2]

. . .

[1]Provisions to implement minimum efficiency standards were under discussion at the time of this writing.
[2]The general question of specific objectives for information programs is a key issue (Wilkie 1978a, b). The EPCA mandates behavior change as a national policy goal.

RESEARCH ISSUES

The study reported here addresses two major questions:
- Will energy consumption labels assist consumers in purchase-related activities?
- Is the reporting format required under the EPCA a good way to disclose energy consumption data?

. . .

Independent Variables

The label format proposed by the EPCA contained a disclosure of average annual dollars of energy use for a given appliance model, plus a comparison with similar models, also in annual dollars. Certain key components of the format thus present interesting questions regarding consumer processing of such information. These include the differential impacts of:
- The presence of energy-use data (energy-use data available versus energy-use data unavailable).
- The presence of comparative energy-use information (comparative information versus no comparative information).
- The unit of measurement [dollars versus kilowatt hours (KWH)].
- The degree of disclosure (overall product energy use versus energy use by each major product feature).

These independent variables relate directly to the research questions under investigation.

Will the disclosure of energy use assist the consumer?
In order to assess the impact of the disclosures, the changed information environment (with energy-use data available) can be compared to the present information environment (with no energy-use data available).

The importance of disclosure formats.
The second major question centers on the development of alternative formats for disclosure. Four specific dimensions emerged as holding particular research interest.

First, the required EPCA disclosure mandated comparative performance information to provide a baseline on relative energy use of competing models. This proposal would seem useful given that applicance models are physically separated, perhaps in brand cluster within a display space, and that some brands and some models will not be carried by a given retail outlet. If, as initial research suggests (e.g., Bettman and Jacoby 1975), consumers prefer to process across brands on a single attribute at a time, this form of comparative information should facilitate better relative judgments about product performance without the normal shopping behavior necessary to personally establish the range of energy use for similar products.

A second issue concerns the unit of measurement employed in the disclosure. . . . The unit of measurement required by the EPCA is dollars (computed by a standard rate per KWH of energy use). This would seem to offer the advantages of (1) being a familiar basis with clear consumer meaning, (2) having already available cognitive rules with which consumers can handle such information, and (3) stimulating a price-quality (cost-benefit) economic judgment presumed useful to conservation behaviors.

On the other hand, there are wide geographic variations in the KWH rates for electricity around the country, as well as significant differences in temperature, humidity, and seasons. These lead to differences in usage rates of some appliances, thus to different amounts of electricity consumed and dollars paid. In addition, there are wide differences in individual usage of certain appliances (e.g., washer, dryer, and air conditioner), which exacerbate this problem. It may be, then, that some form of the more basic KWH unit of measurement would lead to more accurate and useful consumer judgments. This might be especially true in terms of postpurchase use behavior, which is the major thrust of conservation efforts.

A third question concerns the time period over which to accumulate consumption data. The EPCA requirement is to compute and provide energy use on an annual basis. The time period chosen will affect the apparent magnitude of the appliance's energy use, as well as the absolute differences between models and brand alternatives. While the magnification of differences for larger time periods, e.g., yearly or lifetime,[3] may stimulate greater impacts toward energy saving, it could also be that use of monthly data may better reflect the household budgetary impact of product energy use.

The final issue involves the degree, quantity, or specificity of the information disclosed. The EPCA treats each appliance model as a unit that consumes energy; this fits nicely with the purchase choices facing the consumer if these are viewed as discrete alternatives. However, the selection or deletion of a few specific features on certain appliances can have significant effects on total energy consumed. Provision of specific (incremental) energy consumption by each of these features might therefore be a particularly attractive alternative. A potentially strong argument against such specificity is, however, that such detail will not be processed or utilized by consumers.

Implementing the Issues

. . .

Five alternatives were employed in the experiment; a sixth condition, serving as a control, provided no energy label. The experimental conditions, together with the rationale for each condition, are described in Exhibit 1.

METHODOLOGY

Because of the problem orientation of this study, careful consideration was given to three decisions that could have negated the potential usefulness of the study in terms of the energy program. These were (1) the product class to be investigated, (2) the size and characteristics of the sample, and (3) the nature of the experimental tasks.

---

[3] A new concept termed "life cycle cost," incorporating discounted purchase price, energy use, and servicing costs over the entire consumer ownership period for the appliance, has recently been proposed (MIT Report 1974). See Hutton and Wilkie (1979) for issues and a study of the potential of this information form.

Exhibit 1 Treatment conditions

Condition 1 (control)
A comparison condition with no energy consumption data available, reflecting the consumer information environment at time of the study.

Condition 2 (The Energy Act Disclosure)
Energy consumption data in annual dollars with a range of comparative annual dollars for similar products.

Condition 3 (degree of disclosure)
Energy consumption data in annual dollars with a range of comparative annual dollars for similar products, plus a listing of annual energy consumption for each feature.

Condition 4 (unit of measurement)
Energy consumption data in annual kilowatt hours with a range of comparative annual kilowatt hours for similar products.

Condtion 5 (time period)
Energy consumption data in monthly dollars with a range of comparative monthly dollars for similar products.

Condition 6 (energy label without the range)
Energy consumption in annual dollars.

Product Class and Experimental Stimuli

The product class chosen for this research was refrigerator freezers. This is an interesting product in light of the following criteria, which combine public policy priorities with research considerations:

- Relevance of the product class to the energy consumption program. The program deals with major home appliances of which refrigerator freezers represent substantial dollar and per capita volume.
- Energy consumption. Refrigerator freezers represent the single greatest consumer of energy in a household (M.I.T. Report 1974).
- Characteristics of product use. The variability of energy use in refrigerator freezers is related to feature and model combinations, rather than to some unique aspect of product use susceptible to strong variations between households.

- Prominence in the household. Refrigerator freezers occupy a prominent place in the household and are used by a very high proportion of our population.
- State of knowledge of the consuming public. For the most part the basic functions of this appliance are understood, and contributions of additional feature options can be recognized by consumers.

. . .

. . . While brands are obviously an important part of the refrigerator decision, many critical judgments involving energy relate strongly to model choice, i.e., what features to include. This study therefore employed a product evaluation task that focused on model decisions, in contrast to introducing the additional facets that the inclusion of brand names might bring to the problem. . . .

Two focus group interviews were conducted to aid in the determination of which product attributes to include in the study. Based on the discussions, the following feature information was made available to respondents: style, size, price, frost-free, icemaker, insulation, and energy use (where appropriate in the design).

Four models of refrigerators were developed to serve as experimental stimuli (Table 1). . . . Table 2 presents the model energy use as it was provided in each experimental condition.

. . .

Sample

A sample of 180 female respondents participated, with 155 subjects (86 percent) providing complete responses for analysis. The intent was to capture a cross-section of the Gainesville, Florida area population. A master list of social, civic, and church organizations in the area was developed, together with demographic and socioeconomic characteristics of each group. From this list, eight organizations were selected for the study; these included a low-income black church group, a blue collar swim club, two secretarial groups, a Catholic church social, the Jaycee wives, and two Parent-Teacher Organizations, one from a blue collar neighborhood and one from an affluent section. . . . Within each

Table 1 Attribute values of experimental refrigerator models

Attribute	Model 1	Model 2	Model 3	Model 4
Model description	Top freezer style with manual defrost	Top freezer style with frost-free defrost	Side-by-side style with frost-free and an icemaker	Top freezer style with frost-free and an icemaker
Price	$359.00	$439.00	$669.00	$589.00
Size	17 cubic feet 13 fresh food 4 freezer	17 cubic feet 13 fresh food 4 freezer	19 cubic feet 13 fresh food 6 freezer	20 cubic feet 15 fresh food 5 freezer
Frost-free	No	Yes. Frost-free adds $100 to the purchase price (and adds $25 each year to the energy use[a])	Yes. Frost-free adds $100 to the purchase price (and adds $25 each year to the energy use[a])	Yes. Frost-free adds $100 to the purchase price (and adds $25 each year to the energy use[a])
Insulation	Poured insulation. Adds $20 to the purchase price (and subtracts $7.50 each year from energy use[a])	Cut fiberglass-standard	Cut fiberglass-standard	Cut fiberglass-standard
Icemaker	No	No	Yes. Icemaker adds $75 to the purchase price (and $12 each year to the energy use[a])	Yes. Icemaker adds $75 to the purchase price (and $12 each year to the energy use[a])

[a]Present only in the condition that discloses energy use by feature.

session subjects were randomly assigned to the experimental conditions.

Experimental Tasks

A key issue in the design of the experiment was to allow multiple levels of response to be investigated in a realistic manner, consistent with the urging of researchers in marketing (Heeler and Ray 1971; Day 1976). The result was a relatively complex between-subjects design consisting of a series of tasks attuned to different levels of cognitive and behavioral responses. Exhibit 2 presents the flow

of the experimental session; each stage is briefly described in the following pages.

Stage 1—Introduction. Subjects were introduced to the experiment with a brief cover story explaining its purpose as a study interested in consumer opinions and decisions with regard to refrigerator freezers. . . .

Stage 2—Initial model evaluation. The second stage was concerned with the extent to which consumers access energy-use data, and their subsequent responses to the information. Rather than

Table 2 Energy consumption information by model by treatment

Treatment	Model 1	Model 2	Model 3	Model 4
Control	None	None	None	None
Dollars/year plus a comparative range plus by feature	$32.40 each year. Similar models use $32.40 to $50.80 each year	$101.00 each year. Similar models use $60.00 to $108.00 each year	$96.80 each year. Similar models use $93.70 to $168.60 each year	$76.80 each year. Similar models use $75.00 to $135.00 each year
Dollars/year plus a comparative range	$32.40 each year. Similar models use $32.40 to $50.80 each year	$101.00 each year. Similar models use $60.00 to $108.00 each year	$96.80 each year. Similar models use $93.70 to $168.60 each year	$76.80 each year. Similar models use $75.00 to $135.00 each year
KWH/year[a] plus a comparative range	648 KWH each year. Similar models use 648 to 1016 KWH each year	2020 KWH each year. Similar models use 1200 to 2160 KWH each year	1956 KWH each year. Similar models use 1874 to 3372 KWH each year	1572 KWH each year. Similar models use 1500 to 2178 KWH each year
Dollars/month plus a comparative range	$2.20 each month. Similar models use $2.20 to $4.23 each month	$8.42 each month. Similar models use $5.00 to $9.00 each month	$8.15 each month. Similar models use $7.81 to $9.70 each month	$6.55 each month. Similar models use $6.25 to $11.34 each month
Dollars/year	$32.40 each year	$101.00 each year	$96.80 each year	$76.80 each year

[a]Computed by dividing the dollars per year by $0.05 per KWH to obtain KWH per year. $0.05 was the Gainesville, Florida rate at the time this research was conducted.

forcing exposure to the information, this stage involved an information acquisition task modifying the paradigm developed by Jacoby (see Jacoby, Speller, and Kohn 1974a, b).

As in stores, where labels will be available on separate models, the experimental subjects received separate information displays for each of the four refrigerator models, as illustrated in Figure 1. Specific information on each model was available under tabs, with the name of the dimension clearly presented above the tab.

Subjects were introduced to the task by being told they were going to evaluate the four best selling models of a particular brand of refrigerator freezer. . . .

Subjects were then told that certain information would be available on each model. In order to obtain the desired information, they need only turn over the appropriate tab, then place it on the record sheet. The acquisition task was explained and demonstrated to the subjects as "allowing us to follow where your eyes go when you are considering a refrigerator freezer." . . . Subjects kept track of the information on an individual board by placing each acquired tab face down on the adhesive strips in the order of acquisition.

Following the task, which was limited to eight minutes, subjects were asked for their ranked preference and scaled overall impressions of each model, and to rank each model in terms of energy

Exhibit 2   Conduct of the experiment

STAGE 1

Introduction

- Purpose of the experiment.
- Release form.
- General information from the subjects about refrigerators and refrigerator freezers.

↓

STAGE 2

Initial Model Evaluation

- Acquisition of model information.
- Model preferences.
- Overall impressions of the models.
- Feature recall.

↓

STAGE 3

Model Evaluation in the Presence of Information

- Evaluation of each model by feature.
- Comparative advice for each model.

↓

STAGE 4

Refrigerator Choice: A Sequential Building Task

- Feature decisions.
- Feature/energy use judgments.

↓

STAGE 5

Classification and Opinion Items

- Demographics.
- Present refrigerator data.
- Choice of energy use disclosures.

---

use, price, size, and number of features. Each of these responses was based on the subject's recall of information acquired.

Stage 3—Model evaluation in the presence of energy information. This task was explained to the subjects as a "second shopping trip" to see the same models, as they did not have very long to look at the models earlier. The same displays (Figure 1) were then presented again, but with the tabs face up and clearly displayed.

Three sets of questions were employed in this stage. First, subjects were asked to evaluate each model, feature by feature, on bipolar good/bad scales. This was intended to allow for research inferences regarding the communicability and direct-impact of the energy-use data.

A second set of measures was designed to tap the impact of the comparative disclosure manipulation, which was complicated by the danger of stimulating demand artifacts. Therefore, a special cover story was developed to introduce the measures:

> A good friend is in the market for a refrigerator freezer and is looking among name brands, one of which is the brand which produces the models you have been looking at. Your friend needs to buy a new refrigerator very soon. She sold her old one when she sold her home, and her new home does not have a refrigerator with it. Your friend has hurriedly called the major appliance dealers and found out that she is too late for the sales. Since she cannot get a "deal" your friend knows that the purchase prices are about the same for the brands she is looking at. Your friend does not have the time to shop so she is calling her friends, who know a lot about refrigerator freezers, for advice. Since you know about the 4 models produced by this brand, your friend is calling you. One of the models your friend wants is the same as one of the models you have just evaluated (questions later used each model as the one assumed to be desired by the friend). In order to give your advice you can use the information on the models.

Three scales were designed to tap judgments (advice to friend) emanating from the comparative disclosures:

- Likelihood of finding a better value if friend shops around.
- Going to other stores being "worth the effort."
- Degree of encouragement/discouragement of friend's decision to buy this brand's model.

A third set of evaluations was completed at this stage, reflecting "subjective state" judgments (Jacoby et al., 1974a). These asked for feelings about the various dimensions of information available on the models in terms of usefulness and complexity.

Stage 4—Refrigerator choice: A sequential building task. The fourth stage was the opera-

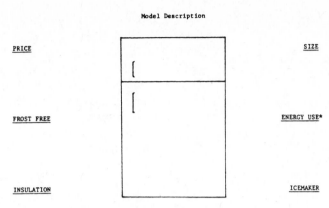

Figure 1 Sample model display for the acquisition task.

tionalization of the choice dimension in a rather unique fashion.[4] Feature choices were simulated in the form of a "building" task. Subjects were told that the researchers wanted to allow them more flexibility in expressing their desires than had been possible when restricted to only four models. They would now be able to design their own refrigerator for their home and budget. The following feature decisions were provided in a specified order, with each feature choice containing certain alternatives:

- Total size—16, 17, 18, 19, 20, or 20+ cubic feet.
- Style—side by side, top freezer, or bottom freezer.
- Color—white or color.
- Insulation—poured insulation or cut fiberglass.
- Defrost—manual, partial automatic, or frost-free.
- Icemaker—yes or no.
- Shelves—stationary wire, adjustable wire, or stationary glass.
- Power miser—yes or no.
- Cold water dispenser—yes or no.

The subjects were to build their models feature by feature. Each feature had the "contribution to purchase price" of that alternative. It is important to note, however, that no energy-use information

[4]The idea for this operationalization arose in discussion with Joel B. Cohen, University of Florida. It is believed that it was first employed in a housing study by Battelle Memorial Institute.

was available in this task. If the energy-use data were to impact, they would have to, in some sense, be retained from earlier exposures. This was seen to be a stringent test of impact on the choice level.

Stage 5—Classification and opinion items. The final questions were on demographics and product ownership. In addition, the participants were asked for their opinions of alternative units of measurement and time periods to be used for the labels.

RESULTS

Impacts of Energy-Use Information
The major comparison made in these analyses is between the control group and the disclosure groups. Evidence on information impact is provided by four major topics: the initial accessing of information, the impacts of initial availability of information, a direct evaluation with the information present, and the direct "choices" made in the building task.

Did the subjects access the energy-use information? Results of the information acquisition task (Table 3) showed no significant differences between the control group and the disclosure group on any of the acquisition measures. Results are therefore presented as sample means. The availability of new energy information apparently did not stimulate subjects to increase the alterna-

Table 3   Information acquisition task

Overall acquisition	Means[a]
Number of models examined (of 4)	2.7
Number of information tabs acquired[b]	10.4
Range of information tabs acquired	1–25
Percent of available information acquired[c]	45%
Number of energy information tabs acquired	1.8
Percent energy information acquired (of available)	46%

By attribute (percent of subjects with ≥1 acquisition)	Percent
Price	73
Size	70
Energy use	64
Frost-free	60
Icemaker	57
Insulation	47

By model	1 (%)	2 (%)	3 (%)	4 (%)	Total (%)
Percent of total acquisitions	12	22	33	33	100
Percent of energy-use acquisitions	15	18	35	33	100

[a]No significant differences between control and disclosure groups. Results are combined here ($n = 155$).
[b]Out of an average of 23.2 available.
[c]Disclosure conditions only ($n = 129$).

tives on which to seek information, nor to engage in a greater amount of total information acquisition. . . .

Acquisition of energy information reflects the overall acquisition rate, perhaps indicating that the energy information was treated as a normal element of the environment. Examination of the specific attributes selected tends to bear out this conclusion. Energy use fits into a comfortable third position, behind price and size, but ahead of the three features. Turning the data slightly, however, provides some cause for concern; for each given attribute, such as price, size, or energy, over one-

fourth of the sample did *not* obtain *any* information on *any* of the four models.

The third section of Table 3 reflects results by model, and lends support to the meaning of the task, in that the bulk of subjects' attention was going to the two models representing largest sales in the actual marketplace. The streamlined, bare-bones version (Model 1) received little attention. The acquisition of energy information reflects this pattern.

Impacts of initial acquisition.   Beyond the simple act of acquiring the information, interest was focused on the effects of such information on consumer ability to comprehend the data, and impacts on evaluations and preferences for the various models. Three analyses were conducted in this regard. All measures were taken after the information boards had been removed from vision, thus providing a reasonably stringent test of impacts.

The first analysis concerned learning, or subjects' ability to exactly rank the models in terms of energy use. As expected, the control group was completely unable to do so (the correct ranking was Model 1, 4, 3, 2). Approximately 15 percent of the disclosure subjects reported this ranking, a statistically significant difference. At the absolute level, however, this is not high, reflecting in part the fact that many participants had not acquired much of the energy information.

The other two analyses involved evaluations of models following the information acquisition task. The expectation, in light of program goals, was that the models high in energy use would be less favorably evaluated. The crucial between-group comparisons are for the high energy-use models—Model 2 ($101 per year) and Model 3 ($96.80 per year).

Model 3, a comparatively very efficient machine given its size and features, was not evaluated differently by the control and disclosure groups. For Model 2 however—the highly inefficient machine—a mean of 1.5 on "overall impression" was provided by the control group, versus 0.0 from disclosure subjects (+3 to −3 scale, $\alpha \leq 0.001$). Twenty-five percent of control group subjects

Table 4 Evaluation of energy performance with information display present (disclosure conditions only)

Measure	Model 1	Model 2	Model 3	Model 4
Mean evaluation[a]	+2.4	−1.2	+0.4	+1.6
Ranked evaluation	1	4	3	2
Actual usage cost	$32.40	$101	$96.80	$76.80
Relative energy cost[b]	100	168	103	102
Actual cost ranks	1	4	3	2

[a]Response scale was bad (−3) to good (+3).
[b]Indexed against cost efficient similar model available in market.

ranked it first in preference, versus 14 percent of those in the disclosure group ($\alpha \leq 0.09$).

. . .

Evaluation of energy performance with information present. In order to afford less stringent tests of impact, subjects were then given a completed information display for each of the four models and asked to rate the models on various attributes, including energy performance.

Results for this rating show that Model 2 is clearly recognized as inferior on this dimension, while Model 1 is rated very high (Table 4). In addition to relative efficiency, then, it would appear that absolute costs are also employed in consumers' ratings, as evidenced by the disparity in ratings for Models 3 and 4. With respect to the energy labeling program, this result provides strong support for a narrow reading of the objectives for these labels; if the labels are intended primarily to communicate energy performance information, they appear to do so quite well when consumers read them for this purpose.

Demand for Product Features

On the building task, subjects in the disclosure conditions chose significantly smaller refrigerator freez-

ers than those in the control group (18.9 versus 19.6 cubic feet; $\alpha < 0.01$). Beyond this, the groups did not differ significantly on the five feature choices. To summarize the net effect of all the choices, we calculated the total energy use of each model as "built" by each subject. The means, $81.59 for the control group versus $79.68 for the disclosure group, were not significantly different.

In sum, this task does not lend strong support to the argument that consumers will evidence strong and immediate shifts in purchasing as a result of the availability of this information. It should be noted, however, that the energy information was *not* available to subjects while undertaking this task (again because of concern with demand characteristics); this could have understated a stimulatory impact of the labels at time of choice.

Is the EPCA Format Best?

As described earlier, the five disclosure conditions differed in terms of the unit of measure, time period, degree of disclosure, and whether a comparison was available. . . .

Unit of measurement. The expected differences between the disclosure formats varying the unit of measurement—KWH versus dollars—did not materalize. Uniformly, across all levels of impact, the unit of measurement did not result in response differences.

Time period for computing energy consumption. The magnitude of the disclosure did not result in consistent differences. Only one measure appeared affected by the monthly versus yearly comparison; the good/bad evaluations of energy performance indicated that the monthly condition did not lead to discrimination between the models as well as did yearly figures.

Degree of disclosure. This manipulation provided energy consumption on an incremental basis for each major feature of the appliance. Results do not indicate that consumer reaction was positive.

Comparative disclosures. This aspect of the format included the range of energy use for similar models. As described earlier, this was assessed with a special task involving advice to the neighbor. The critical judgments in this task involved Model 2. Consumers provided with a comparative range in addition to dollars per year data showed a tendency to advise further "shopping around," while those given only dollars per year were slightly negative on this measure (+0.3 versus −0.5 on a −3 to +3 scale; $\alpha < 0.09$). Measures of "better value" elsewhere and encouragement of immediate purchase were not significantly different though sample means were in expected directions. In a secondary set of analyses, responses for the other three models—all comparatively good performers on energy—showed no differences with regard to these judgments.

SUMMARY AND IMPLICATIONS

This experiment examined several issues on consumer response to the new federal program mandating energy use by major home appliances. Primary interest concerned the potential of the label to aid consumer decisions and the selection of a format to convey energy-use data on the labels. The empirical findings may be briefly summarized as follows:

- The profile of consumer response to this energy-use information indicates a potential impact consistent with the goals of the program, i.e., a shift away from energy inefficient appliances.
- In the "initial shopping visit to a well-known local appliance store," results showed significant effects of the label on model preference and overall impressions, with respect to the energy inefficient model.
- Respondents, on a second "shopping trip," made reasonably accurate judgments about the efficiency of the various models' energy performance. Even when models were evaluated high or low overall, subjects would characterize energy efficiency correctly.
- The strongest test was a choice task asking respondents to "build" their own refrigerators by considering and choosing a set of features. The results were generally nonsignificant.

- Information format analyses provided no consistent differential effects on the dependent measures used in this study.

It is necessary to temper these conclusions by noting that the study was not conducted in a field setting and most subjects were not actively seeking a refrigerator at the time. . . .

It is also useful to examine why, when the preponderance of results were nonsignificant, a reasonably positive conclusion is advanced regarding the potential impact of this information. The pattern of nonsignificant findings was primarily associated with four factors, each of which deserves brief mention:

1. The three energy efficient models provided no differences on any of the tasks. This implies that the introduction of favorable energy information does not impact nearly as strongly as negative energy information (Model 2), suggesting that consumers may implicitly assume satisfactory energy efficiency in the absence of explicit information.
2. The different format options do not appear to be of crucial importance, at least within the framework of this study.
3. The behavior task, together with the strength of desires for certain features, evidenced little information impact. This finding is consistent with the bulk of research evidence in consumer information to date (Day 1976).
4. Individual consumer differences were quite evident in conducting the sessions and manifested themselves as high variance in the data. This suggests that informational impacts will not be present for the entire population.

This research represents an example of a blending of policy setting and experimental design considerations. The goal for this study was not to design the perfect label, but to investigate some interesting and potentially important issues involving this new form of information. Demand characteristics (Sawyer 1975) are a key problem for future consumer information research in public policy. Researchers must carefully deal with the problem that consumers have never encountered the new information of interest in the survey or experiment, as well as with the more general issues of time and learning (Wilkie 1974a). The staged set of tasks employed here may prove to be a useful start for future research aimed at similar issues.

REFERENCES

Association of Home Appliance Manufacturers (1976), *The 1976 Director of Certified Refrigerator Freezers*, Chicago: Association of Home Appliance Manufacturers.

Bettman, James, and Jacoby, Jacob (1976), "Patterns of Processing in Consumer Information Acquisition," in *Advances in Consumer Research:* Vol. 3, ed. Beverlee B. Anderson, Chicago: Association for Consumer Research, pp. 315–20.

Campbell, Donald T., and Fiske, Donald W. (1959), "Convergent and Discriminant Validation by the Multi-Trait Multi-Method Matrix," *Psychological Bulletin*, 56, 81–105.

Hays, William L. (1963), *Statistics*, New York: Holt, Rinehart, and Winston.

Heeler, Roger M., and Ray, Michael L. (1972), "Measure Validation in Marketing," *Journal of Marketing Research*, 9, 361–70.

Hutton, R. Bruce, and Wilkie, William L. (1979), "Life Cycle Cost: Impact on Consumer Response to New Product Information," working paper, Department of Marketing, University of Denver.

Jacoby, Jacob, Speller, Donald E., and Kohn, Carol A. (1974a) "Brand Choice as a Function of Information Load," *Journal of Marketing Research*, 11, 63–9.

———, Speller, Donald E., and Kohn, Carol A. (1974b), "Brand Choice as a Function of Information Load:

Replication and Extension," *Journal of Consumer Research*, 1, 33–42.

McNeill, Dennis L. (1977), "An Investigation of Issues Surrounding the Disclosure of Energy Use Data on Major Home Appliances," unpublished Ph.D. dissertation, University of Florida.

Millstein, Jeffrey (1977), Statement Made to Consumer Research Interagency Group, Washington, D.C.

Massachusetts Institute of Technology Report (1974), *The Productivity of Servicing Consumer Durable Products*, Cambridge, Mass.: Center for Policy Alternatives, M.I.T.

Response Analysis Corporation (1977), "Communication Effectiveness of Energy Consumption Labels for Major Appliances," unpublished report, Washington, D.C.: Federal Trade Commission.

Sawyer, Alan G. (1975), "Demand Artifacts in Laboratory Experiments in Consumer Research," *Journal of Consumer Research*, 1, 20–30.

Wilkie, William L. (1973), "Consumer Research and the FTC," *Association for Consumer Research Newsletter*, p. 3.

———, (1974a), "Analysis of Effects of Information Load," *Journal of Marketing Research*, 11, 462–6.

———, and Gardner, David M., (1974), "The Role of Marketing Research in Public Policy Decision Making," *Journal of Marketing*, 38, 38–47.

———, (1978a), "Consumer Information Processing and Public Policy Research," in *Marketing and the Public Interest: Essays in Honor of E. T. Grether*, ed. John Cady, Cambridge, Mass.: Marketing Science Institute, pp. 223–37.

———, (1978b), "Consumer Information Processing: Issues for Public Policymakers," in *Consumer Research for Consumer Policy*, eds. M. Denny and R. Lund, Cambridge, Mass.: Center for Policy Alternatives, M.I.T., pp. 88–117.

SECTION XV

CONSUMER RESEARCH

Throughout this book articles that report the results of research have been included to indicate what is known about consumer behavior. In this section we turn to descriptions of how research can and should be conducted. When we hear someone describe a particularly interesting or unusual piece of gossip, we often ask, "How did you find that out?" or "Who told you that?" Similarly in reading reports of the findings of consumer research, it is just as important to ask, "How did the researchers find this out?" as it is to ask, "What did they discover?"

We can believe that the research results are true only if the research meets certain standards. To determine if these standards were met we must carefully read the description of how the research was conducted. Good research must meet the standards of nonbias, validity, reliability, and sampling and data collection that are appropriate for the research questions being addressed. These standards are described in the two articles in this section.

But first we must ask why research is necessary at all in consumer behavior. The primary reason is that there is much that is not known about the subject. We might speculate as to what makes consumers behave as they do, but only research that is carried out scientifically can provide information that is valid, reliable, and judged to have high probability to reflect the true state of things. Second, there are many new areas of consumer behavior that have only recently drawn the attention of consumer behavior researchers. These include public policy topics such as the utilization of information by consumers as well as not-for-profit organizations, such as health clinics and universities, which are discovering they can learn more about their interaction with their users through consumer behavior research. Finally, but not least in importance, is the need to monitor changes in consumer behavior constantly in order to be able to modify marketing strategies accordingly.

"RESEARCH METHODS IN CONSUMER BEHAVIOR"

Many methods are discussed in the Cipkala paper. Most of the terms are defined and explained in the article. For introductory purposes, a brief outline of the methods discussed is presented here. This outline can be used by the reader as a guide for points to look for in reading the paper.

In addition, readers should use this outline and the paper as a way to check their understanding of consumer behavior research methods. Before reading further, think of five different questions that could be answered by conducting research (e.g., "What is the relationship between social class and early adoption propensity?"). Then decide which of the methods discussed in the Cipkala paper could possibly be used to answer each of these questions. Which methods are best or more appropriate for each of the questions? Why?

Outline of Research Methods

I. Secondary data collection
II. Primary data collection
    A. Surveys
        1. Means of conducting
            a. Personal interview
            b. Mail questionnaire
            c. Telephone interview
        2. Objectives
            a. Disguised
            b. Nondisguised
        3. Sequence of questions
            a. Structured
            b. Nonstructured
    B. Observation
        1. Personalness
            a. Personal
            b. Mechanical
        2. Reactivity
            a. Reactive
            b. Nonreactive
    C. Experimentation
        1. Where conducted
            a. Laboratory
            b. Field
         2. Validity
            a. Internal
            b. External

3. Design
    a. After-only
    b. Before-after
    c. Before-after with control
    d. Four group-six study (Solomon four group)
    e. After-only with control
    f. Panel
    g. Factorial
    h. Latin square

"DESIGNING RESEARCH FOR APPLICATION"

In conducting research, the researcher usually expects that the findings will be useful beyond the context of the specific study. In fields such as marketing, research results may be immediately applied if the research carries this kind of generalizability. Nevertheless, much consumer research is not generalizable.

Calder, Phillips, and Tybout point out that generalizability is not a single issue, but that two distinct types of application of research results may exist. A researcher concerned with effects application is primarily interested in whether or not specific effects can be transferred from the laboratory (or the experiment) to the real world. In this case, the researcher is not particularly interested in a broader theoretical understanding of the causes behind the effects. For example, the advertising manager learns that a certain advertisement led to a sales increase in the test market. He/she then decides to use the advertisement regionally, reasoning that the effect in the test can be obtained in a wider population.

On the other hand, the researcher may be interested in theoretical application. The theory derived or verified through research should be generalizable, but the specific context and the specific effect is not of great interest. The researcher may develop a theory relating stimulus and response. The marketer can then apply the theory in a specific context, for example, consumer products advertising, but the theory is not tied to this context.

Ensuring that research results are generalizable in either effect or theory application is difficult. Furthermore, criteria for applicability differ in each case. The authors discuss the differences between theory and effects application and discuss how research might be designed in order to ensure that the desired type of applicability can be achieved.

RESEARCH METHODS IN CONSUMER BEHAVIOR

JOHN CIPKALA

INTRODUCTION

To put the notion of research methods in consumer behavior in proper perspective, it is important to clarify the terms research and methods. Webster's New Collegiate Dictionary defines research as "an investigation aimed at the discovery and interpretation of facts, revision of accepted theories or laws in the light of new factors, or practiced application of such new or revised theories or laws." For example, one common goal of any discipline is expanding its knowledge base. Researchers often begin by examining the present state of knowledge in a particular area and then follow with empirical studies to test hypotheses about some aspect of the relevant theory. If the research is sound, the results from the empirical studies will not only advance the knowledge in the discipline, but also will generate further research in related areas. Thus, there seems to be little doubt that research is vital to understanding more about any discipline.

Methods in consumer behavior are the means of gathering data. For example, "methods include such procedures as the making of observations and measurements, performing experiments, building models and theories, or providing explanations and making predictions" (Miller, 1970, p. 65).

The research process can be divided into seven steps:

1. A definition of the problem and/or research objectives.
2. The construction of a theoretical framework.
3. The development of hypotheses.
4. The selection and execution of a research design.
5. The analysis and interpretation of results.
6. A written report.
7. Research utilization.

The role of methods in consumer behavior research is in research design. Research design includes the plan, structure, and strategy of investigation to obtain answers to research questions. The plan is the overall scheme of the research and includes an outline of what the researcher will do from formulating the hypotheses and their operational implications to the final analysis of the task. The structure of the research is more specific. It is the outline of the relationships among the variables. Strategy is also more specific than the plan of the investigation. It includes the methods to be used to gather and analyze the data. Thus, strategy determines how the research will be tackled (Kerlinger, 1973, p. 300).

There are two types of data: primary data and secondary data. Secondary data are data already existing, having been originally collected for some purpose other than the project at hand. Examples of secondary data are the data found in government publications, libraries, and the results from other studies in consumer behavior. Primary data, in contrast, are original data collected specifically for the current research project, such as when a researcher stands in a supermarket and observes whether people use shopping lists and also in what order they go to the various departments. Of course, secondary data sources always ought to be exhausted before gathering primary data. The emphasis in this chapter will be upon the collection of primary data, since most studies in consumer behavior research require a significant collection of primary data. The remainder of this chapter will discuss the major methods of gathering primary data, some of the common statistics employed, and, finally, some conclusions about the state of research methods in consumer behavior.

METHODS OF GATHERING PRIMARY DATA[1]

There are three principal methods of gathering primary data: survey, observation, and experimentation. Normally, not all three methods are used in the same project. The choice of methods will depend largely upon the availability of time, money, and personnel. However, to increase the validity of the data, sometimes more than one method for gathering data is used.

Survey
A survey is a study of a population by selecting and studying samples chosen from the population. The

[1]For a more comprehensive discussion of the basic methods of gathering primary data, see Zaltman and Burger (1978).

purpose of many surveys is simply to provide someone with information. The information may be descriptive (e.g., how families of different sizes spend their income), or explanatory (e.g., determining how and why attitudes toward education influence voting behavior on a school bond issue).

The instrument for collecting data in surveys is the interview or questionnaire. An interview is an interpersonal contact between an interviewer and a respondent in order to obtain answers pertinent to some research problem. Surveys may be conducted on a personal face-to-face basis, over the telephone, or by mail. The instrument may be structured or nonstructured; that is, the questions, their sequence and wording, may or may not be fixed. These different types of instruments can be evaluated on the following criteria: (1) flexibility, (2) amount of information to be obtained. (3) accuracy of information, (4) speed, (5) cost, and (6) administration.

The personal interview is a face-to-face contact between an interviewer and a respondent. This interviewing may be conducted in a number of settings, such as the home of the respondent, the office of the respondent or of the interviewer, in the street, or virtually any meeting place. The personal interview may be on either an individual basis or in a group. Group interviews are called focus group interviews when the interviewer focuses attention upon a given experience and its effects.

Personal interviews are probably the most flexible of all interviews. The interviewer is able to alter the form, content, and order of questioning in order to probe deeper or ask unplanned questions. More information is usually possible relative to the telephone or mail interview. Virtually every subject lends itself to personal interviewing. In addition to probing, the interviewer may also obtain supplementary information by observing, for example, the respondent's standard of living, home, and neighborhood. Finally, a statistically sound sample is ordinarily more easily obtainable with personal interviewing than with the telephone or mail interview. However, there is also the accompanying problem of interviewer bias. If, for example, the interviewer does not always ask a particular question in the same way, respondents will get different stimuli which will produce additional variations in their responses.

The other major limitations of personal interviewing are its relatively high cost and the difficulties of administration. Not only is personal interviewing expensive, but it is also time consuming. Lastly, personal interviewing requires much administration since interviewers must be selected, trained, and supervised.[2]

Surveys conducted by mail involve mailing a list of questions to potential respondents and having them return the completed form by mail. Unlike the personal interview, there is no interviewer bias since the manner in which questions are posed is uniform. Mail interviewing also lends itself to wide geographic coverage at a rather low cost, particularly because there are virtually no expenses beyond the cost of stamps, paper, and envelopes. Also, since respondents may answer the questions in their leisure time, responses can be more carefully thought out. Because respondents remain anonymous, they will probably give true answers since they do not feel any need to impress the interviewer or feel embarrassed. Finally, it is easier to reach some groups by mail than by the personal interview or telephone.

Mail surveys offer little flexibility since there can be no probing or observing for supplemental information. Also, not much information can be obtained because questions must be few and simple in order to increase the probability of return. Another problem of interviewing by mail is the rather slow return time. Leisure time allows the respondent to wait a week or two (or even a couple of months) before responding. In many cases, the respondent doesn't even answer, creating the problem of sample representativeness (often referred to as nonrespondent bias). If those people who did not respond would have responded differently from those who did respond, then generalizing the results from the sample to the population would be incorrect. Another major problem with mail interviewing is the compilation of a good mailing list,

especially in broad-scale surveys. Mailing lists for baby shoes, for example, can be very good since newspapers print the names of newborns and their parents daily. A mailing list for cable television subscribers is probably more difficult to obtain.[3]

The telephone survey includes interviews conducted over the telephone. It is more flexible than the mail survey, but less flexible than the personal interview. Telephone interviewers can clarify questions and probe beyond basic questions, but obtaining supplementary information by observation is impossible. Similarly, more information can be obtained by telephone interviewing than by mail interviewing, but less than by personal interviewing. Telephone interviewers can probe to obtain more information, but only on a limited basis because respondents normally do not want to talk by phone for more than just a few minutes. Because of the timeliness of telephone interviewing, the information obtained can be very accurate. For example, suppose a telephone interviewer were to call a person's home and ask whether the person is watching television and, if so, which television show and who the sponsor is. The response given is surely more accurate than, say, the answer to a mail interviewer who asks the questions: which television program did you watch last Tuesday at 8:30 p.m. and who was the sponsor? Telephone interviewing is also relatively inexpensive. Despite long-distance phone calling, costs can be kept at a low level since there are no travel expenses and only a few interviewers from a central location are required.

Although only a few interviewers are required and although wide geographic coverage is feasible, there remains one major limitation to the telephone survey. It is virtually impossible to get a very good cross-section of the population. Some people do not have phones, some have unlisted numbers, some are not at home when the interviewer calls, and others simply refuse to respond. Table 1 summarizes the advantages and disadvantages of these three types of surveys.

---

[2]For a more complete listing of the advantages and disadvantages of personal interviewing, see Miller (1970, pp. 86–88).

[3]For a more complete listing of the advantages and disadvantages of mail interviewing, see Miller (1970, pp. 76–77).

Table 1 Advantages and Disadvantages of Three Survey Types

Criteria	Type of Survey		
	Personal Interview	Mail Survey	Telephone Interview
1. Flexibility	Most flexible; much probing possible	Little flexibility; no probing possible	Medium amount of flexibility
2. Amount of information obtained	Much information can be obtained	Can only have a few simple questions	Medium amount of information
3. Accuracy of information	Depends on specific questions—can be high or low	Fairly high if anonymous	Depends on specific questions—can be high or low
4. Speed	Time consuming to conduct	Slow return time	Medium amount of time required
5. Cost	High	Low	Medium
6. Administration	Difficult; requires much supervision	No interviewers required; questionnaire must be easily understood	Requires some supervision

In all three types of surveys, someone fills out a questionnaire. In a mail survey the respondent reads questions and then writes down the answers. In personal and telephone interviews the interviewer asks the questions (either from memory or from a piece of paper). The respondent gives verbal answers, and the interviewer writes them down (either immediately or later). The questionnaire is the interview schedule, a formal list of questions used to conduct a survey. The importance of the questionnaire and the difficulty of designing it cannot be overemphasized. Payne (1951) devotes an entire book to the preparation of questionnaires. In addition, Moser and Kalton contend that "No survey can be better than its questionnaire, a cliche which expresses the truth that no matter how efficient the sample design or sophisticated the analysis, ambiguous questions will produce noncomparable answers, leading questions biased answers, and vague questions vague answers. De-

sign of the questionnaire must begin at the start of the planning stages and will not end until the pilot surveys are completed" (1972, p. 308).

One procedure for questionnaire construction is set forth by Boyd and Westfall (1972, pp. 288–316). First, it is necessary to determine what information is needed to answer the research questions. Second, what type of survey should be used—personal interview, mail, or telephone? Next, the questionnaire designer must determine the content and necessity of each question and try to determine whether the respondents can and will answer it. Is the question necessary? Are several questions needed instead of one? One of the biggest mistakes in questionnaire design is to throw in a hodgepodge of questions because "they might turn up something interesting." Fourth, the type of question to use must be determined—open-ended, multiple choice, etc. Fifth, the wording of the questionnaire must be decided. It is imperative at this step to define the issue, to use simple words, to avoid ambiguous and leading questions, and to decide whether to use an objective or subjective question, a positive or negative question. The sixth step is deciding on the sequence of questions. Opening questions must win the interest of the respondent. Difficult questions usually should be saved for the body or end of the questionnaire. After respondents have answered a number of questions, they are apt to be more at ease with the interviewing process and will be less likely to balk at personal questions such as those relating to income and knowledge. It is also important to consider the influence of succeeding questions. If mentioning the sponsor of the survey would bias the answers, then any questions suggesting the sponsor ought to be left at the end of the questionnaire. Finally, questions ought to follow one another in a logical order—that is, an order which is logical to the respondent! Seventh, the questionnaire designer must determine the physical form, layout, and method of reproduction. For mail surveys, cover letters stating the nature and purpose of the survey are often very useful in gaining the cooperation of respondents. Questionnaires must be legal, letter, or postcard size. Questions should not be crowded together on a page, and sufficient space must be provided for answering the questions. The next step is to prepare a preliminary draft and pretest it under field conditions. No matter how hard the researcher tries, it seems inevitable that something has been left out, is not necessary, or is ambiguous. Lastly, the questionnaire must be revised and a final draft prepared.

Questionnaire studies can also be classified by disguise and structure, depending upon, respectively, whether the objectives are clear to the respondent and whether a prescribed sequence of questions is followed (Boyd and Westfall, 1972, pp. 136–143). Using these two bases for classification, four types of questionnaire studies can be identified as shown in the figure.

Most questionnaire studies are structured-nondisguised (Type A). The objectives of the questionnaire are made clear to the respondent. A formal list of questions is asked directly and in a predeter-

	Structured	Nonstructured
Nondisguised	A	B
Disguised	C	D

mined sequence. Answers are frequently limited to a list of alternatives. The structured-nondisguised questionnaire is speedy, it permits an easy tabulation of the data, and it is reliable, since interviewer bias is at a minimum. However, it is also rather inflexible, since probing is not possible.

The nonstructured-nondisguised questionnaire (Type B) is used for the purpose of allowing the respondent to talk freely about some subject of interest. It employs the psychoanalytic technique of depth interviewing, a technique where the interviewer tries to put respondents at ease and encourage them to express any ideas they have about the subject. For example, a fixed list of direct questions dealing with motives seldom generates useful answers. People often cannot articulate their motives or, if they can, may be embarrassed to do so. For example, the family that bought a new Cadillac as a status symbol may respond in direct questioning that the car is really very economical in the long run. The nonstructured-nondisguised questionnaire therefore attempts to ask questions in such a way that status considerations, for instance, may be mentioned. With nonstructured-nondisguised questionnaires, there is the major problem concerning the validity and reliability of the interviewer's interpretations. Different interviewers may interpret the same information quite differently.

In order to circumvent the problems of socially acceptable responses, false answers, or answers which cannot be articulated, disguised methods of gathering data are used (Types C and D). Projective techniques, where individuals reflect themselves in interpreting a situation, are commonly used for this purpose. Three common projective techniques are word associations, sentence completion, and story telling. In word association, a series of words is read one at a time to the respondent who, in turn, says the first thing that comes to his or her mind. Sentence completion, as the term suggests, requires the respondent to complete an incomplete sentence. In story telling, the respondent is shown a picture and is then asked to tell a story about it.

Structured-disguised questioning (Type C) has many of the characteristics discussed above. The questioning is speedy, the answers are easy to tabulate, and there is less chance for interviewer bias; however, the questioning is less flexible and is limited to the collection of factual information. An illustration of the structured-disguised type of questioning might be a test for political party preferences. Psychological theory posits that an individual's knowledge, perception, and memory are conditioned by attitudes. Therefore, it would be reasonable to expect that Democrats listen to more speeches by other Democrats than by Republicans and, thus, Democrats have more information about Democratic candidates than about Republican candidates. A straightforward question, such as "Are you a Republican or a Democrat?" might get a biased answer. Instead, a simple test of information about the candidates would probably better distinguish Republicans from Democrats.

Observation

The survey method of gathering primary data is rather inexpensive, speedy, and versatile enough to apply to almost all types of problems. When people are unwilling or unable to respond or when the questioning process influences the results (for example, giving socially acceptable answers or saying what the interviewer wants to hear), the observation method of gathering primary data can be used. In the observation method, data is collected by observing some action of the respondent rather than asking for information. The underlying premise is that the person is unaware of being observed and, hence, will behave in the usual manner, or if aware of being observed, at least over time can only behave in his or her ordinary manner.

Observation studies can be classified according to two dimensions: personalness and reactivity.

This classification scheme may be diagrammed as follows:

| | | Reactivity | |
		Nonreactive	Reactive
Personalness	Personal	Personal Nonreactive	Personal Reactive
	Mechanical	Mechanical Nonreactive	Mechanical Reactive

Each cell is discussed below.

In personal nonreactive (unobtrusive) observation, information is obtained by a researcher without any interaction with the respondent. Numerous examples have been cited (Webb, et al., 1966) from the literature in consumer behavior research. One investigator measured the level of whiskey consumption in a tavern which was officially "dry" by counting empty bottles in trash cans. The degree of fear induced by a ghost-story-telling session was measured by noting the shrinking diameter of a circle of seated children. Finally, to determine where their customers came from, store owners have recorded license numbers of cars in the parking lot and then traced the addressed of the owners through the license bureau.

The personal reactive observation method obtains information by a researcher interacting with the respondent. The interaction may be simple and direct. For example, "in an effort to find ways of improving the service in a retail store, an observer may mingle with the customers in the store and look for activities that suggest service problems" (Boyd and Westfall, 1972, p. 162).

The interaction may also be contrived, such as an observer posing as a customer and bargaining with the salesperson over price in order to test the salesperson's selling abilities. An interesting contrived observation is the lost letter technique. To measure the relative interest in a political candidate in different geographical areas, a researcher may stamp and address fifty letters to:

Educators for President Jimmy Carter
% John Dobson
136 Market Street
Pittsburgh, Pennsylvania 15216

By dropping these letters on the sidewalk on various streets (i.e., "losing" them before they were placed in the mailbox), and also by "losing" in the same areas another set of fifty letters with the same address except for the first line, the observer could then determine the proportion of letters returned from both the experimental and control groups in each area.

Another type of personal reactive research is participant observation. Here the observer joins in the life of the group being studied. The participant-observer watches what happens to the members and how they behave. This type of researcher also engages in conversations with them to find out their reactions to, and interpretations of, the events that have occurred. The observer's task is to take on a position in which he or she can get a complete and unbiased picture of the life of the group. If the observer can become so accepted as part of the group that its members forget about being observed, he or she will naturally get a more authentic picture of its behavior (McCall and Simmons, 1969).

Mechanical observations use a piece of apparatus to do the recording. The recording apparatus may be either reactive or nonreactive with the respondent. A very common use of mechanical observation is the A. C. Nielsen Company audiometer which is attached to the TV set or radio to identify which channel is being watched or listened to. Two-way mirrors are non-reactive mechanical observation, since there is no interaction with the person being observed. Tape recorders and cameras may be either reactive or nonreactive, depending upon the physical facility and the purposes of the research. When the respondent speaks into a tape recorder, the research is said to be nonreactive. However, if the tape recorder asks questions, then it is reactive.

The observation method has several merits. First, information is often obtained in a natural rather than an artificial setting. It can be highly accurate, since it removes any conjecture about what the respondent does in a given situation. With the ease of mechanical devices, more detailed and permanent information is possible. A major drawback, however, can be observer bias (analogous to interviewer bias in the survey method). Finally, it can be very expensive, since at times there may be simply nothing to observe.

Experimentation

Experimentation is a research process in which one or more variables are manipulated under conditions that permit the collection of data which shows the effects of these variables. The underlying premise of experimentation is that small-scale experiments will furnish valuable information in designing or testing a large-scale consumer behavior program.

The basic structure of experimentation is quite simple. First, a hypothesis is formulated: "if X, then Y." For example, if advertising, X, is used, more sales, Y, will be generated. Next, depending upon the purpose of the experiment, X is either manipulated or measured. Then Y is observed to see if there is a concomitant variation as a result of the variation in X. If there is, then there is evidence of the validity of the hypothesis. Finally, to achieve control of both the extraneous variables[4] and the experimental variables, the experimenter will randomly assign subjects to groups and will actively manipulate X.

Experiments can be conducted either in the laboratory or in the field. The laboratory experiment is a research study in which the variance of all or nearly all of the extraneous variables is kept at a minimum. This control is achieved by isolating the experiment in a physical setting apart from the routine of ordinary living and by manipulating one or more experimental variables under rigorously specified conditions. An illustration of a lab experiment might be an artificial store setup, in, say, a hotel ballroom where food shoppers are asked to go through the artificial store and select products as *if* they were on a regular shopping trip. If prices are varied and if actual selections are comparable to purchases in a real store setting, then the price which generated the greatest sales, for example, can be determined.

---

[4]An extraneous variable is a variable which has an effect on the experimental outcome which confounds the effect of the experimental variable. See the following discussion of factors jeopardizing internal and external validity.

A field experiment is a research study conducted in an everyday setting in which one or more experimental variables are manipulated under as carefully controlled conditions as possible. The contrast between the laboratory experiment and field experiment is not precise—often the differences are matters of degree. Where the laboratory experiment has a maximum of control, most field studies are conducted with less control, a factor that is often a serious limitation to the experiment. However, this limitation of control in field experiments is sometimes compensated for by the natural settings which permit consumers to behave in their normal manner. The artificiality of laboratory experiments, in contrast, often allows consumers to behave differently than normal which, consequently, can invalidate the results of the experiment.

Two very serious issues in experimentation are internal and external validity. Internal validity asks the question: "Did the experimental variable in fact make a difference in the experiment?" It may be that the extraneous variables, instead of the experimental variables, were the source of the experimental outcomes. There are seven major factors which can jeopardize internal validity.[5] If not controlled, these factors will invalidate the results. They are as follows:

1. History. Events specific to the experiment can occur between the first and second measurement of the experimental variable. For example, attitudes and preferences toward a particular product may change over time, perhaps as the result of television advertising or news articles. More consumers may purchase a domestic automobile after a price decrease than before the price change, not because of the price decrease itself, but rather because there was strong sentiment not to buy foreign products.

2. Maturation. Like history, maturation is a function of time. However, instead of events specific to the experiment occurring, maturation is concerned with general types of events occurring, particularly the biological and psychological processes of the respondent (such as growing older, hungrier, wiser, more tired, and more bored). Though a consumer's last car was a sports car, he may not purchase another one because he is older and feels it doesn't fit his image, regardless of price, styling, and the like.

3. Testing. Testing refers to the effect of a pretest. If a group of food shoppers were asked to report on a weekly basis the grocery items they purchased and the amount spent, they may in time become very concerned about being thrifty, and also very conscious about what specific brands they purchase. As a result, they may alter their normal purchasing behavior. Thus, pretests can influence future behavior and thereby confound the effects of the experimental variable.

4. Instrumentation. It is possible that over the duration of the experiment the calibration of the measuring device or the way observers score responses may change. At one point, consumers may be designated as brand loyal if they purchase the same brand three times successively. Later, the same experimenter or even a different experimenter may categorize a consumer as being brand loyal if four out of five purchases were of the same brand.

5. Statistical regression. Due to chance, low scorers on a pretest may score higher on a post-test when, in fact, no real change has taken place as a result of the experimental variable. Such a phenomenon occurs because there is no *perfect* relationship between the pretest and post-test.

6. Selection. The effect of the experimental variable may be confounded by the way respondents are selected for an experiment. For example, if a researcher advertises in a newspaper that subjects are being recruited for some research on product dissatisfaction and that participating subjects will receive $5, there may be bias in the sample which results. The researcher is likely to get subjects who want $5 (and, therefore, may not value their time very highly) and subjects who are

---

[5]For a very comprehensive treatment, see Campbell and Stanley (1963).

particularly interested in product dissatisfaction (maybe they have had an unusually bad experience).

7. Mortality.   Differences other than the experimental effects can arise because people drop out of the experiment. It is extremely unlikely that replacements will be exactly equivalent to those who left and, in many cases, replacements are not even recruited. In experimentally testing a group of consumers for packaging preferences, preferences may be overstated if those who dropped out of the experiment didn't like the packaging.

External validity is a second major issue in experimentation. It is concerned with how the experimental results can be generalized to other populations and settings. There are four major factors which can jeopardize external validity.[6]

1. The interaction of testing and the experimental variable.   A pretest might increase or decrease the respondent's sensitivity to the experimental variable. Therefore, the results obtained from the pretested population will probably not be representative of the effects of the experimental variable for the nonpretested population.

2. The interaction of selection and the experimental variable.   It is possible that the experimental results are valid only for the specific population of the experiment. This possibility becomes more tenable as subjects become harder to find.

3. The interaction of experimental arrangements.   A common reason for not being able to generalize experimental results is the artificiality of the experimental setting (such as the hotel ballroom acting as a mock-up supermarket) and subjects' knowledge that they are participating in a experiment. When subjects know they are playacting, being observed, and acting as guinea pigs, they may be less likely to behave as they usually do.

4. The interaction of multiple experimental variables.   Where many experimental variables are used on the same subject, the effects of each experimental treatment[7] become difficult to erase. The subject probably remembers previous actions and responses and, consequently, it may be impossible to isolate the effects of the current stimuli from the previous experimental stimuli.

Experiments may be designed in many ways, depending upon the nature and purpose of the research. Some of the major experimental designs are discussed below. The notation of Campbell and Stanley (1963) is used where:

X_i represents the *i*th treatment of the experimental variable;

O_i represents the *i*th observation or measurement;

R represents a random assignment of subjects to treatments;

X and O in the same row represent a treatment and observation of the same subject;

E represents the effect of the experimental variable.

Time sequence is represented horizontally.

A very simple design is the "after only" ("one shot") design, diagrammed as

$$X \quad O$$
$$E = O$$

First, a treatment of the experimental variable is applied to a group of subjects and then an observation or measurement is made. Studies having such designs can be of little scientific value because of the total absence of control. The experimenter cannot be sure what the effect of the experimental variable is because there is nothing with which to compare it. The design does not allow the experimenter to know whether or not subjects not receiving the treatment behave exactly as those who did receive the treatment. "After only" designs therefore are usually limited to exploratory studies, where the purpose is only to generate hypotheses and ideas for testing.

[6]For a more comprehensive discussion, see Campbell and Stanley (1963).

[7]An experimental treatment is a specific manipulation of the experimental variable.

A second design is the "before-after" ("one group pretest post-test") design. It is denoted as

$$O_1 X O_2$$
$$E = O_2 - O_1$$

In this design, an observation or measurement is made both before and after a specific treatment is applied to the subjects. Though often judged as better than the "after-only" design, the "before-after" design still has many problems of internal validity, namely history, maturation, testing, instrumentation, and statistical regression. Also, the experimenter still cannot be sure whether or not subjects not exposed to the experimental variable might also show the change reflected by the difference between the two observations.

The "before-after with control" ("pretest post-test control group") design eliminates many of the above problems. It is a very common design in consumer behavior research and is diagrammed as:

$$R\ O_1\ X\ O_2$$
$$R\ O_3\quad O_4$$
$$E = (O_2 - O_1) - (O_4 - O_3).$$

In addition to observations or measurements before and after the experimental treatment is applied, this design also permits a comparison of those subjects who received the treatments with those who did not. The experimental group (those subjects who receive the treatments) and the control group (those subjects who do not receive the treatments) are selected in such a way that they are as similar as possible. Matching subjects on such characteristics as age, sex, income, and attitudes is one method of achieving similarity of groups, but this method is difficult to apply, since it is usually impossible to find two groups or even two people who are exactly alike. An alternative and more feasible method of achieving similarity of groups is randomization. By randomly assigning all subjects to the experimental and control groups, it is presumed that there will be a similar distribution of subject types in each group. This principle of randomization also minimizes the effect of selection as a confounding factor to determining the effect of

the experimental variable. However, the mortality factor still remains.

The "four group-six study" ("Solomon four group") design can be diagrammed as:

$$R\ O_1\ X\ O_2$$
$$R\ O_3\quad O_4$$
$$R\quad\ \ X\ O_5$$
$$R\quad\quad\ O_6$$
$$E = \left[\left(O_5 - \frac{O_1 + O_3}{2}\right) - \left(O_6 - \frac{O_1 + O_3}{2}\right)\right]$$

This design is a combination of the previous designs: the top half of this design is equivalent to the "before-after with control group" design; the third row is simply the "after-only" design; and the last row is just an observation or measurement of a fourth group of subjects at the same time that O_2, O_4, and O_5 are obtained. The "four group-six study" design is ideal for experiments in which data are collected from individuals in such a way that they realize it is being done—it eliminates the testing effect. Unfortunately, this design has little practical value. Since six observations are required, the difficulty of obtaining a large number of subjects and the time and expense involved often makes this design impractical for many consumer behavior studies. However, it can serve as an ideal against which to compare other proposed designs.

In some of the designs presented, pretests were used. Suppose that pretests are not possible or feasible because of such reasons as time, money, and availability of subjects. In some cases, the "after-only with control" design, diagrammed

$$R\ X\ O_1$$
$$R\quad O_2$$
$$E = O_2 - O_1$$

may be used. Again, the experimental and control groups are selected in a way, such as by randomization, to be as alike as possible. The experimental effect then is simply the difference between the two observations or measurements.

A variation of the "before-after" design is the "panel" design. One type of panel design appears as:

$$O_1\ O_2\ X_1\ O_3\ X_2\ O_4\ O_5\ X_3\ O_6$$

The treatment effect of, say, X_2 would be computed as:

$$E \text{ (treatment } X_2) = O_4 - O_3$$

A sample of subjects is recruited and information is obtained from the members continuously or at intervals over a period of time. The members of the panel typically are asked to record in a diary their purchasing behavior relevant to the experiment. The drawback to panel designs, however, is that the experimenter must select the sample such that it is representative of the population and that the subjects properly, honestly, and conscientiously record entries in their diary.

Factorial designs, unlike the above designs, permit the experimenter to test two or more experimental variables at the same time. This design allows the determination of not only the main effects of each experimental variable, but also of the interactions between variables. A factorial design, for example, might be used to determine the proper concentration of sugar and carbonation in soft drinks. Suppose there are four levels of carbonation and three levels of sugar, as below:

		Carbonation			
		1	2	3	4
	1	a	b	c	d
Sugar	2	e	f	g	h
	3	i	j	k	l

If the experimenter were to test each combination of carbonation and sugar on the same group of subjects, then the best combination could be determined by simply observing the highest score on some scaled measure of likes and preferences (or the greatest sales if each of the twelve types were actually sold in the marketplace under similar conditions).

Unfortunately, many tests are required for such experiments. A Latin square design can economize on the number of studies necessary, although at the expense of larger errors. Suppose an experi-

menter wanted to test the effects of three variables, such as the effects of packaging, test city, and price, as shown below:

		Packaging			
		1	2	3	4
	1	A	B	C	D
Test	2	B	A	D	C
city	3	C	D	A	B
	4	D	C	B	A

This arrangement has the same number of levels (four) for each variable and may be viewed as sixteen "after-only" designs. The four different prices are represented by the letters A, B. C, and D. Each price is tested once and only once with each of the test cities and with each of the different types of packaging.[8] The sum of the sales associated with all four of any one letter, i.e., one specific price, could be compared with the total sales associated with all four of any other letter to determine which price to charge. However, if there were an interaction between test city and packaging (such as one city being out of stock of one of the packaging types due to a delivery strike), then the results from this design could not be generalized to other test cities and packaging types. In order to generalize the results, there must not be any interactions among the variables. Thus, the savings in fewer test cells (sixteen instead of sixty-four with the usual factorial design) can result in confounding the effect of price with an interaction effect of test city and packaging.

The experimental method, in summary, has its strength and weaknesses. Its principal strength is the ability to determine cause and effect, often in very realistic and natural settings. Unfortunately, however, it also frequently requires much time, money, and administration, especially in selecting subjects and controlling for extraneous variables.

---

[8]Note, however, that each price is not tested with each of the possible test city—packaging levels. For example, the fourth test city and the second type of packaging receive only one price treatment, C.

SUMMARY

Researchers in consumer behavior have an arsenal of methods and techniques available to them. To use these methods and techniques effectively and efficiently, it is important that the researcher clearly understand their assumptions, purposes, and limitations. New techniques will undoubtedly evolve in the future, but probably the most significant advances in research methods in consumer behavior over the short run will come from new applications of existing methods. As researchers become more familiar with methods and techniques, they will become better able to apply the proper mix of techniques which is necessary to plan, design, analyze, and interpret solutions to research problems.

REFERENCES

Boyd, Harper W., Jr., and Westfall, Ralph (1972), *Marketing Research: Text and Cases,* Homewood, Ill.: Irwin.

Campbell, Donald T., and Stanley, Julian C. (1963), *Experimental and Quasi-Experimental Designs for Research,* Chicago: Rand McNally.

Kerlinger, Fred N. (1973) *Foundations of Behavioral Research,* New York: Holt, Rinehart and Winston.

McCall, George J., and Simmons, I. L. eds. (1969), *Issues in Participant Observation,* Reading, Mass.: Addison-Wesley.

Miller, Delbert C. (1970), *Handbook of Research Design and Social Measurement,* New York: David McKay Co.,

Moser, C. A., and Kalton, G. (1972), *Survey Methods in Social Investigation,* New York: Basic Books.

Payne, Stanley L. (1951), *The Art of Asking Questions,* Princeton, N.J.: Princeton University Press.

Webb, Eugene J., et al. (1966), *Unobtrusive Measures: Nonreactive Research in the Social Sciences,* Chicago: Rand McNally.

Zaltman, Gerald, and Burger, Philip C. (1975), *Marketing Research: Fundamentals and Dynamics,* 2nd ed., Hinsdale, Ill.: Dryden Press.

DESIGNING RESEARCH FOR APPLICATION

BOBBY J. CALDER
LYNN W. PHILLIPS
ALICE M. TYBOUT

There is always the expectation in conducting research that the findings ultimately will be useful in addressing situations beyond the one studied. Yet, there exists a concern that much of consumer research, and behavioral research in general, is not generalizable. It frequently is argued that research procedures, particularly the use of student subjects and laboratory settings, necessarily limit the application of findings. Underlying this contention is a failure to recognize that generalizability is not a single issue. Two distinct types of application may be identified in consumer research.

The first type of generalizability, which we term *effects application*, maps observed data directly into events beyond the research setting. That is, the specific effects obtained are expected to mirror findings that would be observed if data were collected for other populations and settings in the real world.[1] The second type, which we term *theory application*, uses only scientific theory to explain events beyond the research setting. Effects observed in the research are employed to assess the status of theory. But, it is the theoretical explanation that is expected to be generalizable and not the particular effects obtained.

DISTINGUISHING RESEARCH GOALS

Effects application and theory application have common elements as well as distinguishing features. Research seeking either type of generalizability necessarily involves some framework or reasoning that might be loosely referred to as "theory." And in both instances, research entails observations of some "effects" related to the theoretical framework. The distinction lies in whether the researcher's primary goal is to apply the specific effects observed or to apply a more general theoretical understanding.

Effects application is based on a desire for knowledge about the events and relationships in a particular real-world situation. The primary goal of

Source: Bobby J. Calder, Lynn W. Phillips, and Alice M. Tybout, "Designing Research for Application," *Journal of Consumer Research*, Vol. 8, September, 1981, pp. 197–207. Reprinted with permission.

[1]The term "real world" is employed in reference to all situations not constructed for, or altered by, the conduct of research. It is not meant to imply that research settings do not have their own reality.

this type of research (here-after referred to as "effects research") is to obtain findings that can be applied directly to the situation of interest. A theoretical framework may be used to identify and measure effects.[2] But it is the effects themselves that are generalized rather than being linked by inference to theoretical constructs and the hypothesized theoretical network then used to deduce patterns of outcomes.

Application of effects calls for correspondence procedures. It is necessary to assess effects in a research setting that corresponds to a real-world situation. Complete correspondence is difficult to achieve, however. The mere fact of data collection usually distinguishes the research setting from its real-world counterpart. And, because interest rarely is limited to present situations, temporal differences often exist as well. These differences, and others, between the research setting and the real world are inevitable. Effects application, nonetheless, is characterized by the premise that there is *sufficient* correspondence to expect the effects observed to be repeated in the real world.

In contrast, theory application is based on a desire for scientific knowledge about events and relationships that occur in a variety of real-world situations. The primary goal of such research (hereafter referred to as "theory research") is to identify scientific theories that provide a general understanding of the real world. Theory applications call for falsification test procedures. These procedures are used to test a theory by creating a context and measuring effects within that context that have the potential to disprove or refute the theory. The research context and effects are not of interest in their own right. Their significance lies in the information that they provide about the theory's adequacy. Theories that repeatedly survive rigorous falsification attempts are accepted as scientific explanation (subject to further more strigent testing), and are candidates for application.[3] Scientific theories typically are universal and, therefore, can explain any real-world situation within their domain.

The actual application of theory entails using the scientific explanation to design a program or intervention predicted to have some effect in the real world. In a marketing context, the intervention may take the form of a product, price, communication strategy, etc. It is crucial to note that, whatever the strategy, the process of translating from theory to intervention is necessarily a creative one. Theories neither specify how their abstract constructs can be embodied in real-world interventions nor identify the level(s) that uncontrolled theoretical variables will assume in a particular application. Moreover, theories are always incomplete—they deal with a subset of variables that exist in the real world. Consequently, the design process must rely on some assumptions about the operation of both theoretical and nontheoretical variables.

Because intervention design is creative, basing an intervention on theory that has survived rigorous falsification attempts is not sufficient to ensure that the intervention will yield the theoretically predicted outcome. Separate falsification procedures are required to test a theory and a theory-based intervention. Perhaps an example can best illustrate this. Theories of aerodynamics explain the processes underlying flight. It is not possible, however, to design an airplane solely from aerodynamic theory. Any number of stress studies and the like are necessary to calibrate the theory to conditions in a particular real-world situation. These studies, which we term efforts at intervention falsification, systematically subject the inter-

[2]The theoretical framework underlying effects research can be either scientific (i.e., a general theory that has survived rigorous testing) or intuitive (i.e., a theory generated to address a particular situation, which may be consistent with informal observations, but which has not undergone any rigorous testing). This is in contrast to theory research, which is restricted to the examination of general scientific theories. Although we subscribe to the view that scientific theory has advantages over intuitive theory even in effects research, this is obviously a debatable issue. Moreover, because this issue is only tangentially related to ones surrounding the conduct and application of effects research, we leave its discussion to some other forum.

[3]It should be noted that the view of theory testing outlined here is a falsificationist one (Popper 1959, 1963). Theories are not proven. They are accepted pending further research. Although many issues surround the falsificationist perspective (Kuhn 1970, Lakatos 1970), they are largely peripheral to the concerns of this paper. The important point is that theory tests must attempt to expose theories to refutation by data, and must be conservative in accepting theories that escape refutation.

Exhibit 1 Summary of two approaches to applicability

	Effects application	*Theory application*
Research goal	To obtain findings that can be generalized directly to a real-world situation of interest.	To obtain scientific theory that can be generalized through the design of theory-based interventions that are viable in the real world.
Research procedure	Generalizing effects requires procedures to ensure that the research setting accurately reflects the real world. These are termed *correspondence procedures*.	Generalizing theory requires two stages of *falsification procedures*. First, *theory falsification procedures* are used to ensure that the abstract theoretical explanation is rendered fully testable. Theories that survive rigorous attempts at falsification are accepted and accorded scientific status.
		Accepted theory is used as a framework for designing an intervention. Then, *intervention falsification procedures* are used to test the intervention under conditions that could cause it to fail in the real world. Only interventions surviving these tests are implemented.

vention to conditions that might cause it to fail in a particular situation. If the intervention does not perform as predicted by the theory, then its weaknesses are exposed. As in theory testing, failures are more informative than successes. But, the failure of an intervention need not imply inadequacies in the theory. Indeed, failure of the theoretical explanation can be implied only when theory falsification procedures are employed.[4] Theory falsification procedures are, thus, the foundation of any effort to apply theory.

If it succeeds, confidence that the intervention is viable increases. As a result, the intervention may be used in the real world. In contrast to effects application, however, *no attempt is made to generalize any particular outcomes observed in testing the theory or the intervention*. It is only the theoretical relationship that the intervention is presumed to represent that is applied beyond the research setting.

The goals of research leading to effects application and to theory application are summarized in Exhibit 1. As we have indicated, different research procedures are necessary to achieve each of these goals. We now examine these research procedures in greater detail.

COMPARISON OF CORRESPONDENCE AND FALSIFICATION PROCEDURES

Effects application relies on research methods not only different from, but also largely incompatible with, the methods leading to theory application. The former requires correspondence procedures to ensure that all features of the real world are represented in the research setting. The latter requires falsification procedures to ensure, first, that the abstract scientific explanation is rendered fully testable, and, second, that the concrete theory-based intervention is viable under conditions pre-

[4]This is not to say that intervention-falsification procedures might not sometimes suggest theory-falsification procedures. Nor does it mean that in some cases the two procedures might not be identical.

Exhibit 2 Comparison of research procedures optimal for correspondence, theory falsification, and intervention falsification

Methodological issues	Correspondence procedures	Falsification procedures	
		Theory	Intervention
Selection of respondents	Use a sample statistically representative of the real-world population.	Use a sample homogeneous on nontheoretical variables.	Use a sample that encompasses individual differences that might influence performance of the intervention.
Operationalization of key variables	Operationalize variables in the research to parallel those in the real world.	Ensure that empirical operationalization of theoretical constructs cannot be construed in terms of other constructs.	Operationalize variables to reflect the manner in which an intervention is to be implemented in the real world.
Selection of a research setting	Choose a research setting statistically representative of the environmental variation present in the real world.	Choose a setting that allows operationalization of theoretical constructs and is free of extraneous sources of variation.	Choose a setting encompassing environmental heterogeneity that might influence the performance of the intervention.
Selection of a research design	Use a design that preserves the correspondence between the research environment and provides the type of information required for decision making (e.g., descriptive, correlational, causal).	Use a design that affords the strongest possible inferences about the relationships between theoretical constructs.	Use a design that affords the strongest possible test of the intervention subject to constraints imposed by the need to represent real-world variation.

sent in the real world. Exhibit 2 summarizes the procedures we will discuss.

Selecting Respondents

When effects application is the goal, correspondence procedures require that research participants match individuals in the real world setting of interest. Ideally, this is accomplished by carefully defining the relevant population for the effects of interest, and then employing in the investigation a strictly representative sample of individuals from this target population.[5] This procedure is necessary if any generalization from the sample to the population is to be statistically valid. But, because strict statistical sampling often is not feasible, other procedures may be invoked to enhance the representativeness of individuals in the research. For example, it may be possible to replicate the study with

---

[5]Although for ease in exposition we use the term "individuals" to refer to respondents, the issues discussed apply equally when the units of analysis are groups.

different subgroups of the target population. Alternatively, one might purposively sample individuals who vary on important dimensions that characterize members of the target population. Some degree of representativeness could even be achieved by sampling only the most prevalent type of individual in the target population (Cook and Campbell 1975).

The underlying theoretical framework may be useful in determining important dimensions for any nonrepresentative sample. When alternatives to statistical sampling are employed, however, the application of the results must rest on belief that the sample(s) accurately reflects the population and not on any statistical principle. Thus, confidence in generalizing is severely weakened when statistical sampling is not used.

The criteria are quite different when theory application is the goal. The theory falsification procedures, which underlie this type of generalization, require only that research participants be selected to provide a rigorous test of the theory at issue. Because most scientific theories are universal in scope, any respondent group can provide a test of the theory's predictions (Kruglanski 1973, Webster and Kervin 1971).[6] The ideal theory falsification procedure, however, is to employ maximally homogeneous respondents.[7] This entails sampling from groups of individuals that are similar on dimensions likely to influence the variables of theoretical interest. (For example, for some theories, students or housewives with similar profiles on relevant dimensions may qualify as homogeneous respondents.)

Homogeneous respondents are desired for two reasons. First, they permit more exact theoretical predictions than may be possible with a heterogeneous group. For instance, by employing a homogeneous student sample it might be possible to predict that purchases of particular product known to be used by students would decrease with advertising exposure. In contrast, if a more heterogeneous sample were selected it might be possible only to predict a decline in some broad category of products. The greater variability in behavior associated with a heterogeneous group makes precise predictions more difficult. This makes failure of the theory harder to detect. Thus, heterogeneous respondents may weaken the theory test.

Homogeneous respondents also are preferred because they decrease the chance of making a false conclusion about whether there is covariation between the variables under study. When respondents are heterogeneous with respect to characteristics that affect their responses, the error variance is increased and the significant relationsips declines. Thus, heterogeneous respondents constitute a threat to statistical conclusion validity (Cook and Campbell 1975). They increase the chance of making a Type II error and concluding that a theory was discomfirmed when, in fact, the theoretical relationship existed but was obscured by variability in the data attributable to nontheoretical constructs. By selecting maximally homogeneous samples, or by conducting full or partial replications of the research for each level or "block" of a respondent characteristic believed to inflate error variance, these random sources of error can be controlled, and the likelihood of making a Type II error decreased (Cook and Campbell 1975, Winer 1971). As a result, the researcher can be more confident that any negative results reflect failure of the theoretical explanation.

It should be noted that nothing in the theory falsification procedure rules out statistical sampling from a relevant population. But a representative sample is not required because *statistical* generalization of the findings is *not* the goal. It is the theory that is applied beyond the research setting. The research sample need only allow a test of the theory. And, any sample within the theory's domain

---

[6]Although any respondent group can be used to test a universal theory, characteristics of the particular group chosen affect, or are affected by, the operationalizations of theory variables. Operationalizations that are relevant for the subject population (Ferber 1977) should be employed to avoid the possibility that Type II errors will weaken the theory test.

[7]An exception to this preference for homogeneity occurs when an individual difference variable that cannot be manipulated by the researcher (e.g., extroversion) is of theoretical interest. Here, testing the theory requires that variability be achieved by sampling individuals who differ on the dimension of interest. This exception is consistent with providing the strongest possible test of the theory.

(e.g., any relevant sample), not just a representative one, can provide such a test.

In summary, effects application requires correspondence between the research sample and the population of interest. This is best achieved through statistical sampling. Only such sampling justifies statistical generalization of the research findings. In contrast, theory application requires a research sample that permits falsification of the theory. Although any sample in the theory's domain can potentially falsify the theory, homogeneous samples are preferred because they typically provide a stronger test of the theory. Only the theory is applied and its applicability is determined by its scientific status, not by statistical sampling principles.

Operationalizing Independent and Dependent Variables

Whether the goal is effects application or theory application, valid operationalizations of the independent and dependent variables are necessary. The two types of application differ, however, in the nature of the variables they strive to capture and, thus, in their criteria and procedures for achieving this objective. When the goal is theory application, theory falsification procedures require that the operationalization of constructs (i.e., the independent and dependent variables) render the theory testable. This involves making certain that there is a high degree of correspondence between the empirical operationalizations and the abstract concepts they intend to represent, and that the empirical indicators used to represent the theory's constructs cannot be construed in terms of other constructs. This is necessary to ensure that any failure to disconfirm the theory is not due to the use of empirical operationalizations not measuring the theoretical constructs and, thus, not testing the relationship of interest. This mislabeling of operationalizations in the theory-relevant terms is referred to as a threat to the construct validity of research results (Cook and Campbell 1975).[8]

Attaining construct validity in theory research requires rigorous definition of the theoretical constructs so that empirical measures can be tailored to them. Further, because single exemplars of any construct always contain measurement components that are irrelevant to the theoretical construct of interest, validity is enhanced by employing multiple operationalizations of each construct (Campbell and Fiske 1959, Cook and Campbell 1975). Multiple exemplars of each construct should demonstrably share common variance attributable to the target construct, and should differ from each other in unique ways (Campbell and Fiske 1959). Such "multiple operationalism" allows one to test whether a theoretical relationship holds even though measurement error is present in each operationalization (Bagozzi 1979).

When the goal is effects application, the operationalization of variables is determined by the need for correspondence. Indices of the independent and dependent variables in the research setting are chosen to parallel events in the real world. They are not tailored to abstract theoretical constructs that these variables may be presumed to represent.

Similarity between the operationalizations of variables and their real-world counterparts is maximized by using naturally occurring events in the target setting as independent variables, and naturally occurring behaviors in the target setting as dependent variables (Tunnell 1977, Webb, Campbell, Schwartz, and Sechrest 1966). Events and behaviors are considered to be "natural" if they occur in the real world. This does not necessarily imply that such events will be uncontrolled by the researcher. Price, advertising strategy, etc., are determined by decision-makers; thus, their systematic variation for research purposes would not compromise naturalness, provided that their variations reflected any real-world constraints (e.g., any practical constraints preventing disentangling related components of a marketing program in the real world). On occasion, however, the researcher may be concerned with effects on variables for which no naturally occurring measures are available, e.g., attitudes. Then, measures must be designed to assess these variables, while still preserving the correspondence between the research setting and the real world. Generally, this is achieved by making

---

[8]For a more comprehensive discussion of construct validity, see Bagozzi (1979, Chap. 5).

these measures as unobtrusive as possible. Regardless of the variables being examined, measurement error is a concern. Therefore, multiple measures of variables also are desirable in research leading to effects application.

The objectives when operationalizing variables for theory research are largely incompatible with the objectives when operationalizing variables for effects research. As just noted, the correspondence needed for effects application is achieved best by employing naturally occurring events and behaviors as variables, whenever possible. However, naturally occurring events and behaviors generally are inappropriate variables in research testing theory. They do not permit the researcher much latitude in tailoring operationalizations to theoretical constructs. Moreover, naturally occurring events often serve as indicators of a complex package of several theoretically distinct constructs. Rarely can they be taken as indicators of a single unidimensional construct. Theory falsification procedures aim to untangle these packages into several distinct variables that can be labeled in theoretical terms. Correspondence procedures aim to preserve these packages as single variables to reflect events in the real world more accurately. Thus, these two types of construct validity typically cannot be pursued simultaneously.

Choosing a Research Setting

The goals of effects application and theory application also imply different criteria in choosing a research setting. The correspondence procedures associated with effects application lead to maximizing the similarity between the research setting and the real-world situation of interest (Ellsworth 1977, Tunnel 1977). This real-world situation usually is heterogeneous on a number of background factors. For example, it may include variation in the time of day, the season, the complexity of the products involved, or the characteristics of salespersons who deliver influence attempts. To enhance transfer of the research findings to the real world, the research setting must reflect the heterogeneity of the background factors. Ideally, a random sampling of background factors present in the real world would be employed (Brunswik 1956). From

a statistical perspective, only this method of treating the heterogeneity in such factors allows generalizing the results from the research to the real world.

Often it is infeasible, if not impossible, to represent systematically all the variation in the real-world setting within a single study. In such circumstances, the researcher may try to identify the background factors most likely to impact the effects of interest. The underlying theoretical framework may be used for this purpose. Then, these factors may be represented in several ways. The study may be replicated in settings representing different levels of these background factors. Alternatively, variation on significant factors may be built into a single study without randomly sampling such factors. Or, some degree of representativeness might be achieved by including only the most frequent or typical setting factor(s) found in the real world (Cook and Campbell 1975). When these approaches are employed, however, generalization of the effects must rest on judgment that all important background factors have been properly represented, and not on a statistical principle.

Regardless of which procedure for treating setting heterogeneity is followed, representativeness is best achieved through field research. Field research refers to "any setting which respondents do not perceive to have been set up for the primary purpose of conducting research" (Cook and Campbell 1975, p. 224). The idea is to conduct the research in the real world with as little intrusion as possible. When effects research must be conducted in nonfield (i.e., laboratory) contexts, efforts should be made to incorporate the critical background factors from the real-world setting into the laboratory setting (Sawyer, Worthing, and Sendak 1979).

The theory falsification procedures associated with theory application lead to selection of an entirely different research setting. To test a theory, its constructs must be tied to a particular set of observables in a specific circumstance. It is not important, however, that these events be representative of some set of events that occur in another setting. Rather, the particular events at issue in the research setting are only important as operationalizations of the theory. What is required is that a theory's operationalization in the test setting allow it to be falsified. Typically, this involves choosing a research setting relatively free of extraneous sources of variation, e.g., free of variation on variables not of theoretical interest, and free of variation in treatment implementation. Extraneous variation can produce spurious effects on the dependent variable, and, at a minimum, inflates error variance (Cook and Campbell 1975). To the extent that theoretically irrelevant factors are at work, significant relationships between the phenomena under study may be obscured and the risk of Type II error may be increased. Insulated test settings minimize such irrelevancies.

Most often, the best procedure for reducing the number of random irrelevancies is to employ a controlled laboratory setting. In contrast to field settings, laboratory settings facilitate the use of standardized procedures and treatment implementation, and allow the researcher to control rigorously the stimuli impinging upon respondents. Moreover, laboratory settings possess other inherent advantages, relative to field settings, in conducting the strongest possible test of a theory. Homogeneous respondents are obtained more easily in the laboratory, because the investigator typically has greater control over who participates in a study. Similarly, the laboratory provides greater latitude for tailoring empirical operationalizations to the constructs they are meant to represent, because operationalizations in the laboratory are only limited by the ingenuity of the investigator, and not by naturally occurring variation and real-world constraints. And, the laboratory possesses greater potential for achieving multiple operationalizations of independent and dependent variables, because the expense associated with exposing individuals to a number of independent variables and administering a number of dependent variable responses typically is lower for the laboratory than for the field. Thus, laboratory settings generally are better geared to achieving high degrees of statistical conclusion validity and theoretical construct validity.

The advantages of the laboratory in terms of increasing statistical power and enhancing construct validity are not without limit. Tests of certain theoretical hypotheses may lead to the field if they involve variables not easily examined in laboratory settings. Thus, the advantages of insulated settings may sometimes have to be given up in order to achieve adequate empirical realizations of a theory's constructs. Nevertheless, such limits to the utility of employing laboratory settings in theory tests do not contradict our thesis. They simply reaffirm the general rule that settings yielding the strongest test of the theory should be employed when the goal is theory application. In many cases, this will be the laboratory.

Selecting a Research Design

The choice of a research setting either determines or is determined by the research design to be used. For example, laboratory research is usually associated with "true" experimental designs wherein respondents are randomly assigned to treatments (Campbell and Stanley 1966, Cook and Campbell 1975). When the goal is theory application, and theory testing is being conducted, true experimental designs are preferred because they allow the strongest test. Unlike other designs, such as the survey method or the case study, true experiments permit the investigator to minimize the possibility that third variables cause any observed relation between the independent and dependent variables. This is necessary to ensure that any failure to disconfirm the theory linking the variables is not due to the spurious impact of irrelevant third variables. Moreover, true experiments allow the investigator to establish that the independent variable precedes the dependent variable in time, thus ruling out the possibility that the dependent variable initiates changes in the independent variable, rather than vice versa. The capacity for establishing temporal antecedence and for ruling out third variable rival explanations enables true experiments to eliminate most plausible threats to internal validity, i.e., threats to the conclusion that a demonstrated statistical relationship between the independent and dependent variables implies causality (Cook and Campbell 1975). This is a critical aspect of theory falsification procedures because most theories are stated in a causal framework. True experiments, by ranking higher than other research designs on internal validity, allow the strongest test of causality.[9]

The general preference for true experimental procedures does not mean that all research testing theory will employ such designs. On occasion, the independent variable(s) of interest is not subject to manipulation by the researcher, and conditions prevent random assignment of respondents to different treatments. When this occurs, correlational or quasi-experimental designs must be employed. In certain cases, these designs permit causal inferences (Bagozzi 1979, Cook and Campbell 1975), and even when they do not, they are often of sufficient probing value to be worth employing. However, research designs of less efficiency than true experiments should be used only when true experiments are not feasible (Campbell and Stanley 1966). This is in keeping with the criterion that the research design chosen be the one that offers the strongest test of the theory.

When the goal is effects application, the need for correspondence necessitates different research design priorities. The design depends on the nature of the event structure of interest and the particular information needed regarding that structure. If it is important to establish the causal sequence of the events in the real world, then true experiments are preferred whenever possible. Yet, true experiments may not be feasible to examine certain variables. And, true experiments may seriously compromise the naturalness of the research setting. In these circumstances, or when causal statements regarding the event structure are not required as a basis for decision making, research seeking effects application should opt for correlational or quasi-experimental designs. Such designs are far less intrusive and, hence, enhance correspondence between the research setting and the real-world situation.

Summary

Effects application and theory application differ sharply in the research procedures upon which they depend. When *effects application* is the goal, correspondence procedures are required to ensure that the findings are generalizable to some real-world situation of interest. These procedures allow *nothing* to be done that might cause an important mis-match between the research and the real-world situation. Ideally, this goal is achieved by employing a representative sample of respondents, using natural events and behaviors as variables in a field context, and selecting a research design that preserves the natural setting (see Exhibit 2). To the extent that similarity between the research and the real-world is achieved, the empirical outcomes observed may be applied in the real world.

When theory application is the goal, falsification procedures are required to assess the scientific status of the theory. These procedures allow *anything* to be done that will ensure a rigorous test of the theory. Such a test is provided when internal, construct, and statistical-conclusion validity are maximized. As summarized in Exhibit 2, this entails selecting homogeneous respondent samples, tailoring multiple empirical operationalizations to the abstract theoretical concepts that they are meant to represent, and conducting true experiments in laboratory or other settings that are relatively free of extraneous sources of variation. If research provides a strong test of the theory, and if the theory escapes refutation, then the theory is accepted as a scientific explanation of real-world events.

Theory application is done through the design of a theory-based intervention. But, before such an intervention is implemented in the real world, intervention falsification procedures are required to test its performance. Like theory falsification procedures, intervention falsification procedures seek the most rigorous test possible. But, in contrast to a theory test, a rigorous intervention test is not provided by minimizing variation on nontheoretical factors. Instead, such a test is obtained by exposing

---

[9]The major threats to internal validity that remain in laboratory experiments are participants uncovering the hypothesis and responding to it rather than to the independent variables alone, or participants responding to demand characteristics, i.e., to inadvertent cues given by the experimenter regarding the appropriate behavior. Procedures such as carefully constructed cover stories, between subjects' designs, and "blind" experimenters can be used to reduce the plausibility of these threats; see Rosenthal and Rosnow (1969a) for a discussion of these procedures.

the intervention to real-world variability that might cause it to fail. Thus, internal, construct, and statistical-conclusion validity are pursued within limits created by the need to reflect important dimensions of the real world. As summarized in Exhibit 2, this entails selecting research respondents and choosing a research setting that are heterogeneous on variables likely to affect intervention outcomes, operationalizing variables to reflect the manner in which the intervention would be implemented in the real world, and employing the most rigorous research design possible given the need to capture aspects of real-world variability. Only interventions that yield outcomes predicted by the theory in such a test situation are applied in the real world.

Although superficially similar, intervention falsification procedures and correspondence procedures are distinct. Correspondence procedures demand that the research provide an *accurate representation* of the real-world situation of interest. This is necessary because the goal is to apply the particular effects observed in the research to the real world. Intervention falsification procedures only require that the research subject the intervention to *levels of variability* that it might encounter in the real world. The research need not mirror the real world because it is the theoretical relationship represented by the intervention, and not the particular effects observed in the research, that is applied.

THE METHODOLOGICAL LITERATURE

Much confusion in the methodological literature has resulted from a lack of realization that different procedures are optimal for achieving the two types of generalizability. This confusion is particularly evident in criticism of laboratory studies with student respondents. It is instructive to review this criticism with the research procedures underlying effects application and theory application in mind.

Objections to laboratory studies have traditionally centered on the "artificiality" of the findings obtained (Aronson and Carlsmith 1968, Opp 1970, Webster and Kervin 1971). But in recent years these objections have manifested themselves in two specific lines of criticism (Kruglanski 1975). One has been the concern that because much re-

search employs student, volunteer, and other convenience samples, it cannot be generalized to broader population groups. A second major line of criticism has been the argument that, because the laboratory is characterized by unique features not found in the real world, laboratory studies necessarily yield nongeneralizable results.

When effects application is the goal, the above concerns are well-founded. Correspondence between the subjects and the setting used in the research and those in the real world is a necessary condition for effects application. To the extent that the use of student or convenience samples and laboratory settings undermines this correspondence, applicability of the effects observed is limited. Thus, procedures that enhance the match between the research environment and the real world, such as the use of relevant representative samples and field settings, are appropriate when effects application is desired.

Yet, when the goal is theory application, the call for research subjects and settings representative of the real world is inappropriate. The foundation of theory application is rigorous theory testing. It is a mistake to assume that the people and events in a theory test must reflect people and events in some real-world situation. Rather, the test circumstance simply must provide the strongest test of the theory possible. Features of the test are only constrained by the requirement that they not undermine the degree to which any demonstrated construct relationship can be generalized to other settings not ruled out by the theory. Any sample is relevant if it permits operationalization within the domain of the theory. Homogeneous convenience samples may thus be employed in theory research. In fact, homogeneous samples are preferred because their use enables more precise predictions and enhances statistical-conclusion validity, thereby increasing the rigor of the theory test.

Similarly, laboratory settings generally are desirable in theory testing research. The controlled environment of the laboratory typically allows the researcher to employ true experimental designs, to tailor variables to abstract theoretical constructs, and to minimize extraneous sources of variation. These features lead to high internal, construct, and statistical-conclusion validity, thereby providing a strong theory test.

The only damaging criticisms of the laboratory setting are those that specify why its unrealistic features might operate as plausible threats to internal, construct, or statistical-conclusion validity. For example, if the artificiality of the laboratory facilitates participants in guessing the experimental hypothesis, then internal validity may be threatened and the theory test weakened. If valid arguments can be made to this effect, generalizability of the observed construct relationship is impaired. Otherwise, the use of insulated environments, standardized procedures, and other "unrealistic" features may constitute perfectly acceptable theory-testing procedures.

Recommendations for alternatives to the controlled laboratory settings, such as the suggestions that true experiments be conducted in field settings or that real-world features be introduced into the laboratory, are detrimental to achieving a rigorous theory test. Conducting true experiments in field settings is likely to reduce internal validity because there are numerous obstacles to forming and maintaining randomly constituted groups in the field (Cook and Campbell, 1975). Construct validity also may be lower because tailoring operationalizations to abstract constructs may be difficult in the field. In addition, statistical-conclusion validity is likely to suffer because the field affords less opportunity for using standardized procedures and controlling stimuli.

Likewise, attempts to incorporate real-world features into the laboratory may undermine construct and statistical-conclusion validity. These features can represent plausible sources of distortion regarding the theoretical labeling of the independent variables, as well as uncontrolled sources of error variance in dependent variable responses (Aronson and Carlsmith 1968; Cook and Campbell 1975, Webster and Kervin 1971). Thus, because these strategies could potentially decrease the internal, construct, and statistical-conclusion validity of research results, they should be avoided in theory-testing research whenever possible. Their implementation could compromise the severity of the theory test.

The conclusion is not that variation in people and events found in the real world is irrelevant to theory application, however. On the contrary, it simply assumes a different role than in effects application. In theory application, accepted theory is used to design an intervention. This intervention, then, must be shown to perform successfully in the face of variability that it is likely to encounter in the real world. To test the performance of an intervention, it may be implemented in an uncontrolled environment such as a field setting, or it may be exposed to extreme levels of important variables in a controlled (laboratory) environment. But, as we observed earlier, the test environment need not be *representative* of any particular real-world situation (as is the case when effects application is sought); it only must expose the intervention to stress that could cause it to fail. Repeated failure of interventions based on a particular theory may suggest the need for a better explanation. However, testing procedures for any new theory remain controlled. The applicability of an explanation is never improved by weakening its test.

PHILOSOPHIES UNDERLYING THE TWO TYPES OF APPLICABILITY

Clarification of the procedural implications of the two types of applicability does much to resolve the confusion in the methodological literature. The distinction between effects application and theory application is more than a procedural one, however. Also at stake are two basic philosophies of how to go about application. Discussion rarely gets beyond the vague perception of research pursuing effects application as "intuitively practical" and research pursuing theory application as research "academically respectable." Not surprisingly, many studies end up trying to embrace both, with little appreciation that they represent different philosophies. Accordingly, it is appropriate to end the present discussion with an *explicit* statement of the philosophical rationale underlying each approach to applications.

Traditionally, the application of effects has rested philosophically on the principle of induction. The notion that observed effects will be repeated in the real world, given the use of correspondence procedures, is an inductive argument. The observation that something has happened is said to imply that it (or something similar) will happen again.

It must be pointed out, however, that, although intuitively plausible, induction turns out, on close examination, to be an extremely hollow form of argument. Induction actually has no basis in logic. With any logical argument, true premises should yield true conclusions. Yet even though the sun has come up every day so far, whether or not it comes up tomorrow is not a matter of logical necessity. True premises may yield a false conclusion. Induction is not a logical argument.

The intuitive appeal of an inductive argument is such that many researchers are willing to subscribe to it as a matter of experience, if not logic. After all, the sun appears to come up every day. Even the appeal from experience, however, is suspect. It amounts to using induction to justify itself. Because induction has seemed to work before, it will work in the future. The circularity of such reasoning is devastating in the case of effects application. The researcher has only a few observations on which to base conclusions. Conclusions about the real world must really be based on an uncritical faith in induction rather than any experiences with observations.

It might seem that the problem of induction could be escaped by resorting to probabilistic conclusions. Given observed effects, the occurence of a real-world event is not proven, but it made more highly probable. Under any standard concept of probability, however, this turns out to be not very helpful. In principle, the researcher could observe an effect an infinite number of times. The number of observations actually available in obviously finite. Thus, the probability of any effect must be zero if the number of possible observations of the effect is infinite. Probabilities are not meaningful in the context of infinite possibility.

Our conclusion must be that effects application rests on very soft grounds. While this approach appears to be the epitome of rigorous application, it is mostly a matter of blind faith. Induction itself cannot support going from observed effects to conclusions about the real world.

Effects application might better be viewed as reasoning by analogy. There is no logical principle involved. Rather, outcomes observed in the research are related to outcomes of the real world. If the research conditions seem to be analogous to events in the real world, then the analogy is completed by concluding that observed effects will hold in the real world. Reasoning by analogy depends, not on logic, but on the researcher's insight. Although correspondence procedures may provide some basis for analogy, this process is ultimately qualitative in nature.[10] This argument cannot be pursued here; however, it is our opinion that effects application could be improved by the increased use of qualitative methods (Calder 1977).

In contrast to effects application, theory application rests on the logical principle that it is possible for observed effects to contradict a theory thereby falsifying it. Theories are tested in situations where they can possibly fail. Only those that survive these tests, then, are accepted and are candidates for application.

The logical principle of falsification requires that theory testing be bound to formal methodological procedures. These procedures are designed to expose the theory to refutation, and should follow directly from the theoretical explanation itself. It is only where theory fully dictates observation that observation can contradict theory. Thus, qualitative methods are not essential in testing theory.

The falsification procedures employed to test theory are not sufficient to ensure successful theory application, however. Accepted theories can provide only a framework for designing interventions. These interventions also must be tested before they are applied in the real world. Again the logic of falsification is invoked. Research procedures are designed to expose the intervention to refutation. These procedures should follow directly from the underlying theory *and* the real-world circumstances that the intervention will face. If the intervention performs as predicted by the theory, it may be implemented. If, however, the intervention

---

[10]See Wright and Kriewall (1980) for an empirical demonstration of the need for effects research to capture individuals' "state-of-mind" in the real-world setting of interest.

does not lead to expected outcomes, it must be modified. Careful assessment of theoretical and nontheoretical variables as part of the testing process may provide insight for this redesign.

Application of theory often stops short of efforts to falsify interventions. It is mistakenly assumed that accepted theories will yield usable interventions without further work. But, whereas such theories do provide efficient frameworks for design, testing the intervention designed is still necessary. Theory application in consumer research would be greatly improved by recognition of the need for, and role of, intervention falsification procedures.[11]

CONCLUSION

Consumer researchers pursue two distinct types of generalizability. One involves the application of specific effects observed in a research setting. The other involves the application of a general scientific theory. Although both types of generalization are tenable, it is important to determine which will be the primary goal prior to designing a study. Effects application and theory application are based on different philosophical assumptions and, therefore, require different research procedures.

Effects application rests on the presumption of correspondence between the research and some real-world situation of interest. If these two situations are analogous, then the outcomes observed in one can be expected to occur in the other. When effects application is the goal, the research subjects, setting, and variables examined must be representative of their real-world counterparts. Any procedures likely to impair the match between the research and the real world, such as convenience samples and laboratory settings, should be avoided. Because objective correspondence is impossible to achieve fully, and can never ensure equivalent *experience*, qualitative insight may assist the researcher in judging whether or not the research experience matches that of the real world.

Theory application rests on the acceptance of the scientific explanation itself. This acceptance is determined by the logical principle of falsification. Theories that survive rigorous efforts at disproof are accepted. The only requirement for research testing theory is that it provide the strongest test possible. Because homogeneous samples and laboratory settings settings often lead to a stronger test of the theory than heterogeneous samples and field settings, they may be preferred in this type of research. But, theory tests alone are not sufficient for theory application. Accepted theories must be calibrated to the real world through the design and testing of interventions.

In sum, the research procedures optimal for effects application and theory application as incompatible. This does not mean that there cannot be synergy between research pursuing each type of applicability. It does mean that research procedures can only be evaluated with reference to the type of generalizability being pursued. To do otherwise only leads to needless criticism and poor communication within the discipline.

REFERENCES

Aronson, Elliot, and Carlsmith, J. Merrill (1968), "Experimentation in Social Psychology," in *Handbook of Social Psychology,* vol. 2, eds. Gardner Lindzey and Elliot Aronson, Reading, Mass.: Addison-Wesley.

Bagozzi, Richard (1979). *Causal Models in Marketing,* New York: John Wiley & Sons.

Brunswik, Egon (1956), *Perception and the Representative Design of Psychological Experiments,* 2nd ed., Berkeley: University of California Press.

Calder, Bobby J. (1977), "Focus Groups and the Nature of Qualitative Marketing Research," *Journal of Marketing Research,* 14, 353–64.

Campbell, Donald, and Fiske, Donald (1959), "Convergent and Discriminant Validation by the Multitrait-Multimethod Matrix," *Psychological Bulletin,* 56, 81–105.

———, and Stanley, John (1966), *Experimental and Quasi-experimental Designs for Research.* Chicago: Rand McNally.

Cartwright, Dorwin, and Zander, Alvin (1968). *Group Dynamics,* New York: Harper and Row.

---

[11]O'Shaughnessy and Ryan's (1979) discussion of the distinction between science and technology in some ways parallels and complements our discussion of the difference between theory testing and intervention design and testing.

Cook, Thomas, and Campbell, Donald (1975). "The Design and Conduct of Experiments and Quasi-experiments in Field Settings," in *Handbook of Industrial and Organizational Research,* ed. Martin Dunnette, Chicago: Rand McNally.

Ellsworth, Phoebe (1977), "From Abstract Ideas to Concrete Instances: Some Guidelines for Choosing Natural Research Settings," *American Psychologist,* 32, 604–15.

Ferber, Robert (1977), "Research by Convenience," *Journal of Consumer Research,* 4, 57–8.

Kruglanski, Arie (1973), "Much Ado About the 'Volunteer Artifacts,'" *Journal of Personality and Social Psychology.* 28, 348–54.

―――― (1975), "The Two Meanings of External Invalidity," *Human Relations,* 28, 653–9.

Kuhn, Thomas (1970), *The Structure of Scientific Revolutions.* Chicago: University of Chicago Press.

Lakatos, Imre (1970), "Falsification and the Methodology of Science Research Programs," in *Criticism and the Growth of Knowledge,* eds. Imre Lakatos and Alan Musgrave, London: Cambridge University Press.

Opp, Karl-Dieter (1970). "The Experimental Methods in the Social Sciences: Some Problems and Proposals for its More Effective Use," *Quality and Quantity,* 34, 39–54.

O'Shaughnessy, John, and Ryan, Mike (1979), "Marketing Science and Technology," in *Conceptual and Theoretical Developments in Marketing,* eds. O. C. Ferrell, Stephen Brown, and Charles Lamb, Chicago: American Marketing Association.

Popper, Karl R. (1959). *The Logic of Scientific Discovery,* New York: Harper Torchbooks.

―――― (1963), *Conjectures and Refutations,* New York: Harper Torchbooks.

Rosenthal, Robert, and Rosnow, Ralph (1969a), *Artifact in Behavioral Research,* New York: Academic Press.

Sawyer, Alan, Worthing, Parker, and Sendak, Paul (1979). "The Role of Laboratory Experiments to Test Marketing Strategies," *Journal of Marketing,* 43, 60–7.

Tunnell, Gilbert (1977), "Three Dimensions of Naturalness: An Expanded Definition of Field Research." *Psychological Bulletin,* 84, 426–77.

Webb, Eugene, Campbell, Donald, Schwartz, Richard, and Sechrest, Lee (1966). *Unobtrusive Measures: Nonreactive Research in the Social Sciences,* Chicago: Rand McNally.

Webster, Murray, and Kervin, John (1971). "Artificiality in Experimental Sociology," *Canadian Review of Sociology and Anthropology,* 8, 263–72.

Winer, B. J. (1971), *Statistical Principles in Experimental Design,* New York: McGraw-Hill.

Wright, Peter, and Kriewall, Mary Ann (1980), "State-of-Mind Effects on the Accuracy with which Utility Functions Predict Marketplace Choice," *Journal of Marketing Research,* 17, 277–94.

INDEX

Page numbers in *italic* indicate pages on which the full reference appears.